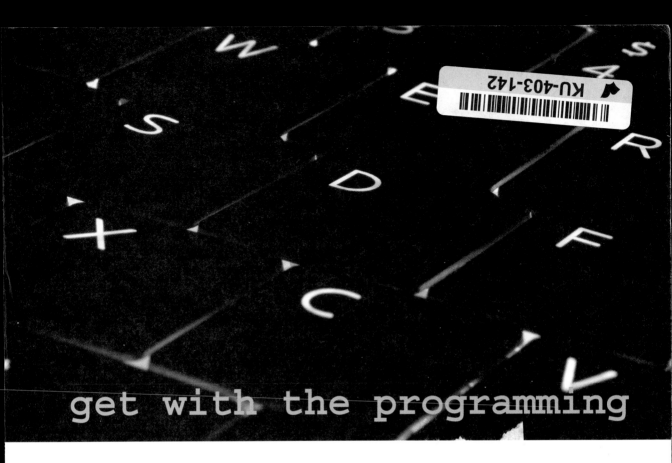

get with the programming

Through the power of practice and immediate personalized feedback, MyProgrammingLab improves your performance.

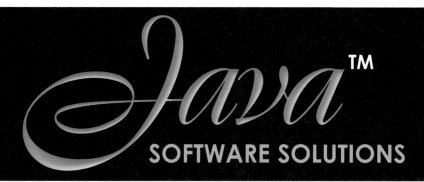

Seventh Edition

Java™
SOFTWARE SOLUTIONS

FOUNDATIONS OF PROGRAM DESIGN

JOHN LEWIS
Virginia Tech

•

WILLIAM LOFTUS
Accenture

International Edition contributions by
S. Abirami
Anna University

Addison-Wesley
Boston   Columbus   Indianapolis   New York   San Francisco   Upper Saddle River
Amsterdam   Cape Town   Dubai   London   Madrid   Milan   Munich   Paris   Montreal   Toronto
Delhi   Mexico City   São Paulo   Sydney   Hong Kong   Seoul   Singapore   Taipei   Tokyo

Editorial Director:	Marcia Horton	Publishing Assistant, International Edition:	Shokhi Shah
Editor-in-Chief:	Michael Hirsch	Senior Operations Supervisor:	Alan Fischer
Editorial Assistant:	Stephanie Sellinger	Manufacturing Buyer:	Lisa McDowell
Vice President Marketing:	Patrice Jones	Art Director:	Linda Knowles
Marketing Manager:	Yezan Alayan	Cover Designer:	Suzanne Harbison
Marketing Coordinator:	Kathryn Ferranti	Image Permission Coordinator:	Rita Wenning
Vice President, Production:	Vince O'Brien	Cover Photograph:	© Creative Crop/Digital Vision/Getty Images
Managing Editor:	Jeff Holcomb		
Production Project Manager:	Heather McNally	Media Editor:	Daniel Sandin
Publisher, International Edition:	Angshuman Chakraborty	Media Project Manager:	Wanda Rockwell
		Full-Service Project Management:	Rose Kernan, Nesbitt Graphics, Inc.
Acquisitions Editor, International Edition:	Arunabha Deb		
		Cover Printer:	Coral Graphics Services, Inc.

Pearson Education Limited
Edinburgh Gate
Harlow
Essex CM20 2JE
England

and Associated Companies throughout the world

Visit us on the World Wide Web at: www.pearsoninternationaleditions.com

© Pearson Education Limited 2012

The rights of John Lewis and William Loftus to be identified as authors of this work have been asserted by them in accordance with the Copyright, Designs and Patents Act 1988.

Authorized adaptation from the United States edition, entitled Java Software Solutions, Foundations of Program Design, 7th edition, *ISBN 978-0-13-214918-1by John Lewis and William Loftus published by Pearson Education © 2012.*

ISBN 10: 0-273-75147-6

ISBN 13: 978-0-273-75147-2

British Library Cataloguing-in-Publication Data

A catalogue record for this book is available from the British Library

10 9 8 7 6 5 4 3 2 1   14 13 12 11 10

Typeset in Sabon LT Std by Glyph International

Printed and bound by Quad/Graphics Book Services, Taunton in The United States of America

The publisher's policy is to use paper manufactured from sustainable forests.

This book is dedicated to our families.
Sharon, Justin, Kayla, Nathan, and Samantha Lewis
and
Veena, Isaac, and Dévi Loftus

Preface

Welcome to the Seventh Edition of *Java Software Solutions: Foundations of Program Design*. We are pleased that this book has served the needs of so many students and faculty over the years. This edition has been tailored further to improve the coverage of topics key to introductory computing.

New to This Edition

- Split Chapter 5 of the 6th edition into two for better coverage and flow.
- Moved the coverage of the `ArrayList` class earlier in the book to permit more interesting projects earlier.
- Improved the discussion of an array as a programming construct.
- Improved the discussions of visibility modifiers, especially regarding the `protected` modifier.
- Replaced and updated examples throughout the book.
- Replaced, updated, and added exercises and programming projects.
- Available with MyProgrammingLab (see details later in this Preface).

Feedback from both instructors and students continues to make it clear that we have hit the mark with the overall vision of the book. The emphasis remains on presenting underlying core concepts in a clear and gradual manner. The Graphics Track sections in each chapter still segregate the coverage of graphics and graphical user interfaces, giving extreme flexibility in how that material gets covered. The casual writing style and entertaining examples still rule the day.

The enhancements in this edition are designed to allow the instructor more flexibility in topic coverage. In an attempt to cover all issues related to conditionals and loops, Chapter 5 in the previous edition had become very large and a bit too encyclopedic. In this edition that chapter has been carefully redesigned into two, giving the coverage of those topics a better flow. The new organization allows more interesting examples to be explored earlier.

One effect of this reorganization is that it allowed us to bring the coverage of the `ArrayList` class earlier in the book. Although arrays are used internally to implement the `ArrayList` class, there is no reason to wait for arrays to be covered to introduce the `ArrayList` class. Like many other classes in the Java API, the `ArrayList` class can be used without needing to know how it works internally. An `ArrayList` object can be used for its (very valuable) functionality as soon as loops are available. The new organization in this edition does exactly that. If the instructor chooses, coverage of `ArrayList` can still be deferred as it has been before, but now the option is there to introduce them earlier.

In addition to these changes, various discussions throughout the book have been revamped and improved. For example, the explanation of the effects of the `protected` visibility modifier has enhanced to clarify its use. Furthermore, throughout the book older examples have been rejuvenated, and end-of-chapter exercises and programming projects have been augmented.

Cornerstones of the Text

This text is based on the following basic ideas that we believe make for a sound introductory text:

- *True object-orientation.* A text that really teaches a solid object-oriented approach must use what we call object-speak. That is, all processing should be discussed in object-oriented terms. That does not mean, however, that the first program a student sees must discuss the writing of multiple classes and methods. A student should learn to use objects before learning to write them. This text uses a natural progression that culminates in the ability to design real object-oriented solutions.

- *Sound programming practices.* Students should not be taught how to program; they should be taught how to write good software. There's a difference. Writing software is not a set of cookbook actions, and a good program is more than a collection of statements. This text integrates practices that serve as the foundation of good programming skills. These practices are used in all examples and are reinforced in the discussions. Students learn how to solve problems as well as how to implement solutions. We introduce and integrate basic software engineering techniques throughout the text. The **Software Failure** vignettes reiterate these lessons by demonstrating the perils of not following these sound practices.

- *Examples.* Students learn by example. This text is filled with fully implemented examples that demonstrate specific concepts. We have intertwined small, readily understandable examples with larger, more realistic ones. There is a balance between graphics and nongraphics programs. The **VideoNotes** provide additional examples in a live presentation format.

■ *Graphics and GUIs.* Graphics can be a great motivator for students, and their use can serve as excellent examples of object-orientation. As such, we use them throughout the text in a well-defined set of sections that we call the Graphics Track. This coverage includes the use of event processing and GUIs. Students learn to build GUIs in the appropriate way by using a natural progression of topics. The Graphics Track can be avoided entirely for those who do not choose to use graphics.

Chapter Breakdown

Chapter 1 (Introduction) introduces computer systems in general, including basic architecture and hardware, networking, programming, and language translation. Java is introduced in this chapter, and the basics of general program development, as well as object-oriented programming, are discussed. This chapter contains broad introductory material that can be covered while students become familiar with their development environment.

Chapter 2 (Data and Expressions) explores some of the basic types of data used in a Java program and the use of expressions to perform calculations. It discusses the conversion of data from one type to another and how to read input interactively from the user with the help of the standard Scanner class.

Chapter 3 (Using Classes and Objects) explores the use of predefined classes and the objects that can be created from them. Classes and objects are used to manipulate character strings, produce random numbers, perform complex calculations, and format output. Enumerated types are also discussed.

Chapter 4 (Writing Classes) explores the basic issues related to writing classes and methods. Topics include instance data, visibility, scope, method parameters, and return types. Encapsulation and constructors are covered as well. Some of the more involved topics are deferred to or revisited in Chapter 6.

Chapter 5 (Conditionals and Loops) covers the use of boolean expressions to make decisions. Then the if statement and while loop are explored in detail. Once loops are established, the concept of an iterator is introduced and the Scanner class is revisited for additional input parsing and the reading of text files. Finally, the ArrayList class introduced, which provides the option for managing a large number of objects.

Chapter 6 (More Conditionals and Loops) examines the rest of Java's conditional (switch) and loop (do, for) statements. All related statements for conditionals and loops are discussed, including the enhanced version of the for loop. The for-each loop is also used to process iterators and ArrayList objects.

Chapter 7 (Object-Oriented Design) reinforces and extends the coverage of issues related to the design of classes. Techniques for identifying the classes and objects needed for a problem and the relationships among them are discussed. This chapter also covers static class members, interfaces, and the design of enumerated type classes. Method design issues and method overloading are also discussed.

Chapter 8 (Arrays) contains extensive coverage of arrays and array processing. The nature of an array as a low-level programming structure is contrasted to the higher-level object management approach. Additional topics include command-line arguments, variable length parameter lists, and multidimensional arrays.

Chapter 9 (Inheritance) covers class derivations and associated concepts such as class hierarchies, overriding, and visibility. Strong emphasis is put on the proper use of inheritance and its role in software design.

Chapter 10 (Polymorphism) explores the concept of binding and how it relates to polymorphism. Then we examine how polymorphic references can be accomplished using either inheritance or interfaces. Sorting is used as an example of polymorphism. Design issues related to polymorphism are examined as well.

Chapter 11 (Exceptions) explores the class hierarchy from the Java standard library used to define exceptions, as well as the ability to define our own exception objects. We also discuss the use of exceptions when dealing with input and output and examine an example that writes a text file.

Chapter 12 (Recursion) covers the concept, implementation, and proper use of recursion. Several examples from various domains are used to demonstrate how recursive techniques make certain types of processing elegant.

Chapter 13 (Collections) introduces the idea of a collection and its underlying data structure. Abstraction is revisited in this context and the classic data structures are explored. Generic types are introduced as well. This chapter serves as an introduction to a CS2 course.

Supplements

Student Online Resources
These student resources can be accessed at the book's Companion Website, www.pearsoninternationaleditions.com/lewis:

- Source Code for all the programs in the text
- Links to Java development environments
- VideoNotes: short step-by-step videos demonstrating how to solve problems from design through coding. VideoNotes allow for self-paced

instruction with easy navigation including the ability to select, play, re-wind, fast-forward, and stop within each VideoNote exercise. Margin icons in your textbook let you know when a VideoNote video is available for a particular concept or homework problem.

Online Practice and Assessment

MyProgrammingLab helps students fully grasp the logic, semantics, and syntax of programming. Through practice exercises and immediate, personalized feed-back, MyProgrammingLab improves the programming competence of beginning students who often struggle with the basic concepts and paradigms of popular high-level programming languages.

A self-study and homework tool, MyProgrammingLab consists of hundreds of small practice problems organized around the structure of this textbook. For students, the system automatically detects errors in the logic and syntax of their code submissions and offers targeted hints that enable students to figure out what went wrong—and why. For instructors, a comprehensive gradebook tracks cor-rect and incorrect answers and stores the code submitted by students for review.

MyProgrammingLab is offered to users of this book in partnership with Turing's Craft, the makers of the CodeLab interactive programming exer-cise system. For a full demonstration, to see feedback from instructors and students, or to get started using MyProgrammingLab in your course, visit www.pearsoninternationaleditions.com/myprogramminglab.

Instructor Resources

The following supplements are available to qualified instructors only. Visit the Pearson Education Instructor Resource Center www.pearsoninternationaleditions .com/lewis

- Presentation Slides—in PowerPoint.
- Solutions—includes solutions to exercises and programming projects.
- Test Bank with powerful test generator software—includes a wealth of free response, multiple-choice, and true/false type questions.
- Lab Manual—lab exercises are designed to accompany the topic progression in the text.

Features

Key Concepts. Throughout the text, the Key Concept boxes highlight funda-mental ideas and important guidelines. These concepts are summarized at the end of each chapter.

Listings. All programming examples are presented in clearly labeled listings, followed by the program output, a sample run, or screen shot display as appropriate. The code is colored to visually distinguish comments and reserved words.

Syntax Diagrams. At appropriate points in the text, syntactic elements of the Java language are discussed in special highlighted sections with diagrams that clearly identify the valid forms for a statement or construct. Syntax diagrams for the entire Java language are presented in Appendix L.

Graphics Track. All processing that involves graphics and graphical user interfaces is discussed in one or two sections at the end of each chapter that we collectively refer to as the Graphics Track. This material can be skipped without loss of continuity, or focused on specifically as desired. The material in any Graphics Track section relates to the main topics of the chapter in which it is found. Graphics Track sections are indicated by a brown border on the edge of the page.

Summary of Key Concepts. The Key Concepts presented throughout a chapter are summarized at the end of the chapter.

Self-Review Questions and Answers. These short-answer questions review the fundamental ideas and terms established in the preceding section. They are designed to allow students to assess their own basic grasp of the material. The answers to these questions can be found at the end of the book in Appendix N.

Exercises. These intermediate problems require computations, the analysis or writing of code fragments, and a thorough grasp of the chapter content. While the exercises may deal with code, they generally do not require any online activity.

Programming Projects. These problems require the design and implementation of Java programs. They vary widely in level of difficulty.

MyProgrammingLab. Many of the problems in the book can be done online in MyProgrammingLab. Through practice exercises and immediate, personalized feedback, MyProgrammingLab improves the programming competence of beginning students who often struggle with the basic concepts and paradigms of popular high-level programming languages.

VideoNotes. Presented by the author, VideoNotes explain topics visually through informal videos in an easy-to-follow format, giving students the extra help they need to grasp important concepts. Look for this VideoNote icon to see which in-chapter topics and end-of-chapter Programming Projects are available as VideoNotes.

Software Failures. These between-chapter vignettes discuss real-world flaws in software design, encouraging students to adopt sound design practices from the beginning.

Acknowledgments

I am most grateful to the faculty and students from around the world who have provided their feedback on previous editions of this book. I am pleased to see the depth of the faculty's concern for their students and the students' thirst for knowledge. Your comments and questions are always welcome.

I am particularly thankful for the assistance, insight, and attention to detail of Robert Burton from Brigham Young University. For years, Robert has consistently provided valuable feedback that helps shape and evolve this textbook. Recently he also performed a revision of the material in Chapter 1 about personal computing systems that brought it back to a state-of-the-art discussion.

Brian Fraser of Simon Fraser University also has recently provided some excellent feedback that helped clarify some issues in this edition. Such interaction with computing educators is incredibly valuable.

I also want to thank Dan Joyce from Villanova University, who developed the Self-Review questions, ensuring that each relevant topic had enough review material, as well as developing the answers to each.

I continue to be amazed at the talent and effort demonstrated by the team at Pearson Addison-Wesley. Michael Hirsch, our editor, has amazing insight and commitment. His assistant, Stephanie Sellinger, is a source of consistent and helpful support. Marketing Manager Yez Alayan makes sure that instructors understand the pedagogical advantages of the text. The cover was designed by the skilled talents of Suzanne Harbison. Jeff Holcomb and Heather McNally led the production effort. The Addison-Wesley folks were supported by a phenomenal team at Nesbitt Graphics, including Jerilyn Bockorick for the interior design, Rose Kernan for project management, Diane Paluba for production coordination. We thank all of these people for ensuring that this book meets the highest quality standards.

Special thanks go to the following people who provided valuable advice to us about this book via their participation in focus groups, interviews, and reviews. They, as well as many other instructors and friends, have provided valuable feedback. They include:

Elizabeth Adams	James Madison University
David Atkins	University of Oregon
Lewis Barnett	University of Richmond
Thomas W. Bennet	Mississippi College
Gian Mario Besana	DePaul University
Hans-Peter Bischof	Rochester Institute of Technology
Robert Burton	Brigham Young University
John Chandler	Oklahoma State University

Robert Cohen	University of Massachusetts, Boston
Dodi Coreson	Linn Benton Community College
James H. Cross II	Auburn University
Eman El-Sheikh	University of West Florida
Christopher Eliot	University of Massachusetts, Amherst
Wanda M. Eanes	Macon State College
Stephanie Elzer	Millersville University
Matt Evett	Eastern Michigan University
Marj Feroe	Delaware County Community College, Pennsylvania
John Gauch	University of Kansas
Chris Haynes	Indiana University
James Heliotis	Rochester Institute of Technology
Laurie Hendren	McGill University
Mike Higgs	Austin College
Stephen Hughes	Roanoke College
Saroja Kanchi	Kettering University
Karen Kluge	Dartmouth College
Jason Levy	University of Hawaii
Peter MacKenzie	McGill University
Blayne Mayfield	Oklahoma State University
Gheorghe Muresan	Rutgers University
Laurie Murphy	Pacific Lutheran University
Dave Musicant	Carleton College
Faye Navabi-Tadayon	Arizona State University
Lawrence Osborne	Lamar University
Barry Pollack	City College of San Francisco
B. Ravikumar	University of Rhode Island
David Riley	University of Wisconsin (La Crosse)
Jerry Ross	Lane Community College
Patricia Roth	Southeastern Polytechnic State University
Carolyn Schauble	Colorado State University
Arjit Sengupta	Georgia State University
Bennet Setzer	Kennesaw State University
Vijay Srinivasan	JavaSoft, Sun Microsystems, Inc.
Stuart Steiner	Eastern Washington University
Katherine St. John	Lehman College, CUNY
Alexander Stoytchev	Iowa State University
Ed Timmerman	University of Maryland, University College
Shengru Tu	University of New Orleans
Paul Tymann	Rochester Institute of Technology
John J. Wegis	JavaSoft, Sun Microsystems, Inc.

Linda Wilson	Dartmouth College
David Wittenberg	Brandeis University
Wang-Chan Wong	California State University (Dominguez Hills)

Thanks also go to my friends and former colleagues at Villanova University who have provided so much wonderful feedback. They include Bob Beck, Cathy Helwig, Anany Levitin, Najib Nadi, Beth Taddei, and Barbara Zimmerman.

Special thanks go to Pete DePasquale of The College of New Jersey for the design and evolution of the PaintBox project, as well as the original Java Class Library appendix.

Many other people have helped in various ways. They include Ken Arnold, Mike Czepiel, John Loftus, Sebastian Niezgoda, and Saverio Perugini. Our apologies to anyone we may have omitted.

The ACM Special Interest Group on Computer Science Education (SIGCSE) is a tremendous resource. Their conferences provide an opportunity for educators from all levels and all types of schools to share ideas and materials. If you are an educator in any area of computing and are not involved with SIGCSE, you're missing out.

The publishers would like to thank Arindam Chatterjee and Salil Joshi for reviewing content for the International Edition.

Contents

Preface   **7**

Chapter 1   **Introduction**   **27**

1.1   **Computer Processing**   28
     Software Categories   29
     Digital Computers   30
     Binary Numbers   33

1.2   **Hardware Components**   36
     Computer Architecture   37
     Input/Output Devices   38
     Main Memory and Secondary Memory   39
     The Central Processing Unit   43

1.3   **Networks**   46
     Network Connections   46
     Local-Area Networks and
         Wide-Area Networks 48
     The Internet   49
     The World Wide Web   50
     Uniform Resource Locators   51

1.4   **The Java Programming Language**   52
     A Java Program   53
     Comments   55
     Identifiers and Reserved Words   57
     White Space   59

1.5   **Program Development**   62
     Programming Language Levels   62
     Editors, Compilers, and Interpreters   64
     Development Environments   66
     Syntax and Semantics   67
     Errors   68

	1.6	**Object-Oriented Programming**	**70**
		Problem Solving	71
		Object-Oriented Software Principles	72

Chapter 2		**Data and Expressions**	**83**

	2.1	**Character Strings**	**84**
		The print and println Methods	84
		String Concatenation	86
		Escape Sequences	89
	2.2	**Variables and Assignment**	**91**
		Variables	91
		The Assignment Statement	93
		Constants	95
	2.3	**Primitive Data Types**	**97**
		Integers and Floating Points	97
		Characters	99
		Booleans	100
	2.4	**Expressions**	**101**
		Arithmetic Operators	101
		Operator Precedence	102
		Increment and Decrement Operators	106
		Assignment Operators	107
	2.5	**Data Conversion**	**109**
		Conversion Techniques	111
	2.6	**Interactive Programs**	**113**
		The Scanner Class	113
	2.7	**Graphics**	**118**
		Coordinate Systems	118
		Representing Color	120
	2.8	**Applets**	**121**
		Executing Applets Using the Web	124
	2.9	**Drawing Shapes**	**125**
		The Graphics Class	125
		Software Failure:	
		NASA Mars Climate Orbiter	
		and Polar Lander	137

Chapter 3	**Using Classes and Objects**	**139**
3.1	Creating Objects	140
	Aliases	142
3.2	The String Class	144
3.3	Packages	148
	The import Declaration	150
3.4	The Random Class	152
3.5	The Math Class	155
3.6	Formatting Output	158
	The NumberFormat Class	158
	The DecimalFormat Class	160
	The printf Method	161
3.7	Enumerated Types	164
3.8	Wrapper Classes	167
	Autoboxing	169
3.9	Components and Containers	169
	Frames and Panels	170
3.10	Nested Panels	174
3.11	Images	177

Chapter 4	**Writing Classes**	**185**
4.1	Classes and Objects Revisited	186
4.2	Anatomy of a Class	188
	Instance Data	193
	UML Class Diagrams	193
4.3	Encapsulation	195
	Visibility Modifiers	196
	Accessors and Mutators	197
4.4	Anatomy of a Method	198
	The return Statement	200
	Parameters	201

	Local Data	201
	Bank Account Example	202
4.5	Constructors Revisited	207
4.6	Graphical Objects	208
4.7	Graphical User Interfaces	217
4.8	Buttons	218
4.9	Text Fields	222

Software Failure:
Denver Airport Baggage
Handling System   231

Chapter 5	**Conditionals and Loops**	**233**
5.1	Boolean Expressions	234
	Equality and Relational Operators	235
	Logical Operators	236
5.2	The if Statement	239
	The if-else Statement	242
	Using Block Statements	245
	Nested if Statements	249
5.3	Comparing Data	252
	Comparing Floats	252
	Comparing Characters	253
	Comparing Objects	254
5.4	The while Statement	256
	Infinite Loops	260
	Nested Loops	262
	The break and continue Statements	265
5.5	Iterators	267
	Reading Text Files	268
5.6	The ArrayList Class	271
5.7	Determining Event Sources	274

	5.8	**Check Boxes and Radio Buttons**	**277**
		Check Boxes	277
		Radio Buttons	281
		Software Failure:	
		Therac-25	293

Chapter 6		**More Conditionals and Loops**	**295**
	6.1	**The switch Statement**	**296**
	6.2	**The Conditional Operator**	**300**
	6.3	**The do Statement**	**301**
	6.4	**The for Statement**	**305**
		The for-each Loop	308
		Comparing Loops	310
	6.5	**Drawing with Loops and Conditionals**	**311**
	6.6	**Dialog Boxes**	**317**

Chapter 7		**Object-Oriented Design**	**327**
	7.1	**Software Development Activities**	**328**
	7.2	**Identifying Classes and Objects**	**329**
		Assigning Responsibilities	331
	7.3	**Static Class Members**	**331**
		Static Variables	332
		Static Methods	332
	7.4	**Class Relationships**	**336**
		Dependency	336
		Dependencies Among Objects	
		of the Same Class	336
		Aggregation	342
		The this Reference	346
	7.5	**Interfaces**	**348**
		The Comparable Interface	353
		The Iterator Interface	354

7.6	**Enumerated Types Revisited**	**355**
7.7	**Method Design**	**358**
	Method Decomposition	359
	Method Parameters Revisited	364
7.8	**Method Overloading**	**369**
7.9	**Testing**	**371**
	Reviews	372
	Defect Testing	372
7.10	**GUI Design**	**375**
7.11	**Layout Managers**	**376**
	Flow Layout	378
	Border Layout	382
	Grid Layout	385
	Box Layout	387
7.12	**Borders**	**391**
7.13	**Containment Hierarchies**	**395**
	Software Failure:	
	2003 Northeast Blackout	403

Chapter 8	**Arrays**	**405**
8.1	**Array Elements**	**406**
8.2	**Declaring and Using Arrays**	**407**
	Bounds Checking	410
	Alternate Array Syntax	415
	Initializer Lists	415
	Arrays as Parameters	416
8.3	**Arrays of Objects**	**418**
8.4	**Command-Line Arguments**	**428**
8.5	**Variable Length Parameter Lists**	**430**
8.6	**Two-Dimensional Arrays**	**434**
	Multidimensional Arrays	438

	8.7	Polygons and Polylines	439
		The Polygon Class	442
	8.8	Mouse Events	444
	8.9	Key Events	453
		Software Failure:	
		LA Air Traffic Control	467

Chapter 9   Inheritance   469

	9.1	Creating Subclasses	470
		The **protected** Modifier	473
		The **super** Reference	476
		Multiple Inheritance	479
	9.2	Overriding Methods	481
		Shadowing Variables	483
	9.3	Class Hierarchies	484
		The Object Class	486
		Abstract Classes	487
		Interface Hierarchies	489
	9.4	Visibility	489
	9.5	Designing for Inheritance	492
		Restricting Inheritance	493
	9.6	The Component Class Hierarchy	494
	9.7	Extending Adapter Classes	497
	9.8	The Timer Class	501
		Software Failure:	
		Ariane 5 Flight 501	511

Chapter 10   Polymorphism   513

	10.1	Late Binding	514
	10.2	Polymorphism via Inheritance	515

10.3	Polymorphism via Interfaces	528
10.4	Sorting	530
	Selection Sort	531
	Insertion Sort	537
	Comparing Sorts	538
10.5	Searching	539
	Linear Search	539
	Binary Search	541
	Comparing Searches	545
10.6	Designing for Polymorphism	545
10.7	Event Processing	547
10.8	File Choosers	548
10.9	Color Choosers	551
10.10	Sliders	553

Chapter 11 Exceptions 563

11.1	Exception Handling	564
11.2	Uncaught Exceptions	565
11.3	The try-catch Statement	566
	The finally Clause	570
11.4	Exception Propagation	571
11.5	The Exception Class Hierarchy	575
	Checked and Unchecked Exceptions	578
11.6	I/O Exceptions	579
11.7	Tool Tips and Mnemonics	583
11.8	Combo Boxes	590
11.9	Scroll Panes	595
11.10	Split Panes	598

Chapter 12	**Recursion**		**609**
	12.1	Recursive Thinking	610
		Infinite Recursion	610
		Recursion in Math	611
	12.2	Recursive Programming	612
		Recursion vs. Iteration	615
		Direct vs. Indirect Recursion	615
	12.3	Using Recursion	616
		Traversing a Maze	617
		The Towers of Hanoi	622
	12.4	Recursion in Graphics	627
		Tiled Pictures	627
		Fractals	630
Chapter 13	**Collections**		**643**
	13.1	Collections and Data Structures	644
		Separating Interface from Implementation	644
	13.2	Dynamic Representations	645
		Dynamic Structures	645
		A Dynamically Linked List	646
		Other Dynamic List Representations	651
	13.3	Linear Data Structures	653
		Queues	653
		Stacks	654
	13.4	Non-Linear Data Structures	657
		Trees	657
		Graphs	658
	13.5	The Java Collections API	660
		Generics	660

Appendix A	Glossary	667
Appendix B	Number Systems	691
Appendix C	The Unicode Character Set	699
Appendix D	Java Operators	703
Appendix E	Java Modifiers	709
Appendix F	Java Coding Guidelines	713
Appendix G	Java Applets	719
Appendix H	Regular Expressions	721
Appendix I	Javadoc Documentation Generator	723
Appendix J	The PaintBox Project	729
Appendix K	GUI Events	741
Appendix L	Java Syntax	745
Appendix M	The Java Class Library	759
Appendix N	Answers to Self-Review Questions	761
Index		815

Introduction

1

- Describe the relationship between hardware and software.
- Define various types of software and how they are used.
- Identify the core hardware components of a computer and explain their roles.
- Explain how the hardware components interact to execute programs and manage data.
- Describe how computers are connected into networks to share information.
- Introduce the Java programming language.
- Describe the steps involved in program compilation and execution.
- Present an overview of object-oriented principles.

This book is about writing well-designed software. To understand software, we must first have a fundamental understanding of its role in a computer system. Hardware and software cooperate in a computer system to accomplish complex tasks. The purpose of various hardware components, and the way those components are connected into networks, are important prerequisites to the study of software development. This chapter first discusses basic computer processing and then begins our exploration of software development by introducing the Java programming language and the principles of object-oriented programming.

1.1 Computer Processing

We begin our exploration of computer systems with an overview of computer processing, defining some fundamental terminology and showing how the key pieces of a computer system interact.

A computer system is made up of hardware and software. The *hardware* components of a computer system are the physical, tangible pieces that support the computing effort. They include chips, boxes, wires, keyboards, speakers, disks, memory cards, USB flash drives (also called jump drives), cables, plugs, printers, mice, monitors, routers, and so on. If you can physically touch it and it can be considered part of a computer system, then it is computer hardware.

> **KEY CONCEPT**
>
> A computer system consists of hardware and software that work in concert to help us solve problems.

The hardware components of a computer are essentially useless without instructions to tell them what to do. A *program* is a series of instructions that the hardware executes one after another. *Software* consists of programs and the data those programs use. Software is the intangible counterpart to the physical hardware components. Together they form a tool that we can use to help solve problems.

The key hardware components in a computer system are

- central processing unit (CPU)
- input/output (I/O) devices
- main memory
- secondary memory devices

Each of these hardware components is described in detail in the next section. For now, let's simply examine their basic roles. The *central processing unit* (CPU) is the device that executes the individual commands of a program. *Input/output (I/O) devices*, such as the keyboard, mouse, and monitor, allow a human being to interact with the computer.

Programs and data are held in storage devices called memory, which fall into two categories: main memory and secondary memory. *Main memory* is the storage device that holds the software while it is being processed by the CPU. *Secondary memory* devices store software in a relatively permanent manner. The most important secondary memory device of a typical computer system is the hard disk that resides inside the main computer box. A USB flash drive is also an important secondary memory device. A typical USB flash drive cannot store nearly as much information as a hard disk. USB flash drives have the advantage of portability; they can be removed temporarily or moved from computer to computer as needed. Another portable secondary memory device is the compact disc (CD).

Figure 1.1 shows how information moves among the basic hardware components of a computer. Suppose you have an executable program you wish to run.

FIGURE 1.1   A simplified view of a computer system

The program is stored on some secondary memory device, such as a hard disk. When you instruct the computer to execute your program, a copy of the program is brought in from secondary memory and stored in main memory. The CPU reads the individual program instructions from main memory. The CPU then executes the instructions one at a time until the program ends. The data that the instructions use, such as two numbers that will be added together, also are stored in main memory. They are either brought in from secondary memory or read from an input device such as the keyboard. During execution, the program may display information to an output device such as a monitor.

> **KEY CONCEPT**
> The CPU reads the program instructions from main memory, executing them one at a time until the program ends.

The process of executing a program is fundamental to the operation of a computer. All computer systems basically work in the same way.

Software Categories

Software can be classified into many categories using various criteria. At this point we will simply differentiate between system programs and application programs.

The *operating system* is the core software of a computer. It performs two important functions. First, it provides a *user interface* that allows the user to interact with the machine. Second, the operating system manages computer resources such as the CPU and main memory. It determines when programs are allowed to run, where they are loaded into memory, and how hardware devices communicate. It is the operating system's job to make the computer easy to use and to ensure that it runs efficiently.

Several popular operating systems are in use today. The Windows operating system was developed for personal computers by Microsoft, which has captured an operating system market share of almost 90%. Various versions of the Unix operating system are also quite

> **KEY CONCEPT**
> The operating system provides a user interface and manages computer resources.

popular, especially in larger computer systems. A version of Unix called Linux was developed as an open source project, which means that many people contributed to its development and its code is freely available. Because of that, Linux has become a particular favorite among some users. Mac OS X is an operating system used for computing systems developed by Apple Computers.

An *application* is a generic term for just about any software other than the operating system. Word processors, missile control systems, database managers, Web browsers, and games all can be considered application programs. Each application program has its own user interface that allows the user to interact with that particular program.

The user interface for most modern operating systems and applications is a *graphical user interface* (GUI, pronounced "gooey"), which, as the name implies, make use of graphical screen elements. Among many others, these elements include

- *windows,* which are used to separate the screen into distinct work areas
- *icons,* which are small images that represent computer resources, such as a file
- *menus, checkboxes, and radio buttons,* which provide the user with selectable options
- *sliders,* which allow the user to select from a range of values
- *buttons,* which can be "pushed" with a mouse click to indicate a user selection

The mouse is the primary input device used with GUIs; thus, GUIs are sometimes called *point-and-click interfaces.* The screen shot in Figure 1.2 shows an example of a GUI.

> **KEY CONCEPT**
> As far as the user is concerned, the interface is the program.

The interface to an application or operating system is an important part of the software because it is the only part of the program with which the user interacts directly. To the user, the interface *is* the program. Throughout this book we discuss the design and implementation of graphical user interfaces.

The focus of this book is the development of high-quality application programs. We explore how to design and write software that will perform calculations, make decisions, and present results textually or graphically. We use the Java programming language throughout the text to demonstrate various computing concepts.

Digital Computers

Two fundamental techniques are used to store and manage information: analog and digital. *Analog* information is continuous, in direct proportion to the source of the information. For example, an alcohol thermometer is an analog device

FIGURE 1.2   An example of a graphical user interface (GUI)

for measuring temperature. The alcohol rises in a tube in direct proportion to the temperature outside the tube. Another example of analog information is an electronic signal used to represent the vibrations of a sound wave. The signal's voltage varies in direct proportion to the original sound wave. A stereo amplifier sends this kind of electronic signal to its speakers, which vibrate to reproduce the sound. We use the term analog because the signal is directly analogous to the information it represents. Figure 1.3 graphically depicts a sound wave captured by a microphone and represented as an electronic signal.

Digital technology breaks information into discrete pieces and represents those pieces as numbers. The music on a compact disc is stored digitally, as a series of numbers. Each number represents the voltage level of one specific instance of the recording. Many of these measurements are taken in a short period of time, perhaps 44,000 measurements every second. The number of measurements per second is called the *sampling rate*. If samples are taken often enough, the discrete voltage measurements

KEY CONCEPT

Digital computers store information by breaking it into pieces and representing each piece as a number.

Sound wave   Analog signal of the sound wave

FIGURE 1.3   A sound wave and an electronic analog signal
that represents the wave

can be used to generate a continuous analog signal that is "close enough" to the
original. In most cases, the goal is to create a reproduction of the original signal
that is good enough to satisfy the human senses.

Figure 1.4 shows the sampling of an analog signal. When analog information
is converted to a digital format by breaking it into pieces, we say it has been
digitized. Because the changes that occur in a signal between samples are lost, the
sampling rate must be sufficiently fast.

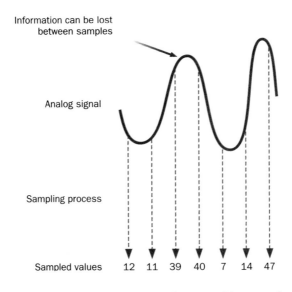

Information can be lost
between samples

Analog signal

Sampling process

Sampled values   12   11   39   40   7   14   47

FIGURE 1.4   Digitizing an analog signal by sampling

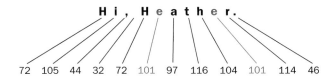

FIGURE 1.5   Text is stored by mapping each character to a number

Sampling is only one way to digitize information. For example, a sentence of text is stored on a computer as a series of numbers, where each number represents a single character in the sentence. Every letter, digit, and punctuation symbol has been assigned a number. Even the space character is assigned a number. Consider the following sentence:

Hi, Heather.

The characters of the sentence are represented as a series of 12 numbers, as shown in Figure 1.5. When a character is repeated, such as the uppercase 'H', the same representation number is used. Note that the uppercase version of a letter is stored as a different number from the lowercase version, such as the 'H' and 'h' in the word Heather. They are considered separate and distinct characters.

Modern electronic computers are digital. Every kind of information, including text, images, numbers, audio, video, and even program instructions is broken into pieces. Each piece is represented as a number. The information is stored by storing those numbers.

Binary Numbers

A digital computer stores information as numbers, but those numbers are not stored as *decimal* values. All information in a computer is stored and managed as *binary* values. Unlike the decimal system, which has 10 digits (0 through 9), the binary number system has only two digits (0 and 1). A single binary digit is called a *bit*.

All number systems work according to the same rules. The *base value* of a number system dictates how many digits we have to work with and indicates the place value of each digit in a number. The decimal number system is base 10, whereas the binary number system is base 2. Appendix B contains a detailed discussion of number systems.

Modern computers use binary numbers because the devices that store and move information are less expensive and more reliable if they have to represent only one of two possible values. Other than this characteristic, there is nothing special about the binary number

> **KEY CONCEPT**
>
> Binary is used to store and move information in a computer because the devices that store and manipulate binary data are inexpensive and reliable.

system. Computers have been created that use other number systems to store and move information, but they aren't as convenient.

Some computer memory devices, such as hard drives, are magnetic in nature. Magnetic material can be polarized easily to one extreme or the other, but intermediate levels are difficult to distinguish. Therefore, magnetic devices can be used to represent binary values quite effectively—a magnetized area represents a binary 1 and a demagnetized area represents a binary 0. Other computer memory devices are made up of tiny electrical circuits. These devices are easier to create and are less likely to fail if they have to switch between only two states. We're better off reproducing millions of these simple devices than creating fewer, more complicated ones.

Binary values and digital electronic signals go hand in hand. They improve our ability to transmit information reliably along a wire. As we've seen, an analog signal has continuously varying voltage with infinitely many states, but a digital signal is *discrete*, which means the voltage changes dramatically between one extreme (such as +5 volts) and the other (such as –5 volts). At any point, the voltage of a digital signal is considered to be either "high," which represents a binary 1, or "low," which represents a binary 0. Figure 1.6 compares these two types of signals.

As a signal moves down a wire, it gets weaker and degrades due to environmental conditions. That is, the voltage levels of the original signal change slightly. The trouble with an analog signal is that as it fluctuates, it loses its original information. Since the information is directly analogous to the signal, any change in the signal changes the information. The changes in an analog signal cannot be recovered because the degraded signal is just as valid as the original. A digital signal degrades just as an analog signal does, but because the digital signal is originally at one of two extremes, it can be reinforced before any information is lost. The voltage may change slightly from its original value, but it still can be interpreted correctly as either high or low.

The number of bits we use in any given situation determines the number of unique items we can represent. A single bit has two possible values, 0 and 1, and

Analog signal   Digital signal

FIGURE 1.6   An analog signal vs. a digital signal

therefore can represent two possible items or situations. If we want to represent the state of a light bulb (off or on), one bit will suffice, because we can interpret 0 as the light bulb being off and 1 as the light bulb being on. If we want to represent more than two things, we need more than one bit.

Two bits, taken together, can represent four possible items because there are exactly four permutations of two bits: 00, 01, 10, and 11. Suppose we want to represent the gear that a car is in (park, drive, reverse, or neutral). We would need only two bits, and could set up a mapping between the bit permutations and the gears. For instance, we could say that 00 represents park, 01 represents drive, 10 represents reverse, and 11 represents neutral. In this case, it wouldn't matter if we switched that mapping around, though in some cases the relationships between the bit permutations and what they represent are important.

Three bits can represent eight unique items, because there are eight permutations of three bits. Similarly, four bits can represent 16 items, five bits can represent 32 items, and so on. Figure 1.7 shows the relationship between the number of bits used and the number of items they can represent. In general, N bits can represent 2^N unique items. For every bit added, the number of items that can be represented doubles.

> **KEY CONCEPT**
>
> There are exactly 2^N permutations of N bits. Therefore, N bits can represent up to 2^N unique items.

1 bit 2 items	2 bits 4 items	3 bits 8 items	4 bits 16 items	5 bits 32 items	
0	00	000	0000	00000	10000
1	01	001	0001	00001	10001
	10	010	0010	00010	10010
	11	011	0011	00011	10011
		100	0100	00100	10100
		101	0101	00101	10101
		110	0110	00110	10110
		111	0111	00111	10111
			1000	01000	11000
			1001	01001	11001
			1010	01010	11010
			1011	01011	11011
			1100	01100	11100
			1101	01101	11101
			1110	01110	11110
			1111	01111	11111

FIGURE 1.7 The number of bits used determines the number of items that can be represented

We've seen how a sentence of text is stored on a computer by mapping characters to numeric values. Those numeric values are stored as binary numbers. Suppose we want to represent character strings in a language that contains 256 characters and symbols. We would need to use eight bits to store each character because there are 256 unique permutations of eight bits (2^8 equals 256). Each bit permutation, or binary value, is mapped to a specific character.

How many bits would be needed to represent 195 countries of the world? Seven wouldn't be enough, because 2^7 equals 128. Eight bits would be enough, but some of the 256 permutations would not be mapped to a country.

Ultimately, representing information on a computer boils down to the number of items there are to represent and determining the way those items are mapped to binary values.

---

myprogramminglab

SELF-REVIEW QUESTIONS *(see answers in Appendix N)*

SR 1.1   What is hardware? What is software?

SR 1.2   What are the two primary functions of an operating system?

SR 1.3   The music on a CD is created using a sampling rate of 44,000 measurements per second. Each measurement is stored as a number that represents a specific voltage level. How many such numbers are used to store a three-minute long song? How many such numbers does it take to represent one hour of music?

SR 1.4   What happens to information when it is stored digitally?

SR 1.5   How many unique items can be represented with the following?

a. 2 bits
b. 4 bits
c. 5 bits
d. 7 bits

SR 1.6   Suppose you want to represent each of the 50 states of the United States using a unique permutation of bits. How many bits would be needed to store each state representation? Why?

1.2 Hardware Components

Let's examine the hardware components of a computer system in more detail. Consider the computer described in Figure 1.8. What does it all mean? Is the system capable of running the software you want it to? How does it compare with other systems? These terms are explained throughout this section.

- 3.07 GHz Intel Core i7 processor

- 4 GB RAM

- 750 GB Hard Drive

- 16x Blu-ray / HD DVD-ROM & 16X DVD±R DVD Burner

- 17" Flat Screen Video Display with 1280 x 1024 resolution

- Network Card

FIGURE 1.8   The hardware specification of a particular computer

Computer Architecture

The architecture of a house defines its structure. Similarly, we use the term *computer architecture* to describe how the hardware components of a computer are put together. Figure 1.9 illustrates the basic architecture of a generic computer system. Information travels between components across a group of wires called a *bus*.

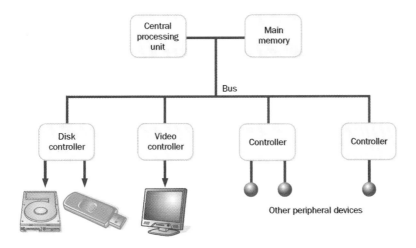

FIGURE 1.9   Basic computer architecture

The CPU and the main memory make up the core of a computer. As we mentioned earlier, main memory stores programs and data that are in active use, and the CPU methodically executes program instructions one at a time.

Suppose we have a program that computes the average of a list of numbers. The program and the numbers must reside in main memory while the program runs. The CPU reads one program instruction from main memory and executes it. If an instruction needs data, such as a number in the list, to perform its task, the CPU reads that information as well. This process repeats until the program ends. The average, when computed, is stored in main memory to await further processing or long-term storage in secondary memory.

Almost all devices in a computer system other than the CPU and main memory are called *peripherals*; they operate at the periphery, or outer edges, of the system (although they may be in the same box). Users don't interact directly with the CPU or main memory. Although they form the essence of the machine, the CPU and main memory would not be useful without peripheral devices.

Controllers are devices that coordinate the activities of specific peripherals. Every device has its own particular way of formatting and communicating data, and part of the controller's role is to handle these idiosyncrasies and isolate them from the rest of the computer hardware. Furthermore, the controller often handles much of the actual transmission of information, allowing the CPU to focus on other activities.

Input/output (I/O) devices and secondary memory devices are considered peripherals. Another category of peripherals consist of *data transfer devices*, which allow information to be sent and received between computers. The computer specified in Figure 1.8 includes a network card, also called a wireless network interface controller (WNIC), which connects to a radio-based computer network.

In some ways, secondary memory devices and data transfer devices can be thought of as I/O devices because they represent a source of information (input) and a place to send information (output). For our discussion, however, we define I/O devices as those devices that allow the user to interact with the computer.

Input/Output Devices

Let's examine some I/O devices in more detail. The most common input devices are the keyboard and the mouse. Others include

- *bar code readers*, such as the ones used at a retail store checkout
- *microphones*, used by voice recognition systems that interpret voice commands
- *virtual reality devices*, such as handheld devices that interpret the movement of the user's hand

- *scanners*, which convert text, photographs, and graphics into machine-readable form

Monitors and printers are the most common output devices. Others include

- *plotters*, which move pens across large sheets of paper (or vice versa)
- *speakers*, for audio output
- *goggles*, for virtual reality display

Some devices can provide both input and output capabilities. A *touch screen* system can detect the user touching the screen at a particular place. Software can then use the screen to display text and graphics in response to the user's touch. Touch screens have become commonplace for handheld devices.

The computer described in Figure 1.8 includes a monitor with a 17-inch diagonal display area. It is a flat screen, which makes use of liquid crystal display (LCD) technology, unlike the older cathode ray tube (CRT) monitors that required substantial voltage and generally were not portable. A picture is represented in a computer by breaking it up into separate picture elements, or *pixels*. The monitor might display a grid of 1280 by 1024 pixels. Representing and managing graphical data is discussed in more detail in Chapter 2.

Main Memory and Secondary Memory

Main memory is made up of a series of small, consecutive *memory locations*, as shown in Figure 1.10. Associated with each memory location is a unique number called an *address*.

> **KEY CONCEPT**
> An address is a unique number associated with a memory location.

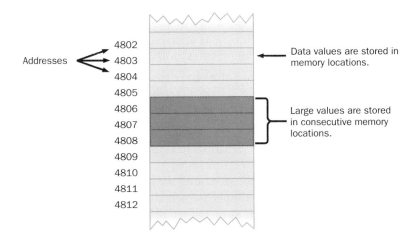

FIGURE 1.10   Memory locations

Unit	Symbol	Number of Bytes
byte		$2^0 = 1$
kilobyte	KB	$2^{10} = 1024$
megabyte	MB	$2^{20} = 1,048,576$
gigabyte	GB	$2^{30} = 1,073,741,824$
terabyte	TB	$2^{40} = 1,099,511,627,776$
petabyte	PB	$2^{50} = 1,125,899,906,842,624$

FIGURE 1.11   Units of binary storage

When data is stored in a memory location, it overwrites and destroys any information that was previously stored at that location. However, the process of reading data from a memory location does not affect it.

On many computers, each memory location consists of eight bits, or one *byte*, of information. If we need to store a value that cannot be represented in a single byte, such as a large number, then multiple, consecutive bytes are used to store the data.

The *storage capacity* of a device such as main memory is the total number of bytes it can hold. Devices can store thousands or millions of bytes, so you should become familiar with larger units of measure. Because computer memory is based on the binary number system, all units of storage are powers of two. A *kilobyte* (KB) is 1024, or 2^{10}, bytes. Some larger units of storage are a *megabyte* (MB), a *gigabyte* (GB), a *terabyte* (TB), and a *petabyte* (PB) as listed in Figure 1.11. It's usually easier to think about these capacities by rounding them off. For example, most computer users think of a kilobyte as approximately one thousand bytes, a megabyte as approximately one million bytes, and so forth.

KEY CONCEPT

Main memory is volatile, meaning the stored information is maintained only as long as electric power is supplied.

Many personal computers have four gigabytes of main memory, or RAM, such as the system described in Figure 1.8 (we discuss RAM in more detail later in this chapter). A large main memory allows large programs or multiple programs to run efficiently, because they don't have to retrieve information from secondary memory as often.

Main memory is usually *volatile*, meaning that the information stored in it will be lost if its electric power supply is turned off. When you are working on a computer, you should often save your work onto a secondary memory device such as a USB flash drive in case the power goes out. Secondary memory devices are usually *nonvolatile*; the information is retained even if the power supply is turned off.

The cache is used by the central processing unit (CPU) to reduce the average access time to instructions and data. The cache is a small, fast memory that stores the contents of the most frequently used main memory locations. Contemporary CPUs include an instruction cache to speed up the fetching of executable instructions and a data cache to speed up the fetching and storing of data.

The most common secondary storage devices are *hard disks* and USB *flash drives*. A typical USB flash drive stores between 1 GB and 256 GB of information. The storage capacities of hard drives vary, but on personal computers, capacities typically range between 120 GB and 500 GB, such as in the system described in Figure 1.8. Some hard disks can store 2 TB of data.

A USB flash drive consists of a small printed circuit board carrying the circuit elements and a USB connector, insulated electrically and protected inside a plastic, metal, or rubberized case, which can be carried in a pocket or on a key chain, for example.

A disk is a magnetic medium on which bits are represented as magnetized particles. A read/write head passes over the spinning disk, reading or writing information as appropriate. A hard disk drive might actually contain several disks in a vertical column with several read/write heads, such as the one shown in Figure 1.12.

To get an intuitive feel for how much information these devices can store, consider that all the information in this book, including pictures and formatting, requires about 7 MB of storage.

Magnetic tapes also have been used as secondary storage but are considerably slower than hard disk and USB flash drives because of the way information is accessed. A hard disk is a *direct access device* since the read/write head can move, in general, directly to the information needed. A USB flash drive is also a direct access

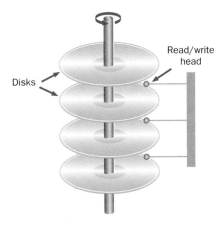

FIGURE 1.12   A hard disk drive with multiple disks and read/write heads

device, but nothing moves mechanically. The terms direct access and *random access* are often used interchangeably. However, information on a tape can be accessed only after first getting past the intervening data. A tape must be rewound or fast-forwarded to get to the appropriate position. A tape is therefore considered a *sequential access device*. For these reasons, tapes largely have fallen out of use as a computing storage device, just as audio cassettes have been supplanted by compact discs.

Two other terms are used to describe memory devices: *random access memory* (RAM) and *read-only memory* (ROM). It's important to understand these terms because they are used often and their names can be misleading. The terms RAM and main memory are basically interchangeable, describing the memory where active programs and data are stored. ROM can refer to chips on the computer motherboard or to portable storage such as a compact disc. ROM chips typically store software called BIOS (basic input/output system) that provide the preliminary instructions needed when the computer is turned on initially. After information is stored on ROM, generally it is not altered (as the term *read-only* implies) during typical computer use. Both RAM and ROM are direct (or random) access devices.

KEY CONCEPT

The surface of a CD has both smooth areas and small pits. A pit represents a binary 1 and a smooth area represents a binary 0.

A *CD-ROM* is a portable secondary memory device. CD stands for compact disc. It is called ROM because information is stored permanently when the CD is created and cannot be changed. Like its musical CD counterpart, a CD-ROM stores information in binary format. When the CD is initially created, a microscopic pit is pressed into the disc to represent a binary 1, and the disc is left smooth to represent a binary 0. The bits are read by shining a low-intensity laser beam onto the spinning disc. The laser beam reflects strongly from a smooth area on the disc but weakly from a pitted area. A sensor receiving the reflection determines whether each bit is a 1 or a 0 accordingly. A typical CD-ROM's storage capacity ranges between 650 and 900 MB.

Variations on basic CD technology emerged quickly. Most personal computers are equipped with a *CD-Recordable* (CD-R) drive. A CD-R can be used to create a CD for music or for general computer storage. Once created, you can use a CD-R disc in a standard CD player, but you can't change the information on a CD-R disc once it has been "burned." Music CDs that you buy are pressed from a mold, whereas CD-Rs are burned with a laser.

A *CD-Rewritable* (CD-RW) disc can be erased and reused. It can be reused because the pits and flat surfaces of a normal CD are simulated on a CD-RW by coating the surface of the disc with a material that, when heated to one temperature becomes amorphous (and therefore nonreflective) and when heated to a different temperature becomes crystalline (and therefore reflective). The CD-RW media doesn't work in all players, but CD-RW drives can create both CD-R and CD-RW discs.

KEY CONCEPT

A rewritable CD simulates the pits and smooth areas of a regular CD by using a coating that can be made amorphous or crystalline as needed.

CDs were initially a popular format for music; they later evolved to be used as a general computer storage device. Similarly, the *DVD* format was originally created for video and is now making headway as a general format for computer data. DVD once stood for digital video disc or digital versatile disc, but now the acronym generally stands on its own. A DVD has a tighter format (more bits per square inch) than a CD and can therefore store much more information. DVD-ROMs eventually may replace CD-ROMs completely because there is a compatible migration path, meaning that a DVD drive can read a CD-ROM. Similar to CD-R and CD-RW, there are DVD-R and DVD-RW discs. The drive listed in Figure 1.8 allows the user to read and write CD-RW discs and read DVD-ROMs, including the ability to play music CDs and watch DVD videos.

The speed of a CD or DVD is expressed in multiples of x, which represents a data transfer speed of 153,600 bytes of data per second for a CD; nine times that speed, or about 1.5 megabytes of data per second, for a DVD; and three times the speed of a DVD, or 4.5 megabytes of data per second, for a Blu-ray disc. The drive described in Figure 1.8 has a maximum data access speed of $16x$, or about 72 MB of data per second. A dual-layer Blu-ray disc has a storage capacity of 50 GB.

The capacity of storage devices changes continually as technology improves. A general rule in the computer industry suggests that storage capacity approximately doubles every 18 months. However, this progress eventually will slow down as capacities approach absolute physical limits.

The Central Processing Unit

The central processing unit (CPU) interacts with main memory to perform all fundamental processing in a computer. The CPU interprets and executes instructions, one after another, in a continuous cycle. It is made up of three important components, as shown in Figure 1.13. The *control unit* coordinates the processing steps, the *registers* provide a small amount of storage space in the CPU itself, and the *arithmetic/logic unit* performs calculations and makes decisions. The registers are the smallest, fastest cache in the system.

The control unit coordinates the transfer of data and instructions between main memory and the registers in the CPU. It also coordinates the execution of the circuitry in the arithmetic/logic unit to perform operations on data stored in particular registers.

In most CPUs, some registers are reserved for special purposes. For example, the *instruction register* holds the current instruction being executed. The *program counter* is a register that holds the address of the next instruction to be executed. In addition to these and other special-purpose registers, the CPU also

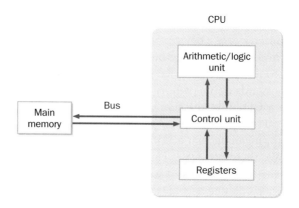

FIGURE 1.13   CPU components and main memory

contains a set of general-purpose registers that are used for temporary storage of values as needed.

The concept of storing both program instructions and data together in main memory is the underlying principle of the *von Neumann architecture* of computer design, named after John von Neumann, a Hungarian-American mathematician who first advanced this programming concept in 1945. These computers continually follow the *fetch-decode-execute* cycle depicted in Figure 1.14. An instruction is fetched from main memory at the address stored in the program counter and is

> **KEY CONCEPT**
> The fetch-decode-execute cycle forms the foundation of computer processing.

put into the instruction register. The program counter is incremented at this point to prepare for the next cycle. Then the instruction is decoded electronically to determine which operation to carry out. Finally, the control unit activates the correct circuitry to carry out the instruction, which may load a data value into a register or add two values together, for example.

The CPU is constructed on a chip called a *microprocessor*, a device that is part of the main circuit board of the computer. This board also contains ROM chips

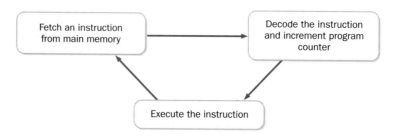

FIGURE 1.14   The continuous fetch-decode-execute cycle

and communication sockets to which device controllers, such as the controller that manages the video display, can be connected.

Another crucial component of the main circuit board is the *system clock*. The clock generates an electronic pulse at regular intervals, which synchronizes the events of the CPU. The rate at which the pulses occur is called the *clock speed*, and it varies depending on the processor. The computer described in Figure 1.8 includes an Intel Core i7 processor that runs at a clock speed of 3.07 gigahertz (GHz), or approximately 3.1 billion pulses per second. The speed of the system clock provides a rough measure of how fast the CPU executes instructions. Similar to storage capacities, the speed of processors is constantly increasing with advances in technology.

SELF-REVIEW QUESTIONS *(see answers in Appendix N)*   myprogramming**lab**

SR 1.7   How many bytes are in each of the following?

  a. 3 KB
  b. 2 MB
  c. 4 GB

SR 1.8   How many bits are there in each of the following?

  a. 8 bytes
  b. 2 KB
  c. 4 MB

SR 1.9   The music on a CD is created using a sampling rate of 44,000 measurements per second. Each measurement is stored as a number that represents a specific voltage level. Suppose each of these numbers requires two bytes of storage space. How many MB does it take to represent one hour of music?

SR 1.10   What are the two primary hardware components in a computer? How do they interact?

SR 1.11   What is a memory address?

SR 1.12   What does volatile mean? Which memory devices are volatile and which are nonvolatile?

SR 1.13   Select the word from the following list that best matches each of the following phrases:

  controller, CPU, main, network card, peripheral, RAM, register, ROM, secondary

  a. Almost all devices in a computer system, other than the CPU and the main memory, are categorized as this.

b. A device that coordinates the activities of a peripheral device.

c. Allows information to be sent and received.

d. This type of memory is usually volatile.

e. This type of memory is usually nonvolatile.

f. This term basically is interchangeable with the term "main memory."

g. Where the fundamental processing of a computer takes place.

1.3 Networks

A single computer can accomplish a great deal, but connecting several computers together into networks can dramatically increase productivity and facilitate the sharing of information. A *network* consists of two or more computers connected together so they can exchange information. Using networks has become the normal mode of commercial computer operation. New technologies are emerging every day to capitalize on the connected environments of modern computer systems.

> **KEY CONCEPT**
>
> A network consists of two or more computers connected together so that they can exchange information.

Figure 1.15 shows a simple computer network. One of the devices on the network is a printer, which allows any computer connected to the network to print a document on that printer. One of the computers on the network is designated as a *file server*, which is dedicated to storing programs and data that are needed by many network users. A file server usually has a large amount of secondary memory. When a network has a file server, each individual computer doesn't need its own copy of a program.

Network Connections

If two computers are directly connected, they can communicate in basically the same way that information moves across wires inside a single machine. When

FIGURE 1.15   A simple computer network

FIGURE 1.16   Point-to-point connections

connecting two geographically close computers, this solution works well and is called a *point-to-point connection*. However, consider the task of connecting many computers together across large distances. If point-to-point connections are used, every computer is directly connected by a wire to every other computer in the network. A separate wire for each connection is not a workable solution because every time a new computer is added to the network, a new communication line will have to be installed for each computer already in the network. Furthermore, a single computer can handle only a small number of direct connections.

Figure 1.16 shows multiple point-to-point connections. Consider the number of communication lines that would be needed if two or three additional computers were added to the network.

Compare the diagrams in Figure 1.15 and Figure 1.16. All of the computers shown in Figure 1.15 share a single communication line. Each computer on the network has its own *network address*, which uniquely identifies it. These addresses are similar in concept to the addresses in main memory except that they identify individual computers on a network instead of individual memory locations inside a single computer. A message is sent across the line from one computer to another by specifying the network address of the computer for which it is intended.

Sharing a communication line is cost effective and makes adding new computers to the network relatively easy. However, a shared line introduces delays. The computers on the network cannot use the communication line at the same time. They have to take turns sending information, which means they have to wait when the line is busy.

> **KEY CONCEPT**
> Sharing a communication line creates delays, but it is cost effective and simplifies adding new computers to the network.

One technique to improve network delays is to divide large messages into segments, called *packets,* and then send the individual packets across the network intermixed with pieces of other messages sent by other users. The packets are collected at the destination and reassembled into the original message. This situation is similar to a group of people using a conveyor belt to move a set of boxes from one place to another. If only one person were allowed to use the conveyor belt at a time, and that person had a large number of boxes to move, the others would be waiting a long time before they could use it. By taking turns, each person can put one box on at a time, and they all can get their work done. It's not as fast as having a conveyor belt of your own, but it's not as slow as having to wait until everyone else is finished.

Local-Area Networks and Wide-Area Networks

A *local-area network* (LAN) is designed to span short distances and connect a relatively small number of computers. Usually a LAN connects the machines in only one building or in a single room. LANs are convenient to install and manage and are highly reliable. As computers became increasingly small and versatile, LANs provided an inexpensive way to share information throughout an organization. However, having a LAN is like having a telephone system that allows you to call only the people in your own town. We need to be able to share information across longer distances.

> **KEY CONCEPT**
>
> A local-area network (LAN) is an effective way to share information and resources throughout an organization.

A *wide-area network* (WAN) connects two or more LANs, often across long distances. Usually one computer on each LAN is dedicated to handling the communication across a WAN. This technique relieves the other computers in a LAN from having to perform the details of long-distance communication. Figure 1.17 shows several LANs connected into a WAN. The LANs connected by a WAN are often owned by different companies or organizations and might even be located in different countries.

LAN

One computer in a LAN

Long-distance connection

FIGURE 1.17   LANs connected into a WAN

The impact of networks on computer systems has been dramatic. Computing resources can now be shared among many users, and computer-based communication across the entire world is common. In fact, the use of networks is now so pervasive that some computers require network resources in order to operate.

The Internet

Throughout the 1970s, an agency in the Department of Defense known as the Advanced Research Projects Agency (ARPA) funded several projects to explore network technology. One result of these efforts was the ARPANET, a WAN that eventually became known as the Internet. The *Internet* is a network of networks. The term Internet comes from the WAN concept of *internetworking*—connecting many smaller networks together.

From the late 1980s through the present day, the Internet has grown incredibly. In 1983, there were fewer than 600 computers connected to the Internet. At the present time, the Internet serves billions of users worldwide. As more and more computers connect to the Internet, the task of keeping up with the larger number of users and heavier traffic has been difficult. New technologies have replaced the ARPANET several times since the initial development, each time providing more capacity and faster processing.

> **KEY CONCEPT**
> The Internet is a wide-area network (WAN) that spans the globe.

A *protocol* is a set of rules that governs how two things communicate. The software that controls the movement of messages across the Internet must conform to a set of protocols called TCP/IP (pronounced by spelling out the letters, T-C-P-I-P). TCP stands for *Transmission Control Protocol,* and IP stands for *Internet Protocol.* The IP software defines how information is formatted and transferred from the source to the destination. The TCP software handles problems such as pieces of information arriving out of their original order or information getting lost, which can happen if too much information converges at one location at the same time.

Every computer connected to the Internet has an *IP address* that uniquely identifies it among all other computers on the Internet. An example of an IP address is 204.192.116.2. Fortunately, the users of the Internet rarely have to deal with IP addresses. The Internet allows each computer to be given a name. Like IP addresses, the names must be unique. The Internet name of a computer is often referred to as its *Internet address.* An example of Internet address is `hector.vt.edu`.

> **KEY CONCEPT**
> Every computer connected to the Internet has an IP address that uniquely identifies it.

The first part of an Internet address is the local name of a specific computer. The rest of the address is the *domain name,* which indicates the organization to which the computer belongs. For example, `vt.edu` is the domain name for the network of computers at Virginia Tech, and `hector` is the name of a particular computer on that campus. Because the domain names are unique, many organizations can have a computer named hector without confusion. Individual departments might be assigned *subdomains* that are added to the basic domain name to uniquely distinguish their set of computers within the larger organization. For example, the cs.vt.edu subdomain is devoted to the Department of Computer Science at Virginia Tech.

The last part of each domain name, called a *top-level domain* (TLD), usually indicates the type of organization to which the computer belongs. The TLD edu typically indicates an educational institution. The TLD com often refers to a commercial business. Another common TLD is org, usually used by nonprofit organizations. During an international meeting held in Paris in 2008, a process was started for introducing generic top-level domains (gTLD). The new rules could result in hundreds of new gTLDs. Many computers, especially those outside of the United States, use a country-code top-level domain (ccTLD) that denotes the country of origin, such as uk for the United Kingdom or au for Australia.

When an Internet address is referenced, it gets translated to its corresponding IP address, which is used from that point on. The software that does this translation is called the *Domain Name System* (DNS). Each organization connected to the Internet operates a *domain server* that maintains a list of all computers at that organization and their IP addresses. It works somewhat like telephone directory assistance in that you provide the name, and the domain server gives back a number. If the local domain server does not have the IP address for the name, it contacts another domain server that does.

The Internet has revolutionized computer processing. Initially, the primary use of interconnected computers was to send electronic mail, but Internet capabilities continue to improve. One of the most significant uses of the Internet is the World Wide Web.

The World Wide Web

The Internet gives us the capability to exchange information. The *World Wide Web* (also known as WWW or simply the Web) makes the exchange of information easy for humans. Web software provides a common user interface through which many different types of information can be accessed with the click of a mouse.

> **KEY CONCEPT**
> The World Wide Web is software that makes sharing information across a network easy for humans.

The Web is based on the concepts of hypertext and hypermedia. The term *hypertext* was coined in 1965 by Ted Nelson. It describes a way to organize information so that the flow of ideas was not constrained to a linear progression. Paul Otlet (1868–1944), considered by some to be the father of information science, envisioned that concept as a way to manage large amounts of information. The underlying idea is that documents can be linked at various points according to natural relationships so that the reader can jump from one document to another, following the appropriate path for that reader's needs. When other media components are incorporated, such as graphics, sound, animations, and video, the resulting organization is called *hypermedia*.

The terms Internet and World Wide Web are sometimes used interchangeably, but there are important differences between the two. The Internet makes it possible to communicate via computers around the world. The Web makes that communication a straightforward and enjoyable activity. The Web is essentially a distributed information service and is based on a set of software applications. It is not a network. Although it is used effectively with the Internet, it is not inherently bound to it. The Web can be used on a LAN that is not connected to any other network or even on a single machine to display HTML documents.

A *browser* is a software tool that loads and formats Web documents for viewing. *Mosaic,* the first graphical interface browser for the Web, was released in 1993. The designer of a Web document defines to other Web information that might be anywhere on the Internet. Some of the people who developed Mosaic went on to found the Netscape Communications Corporation and create the Netscape Navigator browser. Popular contemporary browsers include Internet Explorer, Mozilla Firefox, Apple Safari, Google Chrome, and Opera.

A computer dedicated to providing access to Web documents is called a *Web server*. Browsers load and interpret documents provided by a Web server. Many such documents are formatted using the *HyperText Markup Language* (HTML). The Java programming language has an intimate relationship with Web processing, because links to Java programs can be embedded in HTML documents and executed through Web browsers. We explore this relationship in more detail in Chapter 2.

Uniform Resource Locators

Information on the Web is found by identifying a *Uniform Resource Locator* (URL, pronounced by spelling out the letters U-R-L). A URL uniquely specifies documents and other information for a browser to obtain and display. The following is an example URL:

```
http://www.google.com
```

The Web site at this particular URL is the home of the well-known Google *search engine*, which enables you to search the Web for information using particular words or phrases.

A URL contains several pieces of information. The first piece is a protocol, which determines the way the browser transmits and

> **KEY CONCEPT**
> A URL uniquely specifies documents and other information found on the Web for a browser to obtain and display.

processes information. The second piece is the Internet address of the machine on which the document is stored. The third piece of information is the file name or resource of interest. If no file name is given, as is the case with the Google URL, the Web server usually provides a default page (such as index.html).

Let's look at another example URL:

```
http://www.whitehouse.gov/photos-and-video/photogallery/photo-day
```

In this URL, the protocol is http, which stands for *HyperText Transfer Protocol*. The machine referenced is www (a typical reference to a Web server), found at domain whitehouse.gov. Finally, photos-and-video/photogallery/photo-day represents a file (or a reference that generates a file) to be transferred to the browser for viewing. Many other forms for URLs exist, but this form is the most common.

myprogramming**lab**

SELF-REVIEW QUESTIONS *(see answers in Appendix N)*

SR 1.14 What is a file server?

SR 1.15 What is the total number of communication lines needed for a fully connected point-to-point network of five computers? Six computers?

SR 1.16 Describe a benefit of having computers on a network share a communication line. Describe a cost/drawback of sharing a communication line.

SR 1.17 What is the etymology of the word Internet?

SR 1.18 The TCP/IP set of protocols describes communication rules for software that uses the Internet. What does TCP stand for? What does IP stand for?

SR 1.19 Explain the parts of the following URLs:

a. duke.csc.villanova.edu/jss/examples.html
b. java.sun.com/products/index.html

1.4 The Java Programming Language

Let's now turn our attention to the software that makes a computer system useful. A program is written in a particular *programming language* that uses specific words and symbols to express the problem solution. A programming language defines a set of rules that determines exactly how a programmer can combine the words and symbols of the language into *programming statements,* which are the instructions that are carried out when the program is executed.

Since the inception of computers, many programming languages have been created. We use the Java language in this book to demonstrate various programming concepts and techniques. Although our main goal is to learn these underlying software development concepts, an important side effect will be to become proficient in the development of Java programs.

Java is a relatively new programming language as compared with many others. It was initiated in 1991 by James Gosling at Sun Microsystems as one of his many set-top box projects. The language initially was called Oak, then Green, and ultimately Java. Java was introduced to the public in 1995 and has gained tremendous popularity since. In 2010, Sun Microsystems was purchased by Oracle.

Java has undergone various changes since its creation. There are variations of the Java Platform, including the Standard Edition, which is the mainstream version of the language and the associated tools; the Enterprise Edition, which includes extra libraries to support large-scale system development; and the Micro Edition, which is specifically for developing software for portable devices such as cell phones. This book focuses on the Standard Edition.

Some parts of early Java technologies have been *deprecated*, which means they are considered old-fashioned and should not be used. When it is important, we point out deprecated elements and discuss their preferred alternatives.

One reason Java attracted some initial attention was because it was the first programming language to deliberately embrace the concept of writing programs (called applets) that can be executed using the Web. Since then, the techniques for creating a Web page that has dynamic, functional capabilities have expanded dramatically.

Java is an *object-oriented programming language*. Objects are the fundamental elements that make up a program. The principles of object-oriented software development are the cornerstone of this book. We explore object-oriented programming concepts later in this chapter and throughout the rest of the book.

> **KEY CONCEPT**
>
> This book focuses on the principles of object-oriented programming.

The Java language is accompanied by a library of extra software that we can use when developing programs. This software is referred to as the *Java API*, which stands for Application Programmer Interface, or simply the *standard class library*. The Java API provides the ability to create graphics, communicate over networks, and interact with databases, among many other features. The Java API is huge and quite versatile. We won't be able to cover all aspects of the library, though we will explore several of them.

Java is used in commercial environments all over the world. It is one of the fastest growing programming technologies of all time. So not only is it a good language in which to learn programming concepts, it is also a practical language that will serve you well in the future.

A Java Program

Let's look at a simple but complete Java program. The program in Listing 1.1 prints two sentences to the screen. This particular program prints a quote by Abraham Lincoln. The output is shown below the program listing.

LISTING 1.1

```
//********************************************************************
//  Lincoln.java        Author: Lewis/Loftus
//
//  Demonstrates the basic structure of a Java application.
//********************************************************************

public class Lincoln
{
   //-----------------------------------------------------------
   //  Prints a presidential quote.
   //-----------------------------------------------------------
   public static void main (String[] args)
   {
      System.out.println ("A quote by Abraham Lincoln:");

      System.out.println ("Whatever you are, be a good one.");
   }
}
```

OUTPUT

```
A quote by Abraham Lincoln:
Whatever you are, be a good one.
```

All Java applications have a similar basic structure. Despite its small size and simple purpose, this program contains several important features. Let's carefully dissect it and examine its pieces.

KEY CONCEPT

Comments do not affect a program's processing; instead, they serve to facilitate human comprehension.

The first few lines of the program are comments, which start with the // symbols and continue to the end of the line. Comments don't affect what the program does but are included to make the program easier to understand by humans. Programmers can and should include comments as needed throughout a program to clearly identify the purpose of the program and describe any special processing. Any written comments or documents, including a user's guide and technical references, are called *documentation*. Comments included in a program are called *inline documentation*.

The rest of the program is a *class definition*. This class is called Lincoln, though we could have named it just about anything we wished. The class definition runs from the first opening brace ({) to the final closing brace (}) on the last line of the program. All Java programs are defined using class definitions.

VideoNote

Overview of program elements.

Inside the class definition are some more comments describing the purpose of the `main` method, which is defined directly below the comments. A *method* is a group of programming statements that is given a name. In this case, the name of the method is `main` and it contains only two programming statements. Like a class definition, a method is also delimited by braces.

All Java applications have a `main` method, which is where processing begins. Each programming statement in the `main` method is executed, one at a time in order, until the end of the method is reached. Then the program ends, or *terminates*. The `main` method definition in a Java program is always preceded by the words `public`, `static`, and `void`, which we examine later in the text. The use of `String` and `args` does not come into play in this particular program. We describe these later also.

The two lines of code in the `main` method invoke another method called `println` (pronounced print line). We *invoke*, or *call*, a method when we want it to execute. The `println` method prints the specified characters to the screen. The characters to be printed are represented as a *character string*, enclosed in double quote characters ("). When the program is executed, it calls the `println` method to print the first statement, calls it again to print the second statement, and then, because that is the last line in the `main` method, the program terminates.

The code executed when the `println` method is invoked is not defined in this program. The `println` method is part of the `System.out` object, which is part of the Java standard class library. It's not technically part of the Java language, but is always available for use in any Java program. We explore the `println` method in more detail in Chapter 2.

Comments

Let's examine comments in more detail. Comments are the only language feature that allows programmers to compose and communicate their thoughts independent of the code. Comments should provide insight into the programmer's original intent. A program is often used for many years, and often many modifications are made to it over time. The original programmer often will not remember the details of a particular program when, at some point in the future, modifications are required. Furthermore, the original programmer is not always available to make the changes; thus, someone completely unfamiliar with the program will need to understand it. Good documentation is therefore essential.

As far as the Java programming language is concerned, the content of comments can be any text whatsoever. Comments are ignored by the computer; they do not affect how the program executes.

The comments in the `Lincoln` program represent one of two types of comments allowed in Java. The comments in `Lincoln` take the following form:

```
// This is a comment.
```

This type of comment begins with a double slash (//) and continues to the end of the line. You cannot have any characters between the two slashes. The computer ignores any text after the double slash to the end of the line. A comment can follow code on the same line to document that particular line, as in the following example:

```
System.out.println ("Monthly Report"); // always use this title
```

The second form a Java comment may have is the following:

```
/* This is another comment. */
```

This comment type does not use the end of a line to indicate the end of the comment. Anything between the initiating slash-asterisk (/*) and the terminating asterisk-slash (*/) is part of the comment, including the invisible *newline* character that represents the end of a line. Therefore, this type of comment can extend over multiple lines. No space can be between the slash and the asterisk.

If there is a second asterisk following the /* at the beginning of a comment, the content of the comment can be used to automatically generate external documentation about your program by using a tool called *javadoc*. More information about javadoc is given in Appendix I.

The two basic comment types can be used to create various documentation styles, such as:

```
// This is a comment on a single line.

//-----------------------------------------------------------
// Some comments such as those above methods or classes
// deserve to be blocked off to focus special attention
// on a particular aspect of your code. Note that each of
// these lines is technically a separate comment.
//-----------------------------------------------------------

/*
   This is one comment
   that spans several lines.
*/
```

Programmers often concentrate so much on writing code that they focus too little on documentation. You should develop good commenting practices and follow them habitually. Comments should be well written, often in complete sentences.

They should not belabor the obvious but should provide appropriate insight into the intent of the code. The following examples are *not* good comments:

```
System.out.println ("hello"); // prints hello
System.out.println ("test");  // change this later
```

The first comment paraphrases the obvious purpose of the line and does not add any value to the statement. It is better to have no comment than a useless one. The second comment is ambiguous. What should be changed later? When is later? Why should it be changed?

> **KEY CONCEPT**
> Inline documentation should provide insight into your code. It should not be ambiguous or belabor the obvious.

Identifiers and Reserved Words

The various words used when writing programs are called *identifiers*. The identifiers in the Lincoln program are class, Lincoln, public, static, void, main, String, args, System, out, and println. These fall into three categories:

- words that we make up when writing a program (Lincoln and args)
- words that another programmer chose (String, System, out, println, and main)
- words that are reserved for special purposes in the language (class, public, static, and void)

While writing the program, we simply chose to name the class Lincoln, but we could have used one of many other possibilities. For example, we could have called it Quote, or Abe, or GoodOne. The identifier args (which is short for arguments) is often used in the way we use it in Lincoln, but we could have used just about any other identifier in its place.

The identifiers String, System, out, and println were chosen by other programmers. These words are not part of the Java language. They are part of the Java standard library of predefined code, a set of classes and methods that someone has already written for us. The authors of that code chose the identifiers in that code—we're just making use of them.

Reserved words are identifiers that have a special meaning in a programming language and can only be used in predefined ways. A reserved word cannot be used for any other purpose, such as naming a class or method. In the Lincoln program, the reserved words used are class, public, static, and void. Throughout the book, we show Java reserved words in blue type. Figure 1.18 lists all of the Java reserved words in alphabetical order. The words marked with an asterisk have been reserved, but currently have no meaning in Java.

An identifier that we make up for use in a program can be composed of any combination of letters, digits, the underscore character (_), and the dollar sign ($), but it cannot begin with a digit. Identifiers may be of any length.

abstract	default	goto*	package	this
assert	do	if	private	throw
boolean	double	implements	protected	throws
break	else	import	public	transient
byte	enum	instanceof	return	true
case	extends	int	short	try
catch	false	interface	static	void
char	final	long	strictfp	volatile
class	finally	native	super	while
const*	float	new	switch	
continue	for	null	synchronized	

FIGURE 1.18   Java reserved words

Therefore, total, label7, nextStockItem, NUM_BOXES, and $amount are all valid identifiers, but 4th_word and coin#value are not valid.

Both uppercase and lowercase letters can be used in an identifier, and the difference is important. Java is *case sensitive,* which means that two identifier names that differ only in the case of their letters are considered to be different identifiers. Therefore, total, Total, ToTaL, and TOTAL are all different identifiers. As you can imagine, it is not a good idea to use multiple identifiers that differ only in their case, because they can be easily confused.

Identifier

An identifier is a letter followed by zero or more letters and digits. A Java Letter includes the 26 English alphabetic characters in both uppercase and lowercase, the $ and _ (underscore) characters, as well as alphabetic characters from other languages. A Java Digit includes the digits 0 through 9.

Examples:

```
total
MAX_HEIGHT
num1
Keyboard
System
```

Although the Java language doesn't require it, using a consistent case format for each kind of identifier makes your identifiers easier to understand. There are various Java conventions regarding identifiers that should be followed, though technically they don't have to be. For example, we use *title case* (uppercase for the first letter of each word) for class names. Throughout the text, we describe the preferred case style for each type of identifier when it is first encountered.

KEY CONCEPT

Java is case sensitive. The uppercase and lowercase versions of a letter are distinct.

While an identifier can be of any length, you should choose your names carefully. They should be descriptive but not verbose. You should avoid meaningless names such as a or x. An exception to this rule can be made if the short name is actually descriptive, such as using x and y to represent (x, y) coordinates on a two-dimensional grid. Likewise, you should not use unnecessarily long names, such as the identifier theCurrentItemBeingProcessed. The name currentItem would serve just as well. As you might imagine, the use of identifiers that are verbose is a much less prevalent problem than the use of names that are not descriptive.

You should always strive to make your programs as readable as possible. Therefore, you should always be careful when abbreviating words. You might think curStVal is a good name to represent the current stock value, but another person trying to understand the code may have trouble figuring out what you meant. It might not even be clear to you two months after writing it.

KEY CONCEPT

Identifier names should be descriptive and readable.

White Space

All Java programs use *white space* to separate the words and symbols used in a program. White space consists of blanks, tabs, and newline characters. The phrase "white space" refers to the fact that, on a white sheet of paper with black printing, the space between the words and symbols is white. The way a programmer uses white space is important because it can be used to emphasize parts of the code and can make a program easier to read.

Except when it's used to separate words, the computer ignores white space. It does not affect the execution of a program. This fact gives programmers a great deal of flexibility in how they format a program. The lines of a program should be divided in logical places, and certain lines should be indented and aligned so that the program's underlying structure is clear.

KEY CONCEPT

Appropriate use of white space makes a program easier to read and understand.

Because white space is ignored, we can write a program in many different ways. For example, taking white space to one extreme, we could put as many words as possible on each line. The code in Listing 1.2, the Lincoln2 program, is formatted quite differently from Lincoln but prints the same message.

LISTING 1.2

```
//********************************************************************
//  Lincoln2.java         Author: Lewis/Loftus
//
//  Demonstrates a poorly formatted, though valid, program.
//********************************************************************

public class Lincoln2{public static void main(String[]args){
System.out.println("A quote by Abraham Lincoln:");
System.out.println("Whatever you are, be a good one.");}}
```

OUTPUT

```
A quote by Abraham Lincoln:
Whatever you are, be a good one.
```

Taking white space to the other extreme, we could write almost every word and symbol on a different line with varying amounts of spaces, such as Lincoln3, shown in Listing 1.3.

> **KEY CONCEPT**
> You should adhere to a set of guidelines that establish the way you format and document your programs.

All three versions of Lincoln are technically valid and will execute in the same way, but they are radically different from a reader's point of view. Both of the latter examples show poor style and make the program difficult to understand. You may be asked to adhere to particular guidelines when you write your programs. A software development company often has a programming style policy that it requires its programmers to follow. In any case, you should adopt and consistently use a set of style guidelines that increase the readability of your code.

LISTING 1.3

```
//********************************************************************
//  Lincoln3.java         Author: Lewis/Loftus
//
//  Demonstrates another valid program that is poorly formatted.
//********************************************************************
          public           class
     Lincoln3
   {
                   public
   static
      void
   main
```

LISTING 1.3   *continued*

```
        (
String
        []
    args                        )
  {
  System.out.println    (
"A quote by Abraham Lincoln:"           )
    ;          System.out.println
              (
      "Whatever you are, be a good one."
      )
    ;
}
          }
```

OUTPUT

```
A quote by Abraham Lincoln:
Whatever you are, be a good one.
```

SELF-REVIEW QUESTIONS *(see answers in Appendix N)*   myprogramminglab

SR 1.20 When was the Java programming language developed? By whom? When was it introduced to the public?

SR 1.21 Where does processing begin in a Java application?

SR 1.22 What do you predict would be the result of the following line in a Java program?

```
System.out.println("Hello");  // prints hello
```

SR 1.23 What do you predict would be the result of the following line in a Java program?

```
// prints hello  System.out.println("Hello");
```

SR 1.24 Which of the following are not valid Java identifiers? Why?

a. RESULT
b. result
c. 12345
d. x12345y
e. black&white
f. answer_7

SR 1.25 Suppose a program requires an identifier to represent the sum of the test scores of a class of students. For each of the following names, state whether or not each is a good name to use for the identifier. Explain your answers.

    a. x
    b. scoreSum
    c. sumOfTheTestScoresOfTheStudents
    d. smTstScr

SR 1.26 What is white space? How does it affect program execution? How does it affect program readability?

1.5 Program Development

The process of getting a program running involves various activities. The program has to be written in the appropriate programming language, such as Java. That program has to be translated into a form that the computer can execute. Errors can occur at various stages of this process and must be fixed. Various software tools can be used to help with all parts of the development process as well. Let's explore these issues in more detail.

Programming Language Levels

Suppose a particular person is giving travel directions to a friend. That person might explain those directions in any one of several languages, such as English, Russian, or Italian. The directions are the same no matter which language is used to explain them, but the manner in which the directions are expressed is different. The friend must be able to understand the language being used in order to follow the directions.

Similarly, a problem can be solved by writing a program in one of many programming languages, such as Java, Ada, C, C++, C#, Pascal, and Smalltalk. The purpose of the program is essentially the same no matter which language is used, but the particular statements used to express the instructions, and the overall organization of those instructions, vary with each language. A computer must be able to understand the instructions in order to carry them out.

Programming languages can be categorized into the following four groups. These groups basically reflect the historical development of computer languages.

- machine language
- assembly language

- high-level languages
- fourth-generation languages

In order for a program to run on a computer, it must be expressed in that computer's *machine language*. Each type of CPU has its own language. For that reason, we can't run a program specifically written for a Sun Workstation, with its Sparc processor, on a Dell PC, with its Intel processor.

Each machine language instruction can accomplish only a simple task. For example, a single machine language instruction might copy a value into a register or compare a value to zero. It might take four separate machine language instructions to add two numbers together and to store the result. However, a computer can do millions of these instructions in a second, and therefore many simple commands can be executed quickly to accomplish complex tasks.

> **KEY CONCEPT**
> All programs must be translated to a particular CPU's machine language in order to be executed.

Machine language code is expressed as a series of binary digits and is extremely difficult for humans to read and write. Originally, programs were entered into the computer by using switches or some similarly tedious method. Early programmers found these techniques to be time consuming and error prone.

These problems gave rise to the use of *assembly language*, which replaced binary digits with *mnemonics*, short English-like words that represent commands or data. It is much easier for programmers to deal with words than with binary digits. However, an assembly language program cannot be executed directly on a computer. It must first be translated into machine language.

Generally, each assembly language instruction corresponds to an equivalent machine language instruction. Therefore, similar to machine language, each assembly language instruction accomplishes only a simple operation. Although assembly language is an improvement over machine code from a programmer's perspective, it is still tedious to use. Both assembly language and machine language are considered *low-level languages*.

Today, most programmers use a *high-level language* to write software. A high-level language is expressed in English-like phrases, and thus is easier for programmers to read and write. A single high-level language programming statement can accomplish the equivalent of many—perhaps hundreds—of machine language instructions. The term high-level refers to the fact that the programming statements are expressed in a way that is far removed from the machine language that is ultimately executed. Java is a high-level language, as are Ada, C++, Smalltalk, and many others.

> **KEY CONCEPT**
> High-level languages allow a programmer to ignore the underlying details of machine language.

Figure 1.19 shows equivalent expressions in a high-level language, assembly language, and machine language. The expressions add two numbers together. The assembly language and machine language in this example are specific to a Sparc processor.

High-Level Language	Assembly Language	Machine Language
a + b	ld [%fp-20], %o0	...
	ld [%fp-24], %o1	1101 0000 0000 0111
	add %o0, %o1, %o0	1011 1111 1110 1000
		1101 0010 0000 0111
		1011 1111 1110 1000
		1001 0000 0000 0000
		...

FIGURE 1.19   A high-level expression and its assembly language and machine language equivalent

The high-level language expression in Figure 1.19 is readable and intuitive for programmers. It is similar to an algebraic expression. The equivalent assembly language code is somewhat readable, but it is more verbose and less intuitive. The machine language is basically unreadable and much longer. In fact, only a small portion of the binary machine code to add two numbers together is shown in Figure 1.19. The complete machine language code for this particular expression is over 400 bits long.

A high-level language insulates programmers from needing to know the underlying machine language for the processor on which they are working. But high-level language code must be translated into machine language in order to be executed.

Some programming languages are considered to operate at an even higher level than high-level languages. They might include special facilities for automatic report generation or interaction with a database. These languages are called *fourth-generation languages,* or simply 4GLs, because they followed the first three generations of computer programming: machine, assembly, and high-level.

Editors, Compilers, and Interpreters

Several special-purpose programs are needed to help with the process of developing new programs. They are sometimes called software tools because they are used to build programs. Examples of basic software tools include an editor, a compiler, and an interpreter.

Initially, you use an *editor* as you type a program into a computer and store it in a file. There are many different editors with many different features. You should become familiar with the editor you will use regularly because it can dramatically affect the speed at which you enter and modify your programs.

FIGURE 1.20   Editing and running a program

Figure 1.20 shows a very basic view of the program development process. After editing and saving your program, you attempt to translate it from high-level code into a form that can be executed. That translation may result in errors, in which case you return to the editor to make changes to the code to fix the problems. Once the translation occurs successfully, you can execute the program and evaluate the results. If the results are not what you want, or if you want to enhance your existing program, you again return to the editor to make changes.

The translation of source code into (ultimately) machine language for a particular type of CPU can occur in a variety of ways. A *compiler* is a program that translates code in one language to equivalent code in another language. The original code is called *source code*, and the language into which it is translated is called the *target language*. For many traditional compilers, the source code is translated directly into a particular machine language. In that case, the translation process occurs once (for a given version of the program), and the resulting executable program can be run whenever needed.

An *interpreter* is similar to a compiler but has an important difference. An interpreter interweaves the translation and execution activities. A small part of the source code, such as one statement, is translated and executed. Then another statement is translated and executed, and so on. One advantage of this technique is that it eliminates the need for a separate compilation phase. However, the program generally runs more slowly because the translation process occurs during each execution.

The process generally used to translate and execute Java programs combines the use of a compiler and an interpreter. This process is pictured in Figure 1.21. The Java compiler translates Java source code into Java *bytecode,* which is a representation of the program in a low-level form similar to machine language code. The Java interpreter reads Java bytecode and executes it on a specific machine. Another compiler could translate the bytecode into a particular machine language for efficient execution on that machine.

> **KEY CONCEPT**
> A Java compiler translates Java source code into Java bytecode, a low-level, architecture-neutral representation of the program.

The difference between Java bytecode and true machine language code is that Java bytecode is not tied to any particular processor type. This approach has the

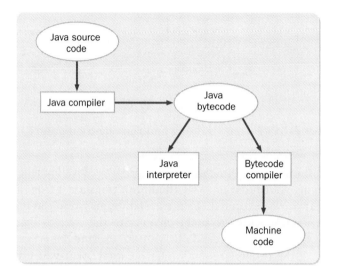

FIGURE 1.21   The Java translation and execution process

distinct advantage of making Java *architecture neutral,* and therefore easily portable from one machine type to another. The only restriction is that there must be a Java interpreter or a bytecode compiler for each processor type on which the Java bytecode is to be executed.

Since the compilation process translates the high-level Java source code into a low-level representation, the interpretation process is more efficient than interpreting high-level code directly. Executing a program by interpreting its bytecode is still slower than executing machine code directly, but it is fast enough for most applications. Note that for efficiency, Java bytecode could be compiled into machine code.

Development Environments

A software *development environment* is the set of tools used to create, test, and modify a program. Some development environments are available for free while others, which may have advanced features, must be purchased. Some environments are referred to as *integrated development environments* (IDEs) because they integrate various tools into one software program and provide a convenient graphical user interface.

Any development environment will contain certain key tools, such as a Java compiler and interpreter. Some will include a *debugger,* which helps you find

errors in a program. Other tools that may be included are documentation genera-
tors, archiving tools, and tools that help you visualize your program structure.

VideoNote

Comparison of Java
IDEs.

Included in the download of the Java Standard Edition is the Java *Software
Development Kit* (SDK), which is sometimes referred to simply as the *Java
Development Kit* (JDK). The Java SDK contains the core development tools
needed to get a Java program up and running, but it is not an integrated environment. The commands for compilation and interpretation are executed on the
command line. That is, the SDK does not have a GUI. It also does not include an
editor, although any editor that can save a document as simple text can be used.

One of the most popular Java IDEs is called Eclipse (see www.eclipse.org).
Eclipse is an *open source* project, meaning that it is developed by a wide collection
of programmers and is available for free. Other popular Java IDEs include jEdit
(www.jedit.org), DrJava (drjava.sourceforge.net), jGRASP (www.jgrasp.com), and
BlueJ (www.bluej.org).

Various other Java development environments are available. A
Web search will unveil dozens of them. The choice of which development environment to use is important. The more you know about
the capabilities of your environment, the more productive you can
be during program development.

> **KEY CONCEPT**
> Many different development environ-
> ments exist to help you create and
> modify Java programs.

Syntax and Semantics

Each programming language has its own unique *syntax*. The syntax rules of a
language dictate exactly how the vocabulary elements of the language can be
combined to form statements. These rules must be followed in order to create a
program. We've already discussed several Java syntax rules. For instance, the fact
that an identifier cannot begin with a digit is a syntax rule. The fact that braces
are used to begin and end classes and methods is also a syntax rule. Appendix L
formally defines the basic syntax rules for the Java programming language, and
specific rules are highlighted throughout the text.

During compilation, all syntax rules are checked. If a program is not syntactically correct, the compiler will issue error messages and will not produce bytecode. Java has a similar syntax to the programming languages C and C++, and
therefore the look and feel of the code is familiar to people with a background in
those languages.

The *semantics* of a statement in a programming language define what will
happen when that statement is executed. Programming languages are generally
unambiguous, which means the semantics of a program are well defined. That is,
there is one and only one interpretation for each statement. On the other hand,
the *natural languages* that humans use to communicate, such as English and

Italian, are full of ambiguities. A sentence can often have two or more different meanings. For example, consider the following sentence:

```
Time flies like an arrow.
```

The average human is likely to interpret this sentence as a general observation: that time moves quickly in the same way that an arrow moves quickly. However, if we interpret the word *time* as a verb (as in "run the 50-yard dash and I'll time you") and the word *flies* as a noun (the plural of fly), the interpretation changes completely. We know that arrows don't time things, so we wouldn't normally interpret the sentence that way, but it is a valid interpretation of the words in the sentence. A computer would have a difficult time trying to determine which meaning is intended. Moreover, this sentence could describe the preferences of an unusual insect known as a "time fly," which might be found near an archery range. After all, fruit flies like a banana.

The point is that one specific English sentence can have multiple valid meanings. A computer language cannot allow such ambiguities to exist. If a programming language instruction could have two different meanings, a computer would not be able to determine which one should be carried out.

Errors

Several different kinds of problems can occur in software, particularly during program development. The term computer error is often misused and varies in meaning depending on the situation. From a user's point of view, anything that goes awry when interacting with a machine can be called a computer error. For example, suppose you charged a $23 item to your credit card, but when you received the bill, the item was listed at $230. After you have the problem fixed, the credit card company apologizes for the "computer error." Did the computer arbitrarily add a zero to the end of the number, or did it perhaps multiply the value by 10? Of course not. A computer follows the commands we give it and operates on the data we provide. If our programs are wrong or our data inaccurate, then we cannot expect the results to be correct. A common phrase used to describe this situation is "garbage in, garbage out."

You will encounter three kinds of errors as you develop programs:

- compile-time error
- run-time error
- logical error

The compiler checks to make sure you are using the correct syntax. If you have any statements that do not conform to the syntactic rules of the language, the compiler will produce a *syntax error*. The compiler also tries to find other problems, such as the use of incompatible types of data. The syntax might be technically correct, but you may be attempting to do something that the language doesn't semantically allow. Any error identified by the compiler is called a *compile-time error*. If a compile-time error occurs, an executable version of the program is not created.

> **KEY CONCEPT**
>
> A Java program must be syntactically correct or the compiler will not produce bytecode.

The second kind of problem occurs during program execution. It is called a *run-time error* and causes the program to terminate abnormally. For example, if we attempt to divide by zero, the program will "crash" and halt execution at that point. Because the requested operation is undefined, the system simply abandons its attempt to continue processing your program. The best programs are *robust*; that is, they avoid as many run-time errors as possible. For example, the program code could guard against the possibility of dividing by zero and handle the situation appropriately if it arises. In Java, many run-time problems are called *exceptions* that can be caught and dealt with accordingly.

VideoNote

Examples of various error types.

The third kind of software problem is a *logical error*. In this case, the software compiles and executes without complaint, but it produces incorrect results. For example, a logical error occurs when a value is calculated incorrectly or when a graphical button does not appear in the correct place. A programmer must test the program thoroughly, comparing the expected results to those that actually occur. When defects are found, they must be traced back to the source of the problem in the code and corrected. The process of finding and correcting defects in a program is called *debugging*. Logical errors can manifest themselves in many ways, and the actual root cause might be difficult to discover.

SELF-REVIEW QUESTIONS *(see answers in Appendix N)*

myprogramminglab

SR 1.27 We all know that computers are used to perform complex jobs. In this section, you learned that a computer's instructions can do only simple tasks. Explain this apparent contradiction.

SR 1.28 What is the relationship between a high-level language and a machine language?

SR 1.29 What is Java bytecode?

SR 1.30 Select the word from the following list that best matches each of the following phrases:

assembly, compiler, high-level, IDE, interpreter, Java, low-level, machine

a. A program written in this type of language can run directly on a computer.

    b. Generally, each language instruction in this type of language corresponds to an equivalent machine language instruction.

    c. Most programmers write their programs using this type of language.

    d. Java is an example of this type of language.

    e. This type of program translates code in one language to code in another language.

    f. This type of program interweaves the translation of code and the execution of the code.

SR 1.31 What do we mean by the syntax and semantics of a programming language?

SR 1.32 Categorize each of the following situations as a compile-time error, run-time error, or logical error.

    a. Misspelling a Java reserved word.

    b. Calculating the average of an empty list of numbers by dividing the sum of the numbers on the list (which is zero) by the size of the list (which is also zero).

    c. Printing a student's high test grade when the student's average test grade should have been output.

1.6 Object-Oriented Programming

As we stated earlier in this chapter, Java is an object-oriented (OO) language. As the name implies, an *object* is a fundamental entity in a Java program. This book is focused on the idea of developing software by defining objects that interact with each other.

The principles of object-oriented software development have been around for many years, essentially as long as high-level programming languages have been used. The programming language Simula, developed in the 1960s, had many characteristics that define the modern OO approach to software development. In the 1980s and 1990s, object-oriented programming became wildly popular, due in large part to the development of programming languages such as C++ and Java. It is now the dominant approach used in commercial software development.

One of the most attractive characteristics of the object-oriented approach is the fact that objects can be used quite effectively to represent real-world entities. We can use a software object to represent an employee in a company, for instance. We'd create one object per employee, each with behaviors and characteristics that we need to represent. In this way, object-oriented programming allows us to map our programs to the real situations that the programs represent. That is, the object-oriented approach makes it easier to solve problems, which is the point of writing a program in the first place.

KEY CONCEPT
Object-oriented programming helps us solve problems, which is the purpose of writing a program.

Let's discuss the general issues related to problem solving, and then explore the specific characteristics of the object-oriented approach that helps us solve those problems.

Problem Solving

In general, problem solving consists of multiple steps:

1. Understanding the problem.
2. Designing a solution.
3. Considering alternatives to the solution and refining the solution.
4. Implementing the solution.
5. Testing the solution and fixing any problems that exist.

Although this approach applies to any kind of problem solving, it works particularly well when developing software. These steps aren't purely linear. That is, some of the activities will overlap others. But at some point, all of these steps should be carefully addressed.

The first step, understanding the problem, may sound obvious, but a lack of attention to this step has been the cause of many misguided software development efforts. If we attempt to solve a problem we don't completely understand, we often end up solving the wrong problem or at least going off on improper tangents. Each problem has a *problem domain*, the real-world issues that are key to our solution. For example, if we are going to write a program to score a bowling match, then the problem domain includes the rules of bowling. To develop a good solution, we must thoroughly understand the problem domain.

The key to designing a problem solution is breaking it down into manageable pieces. A solution to any problem can rarely be expressed as one big task. Instead, it is a series of small cooperating tasks that interact to perform a larger task. When developing software, we don't write one big program. We design separate pieces that are responsible for certain parts of the solution, and then integrate them with the other parts.

KEY CONCEPT
Program design involves breaking a solution down into manageable pieces.

Our first inclination toward a solution may not be the best one. We must always consider alternatives and refine the solution as necessary. The earlier we consider alternatives, the easier it is to modify our approach.

Implementing the solution is the act of taking the design and putting it in a usable form. When developing a software solution to a problem, the implementation stage is the process of actually writing the program. Too often programming is thought of as writing code. But in most cases, the act of designing the program should be far more interesting and creative than the process of implementing the design in a particular programming language.

At many points in the development process, we should test our solution to find any errors that exist so that we can fix them. Testing cannot guarantee that there aren't still problems yet to be discovered, but it can raise our confidence that we have a viable solution.

Throughout this text we explore techniques that allow us to design and implement elegant programs. Although we will often get immersed in these details, we should never forget that our primary goal is to solve problems.

Object-Oriented Software Principles

Object-oriented programming ultimately requires a solid understanding of the following terms:

- object
- attribute
- method
- class
- encapsulation
- inheritance
- polymorphism

In addition to these terms, there are many associated concepts that allow us to tailor our solutions in innumerable ways. This book is designed to help you evolve your understanding of these concepts gradually and naturally. This section provides an overview of these ideas at a high level to establish some terminology and provide the big picture.

We mentioned earlier that an *object* is a fundamental element in a program. A software object often represents a real object in our problem domain, such as a bank account. Every object has a *state* and a set of *behaviors*. By "state" we mean state of being—fundamental characteristics that currently define the object. For example, part of a bank account's state is its current balance. The behaviors of an object are the activities associated with the object. Behaviors associated with a bank account probably include the ability to make deposits and withdrawals.

In addition to objects, a Java program also manages primitive data. *Primitive data* includes fundamental values such as numbers and characters. Objects usually represent more interesting or complex entities.

An object's *attributes* are the values it stores internally, which may be represented as primitive data or as other objects. For example, a bank account object may store a floating point number (a primitive value) that represents the balance of the account. It may contain other attributes, such as the name of the account owner. Collectively, the values of an object's attributes define its current state.

> **KEY CONCEPT**
> Each object has a state, defined by its attributes, and a set of behaviors, defined by its methods.

As mentioned earlier in this chapter, a *method* is a group of programming statements that is given a name. When a method is invoked, its statements are executed. A set of methods is associated with an object. The methods of an object define its potential behaviors. To define the ability to make a deposit into a bank account, we define a method containing programming statements that will update the account balance accordingly.

An object is defined by a *class*. A class is the model or blueprint from which an object is created. Consider the blueprint created by an architect when designing a house. The blueprint defines the important characteristics of the house—its walls, windows, doors, electrical outlets, and so on. Once the blueprint is created, several houses can be built using it, as depicted in Figure 1.22.

In one sense, the houses built from the blueprint are different. They are in different locations, have different addresses, contain different furniture, and are inhabited by different people. Yet in many ways they are the "same" house. The

FIGURE 1.22   A class is used to create objects just as a house blueprint is used to create different, but similar, houses

layout of the rooms and other crucial characteristics are the same in each. To create a different house, we would need a different blueprint.

A class is a blueprint of an object. It establishes the kind of data an object of that type will hold and defines the methods that represent the behavior of such objects. However, a class is not an object any more than a blueprint is a house. In general, a class contains no space to store data. Each object has space for its own data, which is why each object can have its own state.

KEY CONCEPT

A class is a blueprint of an object. Multiple objects can be created from one class definition.

Once a class has been defined, multiple objects can be created from that class. For example, once we define a class to represent the concept of a bank account, we can create multiple objects that represent specific, individual bank accounts. Each bank account object would keep track of its own balance.

An object should be *encapsulated,* which means it protects and manages its own information. That is, an object should be self-governing. The only changes made to the state of the object should be accomplished by that object's methods. We should design objects so that other objects cannot "reach in" and change their states.

Classes can be created from other classes by using *inheritance.* That is, the definition of one class can be based on another class that already exists. Inheritance is a form of *software reuse,* capitalizing on the similarities between various kinds of classes that we may want to create. One class can be used to derive several new classes. Derived classes can then be used to derive even more classes. This creates a hierarchy of classes, where the attributes and methods defined in one class are inherited by its children, which in turn pass them on to their children, and so on. For example, we might create a hierarchy of classes that represent various types of accounts. Common characteristics are defined in high-level classes, and specific differences are defined in derived classes.

Polymorphism is the idea that we can refer to multiple types of related objects over time in consistent ways. It gives us the ability to design powerful and elegant solutions to problems that deal with multiple objects.

Some of the core object-oriented concepts are depicted in Figure 1.23. We don't expect you to understand these ideas fully at this point. Most of this book is designed to flesh out these ideas. This overview is intended only to set the stage.

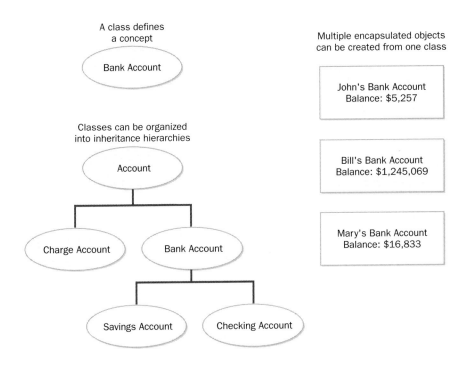

FIGURE 1.23   Various aspects of object-oriented software

myprogramminglab

SELF-REVIEW QUESTIONS *(see answers in Appendix N)*

SR 1.33   List the five general steps required to solve a problem.

SR 1.34   Why is it important to consider more than one approach to solving a problem? Why is it important to consider alternatives early in the process of solving a problem?

SR 1.35   What are the primary concepts that support object-oriented programming?

Summary of Key Concepts

- A computer system consists of hardware and software that work in concert to help us solve problems.

- The CPU reads the program instructions from main memory, executing them one at a time until the program ends.

- The operating system provides a user interface and manages computer resources.

- As far as the user is concerned, the interface *is* the program.

- Digital computers store information by breaking it into pieces and representing each piece as a number.

- Binary is used to store and move information in a computer because the devices that store and manipulate binary data are inexpensive and reliable.

- There are exactly 2^N permutations of N bits. Therefore, N bits can represent up to 2^N unique items.

- The core of a computer is made up of main memory, which stores programs and data, and the CPU, which executes program instructions one at a time.

- An address is a unique number associated with a memory location.

- Main memory is volatile, meaning the stored information is maintained only as long as electric power is supplied.

- The surface of a CD has both smooth areas and small pits. A pit represents a binary 1 and a smooth area represents a binary 0.

- A rewritable CD simulates the pits and smooth areas of a regular CD by using a coating that can be made amorphous or crystalline as needed.

- The fetch-decode-execute cycle forms the foundation of computer processing.

- A network consists of two or more computers connected together so that they can exchange information.

- Sharing a communication line creates delays, but it is cost effective and simplifies adding new computers to the network.

- A local-area network (LAN) is an effective way to share information and resources throughout an organization.

- The Internet is a wide-area network (WAN) that spans the globe.

- Every computer connected to the Internet has an IP address that uniquely identifies it.

- The World Wide Web is software that makes sharing information across a network easy for humans.
- A URL uniquely specifies documents and other information found on the Web for a browser to obtain and display.
- This book focuses on the principles of object-oriented programming.
- Comments do not affect a program's processing; instead, they serve to facilitate human comprehension.
- Inline documentation should provide insight into your code. It should not be ambiguous or belabor the obvious.
- Java is case sensitive. The uppercase and lowercase versions of a letter are distinct.
- Identifier names should be descriptive and readable.
- Appropriate use of white space makes a program easier to read and understand.
- You should adhere to a set of guidelines that establish the way you format and document your programs.
- All programs must be translated to a particular CPU's machine language in order to be executed.
- High-level languages allow a programmer to ignore the underlying details of machine language.
- A Java compiler translates Java source code into Java bytecode, a low-level, architecture-neutral representation of the program.
- Many different development environments exist to help you create and modify Java programs.
- Syntax rules dictate the form of a program. Semantics dictate the meaning of the program statements.
- The programmer is responsible for the accuracy and reliability of a program.
- A Java program must be syntactically correct or the compiler will not produce bytecode.
- Object-oriented programming helps us solve problems, which is the purpose of writing a program.
- Program design involves breaking a solution down into manageable pieces.
- Each object has a state, defined by its attributes, and a set of behaviors, defined by its methods.
- A class is a blueprint of an object. Multiple objects can be created from one class definition.

Exercises

myprogramminglab

Visit www.myprogramminglab.com to complete many of these Exercises online and get instant feedback.

EX 1.1 Describe the hardware components of your personal computer or of a computer in a lab to which you have access. Include the processor type and speed, storage capacities of main and secondary memory, and types of I/O devices. Explain how you determined your answers.

EX 1.2 What is the base value of the binary number system?

EX 1.3 How many unique items can be represented with each of the following?

a. 1 bit

b. 3 bits

c. 6 bits

d. 8 bits

e. 10 bits

f. 16 bits

EX 1.4 If an image is made up of 256 possible colors, how many bits would be needed to store each pixel of the image? Why?

EX 1.5 If a language uses 26 characters, 14 symbols and 10 numerals, how many bits would be required to represent that language? Why?

EX 1.6 How many kilobytes are required to represent the following?

a. 10 MB

b. 1 GB

c. 2 TB

d. 1 PB

EX 1.7 Explain the difference between main memory and secondary memory.

EX 1.8 How do sequential access devices differ from direct access devices? Give examples.

EX 1.9 Determine how your computer, or a computer in a lab to which you have access, is connected to others across a network. Is it linked to the Internet? Draw a diagram to show the basic connections in your environment.

EX 1.10 List two IP addresses you are familiar with. What relationship do IP addresses share with the Domain Name System?

EX 1.11 What is the total number of communication lines needed for a fully connected point-to-point network of eight computers? Nine computers? Ten computers? What is a general formula for determining this result?

EX 1.12 Explain the difference between hypertext and hypermedia.

EX 1.13 List and explain the parts of the URLs below:

a. http://openeducationnews.org

b. www.mail.yahoo.com

c. http://www.management.uottawa.ca/csi1301

EX 1.14 Use a Web browser to access information through the Web about the following topics. For each one, explain the process you used to find the information and record the specific URLs you found.

a. the Philadelphia Phillies baseball team

b. wine production in California

c. the subway systems in two major cities

d. vacation opportunities in the Caribbean

EX 1.15 What are reserved words? Give examples of reserved words found in Java.

EX 1.16 Which of the following are valid Java identifiers? If not, why?

a. `Color`

b. `System`

c. `123abc`

d. `Variable1`

e. `METHOD`

f. `Low%`

g. `Add one`

EX 1.17 How would the following comment statements be interpreted?

a. `// This is the first program.`

b. `/*  This program deals with`
      `the area calculation of a rectangle`

   `*/`

EX 1.18 Is Java case sensitive or insensitive? Explain your answer.

EX 1.19 What is a programming language? How can programming languages be categorized? Are all the groups required? Which programming languages would a programmer find easiest to use when solving a problem? Why?

EX 1.20 Categorize each of the following situations as a compile-time error, run-time error, or logical error.

a. multiplying two numbers when you meant to add them

b. dividing by zero

c. forgetting a semicolon at the end of a programming statement

d. spelling a word incorrectly in the output

e. producing inaccurate results

f. typing a { when you should have typed a (

Programming Projects

myprogramminglab

Visit www.myprogramminglab.com to complete many of these Programming Projects online and get instant feedback.

PP 1.1 What would the output of the following application be? How would you indicate the name of this application?

```
public class Test
{
    public static void main (String[] args)
    {

        System.out.println ("Welcome to Java");
    }
}
```

PP 1.2 Introduce the following errors, one at a time, to the program from PP 1.1. Record any error messages that the compiler produces. Fix the previous error each time before you introduce a new one. If no error messages are produced, explain why. Try to predict what will happen before you make each change.

a. change Test to test

b. change Emergency to emergency

c. remove the first quotation mark in the string

d. remove the last quotation mark in the string

e. change main to man

f. change `println` to `bogus`

g. remove the semicolon at the end of the `println` statement

h. remove the last brace in the program

VideoNote

Developing a solution for PP 1.2.

PP 1.3   Write an application that prints, on separate lines, your name, your birthday, your hobbies, your favorite book, and your favorite movie. Label each piece of information in the output.

PP 1.4   Write an application that prints the phrase `Knowledge is Power`:

a. on one line

b. on three lines, one word per line, with the words centered relative to each other

c. inside a box made up of the characters = and |

PP 1.5   Write an application that prints a list of four or five web sites that you enjoy. Print both the site name and the URL.

PP 1.6   Write an application that prints the first few verses of a song (your choice). Label the chorus.

PP 1.7   Write an application that prints the outline of a tree using asterisk (*) characters.

PP 1.8   Write an application that prints a paragraph from a novel of your choice.

PP 1.9   Write an application that prints the following diamond shape. Don't print any unneeded characters. (That is, don't make any character string longer than it has to be.)

```
    *
   ***
  *****
 *******
*********
 *******
  *****
   ***
    *
```

PP 1.10 Write an application that displays your initials in large block letters. Make each large letter out of the corresponding regular character. For example:

```
JJJJJJJJJJJJJJJ     AAAAAAAAA     LLLL
JJJJJJJJJJJJJJJ     AAAAAAAAAA    LLLL
          JJJJ      AAA     AAA   LLLL
          JJJJ      AAA     AAA   LLLL
          JJJJ      AAAAAAAAAA    LLLL
J         JJJJ      AAAAAAAAAA    LLLL
JJ        JJJJ      AAA     AAA   LLLL
  JJJJJJJJJJJJ      AAA     AAA   LLLLLLLLLLLLL
   JJJJJJJJJ        AAA     AAA   LLLLLLLLLLLLL
```

Data and Expressions

2

CHAPTER OBJECTIVES

- Discuss the use of character strings, concatenation, and escape sequences.
- Explore the declaration and use of variables.
- Describe the Java primitive data types.
- Discuss the syntax and processing of expressions.
- Define the types of data conversions and the mechanisms for accomplishing them.
- Introduce the Scanner class to create interactive programs.
- Explore basic graphics concepts and the techniques for drawing shapes.
- Introduce the concept of a Java applet.

This chapter explores some of the basic types of data used in a Java program and the use of expressions to perform calculations. It discusses the conversion of data from one type to another and how to read input interactively from the user running a program. This chapter also begins the Graphics Track for the book, in which we introduce the concepts of graphical programming, explore the relationship between Java and the Web, and delve into Java's abilities to manipulate color and draw shapes.

2.1 Character Strings

In Chapter 1 we discussed the basic structure of a Java program, including the use of comments, identifiers, and white space, using the Lincoln program as an example. Chapter 1 also included an overview of the various concepts involved in object-oriented programming, such as objects, classes, and methods. Take a moment to review these ideas if necessary.

A character string is an object in Java, defined by the class String. Because strings are so fundamental to computer programming, Java provides the ability to use a *string literal*, delimited by double quotation characters, as we've seen in previous examples. We explore the String class and its methods in more detail in Chapter 3. For now, let's explore the use of string literals in more detail.

The following are all examples of valid string literals:

```
"The quick brown fox jumped over the lazy dog."
"602 Greenbriar Court, Chalfont PA 18914"
"x"
""
```

A string literal can contain any valid characters, including numeric digits, punctuation, and other special characters. The last example in the list above contains no characters at all.

The print and println Methods

In the Lincoln program in Chapter 1, we invoked the println method as follows:

```
System.out.println ("Whatever you are, be a good one.");
```

This statement demonstrates the use of objects. The System.out object represents an output device or file, which by default is the monitor screen. To be more precise, the object's name is out and it is stored in the System class. We explore that relationship in more detail at the appropriate point in the text.

The println method is a service that the System.out object performs for us. Whenever we request it, the object will print a character string to the screen. We can say that we send the println message to the System.out object to request that some text be printed.

Each piece of data that we send to a method is called a *parameter*. In this case, the println method takes only one parameter: the string of characters to be printed.

The System.out object also provides another service we can use: the print method. The difference between print and println is small but important. The println method prints the information sent to it, then moves to the beginning of the next line. The print method is similar to println, but does not advance to the next line when completed.

KEY CONCEPT

The print and println methods represent two services provided by the System.out object.

The program shown in Listing 2.1 is called Countdown, and it invokes both the print and println methods.

Carefully compare the output of the Countdown program, shown at the bottom of the program listing, to the program code. Note that the word Liftoff is printed on the same line as the first few words, even though it is printed using the println method. Remember that the println method moves to the beginning of the next line *after* the information passed to it has been printed.

LISTING 2.1

```
//********************************************************************
//  Countdown.java       Author: Lewis/Loftus
//
//  Demonstrates the difference between print and println.
//********************************************************************
public class Countdown
{
   //-----------------------------------------------------------------
   //  Prints two lines of output representing a rocket countdown.
   //-----------------------------------------------------------------
   public static void main (String[] args)
   {
      System.out.print ("Three... ");
      System.out.print ("Two... ");
      System.out.print ("One... ");
      System.out.print ("Zero... ");
      System.out.println ("Liftoff!"); // appears on first output line
      System.out.println ("Houston, we have a problem.");
   }
}
```

OUTPUT

```
Three... Two... One... Zero... Liftoff!
Houston, we have a problem.
```

String Concatenation

A string literal cannot span multiple lines in a program. The following program statement is improper syntax and would produce an error when attempting to compile:

```
// The following statement will not compile
System.out.println ("The only stupid question is
the one that is not asked.");
```

When we want to print a string that is too long to fit on one line in a program, we can rely on *string concatenation* to append one string to the end of another. The string concatenation operator is the plus sign (+). The following expression concatenates one character string to another, producing one long string:

```
"The only stupid question is " + "the one that is not asked."
```

The program called Facts shown in Listing 2.2 contains several println statements. The first one prints a sentence that is somewhat long and will not fit on one line of the program. Since a character literal cannot span two lines in a program, we split the string into two and use string concatenation to append them. Therefore, the string concatenation operation in the first println statement results in one large string that is passed to the method to be printed.

Note that we don't have to pass any information to the println method, as shown in the second line of the Facts program. This call does not print any visible characters, but it does move to the next line of output. So in this case calling println with no parameters has the effect of printing a blank line.

The last three calls to println in the Facts program demonstrate another interesting thing about string concatenation: Strings can be concatenated with numbers. Note that the numbers in those lines are not enclosed in double quotes and are therefore not character strings. In these cases, the number is automatically converted to a string, and then the two strings are concatenated.

Because we are printing particular values, we simply could have included the numeric value as part of the string literal, such as:

```
"Speed of ketchup: 40 km per year"
```

Digits are characters and can be included in strings as needed. We separate them in the Facts program to demonstrate the ability to concatenate a string and a number. This technique will be useful in upcoming examples.

As you can imagine, the + operator is also used for arithmetic addition. Therefore, what the + operator does depends on the types of data on which it

LISTING 2.2

```java
//********************************************************************
//  Facts.java        Author: Lewis/Loftus
//
//  Demonstrates the use of the string concatenation operator and the
//  automatic conversion of an integer to a string.
//********************************************************************

public class Facts
{
   //-----------------------------------------------------------------
   //  Prints various facts.
   //-----------------------------------------------------------------
   public static void main (String[] args)
   {
      // Strings can be concatenated into one long string
      System.out.println ("We present the following facts for your "
                          + "extracurricular edification:");

      System.out.println ();

      // A string can contain numeric digits
      System.out.println ("Letters in the Hawaiian alphabet: 12");

      // A numeric value can be concatenated to a string
      System.out.println ("Dialing code for Antarctica: " + 672);

      System.out.println ("Year in which Leonardo da Vinci invented "
                          + "the parachute: " + 1515);

      System.out.println ("Speed of ketchup: " + 40 + " km per year");
   }
}
```

OUTPUT

```
We present the following facts for your extracurricular edification:

Letters in the Hawaiian alphabet: 12
Dialing code for Antarctica: 672
Year in which Leonardo da Vinci invented the parachute: 1515
Speed of ketchup: 40 km per year
```

operates. If either or both of the operands of the + operator are strings, then string concatenation is performed.

The Addition program shown in Listing 2.3 demonstrates the distinction between string concatenation and arithmetic addition. The Addition program uses the + operator four times. In the first call to println, both + operations perform string concatenation, because the operators are executed left to right. The first operator concatenates the string with the first number (24), creating a larger string. Then that string is concatenated with the second number (45), creating an even larger string, which gets printed.

In the second call to println, we use parentheses to group the + operation with the two numeric operands. This forces that operation to happen first. Because both operands are numbers, the numbers are added in the arithmetic

LISTING 2.3

```java
//********************************************************************
//  Addition.java        Author: Lewis/Loftus
//
//  Demonstrates the difference between the addition and string
//  concatenation operators.
//********************************************************************

public class Addition
{
   //-----------------------------------------------------------------
   //  Concatenates and adds two numbers and prints the results.
   //-----------------------------------------------------------------
   public static void main (String[] args)
   {
      System.out.println ("24 and 45 concatenated: " + 24 + 45);

      System.out.println ("24 and 45 added: " + (24 + 45));
   }
}
```

OUTPUT

```
24 and 45 concatenated: 2445
24 and 45 added: 69
```

sense, producing the result 69. That number is then concatenated with the string, producing a larger string that gets printed.

We revisit this type of situation later in this chapter when we formalize the precedence rules that define the order in which operators get evaluated.

Escape Sequences

Because the double quotation character (") is used in the Java language to indicate the beginning and end of a string, we must use a special technique to print the quotation character. If we simply put it in a string ("""), the compiler gets confused because it thinks the second quotation character is the end of the string and doesn't know what to do with the third one. This results in a compile-time error.

VideoNote

Example using strings and escape sequences.

To overcome this problem, Java defines several *escape sequences* to represent special characters. An escape sequence begins with the backslash character (\), which indicates that the character or characters that follow should be interpreted in a special way. Figure 2.1 lists the Java escape sequences.

> **KEY CONCEPT**
>
> An escape sequence can be used to represent a character that would otherwise cause compilation problems.

The program in Listing 2.4, called `Roses`, prints some text resembling a poem. It uses only one `println` statement to do so, despite the fact that the poem is several lines long. Note the escape sequences used throughout the string. The \n escape sequence forces the output to a new line, and the \t escape sequence represents a tab character. The \" escape sequence ensures that the quote character is treated as part of the string, not the termination of it, which enables it to be printed as part of the output.

Escape Sequence	Meaning
\b	backspace
\t	tab
\n	newline
\r	carriage return
\"	double quote
\'	single quote
\\	backslash

FIGURE 2.1   Java escape sequences

LISTING 2.4

```
//********************************************************************
//  Roses.java        Author: Lewis/Loftus
//
//  Demonstrates the use of escape sequences.
//********************************************************************

public class Roses
{
   //-----------------------------------------------------------------
   //  Prints a poem (of sorts) on multiple lines.
   //-----------------------------------------------------------------
   public static void main (String[] args)
   {
      System.out.println ("Roses are red,\n\tViolets are blue,\n" +
         "Sugar is sweet,\n\tBut I have \"commitment issues\",\n\t" +
         "So I'd rather just be friends\n\tAt this point in our " +
         "relationship.");
   }
}
```

OUTPUT

```
Roses are red,
        Violets are blue,
Sugar is sweet,
        But I have "commitment issues",
        So I'd rather just be friends
        At this point in our relationship.
```

myprogramminglab | SELF-REVIEW QUESTIONS *(see answers in Appendix N)*

SR 2.1   What is a string literal?

SR 2.2   What is the difference between the print and println methods?

SR 2.3   What is a parameter?

SR 2.4   What output is produced by the following code fragment?

```
System.out.println ("One ");
System.out.print ("Two ");
System.out.println ("Three ");
```

SR 2.5 What output is produced by the following code fragment?

```
System.out.print ("Ready ");
System.out.println ();
System.out.println ("Set ");
System.out.println ();
System.out.println ("Go ");
```

SR 2.6 What output is produced by the following statement? What is produced if the inner parentheses are removed?

```
System.out.println ("It is good to be " + (5 + 5));
```

SR 2.7 What is an escape sequence? Give some examples.

SR 2.8 Write a single println statement that will output the following exactly as shown (including line breaks and quotation marks).

> "I made this letter longer than usual because I lack the time to make it short."
> Blaise Pascal

2.2 Variables and Assignment

Most of the information we manage in a program is represented by variables. Let's examine how we declare and use them in a program.

Variables

A *variable* is a name for a location in memory used to hold a data value. A variable declaration instructs the compiler to reserve a portion of main memory space large enough to hold a particular type of value and indicates the name by which we refer to that location.

> **KEY CONCEPT**
> A variable is a name for a memory location used to hold a value of a particular data type.

Consider the program PianoKeys, shown in Listing 2.5. The first line of the main method is the declaration of a variable named keys that holds an integer (int) value. The declaration also gives keys an initial value of 88. If an initial value is not specified for a variable, the value is undefined. Most Java compilers give errors or warnings if you attempt to use a variable before you've explicitly given it a value.

The keys variable, with its value, could be pictured as follows:

keys | 88 |

Local Variable Declaration

Variable Declarator

A variable declaration consists of a Type followed by a list of variables. Each variable can be initialized in the declaration to the value of the specified Expression. If the final modifier precedes the declaration, the identifiers are declared as named constants whose values cannot be changed once set.

Examples:

```
int total;
double num1, num2 = 4.356, num3;
char letter = 'A', digit = '7';
final int MAX = 45;
```

LISTING 2.5

```
//********************************************************************
//  PianoKeys.java        Author: Lewis/Loftus
//
//  Demonstrates the declaration, initialization, and use of an
//  integer variable.
//********************************************************************

public class PianoKeys
{
    //-----------------------------------------------------------------
    //  Prints the number of keys on a piano.
    //-----------------------------------------------------------------
    public static void main (String[] args)
```

LISTING 2.5   *continued*

```
    {
        int keys = 88;
        System.out.println ("A piano has " + keys + " keys.");
    }
}
```

OUTPUT

```
A piano has 88 keys.
```

In the PianoKeys program, two pieces of information are used in the call to the println method. The first is a string, and the second is the variable keys. When a variable is referenced, the value currently stored in it is used. Therefore, when the call to println is executed, the value of keys, which is 88, is obtained. Because that value is an integer, it is automatically converted to a string and concatenated with the initial string. The concatenated string is passed to println and printed.

A variable declaration can have multiple variables of the same type declared on one line. Each variable on the line can be declared with or without an initializing value. For example:

```
int count, minimum = 0, result;
```

The Assignment Statement

Let's examine a program that changes the value of a variable. Listing 2.6 shows a program called Geometry. This program first declares an integer variable called sides and initializes it to 7. It then prints out the current value of sides.

The next line in main changes the value stored in the variable sides:

```
sides = 10;
```

This is called an *assignment statement* because it assigns a value to a variable. When executed, the expression on the right-hand side of the assignment operator (=) is evaluated, and the result is stored in the memory location indicated by the variable on the left-hand side. In this example, the expression is simply a number, 10. We discuss expressions that are more involved than this in the next section.

LISTING 2.6

```java
//********************************************************************
//  Geometry.java       Author: Lewis/Loftus
//
//  Demonstrates the use of an assignment statement to change the
//  value stored in a variable.
//********************************************************************

public class Geometry
{
   //-----------------------------------------------------------------
   //  Prints the number of sides of several geometric shapes.
   //-----------------------------------------------------------------
   public static void main (String[] args)
   {
      int sides = 7;  // declaration with initialization
      System.out.println ("A heptagon has " + sides + " sides.");

      sides = 10;  // assignment statement
      System.out.println ("A decagon has " + sides + " sides.");

      sides = 12;
      System.out.println ("A dodecagon has " + sides + " sides.");
   }
}
```

OUTPUT

```
A heptagon has 7 sides.
A decagon has 10 sides.
A dodecagon has 12 sides.
```

KEY CONCEPT

Accessing data leaves it intact in memory, but an assignment statement overwrites the old data.

A variable can store only one value of its declared type. A new value overwrites the old one. In this case, when the value 10 is assigned to sides, the original value 7 is overwritten and lost forever, as follows:

After initialization: sides | 7 |

After first assignment: sides | 10 |

Basic Assignment

The basic assignment statement uses the assignment operator (=) to store the result of the Expression into the specified Identifier, usually a variable.

Examples:

```
total = 57;
count = count + 1;
value = (min / 2) * lastValue;
```

When a reference is made to a variable, such as when it is printed, the value of the variable is not changed. This is the nature of computer memory: Accessing (reading) data leaves the values in memory intact, but writing data replaces the old data with the new.

The Java language is *strongly typed,* meaning that we are not allowed to assign a value to a variable that is inconsistent with its declared type. Trying to combine incompatible types will generate an error when you attempt to compile the program. Therefore, the expression on the right-hand side of an assignment statement must evaluate to a value compatible with the type of the variable on the left-hand side.

> **KEY CONCEPT**
> We cannot assign a value of one type to a variable of an incompatible type.

Constants

Sometimes we use data that is constant throughout a program. For instance, we might write a program that deals with a theater that can hold no more than 427 people. It is often helpful to give a constant value a name, such as MAX_OCCUPANCY, instead of using a literal value, such as 427, throughout the code. The purpose and meaning of literal values such as 427 is often confusing to someone reading the code. By giving the value a name, you help explain its role in the program.

Constants are identifiers and are similar to variables except that they hold a particular value for the duration of their existence. Constants are, to use the English meaning of the words, not variable. Their value doesn't change.

> **KEY CONCEPT**
> Constants hold a particular value for the duration of their existence.

In Java, if you precede a declaration with the reserved word final, the identifier is made a constant. By convention, uppercase letters are used when naming constants to distinguish them from regular variables, and individual words are separated using the underscore character. For example, the constant describing the maximum occupancy of a theater could be declared as follows:

```
final int MAX_OCCUPANCY = 427;
```

The compiler will produce an error message if you attempt to change the value of a constant once it has been given its initial value. This is another good reason to use constants. Constants prevent inadvertent coding errors because the only valid place to change their value is in the initial assignment.

There is a third good reason to use constants. If a constant is used throughout a program and its value needs to be modified, then you have to change it in only one place. For example, if the capacity of the theater changes (because of a renovation) from 427 to 535, then you have to change only one declaration, and all uses of MAX_OCCUPANCY automatically reflect the change. If the literal 427 had been used throughout the code, each use would have to be found and changed. If you were to miss any uses of the literal value, problems would surely arise.

SELF-REVIEW QUESTIONS *(see answers in Appendix N)*

SR 2.9   What is a variable declaration?

SR 2.10   Given the following variable declarations, answer each question.

```
int count = 0, value, total;
final int MAX_VALUE = 100;
int myValue = 50;
```

a. How many variables are declared?
b. What is the type of these declared variables?
c. Which of the variables are given an initial value?
d. Based on the above declarations, is the following assignment statement legal? Explain.

```
myValue = 100;
```

e. Based on the above declarations is the following assignment statement legal? Explain.

```
MAX_VALUE = 50;
```

SR 2.11   Your program needs a variable of type int to hold the number of CDs in a music collection. The initial value should be zero. Write a declaration statement for the variable.

SR 2.12   Your program needs a variable of type int to hold the number of feet in a mile (5,280). Write a declaration statement for the variable.

SR 2.13   Briefly describe three reasons for using a constant in a program instead of a literal value.

2.3 Primitive Data Types

There are eight *primitive data types* in Java: four subsets of integers, two subsets of floating point numbers, a character data type, and a boolean data type. Everything else is represented using objects. Let's examine these eight primitive data types in some detail.

Integers and Floating Points

Java has two basic kinds of numeric values: integers, which have no fractional part, and floating points, which do. There are four integer data types (byte, short, int, and long) and two floating point data types (float and double). All of the numeric types differ by the amount of memory space used to store a value of that type, which determines the range of values that can be represented. The size of each data type is the same for all hardware platforms. All numeric types are *signed*, meaning that both positive and negative values can be stored in them. Figure 2.2 summarizes the numeric primitive types.

> **KEY CONCEPT**
> Java has two kinds of numeric values: integer and floating point. There are four integer data types and two floating point data types.

Recall from our discussion in Chapter 1 that a bit can be either a 1 or a 0. Because each bit can represent two different states, a string of N bits can be used to represent 2^N different values. Appendix B describes number systems and these kinds of relationships in more detail.

When designing programs, we sometimes need to be careful about picking variables of appropriate size so that memory space is not wasted. This occurs in situations where memory space is particularly restricted, such as a program that runs on a personal data assistant (PDA). In such cases, we can choose a variable's data type accordingly. For example, if the value of a particular variable will not

Type	Storage	Min Value	Max Value
byte	8 bits	−128	127
short	16 bits	−32,768	32,767
int	32 bits	−2,147,483,648	2,147,483,647
long	64 bits	−9,223,372,036,854,775,808	9,223,372,036,854,775,807
float	32 bits	Approximately −3.4E+38 with 7 significant digits	Approximately 3.4E+38 with 7 significant digits
double	64 bits	Approximately −1.7E+308 with 15 significant digits	Approximately 1.7E+308 with 15 significant digits

FIGURE 2.2   The Java numeric primitive types

vary outside of a range of 1 to 1000, then a two-byte integer (short) is large enough to accommodate it. On the other hand, when it's not clear what the range of a particular variable will be, we should provide a reasonable, even generous, amount of space. In most situations memory space is not a serious restriction, and we can usually afford generous assumptions.

Note that even though a float value supports very large (and very small) numbers, it has only seven significant digits. Therefore, if it is important to accurately maintain a value such as 50341.2077, we need to use a double.

As we've already discussed, a *literal* is an explicit data value used in a program. The various numbers used in programs such as Facts and Addition and PianoKeys are all *integer literals*. Java assumes all integer literals are of type int, unless an L or l is appended to the end of the value to indicate that it should be considered a literal of type long, such as 45L.

Likewise, Java assumes that all *floating point literals* are of type double. If we need to treat a floating point literal as a float, we append an F or f to the end of the value, as in 2.718F or 123.45f. Numeric literals of type double can be followed by a D or d if desired.

Decimal Integer Literal

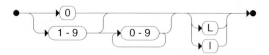

An integer literal is composed of a series of digits followed by an optional suffix to indicate that it should be considered a integer. Negation of a literal is considered a separate operation.

Examples:

```
5
2594
4920328L
```

The following are examples of numeric variable declarations in Java:

```
int answer = 42;
byte smallNumber1, smallNumber2;
long countedStars = 86827263927L;
float ratio = 0.2363F;
double delta = 453.523311903;
```

Characters

Characters are another fundamental type of data used and managed on a computer. Individual characters can be treated as separate data items, and, as we've seen in several examples, they can be combined to form character strings.

A *character literal* is expressed in a Java program with single quotes, such as 'b' or 'J' or ';'. You will recall that *string literals* are delineated using double quotation marks, and that the String type is not a primitive data type in Java; it is a class name. We discuss the String class in detail in the next chapter.

Note the difference between a digit as a character (or part of a string) and a digit as a number (or part of a larger number). The number 602 is a numeric value that can be used in an arithmetic calculation. But in the string "602 Greenbriar Court" the 6, 0, and 2 are characters, just like the rest of the characters that make up the string.

The characters we can manage are defined by a *character set*, which is simply a list of characters in a particular order. Each programming language supports a particular character set that defines the valid values for a character variable in that language. Several character sets have been proposed, but only a few have been used regularly over the years. The *ASCII character set* is a popular choice. ASCII stands for the American Standard Code for Information Interchange. The basic ASCII set uses seven bits per character, providing room to support 128 different characters, including:

- uppercase letters, such as 'A', 'B', and 'C'
- lowercase letters, such as 'a', 'b', and 'c'
- punctuation, such as the period ('.'), semicolon (';'), and comma (',')
- the digits '0' through '9'
- the space character, ' '
- special symbols, such as the ampersand ('&'), vertical bar ('|'), and backslash ('\')
- control characters, such as the carriage return, null, and end-of-text marks

The *control characters* are sometimes called nonprinting or invisible characters because they do not have a specific symbol that represents them. Yet they are as valid as any other character and can be stored and used in the same ways. Many control characters have special meaning to certain software applications.

As computing became a worldwide endeavor, users demanded a more flexible character set containing other language alphabets. ASCII was extended to use eight bits per character, and the number of characters in the set doubled to 256. The extended ASCII contains many accented and diacritical characters used in languages other than English.

> **KEY CONCEPT**
> Java uses the 16-bit Unicode character set to represent character data.

However, even with 256 characters, the ASCII character set cannot represent the world's alphabets, especially given the various Asian alphabets and their many thousands of ideograms. Therefore, the developers of the Java programming language chose the *Unicode character set*, which uses 16 bits per character, supporting 65,536 unique characters (and techniques that allow even more characters to be represented using multiple bytes). The characters and symbols from many languages are included in the Unicode definition. ASCII is a subset of the Unicode character set, comprising the first 256 characters. Appendix C discusses the Unicode character set in more detail.

A character set assigns a particular number to each character, so by definition the characters are in a particular order. This is referred to as lexicographic order. In the ASCII and Unicode ordering, the digit characters '0' through '9' are continuous (no other characters intervene) and in order. Similarly, the lowercase alphabetic characters 'a' through 'z' are continuous and in order, as are the uppercase alphabetic characters 'A' through 'Z'. These characteristics make it relatively easy to keep things in alphabetical order.

In Java, the data type char represents a single character. The following are some examples of character variable declarations in Java:

```
char topGrade = 'A';
char symbol1, symbol2, symbol3;
char terminator = ';', separator = ' ';
```

Booleans

A boolean value, defined in Java using the reserved word boolean, has only two valid values: true and false. A boolean variable is usually used to indicate whether a particular condition is true, but it can also be used to represent any situation that has two states, such as a light bulb being on or off.

A boolean value cannot be converted to any other data type, nor can any other data type be converted to a boolean value. The words true and false are reserved in Java as *boolean literals* and cannot be used outside of this context.

The following are some examples of boolean variable declarations in Java:

```
boolean flag = true;
boolean tooHigh, tooSmall, tooRough;
boolean done = false;
```

myprogramminglab | SELF-REVIEW QUESTIONS *(see answers in Appendix N)*

SR 2.14   What is primitive data? How are primitive data types different from objects?

SR 2.15   How many values can be stored in an integer variable?

SR 2.16   What are the four integer data types in Java? How are they different?

SR 2.17   What type does Java automatically assign to an integer literal? How can you indicate that an integer literal should be considered a different type?

SR 2.18   What type does Java automatically assign to a floating point literal? How can you indicate that a floating point literal should be considered a different type?

SR 2.19   What is a character set?

SR 2.20   How many characters are supported by the ASCII character set, the extended ASCII character set, and the Unicode character set?

2.4 Expressions

An *expression* is a combination of one or more operators and operands that usually perform a calculation. The value calculated does not have to be a number, but it often is. The operands used in the operations might be literals, constants, variables, or other sources of data. The manner in which expressions are evaluated and used is fundamental to programming. For now we will focus on arithmetic expressions that use numeric operands and produce numeric results.

> **KEY CONCEPT**
> Expressions are combinations of operators and operands used to perform a calculation.

Arithmetic Operators

The usual arithmetic operations are defined for both integer and floating point numeric types, including addition (+), subtraction (−), multiplication (*), and division (/). Java also has another arithmetic operation: The *remainder operator* (%) returns the remainder after dividing the second operand into the first. The remainder operator is sometimes called the modulus operator. The sign of the result of a remainder operation is the sign of the numerator. Therefore:

Operation	Result
17 % 4	1
−20 % 3	−2
10 % −5	0
3 % 8	3

VideoNote

Review of primitive data
and expressions.

As you might expect, if either or both operands to any numeric operator are floating point values, the result is a floating point value. However, the division operator produces results that are less intuitive, depending on the types of the operands. If both operands are integers, the / operator performs *integer division*, meaning that any fractional part of the result is discarded. If one or the other or both operands are floating point values, the / operator performs *floating point division*, and the fractional part of the result is kept. For example, the result of 10/4 is 2, but the results of 10.0/4 and 10/4.0 and 10.0/4.0 are all 2.5.

A *unary operator* has only one operand, while a *binary operator* has two. The + and − arithmetic operators can be either unary or binary. The binary versions accomplish addition and subtraction, and the unary versions represent positive and negative numbers. For example, −1 is an example of using the unary negation operator to make the value negative. The unary + operator is rarely used.

Java does not have a built-in operator for raising a value to an exponent. However, the Math class provides methods that perform exponentiation and many other mathematical functions. The Math class is discussed in Chapter 3.

Operator Precedence

Operators can be combined to create more complex expressions. For example, consider the following assignment statement:

```
result = 14 + 8 / 2;
```

> **KEY CONCEPT**
>
> Java follows a well-defined set of precedence rules that governs the order in which operators will be evaluated in an expression.

The entire right-hand side of the assignment is evaluated, and then the result is stored in the variable. But what is the result? If the addition is performed first, the result is 11; if the division operation is performed first, the result is 18. The order of operator evaluation makes a big difference. In this case, the division is performed before the addition, yielding a result of 18.

Note that in this and subsequent examples, we use literal values rather than variables to simplify the expression. The order of operator evaluation is the same if the operands are variables or any other source of data.

All expressions are evaluated according to an *operator precedence hierarchy* that establishes the rules that govern the order in which operations are evaluated. The arithmetic operators generally follow the same rules you learned in algebra. Multiplication, division, and the remainder operator all have equal precedence and are performed before (have higher precedence than) addition and subtraction. Addition and subtraction have equal precedence.

Any arithmetic operators at the same level of precedence are performed left to right. Therefore we say the arithmetic operators have a *left-to-right association*.

Precedence, however, can be forced in an expression by using parentheses. For instance, if we really wanted the addition to be performed first in the previous example, we could write the expression as follows:

```
result = (14 + 8) / 2;
```

Any expression in parentheses is evaluated first. In complicated expressions, it is good practice to use parentheses, even when it is not strictly necessary, to make it clear how the expression is evaluated.

Parentheses can be nested, and the innermost nested expressions are evaluated first. Consider the following expression:

```
result = 3 * ((18 - 4) / 2);
```

In this example, the result is 21. First, the subtraction is performed, forced by the inner parentheses. Then, even though multiplication and division are at the same level of precedence and usually would be evaluated left to right, the division is performed first because of the outer parentheses. Finally, the multiplication is performed.

After the arithmetic operations are complete, the computed result is stored in the variable on the left-hand side of the assignment operator (=). In other words, the assignment operator has a lower precedence than any of the arithmetic operators.

The evaluation of a particular expression can be shown using an *expression tree*, such as the one in Figure 2.3. The operators are executed from the bottom up, creating values that are used in the rest of the expression. Therefore, the operations lower in the tree have a higher precedence than those above, or they are forced to be executed earlier using parentheses.

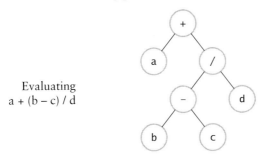

Evaluating
a + (b − c) / d

FIGURE 2.3   An expression tree

Precedence Level	Operator	Operation	Associates
1	+	unary plus	R to L
	−	unary minus	
2	*	multiplication	L to R
	/	division	
	%	remainder	
3	+	addition	L to R
	−	subtraction	
	+	string concatenation	
4	=	assignment	R to L

FIGURE 2.4   Precedence among some of the Java operators

The parentheses used in expressions are actually operators themselves. Parentheses have a higher precedence than almost any other operator. Figure 2.4 shows a precedence table with the relationships between the arithmetic operators, parentheses, and the assignment operator. Appendix D includes a full precedence table showing all Java operators.

For an expression to be syntactically correct, the number of left parentheses must match the number of right parentheses and they must be properly nested. The following examples are *not* valid expressions:

```
result = ((19 + 8) % 3) - 4);   // not valid
result = (19 (+ 8 %) 3 - 4);    // not valid
```

Keep in mind that when a variable is referenced in an expression, its current value is used to perform the calculation. In the following assignment statement, the current value of the variable count is added to the current value of the variable total, and the result is stored in the variable sum:

```
sum = count + total;
```

The original value contained in sum before this assignment is overwritten by the calculated value. The values stored in count and total are not changed.

The same variable can appear on both the left-hand side and the right-hand side of an assignment statement. Suppose the current value of a variable called count is 15 when the following assignment statement is executed:

```
count = count + 1;
```

Because the right-hand expression is evaluated first, the original value of count is obtained and the value 1 is added to it, producing the result 16. That result is then stored in the variable count, overwriting the original value of 15 with the new value of 16. Therefore, this assignment statement *increments*, or adds 1 to, the variable count.

Let's look at another example of expression processing. The program in Listing 2.7, called TempConverter, converts a particular Celsius temperature value to its equivalent Fahrenheit value using an expression that computes the following formula:

$$\text{Fahrenheit} = \frac{9}{5}\ \text{Celsius} + 32$$

LISTING 2.7

```java
//********************************************************************
//  TempConverter.java       Author: Lewis/Loftus
//
//  Demonstrates the use of primitive data types and arithmetic
//  expressions.
//********************************************************************

public class TempConverter
{
   //-----------------------------------------------------------------
   //  Computes the Fahrenheit equivalent of a specific Celsius
   //  value using the formula F = (9/5)C + 32.
   //-----------------------------------------------------------------
   public static void main (String[] args)
   {
      final int BASE = 32;
      final double CONVERSION_FACTOR = 9.0 / 5.0;

      double fahrenheitTemp;
      int celsiusTemp = 24;   // value to convert

      fahrenheitTemp = celsiusTemp * CONVERSION_FACTOR + BASE;

      System.out.println ("Celsius Temperature: " + celsiusTemp);
      System.out.println ("Fahrenheit Equivalent: " + fahrenheitTemp);
   }
}
```

OUTPUT

```
Celsius Temperature: 24
Fahrenheit Equivalent: 75.2
```

Note that in the temperature conversion program, the operands to the division operation are floating point literals to ensure that the fractional part of the number is kept. The precedence rules dictate that the multiplication happens before the addition in the final conversion computation.

The TempConverter program is not very useful because it converts only one data value that we included in the program as a constant (24 degrees Celsius). Every time the program is run it produces the same result. A far more useful version of the program would obtain the value to be converted from the user each time the program is executed. Interactive programs that read user input are discussed later in this chapter.

Increment and Decrement Operators

There are two other useful arithmetic operators. The *increment operator* (++) adds 1 to any integer or floating point value. The two plus signs that make up the operator cannot be separated by white space. The *decrement operator* (--) is similar except that it subtracts 1 from the value. They are both unary operators because they operate on only one operand. The following statement causes the value of count to be incremented:

```
count++;
```

The result is stored back into the variable count. Therefore it is functionally equivalent to the following statement, which we discussed in the previous section:

```
count = count + 1;
```

The increment and decrement operators can be applied after the variable (such as count++ or count--), creating what is called the *postfix form* of the operator. They can also be applied before the variable (such as ++count or --count), in what is called the *prefix form*. When used alone in a statement, the prefix and postfix forms are functionally equivalent. That is, it doesn't matter if you write

```
count++;
```

or

```
++count;
```

However, when such a form is written as a statement by itself, it is usually written in its postfix form.

When the increment or decrement operator is used in a larger expression, it can yield different results depending on the form used. For example, if the variable count currently contains the value 15, the following statement assigns the value 15 to total and the value 16 to count:

```
total = count++;
```

However, the following statement assigns the value 16 to both total and count:

```
total = ++count;
```

The value of count is incremented in both situations, but the value used in the larger expression depends on whether a prefix or postfix form of the increment operator is used.

Because of the subtle differences between the prefix and postfix forms of the increment and decrement operators, they should be used with care. As always, favor the side of readability.

Assignment Operators

As a convenience, several *assignment operators* have been defined in Java that combine a basic operation with assignment. For example, the += operator can be used as follows:

```
total += 5;
```

This performs the same operation as the following statement:

```
total = total + 5;
```

The right-hand side of the assignment operator can be a full expression. The expression on the right-hand side of the operator is evaluated, then that result is added to the current value of the variable on the left-hand side, and that value is stored in the variable. Therefore, the following statement:

```
total += (sum - 12) / count;
```

is equivalent to:

```
total = total + ((sum - 12) / count);
```

Many similar assignment operators are defined in Java, including those that perform subtraction (-=), multiplication (*=), division (/=), and remainder (%=). The entire set of Java operators is discussed in Appendix D.

All of the assignment operators evaluate the entire expression on the right-hand side first, then use the result as the right operand of the other operation. Therefore, the following statement:

```
result *= count1 + count2;
```

is equivalent to:

```
result = result * (count1 + count2);
```

Likewise, the following statement:

```
result %= (highest - 40) / 2;
```

is equivalent to:

```
result = result % ((highest - 40) / 2);
```

Some assignment operators perform particular functions depending on the types of the operands, just as their corresponding regular operators do. For example, if the operands to the += operator are strings, then the assignment operator performs string concatenation.

SELF-REVIEW QUESTIONS *(see answers in Appendix N)*

SR 2.21 What is the result of 19%5 when evaluated in a Java expression? Explain.

SR 2.22 What is the result of 13/4 when evaluated in a Java expression? Explain.

SR 2.23 If an integer variable diameter currently holds the value 5, what is its value after the following statement is executed? Explain.

```
diameter = diameter * 4;
```

SR 2.24 What is operator precedence?

SR 2.25 What is the value of each of the following expressions?

```
a. 15 + 7 * 3
b. (15 + 7) * 3
c. 3 * 6 + 10 / 5 + 5
d. 27 % 5 + 7 % 3
e. 100 / 2 / 2 / 2
f. 100 / ( 2 / 2) / 2
```

SR 2.26 For each of the following expressions state whether they are valid or invalid. If invalid, explain why.

```
a. result = ( 5 + 2 );
b. result = ( 5 + 2 * ( 15 - 3 );
c. result = ( 5 + 2 (;
d. result = ( 5 + 2 ( 4 ) );
```

SR 2.27 What value is contained in the integer variable `result` after the following sequence of statements is executed?

```
result = 27;
result = result + 3;
result = result / 7;
result = result * 2;
```

SR 2.28 What value is contained in the integer variable `result` after the following sequence of statements is executed?

```
int base;
int result;
base = 5;
result = base + 3;
base = 7;
```

SR 2.29 What is an assignment operator?

SR 2.30 If an integer variable `weight` currently holds the value 100, what is its value after the following statement is executed? Explain.

```
weight -= 17;
```

2.5 Data Conversion

Because Java is a strongly typed language, each data value is associated with a particular type. It is sometimes helpful or necessary to convert a data value of one type to another type, but we must be careful that we don't lose important information in the process. For example, suppose a short variable that holds the number 1000 is converted to a byte value. Because a byte does not have enough bits to represent the value 1000, some bits would be lost in the conversion, and the number represented in the byte would not keep its original value.

A conversion between one primitive type and another falls into one of two categories: widening conversions and narrowing conversions. *Widening conversions* are the safest because they usually do not lose information. They are called widening conversions because they go from one data type to another type that uses an equal or greater amount of space to store the value. Figure 2.5 lists the Java widening conversions.

For example, it is safe to convert from a byte to a short because a byte is stored in 8 bits and a short is stored in 16 bits. There is no loss of information. All widening conversions that go from an integer type to another integer type, or from a floating point type to another floating point type, preserve the numeric value exactly.

From	To
byte	short, int, long, float, or double
short	int, long, float, or double
char	int, long, float, or double
int	long, float, or double
long	float or double
float	double

FIGURE 2.5   Java widening conversions

KEY CONCEPT

Narrowing conversions should be avoided because they can lose information.

Although widening conversions do not lose any information about the magnitude of a value, the widening conversions that result in a floating point value can lose precision. When converting from an int or a long to a float, or from a long to a double, some of the least significant digits may be lost. In this case, the resulting floating point value will be a rounded version of the integer value, following the rounding techniques defined in the IEEE 754 floating point standard.

Narrowing conversions are more likely to lose information than widening conversions are. They often go from one type to a type that uses less space to store a value, and therefore some of the information may be compromised. Narrowing conversions can lose both numeric magnitude and precision. Therefore, in general, they should be avoided. Figure 2.6 lists the Java narrowing conversions.

An exception to the space-shrinking situation in narrowing conversions is when we convert a byte (8 bits) or short (16 bits) to a char (16 bits). These are still

From	To
byte	char
short	byte or char
char	byte or short
int	byte, short, or char
long	byte, short, char, or int
float	byte, short, char, int, or long
double	byte, short, char, int, long, or float

FIGURE 2.6   Java narrowing conversions

considered narrowing conversions, because the sign bit is incorporated into the new character value. Since a character value is unsigned, a negative integer will be converted into a character that has no particular relationship to the numeric value of the original integer.

Note that `boolean` values are not mentioned in either widening or narrowing conversions. A `boolean` value cannot be converted to any other primitive type and vice versa.

Conversion Techniques

In Java, conversions can occur in three ways:

- assignment conversion
- promotion
- casting

Assignment conversion occurs when a value of one type is assigned to a variable of another type during which the value is converted to the new type. Only widening conversions can be accomplished through assignment. For example, if money is a `float` variable and dollars is an `int` variable, then the following assignment statement automatically converts the value in dollars to a `float`:

```
money = dollars;
```

Therefore, if dollars contains the value 25, after the assignment, money contains the value 25.0. However, if we attempt to assign money to dollars, the compiler will issue an error message alerting us to the fact that we are attempting a narrowing conversion that could lose information. If we really want to do this assignment, we have to make the conversion explicit by using a cast.

Conversion via *promotion* occurs automatically when certain operators need to modify their operands in order to perform the operation. For example, when a floating point value called sum is divided by an integer value called count, the value of count is promoted to a floating point value automatically, before the division takes place, producing a floating point result:

```
result = sum / count;
```

A similar conversion is taking place when a number is concatenated with a string. The number is first converted (promoted) to a string, then the two strings are concatenated.

Casting is the most general form of conversion in Java. If a conversion can be accomplished at all in a Java program, it can be accomplished using a cast. A cast is a Java operator that is specified by a type name in parentheses. It is placed in front of the value to be converted. For example, to convert money to an integer value, we could put a cast in front of it:

```
dollars = (int) money;
```

The cast returns the value in money, truncating any fractional part. If money contained the value 84.69, then after the assignment, dollars would contain the value 84. Note, however, that the cast does not change the value in money. After the assignment operation is complete, money still contains the value 84.69.

Casts are helpful in many situations where we need to treat a value temporarily as another type. For example, if we want to divide the integer value total by the integer value count and get a floating point result, we could do it as follows:

```
result = (float) total / count;
```

First, the cast operator returns a floating point version of the value in total. This operation does not change the value in total. Then, count is treated as a floating point value via arithmetic promotion. Now the division operator will perform floating point division and produce the intended result. If the cast had not been included, the operation would have performed integer division and truncated the answer before assigning it to result. Also note that because the cast operator has a higher precedence than the division operator, the cast operates on the value of total, not on the result of the division.

SELF-REVIEW QUESTIONS *(see answers in Appendix N)*

SR 2.31 Why are widening conversions safer than narrowing conversions?

SR 2.32 Identify each of the following conversions as either a widening conversion or a narrowing conversion.

   a. int to long
   b. int to byte
   c. byte to short
   d. byte to char
   e. short to double

SR 2.33 Assuming result is a float variable and value is an int variable, what type of variable will value be after the following assignment statement is executed? Explain.

```
result = value;
```

SR 2.34   Assuming `result` is a `float` variable that contains the value 27.32 and
`value` is an `int` variable that contains the `value` 15, what are the values of each of the variables after the following assignment statement is executed? Explain.

```
value = (int) result;
```

SR 2.35   Given the following declarations, what result is stored by each of the following assignment statements.

```
int iResult, num1 = 17, num2 = 5;
double fResult, val1 = 12.0, val2 = 2.34;

a. iResult = num1 / num2;
b. fResult = num1 / num2;
c. fResult = val1 / num2;
d. fResult = (double) num1 / num2;
e. iResult = (int) val1 / num2;
```

2.6 Interactive Programs

It is often useful to design a program to read data from the user interactively during execution. That way, new results can be computed each time the program is run, depending on the data that is entered.

The Scanner Class

The Scanner class, which is part of the standard Java class library, provides convenient methods for reading input values of various types. The input could come from various sources, including data typed interactively by the user or data stored in a file. The Scanner class can also be used to parse a character string into separate pieces. Figure 2.7 lists some of the methods provided by the Scanner class.

> **KEY CONCEPT**
> The Scanner class provides methods for reading input of various types from various sources.

We must first create a Scanner object in order to invoke its methods. Objects in Java are created using the new operator. The following declaration creates a Scanner object that reads input from the keyboard:

```
Scanner scan = new Scanner (System.in);
```

This declaration creates a variable called scan that represents a Scanner object. The object itself is created by the new operator and a call to a special method

```
Scanner (InputStream source)
Scanner (File source)
Scanner (String source)
        Constructors: sets up the new scanner to scan values from the specified source.

String next()
        Returns the next input token as a character string.

String nextLine()
        Returns all input remaining on the current line as a character string.

boolean nextBoolean()
byte nextByte()
double nextDouble()
float nextFloat()
int nextInt()
long nextLong()
short nextShort()
        Returns the next input token as the indicated type. Throws
        InputMismatchException  if the next token is inconsistent with the type.

boolean hasNext()
        Returns true if the scanner has another token in its input.

Scanner useDelimiter (String pattern)
Scanner useDelimiter (Pattern pattern)
        Sets the scanner's delimiting pattern.

Pattern delimiter()
        Returns the pattern the scanner is currently using to match delimiters.

String findInLine (String pattern)
String findInLine (Pattern pattern)
        Attempts to find the next occurrence of the specified pattern, ignoring delimiters.
```

FIGURE 2.7   Some methods of the Scanner class

called a *constructor* to set up the object. The Scanner constructor accepts a parameter that indicates the source of the input. The System.in object represents the *standard input stream*, which by default is the keyboard. Creating objects using the new operator is discussed further in the next chapter.

Unless specified otherwise, a Scanner object assumes that white space characters (space characters, tabs, and new lines) are used to separate the elements of the input, called *tokens*, from each other. These characters are called the input *delimiters*. The set of delimiters can be changed if the input tokens are separated by characters other than white space.

The next method of the Scanner class reads the next input token as a string and returns it. Therefore, if the input consisted of a series of words separated by spaces, each call to next would return the next word. The nextLine method reads all of the input until the end of the line is found, and returns it as one string.

The program Echo, shown in Listing 2.8, simply reads a line of text typed by the user, stores it in a variable that holds a character string, then echoes it back to the screen.

The import statement above the definition of the Echo class tells the program that we will be using the Scanner class in this program. The Scanner class is part of the java.util class library. The use of the import statement is discussed further in Chapter 3.

Various Scanner methods such as nextInt and nextDouble are provided to read data of particular types. The GasMileage program, shown in Listing 2.9, reads the number of miles traveled as an integer, and the number of gallons of fuel consumed as a double, then computes the gas mileage.

LISTING 2.8

```
//********************************************************************
//  Echo.java         Author: Lewis/Loftus
//
//  Demonstrates the use of the nextLine method of the Scanner class
//  to read a string from the user.
//********************************************************************

import java.util.Scanner;

public class Echo
{
    //-----------------------------------------------------------------
    //  Reads a character string from the user and prints it.
    //-----------------------------------------------------------------
    public static void main (String[] args)
```

LISTING 2.8   *continued*

```java
    {
        String message;
        Scanner scan = new Scanner (System.in);

        System.out.println ("Enter a line of text:");

        message = scan.nextLine();

        System.out.println ("You entered: \"" + message + "\"");
    }
}
```

OUTPUT

```
Enter a line of text:
Set your laser printer on stun!
You entered: "Set your laser printer on stun!"
```

As you can see by the output of the GasMileage program, the calculation produces a floating point result that is accurate to several decimal places. In the next chapter we discuss classes that help us format our output in various ways, including rounding a floating point value to a particular number of decimal places.

LISTING 2.9

```java
//********************************************************************
//  GasMileage.java        Author: Lewis/Loftus
//
//  Demonstrates the use of the Scanner class to read numeric data.
//********************************************************************

import java.util.Scanner;

public class GasMileage
{
    //-----------------------------------------------------------------
    //  Calculates fuel efficiency based on values entered by the
    //  user.
    //-----------------------------------------------------------------
    public static void main (String[] args)
```

LISTING 2.9   *continued*

```java
    {
        int miles;
        double gallons, mpg;

        Scanner scan = new Scanner (System.in);

        System.out.print ("Enter the number of miles: ");
        miles = scan.nextInt();

        System.out.print ("Enter the gallons of fuel used: ");
        gallons = scan.nextDouble();

        mpg = miles / gallons;

        System.out.println ("Miles Per Gallon: " + mpg);
    }
}
```

OUTPUT

```
Enter the number of miles: 328
Enter the gallons of fuel used: 11.2
Miles Per Gallon: 29.28571428571429
```

A Scanner object processes the input one token at a time, based on the methods used to read the data and the delimiters used to separate the input values. Therefore, multiple values can be put on the same line of input or can be separated over multiple lines, as appropriate for the situation.

In Chapter 5 we use the Scanner class to read input from a data file and modify the delimiters it uses to parse the data. Appendix H explores how to use the Scanner class to analyze its input using patterns called *regular expressions*.

VideoNote

Example using the Scanner class.

SELF-REVIEW QUESTIONS *(see answers in Appendix N)*

myprogramminglab

SR 2.36 Identify which line of the GasMileage program does each of the following.

    a. Tells the program that we will be using the Scanner class.
    b. Creates a Scanner object.
    c. Sets up the Scanner object scan to read from the standard input stream.
    d. Reads an integer from the standard input stream.

SR 2.37 Assume you already have instantiated a Scanner object named myScanner and an int variable named value as follows in your program:

```
Scanner myScanner = new Scanner (System.in);
int value = 0;
```

Write program statements that will ask the user to enter their age, and store their response in value.

2.7 Graphics

Graphics play a crucial role in computer systems. Throughout this book we explore various aspects of graphics and discuss how they are accomplished. In fact, the last one or two sections of each chapter are devoted to graphics topics. We refer to this as the *Graphics Track* through the book. These sections can be skipped without losing continuity through the rest of the text, incorporated into the regular flow of the chapters, or explored as a group.

> **KEY CONCEPT**
>
> Graphical data is represented by dividing it into many small pieces called pixels.

A picture, like all other information stored on a computer, must be digitized by breaking the information into pieces and representing those pieces as numbers. In the case of pictures, we break the picture into *pixels* (picture elements). A pixel is a tiny region that represents a very small piece of the picture. The complete picture is stored by storing the color of each individual pixel.

A digitized picture can be reproduced when needed by reassembling its pixels. The more pixels used to represent a picture, the more realistic it looks when it is reproduced. The number of pixels used to represent a picture is called the *picture resolution*. The number of pixels that can be displayed by a monitor is called the *monitor resolution*.

A black and white picture can be stored by representing each pixel using a single bit. If the bit is 0, that pixel is white; if the bit is 1, it is black. Figure 2.8 shows a black and white picture that has been stored digitally and an enlargement of a portion of that picture, which shows the individual pixels.

Coordinate Systems

When drawn, each pixel of a picture is mapped to a pixel on the monitor screen. Each computer system and programming language defines a coordinate system so that we can refer to particular pixels.

FIGURE 2.8   A digitized picture with a small portion magnified

A traditional two-dimensional Cartesian coordinate system has two axes that meet at the origin. Values on either axis can be negative or positive. The Java programming language has a relatively simple coordinate system in which all of the visible coordinates are positive. Figure 2.9 compares a traditional coordinate system to the Java coordinate system.

Each point in the Java coordinate system is represented using an (x, y) pair of values. The top-left corner of any Java drawing area has coordinates $(0, 0)$. The x-axis coordinates get larger as you move to the right, and the y-axis coordinates get larger as you move down.

> **KEY CONCEPT**
>
> Java's coordinate system has the origin in the upper-left corner and all visible coordinates are positive.

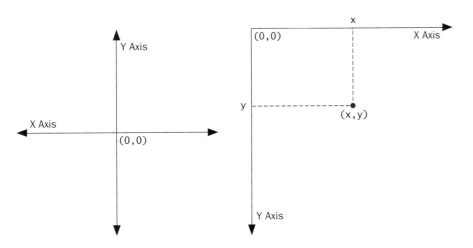

FIGURE 2.9   A traditional coordinate system and the Java coordinate system

As we've seen in previous examples, a Java program does not have to be graphical in nature. However, if it is, each graphical component in the program has its own coordinate system, with the origin (0, 0) in the top-left corner. This consistent approach makes it relatively easy to manage various graphical elements.

Representing Color

Color pictures are divided into pixels, just as black and white pictures are. However, because each pixel can be one of many possible colors, it is not sufficient to represent each pixel using only one bit. There are various ways to represent the color of a pixel. Let's briefly discuss one popular technique.

> **KEY CONCEPT**
>
> Colors are represented in Java using an RGB value—three values that represent the contributions of the primary colors red, green, and blue.

Every color can be represented as a mix of three *primary colors*: red, green, and blue. In Java, as in many other computer languages, colors are specified by three numbers that are collectively referred to as an *RGB value*. RGB stands for Red-Green-Blue. Each number represents the contribution of a primary color. Using one byte (eight bits) to store each of the three numbers, the numbers can range from 0 to 255. The level of each primary color determines the overall color. For example, high values of red and green combined with a low level of blue results in a shade of yellow.

Color	Object	RGB Value
black	Color.black	0, 0, 0
blue	Color.blue	0, 0, 255
cyan	Color.cyan	0, 255, 255
gray	Color.gray	128, 128, 128
dark gray	Color.darkGray	64, 64, 64
light gray	Color.lightGray	192, 192, 192
green	Color.green	0, 255, 0
magenta	Color.magenta	255, 0, 255
orange	Color.orange	255, 200, 0
pink	Color.pink	255, 175, 175
red	Color.red	255, 0, 0
white	Color.white	255, 255, 255
yellow	Color.yellow	255, 255, 0

FIGURE 2.10   Predefined colors in the Color class

In Java, a programmer uses the Color class, which is part of the java.awt package, to define and manage colors. Each object of the Color class represents a single color. The class contains several instances of itself to provide a basic set of predefined colors. Figure 2.10 lists the predefined colors of the Color class. It also contains methods to define and manage many other colors.

> **KEY CONCEPT**
> The Color class contains several predefined colors that are commonly used, and can be used to define many others.

SELF-REVIEW QUESTIONS *(see answers in Appendix N)*

myprogramminglab

SR 2.38   How can a black and white picture be represented using 1s and 0s?

SR 2.39   Three corners of a rectangle drawn using the Java coordinate system have coordinates (3, 4), (3, 7), and (8, 7). What are the coordinates of the fourth corner?

SR 2.40   Two corners of a square drawn using the Java coordinate system have coordinates (5, 10) and (8, 10). What are the coordinates of the other two corners?

SR 2.41   How many bits are needed to store a color picture that is 300 pixels wide and 200 pixels high? Assume color is represented using the RGB technique described in this chapter and that no special compression technique is used.

2.8 Applets

There are two kinds of Java programs: Java applets and Java applications. A Java *applet* is a Java program that is intended to be embedded into an HTML document, transported across a network, and executed using a Web browser. A Java *application* is a stand-alone program that can be executed using a Java interpreter. All programs presented thus far in this book have been Java applications.

> **KEY CONCEPT**
> Applets are Java programs that are usually transported across a network and executed using a Web browser.

The Web enables users to send and receive various types of media, such as text, graphics, and sound, using a point-and-click interface that is extremely convenient and easy to use. A Java applet was the first kind of executable program that could be retrieved using Web software. Java applets are considered just another type of media that can be exchanged across the Web.

Though Java applets are generally intended to be transported across a network, they don't have to be. They can be viewed locally using a Web browser. For that matter, they don't even have to be executed through a Web browser at all. A tool in Sun's Java Software Development Kit called *appletviewer* can be used to interpret and execute an applet. We use appletviewer to display applets in this book. However, usually the point of making a Java applet is to provide a link to it on a Web page and allow it to be retrieved and executed by Web users anywhere in the world.

Java bytecode (not Java source code) is linked to an HTML document and sent across the Web. A version of the Java interpreter embedded in a Web browser is used to execute the applet once it reaches its destination. A Java applet must be compiled into bytecode format before it can be used with the Web.

There are some important differences between the structure of a Java applet and the structure of a Java application. Because the Web browser that executes an applet is already running, applets can be thought of as a part of a larger program. As such they do not have a main method where execution starts. The paint method in an applet is automatically invoked by the applet. Consider the program in Listing 2.10, in which the paint method is used to draw a few shapes and write a quotation by Albert Einstein to the screen.

The two import statements at the beginning of the program explicitly indicate the packages that are used in the program. In this example, we need the JApplet

LISTING 2.10

```java
//********************************************************************
//  Einstein.java        Author: Lewis/Loftus
//
//  Demonstrates a basic applet.
//********************************************************************

import javax.swing.JApplet;
import java.awt.*;

public class Einstein extends JApplet
{
    //-----------------------------------------------------------------
    //  Draws a quotation by Albert Einstein among some shapes.
    //-----------------------------------------------------------------
    public void paint (Graphics page)
    {
        page.drawRect (50, 50, 40, 40);      // square
        page.drawRect (60, 80, 225, 30);     // rectangle
        page.drawOval (75, 65, 20, 20);      // circle
        page.drawLine (35, 60, 100, 120);    // line

        page.drawString ("Out of clutter, find simplicity.", 110, 70);
        page.drawString ("-- Albert Einstein", 130, 100);
    }
}
```

LISTING 2.10   *continued*

DISPLAY

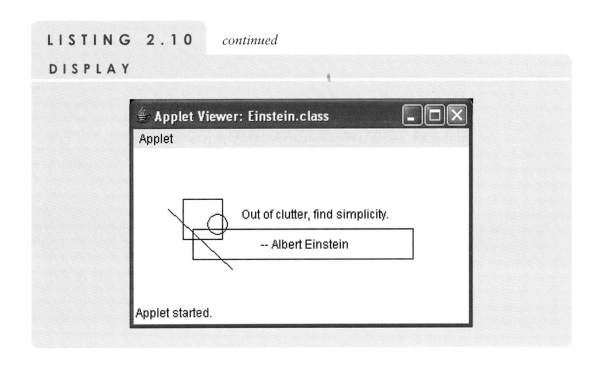

class, which is part of the javax.swing package, and various graphics capabilities defined in the java.awt package. Chapter 3 explores import statements further.

A class that defines an applet extends the JApplet class, as indicated in the header line of the class declaration. This process is making use of the object-oriented concept of inheritance, which we discussed in Chapter 1 and explore in more detail later in the book. Applet classes must also be declared as public.

The paint method is one of several applet methods that have particular significance. It is invoked automatically whenever the graphic elements of the applet need to be painted to the screen, such as when the applet is first run or when another window that was covering it is moved.

Note that the paint method accepts a Graphics object as a parameter. A Graphics object defines a particular *graphics context* with which we can interact. The graphics context passed into an applet's paint method represents the entire applet window. Each graphics context has its own coordinate system. In later examples, we will have multiple components, each with its own graphics context.

A Graphics object allows us to draw various shapes using methods such as drawRect, drawOval, drawLine, and drawString. The parameters passed to the drawing methods specify the coordinates and sizes of the shapes to be drawn. We explore these and other methods that draw shapes in the next section.

Executing Applets Using the Web

In order for the applet to be transmitted over the Web and executed by a browser, it must be referenced in a HyperText Markup Language (HTML) document. An HTML document contains *tags* that specify formatting instructions and identify the special types of media that are to be included in a document. A Java program is considered a specific media type, just as text, graphics, and sound are.

An HTML tag is enclosed in angle brackets. The following is an example of an applet tag:

```
<applet code="Einstein.class" width="350" height="175">
</applet>
```

This tag dictates that the bytecode stored in the file `Einstein.class` should be transported over the network and executed on the machine that wants to view this particular HTML document. The applet tag also indicates the width and height of the applet.

There are other tags that can be used to reference an applet in an HTML file, including the `<object>` tag and the `<embed>` tag. The `<object>` tag is actually the tag that should be used, according to the World Wide Web Consortium (W3C). However, browser support for the `<object>` tag is not consistent. For now, the most reliable solution is to use the `<applet>` tag.

Note that the applet tag refers to the bytecode file of the `Einstein` applet, not to the source code file. Before an applet can be transported using the Web, it must be compiled into its bytecode format. Then, as shown in Figure 2.11, the document can be loaded using a Web browser, which will automatically interpret and execute the applet.

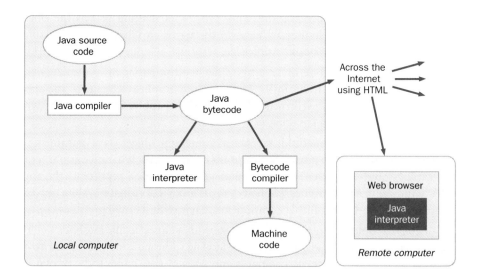

FIGURE 2.11   The Java translation and execution process, including applets

SELF-REVIEW QUESTIONS *(see answers in Appendix N)*   myprogramminglab

SR 2.42   What is the difference between a Java application and a Java applet?

SR 2.43   When is an applet's `paint` method invoked?

SR 2.44   What is wrong with the following HTML applet tag? Explain.

```
<applet code="DrawHouse.java" width="400" height="300">
</applet>
```

2.9 Drawing Shapes

The Java standard class library provides many classes that let us present and manipulate graphical information. The `Graphics` class is fundamental to all such processing.

The Graphics Class

The `Graphics` class is defined in the `java.awt` package. It contains various methods that allow us to draw shapes, including lines, rectangles, and ovals. Figure 2.12 lists some of the fundamental drawing methods of the `Graphics` class.

> **KEY CONCEPT**
> Most shapes can be drawn filled (opaque) or unfilled (as an outline).

Note that these methods also let us draw circles and squares, which are just specific types of ovals and rectangles, respectively. We discuss additional drawing methods of the `Graphics` class later in the book at appropriate points.

The methods of the `Graphics` class allow us to specify whether we want a shape filled or unfilled. An unfilled shape shows only the outline of the shape and is otherwise transparent (you can see any underlying graphics). A filled shape is solid between its boundaries and covers any underlying graphics.

All of these methods rely on the Java coordinate system, which we discussed earlier in this chapter. Recall that point $(0,0)$ is in the upper-left corner, such that x values get larger as we move to the right, and y values get larger as we move down. Any shapes drawn at coordinates that are outside the visible area will not be seen.

> **KEY CONCEPT**
> A bounding rectangle is used to define the position and size of curved shapes such as ovals.

Many of the `Graphics` drawing methods are self-explanatory, but some require a little more discussion. Note, for instance, that an oval drawn by the `drawOval` method is defined by the coordinate of the upper-left corner and dimensions that specify the width and height of a *bounding rectangle*. Shapes with curves, such

```
void drawLine (int x1, int y1, int x2, int y2)
    Paints a line from point (x1, y1) to point (x2, y2).

void drawRect (int x, int y, int width, int height)
    Paints a rectangle with upper left corner (x, y) and dimensions width and
    height.

void drawOval (int x, int y, int width, int height)
    Paints an oval bounded by the rectangle with an upper left corner of (x, y) and
    dimensions width and height.

void drawString (String str, int x, int y)
    Paints the character string str at point (x, y), extending to the right.

void drawArc (int x, int y, int width, int height, int
startAngle, int arcAngle)
    Paints an arc along the oval bounded by the rectangle defined by x, y, width,
    and height.  The arc starts at startAngle and extends for a distance defined by
    arcAngle.

void fillRect (int x, int y, int width, int height)
    Same as their draw counterparts, but filled with the current foreground color.

void fillOval (int x, int y, int width, int height)

void fillArc (int x, int y, int width, int height,
int startAngle, int arcAngle)

Color getColor ()
    Returns this graphics context's foreground color.

void setColor (Color color)
    Sets this graphics context's foreground color to the specified color.
```

FIGURE 2.12   Some methods of the Graphics class

KEY CONCEPT

An arc is a segment of an oval beginning at a specific start angle and extending for a distance specified by the arc angle.

as ovals, are often defined by a rectangle that encompasses their perimeters. Figure 2.13 depicts a bounding rectangle for an oval.

An arc can be thought of as a segment of an oval. To draw an arc, we specify the oval of which the arc is a part and the portion of the oval in which we're interested. The starting point

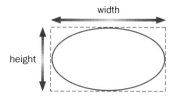

FIGURE 2.13   An oval and its bounding rectangle

of the arc is defined by the *start angle* and the ending point of the arc is defined by the *arc angle*. The arc angle does not indicate where the arc ends, but rather its range. The start angle and the arc angle are measured in degrees. The origin for the start angle is an imaginary horizontal line passing through the center of the oval and can be referred to as 0°, as shown in Figure 2.14.

Every graphics context has a current *foreground color* that is used whenever shapes or strings are drawn. Every surface that can be drawn on has a *background color*. The foreground color is set using the `setColor` method of the `Graphics` class, and the background color is set using the `setBackground` method of the component on which we are drawing, such as the applet.

Listing 2.11 shows an applet called `Snowman`. It uses various drawing and color methods to draw a winter scene featuring a snowman. Review the code carefully to note how each shape is drawn to create the overall picture.

VideoNote

Example using drawn shapes.

Note that the snowman figure is based on two constant values called MID and TOP, which define the midpoint of the snowman (left to right) and the top of the

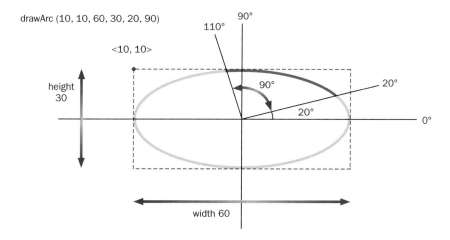

FIGURE 2.14   An arc defined by an oval, a start angle, and an arc angle

LISTING 2.11

```java
//********************************************************************
//  Snowman.java        Author: Lewis/Loftus
//
//  Demonstrates basic drawing methods and the use of color.
//********************************************************************

import javax.swing.JApplet;
import java.awt.*;

public class Snowman extends JApplet
{
    //-----------------------------------------------------------------
    //  Draws a snowman.
    //-----------------------------------------------------------------
    public void paint (Graphics page)
    {
        final int MID = 150;
        final int TOP = 50;

        setBackground (Color.cyan);

        page.setColor (Color.blue);
        page.fillRect (0, 175, 300, 50);   // ground

        page.setColor (Color.yellow);
        page.fillOval (-40, -40, 80, 80);   // sun

        page.setColor (Color.white);
        page.fillOval (MID-20, TOP, 40, 40);        // head
        page.fillOval (MID-35, TOP+35, 70, 50);     // upper torso
        page.fillOval (MID-50, TOP+80, 100, 60);    // lower torso

        page.setColor (Color.black);
        page.fillOval (MID-10, TOP+10, 5, 5);   // left eye
        page.fillOval (MID+5, TOP+10, 5, 5);    // right eye

        page.drawArc (MID-10, TOP+20, 20, 10, 190, 160);    // smile

        page.drawLine (MID-25, TOP+60, MID-50, TOP+40);  // left arm
        page.drawLine (MID+25, TOP+60, MID+55, TOP+60);  // right arm

        page.drawLine (MID-20, TOP+5, MID+20, TOP+5);  // brim of hat
        page.fillRect (MID-15, TOP-20, 30, 25);        // top of hat
    }
}
```

LISTING 2.11 *continued*

DISPLAY

snowman's head. The entire snowman figure is drawn relative to these values. Using constants like these makes it easier to create the snowman and to make modifications later. For example, to shift the snowman to the right or left in our picture, only one constant declaration would have to change.

SELF-REVIEW QUESTIONS *(see answers in Appendix N)*   myprogramminglab

SR 2.45 What is a bounding rectangle?

SR 2.46 Assuming you have a Graphics object called page, write a statement that will draw a square with a side length of 50, such that its upper-left corner is at point (16, 12).

SR 2.47 Assuming you have a Graphics object called page, write a sequence of statements that will draw a blue rectangle with a height of 20 and a width of 40, such that its upper-left corner is at point (30, 35).

SR 2.48 What would be the result of making each of the following changes separately to the Snowman program? You may make the change, compile and run the program, and observe and report the results. Briefly explain what you observe.

a. The value of MID is set to 120 instead of 150.
b. The value of TOP is set to 25 instead of 50.
c. Just before the last two statements of the program (the statements that draw the hat) we include the statement

```
page.setColor (Color.blue);
```

d. In the statement that creates the smile, the 190 is changed to a 10.
e. Just before the statement that creates the upper torso, the foreground color is set to cyan. It is set back to white immediately after the upper torso is created.

Summary of Key Concepts

- The `print` and `println` methods represent two services provided by the `System.out` object.

- An escape sequence can be used to represent a character that would otherwise cause compilation problems.

- A variable is a name for a memory location used to hold a value of a particular data type.

- Accessing data leaves it intact in memory, but an assignment statement overwrites the old data.

- We cannot assign a value of one type to a variable of an incompatible type.

- Constants hold a particular value for the duration of their existence.

- Java has two kinds of numeric values: integer and floating point. There are four integer data types and two floating point data types.

- Java uses the 16-bit Unicode character set to represent character data.

- Expressions are combinations of operators and operands used to perform a calculation.

- Java follows a well-defined set of precedence rules that governs the order in which operators will be evaluated in an expression.

- Narrowing conversions should be avoided because they can lose information.

- The `Scanner` class provides methods for reading input of various types from various sources.

- Graphical data is represented by dividing it into many small pieces called pixels.

- Java's coordinate system has the origin in the upper-left corner and all visible coordinates are positive.

- Colors are represented in Java using an RGB value—three values that represent the contributions of the primary colors red, green, and blue.

- The `Color` class contains several predefined colors that are commonly used, and can be used to define many others.

- Applets are Java programs that are usually transported across a network and executed using a Web browser.

- Most shapes can be drawn filled (opaque) or unfilled (as an outline).

- A bounding rectangle is used to define the position and size of curved shapes such as ovals.

- An arc is a segment of an oval beginning at a specific start angle and extending for a distance specified by the arc angle.

Exercises

Visit www.myprogramminglab.com to complete many of these Exercises online and get instant feedback.

EX 2.1   Explain the following programming statement in terms of objects and the services they provide:

```
System.out.println ("I gotta be me!");
```

EX 2.2   What output is produced by the following code fragment? Explain.

```
a. System.out.print("Java ")
       System.out.print("Programming");
```

```
b. System.out.println("Java ");
       System.out.println("Programming");
```

EX 2.3   Write a single Java program statement to display the text below and explain why it is written like that.

```
"A piano has
            88 keys"
```

EX 2.4   What output is produced by the following code fragments?

```
a. System.out.println ("Result : "+ 40+30);
b. System.out.println ("Result : "+(40+30));
```

EX 2.5   What output is produced by the following code fragments?

```
System.out.println("A \"label\" can contain either \n\ttext,
\n\tan image, or \n\tboth.");
```

EX 2.6   What value is contained in the integer variable value after the following statements are executed?

```
value=16;
value=value+5;
value=value+1;
value=value/3;
```

EX 2.7   What output is contained in the floating point variable value after the following statements are executed?

```
value=2.5f;
value=value*2;
value=value/3;
```

EX 2.8   What result is contained in the integer variable `value` after the following statements are executed?

```
value=10;
value += 10;
value *= value;
value /= value;
value -=10;
```

EX 2.9   Write four different program statements that decrement the value of an integer variable `count`.

EX 2.10 Given the following declarations, what result is stored in each of the listed assignment statements?

```
int iResult, num1 = 25, num2 = 40, num3 = 17, num4 = 5;
double fResult, val1 = 17.0, val2 = 12.78;
```

```
a. iResult = num1 / num4;
b. fResult = num1 / num4;
c. iResult = num3 / num4;
d. fResult = num3 / num4;
e. fResult = val1 / num4;
f. fResult = val1 / val2;
g. iResult = num1 / num2;
h. fResult = (double) num1 / num2;
i. fResult = num1 / (double) num2;
j. fResult = (double) (num1 / num2);
k. iResult = (int) (val1 / num4);
l. fResult = (int) (val1 / num4);
m. fResult = (int) ((double) num1 / num2);
n. iResult = num3 % num4;
o. iResult = num2 % num3;
p. iResult = num3 % num2;
q. iResult = num2 % num4;
```

EX 2.11 For each of the following expressions, indicate the order in which the operators will be evaluated by writing a number beneath each operator.

```
a. a - b - c - d
b. a - b + c - d
c. a + b / c / d
d. a + b / c * d
e. a / b * c * d
f. a % b / c * d
g. a % b % c % d
```

h. a – (b – c) – d
i. (a – (b – c)) – d
j. a – ((b – c) – d)
k. a % (b % c) * d * e
l. a + (b – c) * d – e
m. (a + b) * c + d * e
n. (a + b) * (c / d) % e

EX 2.12 Explain the role of an applet and its significance in Java programs.

EX 2.13 Compare and contrast picture resolution with the monitor resolution used by graphical computer systems.

EX 2.14 How many bits are needed to store a color picture that is 400 pixels wide and 250 pixels high? Assume color is represented using the RGB technique described in this chapter and that no special compression is done.

EX 2.15 Assuming you have a Graphics object called page, write suitable statements to draw a triangle with vertices (100,200), (225, 50) and (275,250).

EX 2.16 Assuming you have a Graphics object called Point, write a suitable statement that will draw a square with a side of 50, whose upper-left corner is at point (30,40).

EX 2.17 Assuming you have a Graphics object called Display, write a code statement to draw an ellipse with major axis 100 and minor axis 50, whose upper-left corner is at point (20,40).

EX 2.18 The following lines of code draw the eyes of the snowman in the Snowman applet. The eyes seem centered on the face when drawn, but the first parameters of each call are not equally offset from the midpoint. Explain.

```
page.fillOval (MID-10, TOP+10, 5, 5);
page.fillOval (MID+5, TOP+10, 5, 5);
```

Programming Projects

Visit www.myprogramminglab.com to complete many of these Programming Projects online and get instant feedback.

PP 2.1 Create a revised version of the Lincoln application from Chapter 1 such that quotes appear around the quotation.

PP 2.2 Write an application that reads five scores (in integers) and prints the total and average of those scores.

PP 2.3   Write an application that prompts for and reads a person's name, age, college, and pet's name. Then print the following paragraph, inserting the appropriate data:

Hello, my name is ***name*** and I am ***age*** years
old. I'm enjoying my time at ***college***, though
I miss my pet ***petname*** very much!

PP 2.4   Write an application that reads two floating point numbers and prints their sum, difference, and product.

PP 2.5   Write an application that converts feet into centimeters. (One foot equals 30.48 centimeters.) Read the feet value from the user as a floating point value and convert it.

PP 2.6   Write an application that converts miles to kilometers. (One mile equals 1.60935 kilometers.) Read the miles value from the user as a floating point value.

PP 2.7   Write an application that prompts for and reads integer values for speed and distance traveled, then prints the time required for the trip as a floating point result.

PP 2.8   Write an application that reads values representing a time duration in hours, minutes, and seconds and then prints the equivalent total number of seconds. (For example, 1 hour, 28 minutes, and 42 seconds is equivalent to 5322 seconds.)

PP 2.9   Create a version of the previous project that reverses the computation. That is, read a value representing a number of seconds, then print the equivalent amount of time as a combination of hours, minutes, and seconds. (For example, 9999 seconds is equivalent to 2 hours, 46 minutes, and 39 seconds.)

VideoNote

Developing a solution of PP 2.10.

PP 2.10   Write an application that determines the value of the coins in a jar and prints the total in dollars and cents. Read integer values that represent the number of quarters, dimes, nickels, and pennies.

PP 2.11   Write an application that prompts for and reads a `double` value representing a monetary amount. Then determine the fewest number of each bill and coin needed to represent that amount, starting with the highest (assume that a ten-dollar bill is the maximum size needed). For example, if the value entered is 47.63 (forty-seven dollars and sixty-three cents), then the program should print the equivalent amount as:

```
4 ten dollar bills
1 five dollar bills
2 one dollar bills
```

```
2 quarters
1 dimes
0 nickles
3 pennies
```

PP 2.12   Write an application that prompts for and reads an integer representing the length of a square's side, then prints the square's perimeter and area.

PP 2.13   Write an application that prompts for and reads the numerator and denominator of a fraction as integers, then prints the decimal equivalent of the fraction.

PP 2.14   Create a revised version of the Snowman applet with the following modifications:

- Add two red buttons to the upper torso.
- Make the snowman frown instead of smile.
- Move the sun to the upper-right corner of the picture.
- Display your name in the upper-left corner of the picture.
- Shift the entire snowman 20 pixels to the right.

PP 2.15   Write an applet that writes your name using the drawString method. Embed a link to your applet in an HTML document and view it using a Web browser.

PP 2.16   Write an applet that draws the Big Dipper. Add some extra stars in the night sky.

PP 2.17   Write an applet that draws some balloons tied to strings. Make the balloons various colors.

PP 2.18   Write an applet that draws the Olympic logo. The circles in the logo should be colored, from left to right, blue, yellow, black, green, and red.

PP 2.19   Write an applet that draws a house with a door (and doorknob), windows, and a chimney. Add some smoke coming out of the chimney and some clouds in the sky.

PP 2.20   Write an applet which draws a smiley face with a nose, eyes, and lips.

PP 2.21   Write an applet that displays your name in shadow text by drawing your name in black, then drawing it again slightly offset in a lighter color.

PP 2.22   Write an applet that shows a pie chart with eight equal slices, all colored differently.

SOFTWARE FAILURE

NASA Mars Climate Orbiter and Polar Lander

What Happened?

As part of a series of missions exploring Mars, NASA launched the Mars Climate Orbiter in December, 1998, and the Mars Polar Lander in January, 1999. The two-spacecraft mission was designed to observe the atmospheric conditions on Mars through each of its seasons. The orbiter and the lander would have collected data about temperature, dust, water vapor, clouds, and the amount of carbon dioxide (CO_2) added and removed from the Martian pole regions.

After its nine-month journey, the orbiter arrived at Mars in September, 1999, and fired its main engines to establish an orbit. The orbiter passed behind the

Artist's conception of the Mars Climate Orbiter

planet (from Earth's perspective) five minutes later as planned, but NASA could not reestablish contact with it after expecting it to emerge. Review of the data showed that the altitude of the orbiter when it was entering orbit was only 57 kilometers, whereas the planned altitude was 140 kilometers. The minimum survivable altitude was between 85 and 100 kilometers. NASA concluded that the orbiter was destroyed by atmospheric friction.

The polar lander arrived at Mars in December, 1999, and all of the data indicated it was on target to make a successful soft landing within 10 kilometers of the target landing site on the Martian south pole. However, NASA lost contact with the lander just after it entered the atmosphere. Multiple attempts to reestablish contact with it over the following weeks and months were unsuccessful.

The total project cost for the orbiter and lander was $327.6 million.

What Caused It?

The root cause of the orbiter's problem was an embarrassing communication issue. The software that guided the navigation of the spacecraft used imperial units of measure (pound-force), while the spacecraft itself expected the data in metric units (newtons). Therefore the desired navigation changes and the actual effects were off by a factor of 4.45. This mismatch resulted in part because one team based in Colorado lead the efforts on the spacecraft, while a California-based team managed issues of navigation.

The cause of the lander's communication problem is unresolved but is not believed to be related to the orbiter's problem. The investigation concluded that the most likely cause was a software error that mistook the vibration caused by the deployment of the lander's legs for the vibration caused by actually landing on the planet's surface. That mistake would have caused the lander's descent engines to cut off while it was still 40 meters above the ground. Other problem scenarios are possible, however.

Lessons Learned

The mismatch of units in the Mars Climate Orbiter shows that seemingly obvious problems can be overlooked in a highly complex system. Mistakes are inevitable, but processes must be in place to catch them before they become critical. The investigation concluded that, in this case, the system for tracking and double-checking interconnected elements between subsystems was not robust enough. There was also inconsistent training of and communication with new members of the team, and some communication lines were too informal. In short, the mission lacked a rigorous total-system view that would have led to the discovery of the mismatched units problem before it was too late.

It's difficult to draw strong conclusions from the lander's problem given that the cause is not clearly understood. The fact that it remains an open question under-scores the need for more evaluation, simulation, and testing in situations where critical resources are at stake.

Source: nasa.gov

Using Classes and Objects

3

CHAPTER OBJECTIVES

- Discuss the creation of objects and the use of object reference variables.
- Explore the services provided by the String class.
- Describe how the Java standard class library is organized into packages.
- Explore the services provided by the Random and Math classes.
- Discuss ways to format output using the NumberFormat and DecimalFormat classes.
- Introduce enumerated types.
- Discuss wrapper classes and the concept of autoboxing.
- Introduce components and containers used in graphical user interfaces.
- Describe a label component and the use of images.

This chapter further explores the use of predefined classes and the objects we can create from them. Using classes and objects for the services they provide is a fundamental part of object-oriented software and sets the stage for writing classes of our own. In this chapter, we use classes and objects to manipulate character strings, produce random numbers, perform complex calculations, and format output. This chapter also introduces the concept of an enumerated type, which is a special kind of class in Java, and discusses the concept of a wrapper class. In the Graphics Track of this chapter, we lay the foundation for developing graphical user interfaces for our programs and discuss how to display images.

3.1 Creating Objects

At the end of Chapter 1 we presented an overview of object-oriented concepts, including the basic relationship between classes and objects. Then in Chapter 2, in addition to discussing primitive data, we provided some examples of using objects for the services they provide. This chapter explores these ideas further.

In previous examples, we've used the `println` method many times. As we mentioned in Chapter 2, the `println` method is a service provided by the `System.out` object, which represents the standard output stream. To be more precise, the identifier `out` is an object variable that is stored in the `System` class. It has been predefined and set up for us as part of the Java standard class library. We can simply use it.

In Chapter 2 we also used the `Scanner` class, which represents an object that allows us to read input from the keyboard or a file. We created a `Scanner` object using the `new` operator. Once the object was created, we were able to use it for the various services it provides. That is, we were able to invoke its methods.

Let's carefully examine the idea of creating an object. In Java, a variable name represents either a primitive value or an object. Like variables that hold primitive types, a variable that refers to an object must be declared. The class used to define an object can be thought of as the type of an object. The declarations of object variables have a similar structure to the declarations of primitive variables.

Consider the following two declarations:

```
int num;
String name;
```

The first declaration creates a variable that holds an integer value, as we've seen many times before. The second declaration creates a `String` variable that holds a *reference* to a `String` object. An object variable doesn't hold an object itself, it holds the address of an object.

Initially, the two variables declared above don't contain any data. We say they are *uninitialized*, which can be depicted as follows:

As we pointed out in Chapter 2, it is always important to make sure a variable is initialized before using it. For an object variable, that means we must make sure it refers to a valid object prior to using it. In most situations, the compiler will issue an error if you attempt to use a variable before initializing it.

An object variable can also be set to null, which is a reserved word in Java. A null reference specifically indicates that a variable does not refer to an object.

Note that, although we've declared a String reference variable, no String object actually exists yet. The act of creating an object using the new operator is called *instantiation*. An object is said to be an *instance* of a particular class. To instantiate an object, we can use the new operator, which returns the address of the new object. The following two assignment statements give values to the two variables declared above:

```
num = 42;
name = new String("James Gosling");
```

After the new operator creates the object, a *constructor* is invoked to help set it up initially. A constructor is a special method that has the same name as the class. In this example, the parameter to the constructor is a string literal that specifies the characters that the string object will hold. After these assignments are executed, the variables can be depicted as:

> **KEY CONCEPT**
> The new operator returns a reference to a newly created object.

```
num        42

name  ─────────────────▶  "James Gosling"
```

Since an object reference variable holds the address of the object, it can be thought of as a *pointer* to the location in memory where the object is held. We could show the numeric address, but the actual address value is irrelevant—what's important is that the variable refers to a particular object.

VideoNote
Creating objects.

After an object has been instantiated, we use the *dot operator* to access its methods. We've used the dot operator many times already, such as in calls to System.out.println. The dot operator is appended directly after the object reference, followed by the method being invoked. For example, to invoke the length method defined in the String class, we can use the dot operator on the name reference variable:

```
count = name.length()
```

The length method does not take any parameters, but the parentheses are still necessary to indicate that a method is being invoked. Some methods produce a value that is *returned* when the method completes. The purpose of the length method of the String class is to determine and return the length of the string (the number of characters it contains). In this example, the returned value is assigned to the variable count. For the string "James Gosling", the length method returns 13, which includes the space between the first and last names. Some methods do not return a value. Other String methods are discussed in the next section.

The act of declaring the object reference variable and creating the object itself can be combined into one step by initializing the variable in the declaration, just as we do with primitive types:

```
String title = new String("Java Software Solutions");
```

Even though they are not primitive types, character strings are so fundamental and so often used that Java defines string literals delimited by double quotation marks, as we've seen in various examples. This is a shortcut notation. Whenever a string literal appears, a String object is created automatically. Therefore the following declaration is valid:

```
String city = "London";
```

That is, for String objects, the explicit use of the new operator and the call to the constructor can be eliminated. In most cases, we will use this simplified syntax.

Aliases

Because an object reference variable stores an address, a programmer must be careful when managing objects. First, let's review the effect of assignment on primitive values. Suppose we have two integer variables, num1, initialized to 5, and num2, initialized to 12:

num1 | 5

num2 | 12

In the following assignment statement, a copy of the value that is stored in num1 is stored in num2:

```
num2 = num1;
```

The original value of 12 in num2 is overwritten by the value 5. The variables num1 and num2 still refer to different locations in memory, and both of those locations now contain the value 5:

num1 | 5

num2 | 5

Now consider the following object declarations:

```
String name1 = "Ada, Countess of Lovelace";
String name2 = "Grace Murray Hopper";
```

Initially, the references name1 and name2 refer to two different String objects:

Now suppose the following assignment statement is executed, copying the value in name1 into name2:

```
name2 = name1;
```

This assignment works the same as the integer assignment—a copy of the value of name1 is stored in name2. But remember, object variables hold the address of an object, and it is the address that gets copied. Originally, the two references referred to different objects. After the assignment, both name1 and name2 contain the same address and therefore refer to the same object:

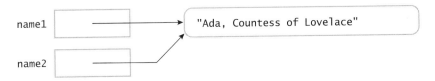

The name1 and name2 reference variables are now *aliases* of each other because they are two names that refer to the same object. All references to the object originally referenced by name2 are now gone; that object cannot be used again in the program.

> **KEY CONCEPT**
> Multiple reference variables can refer to the same object.

One important implication of aliases is that when we use one reference to change an object, it is also changed for the other reference because there is really only one object. Aliases can produce undesirable effects unless they are managed carefully.

All interaction with an object occurs through a reference variable, so we can use an object only if we have a reference to it. When all references to an object are lost (perhaps by reassignment), that object can no longer contribute to the program. The program can no longer invoke its methods or use its variables. At this point the object is called *garbage* because it serves no useful purpose.

Java performs *automatic garbage collection*. When the last reference to an object is lost, the object becomes a candidate for garbage collection. Occasionally, behind the scenes, the Java environment executes a method that "collects" all the objects marked for garbage collection and returns their memory to the system for future use. The programmer does not have to worry about explicitly reclaiming memory that has become garbage.

SELF-REVIEW QUESTIONS *(see answers in Appendix N)*

SR 3.1   What is a null reference?

SR 3.2   What does the new operator accomplish?

SR 3.3   Write a declaration for a String variable called author, and initialize it to the string "Fred Brooks". Draw a graphic representation of the variable and its value.

SR 3.4   Write a code statement that sets the value of an integer variable called size to the length of a String object called name.

SR 3.5   What is an alias? How does it relate to garbage collection?

3.2 The String Class

Let's examine the String class in more detail. Figure 3.1 lists some of the more useful methods of the String class.

Once a String object is created, its value cannot be lengthened or shortened, nor can any of its characters change. Thus we say that a String object is *immutable*. However, several methods in the String class return new String objects that are the result of modifying the original string's value.

Note that some of the String methods refer to the *index* of a particular character. A character in a string can be specified by its position, or index, in the string. The index of the first character in a string is zero, the index of the next character is one, and so on. Therefore, in the string "Hello", the index of the character 'H' is zero and the character at index four is 'o'.

Several String methods are exercised in the program shown in Listing 3.1.

As you examine the StringMutation program, keep in mind that this is not a single String object that changes its data; this program creates five separate String objects using various methods of the String class. Originally, the phrase object is set up:

String (String str)
   Constructor: creates a new string object with the same characters as str.

char charAt (int index)
   Returns the character at the specified index.

int compareTo (String str)
   Returns an integer indicating if this string is lexically before (a negative return value), equal to (a zero return value), or lexically after (a positive return value), the string str.

String concat (String str)
   Returns a new string consisting of this string concatenated with str.

boolean equals (String str)
   Returns true if this string contains the same characters as str (including case) and false otherwise.

boolean equalsIgnoreCase (String str)
   Returns true if this string contains the same characters as str (without regard to case) and false otherwise.

int length ()
   Returns the number of characters in this string.

String replace (char oldChar, char newChar)
   Returns a new string that is identical with this string except that every occurrence of oldChar is replaced by newChar.

String substring (int offset, int endIndex)
   Returns a new string that is a subset of this string starting at index offset and extending through endIndex-1.

String toLowerCase ()
   Returns a new string identical to this string except all uppercase letters are converted to their lowercase equivalent.

String toUpperCase ()
   Returns a new string identical to this string except all lowercase letters are converted to their uppercase equivalent.

FIGURE 3.1   Some methods of the String class

LISTING 3.1

```java
//********************************************************************
//  StringMutation.java       Author: Lewis/Loftus
//
//  Demonstrates the use of the String class and its methods.
//********************************************************************

public class StringMutation
{
   //-----------------------------------------------------------------
   // Prints a string and various mutations of it.
   //-----------------------------------------------------------------
   public static void main (String[] args)
   {
      String phrase = "Change is inevitable";
      String mutation1, mutation2, mutation3, mutation4;

      System.out.println ("Original string: \"" + phrase + "\"");
      System.out.println ("Length of string: " + phrase.length());

      mutation1 = phrase.concat (", except from vending machines.");
      mutation2 = mutation1.toUpperCase();
      mutation3 = mutation2.replace ('E', 'X');
      mutation4 = mutation3.substring (3, 30);

      // Print each mutated string
      System.out.println ("Mutation #1: " + mutation1);
      System.out.println ("Mutation #2: " + mutation2);
      System.out.println ("Mutation #3: " + mutation3);
      System.out.println ("Mutation #4: " + mutation4);

      System.out.println ("Mutated length: " + mutation4.length());
   }
}
```

OUTPUT

```
Original string: "Change is inevitable"
Length of string: 20
Mutation #1: Change is inevitable, except from vending machines.
Mutation #2: CHANGE IS INEVITABLE, EXCEPT FROM VENDING MACHINES.
Mutation #3: CHANGX IS INXVITABLX, XXCXPT FROM VXNDING MACHINXS.
Mutation #4: NGX IS INXVITABLX, XXCXPT F
Mutated length: 27
```

After printing the original phrase and its length, the concat method is executed to create a new string object referenced by the variable mutation1:

mutation1 ⟶ "Change is inevitable, except from vending machines."

Then the toUpperCase method is executed on the mutation1 object, and the resulting string is stored in mutation2:

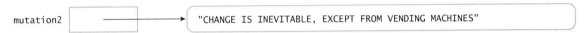

mutation2 ⟶ "CHANGE IS INEVITABLE, EXCEPT FROM VENDING MACHINES"

Notice that the length and concat methods are executed on the phrase object, but the toUpperCase method is executed on the mutation1 object. Any method of the String class can be executed on any String object, but for any given invocation, a method is executed on a particular object. The results of executing toUpperCase on mutation1 would be very different from the results of executing toUpperCase on phrase. Remember, each object has its own state, which often affects the results of method calls.

> **KEY CONCEPT**
>
> Usually a method is executed on a particular object, which affects the results.

Finally, the String object variables mutation3 and mutation4 are initialized by the calls to mutation2.replace and mutation3.substring, respectively:

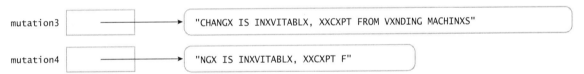

mutation3 ⟶ "CHANGX IS INXVITABLX, XXCXPT FROM VXNDING MACHINXS"

mutation4 ⟶ "NGX IS INXVITABLX, XXCXPT F"

SELF-REVIEW QUESTIONS *(see answers in Appendix N)*   myprogramming**lab**

SR 3.6   Assume s1, s2, and s3 are String variables initialized to "Amanda", "Bobby", and "Chris" respectively. Which String variable or variables are changed by each of the following statements?

```
a. System.out.println (s1);
b. s1 = s3.toLowerCase();
c. System.out.println (s2.replace('B', 'M'));
d. s3 = s2.concat(s1);
```

SR 3.7   What output is produced by the following code fragment?

```
String s1 = "Foundations";
String s2;
System.out.println (s1.charAt(1));
s2 = s1.substring(0, 5);
System.out.println (s2);
```

```
System.out.println (s1.length());
System.out.println (s2.length());
```

SR 3.8 Write a statement that prints the value of a `String` object called `title` in all uppercase letters.

SR 3.9 Write a declaration for a `String` variable called `front`, and initialize it to the first 10 characters of another `String` object called `description`.

3.3 Packages

We mentioned earlier that the Java language is supported by a standard class library that we can make use of as needed. Let's examine that idea further.

A *class library* is a set of classes that supports the development of programs. A compiler or development environment often comes with a class library. Class libraries can also be obtained separately through third-party vendors. The classes in a class library contain methods that are often valuable to a programmer because of the special functionality they offer. In fact, programmers often become dependent on the methods in a class library and begin to think of them as part of the language. However, technically, they are not in the language itself.

The `String` class, for instance, is not an inherent part of the Java language. It is part of the Java standard class library that can be found in any Java development environment. The classes that make up the library were created by employees at Sun Microsystems, the people who created the Java language.

The class library is made up of several clusters of related classes, which are often referred to as the Java APIs, which stands for *application programming interfaces*. For example, we may refer to the Java Database API when we're talking about the set of classes that helps us write programs that interact with a database. Another example of an API is the Java Swing API, which refers to a set of classes that defines special graphical components used in a graphical user interface. Often the entire standard library is referred to generically as the Java API.

The classes of the Java standard class library are also grouped into *packages*. Each class is part of a particular package. The `String` class, for example, is part of the `java.lang` package. The `System` class is part of the `java.lang` package as well. We mentioned in Chapter 2 that the `Scanner` class is part of the `java.util` package.

The package organization is more fundamental and language-based than the API names. Though there is a general correspondence between package and API names, the groups of classes that make up a given API might cross packages. In this book, we primarily refer to classes in terms of their package organization.

Package	Provides support to
java.applet	Create programs (applets) that are easily transported across the Web.
java.awt	Draw graphics and create graphical user interfaces; AWT stands for Abstract Windowing Toolkit.
java.beans	Define software components that can be easily combined into applications.
java.io	Perform a wide variety of input and output functions.
java.lang	General support; it is automatically imported into all Java programs.
java.math	Perform calculations with arbitrarily high precision.
java.net	Communicate across a network.
java.rmi	Create programs that can be distributed across multiple computers; RMI stands for Remote Method Invocation.
java.security	Enforce security restrictions.
java.sql	Interact with databases; SQL stands for Structured Query Language.
java.text	Format text for output.
java.util	General utilities.
javax.swing	Create graphical user interfaces with components that extend the AWT capabilities.
javax.xml.parsers	Process XML documents; XML stands for eXtensible Markup Language.

FIGURE 3.2   Some packages in the Java standard class library

Figure 3.2 describes some of the packages that are part of the Java standard class library. These packages are available on any platform that supports Java software development. Some of these packages support highly specific programming techniques and will not come into play in the development of basic programs.

Various classes of the Java API are discussed throughout this book. For convenience we include in the book some documentation (like Figure 3.2) on the classes we'll use, but it's also very important for you to know how to get more information about the Java API classes. The *online Java API documentation* is an invaluable resource for any Java programmer. It is a Web site that contains pages on each class in the standard Java API, listing and describing the methods in each one.

Figure 3.3 shows one page of this documentation. Links on the side allow you to examine particular packages and jump to particular classes. Take some time

FIGURE 3.3   A page from the online Java API documentation

to get comfortable navigating this site and learning how the information is organized. The entire set of Java API documentation can be downloaded so that you have a local copy always available, or you can rely on the online version.

The `import` Declaration

The classes of the `java.lang` package are automatically available for use when writing a Java program. To use classes from any other package, however, we must either *fully qualify* the reference or use an *import declaration*. Recall that the example programs that use the `Scanner` class include an `import` declaration.

When you want to use a class from a class library in a program, you could use its fully qualified name, including the package name, every time it is referenced. For example, every time you want to refer to the `Scanner` class that is defined in the `java.util` package, you could write `java.util.Scanner`. However, completely specifying the package and class name every time it is needed quickly becomes tiring. Java provides the `import` declaration to simplify these references.

The `import` declaration specifies the packages and classes that will be used in a program so that the fully qualified name is not necessary with each reference. As we've seen, the following is an example of an `import` declaration:

```
import java.util.Scanner;
```

This declaration asserts that the `Scanner` class of the `java.util` package may be used in the program. Once this `import` declaration is made, it is sufficient to use the simple name `Scanner` when referring to that class in the program.

If two classes from two different packages have the same name, `import` declarations will not suffice because the compiler won't be able to figure out which class is being referenced in the flow of the code. When such situations arise, which is rare, the fully qualified names should be used in the code.

Another form of the `import` declaration uses an asterisk (*) to indicate that any class inside the package might be used in the program. Therefore, the following declaration allows all classes in the `java.util` package to be referenced in the program without qualifying each reference:

```
import java.util.*;
```

If only one class of a particular package will be used in a program, it is usually better to name the class specifically in the `import` declaration. However, if two or more will be used, the * notation is usually fine.

The classes of the `java.lang` package are automatically imported because they are fundamental and can be thought of as basic extensions to the language. Therefore, any class in the `java.lang` package, such as `System` and `String`, can be used without an explicit `import` declaration. It's as if all program files automatically contain the following declaration:

> **KEY CONCEPT**
> All classes of the `java.lang` package are automatically imported for every program.

```
import java.lang.*;
```

> myprogramming**lab**

SELF-REVIEW QUESTIONS *(see answers in Appendix N)*

SR 3.10   What is a Java package?

SR 3.11   What does the `java.net` package contain? The `javax.swing` package?

SR 3.12   What package contains the `Scanner` class? The `String` class? The `Random` class? The `Math` class?

SR 3.13   Using the online Java API documentation, describe the `Point` class.

SR 3.14   What does an `import` statement accomplish?

SR 3.15   Why doesn't the `String` class have to be specifically imported into our programs?

3.4 The Random Class

The need for random numbers occurs frequently when writing software. Games often use a random number to represent the roll of a die or the shuffle of a deck of cards. A flight simulator may use random numbers to determine how often a simulated flight has engine trouble. A program designed to help high school students prepare for the SATs may use random numbers to choose the next question to ask.

The Random class, which is part of the java.util class, represents a *pseudorandom number generator*. A random number generator picks a number at random out of a range of values. A program that serves this role is technically pseudorandom, because a program has no means to actually pick a number randomly. A pseudorandom number generator performs a series of complicated calculations, based on an initial *seed value*, and produces a number. Though they are technically not random (because they are calculated), the values produced by a pseudorandom number generator usually appear random, at least random enough for most situations.

KEY CONCEPT

A pseudorandom number generator performs a complex calculation to create the illusion of randomness.

Figure 3.4 lists some of the methods of the Random class. The nextInt method can be called with no parameters, or we can pass it a single integer value. The version that takes no parameters generates a random number across the entire range of int values, including negative numbers. Usually, though, we need a random number within a more specific range. For instance, to simulate the roll of a die, we might want a random number in the range of 1 to 6. The nextInt method returns a value that's in the range from 0 to one less than its parameter. For example, if we pass in 100, we'll get a return value that is greater than or equal to 0 and less than or equal to 99.

```
Random ()
    Constructor: creates a new pseudorandom number generator.

float nextFloat ()
    Returns a random number between 0.0 (inclusive) and 1.0 (exclusive).

int nextInt ()
    Returns a random number that ranges over all possible int values (positive
    and negative).

int nextInt (int num)
    Returns a random number in the range 0 to num-1.
```

FIGURE 3.4   Some methods of the Random class

Note that the value that we pass to the `nextInt` method is also the number of possible values we can get in return. We can shift the range as needed by adding or subtracting the proper amount. To get a random number in the range 1 to 6, we can call `nextInt(6)` to get a value from 0 to 5, and then add 1.

The `nextFloat` method of the `Random` class returns a `float` value that is greater than or equal to 0.0 and less than 1.0. If desired, we can use multiplication to scale the result, cast it into an `int` value to truncate the fractional part, and then shift the range as we do with integers.

The program shown in Listing 3.2 produces several random numbers in various ranges.

LISTING 3.2

```
//********************************************************************
//  RandomNumbers.java       Author: Lewis/Loftus
//
//  Demonstrates the creation of pseudo-random numbers using the
//  Random class.
//********************************************************************

import java.util.Random;

public class RandomNumbers
{
   //-----------------------------------------------------------------
   //  Generates random numbers in various ranges.
   //-----------------------------------------------------------------
   public static void main (String[] args)
   {
      Random generator = new Random();
      int num1;
      float num2;

      num1 = generator.nextInt();
      System.out.println ("A random integer: " + num1);

      num1 = generator.nextInt(10);
      System.out.println ("From 0 to 9: " + num1);

      num1 = generator.nextInt(10) + 1;
      System.out.println ("From 1 to 10: " + num1);
```

LISTING 3.2   *continued*

```
    num1 = generator.nextInt(15) + 20;
    System.out.println ("From 20 to 34: " + num1);

    num1 = generator.nextInt(20) - 10;
    System.out.println ("From -10 to 9: " + num1);

    num2 = generator.nextFloat();
    System.out.println ("A random float (between 0-1): " + num2);

    num2 = generator.nextFloat() * 6;   // 0.0 to 5.999999
    num1 = (int)num2 + 1;
    System.out.println ("From 1 to 6: " + num1);
  }
}
```

OUTPUT

```
A random integer: 1773351873
From 0 to 9: 8
From 1 to 10: 6
From 20 to 34: 20
From -10 to 9: -6
A random float (between 0-1): 0.71058085
From 1 to 6: 3
```

myprogramming**lab**

SELF-REVIEW QUESTIONS *(see answers in Appendix N)*

SR 3.16 Given a Random object called rand, what does the call rand.nextInt() return?

SR 3.17 Given a Random object called rand, what does the call rand.nextInt(20) return?

SR 3.18 Assuming that a Random object has been created called generator, what is the range of the result of each of the following expressions?

a. generator.nextInt(50)
b. generator.nextInt(5) + 10
c. generator.nextInt(10) + 5
d. generator.nextInt(50) - 25

SR 3.19 Assuming that a Random object has been created called generator, write expressions that generate each of the following ranges of integers, including the endpoints. Use the version of the nextInt method that accepts a single integer parameter.

    a. 0 to 30
    b. 10 to 19
    c. –5 to 5

3.5 The Math Class

The Math class provides a large number of basic mathematical functions that are often helpful in making calculations. The Math class is defined in the java.lang package of the Java standard class library. Figure 3.5 lists several of its methods.

All the methods in the Math class are *static methods* (also called *class methods*), which means they can be invoked through the name of the class in which they are defined, without having to instantiate an object of the class first. Static methods are discussed further in Chapter 6.

The methods of the Math class return values, which can be used in expressions as needed. For example, the following statement computes the absolute value of the number stored in total, adds it to the value of count raised to the fourth power, and stores the result in the variable value:

> **KEY CONCEPT**
> All methods of the Math class are static, meaning they are invoked through the class name.

```
value = Math.abs(total) + Math.pow(count, 4);
```

Note that you can pass an integer value to a method that accepts a double parameter. This is a form of assignment conversion, which was discussed in Chapter 2.

The Quadratic program, shown in Listing 3.3, uses the Math class to compute the roots of a quadratic equation. Recall that a quadratic equation has the following general form:

```
ax² + bx + c
```

The Quadratic program reads values that represent the coefficients in a quadratic equation (a, b, and c), and then evaluates the quadratic formula to determine the roots of the equation. The quadratic formula is:

$$roots = \frac{-b \pm \sqrt{b^2 - 4ac}}{2a}$$

VideoNote

Example using the Random and Math classes.

```
static int abs (int num)
   Returns the absolute value of num.

static double acos (double num)

static double asin (double num)

static double atan (double num)
   Returns the arc cosine, arc sine, or arc tangent of num.

static double cos (double angle)

static double sin (double angle)

static double tan (double angle)
   Returns the angle cosine, sine, or tangent of angle, which is measured in
   radians.

static double ceil (double num)
   Returns the ceiling of num, which is the smallest whole number greater than or
   equal to num.

static double exp (double power)
   Returns the value e raised to the specified power.

static double floor (double num)
   Returns the floor of num, which is the largest whole number less than or equal
   to num.

static double pow (double num, double power)
   Returns the value num raised to the specified power.

static double random ()
   Returns a random number between 0.0 (inclusive) and 1.0 (exclusive).

static double sqrt (double num)
   Returns the square root of num, which must be positive.
```

FIGURE 3.5   Some methods of the Math class

Note that this program assumes that the discriminant (the value under the square root) is negative. If it's not negative, the results will not be a valid number, which Java represents as NAN, which stands for Not A Number. In Chapter 5 we will see how we can handle this type of situation gracefully.

LISTING 3.3

```java
//********************************************************************
//  Quadratic.java        Author: Lewis/Loftus
//
//  Demonstrates the use of the Math class to perform a calculation
//  based on user input.
//********************************************************************

import java.util.Scanner;

public class Quadratic
{
   //-----------------------------------------------------------------
   //  Determines the roots of a quadratic equation.
   //-----------------------------------------------------------------
   public static void main (String[] args)
   {
      int a, b, c;  // ax^2 + bx + c
      double discriminant, root1, root2;

      Scanner scan = new Scanner (System.in);

      System.out.print ("Enter the coefficient of x squared: ");
      a = scan.nextInt();

      System.out.print ("Enter the coefficient of x: ");
      b = scan.nextInt();

      System.out.print ("Enter the constant: ");
      c = scan.nextInt();

      // Use the quadratic formula to compute the roots.
      // Assumes a positive discriminant.

      discriminant = Math.pow(b, 2) - (4 * a * c);
      root1 = ((-1 * b) + Math.sqrt(discriminant)) / (2 * a);
      root2 = ((-1 * b) - Math.sqrt(discriminant)) / (2 * a);

      System.out.println ("Root #1: " + root1);
      System.out.println ("Root #2: " + root2);
   }
}
```

LISTING 3.3   *continued*

OUTPUT

```
Enter the coefficient of x squared: 3
Enter the coefficient of x: 8
Enter the constant: 4
Root #1: -0.6666666666666666
Root #2: -2.0
```

myprogramminglab

SELF-REVIEW QUESTIONS *(see answers in Appendix N)*

SR 3.20 What is a class method (also called a static method)?

SR 3.21 What is the value of each of the following expressions?

a. `Math.abs(10) + Math.abs(-10)`
b. `Math.pow(2, 4)`
c. `Math.pow(4, 2)`
d. `Math.pow(3, 5)`
e. `Math.pow(5, 3)`
f. `Math.sqrt(16)`

SR 3.22 Write a statement that prints the sine of an angle measuring 1.23 radians.

SR 3.23 Write a declaration for a `double` variable called `result` and initialize it to 5 raised to the power 2.5.

SR 3.24 Using the online Java API documentation, list three methods of the Math class that are not included in Figure 3.5.

3.6 Formatting Output

The NumberFormat class and the DecimalFormat class are used to format information so that it looks appropriate when printed or displayed. They are both part of the Java standard class library and are defined in the `java.text` package.

The NumberFormat Class

The NumberFormat class provides generic formatting capabilities for numbers. You don't instantiate a NumberFormat object by using the new operator. Instead, you request an object from one of the static methods that you invoke through the class name itself. Figure 3.6 lists some of the methods of the NumberFormat class.

String format (double number)
  Returns a string containing the specified number formatted according to this
  object's pattern.

static NumberFormat getCurrencyInstance()
  Returns a NumberFormat object that represents a currency format for the
  current locale.

static NumberFormat getPercentInstance()
  Returns a NumberFormat object that represents a percentage format for the
  current locale.

FIGURE 3.6   Some methods of the NumberFormat class

Two of the methods in the NumberFormat class, getCurrencyInstance
and getPercentInstance, return an object that is used to format numbers. The
getCurrencyInstance method returns a formatter for monetary values, and
the getPercentInstance method returns an object that formats a percentage.
The format method is invoked through a formatter object and returns a String
that contains the number formatted in the appropriate manner.

The Purchase program shown in Listing 3.4 uses both types of formatters. It
reads in a sales transaction and computes the final price, including tax.

LISTING 3.4

```
//********************************************************************
//  Purchase.java       Author: Lewis/Loftus
//
//  Demonstrates the use of the NumberFormat class to format output.
//********************************************************************

import java.util.Scanner;
import java.text.NumberFormat;

public class Purchase
{
    //----------------------------------------------------------------
    //  Calculates the final price of a purchased item using values
    //  entered by the user.
    //----------------------------------------------------------------
    public static void main (String[] args)
```

LISTING 3.4   *continued*

```java
   {
      final double TAX_RATE = 0.06;  // 6% sales tax

      int quantity;
      double subtotal, tax, totalCost, unitPrice;

      Scanner scan = new Scanner (System.in);

      NumberFormat fmt1 = NumberFormat.getCurrencyInstance();
      NumberFormat fmt2 = NumberFormat.getPercentInstance();

      System.out.print ("Enter the quantity: ");
      quantity = scan.nextInt();

      System.out.print ("Enter the unit price: ");
      unitPrice = scan.nextDouble();

      subtotal = quantity * unitPrice;
      tax = subtotal * TAX_RATE;
      totalCost = subtotal + tax;

      // Print output with appropriate formatting
      System.out.println ("Subtotal: " + fmt1.format(subtotal));
      System.out.println ("Tax: " + fmt1.format(tax) + " at "
                          + fmt2.format(TAX_RATE));
      System.out.println ("Total: " + fmt1.format(totalCost));
   }
}
```

OUTPUT

```
Enter the quantity: 5
Enter the unit price: 3.87
Subtotal: $19.35
Tax: $1.16 at 6%
Total: $20.51
```

The DecimalFormat Class

Unlike the NumberFormat class, the DecimalFormat class is instantiated in the traditional way using the new operator. Its constructor takes a string that represents the pattern that will guide the formatting process. We can then use the

```
DecimalFormat (String pattern)
    Constructor:  creates a new DecimalFormat object with the specified pattern.

void applyPattern (String pattern)
    Applies the specified pattern to this DecimalFormat object.

String format (double number)
    Returns a string containing the specified number formatted according to the
    current pattern.
```

FIGURE 3.7   Some methods of the DecimalFormat class

format method to format a particular value. At a later point, if we want to change the pattern that the formatter object uses, we can invoke the applyPattern method. Figure 3.7 describes these methods.

The pattern defined by the string that is passed to the DecimalFormat constructor can get fairly elaborate. Various symbols are used to represent particular formatting guidelines. The pattern defined by the string "0.###", for example, indicates that at least one digit should be printed to the left of the decimal point and should be a zero if the integer portion of the value is zero. It also indicates that the fractional portion of the value should be rounded to three digits.

This pattern is used in the CircleStats program, shown in Listing 3.5, which reads the radius of a circle from the user and computes its area and circumference. Trailing zeros, such as in the circle's area of 78.540, are not printed.

The printf Method

In addition to print and println, the System class has another output method called printf, which allows the user to print a formatted string containing data values. The first parameter to the method represents the format string, and the remaining parameters specify the values that are inserted into the format string.

For example, the following line of code prints an ID number and a name:

```
System.out.printf ("ID: %5d\tName: %s", id, name);
```

The first parameter specifies the format of the output and includes literal characters that label the output values as well as escape characters such as \t. The pattern %5d indicates that the corresponding numeric value (id) should be printed in a field of five characters. The pattern %s matches the string parameter

LISTING 3.5

```java
//********************************************************************
//  CircleStats.java        Author: Lewis/Loftus
//
//  Demonstrates the formatting of decimal values using the
//  DecimalFormat class.
//********************************************************************

import java.util.Scanner;
import java.text.DecimalFormat;

public class CircleStats
{
   //-----------------------------------------------------------------
   //  Calculates the area and circumference of a circle given its
   //  radius.
   //-----------------------------------------------------------------
   public static void main (String[] args)
   {
      int radius;
      double area, circumference;

      Scanner scan = new Scanner (System.in);

      System.out.print ("Enter the circle's radius: ");
      radius = scan.nextInt();

      area = Math.PI * Math.pow(radius, 2);
      circumference = 2 * Math.PI * radius;

      // Round the output to three decimal places
      DecimalFormat fmt = new DecimalFormat ("0.###");

      System.out.println ("The circle's area: " + fmt.format(area));
      System.out.println ("The circle's circumference: "
                          + fmt.format(circumference));
   }
}
```

OUTPUT

```
Enter the circle's radius: 5
The circle's area: 78.54
The circle's circumference: 31.416
```

name. The values of id and name are inserted into the string, producing a result such as:

```
ID: 24036   Name: Larry Flagelhopper
```

The printf method was added to Java to mirror a similar function used in programs written in the C programming language. It makes it easier for a programmer to translate (or *migrate*) an existing C program into Java.

Older software that still has value is called a *legacy system*. Maintaining a legacy system is often a costly effort because, among other things, it is based on older technologies. But in many cases, maintaining a legacy system is still more cost effective than migrating it to new technology, such as writing it in a newer language. Adding the printf method is an attempt to make such migrations easier, and therefore less costly, by providing the same kind of output statement that C programmers have come to rely on.

> **KEY CONCEPT**
>
> The printf method was added to Java to support the migration of legacy systems.

However, using the printf method is not a particularly clean object-oriented solution to the problem of formatting output, so we avoid its use in this book.

myprogramminglab

SELF-REVIEW QUESTIONS *(see answers in Appendix N)*

SR 3.25 Describe how you request a NumberFormat object for use within a program.

SR 3.26 Suppose that in your program you have a double variable named cost. You want to output the value stored in cost formatted as the currency of the current locale.

    a. Write a code statement that declares and requests a NumberFormat object named moneyFormat that can be used to represent currency in the format of the current locale.

    b. Write a code statement that uses the moneyFormat object and prints the value of cost, formatted as the currency of the current locale.

    c. What would be the output from the statement you wrote in part (b) if the value in cost is 54.89 and your computer's locale is set to the United States? What if your computer's locale is set to the United Kingdom?

SR 3.27 What are the steps to output a floating point value as a percentage using Java's formatting classes?

SR 3.28 Write code statements that prompt for and read in a double value from the user, and then print the result of taking the square root of the absolute value of the input value. Output the result to two decimal places.

3.7 Enumerated Types

Java provides the ability to define an *enumerated type*, which can then be used as the type of a variable when it is declared. An enumerated type establishes all possible values of a variable of that type by listing, or enumerating, them. The values are identifiers, and can be anything desired.

For example, the following declaration defines an enumerated type called Season, whose possible values are winter, spring, summer, and fall:

```
enum Season {winter, spring, summer, fall}
```

There is no limit to the number of values that you can list for an enumerated type. Once the type is defined, a variable can be declared of that type:

```
Season time;
```

> **KEY CONCEPT**
>
> Enumerated types are type-safe, ensuring that invalid values will not be used.

The variable time is now restricted in the values it can take on. It can hold one of the four Season values, but nothing else. Java enumerated types are considered to be *type-safe*, meaning that any attempt to use a value other than one of the enumerated values will result in a compile-time error.

The values are accessed through the name of the type. For example:

```
time = Season.spring;
```

Enumerated types can be quite helpful in situations in which you have a relatively small number of distinct values that a variable can assume. For example, suppose we wanted to represent the various letter grades a student could earn. We might declare the following enumerated type:

```
enum Grade {A, B, C, D, F}
```

Any initialized variable that holds a Grade is guaranteed to have one of those valid grades. That's better than using a simple character or string variable to represent the grade, which could take on any value.

Suppose we also wanted to represent plus and minus grades, such as A– and B+. We couldn't use A– or B+ as values, because they are not valid identifiers (the characters '-' and '+' cannot be part of an identifier in Java). However, the same values could be represented using the identifiers Aminus, Bplus, etc.

Internally, each value in an enumerated type is stored as an integer, which is referred to as its *ordinal value*. The first value in an enumerated type has an ordinal value of 0, the second one has an ordinal value of 1, the third one 2, and so on. The ordinal values are used internally only. You cannot assign a numeric value to an enumerated type, even if it corresponds to a valid ordinal value.

An enumerated type is a special kind of class, and the variables of an enumerated type are object variables. As such, there are a few methods associated with all enumerated types. The `ordinal` method returns the numeric value associated with a particular enumerated type value. The `name` method returns the name of the value, which is the same as the identifier that defines the value.

Listing 3.6 shows a program called `IceCream` that declares an enumerated type and exercises some of its methods. Because enumerated types are special types of classes, they are not defined within a method. They can be defined either at the class level (within the class but outside a method), as in this example, or at the outermost level.

We explore enumerated types further in Chapter 6.

LISTING 3.6

```java
//********************************************************************
//  IceCream.java        Author: Lewis/Loftus
//
//  Demonstrates the use of enumerated types.
//********************************************************************

public class IceCream
{
    enum Flavor {vanilla, chocolate, strawberry, fudgeRipple, coffee,
                 rockyRoad, mintChocolateChip, cookieDough}

    //-----------------------------------------------------------------
    //  Creates and uses variables of the Flavor type.
    //-----------------------------------------------------------------
    public static void main (String[] args)
    {
        Flavor cone1, cone2, cone3;

        cone1 = Flavor.rockyRoad;
        cone2 = Flavor.chocolate;

        System.out.println ("cone1 value: " + cone1);
        System.out.println ("cone1 ordinal: " + cone1.ordinal());
        System.out.println ("cone1 name: " + cone1.name());

        System.out.println ();
        System.out.println ("cone2 value: " + cone2);
        System.out.println ("cone2 ordinal: " + cone2.ordinal());
        System.out.println ("cone2 name: " + cone2.name());
```

LISTING 3.6 *continued*

```
    cone3 = cone1;

    System.out.println ();
    System.out.println ("cone3 value: " + cone3);
    System.out.println ("cone3 ordinal: " + cone3.ordinal());
    System.out.println ("cone3 name: " + cone3.name());
    }
}
```

OUTPUT

```
cone1 value: rockyRoad
cone1 ordinal: 5
cone1 name: rockyRoad

cone2 value: chocolate
cone2 ordinal: 1
cone2 name: chocolate

cone3 value: rockyRoad
cone3 ordinal: 5
cone3 name: rockyRoad
```

myprogramminglab

SELF-REVIEW QUESTIONS *(see answers in Appendix N)*

SR 3.29 Write the declaration of an enumerated type that represents movie ratings.

SR 3.30 Suppose that an enumerated type called CardSuit has been defined as follows:

```
enum CardSuit {clubs, diamonds, hearts, spades}
```

What is the output of the following code sequence?

```
CardSuit card1, card2;
card1 = CardSuit.clubs;
card2 = CardSuit.hearts;
System.out.println (card1);
System.out.println (card2.name());
System.out.println (card1.ordinal());
System.out.println (card2.ordinal());
```

SR 3.31 Why use an enumerated type such as CardSuit defined in the previous question? Why not just use String variables and assign them values such as "hearts"?

3.8 Wrapper Classes

As we've discussed previously, Java represents data by using primitive types (such as int, double, char, and boolean) in addition to classes and objects. Having two categories of data to manage (primitive values and object references) can present a challenge in some circumstances. For example, we might create an object that serves as a container to hold various types of other objects. However, in a specific situation, we may want it to hold a simple integer value. In these cases we need to "wrap" a primitive value into an object.

A *wrapper class* represents a particular primitive type. For instance, the Integer class represents a simple integer value. An object created from the Integer class stores a single int value. The constructors of the wrapper classes accept the primitive value to store. For example:

```
Integer ageObj = new Integer(40);
```

Once this declaration and instantiation are performed, the ageObj object effectively represents the integer 40 as an object. It can be used wherever an object is needed in a program rather than a primitive type.

> **KEY CONCEPT**
>
> A wrapper class allows a primitive value to be managed as an object.

For each primitive type in Java there exists a corresponding wrapper class in the Java class library. All wrapper classes are defined in the java.lang package. Figure 3.8 shows the wrapper class that corresponds to each primitive type.

Note that there is even a wrapper class that represents the type void. However, unlike the other wrapper classes, the Void class cannot be instantiated. It simply represents the concept of a void reference.

Primitive Type	Wrapper Class
byte	Byte
short	Short
int	Integer
long	Long
float	Float
double	Double
char	Character
boolean	Boolean
void	Void

FIGURE 3.8   Wrapper classes in the Java class library

```
Integer (int value)
    Constructor: creates a new Integer object storing the specified value.

byte byteValue ()
double doubleValue ()
float floatValue ()
int intValue ()
long longValue ()
    Return the value of this Integer as the corresponding primitive type.

static int parseTnt (String str)
    Returns the int corresponding to the value stored in the
    specified string.

static String toBinaryString (int num)
static String tohexString (int num)
static String toOctalString (int num)
    Returns a string representation of the specified integer value in the
    corresponding base.
```

FIGURE 3.9   Some methods of the `Integer` class

Wrapper classes also provide various methods related to the management of the associated primitive type. For example, the `Integer` class contains methods that return the `int` value stored in the object and that convert the stored value to other primitive types. Figure 3.9 lists some of the methods found in the `Integer` class. The other wrapper classes have similar methods.

Note that the wrapper classes also contain static methods that can be invoked independent of any instantiated object. For example, the `Integer` class contains a static method called `parseInt` to convert an integer that is stored in a `String` to its corresponding `int` value. If the `String` object `str` holds the string "987", the following line of code converts the string into the integer value 987 and stores that value in the `int` variable num:

```
num = Integer.parseInt(str);
```

The Java wrapper classes often contain static constants that are helpful as well. For example, the `Integer` class contains two constants, `MIN_VALUE` and `MAX_VALUE`, that hold the smallest and largest `int` values, respectively. The other wrapper classes contain similar constants for their types.

Autoboxing

Autoboxing is the automatic conversion between a primitive value and a corresponding wrapper object. For example, in the following code, an int value is assigned to an Integer object reference variable:

```
Integer obj1;
int num1 = 69;
obj1 = num1;   // automatically creates an Integer object
```

The reverse conversion, called unboxing, also occurs automatically when needed. For example:

```
Integer obj2 = new Integer(69);
int num2;
num2 = obj2;   // automatically extracts the int value
```

Assignments between primitive types and object types are generally incompatible. The ability to autobox occurs only between primitive types and corresponding wrapper classes. In any other case, attempting to assign a primitive value to an object reference variable, or vice versa, will cause a compile-time error.

> **KEY CONCEPT**
>
> Autoboxing provides automatic conversions between primitive values and corresponding wrapper objects.

SELF-REVIEW QUESTIONS *(see answers in Appendix N)*

myprogramminglab

SR 3.32 How can we represent a primitive value as an object?

SR 3.33 What wrapper classes correspond to each of the following primitive types: byte, int, double, char, and boolean?

SR 3.34 Suppose that an int variable named number has been declared and initialized and an Integer variable named holdNumber has been declared. Show two approaches in Java for having holdNumber represent the value stored in number.

SR 3.35 Write a statement that prints out the largest possible int value.

3.9 Components and Containers

In the Graphics Track sections of Chapter 2 we introduced the Java capabilities to draw shapes using the Graphics and Color classes from the Java standard class library. We also defined the concept of an applet, a Java program that is intended to be embedded in a Web page and executed through a browser. Recall that, in contrast to applets, Java applications are stand-alone programs that are not executed through the Web.

Most of the example programs we've looked at so far have been Java applications. More specifically, they have been *command-line applications*, which interact with the user only through simple text prompts. A Java application can have graphical components as well. Throughout the rest of the book, in the Graphics Track sections at the end of each chapter, we will explore the capabilities of Java to create programs with graphical user interfaces (GUIs). In this chapter we establish the basic issues regarding graphics-based applications.

A GUI *component* is an object that represents a screen element that is used to display information or to allow the user to interact with the program in a certain way. GUI components include labels, buttons, text fields, scroll bars, and menus.

Java components and other GUI-related classes are defined primarily in two packages: java.awt and javax.swing. (Note the x in javax.swing.) The *Abstract Windowing Toolkit* (AWT) was the original Java GUI package. It still contains many important classes, such as the Color class that we used in Chapter 2. The *Swing* package was added later and provides components that are more versatile than those of the AWT package. Both packages are needed for GUI development, but we will use Swing components whenever there is an option.

> **KEY CONCEPT**
>
> Containers are special GUI components that hold and organize other components.

A *container* is a special type of component that is used to hold and organize other components. Frames and panels are two examples of Java containers. Let's explore them in more detail.

Frames and Panels

A *frame* is a container that is used to display GUI-based Java applications. A frame is displayed as a separate window with its own title bar. It can be repositioned on the screen and resized as needed by dragging it with the mouse. It contains small buttons in the corner of the frame that allow the frame to be minimized, maximized, and closed. A frame is defined by the JFrame class.

> **KEY CONCEPT**
>
> A frame is displayed as a separate window, but a panel can be displayed only as part of another container.

A *panel* is also a container. However, unlike a frame, it cannot be displayed on its own. A panel must be added to another container for it to be displayed. Generally a panel doesn't move unless you move the container that it's in. Its primary role is to help organize the other components in a GUI. A panel is defined by the JPanel class.

We can classify containers as either heavyweight or lightweight. A *heavyweight container* is one that is managed by the underlying operating system on which the program is run, whereas a *lightweight container* is managed by the Java program itself. Occasionally this distinction will be important as we explore GUI development. A frame is a heavyweight component, and a panel is a lightweight component.

Heavyweight components are more complex than lightweight components in general. A frame, for example, has multiple *panes,* which are responsible for various characteristics of the frame window. All visible elements of a Java interface are displayed in a frame's *content pane.*

Generally, we can create a Java GUI-based application by creating a frame in which the program interface is displayed. The interface is often organized onto a primary panel, which is added to the frame's content pane. The components in the primary panel are often organized using other panels as needed.

Containers are generally not useful unless they help us organize and display other components. Let's examine another fundamental GUI component. A *label* is a component that displays a line of text in a GUI. A label can also display an image, a topic discussed later in this chapter. Usually, labels are used to display information or identify other components in the GUI. Labels can be found in almost every GUI-based program.

Let's look at an example that uses frames, panels, and labels. When the program in Listing 3.7 is executed, a new window appears on the screen displaying a phrase. The text of the phrase is displayed using two label components. The labels are organized in a panel, and the panel is displayed in the content pane of the frame.

The JFrame constructor takes a string as a parameter, which it displays in the title bar of the frame. The call to the setDefaultCloseOperation method determines what will happen when the close button (the X) in the corner of the frame is clicked. In most cases we'll simply let that button terminate the program, as indicated by the EXIT_ON_CLOSE constant.

A panel is created by instantiating the JPanel class. The background color of the panel is set using the setBackground method. The setPreferredSize method accepts a Dimension object as a parameter, which is used to indicate the width and height of the component in pixels. The size of many components can be set this way, and most also have setMinimumSize and setMaximumSize methods to help control the look of the interface.

The labels are created by instantiating the JLabel class, passing to its constructor the text of the label. In this program two separate label components are created.

Containers have an add method that allows other components to be added to them. Both labels are added to the primary panel and are from that point on considered to be part of that panel. The order in which components are added to a container often matters. In this case, it determines which label appears above the other.

Finally, the content pane of the frame is obtained using the getContentPane method, immediately after which the add method of the content pane is called to

LISTING 3.7

```java
//********************************************************************
//  Authority.java       Author: Lewis/Loftus
//
//  Demonstrates the use of frames, panels, and labels.
//********************************************************************

import java.awt.*;
import javax.swing.*;

public class Authority
{
    //-----------------------------------------------------------------
    //  Displays some words of wisdom.
    //-----------------------------------------------------------------
    public static void main (String[] args)
    {
        JFrame frame = new JFrame ("Authority");

        frame.setDefaultCloseOperation (JFrame.EXIT_ON_CLOSE);

        JPanel primary = new JPanel();
        primary.setBackground (Color.yellow);
        primary.setPreferredSize (new Dimension(250, 75));

        JLabel label1 = new JLabel ("Question authority,");
        JLabel label2 = new JLabel ("but raise your hand first.");

        primary.add (label1);
        primary.add (label2);

        frame.getContentPane().add(primary);
        frame.pack();
        frame.setVisible(true);
    }
}
```

DISPLAY

add the panel. The pack method of the frame sets its size appropriately based on its contents—in this case the frame is sized to accommodate the size of the panel it contains. This is a better approach than trying to set the size of the frame explicitly, which should change as the components within the frame change. The call to the setVisible method causes the frame to be displayed on the monitor screen.

The Authority program is not interactive. In general, labels do not allow the user to interact with a program. We will examine interactive GUI components in the next chapter.

However, you can interact with the frame itself in various ways. You can move the entire frame to another point on the desktop by grabbing the title bar of the frame and dragging it with the mouse. You can also resize the frame by dragging the bottom-right corner of the frame. Note what happens when the frame is made wider: the second label pops up next to the first label.

Every container is managed by an object called a *layout manager* that determines how the components in the container are laid out. The layout manager is consulted when important things happen to the interface, such as when the frame is resized.

> **KEY CONCEPT**
> Every container is managed by a layout manager.

Unless you specify otherwise, the components in a panel will try to arrange themselves next to one another in a row, and a component will move down to the next row only when the width of the panel won't accommodate it. Experiment with this program to see how the layout manager changes the organization of the labels as the window size is changed. Layout managers are discussed in more detail in the Graphics Track sections of Chapter 7.

SELF-REVIEW QUESTIONS *(see answers in Appendix N)*   **my**programming**lab**

SR 3.36 What is the difference between a frame and a panel?

SR 3.37 Select the term from the following list that best matches each of the following phrases:

container, content pane, frame, heavyweight, label, layout manager, lightweight, panel

a. A component that is used to hold and organize other components.
b. A container displayed in its own window with a title bar.
c. Its primary role is to help organize other components in a GUI; it must be added to another container to be displayed.
d. This type of component is managed by the underlying operating system.
e. This type of component is managed by the Java program itself.
f. The part of a frame that displays visible elements.

g. A component that displays a line of text in a GUI.

h. Determines how the components in a container are arranged on the screen.

SR 3.38   Run the Authority program. Describe what happens if you resize the frame by dragging the bottom-right corner towards the right. Explain.

SR 3.39   Which of the following statements best describes how the GUI of the Authority program is constructed?

- A frame is added to a panel, which is added to two labels.
- Labels are added to a panel, which is added to the content pane of a frame.
- Frames, panels, and labels are added to the foreground.
- A panel displays two labels to the user.

SR 3.40   What is the result of separately making each of the following changes to the Authority program? You may make the change, compile and run the program, and observe and report the results. Briefly explain what you observe.

a. The dimensions passed to the setPreferredSize method are (300, 300) instead of (250, 75).

b. The background color is set to black instead of yellow.

c. The order of the two label instantiation statements is reversed (i.e., first you create label2 as a new JLabel, passing it the string "but raise your hand first.", and then you create label1 as a new JLabel, passing it the string "Question authority,").

d. The order of the two primary add statements is reversed (i.e., first you add label2 to the primary panel, and then you add label1).

3.10 Nested Panels

In the previous section, we saw an example in which two labels were contained in a panel that was contained in a frame. Such relationships make up the *containment hierarchy* of an interface, which can be as intricate as needed to create the visual effect desired.

KEY CONCEPT

Panels can be nested to create an intricate containment hierarchy of components.

In particular, it is common to have multiple layers of nested panels to organize and group components in various ways. While you shouldn't include unnecessary components in the containment hierarchy, don't hesitate to include extra scaffolding in the creation of an interface to help achieve the effect you want.

The program in Listing 3.8, `NestedPanels`, creates two subpanels, each containing a label. Both subpanels are put onto another panel, which is then added to the content pane of the frame.

LISTING 3.8

```
//********************************************************************
//  NestedPanels.java         Author: Lewis/Loftus
//
//  Demonstrates a basic component hierarchy.
//********************************************************************

import java.awt.*;
import javax.swing.*;

public class NestedPanels
{
    //-----------------------------------------------------------------
    //  Presents two colored panels nested within a third.
    //-----------------------------------------------------------------
    public static void main (String[] args)
    {
        JFrame frame = new JFrame ("Nested Panels");
        frame.setDefaultCloseOperation (JFrame.EXIT_ON_CLOSE);

        // Set up first subpanel
        JPanel subPanel1 = new JPanel();
        subPanel1.setPreferredSize (new Dimension(150, 100));
        subPanel1.setBackground (Color.green);
        JLabel label1 = new JLabel ("One");
        subPanel1.add (label1);

        // Set up second subpanel
        JPanel subPanel2 = new JPanel();
        subPanel2.setPreferredSize (new Dimension(150, 100));
        subPanel2.setBackground (Color.red);
        JLabel label2 = new JLabel ("Two");
        subPanel2.add (label2);

        // Set up primary panel
        JPanel primary = new JPanel();
        primary.setBackground (Color.blue);
        primary.add (subPanel1);
        primary.add (subPanel2);
```

LISTING 3.8 *continued*

```
        frame.getContentPane().add(primary);
        frame.pack();
        frame.setVisible(true);
    }
}
```

DISPLAY

Note that the primary panel in the program was not explicitly sized. It sized itself as needed to accommodate the two panels contained in it. Also note that the subpanels have a buffer around them through which the blue of the primary panel can be seen. Such spacing is a function of the layout manager that is used to govern the container and the characteristics set for the components themselves. These issues are explored further in later Graphics Track sections.

VideoNote

Example using frames and panels.

As you did with the previous example, execute and experiment with this one. Resize the frame to see the effect on the components. Note that the size of the subpanels stays fixed, and that the orientation of the two panels changes depending on the width of the primary panel (which expands as the frame expands).

After you are comfortable with the way the components are laid out relative to each other, change the background color of all panels to the same color (say, green) to see how the distinction between panels can be invisible if the interface is designed accordingly.

myprogramminglab

SELF-REVIEW QUESTIONS *(see answers in Appendix N)*

SR 3.41   What is the containment hierarchy of a Java graphical user interface?

SR 3.42   In the `NestedPanels` program, how many panels are created? What are the names of the panel variables?

SR 3.43   In the `NestedPanels` program, which panels are added to another panel? Which panel are they added to? Which panel is explicitly added to the content pane of the frame?

3.11 Images

Images often play an important role in graphics-based software. Java has the ability to use JPEG and GIF images in various ways. The `Graphics` class contains a `drawImage` method that allows you to draw the image just as you would draw a shape or character string. An image can also be incorporated into a label component. Let's explore the relationship between images and labels in more detail.

As we've seen in previous sections, a label defined by the `JLabel` class can be used to provide information to the user or to describe other components in an interface. A `JLabel` can also contain an image. That is, a label can be composed of text, an image, or both.

> **KEY CONCEPT**
> A label can contain text, an image, or both.

The `ImageIcon` class is used to represent an image that is included in a label. The `ImageIcon` constructor takes the name of the image file and loads it into the object. `ImageIcon` objects can be made using either JPEG or GIF images.

The alignment of the text and image within the label can be set explicitly, using either the `JLabel` constructor or specific methods. Similarly, we can set the position of the text relative to the image.

The `LabelDemo` program shown in Listing 3.9 displays several labels. Each label shows its text and image in different orientations.

The third parameter passed to the `JLabel` constructor defines the horizontal positioning of the label within the space allowed for the label in the panel. The `SwingConstants` interface contains several constants used by various Swing components, making it easier to refer to them.

The orientation of the label's text and image is explicitly set using the `setHorizontalTextPosition` and `setVerticalTextPosition` methods. As shown in the case of the first label, the default horizontal position for text is on the right (image on the left), and the default vertical position for text is centered relative to the image.

Don't confuse the horizontal positioning of the label in the container with the setting of the orientation between the text and the image. The third parameter of the constructor determines the first, and the explicit method calls determine the second.

By putting an image in a label, it becomes part of a component that gets laid out with all other components in a container, instead of being drawn in a particular place. This is an appropriate design decision: whether to draw an image using

LISTING 3.9

```java
//********************************************************************
//  LabelDemo.java       Author: Lewis/Loftus
//
//  Demonstrates the use of image icons in labels.
//********************************************************************

import java.awt.*;
import javax.swing.*;

public class LabelDemo
{
   //-----------------------------------------------------------------
   //  Creates and displays the primary application frame.
   //-----------------------------------------------------------------
   public static void main (String[] args)
   {
      JFrame frame = new JFrame ("Label Demo");
      frame.setDefaultCloseOperation (JFrame.EXIT_ON_CLOSE);

      ImageIcon icon = new ImageIcon ("devil.gif");

      JLabel label1, label2, label3;

      label1 = new JLabel ("Devil Left", icon, SwingConstants.CENTER);

      label2 = new JLabel ("Devil Right", icon, SwingConstants.CENTER);
      label2.setHorizontalTextPosition (SwingConstants.LEFT);
      label2.setVerticalTextPosition (SwingConstants.BOTTOM);

      label3 = new JLabel ("Devil Above", icon, SwingConstants.CENTER);
      label3.setHorizontalTextPosition (SwingConstants.CENTER);
      label3.setVerticalTextPosition (SwingConstants.BOTTOM);

      JPanel panel = new JPanel();
      panel.setBackground (Color.cyan);
      panel.setPreferredSize (new Dimension (200, 250));
      panel.add (label1);
      panel.add (label2);
      panel.add (label3);
      frame.getContentPane().add(panel);
      frame.pack();
      frame.setVisible(true);
   }
}
```

SR 3.46 What is the result of separately making each of the following changes to the LabelDemo program? You may make the change, compile and run the program, and observe and report the results. Briefly explain what you observe.

a. Change the third parameter of each of the three JLabel constructor calls to SwingConstants.LEFT.

b. Change the horizontal text position of label2 from LEFT to RIGHT.

c. Change the horizontal text position of label2 from LEFT to BOTTOM.

d. Change the vertical text position of label3 from BOTTOM to CENTER.

Summary of Key Concepts

- The new operator returns a reference to a newly created object.
- Multiple reference variables can refer to the same object.
- Usually a method is executed on a particular object, which affects the results.
- A class library provides useful support when developing programs.
- The Java standard class library is organized into packages.
- All classes of the java.lang package are automatically imported for every program.
- A pseudorandom number generator performs a complex calculation to create the illusion of randomness.
- All methods of the Math class are static, meaning they are invoked through the class name.
- The printf method was added to Java to support the migration of legacy systems.
- Enumerated types are type-safe, ensuring that invalid values will not be used.
- A wrapper class allows a primitive value to be managed as an object.
- Autoboxing provides automatic conversions between primitive values and corresponding wrapper objects.
- Containers are special GUI components that hold and organize other components.
- A frame is displayed as a separate window, but a panel can be displayed only as part of another container.
- Every container is managed by a layout manager.
- Panels can be nested to create an intricate containment hierarchy of components.
- A label can contain text, an image, or both.

Exercises

Visit www.myprogramminglab.com to complete many of these Exercises online and get instant feedback.

myprogramminglab

EX 3.1   Write a statement that prints the length of a String concatenated by two strings, JAVA and PROGRAMMING.

EX 3.2   Write a statement that prints the index of the character 'M' that occurs last in the string PROGRAMMING.

EX 3.3 Write a declaration for a `String` variable called `change` and initialize it to the characters stored in another `String` object called `original` with all `'e'` characters changed to `'j'`.

EX 3.4 What output is produced by the following code fragment?

```
String m1,m2;
m1="Java Strings";
m1=m1.replace('s','z');
m2=m1.toLowerCase();
System.out.println(m2);
```

EX 3.5 What is the difference between these `import` statements?

a. `import java.util.Random;`
b. `import java.util.*;`

EX 3.6 Assuming that a `Random` object has been created called `generator`, what is the range of the result of each of the following expressions?

a. `generator.nextInt(40)`
b. `generator.nextInt(7)  -  3`
c. `generator.nextInt(13)  +  3`
d. `generator.nextInt(6)  -  6`

EX 3.7 Write code to declare and instantiate an object of the `Random` class (call the object reference variable `rand`). Then write a list of expressions using the `nextInt` method that generates random numbers in the following specified ranges, including the endpoints. Use the version of the `nextInt` method that accepts a single integer parameter.

a. 0 to 10
b. 0 to 500
c. 1 to 10
d. 1 to 500
e. 25 to 50
f. −10 to 15

EX 3.8 Write an assignment statement that computes the square root of the sum of the square roots of `num1` and `num2` and assigns the result to `num3`.

EX 3.9 Write a single statement that computes and prints the absolute value of `total`.

EX 3.10 Write code statements to create a `DecimalFormat` object that will round a formatted value to four decimal places and make the letters "Rs" precede the value. Also write a statement that uses the resulting object to print the value of money, properly formatted.

EX 3.11 Write code statements in Java that prompt for and read a `double` value and an `int` value from the user, and print the result by raising the `double` value to the power of the `int` value.

EX 3.12 Write a declaration for an enumerated type that represents the days of the week.

Programming Projects

Visit www.myprogramminglab.com to complete many of these Programming Projects online and get instant feedback.

PP 3.1 Write an application that prompts for and reads the user's name and password, checks whether the given password is strong or not, and prints the result (which would be the nature of the password). A password is considered strong if the same four-letter sequence does not occur in the given user name and password. If this condition is not satisfied, it is a weak password. Both the username and password should contain a minimum of four characters each.

PP 3.2 Write an application that prints the sum of cubes. Prompt for and read two integer values and print the sum of each value raised to the third power.

PP 3.3 Write an application that creates and prints a random phone number of the form XXX–XXX–XXXX. Include the dashes in the output. Do not let the first three digits contain an 8 or 9 (but don't be more restrictive than that), and make sure that the second set of three digits is not greater than 742. *Hint:* Think through the easiest way to construct the phone number. Each digit does not have to be determined separately.

PP 3.4 Write an application that reads the (x,y) coordinates for two points. Compute the distance between the two points using the following formula:

$$\text{Distance} = \sqrt{(x_2 - x_1)^2 + (y_2 - y_1)^2}$$

PP 3.5 Write an application that reads the radius of a sphere and prints its volume and surface area. Use the following formulas. Print the output to four decimal places. *r* represents the radius.

$$\text{Volume} = \frac{4}{3}\pi r^3$$

$$\text{Surface Area} = 4\pi r^2$$

VideoNote

Developing a solution of PP 3.5.

PP 3.6   Write an application that reads the lengths of the sides of a triangle from the user. Compute the area of the triangle using Heron's formula (below), in which s represents half of the perimeter of the triangle and a, b, and c represent the lengths of the three sides. Print the area to three decimal places.

$$\text{Area} = \sqrt{s(s-a)(s-b)(s-c)}$$

PP 3.7   Write an application that generates a random integer in the range 20 to 40, inclusive, and displays the sine, cosine, and tangent of that number.

PP 3.8   Write an application that generates a random integer radius (r) and height (h) for a cylinder in the range 1 to 10, inclusive, and then computes the volume and surface area of the cylinder.

$$\text{Volume} = \pi r^2 h$$

$$\text{Area} = 2\pi rh$$

PP 3.9   Write an application that displays a frame containing two labels that display your name, one for your first name and one for your last. Experiment with the size of the window to see the labels change their orientation to each other.

PP 3.10   Write an application that displays a frame containing two panels. Each panel should contain two images (use four unique images—your choice). Fix the size of the first panel so that both of its images remain side by side. Allow the other panel to change size as needed. Experiment with the size of the window to see the images change orientation. Make sure you understand why the application behaves as it does.

PP 3.11   Modify the LabelDemo program so that it displays a fourth label, with the text of the label centered above the image.

Writing Classes

4

CHAPTER OBJECTIVES

- Discuss the structure and content of a class definition.
- Establish the concept of object state using instance data.
- Describe the effect of visibility modifiers on methods and data.
- Explore the structure of a method definition, including parameters and return values.
- Discuss the structure and purpose of a constructor.
- Explore the creation of graphical objects.
- Introduce the concepts needed to create an interactive graphical user interface.
- Explore some basic GUI components and events.

In Chapter 3, we used classes and objects for the various services they provide. That is, we used the predefined classes in the Java class library that are provided to us to make the process of writing programs easier. In this chapter, we address the heart of object-oriented programming: writing our own classes to define our own objects. This chapter explores the basics of class definitions, including the structure of methods and the scope and encapsulation of data. The Graphics Track sections of this chapter discuss how to write classes that have graphical representations and introduce the issues necessary to create a truly interactive graphical user interface.

4.1 Classes and Objects Revisited

In Chapter 1, we introduced basic object-oriented concepts, including a brief overview of objects and classes. In Chapter 3, we used several predefined classes from the Java standard class library to create objects and use them for the particular functionality they provided.

In this chapter, we turn our attention to writing our own classes. Although existing class libraries provide many useful classes, the essence of object-oriented program development is the process of designing and implementing our own classes to suit our specific needs.

Recall the basic relationship between an object and a class: a class is a blueprint of an object. The class represents the concept of an object, and any object created from that class is a realization of that concept.

For example, from Chapter 3 we know that the String class represents a concept of a character string, and that each String object represents a particular string that contains specific characters.

Let's consider another example. Suppose a class called Student represents a student at a university. An object created from the Student class would represent a particular student. The Student class represents the general concept of a student, and every object created from that class represents an actual student attending the school. In a system that helps manage the business of a university, we would have one Student class and thousands of Student objects.

Recall that an object has a *state*, which is defined by the values of the *attributes* associated with that object. The attributes of a student may include the student's name, address, major, and grade point average. The Student class establishes that each student has these attributes. Each Student object stores the values of these attributes for a particular student. In Java, an object's attributes are defined by variables declared within a class.

An object also has *behaviors*, which are defined by the *operations* associated with that object. The operations of a student would include the ability to update that student's address and compute that student's current grade point average. The Student class defines the operations, such as the details of how a grade point average is computed. These operations can then be executed on (or by) a particular Student object. Note that the behaviors of an object may modify the state of that object. In Java, an object's operations are defined by methods declared within a class.

Figure 4.1 lists some examples of classes, with some attributes and operations that might be defined for objects of those classes. It's up to the program designer to determine what attributes and operations are needed, which depends on the purpose of the program and the role a particular object plays in that purpose. Consider other attributes and operations you might include for these examples.

Class	Attributes	Operations
Student	Name Address Major Grade point average	Set address Set major Compute grade point average
Rectangle	Length Width Color	Set length Set width Set color
Aquarium	Material Length Width Height	Set material Set length Set width Set height Compute volume Compute filled weight
Flight	Airline Flight number Origin city Destination city Current status	Set airline Set flight number Determine status
Employee	Name Department Title Salary	Set department Set title Set salary Compute wages Compute bonus Compute taxes

FIGURE 4.1   Examples of classes and some possible attributes and operations

SELF-REVIEW QUESTIONS *(see answers in Appendix N)*

myprogramminglab

SR 4.1   What is an attribute?

SR 4.2   What is an operation?

SR 4.3   List some attributes and operations that might be defined for a class called Book that represents a book in a library.

SR 4.4   True or False? Explain.

    a. We should use only classes from the Java standard class library when writing our programs—there is no need to define or use other classes.

    b. An operation on an object can change the state of an object.

    c. The current state of an object can affect the result of an operation on that object.

    d. In Java, the state of an object is represented by its methods.

4.2 Anatomy of a Class

In all of our previous examples, we've written a single class containing a single main method. These classes represent small but complete programs. These programs often instantiated objects using predefined classes from the Java class library and used those objects for the services they provide. Those predefined classes are part of the program too, but we never really concern ourselves with them other than to know how to interact with them. We simply trust them to provide the services they promise.

Let's look at another, similar example. The RollingDice class shown in Listing 4.1 contains a main method that instantiates two Die objects (as in the singular of dice). It then rolls the dice and prints the results. It also calls several other methods provided by the Die class, such as the ability to explicitly set and get the current face value of a die.

LISTING 4.1

```java
//********************************************************************
//  RollingDice.java        Author: Lewis/Loftus
//
//  Demonstrates the creation and use of a user-defined class.
//********************************************************************

public class RollingDice
{
   //-----------------------------------------------------------
   //  Creates two Die objects and rolls them several times.
   //-----------------------------------------------------------
   public static void main (String[] args)
   {
      Die die1, die2;
      int sum;

      die1 = new Die();
      die2 = new Die();

      die1.roll();
      die2.roll();
      System.out.println ("Die One: " + die1 + ", Die Two: " + die2);

      die1.roll();
      die2.setFaceValue(4);
```

LISTING   4.1   *continued*

```
        System.out.println ("Die One: " + die1 + ", Die Two: " + die2);

        sum = die1.getFaceValue() + die2.getFaceValue();
        System.out.println ("Sum: " + sum);

        sum = die1.roll() + die2.roll();
        System.out.println ("Die One: " + die1 + ", Die Two: " + die2);
        System.out.println ("New sum: " + sum);
    }
}
```

OUTPUT

```
Die One: 5, Die Two: 2
Die One: 1, Die Two: 4
Sum: 5
Die One: 4, Die Two: 2
New sum: 6
```

The primary difference between this example and previous examples is that the `Die` class is not a predefined part of the Java class library. We have to write the `Die` class ourselves, defining the services we want `Die` objects to perform, if this program is to compile and run.

Every class can contain data declarations and method declarations, as depicted in Figure 4.2. The data declarations represent the data that will be stored in each object of the class. The method declarations define the services that those objects will provide. Collectively, the data and methods of a class are called the *members* of a class.

The classes we've written in previous examples follow this model as well, but contain no data at the class level and contain only one method (the `main` method). We'll continue to define classes like this, such as the `RollingDice` class, to define the starting point of a program.

True object-oriented programming, however, comes from defining classes that represent objects with well-defined state and behavior. For example, at any given moment a `Die` object is showing a particular face value, which we could refer to as the state of the die. A `Die` object also has various methods we can invoke on it, such as the ability to roll the die or get its face value. These methods represent the behavior of a die.

KEY CONCEPT

The heart of object-oriented programming is defining classes that represent objects with well-defined state and behavior.

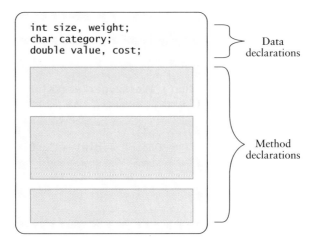

```
int size, weight;
char category;
double value, cost;
```

Data declarations

Method declarations

FIGURE 4.2   The members of a class: data and method declarations

The Die class is shown in Listing 4.2. It contains two data values: an integer constant (MAX) that represents the maximum face value of the die, and an integer variable (faceValue) that represents the current face value of the die. It also contains a constructor called Die and four regular methods: roll, setFaceValue, getFaceValue, and toString.

You will recall from Chapters 2 and 3 that constructors are special methods that have the same name as the class. The Die constructor gets called when the new operator is used to create a new instance of the Die class. The rest of the methods in the Die class define the various services provided by Die objects.

We use a header block of documentation to explain the purpose of each method in the class. This practice is not only crucial for anyone trying to understand the software, it also separates the code visually so that it's easy for the eye to jump from one method to the next while reading the code.

VideoNote
Dissecting the Die class.

Figure 4.3 lists the methods of the Die class. From this point of view, it looks no different from any other class that we've used in previous examples. The only important difference is that the Die class was not provided for us by the Java standard class library. We wrote it ourselves.

The methods of the Die class include the ability to roll the die, producing a new random face value. The roll method returns the new face value to the calling method, but you can also get the current face value at any time using the getFaceValue method. The setFaceValue method sets the face value explicitly, as if you had reached over and turned the die to whatever face you wanted. The toString method of any object gets called automatically whenever you pass the object to a print or println method to obtain a string description of the object

LISTING 4.2

```java
//********************************************************************
//  Die.java        Author: Lewis/Loftus
//
//  Represents one die (singular of dice) with faces showing values
//  between 1 and 6.
//********************************************************************

public class Die
{
   private final int MAX = 6;  // maximum face value

   private int faceValue;  // current value showing on the die

   //-----------------------------------------------------------------
   //  Constructor: Sets the initial face value.
   //-----------------------------------------------------------------
   public Die()
   {
      faceValue = 1;
   }

   //-----------------------------------------------------------------
   //  Rolls the die and returns the result.
   //-----------------------------------------------------------------
   public int roll()
   {
      faceValue = (int)(Math.random() * MAX) + 1;

      return faceValue;
   }

   //-----------------------------------------------------------------
   //  Face value mutator.
   //-----------------------------------------------------------------
   public void setFaceValue (int value)
   {
      faceValue = value;
   }

   //-----------------------------------------------------------------
   //  Face value accessor.
   //-----------------------------------------------------------------
   public int getFaceValue()
```

LISTING 4.2   *continued*

```
    {
        return faceValue;
    }

    //------------------------------------------------------------
    //  Returns a string representation of this die.
    //------------------------------------------------------------
    public String toString()
    {
        String result = Integer.toString(faceValue);

        return result;
    }
}
```

to print. Therefore it's usually a good idea to define a `toString` method for most classes. The definitions of these methods have various parts, and we'll dissect them as we proceed through this chapter.

For the examples in this book, we usually store each class in its own file. Java allows multiple classes to be stored in one file. If a file contains multiple classes, only one of those classes can be declared using the reserved word `public`. Furthermore, the name of the public class must correspond to the name of the file. For instance, class `Die` is stored in a file called `Die.java`.

```
Die()
        Constructor: Sets the initial face value of the die to 1.

int roll()
        Rolls the die by setting the face value to a random number in the appropriate range.

void setFaceValue (int value)
        Sets the face value of the die to the specified value.

int getFaceValue()
        Returns the current face value of the die.

String toString()
        Returns a string representation of the die indicating its current face value.
```

FIGURE 4.3   Some methods of the `Die` class

Instance Data

Note that in the `Die` class, the constant `MAX` and the variable `faceValue` are declared inside the class but not inside any method. The location at which a variable is declared defines its *scope*, which is the area within a program in which that variable can be referenced. By being declared at the class level (not within a method), these variables and constants can be referenced in any method of the class.

Attributes such as the variable `faceValue` are called *instance data* because new memory space is reserved for that variable every time an instance of the class that is created. Each `Die` object has its own `faceValue` variable with its own data space. That's how each `Die` object can have its own state. We see that in the output of the `RollingDice` program: one die has a face value of 5 and the other has a face value of 2. That's possible only because the memory space for the `faceValue` variable is created for each `Die` object.

> **KEY CONCEPT**
> The scope of a variable, which determines where it can be referenced, depends on where it is declared.

We can depict this situation as follows:

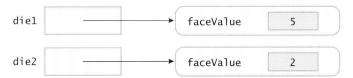

The `die1` and `die2` reference variables point to (that is, contain the address of) their respective `Die` objects. Each object contains a `faceValue` variable with its own memory space. Thus each object can store different values for its instance data.

Java automatically initializes any variables declared at the class level. For example, all variables of numeric types such as `int` and `double` are initialized to zero. However, despite the fact that the language performs this automatic initialization, it is good practice to initialize variables explicitly (usually in a constructor) so that anyone reading the code will clearly understand the intent.

UML Class Diagrams

Throughout this book we use *UML diagrams* to visualize relationships among classes and objects. UML stands for the *Unified Modeling Language*, which has become the most popular notation for representing the design of an object-oriented program.

Several types of UML diagrams exist, each designed to show specific aspects of object-oriented programs. We focus primarily on UML *class diagrams* in this book to show the contents of classes and the relationships among them.

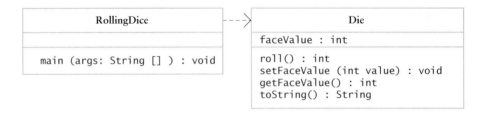

FIGURE 4.4 A UML class diagram showing the classes involved in the
RollingDice program

In a UML diagram, each class is represented as a rectangle, possibly containing three sections to show the class name, its attributes (data), and its operations (methods). Figure 4.4 shows a class diagram containing the classes of the RollingDice program.

The arrow connecting the RollingDice and Die classes in Figure 4.4 indicates that a relationship exists between the classes. A dotted arrow indicates that one class *uses* the methods of the other class. Other types of object-oriented relationships between classes are shown with different types of connecting lines and arrows. We'll discuss these other relationships as we explore the appropriate topics in the book.

Keep in mind that UML is not designed specifically for Java programmers. It is intended to be language independent. Therefore the syntax used in a UML diagram is not necessarily the same as Java. For example, the type of a variable is shown after the variable name, separated by a colon. Return types of methods are shown the same way.

UML diagrams are versatile. We can include whatever appropriate information is desired, depending on the goal of a particular diagram. We might leave out the data and method sections of a class, for instance, if those details aren't relevant for a particular diagram.

UML diagrams allow you to visualize a program's design. As our programs get larger, made up of more and more classes, these visualizations become increasingly helpful. We will explore new aspects of UML diagrams as the situation dictates.

myprogramminglab

SELF-REVIEW QUESTIONS *(see answers in Appendix N)*

SR 4.5   What is the difference between an object and a class?

SR 4.6   Describe the instance data of the Die class.

SR 4.7   Which of the methods defined for the Die class can change the state of a Die object—that is, which of the methods assign values to the instance data?

SR 4.8   What happens when you pass an object to a `print` or `println` method?

SR 4.9   What is the scope of a variable?

SR 4.10 What are UML diagrams designed to do?

4.3 Encapsulation

We mentioned in our overview of object-oriented concepts in Chapter 1 that an object should be *self-governing*. That is, the instance data of an object should be modified only by that object. For example, the methods of the `Die` class should be solely responsible for changing the value of the `faceValue` variable. We should make it difficult, if not impossible, for code outside of a class to "reach in" and change the value of a variable that is declared inside that class. This characteristic is called *encapsulation*.

An object should be encapsulated from the rest of the system. It should interact with other parts of a program only through the specific set of methods that define the services that that object provides. These methods define the *interface* between that object and the program that uses it.

> **KEY CONCEPT**
> An object should be encapsulated, guarding its data from inappropriate access.

Encapsulation is depicted graphically in Figure 4.5. The code that uses an object, sometimes called the *client* of an object, should not be allowed to access variables directly. The client should call an object's methods, and those methods then interact with the data encapsulated within the object. For example, the `main` method in the `RollingDice` program calls the `roll` method of the `Die` objects. The `main` method should not (and in fact cannot) access the `faceValue` variable directly.

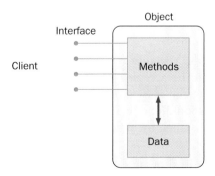

FIGURE 4.5   A client interacting with the methods of an object

In Java, we accomplish object encapsulation using *modifiers*. A modifier is a Java reserved word that is used to specify particular characteristics of a programming language construct. In Chapter 2 we discussed the `final` modifier, which is used to declare a constant. Java has several modifiers that can be used in various ways. Some modifiers can be used together, but some combinations are invalid. We discuss various Java modifiers at appropriate points throughout this book, and all of them are summarized in Appendix E.

Visibility Modifiers

Some of the Java modifiers are called *visibility modifiers* because they control access to the members of a class. The reserved words `public` and `private` are visibility modifiers that can be applied to the variables and methods of a class. If a member of a class has *public visibility*, it can be directly referenced from outside of the object. If a member of a class has *private visibility*, it can be used anywhere inside the class definition but cannot be referenced externally. A third visibility modifier, `protected`, is relevant only in the context of inheritance. We discuss it in Chapter 9.

> **KEY CONCEPT**
>
> Instance variables should be declared with private visibility to promote encapsulation.

Public variables violate encapsulation. They allow code external to the class in which the data is defined to reach in and access or modify the value of the data. Therefore, instance data should be defined with private visibility. Data that is declared as `private` can be accessed only by the methods of the class.

The visibility we apply to a method depends on the purpose of that method. Methods that provide services to the client must be declared with public visibility so that they can be invoked by the client. These methods are sometimes referred to as *service methods*. A `private` method cannot be invoked from outside the class. The only purpose of a `private` method is to help the other methods of the class do their job. Therefore they are sometimes referred to as *support methods*.

The table in Figure 4.6 summarizes the effects of public and private visibility on both variables and methods.

Giving constants public visibility is generally considered acceptable because, although their values can be accessed directly, they cannot be changed because they were declared using the `final` modifier. Keep in mind that encapsulation means that data values should not be able to be *changed* directly by another part of the code. Because constants, by definition, cannot be changed, the encapsulation issue is largely moot.

UML class diagrams can show the visibility of a class member by preceding it with a particular character. A member with public visibility is preceded by a plus sign (+), and a member with private visibility is preceded by a minus sign (-).

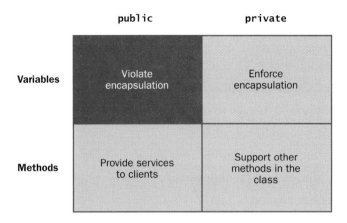

FIGURE 4.6   The effects of public and private visibility

Accessors and Mutators

Because instance data is generally declared with private visibility, a class usually provides services to access and modify data values. A method such as getFaceValue is called an *accessor method* because it provides read-only access to a particular value. Likewise, a method such as setFaceValue is called a *mutator method* because it changes a particular value.

> **KEY CONCEPT**
>
> Most objects contain accessor and mutator methods to allow the client to manage data in a controlled manner.

Generally, accessor method names have the form getX, where X is the value to which it provides access. Likewise, mutator method names have the form setX, where X is the value they are setting. Therefore these types of methods are sometimes referred to as "getters" and "setters."

For example, if a class contains the instance variable height, it should also probably contain the methods getHeight and setHeight. Note that this naming convention capitalizes the first letter of the variable when used in the method names, which is consistent with how method names are written in general.

Some methods may provide accessor and/or mutator capabilities as a side effect of their primary purpose. For example, the roll method of the Die class changes the faceValue of the die and returns that new value as well. Note that the code of the roll method is careful to keep the face value of the die in the valid range (1 to MAX). Service methods must be carefully designed to permit only appropriate access and valid changes.

This points out a flaw in the design of the Die class. Note that there is no restriction on the setFaceValue method—a client could use it to set the die value to a number such as 20, which is outside the valid range. The code of the setFaceValue method should allow only valid modifications to the face value of a die. We explore how that kind of control can be accomplished in the next chapter.

SELF-REVIEW QUESTIONS *(see answers in Appendix N)*

SR 4.11 Objects should be self-governing. Explain.

SR 4.12 What is the interface to an object?

SR 4.13 What is a modifier?

SR 4.14 Why might a constant be given public visibility?

SR 4.15 Describe each of the following:

    a. public method
    b. private method
    c. public variable
    d. private variable

4.4 Anatomy of a Method

We've seen that a class is composed of data declarations and method declarations. Let's examine method declarations in more detail.

As we stated in Chapter 1, a method is a group of programming language statements that is given a name. A *method declaration* specifies the code that is executed when the method is invoked. Every method in a Java program is part of a particular class.

When a method is called, the flow of control transfers to that method. One by one, the statements of that method are executed. When that method is done, control returns to the location where the call was made and execution continues.

The *called method* (the one that is invoked) might be part of the same class as the *calling method* that invoked it. If the called method is part of the same class, only the method name is needed to invoke it. If it is part of a different class, it is invoked through the name of an object of that other class, as we've seen many times. Figure 4.7 shows the flow of execution as methods are called.

We've defined the main method of a program many times in previous examples. Its definition follows the same syntax as all methods. The header of a method includes the type of the return value, the method name, and a list of parameters that the method accepts. The statements that make up the body of the method are defined in a block delimited by braces. The rest of this section discusses issues related to method declarations in more detail.

Method Declaration

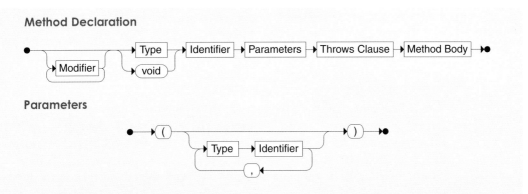

Parameters

A method is defined by optional modifiers, followed by a return Type, followed by an Identifier that determines the method name, followed by a list of Parameters, followed by the Method Body. The return Type indicates the type of value that will be returned by the method, which may be void. The Method Body is a block of statements that executes when the method is invoked. The Throws Clause is optional and indicates the exceptions that may be thrown by this method.

Example:

```
public void instructions (int count)
{
    System.out.println ("Follow all instructions.");
    System.out.println ("Use no more than " + count +
                        " turns.");
}
```

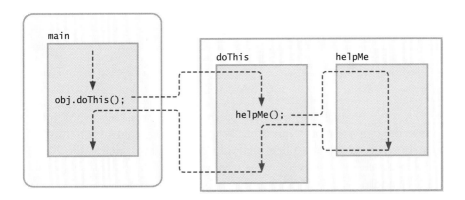

FIGURE 4.7   The flow of control following method invocations

The return Statement

The return type specified in the method header can be a primitive type, class name, or the reserved word void. When a method does not return any value, void is used as the return type, as is always done with the main method. The setFaceValue method of the Die class also has a return type of void.

A method that returns a value must have a *return statement.* When a return statement is executed, control is immediately returned to the statement in the calling method, and processing continues there. A return statement consists of the reserved word return followed by an expression that dictates the value to be returned. The expression must be consistent with the return type in the method header.

The getFaceValue method of the Die class returns an int value that represents the current value of the die. The roll method does the same, returning the new value to which faceValue was just randomly set. The toString method returns a String object.

> **KEY CONCEPT**
> The value returned from a method must be consistent with the return type specified in the method header.

A method that does not return a value does not usually contain a return statement. The method automatically returns to the calling method when the end of the method is reached. Such methods may contain a return statement without an expression.

It is usually not good practice to use more than one return statement in a method, even though it is possible to do so. In general, a method should have one return statement as the last line of the method body, unless that makes the method overly complex.

The value that is returned from a method can be ignored in the calling method. For example, in the main method of the RollingDice class, the value that is returned

Return Statement

A return statement consists of the return reserved word followed by an optional Expression. When executed, control is immediately returned to the calling method, returning the value defined by Expression.

Examples:

```
return;
return distance * 4;
```

from the `roll` method is ignored in several calls, while in others the return value is used in a calculation.

Constructors do not have a return type (not even `void`) and therefore cannot return a value. We discuss constructors in more detail later in this chapter.

Parameters

As we defined in Chapter 2, a parameter is a value that is passed into a method when it is invoked. The *parameter list* in the header of a method specifies the types of the values that are passed and the names by which the called method will refer to those values.

The names of the parameters in the header of the method declaration are called *formal parameters*. In an invocation, the values passed into a method are called *actual parameters*. The actual parameters are also called the *arguments* to the method.

A method invocation and definition always give the parameter list in parentheses after the method name. If there are no parameters, an empty set of parentheses is used, as is the case in the `roll` and `getFaceValue` methods. The `Die` constructor also takes no parameters, although constructors often do.

The formal parameters are identifiers that serve as variables inside the method and whose initial values come from the actual parameters in the invocation. When a method is called, the value in each actual parameter is copied and stored in the corresponding formal parameter. Actual parameters can be literals, variables, or full expressions. If an expression is used as an actual parameter, it is fully evaluated before the method call and the result is passed as the parameter.

> **KEY CONCEPT**
> When a method is called, the actual parameters are copied into the formal parameters.

The only method in the `Die` class that accepts any parameters is the `setFaceValue` method, which accepts a single `int` parameter. The formal parameter name is `value`. In the `main` method, the value of 4 is passed into it as the actual parameter.

The parameter lists in the invocation and the method declaration must match up. That is, the value of the first actual parameter is copied into the first formal parameter, the second actual parameter into the second formal parameter, and so on, as shown in Figure 4.8. The types of the actual parameters must be consistent with the specified types of the formal parameters.

Other details regarding parameter passing are discussed in Chapter 7.

Local Data

As we described earlier in this chapter, the scope of a variable or constant is the part of a program in which a valid reference to that variable can be made. A variable

FIGURE 4.8   Passing parameters from the method invocation to the declaration

can be declared inside a method, making it *local data* as opposed to instance data. Recall that instance data is declared in a class but not inside any particular method.

> **KEY CONCEPT**
>
> A variable declared in a method is local to that method and cannot be used outside of it.

Local data has scope limited to only the method in which it is declared. The variable `result` declared in the `toString` method of the `Die` class is local data. Any reference to `result` in any other method of the `Die` class would have caused the compiler to issue an error message. A local variable simply does not exist outside of the method in which it is declared. On the other hand, instance data, declared at the class level, has a scope of the entire class; any method of the class can refer to it.

Because local data and instance data operate at different levels of scope, it's possible to declare a local variable inside a method with the same name as an instance variable declared at the class level. Referring to that name in the method will reference the local version of the variable. This naming practice obviously has the potential to confuse anyone reading the code, so it should be avoided.

The formal parameter names in a method header serve as local data for that method. They don't exist until the method is called, and they cease to exist when the method is exited. For example, the formal parameter `value` in the `setFaceValue` method comes into existence when the method is called and goes out of existence when the method finishes executing.

Bank Account Example

Let's look at another example of a class and its use. The `Transactions` class shown in Listing 4.3 contains a `main` method that creates a few `Account` objects and invokes their services.

LISTING 4.3

```java
//********************************************************************
//  Transactions.java       Author: Lewis/Loftus
//
//  Demonstrates the creation and use of multiple Account objects.
//********************************************************************

public class Transactions
{
   //-----------------------------------------------------------------
   //  Creates some bank accounts and requests various services.
   //-----------------------------------------------------------------
   public static void main (String[] args)
   {
      Account acct1 = new Account ("Ted Murphy", 72354, 102.56);
      Account acct2 = new Account ("Jane Smith", 69713, 40.00);
      Account acct3 = new Account ("Edward Demsey", 93757, 759.32);

      acct1.deposit (25.85);

      double smithBalance = acct2.deposit (500.00);
      System.out.println ("Smith balance after deposit: " +
                          smithBalance);

      System.out.println ("Smith balance after withdrawal: " +
                          acct2.withdraw (430.75, 1.50));

      acct1.addInterest();
      acct2.addInterest();
      acct3.addInterest();

      System.out.println ();
      System.out.println (acct1);
      System.out.println (acct2);
      System.out.println (acct3);
   }
}
```

OUTPUT

```
Smith balance after deposit: 540.0
Smith balance after withdrawal: 107.75

72354    Ted Murphy       $132.90
69713    Jane Smith       $111.52
93757    Edward Demsey    $785.90
```

The Account class, shown in Listing 4.4, represents a basic bank account. It contains instance data representing the account number, the account's current balance, and the name of the account's owner. Note that instance data can be an object reference variable (not just a primitive type), such as the account owner's name, which is a reference to a String object. The interest rate for the account is stored as a constant.

The constructor of the Account class accepts three parameters that are used to initialize the instance data. The deposit and withdraw methods perform the basic

LISTING 4.4

```java
//********************************************************************
//  Account.java        Author: Lewis/Loftus
//
//  Represents a bank account with basic services such as deposit
//  and withdraw.
//********************************************************************

import java.text.NumberFormat;

public class Account
{
   private final double RATE = 0.035;  // interest rate of 3.5%

   private long acctNumber;
   private double balance;
   private String name;

   //-----------------------------------------------------------------
   // Sets up the account by defining its owner, account number,
   // and initial balance.
   //-----------------------------------------------------------------
   public Account (String owner, long account, double initial)
   {
      name = owner;
      acctNumber = account;
      balance = initial;
   }

   //-----------------------------------------------------------------
   //  Deposits the specified amount into the account. Returns the
   //  new balance.
   //-----------------------------------------------------------------
   public double deposit (double amount)
```

LISTING 4.4   *continued*

```java
   {
      balance = balance + amount;
      return balance;
   }

   //---------------------------------------------------------------
   //  Withdraws the specified amount from the account and applies
   //  the fee. Returns the new balance.
   //---------------------------------------------------------------
   public double withdraw (double amount, double fee)
   {
      balance = balance - amount - fee;

      return balance;
   }

   //---------------------------------------------------------------
   //  Adds interest to the account and returns the new balance.
   //---------------------------------------------------------------
   public double addInterest ()
   {
      balance += (balance * RATE);
      return balance;
   }

   //---------------------------------------------------------------
   //  Returns the current balance of the account.
   //---------------------------------------------------------------
   public double getBalance ()
   {
      return balance;
   }

   //---------------------------------------------------------------
   //  Returns a one-line description of the account as a string.
   //---------------------------------------------------------------
   public String toString ()
   {
      NumberFormat fmt = NumberFormat.getCurrencyInstance();
      return acctNumber + "\t" + name + "\t" + fmt.format(balance);
   }
}
```

transactions on the account, adjusting the balance based on the parameters. There is also an addInterest method that updates the balance by adding in the interest earned. These methods represent valid ways to change the balance, so a classic mutator such as setBalance is not provided.

The status of the three Account objects just after they were created in the Transactions program could be depicted as follows:

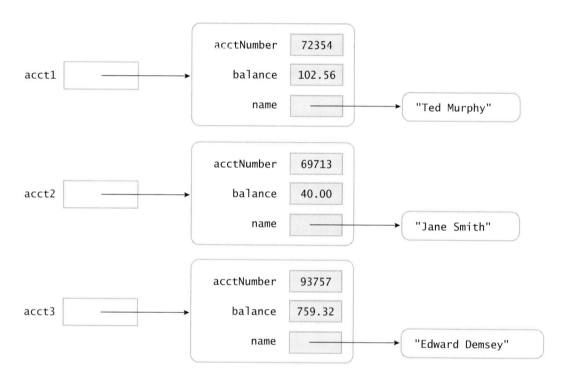

The various methods that update the balance of the account could be more rigorously designed. Checks should be made to ensure that the parameter values are valid, such as preventing the withdrawal of a negative amount (which would essentially be a deposit). This processing is discussed in the next chapter.

SELF-REVIEW QUESTIONS *(see answers in Appendix N)*

SR 4.16 Why is a method invoked through (or on) a particular object? What is the exception to that rule?

SR 4.17 What does it mean for a method to return a value?

SR 4.18 What does the return statement do?

SR 4.19 Is a return statement required?

SR 4.20 Explain the difference between an actual parameter and a formal parameter.

SR 4.21 Write a method called getFaceDown for the Die class that returns the current "face down" value of the die. *Hint:* On a standard die, the sum of any two opposite faces is seven.

SR 4.22 In the Transactions program:

   a. How many Account objects are created?
   b. How many arguments (actual parameters) are passed to the withdraw method when it is invoked on the acct2 object?
   c. How many arguments (actual parameters) are passed to the addInterest method when it is invoked on the acct3 object?

SR 4.23 Which of the Account class methods would you classify as accessor methods? As mutator methods? As service methods?

4.5 Constructors Revisited

As we stated in Chapter 2, a constructor is similar to a method that is invoked when an object is instantiated. When we define a class, we usually define a constructor to help us set up the class. In particular, we often use a constructor to initialize the variables associated with each object.

A constructor differs from a regular method in two ways. First, the name of a constructor is the same name as the class. Therefore the name of the constructor in the Die class is Die, and the name of the constructor in the Account class is Account. Second, a constructor cannot return a value and does not have a return type specified in the method header.

A common mistake made by programmers is to put a void return type on a constructor. As far as the compiler is concerned, putting any return type on a constructor, even void, turns it into a regular method that happens to have the same name as the class. As such, it cannot be invoked as a constructor. This leads to error messages that are sometimes difficult to decipher.

> **KEY CONCEPT**
> A constructor cannot have any return type, even void.

Generally, a constructor is used to initialize the newly instantiated object. For instance, the constructor of the Die class sets the face value of the die to 1 initially. The constructor of the Account class sets the values of the instance variables to the values passed in as parameters to the constructor.

We don't have to define a constructor for every class. Each class has a *default constructor* that takes no parameters. The default constructor is used if we don't provide our own. This default constructor generally has no effect on the newly created object.

SELF-REVIEW QUESTIONS *(see answers in Appendix N)*

SR 4.24 What are constructors used for?

SR 4.25 How are constructors defined?

4.6 Graphical Objects

Some objects have a graphical representation, meaning that their state and behaviors include information about what the object looks like visually. A graphical object might contain data about its size and color, for instance, and it may contain methods to draw it.

In Chapter 3 we instantiated and used graphical components such as frames, panels, labels, and images. Certainly these components can be considered graphical objects. This section examines some of them in more detail and explores how to define our own objects that have graphical characteristics.

The program in Listing 4.5 displays a smiling face and a text caption. The main method in the SmilingFace class does not deal with all of those details, however. Instead, the main method sets up the frame for the program and uses it to display an instantiation of the SmilingFacePanel class.

The SmilingFacePanel class is shown in Listing 4.6. It defines two constants on which the drawing is based (BASEX and BASEY), a constructor that sets up the key aspects of the panel, and a method called paintComponent that draws the face that we see when the program is executed. In this case, instead of adding GUI components to this panel, we are simply drawing on it.

Note that the SmilingFacePanel class extends the JPanel class. As we mentioned in Chapter 2 in our discussion of applets, the extends clause establishes an inheritance relationship. The SmilingFacePanel class inherits the characteristics of the JPanel class. That is, a SmilingFacePanel *is* a JPanel. At this point, that's all you really need to know about inheritance, which is discussed in detail in Chapter 9.

VideoNote

Example using an extended JPanel.

The constructor of the SmilingFacePanel class sets the background color and preferred size of the panel, as well as setting the panel's default font. Note that these calls are not made to some other object, as we did in Chapter 3 when we created a separate JPanel object. When a method is called without being invoked through a particular object, you can think of it as the object "talking to itself." The calls in the constructor are made to the object represented by the SmilingFacePanel class.

LISTING 4.5

```java
//********************************************************************
//  SmilingFace.java       Author: Lewis/Loftus
//
//  Demonstrates the use of a separate panel class.
//********************************************************************

import javax.swing.JFrame;

public class SmilingFace
{
   //-----------------------------------------------------------------
   //  Creates the main frame of the program.
   //-----------------------------------------------------------------
   public static void main (String[] args)
   {
      JFrame frame = new JFrame ("Smiling Face");
      frame.setDefaultCloseOperation (JFrame.EXIT_ON_CLOSE);

      SmilingFacePanel panel = new SmilingFacePanel();

      frame.getContentPane().add(panel);

      frame.pack();
      frame.setVisible(true);
   }
}
```

DISPLAY

LISTING 4.6

```java
//********************************************************************
//  SmilingFacePanel.java       Author: Lewis/Loftus
//
//  Demonstrates the use of a separate panel class.
//********************************************************************

import javax.swing.JPanel;
import java.awt.*;

public class SmilingFacePanel extends JPanel
{
   private final int BASEX = 120, BASEY = 60;  // base point for head

   //-----------------------------------------------------------------
   //  Constructor: Sets up the main characteristics of this panel.
   //-----------------------------------------------------------------
   public SmilingFacePanel ()
   {
      setBackground (Color.blue);
      setPreferredSize (new Dimension(320, 200));
      setFont (new Font("Arial", Font.BOLD, 16));
   }


   //-----------------------------------------------------------------
   //  Draws a face.
   //-----------------------------------------------------------------
   public void paintComponent (Graphics page)
   {
      super.paintComponent (page);

      page.setColor (Color.yellow);
      page.fillOval (BASEX, BASEY, 80, 80);  // head
      page.fillOval (BASEX-5, BASEY+20, 90, 40);  // ears

      page.setColor (Color.black);
      page.drawOval (BASEX+20, BASEY+30, 15, 7);  // eyes
      page.drawOval (BASEX+45, BASEY+30, 15, 7);

      page.fillOval (BASEX+25, BASEY+31, 5, 5);  // pupils
      page.fillOval (BASEX+50, BASEY+31, 5, 5);

      page.drawArc (BASEX+20, BASEY+25, 15, 7, 0, 180);  // eyebrows
      page.drawArc (BASEX+45, BASEY+25, 15, 7, 0, 180);
```

LISTING 4.6   *continued*

```
        page.drawArc (BASEX+35, BASEY+40, 15, 10, 180, 180);   // nose
        page.drawArc (BASEX+20, BASEY+50, 40, 15, 180, 180);   // mouth

        page.setColor (Color.white);
        page.drawString ("Always remember that you are unique!",
                        BASEX-105, BASEY-15);
        page.drawString ("Just like everyone else.", BASEX-45, BASEY+105);
    }
}
```

The paintComponent method accepts a Graphics object as a parameter, which, as we discussed in Chapter 2, represents the graphics context for a component. Graphics are drawn on the panel by making method calls to the panel's graphics context (the page parameter).

Every JPanel object has a paintComponent method that automatically gets called to draw the panel. In this case we are adding to the definition of paintComponent—telling it that in addition to drawing the background of the panel, it should also draw the face and words as defined by the various calls made in the paintComponent method. The first line of the paintComponent method is a call to super.paintComponent, which represents the regular JPanel version of the paintComponent method, which handles the painting of the background. We will almost always use this as the first line of code in a paintComponent method.

Let's look at another example. The Splat class shown in Listing 4.7 contains a main method that creates and displays the frame for the program. Visually, this

LISTING 4.7

```
//********************************************************************
//  Splat.java        Author: Lewis/Loftus
//
//  Demonstrates the use of graphical objects.
//********************************************************************

import javax.swing.*;
import java.awt.*;

public class Splat
{
```

LISTING 4.7 *continued*

```
//-----------------------------------------------------------------
//   Presents a collection of circles.
//-----------------------------------------------------------------
public static void main (String[] args)
{
    JFrame frame = new JFrame ("Splat");
    frame.setDefaultCloseOperation (JFrame.EXIT_ON_CLOSE);

    frame.getContentPane().add(new SplatPanel());

    frame.pack();
    frame.setVisible(true);
}
}
```

DISPLAY

program simply draws a few filled circles. The interesting thing about this program is not what it does, but how it does it—each circle drawn in this program is represented by its own object.

The main method instantiates a SplatPanel object and adds it to the frame. The SplatPanel class is shown in Listing 4.8. Like the SmilingFacePanel class in the previous example, the SplatPanel class is derived from JPanel. It holds as instance data five Circle objects, which are instantiated in the constructor.

LISTING 4.8

```java
//********************************************************************
//  SplatPanel.java        Author: Lewis/Loftus
//
//  Demonstrates the use of graphical objects.
//********************************************************************

import javax.swing.*;
import java.awt.*;

public class SplatPanel extends JPanel
{
    private Circle circle1, circle2, circle3, circle4, circle5;

    //-----------------------------------------------------------------
    //  Constructor: Creates five Circle objects.
    //-----------------------------------------------------------------
    public SplatPanel()
    {
        circle1 = new Circle (30, Color.red, 70, 35);
        circle2 = new Circle (50, Color.green, 30, 20);
        circle3 = new Circle (100, Color.cyan, 60, 85);
        circle4 = new Circle (45, Color.yellow, 170, 30);
        circle5 = new Circle (60, Color.blue, 200, 60);

        setPreferredSize (new Dimension(300, 200));
        setBackground (Color.black);
    }

    //-----------------------------------------------------------------
    //  Draws this panel by requesting that each circle draw itself.
    //-----------------------------------------------------------------
    public void paintComponent (Graphics page)
    {
        super.paintComponent(page);

        circle1.draw(page);
        circle2.draw(page);
        circle3.draw(page);
        circle4.draw(page);
        circle5.draw(page);
    }
}
```

The paintComponent method in the SplatPanel class draws the panel by calling the draw method of each circle. Essentially, the SplatPanel class asks each circle to draw itself.

The Circle class is shown in Listing 4.9. It defines instance data to store the size of the circle, its (x, y) location, and its color. These values are set using the constructor, and the class contains all the appropriate accessor and mutator methods. The draw method of the Circle class simply draws the circle based on the values of its instance data (its current state).

LISTING 4.9

```java
//********************************************************************
//  Circle.java        Author: Lewis/Loftus
//
//  Represents a circle with a particular position, size, and color.
//********************************************************************

import java.awt.*;

public class Circle
{
   private int diameter, x, y;
   private Color color;

   //-----------------------------------------------------------------
   //  Constructor: Sets up this circle with the specified values.
   //-----------------------------------------------------------------
   public Circle (int size, Color shade, int upperX, int upperY)
   {
      diameter = size;
      color = shade;
      x = upperX;
      y = upperY;
   }

   //-----------------------------------------------------------------
   //  Draws this circle in the specified graphics context.
   //-----------------------------------------------------------------
   public void draw (Graphics page)
   {
      page.setColor (color);
      page.fillOval (x, y, diameter, diameter);
   }
```

LISTING 4.9   *continued*

```java
//------------------------------------------------------------------
//  Diameter mutator.
//------------------------------------------------------------------
public void setDiameter (int size)
{
   diameter = size;
}


//------------------------------------------------------------------
//  Color mutator.
//------------------------------------------------------------------
public void setColor (Color shade)
{
   color = shade;
}


//------------------------------------------------------------------
//  X mutator.
//------------------------------------------------------------------
public void setX (int upperX)
{
   x = upperX;
}


//------------------------------------------------------------------
//  Y mutator.
//------------------------------------------------------------------
public void setY (int upperY)
{
   y = upperY;
}


//------------------------------------------------------------------
//  Diameter accessor.
//------------------------------------------------------------------
public int getDiameter ()
{
   return diameter;
}
```

LISTING 4.9 *continued*

```java
//-----------------------------------------------------------------
//  Color accessor.
//-----------------------------------------------------------------
public Color getColor ()
{
    return color;
}

//-----------------------------------------------------------------
//  X accessor.
//-----------------------------------------------------------------
public int getX ()
{
    return x;
}

//-----------------------------------------------------------------
//  Y accessor.
//-----------------------------------------------------------------
public int getY ()
{
    return y;
}
}
```

The Splat program embodies fundamental object-oriented thinking. Each circle manages itself and will draw itself in whatever graphics context you pass it. Each Circle object maintains its own state. The Circle class is defined in a way that can be used in other situations and programs.

myprogramming**lab**

SELF-REVIEW QUESTIONS *(see answers in Appendix N)*

SR 4.26 Where is the "content" of the panel created in the SmilingFace program defined?

SR 4.27 In the SmilingFace program, when and how is the paintComponent method of the panel object invoked?

SR 4.28 Write code that will add a pair of eyeglasses to the smiling face.

SR 4.29 Rewrite the constructor for the Circle class so that it generates a circle with a random diameter that is between 20 and 200 inclusive for the Circle object it sets up. The other attributes of the circle should be provided as parameters to the constructor.

4.7 Graphical User Interfaces

In Chapters 2 and 3 we introduced a few key components that are helpful in the design of graphics-based programs. What we need now is true user interaction, which is the heart of a graphical user interface (GUI). This section introduces the concepts needed to create interactive GUI-based programs. It lays the groundwork for all GUI discussions throughout the book.

At least three kinds of objects are needed to create a graphical user interface in Java:

- components
- events
- listeners

As we mentioned in Chapter 3, a GUI *component* is an object that defines a screen element to display information or allow the user to interact with a program in a certain way. Examples of GUI components include push buttons, text fields, labels, scroll bars, and menus. A *container* is a special type of component that is used to hold and organize other components. We've already used containers such as frames and panels and explored the use of labels as well.

An *event* is an object that represents some occurrence in which we may be interested. Often, events correspond to user actions, such as pressing a mouse button or typing a key on the keyboard. Most GUI components generate events to indicate a user action related to that component. For example, a button component will generate an event to indicate that the button has been pushed. A program that is oriented around a GUI, responding to events from the user, is called *event-driven*.

A *listener* is an object that "waits" for an event to occur and responds in some way when it does. We must carefully establish the relationships among the listener, the event it listens for, and the component that will generate the event.

> **KEY CONCEPT**
> A GUI is made up of components, events that represent user actions, and listeners that respond to those events.

For the most part, we will use components and events that are predefined by classes in the Java class library. We will tailor the behavior of the components, but their basic roles have been established. We will, however, write listener classes to perform whatever actions we desire when events occur.

Specifically, to create a Java program that uses a GUI, we must:

- instantiate and set up the necessary components,
- implement listener classes that define what happens when particular events occur, and
- establish the relationship between the listeners and the components that generate the events of interest.

VideoNote

Overview of GUI development.

In some respects, once you have a basic understanding of event-driven programming, the rest is just detail. There are many types of components you can use that produce many types of events that you may want to acknowledge. But they all work in the same basic way. They all have the same core relationships to one another.

The following sections introduce some more components and present examples of GUI-based programs that allow true user interaction.

myprogramminglab

SELF-REVIEW QUESTIONS *(see answers in Appendix N)*

SR 4.30 What is the relationship between an event and a listener?

SR 4.31 Can we add any kind of listener to any component? Explain.

4.8 Buttons

The `PushCounter` program shown in Listing 4.10 presents the user with a single push button (labeled "`Push Me!`"). Each time the button is pushed, a counter is updated and displayed.

LISTING 4.10

```
//********************************************************************
//  PushCounter.java       Author: Lewis/Loftus
//
//  Demonstrates a graphical user interface and an event listener.
//********************************************************************

import javax.swing.JFrame;

public class PushCounter
{
    //-----------------------------------------------------------------
    //  Creates the main program frame.
    //-----------------------------------------------------------------
    public static void main (String[] args)
    {
        JFrame frame = new JFrame ("Push Counter");
        frame.setDefaultCloseOperation (JFrame.EXIT_ON_CLOSE);
```

LISTING 4.10   *continued*

```
    frame.getContentPane().add(new PushCounterPanel());
    frame.pack();
    frame.setVisible(true);
  }
}
```

DISPLAY

The components used in this program include a button, a label to display the count, a panel to organize the GUI, and a frame to display the panel. The panel is defined by the PushCounterPanel class, shown in Listing 4.11.

A push button is a component that allows the user to initiate an action with a press of the mouse. There are other types of button components that we explore in later chapters. A push button is defined by the JButton class.

LISTING 4.11

```
//********************************************************************
//   PushCounterPanel.java        Author: Lewis/Loftus
//
//   Demonstrates a graphical user interface and an event listener.
//********************************************************************

import java.awt.*;
import java.awt.event.*;
import javax.swing.*;

public class PushCounterPanel extends JPanel
{
   private int count;
   private JButton push;
   private JLabel label;
```

LISTING 4.11 *continued*

```java
//-------------------------------------------------------------------
//  Constructor: Sets up the GUI.
//-------------------------------------------------------------------
public PushCounterPanel ()
{
    count = 0;

    push = new JButton ("Push Me!");
    push.addActionListener (new ButtonListener());

    label = new JLabel ("Pushes: " + count);

    add (push);
    add (label);

    setPreferredSize (new Dimension(300, 40));
    setBackground (Color.cyan);
}

//*******************************************************************
//  Represents a listener for button push (action) events.
//*******************************************************************
private class ButtonListener implements ActionListener
{
    //-------------------------------------------------------------
    // Updates the counter and label when the button is pushed.
    //-------------------------------------------------------------
    public void actionPerformed (ActionEvent event)
    {
        count++;
        label.setText("Pushes: " + count);
    }
}
}
```

The PushCounterPanel constructor sets up the GUI. The call to the JButton constructor takes a String parameter that specifies the text shown on the button. The button and the label are added to the panel.

The only event of interest in this program occurs when the button is pushed. To respond to the event, we must create a listener object for that event, so we must write a class that represents the listener.

A JButton generates an *action event* when it is pushed. Therefore the listener class we write will be an action event listener. In this program, we define a class called ButtonListener to represent the listener for this event.

We could write the ButtonListener class in its own file, or even in the same file but outside of the PushCounterPanel class. However, then we would have to set up a way to communicate between the listener and the components of the GUI that the listener updates. Instead, we define the ButtonListener class as an *inner class,* which is a class defined within another class. As such, it automatically has access to the members of the class that contains it. You should create inner classes only in situations in which there is an intimate relationship between the two classes and in which the inner class is not accessed by any other class. The relationship between a listener and its GUI is one of the few situations in which an inner class is appropriate.

> **KEY CONCEPT**
>
> Listeners are often defined as inner classes because of the intimate relationship between the listener and the GUI components.

Listener classes are written by implementing an *interface,* which is a list of methods that the implementing class must define. The Java standard class library contains interfaces for many types of events. An action listener is created by implementing the ActionListener interface; therefore, we include the implements clause in the ButtonListener class. Interfaces are discussed in more detail in Chapter 7.

The only method listed in the ActionListener interface is the actionPerformed method, so that's the only method that the ButtonListener class must implement. The component that generates the action event (in this case the button) will call the actionPerformed method when the event occurs, passing in an ActionEvent object that represents the event. Sometimes we will use the event object, and other times it is simply sufficient to know that the event occurred. In this case, we have no need to interact with the event object. When the event occurs, the listener increments the count and resets the text of the label by using the setText method.

Remember, we not only have to create a listener for an event, we must also set up the relationship between the listener and the component that will generate the event. To do so, we add the listener to the component by calling the appropriate method. In the PushCounterPanel constructor, we call the addActionListener method, passing in a newly instantiated ButtonListener object.

Review this example carefully, noting how it accomplishes the three key steps to creating an interactive GUI-based program. It creates and sets up the GUI components, creates the appropriate listener for the event of interest, and sets up the relationship between the listener and the component that will generate the event.

SELF-REVIEW QUESTIONS *(see answers in Appendix N)*

SR 4.32 What type of event does a push button (a `JButton` object) generate?

SR 4.33 How would you change the `PushCounterPanel` class so that instead of displaying a count of how many times the button was pushed, it displays a count "trail"? After one push, it displays "01"; after two pushes, it displays "012"; after five pushes, it displays "012345"; and so on.

4.9   Text Fields

Let's look at another example that uses another component: a text field. The `Fahrenheit` program shown in Listing 4.12 presents a GUI that includes a text field into which the user can type a Fahrenheit temperature. When the user presses the Enter (or Return) key, the equivalent Celsius temperature is displayed.

The interface for the `Fahrenheit` program is set up in the `FahrenheitPanel` class. The text field is an object of the `JTextField` class. The `JTextField` constructor takes an integer parameter that specifies the size of the field in number of characters based on the current default font.

The text field and various labels are added to the panel to be displayed. Remember that a panel is governed by a layout manager called flow layout, which puts as many components on a line as it can fit. So if you resize the frame, the orientation of the labels and text field may change. We examine layout managers in detail in Chapter 7, providing more options for controlling the layout of the components.

If the cursor is currently in the text field, the text field component generates an action event when the Enter or Return key is pressed. Therefore we need to set up a listener object to respond to action events. As we did in the `PushCounter` program in the previous section, we define the listener as an inner class that implements the `ActionListener` interface.

The text field component calls the `actionPerformed` method when the user presses the Enter key. The method first retrieves the text from the text field by calling its `getText` method, which returns a character string. The text is converted to an integer using the `parseInt` method of the `Integer` wrapper class. Then the method performs the calculation to determine the equivalent Celsius temperature and sets the text of the appropriate label with the result.

Note that a push button and a text field generate the same kind of event: an action event. So an alternative to the `Fahrenheit` program design is to add a `JButton` object to the GUI that causes the conversion to occur when the user uses the mouse to press the button. For that matter, the same listener object can be

LISTING 4.12

```java
//********************************************************************
//  Fahrenheit.java         Author: Lewis/Loftus
//
//  Demonstrates the use of text fields.
//********************************************************************

import javax.swing.JFrame;

public class Fahrenheit
{
   //-----------------------------------------------------------------
   //  Creates and displays the temperature converter GUI.
   //-----------------------------------------------------------------
   public static void main (String[] args)
   {
      JFrame frame = new JFrame ("Fahrenheit");
      frame.setDefaultCloseOperation (JFrame.EXIT_ON_CLOSE);

      FahrenheitPanel panel = new FahrenheitPanel();

      frame.getContentPane().add(panel);
      frame.pack();
      frame.setVisible(true);
   }
}
```

DISPLAY

LISTING 4.13

```java
//********************************************************************
//  FahrenheitPanel.java       Author: Lewis/Loftus
//
//  Demonstrates the use of text fields.
//********************************************************************

import java.awt.*;
import java.awt.event.*;
import javax.swing.*;

public class FahrenheitPanel extends JPanel
{
    private JLabel inputLabel, outputLabel, resultLabel;
    private JTextField fahrenheit;

    //-----------------------------------------------------------------
    //  Constructor: Sets up the main GUI components.
    //-----------------------------------------------------------------
    public FahrenheitPanel()
    {
        inputLabel = new JLabel ("Enter Fahrenheit temperature:");
        outputLabel = new JLabel ("Temperature in Celsius: ");
        resultLabel = new JLabel ("---");

        fahrenheit = new JTextField (5);
        fahrenheit.addActionListener (new TempListener());

        add (inputLabel);
        add (fahrenheit);
        add (outputLabel);
        add (resultLabel);

        setPreferredSize (new Dimension(300, 75));
        setBackground (Color.yellow);
    }

    //********************************************************************
    //  Represents an action listener for the temperature input field.
    //********************************************************************
    private class TempListener implements ActionListener
```

LISTING 4.13   *continued*

```
    {
        //--------------------------------------------------------------
        //  Performs the conversion when the enter key is pressed in
        //  the text field.
        //--------------------------------------------------------------
        public void actionPerformed (ActionEvent event)
        {
            int fahrenheitTemp, celsiusTemp;

            String text = fahrenheit.getText();

            fahrenheitTemp = Integer.parseInt (text);
            celsiusTemp = (fahrenheitTemp-32) * 5/9;

            resultLabel.setText (Integer.toString (celsiusTemp));
        }
    }
}
```

used to listen to multiple components at the same time. So the listener could be added to both the text field and the button, giving the user the option. Pressing either the button or the Enter key will cause the conversion to be performed. These variations are left as programming projects.

SELF-REVIEW QUESTIONS *(see answers in Appendix N)*   myprogramminglab

SR 4.34   Describe what happens within the Fahrenheit program when a user types a number into the text box of the interface and presses the Enter (or Return) key.

SR 4.35   Change the FahrenheitPanel class so that when the user enters a number in the text field a statement appears in the form "X degrees Fahrenheit = Y degrees Celsius" below the text field. For example, if the user enters 223, the statement "223 degrees Fahrenheit = 106 degrees Celsius" appears instead of "Temperature in Celsius: 106".

Summary of Key Concepts

- The heart of object-oriented programming is defining classes that represent objects with well-defined state and behavior.

- The scope of a variable, which determines where it can be referenced, depends on where it is declared.

- A UML class diagram helps us visualize the contents of and relationships among the classes of a program.

- An object should be encapsulated, guarding its data from inappropriate access.

- Instance variables should be declared with private visibility to promote encapsulation.

- Most objects contain accessor and mutator methods to allow the client to manage data in a controlled manner.

- The value returned from a method must be consistent with the return type specified in the method header.

- When a method is called, the actual parameters are copied into the formal parameters.

- A variable declared in a method is local to that method and cannot be used outside of it.

- A constructor cannot have any return type, even `void`.

- A GUI is made up of components, events that represent user actions, and listeners that respond to those events.

- Listeners are often defined as inner classes because of the intimate relationship between the listener and the GUI components.

Exercises

myprogramminglab

Visit www.myprogramminglab.com to complete many of these Exercises online and get instant feedback.

EX 4.1   For each of the following pairs, which represents a class and which represents an attribute of that class?

     a. Car, Engine
     b. No_of_limbs, Animal
     c. Game, No_of_players
     d. Tour, Place
     e. Festivals, Deity

EX 4.2   List some attributes and operations that might be defined for a class called `WindowFrame` that represents a window.

EX 4.3   List some attributes and operations that might be defined for a class called `Exam` that represents an examination being conducted.

EX 4.4   List some attributes and operations that might be defined for a class called `Student` that represents a student.

EX 4.5   Write a method called `lyrics` that prints the lyrics of a song when invoked. The method should accept no parameters and return no value.

EX 4.6   Write a method called `Cuboid` that accepts three integer parameters (length, breadth, and height) and returns the volume of a cuboid.

EX 4.7   Write a method called `random100` that returns a random integer in the range of 1 to 100 (inclusive).

EX 4.8   Write a method called `randomInRange` that accepts two integer parameters representing a range. The method should return a random integer in the specified range (inclusive). Assume that the first parameter is greater than the second.

EX 4.9   Write a method called `randomColor` that creates and returns a `Color` object that represents a random color. Recall that a `Color` object can be defined by three integer values between 0 and 255, representing the contributions of red, green, and blue (its RGB value).

EX 4.10   Draw a UML class diagram that shows the relationships among the classes used in the `Transactions` program.

EX 4.11   Draw a UML diagram that shows the relationships among the classes used in a `Course Registration` program (it will involve students, teachers and courses).

EX 4.12   Draw a UML diagram that shows the relationships among the classes used in a `Company` program (the company will consist of various employees).

Programming Projects

Visit www.myprogramminglab.com to complete many of these Programming Projects online and get instant feedback.

myprogramminglab

PP 4.1   Design and implement a class called `Shape` which calculates the area of a rectangle when the input is provided. Create a driver class called `Polygon` whose main method instantiates and draws the rectangle by calling the `Shape` object.

VideoNote

Developing a solution
of PP 4.2.

PP 4.2   Design and implement a class called Dog that contains instance
data that represents the dog's name and age. Define the Dog constructor to accept and initialize instance data. Include getter and
setter methods for the name and age. Include a method to compute and return the age of the dog in "person years" (seven times
the dogs age). Include a toString method that returns a one-line
description of the dog. Create a driver class called Kennel, whose
main method instantiates and updates several Dog objects.

PP 4.3   Design and implement a class called Car that contains instance
data that represents the make, model, and year of the car. Define
the Car constructor to initialize these values. Include getter and
setter methods for all instance data, and a toString method that
returns a one-line description of the car. Create a driver class
called CarTest, whose main method instantiates and updates several Car objects.

PP 4.4   Design and implement a class called Box that contains instance
data that represents the height, width, and depth of the box. Also
include a boolean variable called full as instance data that represents whether the box is full or not. Define the Box constructor to accept and initialize the height, width, and depth of the
box. Each newly created Box is empty (the constructor should
initialize full to false). Include getter and setter methods for all
instance data. Include a toString method that returns a one-
line description of the box. Create a driver class called BoxTest,
whose main method instantiates and updates several Box objects.

PP 4.5   Design and implement a class called Book that contains instance
data for the title, author, publisher, and copyright date. Define
the Book constructor to accept and initialize this data. Include
setter and getter methods for all instance data. Include a
toString method that returns a nicely formatted, multi-line
description of the book. Create a driver class called Bookshelf,
whose main method instantiates and updates several Book
objects.

PP 4.6   Design and implement a class called Flight that represents an
airline flight. It should contain instance data that represents the
airline name, flight number, and the flight's origin and destination
cities. Define the Flight constructor to accept and initialize all
instance data. Include getter and setter methods for all instance data.
Include a toString method that returns a one-line description of
the flight. Create a driver class called FlightTest, whose main
method instantiates and updates several Flight objects.

PP 4.7   Design and implement a class called Bulb that represents a light bulb that can be turned on and off. Create a driver class called Lights whose main method instantiates and turns on some Bulb objects.

PP 4.8   Using the Die class defined in this chapter, design and implement a class called PairOfDice, composed of two Die objects. Include methods to set and get the individual die values, a method to roll the dice, and a method that returns the current sum of the two die values. Create a driver class called RollingDice2 to instantiate and use a PairOfDice object.

PP 4.9   Design and implement a class called Building that represents a graphical depiction of a building. Allow the parameters to the constructor to specify the building's width and height. Each building should be colored black and should contain a few random windows of yellow. Create a program that draws a random skyline of buildings.

PP 4.10   Write a program that displays a graphical seating chart for a dinner party. Create a class called Diner (as in one who dines) that stores the person's name, gender, and location at the dinner table. A diner is graphically represented as a circle, color-coded by gender, with the person's name printed in the circle.

PP 4.11   Create a class called Crayon that represents one crayon of a particular color and length (height). Design and implement a program that draws a box of crayons.

PP 4.12   Create a class called Star that represents a five-pointed star. Let the constructor accept the width of the star and the coordinates of the star's top point. Write a program that draws a sky containing stars of various sizes.

PP 4.13   Modify the Fahrenheit program from this chapter so that it displays a button that, when pressed, also causes the conversion calculation to take place. That is, the user will now have the option of either pressing Enter in the text field or pressing the button. Have the listener that is already defined for the text field also listen for the button push.

PP 4.14   Design and implement an application using applets to display an image and to display another image when you erase the first image.

PP 4.15   Design and implement an application that presents two buttons and a label to the user. Label the buttons Increment and

Decrement, respectively. Display a numeric value (initially 50) using the label. Each time the increment button is pushed, increment the value displayed. Likewise, each time the decrement button is pressed, decrement the value displayed.

PP 4.16 Design and implement an application that draws a traffic light and uses a push button to change the state of the light. Derive the drawing surface from the JPanel class and use another panel to organize the drawing surface and the button.

PP 4.17 Develop an application that implements a prototype user interface for composing an email message. The application should have text fields for the To, CC, and Bcc address lists and subject line, and one for the message body. Include a button labeled Send. When the Send button is pushed, the program should print the contents of all fields to standard output using println statements.

Denver Airport Baggage Handling System

What Happened?

The designers of the Denver International Airport had big plans to automate the handling of luggage. With as much as a mile to cover between the airport gates and terminals, the hope was to develop a system that whisked your luggage from the check-in counter to the departing plane and from an arriving plane to baggage collection with minimal human intervention. They thought the system would result in fewer flight delays, less waiting at luggage carousels, and reduced labor costs.

The system was designed and created in the late 1980s and early 1990s. Approximately 26 miles of track were constructed to move bags up and down inclines in gray carts under the control of a central computer.

■ The automated baggage-handling system in Denver resulted in lost luggage and mangled packages.

However, the planned March 1994 opening of the airport was delayed continuously due to failures in the baggage system. During tests, bags were misloaded and misrouted. They fell out of carts when making turns. The system loaded bags into carts that already were full and unloaded them onto belts already jammed with luggage. Bags were damaged by being wedged under carts and dropped onto concrete floors.

The airport finally opened for business in February of 1995. At that point, only one airline—United—agreed to use the automated system. This was a stripped-down version of the system, used only for outgoing flights. No other airline used the system at all. They opted for humans driving luggage carts, just as most airports do today. United finally gave up using the system in 2005.

The original cost of the system was $186 million. The delays cost $1 million a day, surpassing the original costs. When United opted to abandon the system in 2005, it did so despite having a lease on the system through 2025 at $60 million per year.

What Caused It?

The fiasco this project represents is considered to be one of the greatest software engineering and overall system-design failures in history. There were many individual issues that contributed to the problems, but in general, the designers simply had too much faith in the technology they were using. They didn't factor in errors and inefficiencies that always occur in a complex system.

The individual problems included the fact that the software misinterpreted data from photoelectric eyes and, therefore, did not detect a pile of existing bags. When the system was restarted after it crashed, it lost information about the status of carts and didn't know which ones were full or not. Sharp corners were not factored in correctly regarding the speed of the conveyors, resulting in spilled carts. A telescoping belt loader called the lizard tongue—designed to reach into a planes cargo hold and pick up bags without human assistance—failed completely.

Lessons Learned

A project of this scope should not be attempted without many localized tests on the technologies in use. The failures were often a result of multiple variables caused by the system as a whole in operation.

When the system was designed in the late 1980s, it relied on a centralized mainframe to control the system. Such an approach seems ridiculous in today's world of distributed processing, but it is a good example of how a large system can be obsolete by the time it is developed. Today, human baggage handlers with handheld scanners result in a far more fast and accurate delivery system than the best goals of the planned automated system.

Source: The International Herald Tribune

Conditionals and Loops

5

CHAPTER OBJECTIVES

- Define the flow of control through a method.
- Explore boolean expressions that can be used to make decisions.
- Perform basic decision making using if statements.
- Discuss issues pertaining to the comparison of certain types of data.
- Execute statements repetitively using while loops.
- Discuss the concept of an iterator object and use one to read a text file.
- Draw with the aid of conditionals and loops.
- Explore more GUI components and events.

All programming languages have statements that allow you to make decisions to determine what to do next. Some of those statements allow you to repeat a certain activity multiple times. This chapter discusses key Java statements of this type and explores issues related to the comparison of data and objects. It begins with a discussion of boolean expressions, which form the basis of any decision. The Graphics Track sections of this chapter explore new drawing options and some new components and events.

5.1 Boolean Expressions

The order in which statements are executed in a running program is called the *flow of control*. Unless otherwise specified, the execution of a program proceeds in a linear fashion. That is, a running program starts at the first programming statement and moves down one statement at a time until the program is complete. A Java application begins executing with the first line of the main method and proceeds step by step until it gets to the end of the main method.

Invoking a method alters the flow of control. When a method is called, control jumps to the code defined for that method. When the method completes, control returns to the place in the calling method where the invocation was made, and processing continues from there.

> **KEY CONCEPT**
> Conditionals and loops allow us to control the flow of execution through a method.

Within a given method, we can alter the flow of control through the code by using certain types of programming statements. Statements that control the flow of execution through a method fall into two categories: conditionals and loops.

A *conditional statement* is sometimes called a *selection statement*, because it allows us to choose which statement will be executed next. The conditional statements in Java are the if statement, the if-else statement, and the switch statement. We explore the if statement and the if-else statement in this chapter and cover the switch statement in Chapter 6.

Each decision is based on a *boolean expression* (also called a *condition*), which is an expression that evaluates to either true or false. The result of the expression determines which statement is executed next. The following is an example of an if statement:

```
if (count > 20)
    System.out.println ("Count exceeded");
```

> **KEY CONCEPT**
> An if statement allows a program to choose whether to execute a particular statement.

The condition in this statement is count > 20. That expression evaluates to a boolean (true or false) result. Either the value stored in count is greater than 20 or it's not. If it is, the println statement is executed. If it's not, the println statement is skipped and processing continues with whatever code follows it.

The need to make decisions like this comes up all the time in programming situations. For example, the cost of life insurance might be dependent on whether the insured person is a smoker. If the person smokes, we calculate the cost using a particular formula; if not, we calculate it using another. The role of a conditional statement is to evaluate a boolean condition (whether the person smokes) and then to execute the proper calculation accordingly.

A *loop*, or *repetition statement*, allows us to execute a programming statement over and over again. Like a conditional, a loop is based on a boolean expression that determines how many times the statement is executed.

For example, suppose we wanted to calculate the grade point average of every student in a class. The calculation is the same for each student; it is just performed on different data. We would set up a loop that repeats the calculation for each student until there are no more students to process.

Java has three types of loop statements: the while statement, the do statement, and the for statement. Each type of loop statement has unique characteristics that distinguish it from the others. We cover the while statement in this chapter and explore do loops and for loops in Chapter 6.

The boolean expressions on which conditionals and loops are based use equality operators, relational operators, and logical operators to make decisions. Before we discuss the conditional and loop statements in detail, let's explore these operators.

Equality and Relational Operators

The == and != operators are called *equality operators*. They test whether two values are equal or not equal, respectively. Note that the equality operator consists of two equal signs side by side and should not be mistaken for the assignment operator that uses only one equal sign.

The following if statement prints a sentence only if the variables total and sum contain the same value:

```
if (total == sum)
    System.out.println ("total equals sum");
```

Likewise, the following if statement prints a sentence only if the variables total and sum do *not* contain the same value:

```
if (total != sum)
    System.out.println ("total does NOT equal sum");
```

Java also has several *relational operators* that let us decide relative ordering between values. Earlier in this section we used the greater than operator (>) to decide if one value was greater than another. We can ask similar questions using various operators. In Java, relational operators are greater than (>), less than (<), greater than or equal to (>=), and less than or equal to (<=). Figure 5.1 lists the Java equality and relational operators.

Operator	Meaning
==	equal to
!=	not equal to
<	less than
<=	less than or equal to
>	greater than
>=	greater than or equal to

FIGURE 5.1   Java equality and relational operators

The equality and relational operators have precedence lower than the arithmetic operators. Therefore, arithmetic operations are evaluated first, followed by equality and relational operations. As always, parentheses can be used to explicitly specify the order of evaluation.

We'll see more examples of relational operators as we examine conditional and loop statements throughout this chapter.

Logical Operators

In addition to the equality and relational operators, Java has three *logical operators* that produce boolean results. They also take boolean operands. Figure 5.2 lists and describes the logical operators.

The ! operator is used to perform the *logical NOT* operation, which is also called the *logical complement*. The logical complement of a boolean value yields its opposite value. That is, if a boolean variable called found has the value false, then !found is true. Likewise, if found is true, then !found is false. The logical NOT operation does not change the value stored in found.

A logical operation can be described by a *truth table* that lists all possible combinations of values for the variables involved in an expression. Because the logical

Operator	Description	Example	Result
!	logical NOT	! a	true if a is false and false if a is true
&&	logical AND	a && b	true if a and b are both true and false otherwise
||	logical OR	a || b	true if a or b or both are true and false otherwise

FIGURE 5.2   Java logical operators

a	!a
false	true
true	false

FIGURE 5.3   Truth table describing the logical NOT operator

NOT operator is unary, there are only two possible values for its one operand: true or false. Figure 5.3 shows a truth table that describes the ! operator.

The && operator performs a *logical AND* operation. The result is true if both operands are true, but false otherwise. Compare that to the result of the *logical OR* operator (||), which is true if one or the other or both operands are true, but false otherwise.

The AND and OR operators are both binary operators since each uses two operands. Therefore, there are four possible combinations to consider: both operands are true, both are false, one is true and the other false, and vice versa. Figure 5.4 depicts a truth table that shows both the && and || operators.

The logical NOT has the highest precedence of the three logical operators, followed by logical AND, then logical OR.

Consider the following if statement:

```
if (!done && (count > MAX))
   System.out.println ("Completed.");
```

Under what conditions would the println statement be executed? The value of the boolean variable done is either true or false, and the NOT operator reverses that value. The value of count is either greater than MAX or it isn't. The truth table in Figure 5.5 breaks down all of the possibilities.

An important characteristic of the && and || operators is that they are "short-circuited." That is, if their left operand is sufficient to decide the boolean result of the operation, the right operand is not evaluated. This situation can occur with both operators, but for

> **KEY CONCEPT**
> Logical operators are often used to construct sophisticated conditions.

a	b	a && b	a || b
false	false	false	false
false	true	false	true
true	false	false	true
true	true	true	true

FIGURE 5.4   Truth table describing the logical AND and OR operators

done	count > MAX	!done	!done && (count > MAX)
false	false	true	false
false	true	true	true
true	false	false	false
true	true	false	false

FIGURE 5.5   A truth table for a specific condition

different reasons. If the left operand of the && operator is false, then the result of the operation will be false no matter what the value of the right operand is. Likewise, if the left operand of the || is true, then the result of the operation is true no matter what the value of the right operand is.

Sometimes you can capitalize on the fact that the operation is short-circuited. For example, the condition in the following if statement will not attempt to divide by zero if the left operand is false. If count has the value zero, the left side of the && operation is false; therefore. the whole expression is false and the right side is not evaluated.

```
if (count != 0 && total/count > MAX)
    System.out.println ("Testing.");
```

You should consider carefully whether or not to rely on these kinds of subtle programming language characteristics. Not all programming languages work the same way. As we have stressed before, you should favor readability over clever programming tricks. Always strive to make it clear to any reader of the code how the logic of your program works.

myprogramminglab

SELF-REVIEW QUESTIONS *(see answers in Appendix N)*

SR 5.1   What is meant by the flow of control through a program?

SR 5.2   What type of conditions are conditionals and loops based on?

SR 5.3   What are the equality operators? The relational operators? The logical operators?

SR 5.4   Given the following declarations, what is the value of each of the listed boolean expressions?

```
int value1 = 5, value2 = 10;
boolean done = true;
```

a. value1 <= value2
b. (value1 + 5) >= value2
c. value1 < value2 / 2
d. value2 != value1
e. !(value1 == value2)
f. (value1 < value2) || done
g. (value1 > value2) || done
h. (value1 < value2) && !done
i. done || !done
j. ((value1 > value2) || done) && (!done || (value2 > value1))

SR 5.5   What is a truth table?

SR 5.6   Assuming done is a boolean variable and value is an int variable, create a truth table for the expression:

(value > 0) || !done

SR 5.7   Assuming c1 and c2 are boolean variables, create a truth table for the expression:

(c1 && !c2) || (!c1 && c2)

5.2 The if Statement

We've used a basic if statement in earlier examples in this chapter. Let's now explore it in detail.

An *if statement* consists of the reserved word if followed by a boolean expression, followed by a statement. The condition is enclosed in parentheses and must evaluate to true or false. If the condition is true, the statement is executed and processing continues with the next statement. If the condition is false, the statement is skipped and processing continues immediately with the next statement. Figure 5.6 shows this processing.

> **KEY CONCEPT**
> Proper indentation is important for human readability; it shows the relationship between one statement and another.

Consider the following example of an if statement:

```
if (total > amount)
    total = total + (amount + 1);
```

In this example, if the value in total is greater than the value in amount, the assignment statement is executed; otherwise the assignment statement is skipped.

Note that the assignment statement in this example is indented under the header line of the if statement. This communicates that the assignment statement

FIGURE 5.6   The logic of an if statement

is part of the if statement; it implies that the if statement governs whether the assignment statement will be executed. Although this indentation is extremely important for the human reader, it is ignored by the compiler.

The example in Listing 5.1 reads the age of the user and then makes a decision as to whether to print a particular sentence based on the age that is entered. The Age program echoes the age value that is entered in all cases. If the age is less than the value of the constant MINOR, the statement about youth is printed. If the age is equal to or greater than the value of MINOR, the println statement is skipped. In either case, the final sentence about age being a state of mind is printed.

LISTING 5.1

```java
//********************************************************************
//  Age.java        Author: Lewis/Loftus
//
//  Demonstrates the use of an if statement.
//********************************************************************

import java.util.Scanner;

public class Age
{
    //-----------------------------------------------------------------
    //  Reads the user's age and prints comments accordingly.
    //-----------------------------------------------------------------
    public static void main (String[] args)
    {
        final int MINOR = 21;

        Scanner scan = new Scanner (System.in);
```

LISTING 5.1 *continued*

```
        System.out.print ("Enter your age: ");
        int age = scan.nextInt();

        System.out.println ("You entered: " + age);

        if (age < MINOR)
            System.out.println ("Youth is a wonderful thing. Enjoy.");

        System.out.println ("Age is a state of mind.");
    }
}
```

OUTPUT

```
Enter your age: 40
You entered: 40
Age is a state of mind.
```

Let's look at a few more examples of basic if statements. The following if statement causes the variable size to be set to zero if its current value is greater than or equal to the value in the constant MAX:

```
if (size >= MAX)
    size = 0;
```

The condition of the following if statement first adds three values together, then compares the result to the value stored in numBooks:

```
if (numBooks < stackCount + inventoryCount + duplicateCount)
    reorder = true;
```

If numBooks is less than the other three values combined, the boolean variable reorder is set to true. The addition operations are performed before the less than operator, because the arithmetic operators have a higher precedence than the relational operators.

Assuming generator refers to an object of the Random class, the following if statement examines the value returned from a call to nextInt to determine a random winner:

```
if (generator.nextInt(CHANCE) == 0)
    System.out.println ("You are a randomly selected winner!");
```

The odds of this code picking a winner are based on the value of the CHANCE constant. That is, if CHANCE contains 20, the odds of winning are 1 in 20. The fact that the condition is looking for a return value of 0 is arbitrary; any value between 0 and CHANCE-1 would have worked.

The if-else Statement

Sometimes we want to do one thing if a condition is true and another thing if that condition is false. We can add an *else clause* to an if statement, making it an *if-else statement,* to handle this kind of situation. The following is an example of an if-else statement:

```
if (height <= MAX)
    adjustment = 0;
else
    adjustment = MAX - height;
```

> **KEY CONCEPT**
>
> An if-else statement allows a program to do one thing if a condition is true and another thing if the condition is false.

If the condition is true, the first assignment statement is executed; if the condition is false, the second assignment statement is executed. Only one or the other will be executed, because a boolean condition evaluates to either true or false. Note that proper indentation is used again to communicate that the statements are part of the governing if statement.

If Statement

An if statement tests the boolean Expression and, if true, executes the first Statement. The optional else clause identifies the Statement that should be executed if the Expression is false.

Examples:

```
if (tal < 7)
    System.out.println ("Total is less than 7.");

if (firstCh != 'a')
    count++;
else
    count = count / 2;
```

The Wages program shown in Listing 5.2 uses an if-else statement to compute the proper payment amount for an employee.

In the Wages program, if an employee works over 40 hours in a week, the payment amount takes into account the overtime hours. An if-else statement is used to determine whether the number of hours entered by the user is greater than 40. If it is, the extra hours are paid at a rate one and a half times the normal rate. If there are no overtime hours, the total payment is based simply on the number of hours worked and the standard rate.

Let's look at another example of an if-else statement:

```
if (roster.getSize() == FULL)
    roster.expand();
else
    roster.addName (name);
```

LISTING 5.2

```
//********************************************************************
//  Wages.java        Author: Lewis/Loftus
//
//  Demonstrates the use of an if-else statement.
//********************************************************************

import java.text.NumberFormat;
import java.util.Scanner;

public class Wages
{
    //-----------------------------------------------------------------
    //  Reads the number of hours worked and calculates wages.
    //-----------------------------------------------------------------
    public static void main (String[] args)
    {
        final double RATE = 8.25;   // regular pay rate
        final int STANDARD = 40;    // standard hours in a work week

        Scanner scan = new Scanner (System.in);

        double pay = 0.0;

        System.out.print ("Enter the number of hours worked: ");
        int hours = scan.nextInt();
```

LISTING 5.2   *continued*

```
     System.out.println ();

     // Pay overtime at "time and a half"
     if (hours > STANDARD)
        pay = STANDARD * RATE + (hours-STANDARD) * (RATE * 1.5);
     else
        pay = hours * RATE;

     NumberFormat fmt = NumberFormat.getCurrencyInstance();
     System.out.println ("Gross earnings: " + fmt.format(pay));
   }
}
```

OUTPUT

```
Enter the number of hours worked: 46

Gross earnings: $404.25
```

This example makes use of an object called roster. Even without knowing what roster represents, or from what class it was created, we can see that it has at least three methods: getSize, expand, and addName. The condition of the if statement calls getSize and compares the result to the constant FULL. If the condition is true, the expand method is invoked (apparently to expand the size of the roster). If the roster is not yet full, the variable name is passed as a parameter to the addName method.

The program in Listing 5.3 instantiates a Coin object, flips the coin by calling the flip method, then uses an if-else statement to determine which of two sentences gets printed based on the result.

LISTING 5.3

```
//********************************************************************
//  CoinFlip.java        Author: Lewis/Loftus
//
//  Demonstrates the use of an if-else statement.
//********************************************************************
```

LISTING 5.3   *continued*

```java
public class CoinFlip
{
    //-----------------------------------------------------------------
    //  Creates a Coin object, flips it, and prints the results.
    //-----------------------------------------------------------------
    public static void main (String[] args)
    {
        Coin myCoin = new Coin();

        myCoin.flip();

        System.out.println (myCoin);

        if (myCoin.isHeads())
            System.out.println ("You win.");
        else
            System.out.println ("Better luck next time.");
    }
}
```

OUTPUT

```
Tails
Better luck next time.
```

The Coin class is shown in Listing 5.4. It stores two integer constants (HEADS and TAILS) that represent the two possible states of the coin, and an instance variable called face that represents the current state of the coin. The Coin constructor initially flips the coin by calling the flip method, which determines the new state of the coin by randomly choosing a number (either 0 or 1). The isHeads method returns a boolean value based on the current face value of the coin. The toString method uses an if-else statement to determine which character string to return to describe the coin. The toString method is automatically called when the myCoin object is passed to println in the main method.

Using Block Statements

We may want to do more than one thing as the result of evaluating a boolean condition. In Java, we can replace any single statement with a *block statement*.

LISTING 5.4

```java
//********************************************************************
//  Coin.java        Author: Lewis/Loftus
//
//  Represents a coin with two sides that can be flipped.
//********************************************************************

public class Coin
{
   private final int HEADS = 0;
   private final int TAILS = 1;

   private int face;

   //-----------------------------------------------------------------
   //  Sets up the coin by flipping it initially.
   //-----------------------------------------------------------------
   public Coin ()
   {
      flip();
   }

   //-----------------------------------------------------------------
   //  Flips the coin by randomly choosing a face value.
   //-----------------------------------------------------------------
   public void flip ()
   {
      face = (int) (Math.random() * 2);
   }

   //-----------------------------------------------------------------
   //  Returns true if the current face of the coin is heads.
   //-----------------------------------------------------------------
   public boolean isHeads ()
   {
      return (face == HEADS);
   }

   //-----------------------------------------------------------------
   // Returns the current face of the coin as a string.
   //-----------------------------------------------------------------
   public String toString()
   {
      String faceName;
```

```
LISTING   5.4      continued

        if (face == HEADS)
            faceName = "Heads";
        else
            faceName = "Tails";

        return faceName;
    }
}
```

A block statement is a collection of statements enclosed in braces. We've used these braces many times in previous examples to enclose method and class definitions.

The program called Guessing, shown in Listing 5.5, uses an if-else statement in which the statement of the else clause is a block statement.

If the guess entered by the user equals the randomly chosen answer, an appropriate acknowledgment is printed. However, if the answer is incorrect, two statements are printed, one that states that the guess is wrong and one that prints the actual answer. A programming project at the end of this chapter expands the concept of this example into the Hi-Lo game.

Note that if the block braces were not used, the sentence stating that the answer is incorrect would be printed if the answer was wrong, but the sentence revealing the correct answer would be printed in all cases. That is, only the first statement would be considered part of the else clause.

Remember that indentation means nothing except to the human reader. Statements that are not blocked properly can lead to the programmer making improper assumptions about how the code will execute. For example, the following code is misleading:

```
if (depth >= UPPER_LIMIT)
    delta = 100;
else
    System.out.println ("WARNING: Delta is being reset to ZERO");
    delta = 0;  // not part of the else clause!
```

The indentation (not to mention the logic of the code) implies that the variable delta is reset to zero only when depth is less than UPPER_LIMIT. However, without using a block, the assignment statement that resets delta to zero is not governed by the if-else statement at all. It is executed in either case, which is clearly not what is intended.

VideoNote

Examples using conditionals.

LISTING 5.5

```java
//********************************************************************
//  Guessing.java        Author: Lewis/Loftus
//
//  Demonstrates the use of a block statement in an if-else.
//********************************************************************

import java.util.*;

public class Guessing
{
   //-----------------------------------------------------------------
   //  Plays a simple guessing game with the user.
   //-----------------------------------------------------------------
   public static void main (String[] args)
   {
      final int MAX = 10;
      int answer, guess;

      Scanner scan = new Scanner (System.in);
      Random generator = new Random();

      answer = generator.nextInt(MAX) + 1;

      System.out.print ("I'm thinking of a number between 1 and "
                        + MAX + ". Guess what it is: ");

      guess = scan.nextInt();

      if (guess == answer)
         System.out.println ("You got it! Good guessing!");
      else
      {
         System.out.println ("That is not correct, sorry.");
         System.out.println ("The number was " + answer);
      }
   }
}
```

OUTPUT

```
I'm thinking of a number between 1 and 10. Guess what it is: 7
That is not correct, sorry.
The number was 5
```

A block statement can be used anywhere a single statement is called for in Java syntax. For example, the if portion of an if-else statement could be a block, or the else portion could be a block (as we saw in the Guessing program), or both parts could be block statements. For example:

```
if (boxes != warehouse.getCount())
{
    System.out.println ("Inventory and warehouse do NOT match.");
    System.out.println ("Beginning inventory process again!");
    boxes = 0;
}
else
{
    System.out.println ("Inventory and warehouse MATCH.");
    warehouse.ship();
}
```

In this if-else statement, the value of boxes is compared to a value obtained by calling the getCount method of the warehouse object (whatever that is). If they do not match exactly, two println statements and an assignment statement are executed. If they do match, a different message is printed and the ship method of warehouse is invoked.

Nested if Statements

The statement executed as the result of an if statement could be another if statement. This situation is called a *nested if*. It allows us to make another decision after determining the results of a previous decision. The program in Listing 5.6, called MinOfThree, uses nested if statements to determine the smallest of three integer values entered by the user.

Carefully trace the logic of the MinOfThree program, using various input sets with the minimum value in all three positions, to see how it determines the lowest value.

An important situation arises with nested if statements. It may seem that an else clause after a nested if could apply to either if statement. For example:

```
if (code == 'R')
    if (height <= 20)
        System.out.println ("Situation Normal");
    else
        System.out.println ("Bravo!");
```

LISTING 5.6

```
//********************************************************************
//  MinOfThree.java        Author: Lewis/Loftus
//
//  Demonstrates the use of nested if statements.
//********************************************************************

import java.util.Scanner;

public class MinOfThree
{
   //-----------------------------------------------------------------
   //  Reads three integers from the user and determines the smallest
   //  value.
   //-----------------------------------------------------------------
   public static void main (String[] args)
   {
      int num1, num2, num3, min = 0;

      Scanner scan = new Scanner (System.in);

      System.out.println ("Enter three integers: ");
      num1 = scan.nextInt();
      num2 = scan.nextInt();
      num3 = scan.nextInt();

      if (num1 < num2)
         if (num1 < num3)
            min = num1;
         else
            min = num3;
      else
         if (num2 < num3)
            min = num2;
         else
            min = num3;

      System.out.println ("Minimum value: " + min);
   }
}
```

OUTPUT

```
Enter three integers:
45  22  69
Minimum value: 22
```

Is the else clause matched to the inner if statement or the outer if statement? The indentation in this example implies that it is part of the inner if statement, and that is correct. An else clause is always matched to the closest unmatched if that preceded it. However, if we're not careful, we can easily mismatch it in our mind and misalign the indentation. This is another reason why accurate, consistent indentation is crucial.

> **KEY CONCEPT**
>
> In a nested if statement, an else clause is matched to the closest unmatched if.

Braces can be used to specify the if statement to which an else clause belongs. For example, if the previous example should have been structured so that the string "Bravo!" is printed if code is not equal to 'R', we could force that relationship (and properly indent) as follows:

```
if (code == 'R')
{
    if (height <= 20)
        System.out.println ("Situation Normal");
}
else
    System.out.println ("Bravo!");
```

By using the block statement in the first if statement, we establish that the else clause belongs to it.

SELF-REVIEW QUESTIONS *(see answers in Appendix N)*   myprogramminglab

SR 5.8   What output is produced by the following code fragment given the assumptions below?

```
if (num1 < num2)
    System.out.print (" red ");
if ((num1 + 5) < num2)
    System.out.print (" white ");
else
    System.out.print (" blue ");
System.out.println (" yellow ");
```

a. Assuming the value of num1 is 2 and the value of num2 is 10?
b. Assuming the value of num1 is 10 and the value of num2 is 2?
c. Assuming the value of num1 is 2 and the value of num2 is 2?

SR 5.9   How do block statements help us in the construction of conditionals?

SR 5.10   What is a nested if statement?

SR 5.11   For each assumption, what output is produced by the following code fragment?

```
if (num1 >= num2)
{
   System.out.print (" red ");
   System.out.print (" orange ");
}
if ((num1 + 5) >= num2)
   System.out.print (" white ");

else

   if ((num1 + 10) >= num2)
   {
      System.out.print (" black ");
      System.out.print (" blue ");
   }

   else

      System.out.print (" yellow ");
System.out.println(" green ");
```

a. Assuming the value of num1 is 5 and the value of num2 is 4?
b. Assuming the value of num1 is 5 and the value of num2 is 12?
c. Assuming the value of num1 is 5 and the value of num2 is 27?

SR 5.12 Write an expression that will print a message based on the value of the int variable named temperature. If temperature is equal to or less than 50, it prints "It is cool." on one line and "Dress warmly." on the next. If temperature is greater than 80, it prints "It is warm." on one line and "Dress coolly." on the next. If temperature is in between 50 and 80, it prints "It is pleasant." on one line and "Dress pleasantly." on the next.

5.3 Comparing Data

When comparing data using boolean expressions, it's important to understand some nuances that arise depending on the type of data being examined. Let's look at a few key situations.

Comparing Floats

An interesting situation occurs when comparing floating point data. Two floating point values are equal, according to the == operator, only if all the binary digits of their underlying representations match. If the compared values are the results of computation, it may be unlikely that they are exactly equal even if they are close enough for the specific situation. Therefore, you should rarely use the equality operator (==) when comparing floating point values.

A better way to check for floating point equality is to compute the absolute value of the difference between the two values and compare the result to some tolerance level. For example, we may choose a tolerance level of 0.00001. If the two floating point values are so close that their difference is less than the tolerance, then we are willing to consider them equal. Comparing two floating point values, f1 and f2, could be accomplished as follows:

```
if (Math.abs(f1 - f2) < TOLERANCE)
    System.out.println ("Essentially equal.");
```

The value of the constant TOLERANCE should be appropriate for the situation.

Comparing Characters

We know what it means when we say that one number is less than another, but what does it mean to say one character is less than another? As we discussed in Chapter 2, characters in Java are based on the Unicode character set, which defines an ordering of all possible characters that can be used. Because the character 'a' comes before the character 'b' in the character set, we can say that 'a' is less than 'b'.

We can use the equality and relational operators on character data. For example, if two character variables ch1 and ch2 hold two characters, we might determine their relative ordering in the Unicode character set with an if statement as follows:

> **KEY CONCEPT**
>
> The relative order of characters in Java is defined by the Unicode character set.

```
if (ch1 > ch2)
    System.out.println (ch1 + " is greater than " + ch2);
else
    System.out.println (ch1 + " is NOT greater than " + ch2);
```

The Unicode character set is structured so that all lowercase alphabetic characters ('a' through 'z') are contiguous and in alphabetical order. The same is true of uppercase alphabetic characters ('A' through 'Z') and characters that represent digits ('0' through '9'). The digits precede the uppercase alphabetic characters, which precede the lowercase alphabetic characters. Before, after, and in between these groups are other characters. See the chart in Appendix C for details.

Remember that a character and a character string are two different types of information. A char is a primitive value that represents one character. A character string is represented as an object in Java, defined by the String class. While comparing strings is based on comparing the characters in the strings, the comparison is governed by the rules for comparing objects.

Comparing Objects

The Unicode relationships among characters make it easy to sort characters and strings of characters. If you have a list of names, for instance, you can put them in alphabetical order based on the inherent relationships among characters in the character set.

However, you should not use the equality or relational operators to compare String objects. The String class contains a method called equals that returns a boolean value that is true if the two strings being compared contain exactly the same characters and is false otherwise. For example:

```java
if (name1.equals(name2))
    System.out.println ("The names are the same.");
else
    System.out.println ("The names are not the same.");
```

> **KEY CONCEPT**
>
> The compareTo method can be used to determine the relative order of strings.

Assuming that name1 and name2 are String objects, this condition determines whether the characters they contain are an exact match. Because both objects were created from the String class, they both respond to the equals message. Therefore, the condition could have been written as name2.equals(name1), and the same result would occur.

It is valid to test the condition (name1 == name2), but that actually tests to see whether both reference variables refer to the same String object. For any object, the == operator tests whether both reference variables are aliases of each other (whether they contain the same address). That's different from testing to see whether two different String objects contain the same characters.

Keep in mind that a string literal (such as "Nathan") is a convenience and is actually a shorthand technique for creating a String object. An interesting issue related to string comparisons is the fact that Java creates a unique object for string literals only when needed. That is, if the string literal "Hi" is used multiple times in a method, only one String object is created to represent it. Therefore, the conditions of both if statements in the following code are true:

```java
String str = "software";
if (str == "software")
    System.out.println ("References are the same");
if (str.equals("software"))
    System.out.println ("Characters are the same");
```

The first time the string literal "software" is used, a String object is created to represent it and the reference variable str is set to its address. Each subsequent time the literal is used, the original object is referenced.

To determine the relative ordering of two strings, use the compareTo method of the String class. The compareTo method is more versatile than the equals method. Instead of returning a boolean value, the compareTo method returns an integer. The return value is negative if the String object through which the method is invoked precedes (is less than) the string that is passed in as a parameter. The return value is zero if the two strings contain the same characters. The return value is positive if the String object through which the method is invoked follows (is greater than) the string that is passed in as a parameter. For example:

```
int result = name1.compareTo(name2);
if (result < 0)
    System.out.println (name1 + " comes before " + name2);
else
    if (result == 0)
        System.out.println ("The names are equal.");
    else
        System.out.println (name1 + " follows " + name2);
```

Keep in mind that comparing characters and strings is based on the Unicode character set (see Appendix C). This is called a *lexicographic ordering*. If all alphabetic characters are in the same case (upper or lower), the lexicographic ordering will be alphabetic ordering as well. However, when comparing two strings, such as "able" and "Baker", the compareTo method will conclude that "Baker" comes first because all of the uppercase letters come before all of the lowercase letters in the Unicode character set. A string that is the prefix of another, longer string is considered to precede the longer string. For example, when comparing the two strings "horse" and "horsefly", the compareTo method will conclude that "horse" comes first.

SELF-REVIEW QUESTIONS *(see answers in Appendix N)*   myprogramminglab

SR 5.13   Why must we be careful when comparing floating point values for equality?

SR 5.14   How do we compare strings for equality?

SR 5.15   Write an equals method for the Die class of Section 4.2. The method should return true if the Die object it is invoked on has the same facevalue as the Die object passed as a parameter, otherwise it should return false.

SR 5.16   Assume the String variables s1 and s2 have been initialized. Write an expression that prints out the two strings on separate lines in lexicographic order.

5.4 The `while` Statement

As we discussed in the introduction of this chapter, a repetition statement (or loop) allows us to execute another statement multiple times. A *while statement* is a loop that evaluates a boolean condition just as an `if` statement does and executes a statement (called the *body* of the loop) if the condition is true. However, unlike the `if` statement, after the body is executed, the condition is evaluated again. If it is still true, the body is executed again. This repetition continues until the condition becomes false; then processing continues with the statement after the body of the `while` loop. Figure 5.7 shows this processing.

While Statement

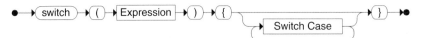

The `while` loop repeatedly executes the specified Statement as long as the boolean Expression is true. The Expression is evaluated first; therefore the Statement might not be executed at all. The Expression is evaluated again after each execution of Statement until the Expression becomes false.

Example:

```
while (total > max)
{
    total = total / 2;
    System.out.println ("Current total: " + total);
}
```

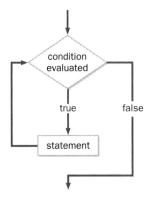

FIGURE 5.7   The logic of a `while` loop

The following loop prints the values from 1 to 5. Each iteration through the loop prints one value, then increments the counter.

```
int count = 1;
while (count <= 5)
{
    System.out.println (count);
    count++;
}
```

Note that the body of the while loop is a block containing two statements. The entire block is repeated on each iteration of the loop.

Let's look at another program that uses a while loop. The Average program shown in Listing 5.7 reads a series of integer values from the user, sums them up, and computes their average.

We don't know how many values the user may enter, so we need to have a way to indicate that the user has finished entering numbers. In this program, we designate zero to be a *sentinel value* that indicates the end of the input. The while loop continues to process input values until the user enters zero. This assumes that zero

LISTING 5.7

```
//********************************************************************
//  Average.java        Author: Lewis/Loftus
//
//  Demonstrates the use of a while loop, a sentinel value, and a
//  running sum.
//********************************************************************

import java.text.DecimalFormat;
import java.util.Scanner;

public class Average
{
    //-----------------------------------------------------------------
    //  Computes the average of a set of values entered by the user.
    //  The running sum is printed as the numbers are entered.
    //-----------------------------------------------------------------
    public static void main (String[] args)
    {
        int sum = 0, value, count = 0;
        double average;

        Scanner scan = new Scanner (System.in);
```

LISTING 5.7   *continued*

```java
        System.out.print ("Enter an integer (0 to quit): ");
        value = scan.nextInt();

        while (value != 0)   // sentinel value of 0 to terminate loop
        {
            count++;

            sum += value;
            System.out.println ("The sum so far is " + sum);

            System.out.print ("Enter an integer (0 to quit): ");
            value = scan.nextInt();
        }

        System.out.println ();

        if (count == 0)
            System.out.println ("No values were entered.");
        else
        {
            average = (double)sum / count;

            DecimalFormat fmt = new DecimalFormat ("0.###");
            System.out.println ("The average is " + fmt.format(average));
        }
    }
}
```

OUTPUT

```
Enter an integer (0 to quit): 25
The sum so far is 25
Enter an integer (0 to quit): 164
The sum so far is 189
Enter an integer (0 to quit): -14
The sum so far is 175
Enter an integer (0 to quit): 84
The sum so far is 259
Enter an integer (0 to quit): 12
The sum so far is 271
Enter an integer (0 to quit): -35
The sum so far is 236
Enter an integer (0 to quit): 0

The average is 39.333
```

is not one of the valid numbers that should contribute to the average. A sentinel value must always be outside the normal range of values entered.

VideoNote

Note that in the Average program, a variable called sum is used to maintain a *running sum*, which means it is the sum of the values entered thus far. The variable sum is initialized to zero, and each value read is added to and stored back into sum.

Examples using while loops.

We also have to count the number of values that are entered so that after the loop concludes we can divide by the appropriate value to compute the average. Note that the sentinel value is not counted. Consider the unusual situation in which the user immediately enters the sentinel value before entering any valid values. The if statement at the end of the program avoids a divide-by-zero error.

Let's examine yet another program that uses a while loop. The WinPercentage program shown in Listing 5.8 computes the winning percentage of a sports team based on the number of games won.

We use a while loop in the WinPercentage program to *validate the input*, meaning we guarantee that the user enters a value that we consider to be valid. In this example, that means that the number of games won must be greater than or equal to zero and less than or equal to the total number of games played. The while loop continues to execute, repeatedly prompting the user for valid input, until the entered number is indeed valid.

LISTING 5.8

```java
//********************************************************************
//  WinPercentage.java       Author: Lewis/Loftus
//
//  Demonstrates the use of a while loop for input validation.
//********************************************************************

import java.text.NumberFormat;
import java.util.Scanner;

public class WinPercentage
{
    //-----------------------------------------------------------------
    //  Computes the percentage of games won by a team.
    //-----------------------------------------------------------------
    public static void main (String[] args)
    {
        final int NUM_GAMES = 12;
        int won;
        double ratio;
```

LISTING 5.8   *continued*

```java
Scanner scan = new Scanner (System.in);

System.out.print ("Enter the number of games won (0 to "
                  + NUM_GAMES + "): ");
won = scan.nextInt();

while (won < 0 || won > NUM_GAMES)
{
    System.out.print ("Invalid input. Please reenter: ");
    won = scan.nextInt();
}

ratio = (double)won / NUM_GAMES;

NumberFormat fmt = NumberFormat.getPercentInstance();

System.out.println ();
System.out.println ("Winning percentage: " + fmt.format(ratio));
    }
}
```

OUTPUT

```
Enter the number of games won (0 to 12): -5
Invalid input. Please reenter: 13
Invalid input. Please reenter: 7

Winning percentage: 58%
```

We generally want our programs to be *robust*, which means that they handle potential problems as elegantly as possible. Validating input data and avoiding errors such as dividing by zero are situations that we should consciously address when designing a program. Loops and conditionals help us recognize and deal with such situations.

Infinite Loops

It is the programmer's responsibility to ensure that the condition of a loop will eventually become false. If it doesn't, the loop body will execute forever, or at least until the program is interrupted. This situation, referred to as an *infinite loop,* is a common mistake.

The following is an example of an infinite loop:

```
int count = 1;
while (count <= 25)   // Warning: this is an infinite loop!
{
    System.out.println (count);
    count = count - 1;
}
```

If you execute this loop, you should be prepared to interrupt it. On most systems, pressing the Control-C keyboard combination (hold down the Control key and press C) terminates a running program.

In this example, the initial value of count is 1, and it is decremented in the loop body. The while loop will continue as long as count is less than or equal to 25. Because count gets smaller with each iteration, the condition will always be true, or at least until the value of count gets so small that an underflow error occurs. The point is that the logic of the code is clearly wrong.

> **KEY CONCEPT**
> We must design our programs carefully to avoid infinite loops.

Let's look at some other examples of infinite loops:

```
int count = 1;
while (count != 50)   // infinite loop
    count += 2;
```

In this code fragment, the variable count is initialized to 1 and is moving in a positive direction. However, note that it is being incremented by 2 each time. This loop will never terminate because count will never equal 50. It begins at 1 and then changes to 3, then 5, and so on. Eventually it reaches 49, then changes to 51, then 53, and continues forever.

Now consider the following situation:

```
double num = 1.0;
while (num != 0.0)   // infinite loop
    num = num - 0.1;
```

Once again, the value of the loop control variable seems to be moving in the correct direction. And, in fact, it seems like num will eventually take on the value 0.0. However, this loop is infinite (at least on most systems), because num will never have a value *exactly* equal to 0.0. This situation is similar to one we discussed earlier in this chapter when we explored the idea of comparing floating point values in the condition of an if statement. Because of the way the values are represented in binary, minute computational errors occur internally, making it problematic to compare two floating point values for equality.

Nested Loops

The body of a loop can contain another loop. This situation is called a *nested loop*. Keep in mind that for each iteration of the outer loop, the inner loop executes completely. Consider the following code fragment. How many times does the string "Here again" get printed?

```
int count1, count2;
count1 = 1;
while (count1 <= 10)
{
    count2 = 1;
    while (count2 <= 50)
    {
        System.out.println ("Here again");
        count2++;
    }
    count1++;
}
```

The println statement is inside the inner loop. The outer loop executes 10 times, as count1 iterates between 1 and 10. The inner loop executes 50 times, as count2 iterates between 1 and 50. For each iteration of the outer loop, the inner loop executes completely. Therefore the println statement is executed 500 times.

As with any loop situation, we must be careful to scrutinize the conditions of the loops and the initializations of variables. Let's consider some small changes to this code. What if the condition of the outer loop were (count1 < 10) instead of (count1 <= 10)? How would that change the total number of lines printed? Well, the outer loop would execute 9 times instead of 10, so the println statement would be executed 450 times. What if the outer loop were left as it was originally defined, but count2 were initialized to 11 instead of 1 before the inner loop? The inner loop would then execute 40 times instead of 50, so the total number of lines printed would be 400.

Let's look at another example that uses a nested loop. A *palindrome* is a string of characters that reads the same forward or backward. For example, the following strings are palindromes:

- radar
- drab bard
- ab cde xxxx edc ba
- kayak
- deified
- able was I ere I saw elba

Note that some palindromes have an even number of characters, whereas others have an odd number of characters. The `PalindromeTester` program shown in Listing 5.9 tests to see whether a string is a palindrome. The user may test as many strings as desired.

The code for `PalindromeTester` contains two loops, one inside the other. The outer loop controls how many strings are tested, and the inner loop scans

LISTING 5.9

```java
//********************************************************************
//  PalindromeTester.java       Author: Lewis/Loftus
//
//  Demonstrates the use of nested while loops.
//********************************************************************

import java.util.Scanner;

public class PalindromeTester
{
   //-----------------------------------------------------------------
   //  Tests strings to see if they are palindromes.
   //-----------------------------------------------------------------
   public static void main (String[] args)
   {
      String str, another = "y";
      int left, right;

      Scanner scan = new Scanner (System.in);

      while (another.equalsIgnoreCase("y")) // allows y or Y
      {
         System.out.println ("Enter a potential palindrome:");
         str = scan.nextLine();

         left = 0;
         right = str.length() - 1;

         while (str.charAt(left) == str.charAt(right) && left < right)
         {
            left++;
            right--;
         }

         System.out.println();
```

LISTING 5.9 *continued*

```
        if (left < right)
            System.out.println ("That string is NOT a palindrome.");
        else
            System.out.println ("That string IS a palindrome.");

        System.out.println();
        System.out.print ("Test another palindrome (y/n)? ");
        another = scan.nextLine();
    }
  }
}
```

OUTPUT

```
Enter a potential palindrome:
radar

That string IS a palindrome.

Test another palindrome (y/n)? y
Enter a potential palindrome:
able was I ere I saw elba

That string IS a palindrome.

Test another palindrome (y/n)? y
Enter a potential palindrome:
abcddcba

That string IS a palindrome.

Test another palindrome (y/n)? y
Enter a potential palindrome:
abracadabra

That string is NOT a palindrome.

Test another palindrome (y/n)? n
```

through each string, character by character, until it determines whether the string is a palindrome.

The variables left and right store the indexes of two characters. They initially indicate the characters on either end of the string. Each iteration of the inner loop compares the two characters indicated by left and right. We fall out of the inner loop when either the characters don't match, meaning the string is not a palindrome, or when the value of left becomes equal to or greater than the value of right, which means the entire string has been tested and it is a palindrome.

Note that the following phrases would not be considered palindromes by the current version of the program:

- A man, a plan, a canal, Panama.
- Dennis and Edna sinned.
- Rise to vote, sir.
- Doom an evil deed, liven a mood.
- Go hang a salami; I'm a lasagna hog.

These strings fail our current criteria for a palindrome because of the spaces, punctuation marks, and changes in uppercase and lowercase. However, if these characteristics were removed or ignored, these strings read the same forward and backward. Consider how the program could be changed to handle these situations. These modifications are included as a programming project at the end of the chapter.

The break and continue Statements

Java includes two statements that affect the processing of conditionals and loops. When a break statement is executed, the flow of execution transfers immediately to the statement after the one governing the current flow. For example, if a break statement is executed within the body of a loop, the execution of the loop is stopped and the statement following the loop is executed. It "breaks" out of the loop.

In Chapter 6 we'll see that using the break statement is usually necessary when writing switch statements. However, it is never necessary to use a break statement in a loop. An equivalent loop can always be written without it. Because the break statement causes program flow to jump from one place to another, using a break in a loop is not good practice. You can and should avoid using the break statement in a loop.

A *continue statement* has a related effect on loop processing. The continue statement is similar to a break, but the loop condition is evaluated again, and the loop body is executed again if it is still true. Like the break statement, the continue statement can always be avoided in a loop, and for the same reasons, it should be.

SELF-REVIEW QUESTIONS *(see answers in Appendix N)*

SR 5.17 What is an infinite loop? Specifically, what causes it?

SR 5.18 What output is produced by the following code fragment?

```
int low = 0, high = 10;
while (low < high)
{
    System.out.println (low);
    low++;
}
```

SR 5.19 What output is produced by the following code fragment?

```
int low = 10, high = 0;
while (low <= high)
{
    System.out.println (low);
    low++;
}
```

SR 5.20 What output is produced by the following code fragment?

```
int low = 0, high = 10;
while (low <= high)
{
    System.out.println (low);
    high = high - low;
}
```

SR 5.21 What output is produced by the following code fragment?

```
int low = 0, high = 10, mid;
while (low <= high)
{
    mid = low;
    while (mid <= high)
    {
        System.out.print (mid + " ");
        mid++;
    }
    System.out.println ();
    low++;
}
```

SR 5.22 Assume the int variable value has been initialized to a positive integer. Write a while loop that prints all of the positive divisors of value. For example, if value is 28, it prints divisors of 28: 1 2 4 7 14 28

SR 5.23 Assume the `int` variable `value` has been initialized to a positive integer. Write a `while` loop that prints all of the positive divisors of each number from one to `value`. For example, if `value` is 4, it prints

>   divisors of 1: 1
>
>   divisors of 2: 1 2
>
>   divisors of 3: 1 3
>
>   divisors of 4: 1 2 4

5.5 Iterators

An *iterator* is an object that has methods that allow you to process a collection of items one at a time. That is, an iterator lets you step through each item and interact with it as needed. For example, your goal may be to compute the dues for each member of a club or print the distinct parts of a URL. The key is that an iterator provides a consistent and simple mechanism for systematically processing a group of items. Since it is inherently a repetitive process, it is closely related to the idea of loops.

> **KEY CONCEPT**
>
> An iterator is an object that helps you process a group of related items.

Technically an iterator object in Java is defined using the `Iterator` interface, which is discussed in Chapter 7. For now it is simply helpful to know that such objects exist and that they can make the processing of a collection of items easier.

Every iterator object has a method called `hasNext` that returns a `boolean` value indicating if there is at least one more item to process. Therefore the `hasNext` method can be used as a condition of a loop to control the processing of each item. An iterator also has a method called `next` to retrieve the next item in the collection to process.

There are several classes in the Java standard class library that define iterator objects. One of these is `Scanner`, a class we've used several times in previous examples to help us read data from the user. The `hasNext` method of the `Scanner` class returns true if there is another input token to process. And, as we've seen previously, it has a `next` method that returns the next input token as a string.

The `Scanner` class also has specific variations of the `hasNext` method, such as the `hasNextInt` and `hasNextDouble` methods, which allow you to determine if the next input token is a particular type. Likewise, as we've seen, there are variations of the `next` method, such as `nextInt` and `nextDouble`, which retrieve values of specific types.

When reading input interactively from the standard input stream, the `hasNext` method of the `Scanner` class will wait until there is input available, then return true. That is, interactive input read from the keyboard is always thought to have more data to process—it just hasn't arrived yet until the user types it in. That's why in previous examples we've used special sentinel values to determine the end of interactive input.

However, the fact that a Scanner object is an iterator is particularly helpful when the scanner is being used to process input from a source that has a specific end point, such as processing the lines of a data file or processing the parts of a character string. Let's examine an example of this type of processing.

Reading Text Files

Suppose we have an input file called urls.inp that contains a list of URLs that we want to process in some way:

www.google.com

www.linux.org/info/gnu.html

thelyric.com/calendar/

www.cs.vt.edu/undergraduate/about

youtube.com/watch?v=EHCRimwRGLs

The program shown in Listing 5.10 reads the URLs from this file and dissects them to show the various parts of the path. It uses a Scanner object to process the input. In fact, it uses multiple Scanner objects—one to read the lines of the data file and another to process each URL string.

LISTING 5.10

```
//********************************************************************
//  URLDissector.java         Author: Lewis/Loftus
//
//  Demonstrates the use of Scanner to read file input and parse it
//  using alternative delimiters.
//********************************************************************

import java.util.Scanner;
import java.io.*;

public class URLDissector
{
    //-----------------------------------------------------------------
    //  Reads urls from a file and prints their path components.
    //-----------------------------------------------------------------
    public static void main (String[] args) throws IOException
    {
```

LISTING 5.10   *continued*

```java
      String url;
      Scanner fileScan, urlScan;

      fileScan = new Scanner (new File("urls.inp"));

      //  Read and process each line of the file
      while (fileScan.hasNext())
      {
         url = fileScan.nextLine();
         System.out.println ("URL: " + url);

         urlScan = new Scanner (url);
         urlScan.useDelimiter("/");

         //  Print each part of the url
         while (urlScan.hasNext())
            System.out.println ("   " + urlScan.next());

         System.out.println();
      }
   }
}
```

OUTPUT

```
URL: www.google.com
  www.google.com

URL: www.linux.org/info/gnu.html
   www.linux.org
   info
   gnu.html

URL: thelyric.com/calendar/
   thelyric.com
   calendar

URL: www.cs.vt.edu/undergraduate/about
   www.cs.vt.edu
   undergraduate
   about

URL: youtube.com/watch?v=EHCRimwRGLs
   youtube.com
   watch?v=EHCRimwRGLs
```

There are two `while` loops in this program, one nested within the other. The outer loop processes each line in the file, and the inner loop processes each token in the current line.

The variable `fileScan` is created as a scanner that operates on the input file named `urls.inp`. Instead of passing `System.in` into the `Scanner` constructor, we instantiate a `File` object that represents the input file and pass it into the `Scanner` constructor. At that point, the `fileScan` object is ready to read and process input from the input file.

If for some reason there is a problem finding or opening the input file, the attempt to create a `File` object will throw an `IOException`, which is why we've added the `throws IOException` clause to the `main` method header. (Processing I/O exceptions is discussed further in Chapter 11.)

The body of the outer `while` loop will be executed as long as the `hasNext` method of the input file scanner returns true—that is, as long as there is more input in the data file to process. Each iteration through the loop reads one line (one URL) from the input file and prints it out.

For each URL, a new `Scanner` object is set up to parse the pieces of the URL string, which is passed into the `Scanner` constructor when instantiating the `urlScan` object. The inner `while` loop prints each token of the URL on a separate line.

> **KEY CONCEPT**
>
> The delimiters used to separate tokens in a Scanner object can be explicitly set as needed.

Recall that, by default, a `Scanner` object assumes that white space (spaces, tabs, and new lines) is used as the delimiters separating the input tokens. That works in this example for the scanner that is reading each line of the input file. However, if the default delimiters do not suffice, as in the processing of a URL in this example, they can be changed.

In this case, we are interested in each part of the path separated by the slash (/) character. A call to the `useDelimiter` method of the scanner sets the delimiter to a slash prior to processing the URL string.

If you want to use more than one alternate delimiter character, or if you want to parse the input in more complex ways, the `Scanner` class can process patterns called *regular expressions*, which are discussed in Appendix H.

myprogramming**lab**

SELF-REVIEW QUESTIONS (*see answers in Appendix N*)

SR 5.24 Devise statements that create each of the following `Scanner` objects.

    a. One for interactive input, which reads from `System.in`.
    b. One that reads from the file "info.dat".
    c. One that reads from the `String` variable `infoString`.

SR 5.25 Assume the `Scanner` object `fileScan` has been initialized to read from a file. Write a `while` loop that calculates the average number of characters per line of the file.

5.6 The ArrayList Class

Now that we have a loop in our arsenal of programming statements, let's introduce a very useful class for managing a set of objects. The ArrayList class is part of the java. util package of the Java standard class library. An ArrayList object stores a list of objects and allows you to refer to each one by an integer *index* value. We will often use loops to scan through the objects in the list and deal with them in one way or another.

Internally, the ArrayList class manages the list using a programming construct called an *array* (hence the name). Arrays are discussed in detail in Chapter 8, but we don't have to know the details of arrays to make use of an ArrayList object. The ArrayList class is part of the Java Collections API, a group of classes that serve to organize and manage other objects. We discuss collection classes further in Chapter 13.

> **KEY CONCEPT**
> An ArrayList object stores a list of objects and lets you access them using an integer index.

Figure 5.8 lists several methods of the ArrayList class. You can add and remove elements in various ways, determine if the list is empty, and obtain the number of elements currently in the list, among several other operations.

Note that the ArrayList class refers to having elements of type E. That is a *generic type* (the E stands for element), which is determined when an ArrayList object is created. So you don't just create an ArrayList object, you create an ArrayList object that will store a particular type of object. The type parameter for a given object is written in angle brackets after the class name. So we can talk about an ArrayList<String> object that manages a list of String objects, or an ArrayList<Book> that manages a list of Book objects.

You can create an ArrayList without specifying the type of element, in which case the ArrayList stores Object references, which means that you can put any type of object in the list. This is usually not a good idea. The point of being able to commit to storing a particular type in a given ArrayList object lets the compiler help you check that only the appropriate types of objects are being stored in the object.

> **KEY CONCEPT**
> When an ArrayList object is created, you specify the type of element that will be stored in the list.

The index values of an ArrayList begin at 0, not 1. So conceptually, for example, an ArrayList of String objects might be managing the following list:

```
0  "Bashful"
1  "Sleepy"
2  "Happy"
3  "Dopey"
4  "Doc"
```

Also note that an ArrayList stores references to objects. You cannot create an ArrayList that stores primitive values such as an int. But that's where wrapper classes come to the rescue again. For example, you can create an ArrayList<Integer> or an ArrayList<Double> as appropriate.

```
ArrayList<E>()
    Constructor: creates an initially empty list.

boolean add (E obj)
    Inserts the specified object to the end of this list.

void add (int index, E obj)
    Inserts the specified object into this list at the specified index.

void clear()
    Removes all elements from this list.

E remove (int index)
    Removes the element at the specified index in this list and returns it.

E get (int index)
    Returns the object at the specified index in this list without removing it.

int indexOf (Object obj)
    Returns the index of the first occurrence of the specified object.

boolean contains (Object obj)
    Returns true if this list contains the specified object.

boolean isEmpty()
    Returns true if this list contains no elements.

int size()
    Returns the number of elements in this list.
```

FIGURE 5.8   Some methods of the `ArrayList<E>` class.

The program shown in Listing 5.11 instantiates an `ArrayList<String>` called band. The method add is used to add several `String` objects to the end of the `ArrayList` in a specific order. Then one particular string is deleted and another is inserted at a particular index. As with any other object, the `toString` method of the `ArrayList` class is automatically called whenever it is sent to the `println` method, which prints all of the elements surrounded by square brackets. The while loop at the end of the program explicitly prints each element on a separate line.

LISTING 5.11

```
//********************************************************************
//  Beatles.java        Author: Lewis/Loftus
//
//  Demonstrates the use of a ArrayList object.
//********************************************************************
```

LISTING 5.11   *continued*

```java
import java.util.ArrayList;

public class Beatles
{
   //-----------------------------------------------------------------
   //  Stores and modifies a list of band members.
   //-----------------------------------------------------------------
   public static void main (String[] args)
   {
      ArrayList<String> band = new ArrayList<String>();

      band.add ("Paul");
      band.add ("Pete");
      band.add ("John");
      band.add ("George");

      System.out.println (band);
      int location = band.indexOf ("Pete");
      band.remove (location);

      System.out.println (band);
      System.out.println ("At index 1: " + band.get(1));
      band.add (2, "Ringo");

      System.out.println ("Size of the band: " + band.size());
      int index = 0;
      while (index < band.size())
      {
         System.out.println (band.get(index));
         index++;
      }
   }
}
```

OUTPUT

```
[Paul, Pete, John, George]
[Paul, John, George]
At index 1: John
Size of the band: 4
Paul
John
Ringo
George
```

SELF-REVIEW QUESTIONS

SR 5.26 What are the advantages of using an `ArrayList` object?

SR 5.27 What type of elements does an `ArrayList` hold?

SR 5.28 Write a declaration for a variable named `dice` that is an `ArrayList` of `Die` objects.

SR 5.29 What output is produced by the following code fragment?

```
ArrayList<String> names = new ArrayList<String>();
names.add ("Andy");
names.add ("Betty");
names.add (1, "Chet");
names.add (1, "Don");
names.remove (2);
System.out.println (names);
```

5.7 Determining Event Sources

In Chapter 4 we began our exploration of creating programs with a truly interactive graphical user interface (GUI). You'll recall that interactive GUIs require that we create listener objects and set up the relationship between listeners and the components that generate the events of interest.

Let's look at an example in which one listener object is used to listen to two different components. The program represented by the `LeftRight` class, shown in Listing 5.12 displays a label and two buttons. When the left button is pressed, the label displays the word Left, and when the right button is pressed, the label displays the word Right.

The `LeftRightPanel` class, shown in Listing 5.13, creates one instance of the `ButtonListener` object, then adds that listener to both buttons. Therefore, when either button is pressed, the `actionPerformed` method of the `ButtonListener` class is invoked.

On each invocation, the `actionPerformed` method uses an `if-else` statement to determine which button generated the event. The `getSource` method is called on the `ActionEvent` object that the button passes into the `actionPerformed` method. The `getSource` method returns a reference to the component that generated the event. The condition of the `if` statement compares the event source to the reference to the left button. If they don't match, then the event must have been generated by the right button.

LISTING 5.12

```
//********************************************************************
//  LeftRight.java        Author: Lewis/Loftus
//
//  Demonstrates the use of one listener for multiple buttons.
//********************************************************************

import javax.swing.JFrame;

public class LeftRight
{
   //-----------------------------------------------------------------
   //  Creates the main program frame.
   //-----------------------------------------------------------------
   public static void main (String[] args)
   {
      JFrame frame = new JFrame ("Left Right");
      frame.setDefaultCloseOperation (JFrame.EXIT_ON_CLOSE);

      frame.getContentPane().add(new LeftRightPanel());

      frame.pack();
      frame.setVisible(true);
   }
}
```

DISPLAY

LISTING 5.13

```java
//********************************************************************
//  LeftRightPanel.java        Author: Lewis/Loftus
//
//  Demonstrates the use of one listener for multiple buttons.
//********************************************************************

import java.awt.*;
import java.awt.event.*;
import javax.swing.*;

public class LeftRightPanel extends JPanel
{
    private JButton left, right;
    private JLabel label;
    private JPanel buttonPanel;

    //-----------------------------------------------------------------
    //  Constructor: Sets up the GUI.
    //-----------------------------------------------------------------
    public LeftRightPanel ()
    {
        left = new JButton ("Left");
        right = new JButton ("Right");

        ButtonListener listener = new ButtonListener();
        left.addActionListener (listener);
        right.addActionListener (listener);

        label = new JLabel ("Push a button");

        buttonPanel = new JPanel();
        buttonPanel.setPreferredSize (new Dimension(200, 40));
        buttonPanel.setBackground (Color.blue);
        buttonPanel.add (left);
        buttonPanel.add (right);

        setPreferredSize (new Dimension(200, 80));
        setBackground (Color.cyan);
        add (label);
        add (buttonPanel);
    }
```

LISTING 5.13   *continued*

```
//**************************************************************
//  Represents a listener for both buttons.
//**************************************************************
private class ButtonListener implements ActionListener
{
    //-----------------------------------------------------------
    //  Determines which button was pressed and sets the label
    //  text accordingly.
    //-----------------------------------------------------------
    public void actionPerformed (ActionEvent event)
    {
        if (event.getSource() == left)
            label.setText("Left");
        else
            label.setText("Right");
    }
}
}
```

We could have created two separate listener classes, one to listen to the left button and another to listen to the right. In that case, the actionPerformed method would not have to determine the source of the event. Whether to have multiple listeners or determine the event source when it occurs is a design decision that should be made depending on the situation.

Note that the two buttons are put on the same panel called buttonPanel, which is separate from the panel represented by the LeftRightPanel class. By putting both buttons on one panel, we can guarantee their visual relationship to each other even when the frame is resized in various ways. For buttons labeled Left and Right, that may be important.

5.8 Check Boxes and Radio Buttons

A push button, as defined by the JButton class, is only one kind of button that we can use in a Java GUI. Two other kinds are check boxes and radio buttons. Let's look at these in detail.

Check Boxes

A *check box* is a button that can be toggled on or off using the mouse, indicating that a particular boolean condition is set or unset. For example, a check box labeled `Collate` might be used to indicate whether the output of a print job should be collated. Although you might have a group of check boxes indicating a set of options, each check box operates independently. That is, each can be set to on or off and the status of one does not influence the others.

The program in Listing 5.14 displays two check boxes and a label. The check boxes determine whether the text of the label is displayed in bold, italic, both, or neither. Any combination of bold and italic is valid. For example, both check boxes could be checked (on), in which case the text is displayed in both bold and italic. If neither is checked, the text of the label is displayed in a plain style.

The GUI for the `StyleOptions` program is embodied in the `StyleOptionsPanel` class shown in Listing 5.15. A check box is represented by the `JCheckBox` class. When a check box changes state from selected (checked) to deselected (unchecked), or vice versa, it generates an *item event*. The `ItemListener` interface contains a single method called `itemStateChanged`. In this example, we use the same listener object to handle both check boxes.

LISTING 5.14

```java
//********************************************************************
//  StyleOptions.java       Author: Lewis/Loftus
//
//  Demonstrates the use of check boxes.
//********************************************************************

import javax.swing.JFrame;

public class StyleOptions
{
   //-----------------------------------------------------------------
   //  Creates and presents the program frame.
   //-----------------------------------------------------------------
   public static void main (String[] args)
   {
      JFrame frame = new JFrame ("Style Options");
      frame.setDefaultCloseOperation (JFrame.EXIT_ON_CLOSE);

      StyleOptionsPanel panel = new StyleOptionsPanel();
      frame.getContentPane().add (panel);

      frame.pack();
      frame.setVisible(true);
   }
}
```

LISTING 5.14   *continued*

DISPLAY

LISTING 5.15

```
//********************************************************************
//  StyleOptionsPanel.java       Author: Lewis/Loftus
//
//  Demonstrates the use of check boxes.
//********************************************************************

import javax.swing.*;
import java.awt.*;
import java.awt.event.*;

public class StyleOptionsPanel extends JPanel
{
   private JLabel saying;
   private JCheckBox bold, italic;

   //-----------------------------------------------------------------
   //  Sets up a panel with a label and some check boxes that
   //  control the style of the label's font.
   //-----------------------------------------------------------------
   public StyleOptionsPanel()
   {
      saying = new JLabel ("Say it with style!");
      saying.setFont (new Font ("Helvetica", Font.PLAIN, 36));

      bold = new JCheckBox ("Bold");
      bold.setBackground (Color.cyan);
```

LISTING 5.15 *continued*

```java
        italic = new JCheckBox ("Italic");
        italic.setBackground (Color.cyan);

        StyleListener listener = new StyleListener();
        bold.addItemListener (listener);
        italic.addItemListener (listener);

        add (saying);
        add (bold);
        add (italic);

        setBackground (Color.cyan);
        setPreferredSize (new Dimension(300, 100));
    }

    //*********************************************************************
    //  Represents the listener for both check boxes.
    //*********************************************************************
    private class StyleListener implements ItemListener
    {
        //------------------------------------------------------------
        //  Updates the style of the label font style.
        //------------------------------------------------------------
        public void itemStateChanged (ItemEvent event)
        {
            int style = Font.PLAIN;

            if (bold.isSelected())
                style = Font.BOLD;

            if (italic.isSelected())
                style += Font.ITALIC;

            saying.setFont (new Font ("Helvetica", style, 36));
        }
    }
}
```

This program also uses the Font class, which represents a particular *character font*. A Font object is defined by the font name, the font style, and the font size. The font name establishes the general visual characteristics of the characters. We are using the Helvetica font in this program. The style of a Java font can be plain, bold, italic, or bold and italic combined. The check boxes in our GUI are set up to change the characteristics of our font style.

The style of a font is represented as an integer, and integer constants defined in the Font class are used to represent the various aspects of the style. The constant PLAIN is used to represent a plain style. The constants BOLD and ITALIC are used to represent bold and italic, respectively. The sum of the BOLD and ITALIC constants indicates a style that is both bold and italic.

The itemStateChanged method of the listener determines what the revised style should be now that one of the check boxes has changed state. It initially sets the style to be plain. Then each check box is consulted in turn using the isSelected method, which returns a boolean value. First, if the bold check box is selected (checked), then the style is set to bold. Then, if the italic check box is selected, the ITALIC constant is added to the style variable. Finally, the font of the label is set to a new font with its revised style.

Note that, given the way the listener is written in this program, it doesn't matter which check box was clicked to generate the event. Both check boxes are processed by the same listener. It also doesn't matter whether the changed check box was toggled from selected to unselected or vice versa. The state of both check boxes is examined if either is changed.

Radio Buttons

A *radio button* is used with other radio buttons to provide a set of mutually exclusive options. Unlike a check box, a radio button is not particularly useful by itself. It has meaning only when it is used with one or more other radio buttons. Only one option out of the group is valid. At any point in time, one and only one button of the group of radio buttons is selected (on). When a radio button from the group is pushed, the other button in the group that is currently on is automatically toggled off.

> **KEY CONCEPT**
>
> Radio buttons operate as a group, providing a set of mutually exclusive options.

The term "radio buttons" comes from the way the buttons worked on an old-fashioned car radio. At any point, one button was pushed to specify the current choice of station; when another was pushed, the current one automatically popped out.

The QuoteOptions program, shown in Listing 5.16, displays a label and a group of radio buttons. The radio buttons determine which quote is displayed in the label. Because only one of the quotes can be displayed at a time, the use of radio buttons is appropriate. For example, if the Comedy radio button is selected, the comedy quote is displayed in the label. If the Philosophy button is then pressed, the Comedy radio button is automatically toggled off and the comedy quote is replaced by a philosophical one.

VideoNote

Examples using check boxes and radio buttons.

LISTING 5.16

```java
//********************************************************************
//  QuoteOptions.java       Author: Lewis/Loftus
//
//  Demonstrates the use of radio buttons.
//********************************************************************

import javax.swing.JFrame;

public class QuoteOptions
{
   //-----------------------------------------------------------------
   //  Creates and presents the program frame.
   //-----------------------------------------------------------------
   public static void main (String[] args)
   {
      JFrame frame = new JFrame ("Quote Options");
      frame.setDefaultCloseOperation (JFrame.EXIT_ON_CLOSE);

      QuoteOptionsPanel panel = new QuoteOptionsPanel();
      frame.getContentPane().add (panel);

      frame.pack();
      frame.setVisible(true);
   }
}
```

DISPLAY

The `QuoteOptionsPanel` class, shown in Listing 5.17, sets up and displays the GUI components. A radio button is represented by the `JRadioButton` class. Because the radio buttons in a set work together, the `ButtonGroup` class is used to define a set of related radio buttons.

Note that each button is added to the button group, and also that each button is added individually to the panel. A `ButtonGroup` object is not a container to organize and display components; it is simply a way to define the group of radio buttons that work together to form a set of dependent options. The `ButtonGroup` object ensures that the currently selected radio button is turned off when another in the group is selected.

A radio button produces an action event when it is selected. The `actionPerformed` method of the listener first retrieves the source of the event using the `getSource` method and then compares it to each of the three radio buttons in turn. Depending on which button was selected, the text of the label is set to the appropriate quote.

LISTING 5.17

```
//********************************************************************
//  QuoteOptionsPanel.java        Author: Lewis/Loftus
//
//  Demonstrates the use of radio buttons.
//********************************************************************

import javax.swing.*;
import java.awt.*;
import java.awt.event.*;

public class QuoteOptionsPanel extends JPanel
{
    private JLabel quote;
    private JRadioButton comedy, philosophy, carpentry;
    private String comedyQuote, philosophyQuote, carpentryQuote;

    //-----------------------------------------------------------------
    //  Sets up a panel with a label and a set of radio buttons
    //  that control its text.
    //-----------------------------------------------------------------
    public QuoteOptionsPanel()
    {
        comedyQuote = "Take my wife, please.";
        philosophyQuote = "I think, therefore I am.";
        carpentryQuote = "Measure twice. Cut once.";
```

LISTING 5.17 *continued*

```java
        quote = new JLabel (comedyQuote);
        quote.setFont (new Font ("Helvetica", Font.BOLD, 24));

        comedy = new JRadioButton ("Comedy", true);
        comedy.setBackground (Color.green);
        philosophy = new JRadioButton ("Philosophy");
        philosophy.setBackground (Color.green);
        carpentry = new JRadioButton ("Carpentry");
        carpentry.setBackground (Color.green);

        ButtonGroup group = new ButtonGroup();
        group.add (comedy);
        group.add (philosophy);
        group.add (carpentry);

        QuoteListener listener = new QuoteListener();
        comedy.addActionListener (listener);
        philosophy.addActionListener (listener);
        carpentry.addActionListener (listener);

        add (quote);
        add (comedy);
        add (philosophy);
        add (carpentry);

        setBackground (Color.green);
        setPreferredSize (new Dimension(300, 100));
    }

    //***********************************************************************
    //  Represents the listener for all radio buttons.
    //***********************************************************************
    private class QuoteListener implements ActionListener
    {
        //--------------------------------------------------------------
        //  Sets the text of the label depending on which radio
        //  button was pressed.
        //--------------------------------------------------------------
        public void actionPerformed (ActionEvent event)
        {
            Object source = event.getSource();
```

LISTING 5.17   *continued*

```
        if (source == comedy)
            quote.setText (comedyQuote);
        else
            if (source == philosophy)
                quote.setText (philosophyQuote);
            else
                quote.setText (carpentryQuote);
    }
  }
}
```

Note that unlike push buttons, both check boxes and radio buttons are *toggle buttons*, meaning that at any time they are either on or off. The difference is in how they are used. Independent options (choose any combination) are controlled with check boxes. Dependent options (choose one of a set) are controlled with radio buttons. If there is only one option to be managed, a check box can be used by itself. As we mentioned earlier, a radio button, on the other hand, makes sense only in conjunction with one or more other radio buttons.

Also note that check boxes and radio buttons produce different types of events. A check box produces an item event, and a radio button produces an action event. The use of different event types is related to the differences in button functionality. A check box produces an event when it is selected or deselected, and the listener could make the distinction if desired. A radio button, on the other hand, produces an event only when it is selected (the currently selected button from the group is deselected automatically).

Summary of Key Concepts

- Conditionals and loops allow us to control the flow of execution through a method.

- An `if` statement allows a program to choose whether to execute a particular statement.

- A loop allows a program to execute a statement multiple times.

- Logical operators are often used to construct sophisticated conditions.

- Proper indentation is important for human readability; it shows the relationship between one statement and another.

- An `if-else` statement allows a program to do one thing if a condition is true and another thing if the condition is false.

- In a nested `if` statement, an `else` clause is matched to the closest unmatched `if`.

- The relative order of characters in Java is defined by the Unicode character set.

- The `compareTo` method can be used to determine the relative order of strings.

- A `while` statement executes the same statement until its condition becomes false.

- We must design our programs carefully to avoid infinite loops.

- An iterator is an object that helps you process a group of related items.

- The delimiters used to separate tokens in a `Scanner` object can be explicitly set as needed.

- An `ArrayList` object stores a list of objects and lets you access them using an integer index.

- When an `ArrayList` object is created, you specify the type of element that will be stored in the list.

- Radio buttons operate as a group, providing a set of mutually exclusive options.

Exercises

myprogramminglab

Visit www.myprogramminglab.com to complete many of these Exercises online and get instant feedback.

EX 5.1   What happens in the `MinOfThree` program if two or more of the values are equal? If exactly two of the values are equal, does it matter whether the equal values are lower or higher than the third?

EX 5.2   What is wrong with the following code fragment? Rewrite it so that it produces correct output.

```
if (total == MAX)
    if (total < sum)
        System.out.println ("total == MAX and < sum.");
else
    System.out.println ("total is not equal to MAX");
```

EX 5.3   What is wrong with the following code fragment? Rewrite it so that it produces correct output.

```
Scanner in=new Scanner(System.in);
int i = in.nextInt( );
if ( i = 5 ) System.out.println( "You entered 5" );
else
    System.out.println( "You entered something other
than 5") ;
```

EX 5.4   What output is produced by the following code fragment?

```
int j,k,num = -4,num1=5;
j= ( num < 0 ? 0 : num * num ) ;
System.out.println("j is "+j) ;
k= ( num1 < 0 ? 0 : num1 * num1 ) ;
System.out.println("k is "+k) ;
```

EX 5.5   What output is produced by the following code fragment?

```
int i=50,j=100;
if (i==50)
{
        if (j==100)
                System.out.println("There are 50 apples
and 100 oranges");
else
{
        System.out.println("There are 50 apples only");
}
    }
System.out.println("There are no apples ");
```

EX 5.6   What output is produced by the following code fragment?

```
int m1=35, m2=40, m3=45, m4=50, m5=55, per ;
per = ( m1+ m2 + m3 + m4+ m5 ) / 5;
if ( per >= 60 )
System.out.println ( "First division" ) ;
```

```
else if ( per >= 50 )
System.out.println( "Second division" ) ;
else if ( per >= 40 )
System.out.println( "Third division" ) ;
else
System.out.println ("fail");
```

EX 5.7   What output is produced by the following code fragment?

```
int i=10;
while(i>0)
      {
System.out.println(i);
i=i-2;
      }
```

EX 5.8   What output is produced by the following code fragment?

```
int x = 4, y = 0, z ;
while ( x >= 0 )
{
if ( x == y )
break ;
else
{
 System.out.println("x is "+x) ;
 System.out.println("y is "+y) ;
}
x-- ; y++;
}
```

EX 5.9   What output is produced by the following code fragment?

```
for(int count =100;count>=2;count-=2)
System.out.println(count);
```

EX 5.10 Write a while loop that verifies that the user enters a positive integer value.

EX 5.11 Transform the following for loop into a while loop (make sure it produces the same output)

```
for(int i=10;i<20;i++)
{
System.out.println(i);
}
```

EX 5.12 Write a method called maxOfTwo that accepts two integer parameters and returns the larger of the two.

EX 5.13 Write a method called `larger` that accepts two floating point parameters (of type `double`) and returns true if the first parameter is greater than the second, and false otherwise.

EX 5.14 Write an `if` statement which verifies whether the user enters a negative integer value or not.

EX 5.15 Write a `while` loop that verifies whether the number entered by the user is odd or not.

EX 5.16 Write a code fragment that reads and prints the sum and average of the values entered by a user until a particular limit value (stored in `limit`) is entered.

EX 5.17 Write a `while` loop to print the even numbers which lie in the range of 35 to 90 (inclusive).

EX 5.18 Write a `while` loop to print the multiples of 5 from 1 to 100.

Programming Projects

Visit www.myprogramminglab.com to complete many of these Programming Projects online and get instant feedback.

myprogramminglab

PP 5.1 Design and implement an application that reads an integer value from the user representing a year. The purpose of the program is to determine if the year is a leap year (and therefore has 29 days in February) in the Gregorian calendar. A year is a leap year if it is divisible by 4, unless it is also divisible by 100 but not 400. For example, the year 2003 is not a leap year, but 2004 is. The year 1900 is not a leap year because it is divisible by 100, but the year 2000 is a leap year because even though it is divisible by 100, it is also divisible by 400. Produce an error message for any input value less than 1582 (the year the Gregorian calendar was adopted).

PP 5.2 Design and implement an application that reads an integer value and prints the sum of all prime numbers which lie between 2 and the input value, both inclusive.

PP 5.3 Design and implement an application that reads an input sentence from the user and prints it, with one word per line.

PP 5.4 Design and implement an application that plays the Hi-Lo guessing game with numbers. The program should pick a random number between 1 and 100 (inclusive), then repeatedly prompt the user to guess the number. On each guess, report to the user that he or she is correct or that the guess is high or low.

VideoNote

Developing a solution of
PP 5.4.

Continue accepting guesses until the user guesses correctly or chooses to quit. Use a sentinel value to determine whether the user wants to quit. Count the number of guesses and report that value when the user guesses correctly. At the end of each game (by quitting or a correct guess), prompt to determine whether the user wants to play again. Continue playing games until the user chooses to stop.

PP 5.5 Create a modified version of the PalindromeTester program so that the spaces, punctuation, and changes in uppercase and lowercase are not considered when determining whether a string is a palindrome. *Hint*: These issues can be handled in several ways. Think carefully about your design.

PP 5.6 Using the Coin class defined in this chapter, design and implement a driver class called FlipRace whose main method creates two Coin objects, then continually flips them both to see which coin first comes up heads three flips in a row. Continue flipping the coins until one of the coins wins the race, and consider the possibility that they might tie. Print the results of each turn, and at the end print the winner and total number of flips that were required.

PP 5.7 Design and implement an application that plays the Rock-Paper-Scissors game against the computer. When played between two people, each person picks one of three options (usually shown by a hand gesture) at the same time, and a winner is determined. In the game, Rock beats Scissors, Scissors beats Paper, and Paper beats Rock. The program should randomly choose one of the three options (without revealing it), then prompt for the user's selection. At that point, the program reveals both choices and prints a statement indicating if the user won, the computer won, or if it was a tie. Continue playing until the user chooses to stop, then print the number of user wins, losses, and ties.

PP 5.8 Design and implement an application that simulates a simple slot machine in which three numbers between 0 and 9 are randomly selected and printed side by side. Print an appropriate statement if all three of the numbers are the same, or if any two of the numbers are the same. Continue playing until the user chooses to stop.

PP 5.9 Design and implement an application that takes a paragraph of text from the user and prints the total number of words and characters present in that paragraph by properly tokenizing the words. (Hint: Spaces can be used as a delimiter for tokenization.)

PP 5.10   Modify the Die class from Chapter 4 so that the setFaceValue method does nothing if the parameter is outside of the valid range of values.

PP 5.11   Modify the Account class from Chapter 4 so that it performs validity checks on the deposit and withdraw operations. Specifically, don't allow the deposit of a negative number or a withdrawal that exceeds the current balance. Print appropriate error messages if these problems occur.

PP 5.12   Design and implement a quiz application which creates additional exercises through random number generation and validates the answer supplied by the user.

PP 5.13   Design and implement a program to process golf scores. The scores of four golfers are stored in a text file. Each line represents one hole, and the file contains 18 lines. Each line contains five values: par for the hole followed by the number of strokes each golfer used on that hole. Determine the winner and produce a table showing how well each golfer did (compared to par).

PP 5.14   Design and implement a program that compares two text input files, line by line, for equality. Print any lines that are not equivalent.

PP 5.15   Design and implement a program that counts the number of punctuation marks in a text input file. Produce a table that shows how many times each symbol occurred.

PP 5.16   Develop a simple tool for calculating basic statistics for a segment of text. The application should have a single window with a scrolling text box (a JTextArea) and a stats box. The stats box should be a panel with a titled border, containing labeled fields that display the number of words in the text box and the average word length, as well as any other statistics that you would like to add. The stats box should also contain a button that, when pressed, recomputes the statistics for the current contents of the text field.

PP 5.17   Using the PairOfDice class from PP 4.7, design and implement a class to play a game called Pig. In this game, the user competes against the computer. On each turn, the current player rolls a pair of dice and accumulates points. The goal is to reach 100 points before your opponent does. If, on any turn, the player rolls a 1, all points accumulated for that round are forfeited and control of the dice moves to the other player. If the player rolls two 1s in one turn, the player loses all points accumulated thus far in the game and loses control of the dice. The player may voluntarily turn over the dice after each roll. Therefore, the player must decide to either roll again (be a pig) and risk losing points, or relinquish control of the dice, possibly allowing the other player to win. Implement the computer player such that it always relinquishes the dice after accumulating 20 or more points in any given round.

PP 5.18 Design and implement a program which generates a 4 × 4 grid with different filled colors in it. Change the colors frequently on those grids.

SOFTWARE FAILURE

Therac-25

What Happened?

The Therac-25 was a radiation therapy machine used to deliver targeted electron or X-ray beams in order to destroy cancerous tissue. While in use, hundreds of patients were given proper treatments using this device. But in six documented cases from 1985 to 1987, the Therac-25 delivered an overdose of radiation resulting in severe disability and death.

In a typical treatment, the patient lies down and the operator adjusts the machine to target the appropriate area of the body. The operator sets the parameters of the treatment on the machine's computer console and pushes a button to deliver the radiation. Patients are told that a typical side effect is minor skin discomfort similar to that of a mild sunburn.

In the accident cases, some patients reported feeling a "tremendous force of heat" or an "electric tingling shock." In one case, the patient lost the use of her shoulder and arm and had to have her left breast removed because of the radiation damage. Several others died of radiation poisoning.

The amount of radiation delivered is measured in rads (radiation absorbed dose). A standard treatment is around 200 rads. It's estimated that the accidents caused 20,000 rads to be administered.

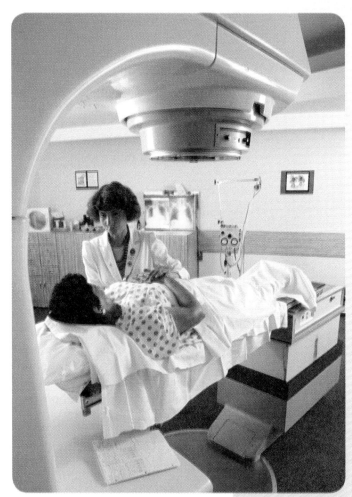

■ Radiation therapy machines deliver precise amounts of targeted radiation.

What Caused It?

The operators were told the Therac-25 had so many safety precautions that it would be "virtually impossible" to overdose a patient. But part of the software used in the Therac-25 was reused from an earlier version of the machine that had included many hardware-based safety precautions. Thus, the hardware features

293

had masked problems with the underlying software. The safety features of the Therac-25 were dominantly software-based, and the lurking problems emerged.

It turned out that if the operator mistyped a parameter and then corrected it in a particular way, the software allowed the machine to deliver the maximum radiation dose without diffusing it properly. It was such a strange error that technicians testing the machine failed to reproduce the problem. At one point, one of the machines that had clearly caused an overdose was put back into service after technicians could find nothing wrong with it.

Analysts say that the software problems were only part of the reason the accidents occurred. While there were fundamental programming errors, there was also inadequate attention to safety issues in general. And one reason the machines were used for so long was that the problems were not reported as accurately and thoroughly as they should have been.

Lessons Learned

Software safety is the dominant issue in this case. When human lives are on the line, it's difficult to imagine not doing everything possible to ensure that your software is as robust as possible. It comes down to risk analysis. How much are you willing to risk that a particular piece of software you're developing still contains an error? For many applications, a problem might cause inconvenience to the user and may have business implications, but other applications literally have people's lives at stake.

This case is also an example of the difficulty of isolating the problem. For hundreds of patients, the Therac-25 provided excellent treatment. One of the initial complaints was dismissed without proper investigation or reporting. Later, when a problem had clearly occurred, it could not be replicated. This was an example of a truly exceptional situation—one that does not occur usually or under normal circumstances.

Source: computingcases.org, IEEE Computer

More Conditionals and Loops

6

CHAPTER OBJECTIVES

- Examine conditional processing using switch statements.
- Discuss the conditional operator.
- Examine alternative repetition statements: the do and for loops.
- Draw graphics with the aid of conditionals and loops.
- Explore the use of dialog boxes.

In Chapter 5 we examined the if statement for making decisions and the while statement for looping. This chapter explores several additional statements in Java for performing similar tasks. In particular, in this chapter we'll explore the switch statement, which allows us to choose among several paths of execution based on a specific value. We'll also explore the do and for loops, which provide logical processing and/or syntax that distinguish them from the while loop. These alternative statements differ in key details, and any particular situation may lend itself to the use of one over another. The Graphics Track sections of this chapter explore the use of conditionals and loops to control our graphics and examine the purpose and use of dialog boxes.

6.1 The switch Statement

Another conditional statement in Java is called the *switch statement,* which causes the executing program to follow one of several paths based on a single value. Similar logic could be constructed with multiple if statements, but in the cases where it is warranted, a switch statement usually makes code easier to read.

The switch statement evaluates an expression to determine a value and then matches that value with one of several possible *cases.* Each case has statements associated with it. After evaluating the expression, control jumps to the statement associated with the first case that matches the value. Consider the following example:

```
switch (idChar)
{
    case 'A':
        aCount = aCount + 1;
        break;
    case 'B':
        bCount = bCount + 1;
        break;
    case 'C':
        cCount = cCount + 1;
        break;
    default:
        System.out.println ("Error in Identification Character.");
}
```

First, the expression is evaluated. In this example, the expression is a simple char variable called idChar. Execution then transfers to the first statement after the case value that matches the result of the expression. Therefore, if idChar contains an 'A', the variable aCount is incremented. If it contains a 'B', the case for 'A' is skipped and processing continues where bCount is incremented. Likewise, if idChar contains a 'C', that case is processed.

> **KEY CONCEPT**
>
> A switch statement matches a character or integer value to one of several possible cases.

If no case value matches that of the expression, execution continues with the optional *default case,* indicated by the reserved word default. If no default case exists, no statements in the switch statement are executed and processing continues with the statement after the switch statement. It is often a good idea to include a default case, even if you don't expect it to be executed.

When a break statement is encountered, processing jumps to the statement following the switch statement. A break statement is usually used to break out of each case of a switch statement. Without a break statement, processing continues into the next case of the switch. Therefore, if the break statement at the end of the 'A' case in the previous example was not there, both the aCount and bCount variables would be incremented when the idChar contains an 'A'. Usually we want to perform only one case, so a break statement is almost always used. Occasionally, though, the "pass through" feature comes in handy.

KEY CONCEPT

A break statement is usually used at the end of each case alternative of a switch statement.

You'll remember that the break statement was briefly mentioned in Chapter 5, because it could be used in other types of loops and conditionals. We warned then that such processing is usually unnecessary and its use is considered by many developers to be bad practice. The switch statement is the exception to this guideline. Using a break statement is the only way to make sure the code for only one case is executed.

The switch statement evaluates the initial Expression and matches its value with one of the cases. Processing continues with the Statement corresponding to that case. The optional default case will be executed if no other case matches.

Example:

```java
switch (numValues)
{
    case 0:
        System.out.println ("No values were entered.");
        break;
    case 1:
        System.out.println ("One value was entered.");
        break;
    case 2:
        System.out.println ("Two values were entered.");
        break;
    default:
        System.out.println ("Too many values were entered.");
}
```

The expression evaluated at the beginning of a switch statement must be of type char, byte, short, or int. In particular, it cannot be a boolean, or a floating point value, or a String. Furthermore, the value of each case must be a constant; it cannot be a variable or other expression. This limits the situations in which a switch statement is appropriate. But when it is appropriate, it usually makes the code easier to read and understand.

Note also that the implicit boolean condition of a switch statement is based on equality. The expression at the beginning of the statement is compared to each case value to determine which one it equals. A switch statement cannot be used to determine other relational operations (such as less than), unless some preliminary processing is done. For example, the GradeReport program in Listing 6.1 prints a comment based on a numeric grade that is entered by the user.

LISTING 6.1

```java
//********************************************************************
//  GradeReport.java       Author: Lewis/Loftus
//
//  Demonstrates the use of a switch statement.
//********************************************************************

import java.util.Scanner;

public class GradeReport
{
   //-----------------------------------------------------------------
   //  Reads a grade from the user and prints comments accordingly.
   //-----------------------------------------------------------------
   public static void main (String[] args)
   {
      int grade, category;

      Scanner scan = new Scanner (System.in);

      System.out.print ("Enter a numeric grade (0 to 100): ");
      grade = scan.nextInt();

      category = grade / 10;

      System.out.print ("That grade is ");

      switch (category)
      {
         case 10:
            System.out.println ("a perfect score. Well done.");
            break;
         case 9:
            System.out.println ("well above average. Excellent.");
            break;
         case 8:
            System.out.println ("above average. Nice job.");
            break;
```

LISTING 6.1   *continued*

```
        case 7:
            System.out.println ("average.");
            break;
        case 6:
            System.out.println ("below average. You should see the");
            System.out.println ("instructor to clarify the material "
                                + "presented in class.");
            break;
        default:
            System.out.println ("not passing.");
    }
  }
}
```

OUTPUT

```
Enter a numeric grade (0 to 100): 86
That grade is above average. Nice job.
```

In GradeReport, the category of the grade is determined by dividing the grade by 10 using integer division, resulting in an integer value between 0 and 10 (assuming a valid grade is entered). This result is used as the expression of the switch, which prints various messages for grades 60 or higher and a default sentence for all other values.

Note that any switch statement could be implemented as a set of nested if statements. However, nested if statements quickly become difficult for a human reader to understand and are error prone to implement and debug. But because a switch can evaluate only equality, sometimes nested if statements are necessary. It depends on the situation.

SELF-REVIEW QUESTIONS *(see answers in Appendix N)*   myprogramminglab

SR 6.1   When a Java program is running, what happens if the expression evaluated for a switch statement does not match any of the case values associated with the statement?

SR 6.2   What happens if a case in a switch statement does not end with a break statement?

SR 6.3   What is the output of the GradeReport program if the user enters "72"? What if the user enters "46"? What if the user enters "123"?

SR 6.4   Transform the following nested `if` statement into an equivalent `switch` statement.

```
if (num1 == 5)
    myChar = 'W';
else
    if (num1 == 6)
        myChar = 'X';
    else
        if (num1 == 7)
            myChar = 'Y';
        else
            myChar = 'Z';
```

6.2 The Conditional Operator

The Java *conditional operator* is similar to an `if-else` statement in some ways. It is a *ternary operator* because it requires three operands. The symbol for the conditional operator is usually written ?:, but it is not like other operators in that the two symbols that make it up are always separated. The following is an example of an expression that contains the conditional operator:

```
(total > MAX) ? total + 1 : total * 2;
```

Preceding the ? is a boolean condition. Following the ? are two expressions separated by the : symbol. The entire conditional expression returns the value of the first expression if the condition is true, and returns the value of the second expression if the condition is false.

Keep in mind that this example is an expression that returns a value. The conditional operator is just that, an operator, not a statement that stands on its own. Usually we want to do something with that value, such as assign it to a variable:

```
total = (total > MAX) ? total + 1 : total * 2;
```

The distinction between the conditional operator and a conditional statement can be subtle. In many ways, the ?: operator lets us form succinct logic that serves as an abbreviated `if-else` statement. The previous statement is functionally equivalent to, but sometimes more convenient than, the following:

```
if (total > MAX)
    total = total + 1;
else
    total = total * 2;
```

Let's look at a couple more examples. Consider the following declaration:

```
int larger = (num1 > num2) ? num1 : num2;
```

If num1 is greater than num2, the value of num1 is returned and used to initialize the variable larger. If not, the value of num2 is returned and used to initialize larger. Similarly, the following statement prints the smaller of the two values:

```
System.out.println ("Smaller: " + ((num1 < num2) ? num1 : num2));
```

The conditional operator is occasionally helpful to evaluate a short condition and return a result. It is not a replacement for an if-else statement, however, because the operands to the ?: operator are expressions, not necessarily full statements. Even when the conditional operator is a viable alternative, you should use it carefully because it may be less readable than an if-else statement.

SELF-REVIEW QUESTIONS *(see answers in Appendix N)*

myprogramminglab

SR 6.5   What is the difference between a conditional operator and a conditional statement?

SR 6.6   Write a declaration that initializes a char variable named id to 'A' if the boolean variable first is true and to 'B' otherwise.

SR 6.7   Express the following logic in a succinct manner using the conditional operator.

```
if (val <= 10)
    System.out.println ("The value is not greater than 10.");
else
    System.out.println ("The value is greater than 10.");
```

6.3 The do Statement

Remember from Chapter 5 that the while statement first examines its condition, then executes its body if that condition is true. The *do statement* is similar to the while statement except that its termination condition is at the end of the loop body. Like the while loop, the do loop executes the statement in the loop body until the condition becomes false. The condition is written at the end of the loop to indicate that it is not evaluated until the loop body is executed. Note that the body of a do loop is always executed at least once. Figure 6.1 shows this processing.

FIGURE 6.1   The logic of a do loop

The following code prints the numbers from 1 to 5 using a do loop. Compare this code with the similar example in Chapter 5 that uses a while loop to accomplish the same task.

```
int count = 0;
do
{
    count++;
    System.out.println (count);
}
while (count < 5);
```

> **KEY CONCEPT**
>
> A do statement executes its loop body at least once.

Note that the do loop begins simply with the reserved word do. The body of the do loop continues until the *while clause* that contains the boolean condition that determines whether the loop body will be executed again. Sometimes it is difficult to determine whether a line of code that begins with the reserved word while is the beginning of a while loop or the end of a do loop.

Let's look at another example of the do loop. The program called ReverseNumber, shown in Listing 6.2, reads an integer from the user and reverses its digits mathematically.

Do Statement

The do loop repeatedly executes the specified Statement as long as the boolean Expression is true. The Statement is executed at least once, then the Expression is evaluated to determine whether the Statement should be executed again.

Example:
```java
do
{
    System.out.print ("Enter a word:");
    word = scan.next();
    System.out.println (word);
}
while (!word.equals("quit"));
```

LISTING 6.2

```java
//********************************************************************
//  ReverseNumber.java       Author: Lewis/Loftus
//
//  Demonstrates the use of a do loop.
//********************************************************************

import java.util.Scanner;

public class ReverseNumber
{
    //-----------------------------------------------------------------
    //  Reverses the digits of an integer mathematically.
    //-----------------------------------------------------------------
    public static void main (String[] args)
    {
        int number, lastDigit, reverse = 0;

        Scanner scan = new Scanner (System.in);

        System.out.print ("Enter a positive integer: ");
        number = scan.nextInt();

        do
        {
            lastDigit = number % 10;
            reverse = (reverse * 10) + lastDigit;
            number = number / 10;
        }
        while (number > 0);

        System.out.println ("That number reversed is " + reverse);
    }
}
```

LISTING 6.2 *continued*

OUTPUT

```
Enter a positive integer: 2896
That number reversed is 6982
```

The do loop in the ReverseNumber program uses the remainder operation to determine the digit in the 1's position, then adds it into the reversed number, then truncates that digit from the original number using integer division. The do loop terminates when we run out of digits to process, which corresponds to the point when the variable number reaches the value zero. Carefully trace the logic of this program with a few examples to see how it works.

If you know you want to perform the body of a loop at least once, then you probably want to use a do statement. A do loop has many of the same properties as a while statement, so it must also be checked for termination conditions to avoid infinite loops.

myprogramminglab

SELF-REVIEW QUESTIONS *(see answers in Appendix N)*

SR 6.8   Compare and contrast a while loop and a do loop.

SR 6.9   What output is produced by the following code fragment?

```
int low = 0, high = 10;
do
{
    System.out.println (low);
    low++;
} while (low < high);
```

SR 6.10   What output is produced by the following code fragment?

```
int low = 10, high = 0;
do
{
    System.out.println (low);
    low++;
} while (low <= high);
```

SR 6.11   Write a do loop to obtain a sequence of positive integers from the user, using zero as a sentinel value. The program should output the sum of the numbers.

6.4 The for Statement

The while and the do statements are good to use when you don't initially know how many times you want to execute the loop body. The *for statement* is another repetition statement that is particularly well suited for executing the body of a loop a specific number of times that can be determined before the loop is executed.

The following code prints the numbers 1 through 5 using a for loop, just as we did using other loop statements in previous examples:

```
for (int count=1; count <= 5; count++)
   System.out.println (count);
```

The header of a for loop contains three parts separated by semicolons. Before the loop begins, the first part of the header, called the *initialization*, is executed. The second part of the header is the boolean condition, which is evaluated before the loop body (like the while loop). If true, the body of the loop is executed, followed by the execution of the third part of the header, which is called the *increment*. Note that the initialization part is executed only once, but the increment part is executed after each iteration of the loop. Figure 6.2 shows this processing.

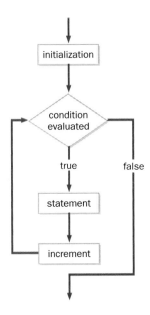

FIGURE 6.2 The logic of a for loop

VideoNote

Examples using for loops.

A for loop can be a bit tricky to read until you get used to it. The execution of the code doesn't follow a "top to bottom, left to right" reading. The increment code executes after the body of the loop even though it is in the header.

In this example, the initialization portion of the for loop header is used to declare the variable count as well as to give it an initial value. We are not required to declare a variable there, but it is common practice in situations where the variable is not needed outside of the loop. Because count is declared in the for loop header, it exists only inside the loop body and cannot be referenced elsewhere. The loop control variable is set up, checked, and modified by the actions in the loop header. It can be referenced inside the loop body, but it should not be modified except by the actions defined in the loop header.

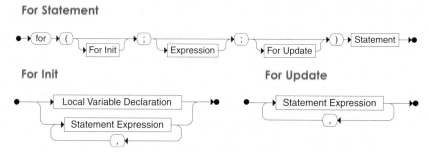

The for statement repeatedly executes the specified Statement as long as the boolean Expression is true. The For Init portion of the header is executed only once, before the loop begins. The For Update portion executes after each execution of Statement.

Examples:

```
for (int value=1; value < 25; value++)
    System.out.println (value + " squared is " + value*value);

for (int num=40; num > 0; num-=3)
    sum = sum + num;
```

The increment portion of the for loop header, despite its name, could decrement a value rather than increment it. For example, the following loop prints the integer values from 100 down to 1:

```
for (int num = 100; num > 0; num--)
    System.out.println (num);
```

In fact, the increment portion of the for loop can perform any calculation, not just a simple increment or decrement. Consider the program shown in Listing 6.3, which prints multiples of a particular value up to a particular limit.

The increment portion of the for loop in the Multiples program adds the value entered by the user after each iteration. The number of values printed per line is controlled by counting the values printed and then moving to the next line whenever count is evenly divisible by the PER_LINE constant.

LISTING 6.3

```java
//********************************************************************
//  Multiples.java         Author: Lewis/Loftus
//
//  Demonstrates the use of a for loop.
//********************************************************************

import java.util.Scanner;

public class Multiples
{
    //-----------------------------------------------------------------
    //  Prints multiples of a user-specified number up to a user-
    //  specified limit.
    //-----------------------------------------------------------------
    public static void main (String[] args)
    {
        final int PER_LINE = 5;
        int value, limit, mult, count = 0;

        Scanner scan = new Scanner (System.in);

        System.out.print ("Enter a positive value: ");
        value = scan.nextInt();

        System.out.print ("Enter an upper limit: ");
        limit = scan.nextInt();

        System.out.println ();
        System.out.println ("The multiples of " + value + " between " +
                            value + " and " + limit + " (inclusive) are:");

        for (mult = value; mult <= limit; mult += value)
        {
            System.out.print (mult + "\t");
```

LISTING 6.3   *continued*

```
    // Print a specific number of values per line of output
    count++;
    if (count % PER_LINE == 0)
        System.out.println();
    }
  }
}
```

OUTPUT

```
Enter a positive value: 7
Enter an upper limit: 400

The multiples of 7 between 7 and 400 (inclusive) are:
7       14      21      28      35
42      49      56      63      70
77      84      91      98      105
112     119     126     133     140
147     154     161     168     175
182     189     196     203     210
217     224     231     238     245
252     259     266     273     280
287     294     301     308     315
322     329     336     343     350
357     364     371     378     385
392     399
```

The Stars program in Listing 6.4 shows the use of nested for loops. The output is a triangle shape made of asterisk characters. The outer loop executes exactly 10 times. Each iteration of the outer loop prints one line of the output. The inner loop performs a different number of iterations depending on the line value controlled by the outer loop. Each iteration of the inner loop prints one star on the current line. Writing programs that print variations on this triangle configuration are included in the programming projects at the end of the chapter.

The for-each Loop

A variation of the for statement, often called the *for-each loop*, is particularly helpful in situations that involve iterators. In Chapter 5 we discussed that some

LISTING 6.4

```java
//********************************************************************
//  Stars.java         Author: Lewis/Loftus
//
//  Demonstrates the use of nested for loops.
//********************************************************************

public class Stars
{
   //-----------------------------------------------------------------
   //  Prints a triangle shape using asterisk (star) characters.
   //-----------------------------------------------------------------
   public static void main (String[] args)
   {
      final int MAX_ROWS = 10;

      for (int row = 1; row <= MAX_ROWS; row++)
      {
         for (int star = 1; star <= row; star++)
            System.out.print ("*");

         System.out.println();
      }
   }
}
```

OUTPUT

```
*
**
***
****
*****
******
*******
********
*********
**********
```

objects are considered to be iterators, which have hasNext and next methods to process each item from a group. If an object has implemented the Iterable interface, then we can use a variation of the for loop to process items using a simplified syntax.

An `ArrayList` object is an `Iterable` object. Therefore, for example, if `library` is an `ArrayList<Book>` object (that is, an `ArrayList` that manages `Book` objects), we can use a `for` loop to process each `Book` object in the collection as follows:

```
for (Book myBook : library)
    System.out.println (myBook);
```

This code can be read as follows: for each `Book` in `library`, print the book object. The variable `myBook` takes the value of each `Book` object in the collection in turn, and the body of the loop can process it appropriately. That succinct for-each loop is essentially equivalent to the following:

```
Book myBook;
while (bookList.hasNext())
{
    myBook = bookList.next();
    System.out.println (myBook);
}
```

This version of the `for` loop can also be used on arrays, which are discussed in Chapter 8. We use the for-each loop as appropriate in various situations throughout the rest of the book.

Comparing Loops

The three basic loop statements (`while`, `do`, and `for`) are functionally equivalent. Any particular loop written using one type of loop can be written using either of the other two loop types. Which type of loop we use depends on the situation.

As we mentioned earlier, the primary difference between a `while` loop and a `do` loop is when the condition is evaluated. If we know we want to execute the loop body at least once, a `do` loop is usually the better choice. The body of a `while` loop, on the other hand, might not be executed at all if the condition is initially false. Therefore, we say that the body of a `while` loop is executed zero or more times, but the body of a `do` loop is executed one or more times.

A `for` loop is like a `while` loop in that the condition is evaluated before the loop body is executed. We generally use a `for` loop when the number of times we want to iterate through a loop is fixed or can be easily calculated. In many situations, it is simply more convenient to separate the code that sets up and controls the loop iterations inside the `for` loop header from the body of the loop.

SR 6.12 When would we use a `for` loop instead of a `while` loop?

SR 6.13 What output is produced by the following code fragment?

```
int value = 0;
for (int num = 10; num <= 40; num += 10)
{
    value = value + num;
}
System.out.println (value);
```

SR 6.14 What output is produced by the following code fragment?

```
int value = 0;
for (int num = 10; num < 40; num += 10)
{
    value = value + num;
}
System.out.println (value);
```

SR 6.15 What output is produced by the following code fragment?

```
int value = 6;
for (int num = 1; num <= value; num ++)
{
    for (int i = 1; i <= (value - num); i++)
        System.out.print (" ");
    for (int i = 1; i <= ((2 * num) - 1); i++)
        System.out.print ("*");
    System.out.println ();
}
```

SR 6.16 Assume `die` is a `Die` object (as defined in Section 4.2). Write a code fragment that will roll `die` 100 times and output the average value rolled.

6.5 Drawing with Loops and Conditionals

Conditionals and loops greatly enhance our ability to generate interesting graphics.

The `Bullseye` program shown in Listing 6.5 draws a target. The drawing actually occurs in the `BullseyePanel` class, shown in Listing 6.6. The `paintComponent`
of the `BullseyePanel` class uses an `if` statement to alternate the colors between
black and white.

Note that each ring is actually drawn as a filled circle (an oval of equal width
and length). Because we draw the circles on top of each other, the inner circles

LISTING 6.5

```java
//********************************************************************
//  Bullseye.java       Author: Lewis/Loftus
//
//  Demonstrates the use of loops to draw.
//********************************************************************

import javax.swing.JFrame;

public class Bullseye
{
   //-----------------------------------------------------------------
   //  Creates the main frame of the program.
   //-----------------------------------------------------------------
   public static void main (String[] args)
   {
      JFrame frame = new JFrame ("Bullseye");
      frame.setDefaultCloseOperation (JFrame.EXIT_ON_CLOSE);

      BullseyePanel panel = new BullseyePanel();

      frame.getContentPane().add(panel);
      frame.pack();
      frame.setVisible(true);
   }
}
```

DISPLAY

LISTING 6.6

```java
//********************************************************************
//  BullseyePanel.java       Author: Lewis/Loftus
//
//  Demonstrates the use of conditionals and loops to guide drawing.
//********************************************************************

import javax.swing.JPanel;
import java.awt.*;

public class BullseyePanel extends JPanel
{
   private final int MAX_WIDTH = 300, NUM_RINGS = 5, RING_WIDTH = 25;

   //-----------------------------------------------------------------
   //  Sets up the bullseye panel.
   //-----------------------------------------------------------------
   public BullseyePanel ()
   {
      setBackground (Color.cyan);
      setPreferredSize (new Dimension(300,300));
   }

   //-----------------------------------------------------------------
   //  Paints a bullseye target.
   //-----------------------------------------------------------------
   public void paintComponent (Graphics page)
   {
      super.paintComponent (page);

      int x = 0, y = 0, diameter = MAX_WIDTH;

      page.setColor (Color.white);

      for (int count = 0; count < NUM_RINGS; count++)
      {
         if (page.getColor() == Color.black)  //  alternate colors
            page.setColor (Color.white);
         else
            page.setColor (Color.black);

         page.fillOval (x, y, diameter, diameter);
```

LISTING 6.6   *continued*

```
        diameter -= (2 * RING_WIDTH);
        x += RING_WIDTH;
        y += RING_WIDTH;
    }

    // Draw the red bullseye in the center
    page.setColor (Color.red);
    page.fillOval (x, y, diameter, diameter);
    }
}
```

cover the inner part of the larger circles, creating the ring effect. At the end, a final red circle is drawn for the bull's-eye.

Let's look at another example. Listing 6.7 shows the Boxes class, which instantiates and displays BoxesPanel, shown in Listing 6.8. The purpose of this program is to draw several randomly sized rectangles in random locations. If the width of a rectangle is below a certain thickness (5 pixels), the box is filled with the color yellow. If the height is less than the same minimal thickness, the box is filled with the color green. Otherwise, the box is drawn, unfilled, in white.

LISTING 6.7

```
//********************************************************************
//  Boxes.java       Author: Lewis/Loftus
//
//  Demonstrates the use of loops to draw.
//********************************************************************

import javax.swing.JFrame;

public class Boxes
{
    //-----------------------------------------------------------------
    //  Creates the main frame of the program.
    //-----------------------------------------------------------------
    public static void main (String[] args)
    {
        JFrame frame = new JFrame ("Boxes");
        frame.setDefaultCloseOperation (JFrame.EXIT_ON_CLOSE);
```

LISTING 6.7   *continued*

```java
    BoxesPanel panel = new BoxesPanel();

    frame.getContentPane().add(panel);
    frame.pack();
    frame.setVisible(true);
    }
}
```

DISPLAY

LISTING 6.8

```java
//********************************************************************
//  BoxesPanel.java        Author: Lewis/Loftus
//
//  Demonstrates the use of conditionals and loops to guide drawing.
//********************************************************************

import javax.swing.JPanel;
import java.awt.*;
import java.util.Random;
```

LISTING 6.8 *continued*

```java
public class BoxesPanel extends JPanel
{
    private final int NUM_BOXES = 50, THICKNESS = 5, MAX_SIDE = 50;
    private final int MAX_X = 350, MAX_Y = 250;
    private Random generator;

    //-----------------------------------------------------------------
    //  Sets up the drawing panel.
    //-----------------------------------------------------------------
    public BoxesPanel ()
    {
        generator = new Random();

        setBackground (Color.black);
        setPreferredSize (new Dimension(400, 300));
    }

    //-----------------------------------------------------------------
    //  Paints boxes of random width and height in a random location.
    //  Narrow or short boxes are highlighted with a fill color.
    //-----------------------------------------------------------------
    public void paintComponent(Graphics page)
    {
        super.paintComponent (page);

        int x, y, width, height;

        for (int count = 0; count < NUM_BOXES; count++)
        {
            x = generator.nextInt(MAX_X) + 1;
            y = generator.nextInt(MAX_Y) + 1;

            width = generator.nextInt(MAX_SIDE) + 1;
            height = generator.nextInt(MAX_SIDE) + 1;

            if (width <= THICKNESS) // check for narrow box
            {
                page.setColor (Color.yellow);
                page.fillRect (x, y, width, height);
            }
            else
                if (height <= THICKNESS) // check for short box
                {
```

LISTING 6.8   *continued*

```
            page.setColor (Color.green);
            page.fillRect (x, y, width, height);
        }
        else
        {
            page.setColor (Color.white);
            page.drawRect (x, y, width, height);
        }
    }
  }
}
```

6.6 Dialog Boxes

A component called a dialog box can be helpful to assist in GUI processing. A *dialog box* is a graphical window that pops up on top of any currently active window so that the user can interact with it. A dialog box can serve a variety of purposes, such as conveying some information, confirming an action, or allowing the user to enter some information. Usually a dialog box has a solitary purpose, and the user's interaction with it is brief.

> **KEY CONCEPT**
>
> A dialog box is a pop-up window that allows brief, specific user interaction to provide information or verify an action.

The Swing package of the Java class library contains a class called JOptionPane that simplifies the creation and use of basic dialog boxes. Figure 6.3 lists some of the methods of JOptionPane.

---

static String showInputDialog (Object msg)
   Displays a dialog box containing the specified message and an input text field. The contents of the text field are returned.

static int showConfirmDialog (Component parent, Object msg)
   Displays a dialog box containing the specified message and Yes/No button options. If the parent component is null, the box is centered on the screen.

static void showMessageDialog (Component parent, Object msg)
   Displays a dialog box containing the specified message. If the parent component is null, the box is centered on the screen.

FIGURE 6.3   Some methods of the JOptionPane class

4

The basic formats for a `JOptionPane` dialog box fall into three categories. A *message dialog box* simply displays an output string. An *input dialog box* presents a prompt and a single input text field into which the user can enter one string of data. A *confirm dialog box* presents the user with a simple yes-or-no question.

Let's look at a program that uses each of these types of dialog boxes. Listing 6.9 shows a program that first presents the user with an input dialog box that requests the user to enter an integer. After the user presses the OK button on the input dialog box, a second dialog box (this time a message dialog box) appears, informing the user whether the number entered was even or odd. After the user dismisses that box, a third dialog box appears, to determine whether the user would like to test another number. If the user presses the button labeled Yes, the series of dialog boxes repeats. Otherwise the program terminates.

LISTING 6.9

```java
//********************************************************************
//  EvenOdd.java        Author: Lewis/Loftus
//
//  Demonstrates the use of the JOptionPane class.
//********************************************************************

import javax.swing.JOptionPane;

public class EvenOdd
{
   //-----------------------------------------------------------------
   // Determines if the value input by the user is even or odd.
   // Uses multiple dialog boxes for user interaction.
   //-----------------------------------------------------------------
   public static void main (String[] args)
   {
      String numStr, result;
      int num, again;

      do
      {
         numStr = JOptionPane.showInputDialog ("Enter an integer: ");
         num = Integer.parseInt(numStr);

         result = "That number is " + ((num%2 == 0) ? "even" : "odd");

         JOptionPane.showMessageDialog (null, result);
         again = JOptionPane.showConfirmDialog (null, "Do Another?");
      }
      while (again == JOptionPane.YES_OPTION);
```

LISTING 6.9   *continued*

```
    }
}
```

DISPLAY

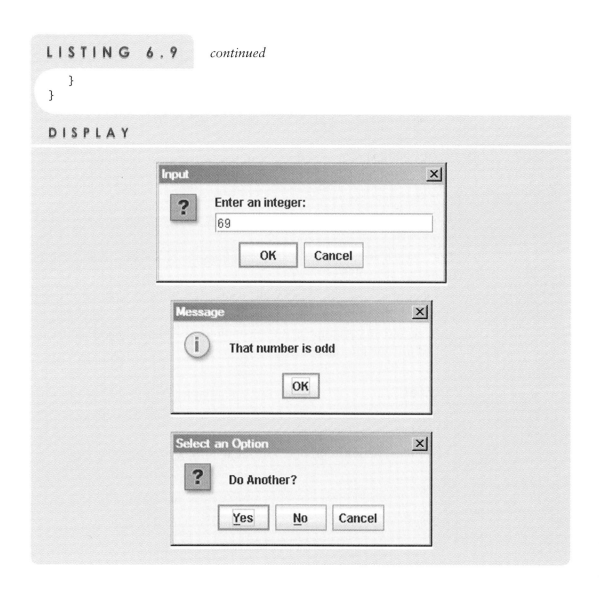

The first parameter to the `showMessageDialog` and the `showConfirmDialog` methods specifies the governing parent component for the dialog box. Using a `null` reference as this parameter causes the dialog box to appear centered on the screen.

Many of the `JOptionPane` methods allow the programmer to tailor the contents of the dialog box. Furthermore, the `showOptionDialog` method can be used to create dialog boxes that combine characteristics of the three basic formats for more elaborate interactions.

Summary of Key Concepts

- A `switch` statement matches a character or integer value to one of several possible cases.
- A `break` statement is usually used at the end of each case alternative of a `switch` statement.
- The conditional operator evaluates to one of two possible values based on a boolean condition.
- A `do` statement executes its loop body at least once.
- A `for` statement is usually used when a loop will be executed a set number of times.
- The for-each version of a `for` loop simplifies the processing of all elements in an `Iterable` object.
- The loop statements are functionally equivalent. Which one you use should depend on the situation.
- A dialog box is a pop-up window that allows brief, specific user interaction to provide information or verify an action.

Exercises

myprogramminglab

Visit www.myprogramminglab.com to complete many of these Exercises online and get instant feedback.

EX 6.1 What output is produced by the following code fragment?

```
for (int num = 0; num <= 200; num += 2)
    System.out.println (num);
```

EX 6.2 What output is produced by the following code fragment?

```
for (int val = 200; val >= 0; val -= 1)
    if (val % 4 != 0)
        System.out.println (val);
```

EX 6.3 Transform the following `while` loop into an equivalent `do` loop (make sure it produces the same output).

```
int num = 1;
while (num < 20)
{
    num++;
    System.out.println (num);
}
```

EX 6.4   Transform the `while` loop from the previous exercise into an equivalent `for` loop (make sure it produces the same output).

EX 6.5   Write a `do` loop that verifies that the user enters an even integer value.

EX 6.6   Write a `for` loop to print the odd numbers from 1 to 99 (inclusive).

EX 6.7   Write a `for` loop to print the multiples of 3 from 300 down to 3.

EX 6.8   Write a code fragment that reads 10 integer values from the user and prints the highest value entered.

EX 6.9   Write a code fragment that determines and prints the number of times the character 'a' appears in a `String` object called `name`.

EX 6.10 Write a code fragment that prints the characters stored in a `String` object called `str` backward.

EX 6.11 Write a code fragment that prints every other character in a `String` object called `word` starting with the first character.

EX 6.12 Write a method called `powersOfTwo` that prints the first 10 powers of 2 (starting with 2). The method takes no parameters and doesn't return anything.

EX 6.13 Write a method called `alarm` that prints the string `"Alarm!"` multiple times on separate lines. The method should accept an integer parameter that specifies how many times the string is printed. Print an error message if the parameter is less than 1.

EX 6.14 Write a method called `sum100` that returns the sum of the integers from 1 to 100, inclusive.

EX 6.15 Write a method called `sumRange` that accepts two integer parameters that represent a range. Issue an error message and return zero if the second parameter is less than the first. Otherwise, the method should return the sum of the integers in that range (inclusive).

EX 6.16 Write a method called `countA` that accepts a `String` parameter and returns the number of times the character 'A' is found in the string.

EX 6.17 Write a method called `reverse` that accepts a `String` parameter and returns a string that contains the characters of the parameter in reverse order. Note that there is a method in the `String` class that performs this operation, but for the sake of this exercise, you are expected to write your own.

Programming Projects

Visit www.myprogramminglab.com to complete many of these Programming Projects online and get instant feedback.

PP 6.1   Design and implement an application that reads an integer value and prints the sum of all even integers between 2 and the input value, inclusive. Print an error message if the input value is less than 2. Prompt accordingly.

PP 6.2   Design and implement an application that reads a string from the user and prints it one character per line.

VideoNote

Developing a solution of PP 6.2

PP 6.3   Design and implement an application that produces a multiplication table, showing the results of multiplying the integers 1 through 12 by themselves.

PP 6.4   Design and implement an application that prints the first few verses of the traveling song "One Hundred Bottles of Beer." Use a loop such that each iteration prints one verse. Read the number of verses to print from the user. Validate the input. The following are the first two verses of the song:

> 100 bottles of beer on the wall
> 100 bottles of beer
> If one of those bottles should happen to fall
> 99 bottles of beer on the wall
>
> 99 bottles of beer on the wall
> 99 bottles of beer
> If one of those bottles should happen to fall
> 98 bottles of beer on the wall

PP 6.5   Using the PairOfDice class from PP 4.7, design and implement an application that rolls a pair of dice 1000 times, counting the number of box cars (two sixes) that occur.

PP 6.6   Using the Coin class defined in this chapter, design and implement a driver class called CountFlips whose main method flips a coin 100 times and counts how many times each side comes up. Print the results.

PP 6.7   Create modified versions of the Stars program to print the following patterns. Create a separate program to produce each pattern. *Hint:* Parts b, c, and d require several loops, some of which print a specific number of spaces.

```
a. **********   b.           *   c. **********   d.          *
   *********                **      *********              ***
   ********                ***      ********              *****
   *******                ****      *******              *******
   ******                *****      ******              *********
   *****                ******      *****              **********
   ****                *******      ****              *******
   ***                ********      ***              *****
   **                *********      **              ***
   *                **********      *              *
```

PP 6.8   Design and implement an application that prints a table show-
           ing a subset of the Unicode characters and their numeric values.
           Print five number/character pairs per line, separated by tab
           characters. Print the table for numeric values from 32 (the space
           character) to 126 (the ~ character), which corresponds to the
           printable ASCII subset of the Unicode character set. Compare
           your output to the table in Appendix C. Unlike the table in
           Appendix C, the values in your table can increase as they go
           across a row.

PP 6.9   Design and implement an application that reads a string from
           the user, then determines and prints how many of each lowercase
           vowel (a, e, i, o, and u) appear in the entire string. Have a sepa-
           rate counter for each vowel. Also count and print the number of
           nonvowel characters.

PP 6.10   Design and implement an application that prints the verses of the
           song "The Twelve Days of Christmas," in which each verse adds
           one line. The first two verses of the song are:

               On the 1st day of Christmas my true love gave to me
               A partridge in a pear tree.
               On the 2nd day of Christmas my true love gave to me
               Two turtle doves, and
               A partridge in a pear tree.

           Use a switch statement in a loop to control which lines get
           printed. *Hint:* Order the cases carefully and avoid the break
           statement. Use a separate switch statement to put the appropri-
           ate suffix on the day number (1st, 2nd, 3rd, etc.). The final verse
           of the song involves all 12 days, as follows:

               On the 12th day of Christmas, my true love gave to me
               Twelve drummers drumming,
               Eleven pipers piping,

> Ten lords a-leaping,
> Nine ladies dancing,
> Eight maids a-milking,
> Seven swans a-swimming,
> Six geese a-laying,
> Five golden rings,
> Four calling birds,
> Three French hens,
> Two turtle doves, and
> A partridge in a pear tree.

PP 6.11 Design and implement a program that draws 20 horizontal, evenly spaced parallel lines of random length.

PP 6.12 Design and implement a program that draws the side view of stair steps from the lower left to the upper right.

PP 6.13 Design and implement a program that draws 100 circles of random color and random diameter in random locations. Ensure that in each case the entire circle appears in the visible area of the applet.

PP 6.14 Design and implement a program that draws 10 concentric circles of random radius.

PP 6.15 Design and implement a program that draws a brick wall pattern in which each row of bricks is offset from the row above and below it.

PP 6.16 Design and implement a program that draws a quilt in which a simple pattern is repeated in a grid of squares.

PP 6.17 Modify the previous problem such that it draws a quilt using a separate class called Pattern that represents a particular pattern. Allow the constructor of the Pattern class to vary some characteristics of the pattern, such as its color scheme. Instantiate two separate Pattern objects and incorporate them in a checkerboard layout in the quilt.

PP 6.18 Design and implement a program that draws a simple fence with vertical, equally spaced slats backed by two horizontal support boards. Behind the fence show a simple house in the background. Make sure the house is visible between the slats in the fence.

PP 6.19 Design and implement a program that draws a rainbow. Use tightly spaced concentric arcs to draw each part of the rainbow in a particular color.

PP 6.20 Design and implement a program that draws 20,000 points in random locations within the visible area. Make the points on the left half of the panel appear in red and the points on the right half of the panel appear in green. Draw each point by drawing a line with a length of only one pixel.

PP 6.21 Design and implement a program that draws 10 circles of random radius in random locations. Fill in the largest circle in red.

PP 6.22 Design and implement an application that uses dialog boxes to obtain two integer values (one dialog box for each value) and display the sum and product of the values. Use another dialog box to see whether the user wants to process another pair of values.

PP 6.23 Redesign and implement a version of the `PalindromeTester` program so that it uses dialog boxes to obtain the input string, display the results, and prompt to continue.

PP 6.24 Design and implement a class called `Card` that represents a standard playing card. Each card has a suit and a face value. Create a program that deals five random cards.

Object-Oriented Design

7

CHAPTER OBJECTIVES

- Establish key issues related to the design of object-oriented software.

- Explore techniques for identifying the classes and objects needed in a program.

- Discuss the relationships among classes.

- Describe the effect of the `static` modifier on methods and data.

- Discuss the creation of a formal object interface.

- Further explore the definition of enumerated type classes.

- Discuss issues related to the design of methods, including method overloading.

- Explore issues related to the design of graphical user interfaces, including layout managers.

This chapter extends our discussion of the design of object-oriented software. We first focus on the stages of software development and the process of identifying classes and objects in the problem domain. We then discuss various issues that affect the design of a class, including static members, class relationships, interfaces, and enumerated types. We also explore design issues at the method level and introduce the concept of method overloading. A discussion of testing strategies rounds out these issues. In the Graphics Track sections of this chapter we focus on GUI design concepts, including layout managers and containment hierarchies.

7.1 Software Development Activities

Creating software involves much more than just writing code. As the problems you tackle get bigger, and the solutions include more classes, it becomes crucial to carefully think through the design of the software. Any proper software development effort consists of four basic *development activities*:

- establishing the requirements
- creating a design
- implementing the design
- testing

It would be nice if these activities, in this order, defined a step-by-step approach for developing software. However, although they may seem to be sequential, they are almost never completely linear in reality. They overlap and interact. Let's discuss each development activity briefly.

Software requirements specify *what* a program must accomplish. They indicate the tasks that a program should perform, not how it performs them. Often requirements are expressed in a document called a *functional specification*.

We discussed in Chapter 1 the basic premise that programming is really about problem solving; we create a program to solve a particular problem. Requirements are the clear expression of that problem. Until we truly know what problem we are trying to solve, we can't actually solve it.

The person or group who wants a software product developed (the *client*) will often provide an initial set of requirements. However, these initial requirements are often incomplete, ambiguous, and perhaps even contradictory. The software developer must work with the client to refine the requirements until all key decisions about what the system will do have been addressed.

Requirements often address user interface issues such as output format, screen layouts, and graphical interface components. Essentially, the requirements establish the characteristics that make the program useful for the end user. They may also apply constraints to your program, such as how fast a task must be performed.

A *software design* indicates *how* a program will accomplish its requirements. The design specifies the classes and objects needed in a program and defines how they interact. It also specifies the relationships among the classes. Low-level design issues deal with how individual methods accomplish their tasks.

A civil engineer would never consider building a bridge without designing it first. The design of software is no less essential. Many problems that occur in software are directly attributable to a lack of good design effort. It has been shown time and again that the effort spent on the design of a program is well worth it, saving both time and money in the long run.

During software design, alternatives need to be considered and explored. Often, the first attempt at a design is not the best solution. Fortunately, changes are relatively easy to make during the design stage.

KEY CONCEPT
The effort put into design is both crucial and cost-effective.

Implementation is the process of writing the source code that will solve the problem. More precisely, implementation is the act of translating the design into a particular programming language. Too many programmers focus on implementation exclusively when actually it should be the least creative of all development activities. The important decisions should be made when establishing the requirements and creating the design.

Testing is the act of ensuring that a program will solve the intended problem given all of the constraints under which it must perform. Testing includes running a program multiple times with various inputs and carefully scrutinizing the results. But it means far more than that. We revisit the issues related to testing in Section 7.9.

SELF-REVIEW QUESTIONS *(see answers in Appendix N)*

myprogramminglab

SR 7.1   Name the four basic activities that are involved in a software development process.

SR 7.2   Who creates/specifies software requirements, the client or the developer? Discuss.

SR 7.3   Compare and contrast the four basic development activities presented in this section with the five general problem-solving steps presented in Section 1.6.

7.2 Identifying Classes and Objects

A fundamental part of object-oriented software design is determining the classes that will contribute to the program. We have to carefully consider how we want to represent the various elements that make up the overall solution. These classes determine the objects that we will manage in the system.

One way to identify potential classes is to identify the objects discussed in the program requirements. Objects are generally nouns. You literally may want to scrutinize a problem description, or a functional specification if available, to identify the nouns found in it. For example, Figure 7.1 shows part of a problem description with the nouns circled.

Of course, not every noun in the problem specification will correspond to a class in your program. This activity is just a starting point that allows you to think about the types of objects a program will manage.

KEY CONCEPT
The nouns in a problem description may indicate some of the classes and objects needed in a program.

> The (user) must be allowed to specify each (product) by its primary (characteristics,) including its (name) and (product number.) If the (bar code) does not match the (product,) then an (error) should be generated to the (message window) and entered into the (error log.) The (summary report) of all (transactions) must be structured as specified in section 7.A.

FIGURE 7.1 A partial problem description with the nouns circled

Remember that a class represents a group of objects with similar behavior. A plural noun in the specification, such as products, may indicate the need for a class that represents one of those items, such as Product. Even if there is only one of a particular kind of object needed in your system, it may best be represented as a class.

Classes that represent objects should generally be given names that are singular nouns, such as Coin, Student, and Message. A class represents a single item from which we are free to create as many instances as we choose.

Another key decision is whether to represent something as an object or as a primitive attribute of another object. For example, we may initially think that an employee's salary should be represented as an integer, and that may work for much of the system's processing. But upon further reflection we might realize that the salary is based on the person's rank, which has upper and lower salary bounds that must be managed with care. Therefore the final conclusion may be that we'd be better off representing all of that data and the associated behavior as a separate class.

Given the needs of a particular program, we want to strike a good balance between classes that are too general and those that are too specific. For example, it may complicate our design unnecessarily to create a separate class for each type of appliance that exists in a house. It may be sufficient to have a single Appliance class, with perhaps a piece of instance data that indicates what type of appliance it is. Then again, it may not. It all depends on what the software is intended to accomplish.

In addition to classes that represent objects from the problem domain, we likely will need classes that support the work necessary to get the job done. For example, in addition to Member objects, we may want a separate class to help us manage all of the members of a club.

Keep in mind that when producing a real system, some of the classes we identify during design may already exist. Even if nothing matches exactly, there may be an old class that's similar enough to serve as the basis for our new class. The existing class may be part of the Java standard class library, part of a solution to a problem we've solved previously, or part of a library that can be bought from a third party. These are all examples of software reuse.

Assigning Responsibilities

Part of the process of identifying the classes needed in a program is the process of assigning responsibilities to each class. Each class represents an object with certain behaviors that are defined by the methods of the class. Any activity that the program must accomplish must be represented somewhere in the behaviors of the classes. That is, each class is responsible for carrying out certain activities, and those responsibilities must be assigned as part of designing a program.

The behaviors of a class perform actions that make up the functionality of a program. Thus we generally use verbs for the names of behaviors and the methods that accomplish them.

Sometimes it is challenging to determine which is the best class to carry out a particular responsibility. Consider multiple possibilities. Sometimes such analysis makes you realize that you could benefit from defining another class to shoulder the responsibility.

It's not necessary in the early stages of a design to identify all the methods that a class will contain. It is often sufficient to assign primary responsibilities and consider how those responsibilities translate to particular methods.

SELF-REVIEW QUESTIONS *(see answers in Appendix N)*

SR 7.4   How can identifying the nouns in a problem specification help you design an object-oriented solution to the problem?

SR 7.5   Is it important to identify and define all of the methods that a class will contain during the early stages of problem solution design? Discuss.

7.3 Static Class Members

We've used static methods in various situations in previous examples in the book. For example, all the methods of the Math class are static. Recall that a static method is one that is invoked through its class name, instead of through an object of that class.

Not only can methods be static, but variables can be static as well. We declare static class members using the static modifier.

VideoNote

Exploring the static modifier.

Deciding whether to declare a method or variable as static is a key step in class design. Let's examine the implications of static variables and methods more closely.

Static Variables

So far, we've seen two categories of variables: local variables that are declared inside a method, and instance variables that are declared in a class but not inside a method. The term *instance variable* is used, because each instance of the class has its own version of the variable. That is, each object has distinct memory space for each variable so that each object can have a distinct value for that variable.

> **KEY CONCEPT**
>
> A static variable is shared among all instances of a class.

A *static variable*, which is sometimes called a *class variable*, is shared among all instances of a class. There is only one copy of a static variable for all objects of the class. Therefore, changing the value of a static variable in one object changes it for all of the others. The reserved word static is used as a modifier to declare a static variable as follows:

```
private static int count = 0;
```

Memory space for a static variable is established when the class that contains it is referenced for the first time in a program. A local variable declared within a method cannot be static.

Constants, which are declared using the final modifier, are often declared using the static modifier. Because the value of constants cannot be changed, there might as well be only one copy of the value across all objects of the class.

Static Methods

In Chapter 3 we briefly introduced the concept of a *static method* (also called a *class method*). Static methods can be invoked through the class name. We don't have to instantiate an object of the class in order to invoke the method. In Chapter 3 we noted that all the methods of the Math class are static methods. For example, in the following line of code the sqrt method is invoked through the Math class name:

```
System.out.println ("Square root of 27: " + Math.sqrt(27));
```

The methods in the Math class perform basic computations based on values passed as parameters. There is no object state to maintain in these situations; therefore, there is no good reason to create an object in order to request these services.

A method is made static by using the static modifier in the method declaration. As we've seen many times, the main method of a Java program must be declared with the static modifier; this is done so that main can be executed by the interpreter without instantiating an object from the class that contains main.

Because static methods do not operate in the context of a particular object, they cannot reference instance variables, which exist only in an instance of a class. The compiler will issue an error if a static method attempts to use a nonstatic variable. A static method can, however, reference static variables, because static variables exist independent of specific objects. Therefore, the main method can access only static or local variables.

The program in Listing 7.1 instantiates several objects of the Slogan class, printing each one out in turn. At the end of the program it invokes a method called getCount through the class name, which returns the number of Slogan objects that were instantiated in the program.

LISTING 7.1

```
//********************************************************************
//  SloganCounter.java       Author: Lewis/Loftus
//
//  Demonstrates the use of the static modifier.
//********************************************************************

public class SloganCounter
{
    //-----------------------------------------------------------------
    //  Creates several Slogan objects and prints the number of
    //  objects that were created.
    //-----------------------------------------------------------------
    public static void main (String[] args)
    {
        Slogan obj;

        obj = new Slogan ("Remember the Alamo.");
        System.out.println (obj);

        obj = new Slogan ("Don't Worry. Be Happy.");
        System.out.println (obj);

        obj = new Slogan ("Live Free or Die.");
        System.out.println (obj);

        obj = new Slogan ("Talk is Cheap.");
        System.out.println (obj);

        obj = new Slogan ("Write Once, Run Anywhere.");
        System.out.println (obj);
```

LISTING 7.1 *continued*

```
    System.out.println();
    System.out.println ("Slogans created: " + Slogan.getCount());
  }
}
```

OUTPUT

```
Remember the Alamo.
Don't Worry. Be Happy.
Live Free or Die.
Talk is Cheap.
Write Once, Run Anywhere.

Slogans created: 5
```

Listing 7.2 shows the Slogan class. The constructor of Slogan increments a static variable called count, which is initialized to zero when it is declared. Therefore, count serves to keep track of the number of instances of Slogan that are created.

The getCount method of Slogan is also declared as static, which allows it to be invoked through the class name in the main method. Note that the only data referenced in the getCount method is the integer variable count, which is static. As a static method, getCount cannot reference any nonstatic data.

The getCount method could have been declared without the static modifier, but then its invocation in the main method would have to have been done through an instance of the Slogan class instead of the class itself.

LISTING 7.2

```
//********************************************************************
//  Slogan.java          Author: Lewis/Loftus
//
//  Represents a single slogan string.
//********************************************************************

public class Slogan
{
   private String phrase;
   private static int count = 0;
```

LISTING 7.2   *continued*

```java
//-----------------------------------------------------------------
//  Constructor: Sets up the slogan and counts the number of
//  instances created.
//-----------------------------------------------------------------
public Slogan (String str)
{
   phrase = str;
   count++;
}

//-----------------------------------------------------------------
//  Returns this slogan as a string.
//-----------------------------------------------------------------
public String toString()
{
   return phrase;
}

//-----------------------------------------------------------------
//  Returns the number of instances of this class that have been
//  created.
//-----------------------------------------------------------------
public static int getCount ()
{
   return count;
}
}
```

SELF-REVIEW QUESTIONS *(see answers in Appendix N)*   myprogramminglab

SR 7.6   What is the difference between a static variable and an instance variable?

SR 7.7   Assume you are defining a BankAccount class whose objects each represent a separate bank account. Write a declaration for a variable of the class that will hold the combined total balance of all the bank accounts represented by the class.

SR 7.8   Assume you are defining a BankAccount class whose objects each represent a separate bank account. Write a declaration for a variable of the class that will hold the minimum balance that each account must maintain.

SR 7.9   What kinds of variables can the main method of any program reference? Why?

7.4 Class Relationships

The classes in a software system have various types of relationships to each other. Three of the more common relationships are dependency, aggregation, and inheritance.

We've seen dependency relationships in many examples in which one class "uses" another. This section revisits the dependency relationship and explores the situation where a class depends on itself. We then explore aggregation, in which the objects of one class contain objects of another, creating a "has-a" relationship. Inheritance, which we introduced in Chapter 1, creates an "is-a" relationship between classes. We defer our detailed examination of inheritance until Chapter 8.

Dependency

In many previous examples, we've seen the idea of one class being dependent on another. This means that one class relies on another in some sense. Often the methods of one class will invoke the methods of the other class. This establishes a "uses" relationship.

Generally, if class A uses class B, then one or more methods of class A invoke one or more methods of class B. If an invoked method is static, then A merely references B by name. If the invoked method is not static, then A must have access to a specific instance of class B in order to invoke the method. That is, A must have a reference to an object of class B.

The way in which one object gains access to an object of another class is an important design decision. It occurs when one class instantiates the objects of another, but that's often the basis of an aggregation relationship. The access can also be accomplished by passing one object to another as a method parameter.

In general, we want to minimize the number of dependencies among classes. The less dependent our classes are on each other, the less impact changes and errors will have on the system.

Dependencies Among Objects of the Same Class

In some cases, a class depends on itself. That is, an object of one class interacts with another object of the same class. To accomplish this, a method of the class may accept as a parameter an object of the same class. Designing such a class drives home the idea that a class represents a particular object.

The concat method of the String class is an example of this situation. The method is executed through one String object and is passed another String object as a parameter. For example:

```
str3 = str1.concat(str2);
```

The String object executing the method (str1) appends its characters to those of the String passed as a parameter (str2). A new String object is returned as a result and stored as str3.

The RationalTester program shown in Listing 7.3 demonstrates a similar situation. A rational number is a value that can be represented as a ratio of two integers (a fraction). The RationalTester program creates two objects representing rational numbers and then performs various operations on them to produce new rational numbers.

LISTING 7.3

```java
//********************************************************************
//  RationalTester.java        Author: Lewis/Loftus
//
//  Driver to exercise the use of multiple Rational objects.
//********************************************************************

public class RationalTester
{
    //-----------------------------------------------------------------
    //  Creates some rational number objects and performs various
    //  operations on them.
    //-----------------------------------------------------------------
    public static void main (String[] args)
    {
        RationalNumber r1 = new RationalNumber (6, 8);
        RationalNumber r2 = new RationalNumber (1, 3);
        RationalNumber r3, r4, r5, r6, r7;

        System.out.println ("First rational number: " + r1);
        System.out.println ("Second rational number: " + r2);

        if (r1.isLike(r2))
            System.out.println ("r1 and r2 are equal.");
        else
            System.out.println ("r1 and r2 are NOT equal.");

        r3 = r1.reciprocal();
        System.out.println ("The reciprocal of r1 is: " + r3);
```

LISTING 7.3 *continued*

```
        r4 = r1.add(r2);
        r5 = r1.subtract(r2);
        r6 = r1.multiply(r2);
        r7 = r1.divide(r2);

        System.out.println ("r1 + r2: " + r4);
        System.out.println ("r1 - r2: " + r5);
        System.out.println ("r1 * r2: " + r6);
        System.out.println ("r1 / r2: " + r7);
    }
}
```

OUTPUT

```
First rational number: 3/4
Second rational number: 1/3
r1 and r2 are NOT equal.
The reciprocal of r1 is: 4/3
r1 + r2: 13/12
r1 - r2: 5/12
r1 * r2: 1/4
r1 / r2: 9/4
```

The RationalNumber class is shown in Listing 7.4. Keep in mind as you examine this class that each object created from the RationalNumber class represents a single rational number. The RationalNumber class contains various operations on rational numbers, such as addition and subtraction.

LISTING 7.4

```
//********************************************************************
//  RationalNumber.java       Author: Lewis/Loftus
//
//  Represents one rational number with a numerator and denominator.
//********************************************************************

public class RationalNumber
{
    private int numerator, denominator;
```

LISTING 7.4   *continued*

```java
//---------------------------------------------------------------
//  Constructor: Sets up the rational number by ensuring a nonzero
//  denominator and making only the numerator signed.
//---------------------------------------------------------------
public RationalNumber (int numer, int denom)
{
    if (denom == 0)
        denom = 1;

    //  Make the numerator "store" the sign
    if (denom < 0)
    {
        numer = numer * -1;
        denom = denom * -1;
    }

    numerator = numer;
    denominator = denom;

    reduce();
}

//---------------------------------------------------------------
//  Returns the numerator of this rational number.
//---------------------------------------------------------------
public int getNumerator ()
{
    return numerator;
}

//---------------------------------------------------------------
//  Returns the denominator of this rational number.
//---------------------------------------------------------------
public int getDenominator ()
{
    return denominator;
}

//---------------------------------------------------------------
//  Returns the reciprocal of this rational number.
//---------------------------------------------------------------
public RationalNumber reciprocal ()
{
    return new RationalNumber (denominator, numerator);
}
```

LISTING 7.4   *continued*

```
//-----------------------------------------------------------
//   Adds this rational number to the one passed as a parameter.
//   A common denominator is found by multiplying the individual
//   denominators.
//-----------------------------------------------------------
public RationalNumber add (RationalNumber op2)
{
    int commonDenominator = denominator * op2.getDenominator();
    int numerator1 = numerator * op2.getDenominator();
    int numerator2 = op2.getNumerator() * denominator;
    int sum = numerator1 + numerator2;

    return new RationalNumber (sum, commonDenominator);
}


//-----------------------------------------------------------
//   Subtracts the rational number passed as a parameter from this
//   rational number.
//-----------------------------------------------------------
public RationalNumber subtract (RationalNumber op2)
{
    int commonDenominator = denominator * op2.getDenominator();
    int numerator1 = numerator * op2.getDenominator();
    int numerator2 = op2.getNumerator() * denominator;
    int difference = numerator1 - numerator2;

    return new RationalNumber (difference, commonDenominator);
}


//-----------------------------------------------------------
//   Multiplies this rational number by the one passed as a
//   parameter.
//-----------------------------------------------------------
public RationalNumber multiply (RationalNumber op2)
{
    int numer = numerator * op2.getNumerator();
    int denom = denominator * op2.getDenominator();

    return new RationalNumber (numer, denom);
}


//-----------------------------------------------------------
//   Divides this rational number by the one passed as a parameter
//   by multiplying by the reciprocal of the second rational.
//-----------------------------------------------------------
```

LISTING 7.4   *continued*

```java
public RationalNumber divide (RationalNumber op2)
{
   return multiply (op2.reciprocal());
}

//-----------------------------------------------------------------
//  Determines if this rational number is equal to the one passed
//  as a parameter. Assumes they are both reduced.
//-----------------------------------------------------------------
public boolean isLike (RationalNumber op2)
{
   return ( numerator == op2.getNumerator() &&
            denominator == op2.getDenominator() );
}

//-----------------------------------------------------------------
//  Returns this rational number as a string.
//-----------------------------------------------------------------
public String toString ()
{
   String result;
   if (numerator == 0)
      result = "0";
   else
      if (denominator == 1)
         result = numerator + "";
      else
      result = numerator + "/" + denominator;
   return result;
}

//-----------------------------------------------------------------
//  Reduces this rational number by dividing both the numerator
//  and the denominator by their greatest common divisor.
//-----------------------------------------------------------------
private void reduce ()
{
   if (numerator != 0)
   {
       int common = gcd (Math.abs(numerator), denominator);

       numerator = numerator / common;
       denominator = denominator / common;
   }
```

LISTING 7.4   *continued*

```
   }

   //-----------------------------------------------------------------
   //  Computes and returns the greatest common divisor of the two
   //  positive parameters. Uses Euclid's algorithm.
   //-----------------------------------------------------------------
   private int gcd (int num1, int num2)
   {
      while (num1 != num2)
         if (num1 > num2)
            num1 = num1 - num2;
         else
            num2 = num2 - num1;

      return num1;
   }
}
```

The methods of the RationalNumber class, such as add, subtract, multiply, and divide, use the RationalNumber object that is executing the method as the first (left) operand and the RationalNumber object passed as a parameter as the second (right) operand.

The isLike method of the RationalNumber class is used to determine if two rational numbers are essentially equal. It's tempting, therefore, to call that method equals, similar to the method used to compare String objects (discussed in Chapter 5). However, in Chapter 9 we will discuss how the equals method is somewhat special due to inheritance, and that it should be implemented in a particular way. So to avoid confusion we call this method isLike for now.

Note that some of the methods in the RationalNumber class, including reduce and gcd, are declared with private visibility. These methods are private because we don't want them executed directly from outside a RationalNumber object. They exist only to support the other services of the object.

Aggregation

Some objects are made up of other objects. A car, for instance, is made up of its engine, its chassis, its wheels, and several other parts. Each of these other parts could be considered a separate object. Therefore we can say that a car is an *aggregation*—it is composed, at least in part, of other objects. Aggregation is sometimes described as a *has-a relationship*. For instance, a car has a chassis.

KEY CONCEPT

An aggregate object is composed of other objects, forming a has-a relationship.

In the software world, we define an *aggregate object* as any object that contains references to other objects as instance data. For example, an Account object contains, among other things, a String object that represents the name of the account owner. We sometimes forget that strings are objects, but technically that makes each Account object an aggregate object.

Aggregation is a special type of dependency. That is, a class that is defined in part by another class is dependent on that class. The methods of the aggregate object generally invoke the methods of the objects from which it is composed.

Let's consider another example. The program StudentBody shown in Listing 7.5 creates two Student objects. Each Student object is composed, in part, of two Address objects, one for the student's address at school and another for the student's home address. The main method does nothing more than create the Student objects and print them out. Once again we are passing objects to the println method, relying on the automatic call to the toString method to create a valid representation of the object that is suitable for printing.

The Student class shown in Listing 7.6 represents a single student. This class would have to be greatly expanded if it were to represent all aspects of a student. We deliberately keep it simple for now so that the object aggregation is clearly shown. The instance data of the Student class includes two references to Address objects. We refer to those objects in the toString method as we create a string representation of the student. By concatenating an Address object to another string, the toString method in Address is automatically invoked.

LISTING 7.5

```
//********************************************************************
//  StudentBody.java        Author: Lewis/Loftus
//
//  Demonstrates the use of an aggregate class.
//********************************************************************

public class StudentBody
{
    //-----------------------------------------------------------------
    //  Creates some Address and Student objects and prints them.
    //-----------------------------------------------------------------
    public static void main (String[] args)
    {
        Address school = new Address ("800 Lancaster Ave.", "Villanova",
                            "PA", 19085);
        Address jHome = new Address ("21 Jump Street", "Lynchburg",
                            "VA", 24551);
```

LISTING 7.5   *continued*

```
      Student john = new Student ("John", "Smith", jHome, school);


      Address mHome = new Address ("123 Main Street", "Euclid", "OH",
                                   44132);
      Student marsha = new Student ("Marsha", "Jones", mHome, school);

      System.out.println (john);
      System.out.println ();
      System.out.println (marsha);
   }
}
```

OUTPUT

```
John Smith
Home Address:
21 Jump Street
Lynchburg, VA 24551
School Address:
800 Lancaster Ave.
Villanova, PA 19085

Marsha Jones
Home Address:
123 Main Street
Euclid, OH 44132
School Address:
800 Lancaster Ave.
Villanova, PA 19085
```

LISTING 7.6

```
//********************************************************************
//   Student.java        Author: Lewis/Loftus
//
//   Represents a college student.
//********************************************************************

public class Student
{
   private String firstName, lastName;
   private Address homeAddress, schoolAddress;
```

LISTING 7.6   *continued*

```java
//-----------------------------------------------------------------
//  Constructor: Sets up this student with the specified values.
//-----------------------------------------------------------------
public Student (String first, String last, Address home,
                Address school)
{
   firstName = first;
   lastName = last;
   homeAddress = home;
   schoolAddress = school;
}

//-----------------------------------------------------------------
//  Returns a string description of this Student object.
//-----------------------------------------------------------------
public String toString()
{
   String result;

   result = firstName + " " + lastName + "\n";
   result += "Home Address:\n" + homeAddress + "\n";
   result += "School Address:\n" + schoolAddress;

   return result;
}
}
```

The Address class is shown in Listing 7.7. It represents a street address. Note that nothing about the Address class indicates that it is part of a Student object. The Address class is kept generic by design and therefore could be used in any situation in which a street address is needed.

LISTING 7.7

```java
//*******************************************************************
//  Address.java       Author: Lewis/Loftus
//
//  Represents a street address.
//*******************************************************************

public class Address
{
```

LISTING 7.7 *continued*

```
    private String streetAddress, city, state;
    private long zipCode;

    //----------------------------------------------------------
    //  Constructor: Sets up this address with the specified data.
    //----------------------------------------------------------
    public Address (String street, String town, String st, long zip)
    {
        streetAddress = street;
        city = town;
        state = st;
        zipCode - zip;
    }

    //----------------------------------------------------------
    // Returns a description of this Address object.
    //----------------------------------------------------------
    public String toString()
    {
        String result;

        result = streetAddress + "\n";
        result += city + ", " + state + " " + zipCode;

        return result;
    }
}
```

The more complex an object, the more likely it will need to be represented as an aggregate object. In UML, aggregation is represented by a connection between two classes, with an open diamond at the end near the class that is the aggregate. Figure 7.2 shows a UML class diagram for the StudentBody program.

Note that in previous UML diagram examples and in Figure 7.2, strings are not represented as separate classes with aggregation relationships, though technically they could be. Strings are so fundamental to programming that often they are represented as though they were a primitive type in a UML diagram.

The this Reference

Before we leave the topic of relationships among classes, we should examine another special reference used in Java programs called the this reference. The word this is a reserved word in Java. It allows an object to refer to itself. As we have discussed, a nonstatic method is invoked through (or by) a particular object

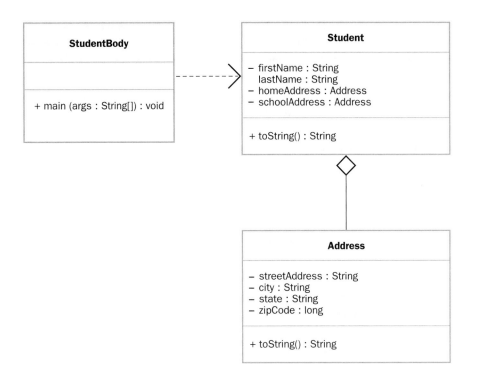

FIGURE 7.2 A UML class diagram showing aggregation

or class. Inside that method, the `this` reference can be used to refer to the currently executing object.

For example, in a class called `ChessPiece` there could be a method called `move`, which could contain the following line:

```
if (this.position == piece2.position)
    result = false;
```

In this situation, the `this` reference is being used to clarify which position is being referenced. The `this` reference refers to the object through which the method was invoked. So when the following line is used to invoke the method, the `this` reference refers to `bishop1`:

```
bishop1.move();
```

However, when a different object is used to invoke the method, the `this` reference refers to that object. Therefore, when the following invocation is used, the `this` reference in the `move` method refers to `bishop2`:

```
bishop2.move();
```

Often, the `this` reference is used to distinguish the parameters of a constructor from their corresponding instance variables with the same names. For example, the constructor of the `Account` class was presented in Chapter 4 as follows:

```java
public Account (String owner, long account, double initial)
{
    name = owner;
    acctNumber = account;
    balance = initial;
}
```

When writing this constructor, we deliberately came up with different names for the parameters to distinguish them from the instance variables `name`, `acctNumber`, and `balance`. This distinction is arbitrary. The constructor could have been written as follows using the `this` reference:

```java
public Account (String name, long acctNumber, double balance)
{
    this.name = name;
    this.acctNumber = acctNumber;
    this.balance = balance;
}
```

In this version of the constructor, the `this` reference specifically refers to the instance variables of the object. The variables on the right-hand side of the assignment statements refer to the formal parameters. This approach eliminates the need to come up with different yet equivalent names. This situation sometimes occurs in other methods but comes up often in constructors.

myprogramming**lab**

SELF-REVIEW QUESTIONS *(see answers in Appendix N)*

SR 7.10   Describe a dependency relationship between two classes.

SR 7.11   Explain how a class can have an association with itself.

SR 7.12   What is an aggregate object?

SR 7.13   What does the `this` reference refer to?

7.5 Interfaces

We've used the term interface to refer to the set of public methods through which we can interact with an object. That definition is consistent with our use of it in this section, but now we are going to formalize this concept using a particular language construct in Java.

LISTING 7.8

```
//********************************************************************
//  Complexity.java         Author: Lewis/Loftus
//
//  Represents the interface for an object that can be assigned an
//  explicit complexity.
//********************************************************************

public interface Complexity
{
    public void setComplexity (int complexity);
    public int getComplexity();
}
```

A Java *interface* is a collection of constants and abstract methods. An *abstract method* is a method that does not have an implementation. That is, there is no body of code defined for an abstract method. The header of the method, including its parameter list, is simply followed by a semicolon. An interface cannot be instantiated.

> **KEY CONCEPT**
>
> An interface is a collection of abstract methods and therefore cannot be instantiated.

Listing 7.8 shows an interface called Complexity. It contains two abstract methods: setComplexity and getComplexity.

An abstract method can be preceded by the reserved word abstract, though in interfaces it usually is not. Methods in interfaces have public visibility by default.

A class *implements* an interface by providing method implementations for each of the abstract methods defined in the interface. A class that implements an interface uses the reserved word implements followed by the interface name in the class header. If a class asserts that it implements a particular interface, it must provide a definition for all methods in the interface. The compiler will produce errors if any of the methods in the interface are not given a definition in the class.

The Question class, shown in Listing 7.9, implements the Complexity interface. Both the setComplexity and getComplexity methods are implemented. They must be declared with the same signatures as their abstract counterparts in the interface. In the Question class, the methods are defined simply to set or return a numeric value representing the complexity level of the question that the object represents.

Note that the Question class also implements additional methods that are not part of the Complexity interface. Specifically, it defines methods called getQuestion, getAnswer, answerCorrect, and toString, which have nothing to do with the interface. The interface guarantees that the class implements certain methods,

LISTING 7.9

```java
//********************************************************************
//  Question.java          Author: Lewis/Loftus
//
//  Represents a question (and its answer).
//********************************************************************

public class Question implements Complexity
{
   private String question, answer;
   private int complexityLevel;

   //-----------------------------------------------------------------
   //  Constructor: Sets up the question with a default complexity.
   //-----------------------------------------------------------------
   public Question (String query, String result)
   {
      question = query;
      answer = result;
      complexityLevel = 1;
   }

   //-----------------------------------------------------------------
   //  Sets the complexity level for this question.
   //-----------------------------------------------------------------
   public void setComplexity (int level)
   {
      complexityLevel = level;
   }

   //-----------------------------------------------------------------
   //  Returns the complexity level for this question.
   //-----------------------------------------------------------------
   public int getComplexity()
   {
      return complexityLevel;
   }

   //-----------------------------------------------------------------
   //  Returns the question.
   //-----------------------------------------------------------------
   public String getQuestion()
   {
      return question;
   }
```

LISTING 7.9   *continued*

```
//-----------------------------------------------------------------
//  Returns the answer to this question.
//-----------------------------------------------------------------
public String getAnswer()
{
   return answer;
}

//-----------------------------------------------------------------
//  Returns true if the candidate answer matches the answer.
//-----------------------------------------------------------------
public boolean answerCorrect (String candidateAnswer)
{
   return answer.equals(candidateAnswer);
}

//-----------------------------------------------------------------
//  Returns this question (and its answer) as a string.
//-----------------------------------------------------------------
public String toString()
{
   return question + "\n" + answer;
}
}
```

but it does not restrict it from having additional ones. It is common for a class that implements an interface to have other methods.

Listing 7.10 shows a program called MiniQuiz, which uses some Question objects.

An interface and its relationship to a class that implements it can be shown in a UML class diagram. An interface is represented similarly to a class node except that the designation <<interface>> is inserted above the interface name. A dotted arrow with a closed arrowhead is drawn from the class to the interface that it implements. Figure 7.3 shows a UML class diagram for the MiniQuiz program.

Multiple classes can implement the same interface, providing alternative definitions for the methods. For example, we could implement a class called Task that also implements the Complexity interface. In it we could choose to manage the complexity of a task in a different way (though it would still have to implement all the methods of the interface).

A class can implement more than one interface. In these cases, the class must provide an implementation for all methods in all interfaces listed. To show that

LISTING 7.10

```java
//********************************************************************
//  MiniQuiz.java        Author: Lewis/Loftus
//
//  Demonstrates the use of a class that implements an interface.
//********************************************************************

import java.util.Scanner;

public class MiniQuiz
{
   //-----------------------------------------------------------------
   //  Presents a short quiz.
   //-----------------------------------------------------------------
   public static void main (String[] args)
   {
      Question q1, q2;
      String possible;

      Scanner scan = new Scanner (System.in);

      q1 = new Question ("What is the capital of Jamaica?",
                         "Kingston");
      q1.setComplexity (4);

      q2 = new Question ("Which is worse, ignorance or apathy?",
                         "I don't know and I don't care");
      q2.setComplexity (10);

      System.out.print (q1.getQuestion());
      System.out.println (" (Level: " + q1.getComplexity() + ")");
      possible = scan.nextLine();
      if (q1.answerCorrect(possible))
         System.out.println ("Correct");
      else
         System.out.println ("No, the answer is " + q1.getAnswer());

      System.out.println();
      System.out.print (q2.getQuestion());
      System.out.println (" (Level: " + q2.getComplexity() + ")");
      possible = scan.nextLine();
      if (q2.answerCorrect(possible))
         System.out.println ("Correct");
      else
```

LISTING 7.10   *continued*

```
        System.out.println ("No, the answer is " + q2.getAnswer());
    }
}
```

OUTPUT

```
What is the capital of Jamaica? (Level: 4)
Kingston
Correct

Which is worse, ignorance or apathy? (Level: 10)
apathy
No, the answer is I don't know and I don't care
```

a class implements multiple interfaces, they are listed in the `implements` clause, separated by commas. For example:

```
class ManyThings implements Interface1, Interface2, Interface3
{
   // contains all methods of all interfaces
}
```

In addition to, or instead of, abstract methods, an interface can also contain constants, defined using the `final` modifier. When a class implements an interface, it gains access to all the constants defined in it.

The interface construct formally defines the ways in which we can interact with a class. It also serves as a basis for a powerful programming technique called polymorphism, which we discuss in Chapter 10.

The Comparable Interface

The Java standard class library contains interfaces as well as classes. The `Comparable` interface, for example, is defined in the `java.lang` package. The `Comparable` interface contains only one method, `compareTo`, which takes an object as a parameter and returns an integer.

The intention of this interface is to provide a common mechanism for comparing one object to another. One object calls the method and passes another as a parameter as follows:

```
if (obj1.compareTo(obj2) < 0)
    System.out.println ("obj1 is less than obj2");
```

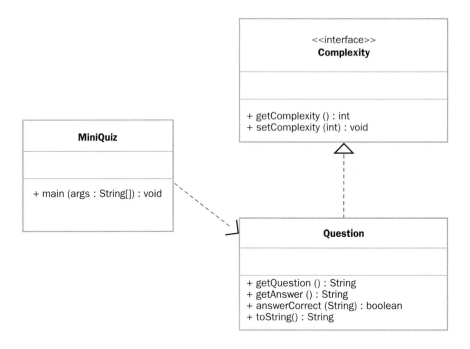

FIGURE 7.3   A UML class diagram for the MiniQuiz program

As specified by the documentation for the interface, the integer that is returned from the compareTo method should be negative if obj1 is less than obj2, 0 if they are equal, and positive if obj1 is greater than obj2. It is up to the designer of each class to decide what it means for one object of that class to be less than, equal to, or greater than another.

In Chapter 5, we mentioned that the String class contains a compareTo method that operates in this manner. Now we can clarify that the String class has this method because it implements the Comparable interface. The String class implementation of this method bases the comparison on the lexicographic ordering defined by the Unicode character set.

The Iterator Interface

The Iterator interface is another interface defined as part of the Java standard class library. It is used by a class that represents a collection of objects, providing a means to move through the collection one object at a time.

In Chapter 5 we defined the concept of an iterator, using a loop to process all elements in the collection. Most iterators, including objects of the Scanner class, are defined using the Iterator interface.

The two primary methods in the Iterator interface are hasNext, which returns a boolean result, and next, which returns an object. Neither of these methods takes any parameters. The hasNext method returns true if there are items left to process, and next returns the next object. It is up to the designer of the class that implements the Iterator interface to decide the order in which objects will be delivered by the next method.

We should note that, according to the spirit of the interface, the next method does not remove the object from the underlying collection; it simply returns a reference to it. The Iterator interface also has a method called remove, which takes no parameters and has a void return type. A call to the remove method removes the object that was most recently returned by the next method from the underlying collection.

SELF-REVIEW QUESTIONS *(see answers in Appendix N)*

`myprogramminglab`

SR 7.14   What is the difference between a class and an interface?

SR 7.15   Define a Java interface called Nameable. Classes that implement this interface must provide a setName method that requires a single String parameter and returns nothing, and a getName method that has no parameters and returns a String.

SR 7.16   True or False? Explain.

   a. A Java interface can include only abstract methods, nothing else.
   b. An abstract method is a method that does not have an implementation.
   c. All of the methods included in a Java interface definition must be abstract.
   d. A class that implements an interface can define only those methods that are included in the interface.
   e. Multiple classes can implement the same interface.
   f. A class can implement more than one interface.
   g. All classes that implement an interface must provide the exact same definitions of the methods that are included in the interface.

7.6 Enumerated Types Revisited

In Chapter 3 we introduced the concept of an enumerated type, which defines a new data type and lists all possible values of that type. We gave an example that defined an enumerated type called Season, which was declared as follows:

```
enum Season {winter, spring, summer, fall}
```

We mentioned that an enumerated type is a special kind of class, and that the values of the enumerated type are objects. The values are, in fact, instances of its own enumerated type. For example, winter is an object of the Season class. Let's explore this concept a bit further.

Suppose we declare a variable of the Season type as follows:

KEY CONCEPT

The values of an enumerated type are static variables of that type.

```
Season time;
```

Because an enumerated type is a special kind of class, the variable time is an object reference variable. Furthermore, as an enumerated type, it can be assigned only the values listed in the Season definition. These values (winter, spring, summer, and fall) are actually references to Season objects that are stored as public static variables within the Season class. Thus we can make an assignment such as the following:

```
time = Season.spring;
```

Now let's take this idea a step further. In Listing 7.11 we redefine the Season type, giving it a more substantial definition. Note that we still use the enum reserved word to declare the enumerated type, and we still list all possible values of the type. In addition, in this definition we add a private String called span, a constructor for the Season class, and a method named getSpan. Each value in the list of values for the enumerated type invokes the constructor, passing it a character string that is then stored in the span variable of each value.

LISTING 7.11

```java
//********************************************************************
//  Season.java          Author: Lewis/Loftus
//
//  Enumerates the values for Season.
//********************************************************************

public enum Season
{
    winter ("December through February"),
    spring ("March through May"),
    summer ("June through August"),
    fall ("September through November");

    private String span;
```

```
LISTING  7.11      continued
```

```
   //---------------------------------------------------------------
   //  Constructor: Sets up each value with an associated string.
   //---------------------------------------------------------------
   Season (String months)
   {
      span = months;
   }

   //---------------------------------------------------------------
   //  Returns the span message for this value.
   //---------------------------------------------------------------
   public String getSpan()
   {
      return span;
   }
}
```

The main method of the SeasonTester class, shown in Listing 7.12, prints each value of the Season enumerated type, as well as the span statement for each. Every enumerated type contains a static method called values that returns a list of all possible values for that type. This list is an iterator, so we can use the enhanced version of a for loop to process each value.

```
LISTING  7.12
```

```
//********************************************************************
//  SeasonTester.java        Author: Lewis/Loftus
//
//  Demonstrates the use of a full enumerated type.
//********************************************************************

public class SeasonTester
{
   //---------------------------------------------------------------
   //  Iterates through the values of the Season enumerated type.
   //---------------------------------------------------------------
   public static void main (String[] args)
   {
```

LISTING 7.12 *continued*

```
    for (Season time : Season.values())
        System.out.println (time + "\t" + time.getSpan());
   }
}
```

OUTPUT

```
winter   December through February
spring   March through May
summer   June through August
fall     September through November
```

KEY CONCEPT

We can add attributes and methods to the definition of an enumerated type.

In addition to the list of possible values defined in every enumerated type, we can include any number of attributes or methods of our own choosing. This provides various opportunities for creative class design.

myprogramming**lab**

SELF-REVIEW QUESTION *(see answer in Appendix N)*

SR 7.17 Using the enumerated type `Season` as defined in this section, what is the output from the following code sequence?

```
Season time1, time2;
time1 = Season.winter;
time2 = Season.summer;
System.out.println (time1);
System.out.println (time2.name());
System.out.println (time1.ordinal());
System.out.println (time2.getSpan());
```

7.7 Method Design

Once you have identified classes and assigned basic responsibilities, the design of each method will determine how exactly the class will define its behaviors. Some methods are straightforward and require little thought. Others are more interesting and require careful planning.

An *algorithm* is a step-by-step process for solving a problem. A recipe is an example of an algorithm. Travel directions are another example of an algorithm. Every method implements an algorithm that determines how that method accomplishes its goals.

An algorithm is often described using *pseudocode,* which is a mixture of code statements and English phrases. Pseudocode provides enough structure to show how the code will operate, without getting bogged down in the syntactic details of a particular programming language or becoming prematurely constrained by the characteristics of particular programming constructs.

This section discusses two important aspects of program design at the method level: method decomposition and the implications of passing objects as parameters.

Method Decomposition

Occasionally, a service that an object provides is so complicated that it cannot reasonably be implemented using one method. Therefore we sometimes need to decompose a method into multiple methods to create a more understandable design. As an example, let's examine a program that translates English sentences into Pig Latin.

> **KEY CONCEPT**
>
> A complex service provided by an object can be decomposed to make use of private support methods.

Pig Latin is a made-up language in which each word of a sentence is modified, in general, by moving the initial sound of the word to the end and adding an "ay" sound. For example, the word *happy* would be written and pronounced *appyhay* and the word *birthday* would become *irthdaybay*. Words that begin with vowels simply have a "yay" sound added on the end, turning the word *enough* into *enoughyay*. Consonant blends such as "ch" and "st" at the beginning of a word are moved to the end together before adding the "ay" sound. Therefore the word *grapefruit* becomes *apefruitgray*.

The `PigLatin` program shown in Listing 7.13 reads one or more sentences, translating each into Pig Latin.

The workhorse behind the `PigLatin` program is the `PigLatinTranslator` class, shown in Listing 7.14. The `PigLatinTranslator` class provides one fundamental service, a static method called `translate`, which accepts a string and translates it into Pig Latin. Note that the `PigLatinTranslator` class does not contain a constructor because none is needed.

LISTING 7.13

```
//********************************************************************
//  PigLatin.java       Author: Lewis/Loftus
//
//  Demonstrates the concept of method decomposition.
//********************************************************************

import java.util.Scanner;
```

LISTING 7.13   *continued*

```java
public class PigLatin
{
   //-----------------------------------------------------------
   //  Reads sentences and translates them into Pig Latin.
   //-----------------------------------------------------------
   public static void main (String[] args)
   {
      String sentence, result, another;

      Scanner scan = new Scanner (System.in);

      do
      {
         System.out.println ();
         System.out.println ("Enter a sentence (no punctuation):");
         sentence = scan.nextLine();

         System.out.println ();
         result = PigLatinTranslator.translate (sentence);
         System.out.println ("That sentence in Pig Latin is:");
         System.out.println (result);

         System.out.println ();
         System.out.print ("Translate another sentence (y/n)? ");
         another = scan.nextLine();
      }
      while (another.equalsIgnoreCase("y"));
   }
}
```

OUTPUT

```
Enter a sentence (no punctuation):
Do you speak Pig Latin
That sentence in Pig Latin is:
oday ouyay eakspay igpay atinlay

Translate another sentence (y/n)? y

Enter a sentence (no punctuation):
Play it again Sam

That sentence in Pig Latin is:
ayplay ityay againyay amsay

Translate another sentence (y/n)? n
```

LISTING 7.14

```java
//********************************************************************
//  PigLatinTranslator.java        Author: Lewis/Loftus
//
//  Represents a translator from English to Pig Latin. Demonstrates
//  method decomposition.
//********************************************************************

import java.util.Scanner;

public class PigLatinTranslator
{
   //-----------------------------------------------------------------
   //  Translates a sentence of words into Pig Latin.
   //-----------------------------------------------------------------
   public static String translate (String sentence)
   {
      String result = "";

      sentence = sentence.toLowerCase();

      Scanner scan = new Scanner (sentence);

      while (scan.hasNext())
      {
         result += translateWord (scan.next());
         result += " ";
      }

      return result;
   }

   //-----------------------------------------------------------------
   //  Translates one word into Pig Latin. If the word begins with a
   //  vowel, the suffix "yay" is appended to the word. Otherwise,
   //  the first letter or two are moved to the end of the word,
   //  and "ay" is appended.
   //-----------------------------------------------------------------
   private static String translateWord (String word)
   {
      String result = "";

      if (beginsWithVowel(word))
         result = word + "yay";
      else
         if (beginsWithBlend(word))
```

LISTING 7.14   *continued*

```java
            result = word.substring(2) + word.substring(0,2) + "ay";
        else
            result = word.substring(1) + word.charAt(0) + "ay";

    return result;
}

//------------------------------------------------------------
//  Determines if the specified word begins with a vowel.
//------------------------------------------------------------
private static boolean beginsWithVowel (String word)
{
    String vowels = "aeiou";

    char letter = word.charAt(0);

    return (vowels.indexOf(letter) != -1);
}

//------------------------------------------------------------
//  Determines if the specified word begins with a particular
//  two-character consonant blend.
//------------------------------------------------------------
private static boolean beginsWithBlend (String word)
{
    return ( word.startsWith ("bl") || word.startsWith ("sc") ||
             word.startsWith ("br") || word.startsWith ("sh") ||
             word.startsWith ("ch") || word.startsWith ("sk") ||
             word.startsWith ("cl") || word.startsWith ("sl") ||
             word.startsWith ("cr") || word.startsWith ("sn") ||
             word.startsWith ("dr") || word.startsWith ("sm") ||
             word.startsWith ("dw") || word.startsWith ("sp") ||
             word.startsWith ("fl") || word.startsWith ("sq") ||
             word.startsWith ("fr") || word.startsWith ("st") ||
             word.startsWith ("gl") || word.startsWith ("sw") ||
             word.startsWith ("gr") || word.startsWith ("th") ||
             word.startsWith ("kl") || word.startsWith ("tr") ||
             word.startsWith ("ph") || word.startsWith ("tw") ||
             word.startsWith ("pl") || word.startsWith ("wh") ||
             word.startsWith ("pr") || word.startsWith ("wr") );
}
}
```

The act of translating an entire sentence into Pig Latin is not trivial. If written in one big method, it would be very long and difficult to follow. A better solution, as implemented in the `PigLatinTranslator` class, is to decompose the `translate` method and use several other support methods to help with the task.

The `translate` method uses a `Scanner` object to separate the string into words. Recall that one role of the `Scanner` class (discussed in Chapter 3) is to separate a string into smaller elements called tokens. In this case, the tokens are separated by space characters so we can use the default white space delimiters. The `PigLatin` program assumes that no punctuation is included in the input.

The `translate` method passes each word to the private support method `translateWord`. Even the job of translating one word is somewhat involved, so the `translateWord` method makes use of two other private methods, `beginsWithVowel` and `beginsWithBlend`.

The `beginsWithVowel` method returns a `boolean` value that indicates whether the word passed as a parameter begins with a vowel. Note that instead of checking each vowel separately, the code for this method declares a string that contains all the vowels, and then invokes the `String` method `indexOf` to determine whether the first character of the word is in the vowel string. If the specified character cannot be found, the `indexOf` method returns a value of −1.

The `beginsWithBlend` method also returns a `boolean` value. The body of the method contains only a `return` statement with one large expression that makes several calls to the `startsWith` method of the `String` class. If any of these calls returns true, then the `beginsWithBlend` method returns true as well.

Note that the `translateWord`, `beginsWithVowel`, and `beginsWithBlend` methods are all declared with private visibility. They are not intended to provide services directly to clients outside the class. Instead, they exist to help the `translate` method, which is the only true service method in this class, to do its job. By declaring them with private visibility, they cannot be invoked from outside this class. If the `main` method of the `PigLatin` class attempted to invoke the `translateWord` method, for instance, the compiler would issue an error message.

Figure 7.4 shows a UML class diagram for the `PigLatin` program. Note the notation showing the visibility of various methods.

Whenever a method becomes large or complex, we should consider decomposing it into multiple methods to create a more understandable class design. First, however, we must consider how other classes and objects can be defined to create better overall system design. In an object-oriented design, method decomposition must be subordinate to object decomposition.

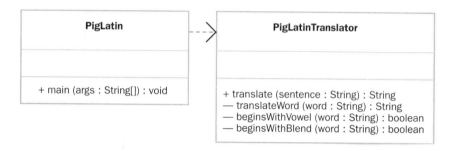

FIGURE 7.4 A UML class diagram for the `PigLatin` program

Method Parameters Revisited

Another important issue related to method design involves the way parameters are passed into a method. In Java, all parameters are passed *by value*. That is, the current value of the actual parameter (in the invocation) is copied into the formal parameter in the method header. We mentioned this issue in Chapter 4; let's examine it now in more detail.

Essentially, parameter passing is like an assignment statement, assigning to the formal parameter a copy of the value stored in the actual parameter. This issue must be considered when making changes to a formal parameter inside a method. The formal parameter is a separate copy of the value that is passed in, so any changes made to it have no effect on the actual parameter. After control returns to the calling method, the actual parameter will have the same value as it did before the method was called.

However, when we pass an object to a method, we are actually passing a reference to that object. The value that gets copied is the address of the object. Therefore, the formal parameter and the actual parameter become aliases of each other. If we change the state of the object through the formal parameter reference inside the method, we are changing the object referenced by the actual parameter, because they refer to the same object. On the other hand, if we change the formal parameter reference itself (to make it point to a new object, for instance), we have not changed the fact that the actual parameter still refers to the original object.

> **KEY CONCEPT**
>
> When an object is passed to a method, the actual and formal parameters become aliases.

The program in Listing 7.15 illustrates the nuances of parameter passing. Carefully trace the processing of this program and note the values that are output. The `ParameterTester` class contains a `main` method that calls the `changeValues` method in a `ParameterModifier` object. Two of the parameters to `changeValues` are `Num` objects, each of which simply stores an integer value. The other parameter is a primitive integer value.

LISTING 7.15

```
//********************************************************************
//  ParameterTester.java        Author: Lewis/Loftus
//
//  Demonstrates the effects of passing various types of parameters.
//********************************************************************

public class ParameterTester
{
   //-----------------------------------------------------------------
   //  Sets up three variables (one primitive and two objects) to
   //  serve as actual parameters to the changeValues method. Prints
   //  their values before and after calling the method.
   //-----------------------------------------------------------------
   public static void main (String[] args)
   {
      ParameterModifier modifier = new ParameterModifier();

      int a1 = 111;
      Num a2 = new Num (222);
      Num a3 = new Num (333);

      System.out.println ("Before calling changeValues:");
      System.out.println ("a1\ta2\ta3");
      System.out.println (a1 + "\t" + a2 + "\t" + a3 + "\n");

      modifier.changeValues (a1, a2, a3);

      System.out.println ("After calling changeValues:");
      System.out.println ("a1\ta2\ta3");
      System.out.println (a1 + "\t" + a2 + "\t" + a3 + "\n");
   }
}
```

OUTPUT

```
Before calling changeValues
a1      a2      a3
111     222     333

Before changing the values:
f1      f2      f3
111     222     333
```

LISTING 7.15   *continued*

```
After changing the values:
f1       f2       f3
999      888      777

After calling changeValues:
a1       a2       a3
111      888      333
```

Listing 7.16 shows the `ParameterModifier` class, and Listing 7.17 shows the `Num` class. Inside the `changeValues` method, a modification is made to each of the three formal parameters: the integer parameter is set to a different value, the value stored in the first `Num` parameter is changed using its `setValue` method, and a new

LISTING 7.16

```java
//********************************************************************
//  ParameterModifier.java       Author: Lewis/Loftus
//
//  Demonstrates the effects of changing parameter values.
//********************************************************************

public class ParameterModifier
{
    //-----------------------------------------------------------------
    //  Modifies the parameters, printing their values before and
    //  after making the changes.
    //-----------------------------------------------------------------
    public void changeValues (int f1, Num f2, Num f3)
    {
        System.out.println ("Before changing the values:");
        System.out.println ("f1\tf2\tf3");
        System.out.println (f1 + "\t" + f2 + "\t" + f3 + "\n");

        f1 = 999;
        f2.setValue(888);
        f3 = new Num (777);

        System.out.println ("After changing the values:");
        System.out.println ("f1\tf2\tf3");
        System.out.println (f1 + "\t" + f2 + "\t" + f3 + "\n");
    }
}
```

LISTING 7.17

```java
//********************************************************************
//  Num.java        Author: Lewis/Loftus
//
//  Represents a single integer as an object.
//********************************************************************

public class Num
{
    private int value;

    //-----------------------------------------------------------------
    //  Sets up the new Num object, storing an initial value.
    //-----------------------------------------------------------------
    public Num (int update)
    {
        value = update;
    }

    //-----------------------------------------------------------------
    //  Sets the stored value to the newly specified value.
    //-----------------------------------------------------------------
    public void setValue (int update)
    {
        value = update;
    }

    //-----------------------------------------------------------------
    //  Returns the stored integer value as a string.
    //-----------------------------------------------------------------
    public String toString ()
    {
        return value + "";
    }
}
```

Num object is created and assigned to the second Num parameter. These changes are reflected in the output printed at the end of the changeValues method.

However, note the final values that are printed after returning from the method. The primitive integer was not changed from its original value, because the change was made to a copy inside the method. Likewise, the last parameter still refers to its original object with its original value. This is because the new Num object created in the method was referred to only by the formal parameter. When the method returned, that formal parameter was destroyed and the Num object it referred to was marked for garbage collection. The only change that is "permanent" is the change made to the state of the second parameter. Figure 7.5 shows the step-by-step processing of this program.

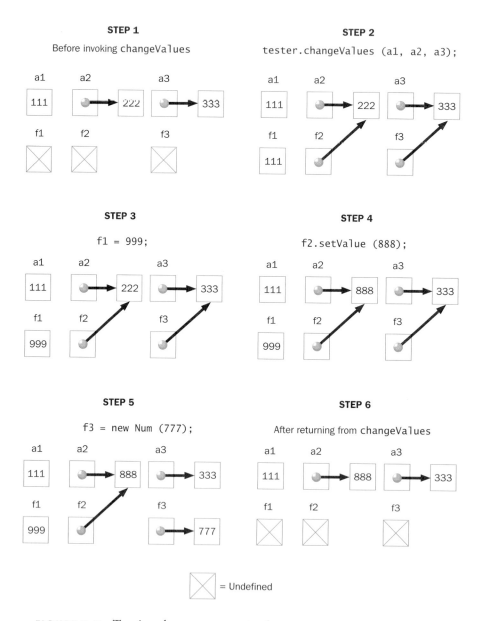

FIGURE 7.5 Tracing the parameters in the ParameterTesting program

SELF-REVIEW QUESTIONS *(see answers in Appendix N)*

SR 7.18 What is method decomposition?

SR 7.19 Answer the following questions about the `PigLatinTranslator` class.

  a. No constructor is defined. Why not?
  b. Some of the defined methods are private. Why?
  c. A `Scanner` object is declared in the `translate` method. What is it used to scan?

SR 7.20 Identify the resultant sequence of calls/returns of `PigLatinTranslator` support methods when `translate` is invoked with the following actual parameters.

  a. `"animal"`
  b. `"hello"`
  c. `"We are the champions"`

SR 7.21 How are objects passed as parameters?

7.8 Method Overloading

As we've discussed, when a method is invoked, the flow of control transfers to the code that defines the method. After the method has been executed, control returns to the location of the call, and processing continues.

Often the method name is sufficient to indicate which method is being called by a specific invocation. But in Java, as in other object-oriented languages, you can use the same method name with different parameter lists for multiple methods. This technique is called *method overloading*. It is useful when you need to perform similar methods on different types of data.

The compiler must still be able to associate each invocation to a specific method declaration. If the method name for two or more methods is the same, additional information is used to uniquely identify the version that is being invoked. In Java, a method name can be used for multiple methods as long as the number of parameters, the types of those parameters, and/or the order of the types of parameters is distinct.

> **KEY CONCEPT**
>
> The versions of an overloaded method are distinguished by the number, type, and order of their parameters.

For example, we could declare a method called `sum` as follows:

```java
public int sum (int num1, int num2)
{
    return num1 + num2;
}
```

Then we could declare another method called sum, within the same class, as follows:

```
public int sum (int num1, int num2, int num3)
{
    return num1 + num2 + num3;
}
```

Now, when an invocation is made, the compiler looks at the number of parameters to determine which version of the sum method to call. For instance, the following invocation will call the second version of the sum method:

```
sum (25, 69, 13);
```

A method's name, along with the number, type, and order of its parameters, is called the method's *signature*. The compiler uses the complete method signature to *bind* a method invocation to the appropriate definition.

The compiler must be able to examine a method invocation to determine which specific method is being invoked. If you attempt to specify two method names with the same signature, the compiler will issue an appropriate error message and will not create an executable program. There can be no ambiguity.

Note that the return type of a method is not part of the method signature. That is, two overloaded methods cannot differ only by their return type. This is because the value returned by a method can be ignored by the invocation. The compiler would not be able to distinguish which version of an overloaded method is being referenced in such situations.

The println method is an example of a method that is overloaded several times, each accepting a single type. The following is a partial list of its various signatures:

VideoNote

Examples of method overloading.

- println (String s)
- println (int i)
- println (double d)
- println (char c)
- println (boolean b)

The following two lines of code actually invoke different methods that have the same name:

```
System.out.println ("Number of students: ");
System.out.println (count);
```

The first line invokes the version of println that accepts a string. The second line, assuming count is an integer variable, invokes the version of println that accepts an integer.

We often use a `println` statement that prints several distinct types, such as:

```
System.out.println ("Number of students: " + count);
```

Remember, in this case the plus sign is the string concatenation operator. First, the value in the variable `count` is converted to a string representation, then the two strings are concatenated into one longer string, and finally the definition of `println` that accepts a single string is invoked.

Constructors can be overloaded, and often are. By providing multiple versions of a constructor, we provide multiple ways to set up an object.

SELF-REVIEW QUESTIONS *(see answers in Appendix N)*

SR 7.22   How are overloaded methods distinguished from each other?

SR 7.23   For each of the following pairs of method headers, state whether or not the signatures are distinct. If not, explain why not.

    a. `String describe (String name, int count)`
       `String describe (int count, String name)`
    b. `void count ( )`
       `int count ( )`
    c. `int howMany (int compareValue)`
       `int howMany (int ceiling)`
    d. `boolean greater (int value1)`
       `boolean greater (int value1, int value2)`

SR 7.24   The `Num` class is defined in Section 7.7. Overload the constructor of that class by defining a second constructor which takes no parameters and sets the `value` attribute to zero.

myprogramminglab

7.9 Testing

The term *testing* can be applied in many ways to software development. Testing certainly includes its traditional definition: the act of running a completed program with various inputs to discover problems. But it also includes any evaluation that is performed by human or machine to assess the quality of the evolving system. These evaluations should occur long before a single line of code is written.

The goal of testing is to find errors. By finding errors and fixing them, we improve the quality of our program. It's likely that later on someone else will find any errors that remain hidden during development. The earlier the errors are found, the easier and cheaper they are to fix. Taking the time to uncover problems as early as possible is almost always worth the effort.

Running a program with specific input and producing the correct results establishes only that the program works for that particular input. As more and more test cases execute without revealing errors, our confidence in the program rises, but we can never really be sure that all errors have been eliminated. There could always be another error still undiscovered. Because of that, it is important to thoroughly test a program in as many ways as possible and with well-designed test cases.

It is possible to prove that a program is correct, but that technique is enormously complex for large systems, and errors can be made in the proof itself. Therefore, we generally rely on testing to determine the quality of a program.

After determining that an error exists, we determine the cause of the error and fix it. After a problem is fixed, we should run previous tests again to make sure that while fixing the problem we didn't create another. This technique is called *regression testing*.

Reviews

One technique used to evaluate design or code is called a *review*, which is a meeting in which several people carefully examine a design document or section of code. Presenting our design or code to others causes us to think more carefully about it and permits others to share their suggestions with us. The participants discuss its merits and problems, and create a list of issues that must be addressed. The goal of a review is to identify problems, not to solve them, which usually takes much more time.

A design review should determine whether the requirements have been addressed. It should also assess the way the system is decomposed into classes and objects. A code review should determine how faithfully the design satisfies the requirements and how faithfully the implementation represents the design. It should identify any specific problems that would cause the design or the implementation to fail in its responsibilities.

Sometimes a review is called a *walkthrough*, because its goal is to step carefully through a document and evaluate each section.

Defect Testing

Since the goal of testing is to find errors, it is often referred to as *defect testing*. With that goal in mind, a good test is one that uncovers any deficiencies in a program. This might seem strange, because we ultimately don't want to have problems in our system. But keep in mind that errors almost certainly exist. Our testing efforts should make every attempt to find them. We want to increase the reliability of our program by finding and fixing the errors that exist, rather than letting users discover them.

A *test case* consists of a set of inputs, user actions, or other initial conditions, along with the expected output. A test case should be appropriately documented so that it can be repeated later as needed. Developers often create a complete *test suite,* which is a set of test cases that covers various aspects of the system.

Because programs operate on a large number of possible inputs, it is not feasible to create test cases for all possible input or user actions. Nor is it usually necessary to test every single situation. Two specific test cases may be so similar that they actually do not test unique aspects of the program. To do both would be a wasted effort. We'd rather execute a test case that stresses the program in some new way. Therefore we want to choose our test cases carefully. To that end, let's examine two approaches to defect testing: black-box testing and white-box testing.

As the name implies, *black-box testing* treats the thing being tested as a black box. In black-box testing, test cases are developed without regard to the internal workings. Black-box tests are based on inputs and outputs. An entire program can be tested using a black-box technique, in which case the inputs are the user-provided information and user actions such as button pushes. A test case is successful only if the input produces the expected output. A single class can also be tested using a black-box technique, which focuses on the system interface (its public methods) of the class. Certain parameters are passed in, producing certain results. Black-box test cases are often derived directly from the requirements of the system or from the stated purpose of a method.

The input data for a black-box test case are often selected by defining equivalence categories. An *equivalence category* is a collection of inputs that are expected to produce similar outputs. Generally, if a method will work for one value in the equivalence category, we have every reason to believe it will work for the others. For example, the input to a method that computes the square root of an integer can be divided into two equivalence categories: nonnegative integers and negative integers. If it works appropriately for one nonnegative value, it will likely work for all nonnegative values. Likewise, if it works appropriately for one negative value, it will likely work for all negative values.

Equivalence categories have defined boundaries. Because all values of an equivalence category essentially test the same features of a program, only one test case inside the equivalence boundary is needed. However, because programming often produces "off by one" errors, the values on and around the boundary should be tested exhaustively. For an integer boundary, a good test suite would include at least the exact value of the boundary, the boundary minus 1, and the boundary plus 1. Test cases that use these cases, plus at least one from within the general field of the category, should be defined.

Let's look at an example. Consider a method whose purpose is to validate that a particular integer value is in the range 0 to 99, inclusive. There are three equivalence categories in this case: values below 0, values in the range of 0 to 99, and values above 99. Black-box testing dictates that we use test values that surround and fall on the boundaries, as well as some general values from the equivalence categories. Therefore, a set of black-box test cases for this situation might be: –500, –1, 0, 1, 50, 98, 99, 100, and 500.

White-box testing, also known as *glass-box testing,* exercises the internal structure and implementation of a method. A white-box test case is based on the logic of the code. The goal is to ensure that every path through a program is executed at least once. A white-box test maps the possible paths through the code and ensures that the test cases cause every path to be executed. This type of testing is often called *statement coverage.*

Paths through code are controlled by various control flow statements that use conditional expressions, such as `if` statements. In order to have every path through the program executed at least once, the input data values for the test cases need to control the values for the conditional expressions. The input data of one or more test cases should cause the condition of an `if` statement to evaluate to `true` in at least one case and to `false` in at least one case. Covering both true and false values in an `if` statement guarantees that both the paths through the `if` statement will be executed. Similar situations can be created for loops and other constructs.

In both black-box and white-box testing, the expected output for each test should be established prior to running the test. It's too easy to be persuaded that the results of a test are appropriate if you haven't first carefully determined what the results should be.

myprogramminglab

SELF-REVIEW QUESTION (*see answer in Appendix N*)

SR 7.25 Select the term from the following list that best matches each of the following phrases:

black-box, defects, regression, review, test case, test suite, walk-through, white-box

a. Running previous test cases after a change is made to a program to help ensure that the change did not introduce an error.
b. A meeting in which several people collectively evaluate an artifact.
c. A review that steps carefully through a document, evaluating each section.
d. The goal of testing is to discover these.

> e. A description of the input and corresponding expected output of a code unit being tested.
> f. A set of test cases that covers various aspects of a system.
> g. With this testing approach, test cases are based solely on requirement specifications.
> h. With this testing approach, test cases are based on the internal workings of the program.

7.10 GUI Design

As we focus on the details that allow us to create GUIs, we may sometimes lose sight of the big picture. As we continue to explore GUI construction, we should keep in mind that our goal is to solve a problem. Specifically, we want to create software that is useful. Knowing the details of components, events, and other language elements gives us the tools to put GUIs together, but we must guide that knowledge with the following fundamental ideas of good GUI design:

- Know the user.
- Prevent user errors.
- Optimize user abilities.
- Be consistent.

> **KEY CONCEPT**
> The design of any GUI should adhere to basic guidelines regarding consistency and usability.

The software designer must understand the user's needs and potential activities in order to develop an interface that will serve that user well. Keep in mind that, to the user, the interface *is* the software. It is the only way the user interacts with the system. As such, the interface must satisfy the user's needs.

Whenever possible, we should design interfaces so that the user can make as few mistakes as possible. In many situations, we have the flexibility to choose one of several components to accomplish a specific task. We should always try to choose components that will prevent inappropriate actions and avoid invalid input. For example, if an input value must be one of a set of particular values, we should use components that allow the user to make only a valid choice. That is, constraining the user to a few valid choices with, for instance, a set of radio buttons is better than allowing the user to type arbitrary and possibly invalid data into a text field. We cover additional components appropriate for specific situations in this chapter.

Not all users are alike. Some are more adept than others at using a particular GUI or GUI components in general. We shouldn't design with only the lowest common denominator in mind. For example, we should provide shortcuts whenever reasonable. That is, in addition to a normal series of actions that will allow a user to accomplish a task, we should also provide redundant ways to accomplish the same task. Using keyboard shortcuts (mnemonics) is a good example. Sometimes these additional mechanisms are less intuitive, but they may be faster for the experienced user.

Finally, consistency is important when dealing with large systems or multiple systems in a common environment. Users become familiar with a particular organization or color scheme; these should not be changed arbitrarily.

myprogramminglab

SELF-REVIEW QUESTIONS *(see answers in Appendix N)*

SR 7.26 What general guidelines for GUI design are presented in this section?

SR 7.27 Why is a good user interface design so important?

7.11 Layout Managers

In addition to the components, events, and listeners that comprise the backbone of a GUI, the most important activity in GUI design is the use of layout managers. A *layout manager* is an object that governs how components are arranged in a container. It determines the size and position of each component and may take many factors into account to do so. Every container has a default layout manager, although we can replace it if we prefer another one.

> **KEY CONCEPT**
>
> The layout manager of a container determines how components are visually presented.

A container's layout manager is consulted whenever a change to the visual appearance of its contents might be needed. When the size of a container is adjusted, for example, the layout manager is consulted to determine how all of the components in the container should appear in the resized container. Every time a component is added to a container, the layout manager determines how the addition affects all of the existing components.

> **KEY CONCEPT**
>
> When changes occur, the components in a container reorganize themselves according to the layout manager's policy.

The table in Figure 7.6 describes several of the predefined layout managers provided by the Java standard class library.

Every layout manager has its own particular properties and rules governing the layout of components. For some layout managers, the order in which you add the components affects their positioning, whereas others provide more specific control. Some layout managers take a component's preferred size or alignment into account, whereas others don't. To develop good GUIs in Java, it is important to become familiar with features and characteristics of various layout managers.

We can use the `setLayout` method of a container to change its layout manager. We've done this a few times in previous examples. For example, the following

Layout Manager	Description
Border Layout	Organizes components into five areas (North, South, East, West and Center).
Box Layout	Organizes components into a single row or column.
Card Layout	Organizes components into one area such that only one is visible at any time.
Flow Layout	Organizes components from left to right, starting new rows as necessary.
Grid Layout	Organizes components into a grid of rows and columns.
GridBag Layout	Organizes components into a grid of cells, allowing components to span more than one cell.

FIGURE 7.6   Some predefined Java layout managers

code sets the layout manager of a JPanel, which has a flow layout by default, so that it uses a border layout instead:

```
JPanel panel = new JPanel();
panel.setLayout (new BorderLayout());
```

Let's explore some of these layout managers in more detail. We'll focus on the most popular layout managers at this point: flow, border, box, and grid. The class presented in Listing 7.18 contains the main method of an application that demonstrates the use and effects of these layout managers.

> **KEY CONCEPT**
> The layout manager for each container can be explicitly set.

The LayoutDemo program introduces the use of a *tabbed pane*, a container that allows the user to select (by clicking on a tab) which of several panes is currently visible. A tabbed pane is defined by the JTabbedPane class. The addTab method creates a tab, specifying the name that appears on the tab and the component to be displayed on that pane when it achieves focus by being "brought to the front" and made visible to the user.

Interestingly, there is an overlap in the functionality provided by tabbed panes and the card layout manager. Similar to the tabbed pane, a card layout allows several layers to be defined, and only one of those layers is displayed at any given point. However, a container managed by a card layout can be adjusted only under program control, whereas tabbed panes allow the user to indicate directly which tab should be displayed.

In this example, each tab of the tabbed pane contains a panel that is controlled by a different layout manager. The first tab simply contains a panel with an introductory message, as shown in Listing 7.19. As we explore each layout manager in more detail, we examine the class that defines the corresponding panel of this program and discuss its visual effect.

LISTING 7.18

```
//********************************************************************
//  LayoutDemo.java       Author: Lewis/Loftus
//
//  Demonstrates the use of flow, border, grid, and box layouts.
//********************************************************************

import javax.swing.*;

public class LayoutDemo
{
   //-----------------------------------------------------------------
   //  Sets up a frame containing a tabbed pane. The panel on each
   //  tab demonstrates a different layout manager.
   //-----------------------------------------------------------------
   public static void main (String[] args)
   {
      JFrame frame = new JFrame ("Layout Manager Demo");
      frame.setDefaultCloseOperation (JFrame.EXIT_ON_CLOSE);

      JTabbedPane tp = new JTabbedPane();
      tp.addTab ("Intro", new IntroPanel());
      tp.addTab ("Flow", new FlowPanel());
      tp.addTab ("Border", new BorderPanel());
      tp.addTab ("Grid", new GridPanel());
      tp.addTab ("Box", new BoxPanel());

      frame.getContentPane().add(tp);
      frame.pack();
      frame.setVisible(true);
   }
}
```

Flow Layout

Flow layout is one of the easiest layout managers to use. The JPanel class uses flow layout by default. Flow layout puts as many components as possible on a row, at their preferred size. When a component cannot fit on a row, it is put on the next row. As many rows as needed are added to fit all components that have been added to the container. Figure 7.7 depicts a container governed by a flow layout manager.

The class in Listing 7.20 represents the panel that demonstrates the flow layout in the LayoutDemo program. It explicitly sets the layout to be a flow layout

LISTING 7.19

```java
//********************************************************************
//  IntroPanel.java       Author: Lewis/Loftus
//
//  Represents the introduction panel for the LayoutDemo program.
//********************************************************************

import java.awt.*;
import javax.swing.*;

public class IntroPanel extends JPanel
{
   //-----------------------------------------------------------------
   //  Sets up this panel with two labels.
   //-----------------------------------------------------------------
   public IntroPanel()
   {
      setBackground (Color.green);

      JLabel l1 = new JLabel ("Layout Manager Demonstration");
      JLabel l2 = new JLabel ("Choose a tab to see an example of " +
                              "a layout manager.");

      add (l1);
      add (l2);
   }
}
```

DISPLAY

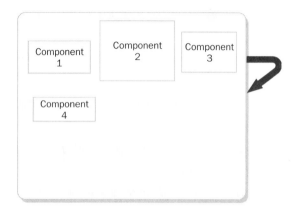

FIGURE 7.7   Flow layout puts as many components as possible on a row

LISTING 7.20

```
//********************************************************************
// FlowPanel.java        Author: Lewis/Loftus
//
// Represents the panel in the LayoutDemo program that demonstrates
// the flow layout manager.
//********************************************************************

import java.awt.*;
import javax.swing.*;

public class FlowPanel extends JPanel
{
   //-----------------------------------------------------------------
   // Sets up this panel with some buttons to show how flow layout
   // affects their position.
   //-----------------------------------------------------------------
   public FlowPanel ()
   {
      setLayout (new FlowLayout());

      setBackground (Color.green);

      JButton b1 = new JButton ("BUTTON 1");
      JButton b2 = new JButton ("BUTTON 2");
      JButton b3 = new JButton ("BUTTON 3");
      JButton b4 = new JButton ("BUTTON 4");
      JButton b5 = new JButton ("BUTTON 5");
```

LISTING 7.20   *continued*

```
        add (b1);
        add (b2);
        add (b3);
        add (b4);
        add (b5);
    }
}
```

DISPLAY

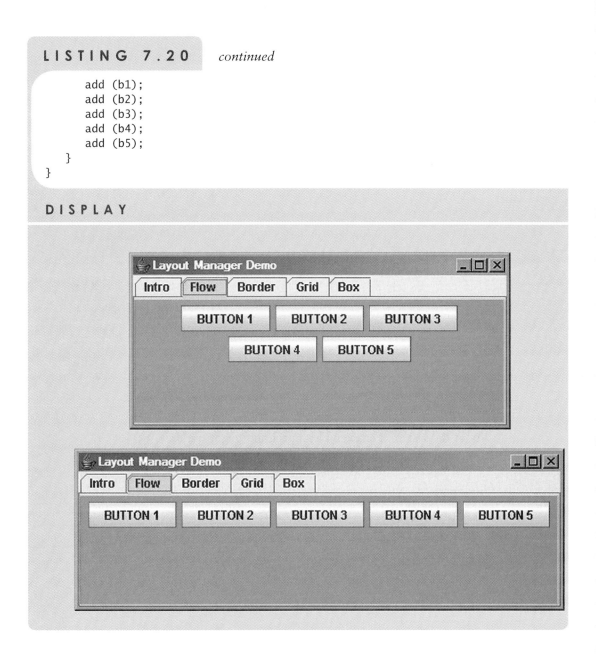

(though in this case that is unnecessary, because JPanel defaults to flow layout). The buttons are then created and added to the panel.

The size of each button is made large enough to accommodate the size of the label that is put on it. As we mentioned earlier, flow layout puts as many of these

VideoNote

Discussion of layout managers.

buttons as possible on one row within the panel, and then starts putting components on another row. When the size of the frame is widened (by dragging the lower-right corner with the mouse, for example), the panel grows as well, and more buttons can fit on a row. When the frame is resized, the layout manager is consulted and the components are reorganized automatically. Note that on each row the components are centered within the window by default.

The constructor of the FlowLayout class is overloaded to allow the programmer to tailor the characteristics of the layout manager. Within each row, components are either centered, left aligned, or right aligned. The alignment defaults to centered. The horizontal and vertical gap size between components also can be specified when the layout manager is created. The FlowLayout class also has methods to set the alignment and gap sizes after the layout manager is created.

Border Layout

A *border layout* has five areas to which components can be added: North, South, East, West, and Center. The areas have a particular positional relationship to each other, as shown in Figure 7.8.

The four outer areas become as big as needed in order to accommodate the component they contain. If no components are added to the North, South, East, or West areas, these areas do not take up any room in the overall layout. The Center area expands to fill any available space.

A particular container might use only a few areas, depending on the functionality of the system. For example, a program might use only the Center, South, and West areas. This versatility makes border layout a very useful layout manager.

The add method for a container governed by a border layout takes as its first parameter the component to be added. The second parameter indicates the area to which it is added. The area is specified using constants defined in the BorderLayout class. Listing 7.21 shows the panel used by the LayoutDemo program to demonstrate the border layout.

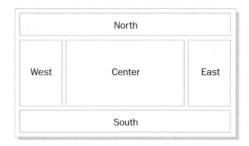

FIGURE 7.8 Border layout organizes components in five areas

LISTING 7.21

```java
//********************************************************************
// BorderPanel.java       Author: Lewis/Loftus
//
// Represents the panel in the LayoutDemo program that demonstrates
// the border layout manager.
//********************************************************************

import java.awt.*;
import javax.swing.*;

public class BorderPanel extends JPanel
{
   //-----------------------------------------------------------------
   // Sets up this panel with a button in each area of a border
   // layout to show how it affects their position, shape, and size.
   //-----------------------------------------------------------------
   public BorderPanel()
   {
      setLayout (new BorderLayout());

      setBackground (Color.green);

      JButton b1 = new JButton ("BUTTON 1");
      JButton b2 = new JButton ("BUTTON 2");
      JButton b3 = new JButton ("BUTTON 3");
      JButton b4 = new JButton ("BUTTON 4");
      JButton b5 = new JButton ("BUTTON 5");

      add (b1, BorderLayout.CENTER);
      add (b2, BorderLayout.NORTH);
      add (b3, BorderLayout.SOUTH);
      add (b4, BorderLayout.EAST);
      add (b5, BorderLayout.WEST);
   }
}
```

LISTING 7.21 *continued*

DISPLAY

In the BorderPanel class constructor, the layout manager of the panel is explicitly set to be border layout. The buttons are then created and added to specific panel areas. By default, each button is made wide enough to accommodate its label and tall enough to fill the area to which it has been assigned. As the frame (and the panel) is resized, the size of each button adjusts as needed, with the button in the Center area filling any unused space.

Each area in a border layout displays only one component. That is, only one component is added to each area of a given border layout. A common error is to add two components to a particular area of a border layout, in which case the first component added is replaced by the second, and only the second is seen when the container is displayed. To add multiple components to an area within a border layout, we first add the components to another container, such as a JPanel, then add the panel to the area.

Note that although the panel used to display the buttons has a green background, no green is visible in the display for Listing 7.21. By default there are no horizontal or vertical gaps between the areas of a border layout. These gaps can be set with an overloaded constructor or with explicit methods of the BorderLayout class. If the gaps are increased, the underlying panel will show through.

Grid Layout

A *grid layout* presents a container's components in a rectangular grid of rows and columns. One component is placed in each grid cell, and all cells are the same size. Figure 7.9 shows the general organization of a grid layout.

The number of rows and columns in a grid layout is established using parameters to the constructor when the layout manager is created. The class in Listing 7.22 shows the panel used by the LayoutDemo program to demonstrate a grid layout. It specifies that the panel should be managed using a grid of two rows and three columns.

As buttons are added to the container, they fill the grid (by default) from left to right and top to bottom. There is no way to explicitly assign a component to a particular location in the grid other than the order in which they are added to the container.

The size of each cell is determined by the container's overall size. When the container is resized, all of the cells change size proportionally to fill the container.

If the value used to specify either the number of rows or the number of columns is zero, the grid expands as needed in that dimension to accommodate the number of components added to the container. The values for the number of rows and columns cannot both be zero.

Component 1	Component 2	Component 3	Component 4
Component 5	Component 6	Component 7	Component 8
Component 9	Component 10	Component 11	Component 12

FIGURE 7.9 Grid layout creates a rectangular grid of equal-sized cells

LISTING 7.22

```java
//********************************************************************
//  GridPanel.java        Author: Lewis/Loftus
//
//  Represents the panel in the LayoutDemo program that demonstrates
//  the grid layout manager.
//********************************************************************

import java.awt.*;
import javax.swing.*;

public class GridPanel extends JPanel
{
    //-----------------------------------------------------------------
    //  Sets up this panel with some buttons to show how grid
    //  layout affects their position, shape, and size.
    //-----------------------------------------------------------------
    public GridPanel()
    {
        setLayout (new GridLayout (2, 3));

        setBackground (Color.green);

        JButton b1 = new JButton ("BUTTON 1");
        JButton b2 = new JButton ("BUTTON 2");
        JButton b3 = new JButton ("BUTTON 3");
        JButton b4 = new JButton ("BUTTON 4");
        JButton b5 = new JButton ("BUTTON 5");

        add (b1);
        add (b2);
        add (b3);
        add (b4);
        add (b5);
    }
}
```

LISTING 7.22   *continued*

DISPLAY

By default, there are no horizontal and vertical gaps between the grid cells. The gap sizes can be specified using an overloaded constructor or with the appropriate GridLayout methods.

Box Layout

A *box layout* organizes components either vertically or horizontally, in one row or one column, as shown in Figure 7.10. It is easy to use, yet when combined with other box layouts, it can produce complex GUI designs similar to those that can be accomplished with a GridBagLayout, which in general is far more difficult to master.

When a BoxLayout object is created, we specify that it will follow either the *X* axis (horizontal) or the *Y* axis (vertical), using constants defined in the BoxLayout class. Unlike other layout managers, the constructor of a BoxLayout takes as its

FIGURE 7.10   Box layout organizes components either vertically or horizontally

first parameter the component that it will govern. Therefore a new BoxLayout object must be created for each component. Listing 7.23 shows the panel used by the LayoutDemo program to demonstrate the box layout.

Components in containers governed by a box layout are organized (top to bottom or left to right) in the order in which they are added to the container.

There are no gaps between the components in a box layout. Unlike previous layout managers we've explored, a box layout does not have a specific vertical or horizontal gap that can be specified for the entire container. Instead, we can add *invisible components* to the container that take up space between other components. The Box class, which is also part of the Java standard class library, contains static methods that can be used to create these invisible components.

The two types of invisible components used in the BoxPanel class are *rigid areas*, which have a fixed size, and *glue*, which specifies where excess space in a container should go. A rigid area is created using the createRigidArea method of the Box class, and takes a Dimension object as a parameter to define the size of the invisible area. Glue is created using the createHorizontalGlue method or createVerticalGlue method, as appropriate.

Note that in our example, the space between buttons separated by a rigid area remains constant even when the container is resized. Glue, on the other hand, expands or contracts as needed to fill the space.

A box layout—more than most of the other layout managers—respects the alignments and the minimum, maximum, and preferred sizes of the components it governs. Therefore, setting the characteristics of the components that go into the container is another way to tailor the visual effect.

LISTING 7.23

```java
//********************************************************************
//  BoxPanel.java       Author: Lewis/Loftus
//
//  Represents the panel in the LayoutDemo program that demonstrates
//  the box layout manager.
//********************************************************************

import java.awt.*;
import javax.swing.*;

public class BoxPanel extends JPanel
{
   //-----------------------------------------------------------------
   // Sets up this panel with some buttons to show how a vertical
   // box layout (and invisible components) affects their position.
   //-----------------------------------------------------------------
   public BoxPanel()
   {
      setLayout (new BoxLayout (this, BoxLayout.Y_AXIS));

      setBackground (Color.green);

      JButton b1 = new JButton ("BUTTON 1");
      JButton b2 = new JButton ("BUTTON 2");
      JButton b3 = new JButton ("BUTTON 3");
      JButton b4 = new JButton ("BUTTON 4");
      JButton b5 = new JButton ("BUTTON 5");

      add (b1);
      add (Box.createRigidArea (new Dimension (0, 10)));
      add (b2);
      add (Box.createVerticalGlue());
      add (b3);
      add (b4);
      add (Box.createRigidArea (new Dimension (0, 20)));
      add (b5);
   }
}
```

LISTING 7.22 *continued*

DISPLAY

SELF-REVIEW QUESTIONS *(see answers in Appendix N)*

SR 7.28   When is a layout manager consulted?

SR 7.29   How does the flow layout manager behave?

SR 7.30   Describe the areas of a border layout.

SR 7.31   What effect does a glue component in a box layout have?

7.12 Borders

Java provides the ability to put a *border* around any Swing component. A border is not a component itself but rather defines how the edge of any component should be drawn and has an important effect on the design of a GUI. A border provides visual cues as to how GUI components are organized and can be used to give titles to components. Figure 7.11 lists the predefined borders in the Java standard class library.

The BorderFactory class is useful for creating borders for components. It has many methods for creating specific types of borders. A border is applied to a component by using the component's setBorder method.

> **KEY CONCEPT**
>
> Borders can be applied to Swing components to group objects and focus attention.

The program in Listing 7.24 demonstrates several types of borders. It simply creates several panels, sets a different border for each, and then displays them in a larger panel by using a grid layout.

Border	Description
Empty Border	Puts buffering space around the edge of a component, but otherwise has no visual effect.
Line Border	A simple line surrounding the component.
Etched Border	Creates the effect of an etched groove around a component.
Bevel Border	Creates the effect of a component raised above the surface or sunken below it.
Titled Border	Includes a text title on or around the border.
Matte Border	Allows the size of each edge to be specified. Uses either a solid color or an image.
Compound Border	A combination of two borders.

FIGURE 7.11   Component borders

LISTING 7.24

```java
//********************************************************************
//  BorderDemo.java        Author: Lewis/Loftus
//
//  Demonstrates the use of various types of borders.
//********************************************************************

import java.awt.*;
import javax.swing.*;
import javax.swing.border.*;

public class BorderDemo
{
   //-----------------------------------------------------------------
   // Creates several bordered panels and displays them.
   //-----------------------------------------------------------------
   public static void main (String[] args)
   {
      JFrame frame = new JFrame ("Border Demo");
      frame.setDefaultCloseOperation (JFrame.EXIT_ON_CLOSE);

      JPanel panel = new JPanel();
      panel.setLayout (new GridLayout (0, 2, 5, 10));
      panel.setBorder (BorderFactory.createEmptyBorder (8, 8, 8, 8));

      JPanel p1 = new JPanel();
      p1.setBorder (BorderFactory.createLineBorder (Color.red, 3));
      p1.add (new JLabel ("Line Border"));
      panel.add (p1);

      JPanel p2 = new JPanel();
      p2.setBorder (BorderFactory.createEtchedBorder ());
      p2.add (new JLabel ("Etched Border"));
      panel.add (p2);

      JPanel p3 = new JPanel();
      p3.setBorder (BorderFactory.createRaisedBevelBorder ());
      p3.add (new JLabel ("Raised Bevel Border"));
      panel.add (p3);

      JPanel p4 = new JPanel();
      p4.setBorder (BorderFactory.createLoweredBevelBorder ());
      p4.add (new JLabel ("Lowered Bevel Border"));
      panel.add (p4);
      JPanel p5 = new JPanel();
```

LISTING 7.24   *continued*

```
        p5.setBorder (BorderFactory.createTitledBorder ("Title"));
        p5.add (new JLabel ("Titled Border"));
        panel.add (p5);

        JPanel p6 = new JPanel();
        TitledBorder tb = BorderFactory.createTitledBorder ("Title");
        tb.setTitleJustification (TitledBorder.RIGHT);
        p6.setBorder (tb);
        p6.add (new JLabel ("Titled Border (right)"));
        panel.add (p6);

        JPanel p7 = new JPanel();
        Border b1 = BorderFactory.createLineBorder (Color.blue, 2);
        Border b2 = BorderFactory.createEtchedBorder ();
        p7.setBorder (BorderFactory.createCompoundBorder (b1, b2));
        p7.add (new JLabel ("Compound Border"));
        panel.add (p7);

        JPanel p8 = new JPanel();
        Border mb = BorderFactory.createMatteBorder (1, 5, 1, 1,
                                                   Color.red);
        p8.setBorder (mb);
        p8.add (new JLabel ("Matte Border"));
        panel.add (p8);

        frame.getContentPane().add (panel);
        frame.pack();
        frame.setVisible(true);
    }
}
```

Let's look at each type of border created in this program. An *empty border* is applied to the larger panel that holds all the others, to create a buffer of space around the outer edge of the frame. The sizes of the top, left, bottom, and right edges of the empty border are specified in pixels. The *line border* is created using a particular color and specifies the line thickness in pixels (3 in this case). The line thickness defaults to 1 pixel if left unspecified. The *etched border* created in this program uses default colors for the highlight and shadow of the etching, but both could be explicitly set if desired.

A *bevel border* can be either raised or lowered. The default coloring is used in this program, although the coloring of each aspect of the bevel can be tailored as

LISTING 7.24 *continued*

DISPLAY

desired, including the outer highlight, inner highlight, outer shadow, and inner shadow. Each of these aspects could be a different color if desired.

A *titled border* places a title on or around the border. The default position for the title is on the border at the top-left edge. Using the setTitleJustification method of the TitledBorder class, this position can be set to many other places above, below, on, or to the left, right, or center of the border.

A *compound border* is a combination of two or more borders. The example in this program creates a compound border using a line border and an etched border. The createCompoundBorder method accepts two borders as parameters and makes the first parameter the outer border and the second parameter the inner border. Combinations of three or more borders are created by first creating a compound border using two borders, then making another compound border using it and yet another one.

A *matte border* specifies the sizes, in pixels, of the top, left, bottom, and right edges of the border. Those edges can be composed of a single color, as they are in this example, or an image icon can be used.

Borders should be used carefully. They can be helpful in drawing attention to appropriate parts of your GUI and can conceptually group related items together. However, if used inappropriately, they can also detract from the elegance of the presentation. Borders should enhance the interface, not complicate or compete with it.

SELF-REVIEW QUESTIONS *(see answers in Appendix N)*   myprogramminglab

SR 7.32 What is the role of the `BorderFactory` class?

SR 7.33 List and briefly describe each of the border types presented in this section.

7.13 Containment Hierarchies

The way components are grouped into containers, and the way those containers are nested within each other, establishes the *containment hierarchy* for a GUI. We introduced this concept in Chapter 3. By carefully designing the containment hierarchy, a GUI can be tailored to have a precise visual effect.

For any Java program, there is generally one primary container, called a *top-level container,* such as a frame or applet. The top-level container of a program often contains one or more other containers, such as panels. These panels may contain other panels to organize the other components as desired.

Each container can have its own layout manager. The final appearance of a GUI is a function of the layout managers chosen for each of the containers and the design of the containment hierarchy. Many combinations are possible, and there is rarely a single best option. As always, we should be guided by the desired system goals and general GUI design guidelines.

> **KEY CONCEPT**
> A GUI's appearance is a function of the containment hierarchy and the layout managers of each container.

Figure 7.12 shows a GUI application that has been annotated to describe its containment hierarchy. Several components used in this program have been discussed previously in this text; others are discussed in later chapters.

Note that in many cases, the use of some containers is not obvious just by looking at the GUI. A panel, in particular, is invisible unless we draw attention to it in some way, such as by giving it a border. We can also use invisible components to provide specific spacing between components. These elements are all part of the containment hierarchy, even though they are not visible to the user.

The entire interface is governed by a border layout with a panel in each area.

North: two labels

East: two labels, a slider, and a combo box with vertical spacing in a box layout

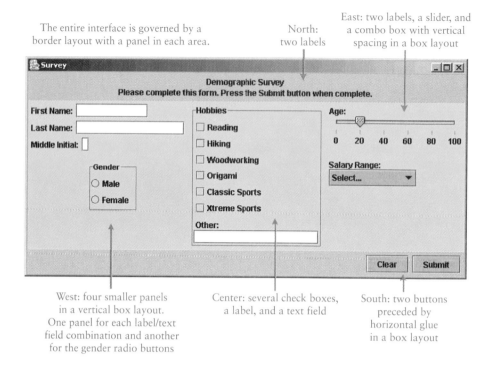

West: four smaller panels in a vertical box layout. One panel for each label/text field combination and another for the gender radio buttons

Center: several check boxes, a label, and a text field

South: two buttons preceded by horizontal glue in a box layout

FIGURE 7.12 The containment hierarchy of a GUI

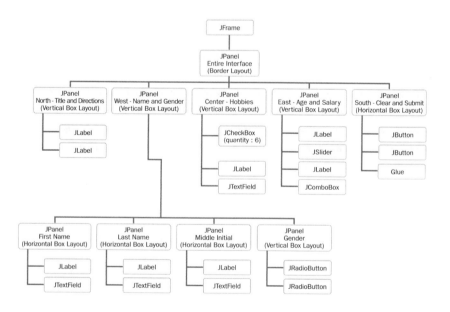

FIGURE 7.13 The containment hierarchy tree

A particular program's containment hierarchy can be represented as a tree structure, such as the one shown in Figure 7.13. The root of the tree is the top-level container. Each level of the tree shows the containers and components held in the containers of the level above.

When changes are made that might affect the visual layout of the components in a program, the layout managers of each container are consulted in turn. The changes in one may affect another. These changes ripple through the containment hierarchy as needed.

SELF-REVIEW QUESTIONS *(see answers in Appendix N)*   myprogramming**lab**

SR 7.34 What is the containment hierarchy for a GUI?

SR 7.35 Draw the containment hierarchy tree for the LeftRight application GUI presented in Chapter 5.

Summary of Key Concepts

- The effort put into design is both crucial and cost effective.

- The nouns in a problem description may indicate some of the classes and objects needed in a program.

- A static variable is shared among all instances of a class.

- An aggregate object is composed of other objects, forming a has-a relationship.

- An interface is a collection of abstract methods and therefore cannot be instantiated.

- The values of an enumerated type are static variables of that type.

- We can add attributes and methods to the definition of an enumerated type.

- A complex service provided by an object can be decomposed to make use of private support methods.

- When an object is passed to a method, the actual and formal parameters become aliases.

- The versions of an overloaded method are distinguished by the number, type, and order of their parameters.

- Testing a program can never guarantee the absence of errors.

- A good test is one that uncovers an error.

- It is not feasible to exhaustively test a program for all possible input and user actions.

- The design of any GUI should adhere to basic guidelines regarding consistency and usability.

- The layout manager of a container determines how components are visually presented.

- When changes occur, the components in a container reorganize themselves according to the layout manager's policy.

- The layout manager for each container can be explicitly set.

- Borders can be applied to Swing components to group objects and focus attention.

- A GUI's appearance is a function of the containment hierarchy and the layout managers of each container.

Exercises

Visit www.myprogramminglab.com to complete many of these Exercises online and get instant feedback.

myprogramminglab

EX 7.1   Write a method called `product` that accepts two integers as input and returns their product.

EX 7.2   Overload the `product` method of Exercise 7.1 so that if three integers are provided as parameters, the method returns the product of all three.

EX 7.3   Overload the `product` method of Exercise 7.1 to accept four integers and return their product.

EX 7.4   Write a method called `StringLength` that takes a string as a parameter and returns the length of the string as an integer by processing it character by character. (Avoid the use of `String` manipulation functions).

EX 7.5   Overload the `StringLength` method from Exercise 7.4 such that if two string parameters are provided, it will return the sum of the lengths of the two strings as an integer.

EX 7.6   Write a method called `drawCircle` that draws a circle based on the method's parameters: a `Graphics` object through which to draw the circle, two integer values representing the (x, y) coordinates of the center of the circle, another integer that represents the circle's radius, and a `Color` object that defines the circle's color. The method does not return anything.

EX 7.7   Overload the `drawCircle` method of Exercise 7.6 such that if the `Color` parameter is not provided, the circle's color will default to black.

EX 7.8   Overload the `drawCircle` method of Exercise 7.6 such that if the radius is not provided, a random radius in the range 10 to 100 (inclusive) will be used.

EX 7.9   Overload the `drawCircle` method of Exercise 7.6 such that if both the color and the radius of the circle are not provided, the color will default to red and the radius will default to 40.

EX 7.10   Does Java handle a `String` as a primitive type or object? Discuss the significance of the `toString` method with an example.

EX 7.11   Discuss when a "review" can be referred to as a "walkthrough" in testing programs.

EX 7.12   What is the `this` reference? Which methods can be invoked through the `this` reference? Discuss.

EX 7.13   Create an interface called `Account` that includes two methods: `getAccount` and `setAccount`. Both methods take the account number as a parameter and return no value. Describe how a class might implement this interface.

EX 7.14   Draw a UML class diagram which depicts the relationship of the classes and the interface of Exercise 7.14.

EX 7.15   Create an interface called `automobile` that has the methods `start` and `stop`. Define two classes, namely `twowheeler` and `fourwheeler`, both of which implement the interface `automobile`.

EX 7.16   Draw a UML class diagram which depicts the relationship of the classes and the interface of Exercise 7.15.

EX 7.17   Which layout organizes components into five areas? Discuss.

EX 7.18   Draw the containment hierarchy tree for the `LayoutDemo` program.

EX 7.19   What visual effect would result by changing the horizontal and vertical gaps on the border layout used in the `LayoutDemo` program? Make the change to test your answer.

EX 7.20   Write the lines of code that will define a compound border using three borders. Use a line border on the inner edge, an etched border on the outer edge, and a raised bevel border in between.

Programming Projects

VideoNote

Developing a solution of PP 7.1.

Visit www.myprogramminglab.com to complete many of these Programming Projects online and get instant feedback.

PP 7.1   Modify the `Account` class from Chapter 4 so that it also permits an account to be opened with just a name and an account number, assuming an initial balance of zero. Modify the `main` method of the `Transactions` class to demonstrate this new capability.

PP 7.2   Modify the `Student` class presented in this chapter as follows. Each student object should also contain the scores for three tests. Provide a constructor that sets all instance values based on parameter values. Overload the constructor such that each test score is assumed to be initially zero. Provide a method called `setTestScore` that accepts two parameters: the test number

(1 through 3) and the score. Also provide a method called getTestScore that accepts the test number and returns the appropriate score. Provide a method called average that computes and returns the average test score for this student. Modify the toString method such that the test scores and average are included in the description of the student. Modify the driver class main method to exercise the new Student methods.

PP 7.3   Design and implement a class called Course that represents a course taken at a school. A course object should keep track of up to five students, as represented by the modified Student class from the previous programming project. The constructor of the Course class should accept only the name of the course. Provide a method called addStudent that accepts one Student parameter (the Course object should keep track of how many valid students have been added to the course). Provide a method called average that computes and returns the average of all students' test score averages. Provide a method called roll that prints all students in the course. Create a driver class with a main method that creates a course, adds several students, prints a roll, and prints the overall course test average.

PP 7.4   Modify the RationalNumber class so that it implements the Comparable interface. To perform the comparison, compute an equivalent floating point value from the numerator and denominator for both RationalNumber objects, then compare them using a tolerance value of 0.0001. Write a main driver to test your modifications.

PP 7.5   Design a Java interface called Priority that includes two methods: setPriority and getPriority. The interface should define a way to establish numeric priority among a set of objects. Design and implement a class called Task that represents a task (such as on a to-do list) that implements the Priority interface. Create a driver class to exercise some Task objects.

PP 7.6   Modify the Task class from PP 7.5 so that it also implements the Complexity interface defined in this chapter. Modify the driver class to show these new features of Task objects.

PP 7.7   Modify the Task class from PPs 7.5 and 7.6 so that it also implements the Comparable interface from the Java standard class library. Implement the interface such that the tasks are ranked by priority. Create a driver class whose main method shows these new features of Task objects.

PP 7.8 Design a Java interface called Lockable that includes the following methods: setKey, lock, unlock, and locked. The setKey, lock, and unlock methods take an integer parameter that represents the key. The setKey method establishes the key. The lock and unlock methods lock and unlock the object, but only if the key passed in is correct. The locked method returns a boolean that indicates whether or not the object is locked. A Lockable object represents an object whose regular methods are protected: if the object is locked, the methods cannot be invoked; if it is unlocked, they can be invoked. Redesign and implement a version of the Coin class from Chapter 5 so that it is Lockable.

PP 7.9 Implement a calculator with numeric keys for the numbers from 0 to 9, along with arithmetic operators (+, -, *, /) and a display box. This should be designed in a GUI using a grid layout.

PP 7.10 Implement a Text Manipulator program which uses GUI to accept a String and displays the total number of words and characters present in that string. Accept the input using a text box and display the results in a label.

PP 7.11 Modify the IntroPanel class of the LayoutDemo program so that it uses a box layout manager. Use invisible components to put space before and between the two labels on the panel.

PP 7.12 Modify the QuoteOptions program from Chapter 5 to change its visual appearance. Present the radio buttons in a vertical column with a surrounding border to the left of the quote label.

PP 7.13 Design and implement a program that displays a numeric keypad that might appear on a phone. Above the keypad buttons, show a label that displays the numbers as they are picked. To the right of the keypad buttons, include another button to clear the display. Use a border layout to manage the overall presentation, and a grid layout to manage the keypad buttons. Put a border around the keypad buttons to group them visually, and a border around the display.

PP 7.14 Design and implement an application that helps a pizza restaurant take orders. Use a tabbed pane for different categories of food (pizza, beverages, special items). Collect information about quantity and size. Display the cost of the order as information is gathered. Use appropriate components for collecting the various kinds of information. Structure the interface carefully using the containment hierarchy and layout managers.

2003 Northeast Blackout

What Happened?

On August 14, 2003, the largest electrical blackout in American history hit the northeastern United States and parts of Canada. Several metropolitan areas were affected, including New York, Cleveland, Detroit, Toronto, and Ottawa. Within a span of three minutes, 21 power plants had shut down, affecting approximately 50 million people.

■ The northeastern United States before and after the blackout.

The typical problems resulted in the blackout areas. Lack of traffic lights caused traffic problems. Trains and elevators were stuck. Airports delayed flights. Water pressure that relied on electric pumps failed. Cell phone usage was disrupted. (Wired telephone usage was still available, but it was overtaxed during the emergency.) Internet traffic slowed due to downed servers and the attempt to reroute messages. Some incidents of looting were reported.

Estimates place the total financial cost of the blackout anywhere between $4 and $8 billion. Nine people died from various causes related to the blackout.

What Caused It?

Many sources of the problem were blamed during the early hours and days after the blackout. Because of the heightened consciousness after the September 11, 2001 attacks, authorities were quick to rule out terrorism. Downed trees and lightning strikes throughout the affected region were blamed. Officials even considered---but quickly ruled out---the "Blaster" computer worm that was spreading at the time.

Over the course of the next few months, a task force sorted out the issues. The initial cause was determined to be in Akron, Ohio, where the FirstEnergy Corp. had failed to keep trees near the power lines trimmed appropriately. On August 14, 2003, tree limbs caused three power lines to fail simultaneously. When such failures occur, the operators at the power control center are responsible for keeping the load balanced. In this case, they failed to do so, because the computer-based alarm system that would have informed them of the problem failed to operate correctly. The load imbalance quickly spread to neighboring power plants, resulting in the cascading blackout.

So although there were various contributing factors, a big part of the problem was the failure of the alarm system. This issue eventually was traced to a race condition bug in the computer General Electric Energys used to monitor alarms.

A race condition in a computer program occurs when two or more processes running concurrently access some shared data. One modifies the data after another has read it, and they both continue processing under the wrong assumptions. In this case, three power lines failing simultaneously caused the race condition that caused the alarm system to fail, which went unnoticed by the operators. Resulting problems caused the entire system to crash shortly thereafter. The backup system crashed for the same reasons. After the bug was discovered, GE issued a patch to correct it.

Lessons Learned

The problems of this event stemmed not from a lack of power but on the inability to get the power where it was needed. This blackout highlighted the poor infrastructure of power lines that exist and the danger of relying on voluntary rules for maintaining the reliability of the power grid.

Regarding the software culpability, race conditions are a known source of failure in concurrent systems and must be tested for thoroughly. Formal analysis is warranted in situations like this one where so much is at stake.

Sources: CNN.com, WashingtonPost.com

Arrays

8

CHAPTER OBJECTIVES

- Define and use arrays for basic data organization.
- Discuss bounds checking and techniques for managing capacity.
- Discuss the issues related to arrays as objects and arrays of objects.
- Explore the use of command-line arguments.
- Describe the syntax and use of variable-length parameter lists.
- Discuss the creation and use of multidimensional arrays.
- Explore mouse and keyboard events.

In our programming efforts, we often want to organize objects or primitive data in a form that is easy to access and modify. The ArrayList class, explored in Chapter 5, was used for exactly that purpose. As the class name implies, an ArrayList is implemented using arrays, which are programming constructs that group data into lists. In this chapter we'll explore the details of arrays, which are a fundamental component of most high-level languages. In the Graphics Track sections of this chapter, we explore methods that let us draw complex multisided figures, and examine the events generated by the mouse and the keyboard.

8.1 Array Elements

An *array* is a simple but powerful programming language construct used to group and organize data. When writing a program that manages a large amount of information, such as a list of 100 names, it is not practical to declare separate variables for each piece of data. Arrays solve this problem by letting us declare one variable that can hold multiple, individually accessible values.

An array is a list of values. Each value is stored at a specific, numbered position in the array. The number corresponding to each position is called an *index* or a *subscript*. Figure 8.1 shows an array of integers and the indexes that correspond to each position. The array is called height; it contains integers that represent several peoples' heights in inches.

In Java, array indexes always begin at zero. Therefore the value stored at index 5 is actually the sixth value in the array. The array shown in Figure 8.1 has 11 values, indexed from 0 to 10.

> **KEY CONCEPT**
> An array of size N is indexed from 0 to N–1.

To access a value in an array, we use the name of the array followed by the index in square brackets. For example, the following expression refers to the ninth value in the array height:

height[8]

According to Figure 8.1, height[8] (pronounced height-sub-eight) contains the value 79. Don't confuse the value of the index, in this case 8, with the value stored in the array at that index, in this case 79.

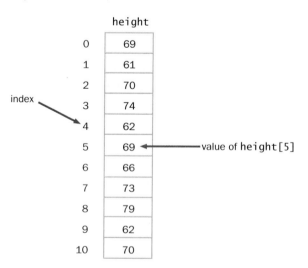

FIGURE 8.1 An array called height containing integer values

The expression `height[8]` refers to a single integer stored at a particular memory location. It can be used wherever an integer variable can be used. Therefore you can assign a value to it, use it in calculations, print its value, and so on. Furthermore, because array indexes are integers, you can use integer expressions to specify the index used to access an array. These concepts are demonstrated in the following lines of code:

```
height[2] = 72;
height[count] = feet * 12;
average = (height[0] + height[1] + height[2]) / 3;
System.out.println ("The middle value is " + height[MAX/2]);
pick = height[rand.nextInt(11)];
```

Arrays are stored contiguously in memory, meaning that the elements are stored one right after the other in memory just as we picture them conceptually. This makes an array extremely efficient in terms of accessing any particular element by its index. Internally, to determine the address of any particular element, the index is multiplied by the size of each element, and added to the memory address of the starting point of the array. That's why array indexes begin at zero instead of one— to make that computation as easy as possible. So from an efficiency point of view, it's as easy to access the 500th element in the array as it is to access the first element.

SELF-REVIEW QUESTIONS *(see answers in Appendix N)*

myprogramminglab

SR 8.1   What is an array?

SR 8.2   How is each element of an array referenced?

SR 8.3   Based on the array shown in Figure 8.1, what are each of the following?

  a. `height[1]`
  b. `height[2] + height[5]`
  c. `height[2 + 5]`
  d. the value stored at index 8
  e. the fourth value
  f. `height.length`

8.2 Declaring and Using Arrays

In Java, arrays are objects. To create an array, the reference to the array must be declared. The array can then be instantiated using the new operator, which allocates memory space to store values. The following code represents the declaration for the array shown in Figure 8.1:

```
int[] height = new int[11];
```

The variable `height` is declared to be an array of integers whose
type is written as `int[]`. All values stored in an array have the same
type (or are at least compatible). For example, we can create an
array that can hold integers or an array that can hold strings, but
not an array that can hold both integers and strings. An array can be
set up to hold any primitive type or any object (class) type. A value stored in an
array is sometimes called an *array element*, and the type of values that an array
holds is called the *element type* of the array.

LISTING 8.1

```java
//********************************************************************
//  BasicArray.java       Author: Lewis/Loftus
//
//  Demonstrates basic array declaration and use.
//********************************************************************

public class BasicArray
{
   //-----------------------------------------------------------------
   //  Creates an array, fills it with various integer values,
   //  modifies one value, then prints them out.
   //-----------------------------------------------------------------
   public static void main (String[] args)
   {
      final int LIMIT = 15, MULTIPLE = 10;

      int[] list = new int[LIMIT];

      // Initialize the array values
      for (int index = 0; index < LIMIT; index++)
         list[index] = index * MULTIPLE;

      list[5] = 999; // change one array value

      // Print the array values
      for (int value : list)
         System.out.print (value + " ");
   }
}
```

OUTPUT

```
0   10   20   30   40   999   60   70   80   90   100   110   120   130   140
```

Note that the type of the array variable (`int[]`) does not include the size of the array. The instantiation of `height`, using the `new` operator, reserves the memory space to store 11 integers indexed from 0 to 10. Once an array is declared to be a certain size, the number of values it can hold cannot be changed.

VideoNote

Overview of arrays.

The example shown in Listing 8.1 creates an array called `list` that can hold 15 integers, which it loads with successive increments of 10. It then changes the value of the sixth element in the array (at index 5). Finally, it prints all values stored in the array.

Figure 8.2 shows the array as it changes during the execution of the `BasicArray` program. It is often convenient to use `for` loops when handling arrays, because the number of positions in the array is constant. Note that a constant called `LIMIT` is used in several places in the `BasicArray` program. This constant is used to declare the size of the array and to control the `for` loop that initializes the array values.

The iterator version of the `for` loop is used to print the values in the array. Recall from Chapter 5 that this version of the `for` loop extracts each value in the

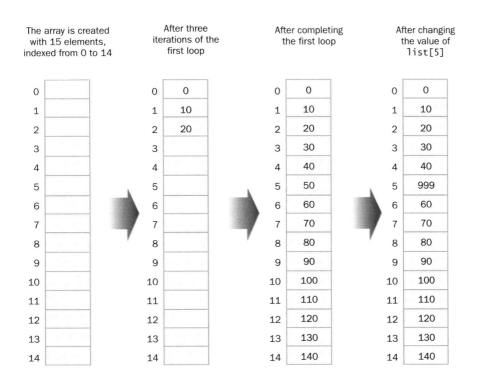

FIGURE 8.2   The array `list` as it changes in the `BasicArray` program

specified iterator. Every Java array is an iterator, so this type of loop can be used whenever we want to process every element stored in an array.

The square brackets used to indicate the index of an array are treated as an operator in Java. Therefore, just like the + operator or the <= operator, the index operator ([]) has a precedence relative to the other Java operators that determines when it is executed. It has the highest precedence of all Java operators.

Bounds Checking

The index operator performs automatic *bounds checking*, which ensures that the index is in range for the array being referenced. Whenever a reference to an array element is made, the index must be greater than or equal to zero and less than the size of the array. For example, suppose an array called prices is created with 25 elements. The valid indexes for the array are from 0 to 24. Whenever a reference is made to a particular element in the array (such as prices[count]), the value of the index is checked. If it is in the valid range of indexes for the array (0 to 24), the reference is carried out. If the index is not valid, an exception called ArrayIndexOutOfBoundsException is thrown.

> **KEY CONCEPT**
> Bounds checking ensures that an index used to refer to an array element is in range.

Of course, in our programs we'll want to perform our own bounds checking. That is, we'll want to be careful to remain within the bounds of the array and process every element we intend to. Because array indexes begin at zero and go up to one less than the size of the array, it is easy to create *off-by-one errors* in a program, which are problems created by processing all but one element or by attempting to index one element too many.

One way to check for the bounds of an array is to use the length constant, which is held in the array object and stores the size of the array. It is a public constant and therefore can be referenced directly. For example, after the array prices is created with 25 elements, the constant prices.length contains the value 25. Its value is set once when the array is first created and cannot be changed. The length constant, which is an integral part of each array, can be used when the array size is needed without having to create a separate constant. Remember that the length of the array is the number of elements it can hold, thus the maximum index of an array is length-1.

Let's look at another example. The program shown in Listing 8.2 reads 10 integers into an array called numbers, and then prints them in reverse order.

Note that in the ReverseOrder program, the array numbers is declared to have 10 elements and therefore is indexed from 0 to 9. The index range is controlled in the for loops by using the length field of the array object. You should carefully set the initial value of loop control variables and the conditions that terminate loops to guarantee that all intended elements are processed and only valid indexes are used to reference an array element.

LISTING 8.2

```java
//********************************************************************
//  ReverseOrder.java          Author: Lewis/Loftus
//
//  Demonstrates array index processing.
//********************************************************************

import java.util.Scanner;

public class ReverseOrder
{
   //-----------------------------------------------------------------
   //  Reads a list of numbers from the user, storing them in an
   //  array, then prints them in the opposite order.
   //-----------------------------------------------------------------
   public static void main (String[] args)
   {
      Scanner scan = new Scanner (System.in);

      double[] numbers = new double[10];

      System.out.println ("The size of the array: " + numbers.length);

      for (int index = 0; index < numbers.length; index++)
      {
         System.out.print ("Enter number " + (index+1) + ": ");
         numbers[index] = scan.nextDouble();
      }

      System.out.println ("The numbers in reverse order:");

      for (int index = numbers.length-1; index >= 0; index--)
         System.out.print (numbers[index] + " ");
   }
}
```

OUTPUT

```
The size of the array: 10
Enter number 1: 18.36
Enter number 2: 48.9
Enter number 3: 53.5
Enter number 4: 29.06
```

LISTING 8.2   *continued*

```
Enter number 5: 72.404
Enter number 6: 34.8
Enter number 7: 63.41
Enter number 8: 45.55
Enter number 9: 69.0
Enter number 10: 99.18
The numbers in reverse order:
99.18  69.0  45.55  63.41  34.8  72.404  29.06  53.5  48.9  18.36
```

The LetterCount example, shown in Listing 8.3, uses two arrays and a String object. The array called upper is used to store the number of times each uppercase alphabetic letter is found in the string. The array called lower serves the same purpose for lowercase letters.

Because there are 26 letters in the English alphabet, both the upper and lower arrays are declared with 26 elements. Each element contains an integer that is initially zero by default. The for loop scans through the string one character at a time. The appropriate counter in the appropriate array is incremented for each character found in the string.

LISTING 8.3

```java
//********************************************************************
//  LetterCount.java       Author: Lewis/Loftus
//
//  Demonstrates the relationship between arrays an strings.
//********************************************************************

import java.util.Scanner;

public class LetterCount
{
   //-----------------------------------------------------------------
   //  Reads a sentence from the user and counts the number of
   //  uppercase and lowercase letters contained in it.
   //-----------------------------------------------------------------
   public static void main (String[] args)
   {
      final int NUMCHARS = 26;
```

LISTING 8.3   *continued*

```java
Scanner scan = new Scanner (System.in);

int[] upper = new int[NUMCHARS];
int[] lower = new int[NUMCHARS];

char current;    // the current character being processed
int other = 0;   // counter for non-alphabetics

System.out.println ("Enter a sentence:");
String line = scan.nextLine();

// Count the number of each letter occurrence
for (int ch = 0; ch < line.length(); ch++)
{
    current = line.charAt(ch);
    if (current >= 'A' && current <= 'Z')
      upper[current-'A']++;
    else
      if (current >= 'a' && current <= 'z')
        lower[current-'a']++;
      else
        other++;
}

// Print the results
System.out.println ();
for (int letter=0; letter < upper.length; letter++)
{
    System.out.print ( (char) (letter + 'A') );
    System.out.print (": " + upper[letter]);
    System.out.print ("\t\t" + (char) (letter + 'a') );
    System.out.println (": " + lower[letter]);
}

System.out.println ();
System.out.println ("Non-alphabetic characters: " + other);
    }
}
```

LISTING 8.3   *continued*

OUTPUT

```
Enter a sentence:
In Casablanca, Humphrey Bogart never says "Play it again, Sam."

A: 0              a: 10
B: 1              b: 1
C: 1              c: 1
D: 0              d: 0
E: 0              e: 3
F: 0              f: 0
G: 0              g: 2
H: 1              h: 1
I: 1              i: 2
J: 0              j: 0
K: 0              k: 0
L: 0              l: 2
M: 0              m: 2
N: 0              n: 4
O: 0              o: 1
P: 1              p: 1
Q: 0              q: 0
R: 0              r: 3
S: 1              s: 3
T: 0              t: 2
U: 0              u: 1
V: 0              v: 1
W: 0              w: 0
X: 0              x: 0
Y: 0              y: 3
Z: 0              z: 0

Non-alphabetic characters: 14
```

VideoNote

Discussion of the
LetterCount example.

Both of the counter arrays are indexed from 0 to 25. We have to map each character to a counter. A logical way to do this is to use upper[0] to count the number of 'A' characters found, upper[1] to count the number of 'B' characters found, and so on. Likewise, lower[0] is used to count 'a' characters, lower[1] is used to count `'b'` characters, and so on. A separate variable called `other` is used to count any nonalphabetic characters that are encountered.

Note that to determine if a character is an uppercase letter we used the boolean expression (`current >= 'A' && current <= 'Z'`). A similar expression is used for determining the lowercase letters. We could have used the static methods `isUpperCase` and `isLowerCase` in the `Character` class to make these determinations but didn't in this example to drive home the point that because characters are based on the Unicode character set, they have a specific numeric value and order that we can use in our programming.

We use the current character to calculate which index in the array to reference. We have to be careful when calculating an index to ensure that it remains within the bounds of the array and matches to the correct element. Remember that in the Unicode character set, the uppercase and lowercase alphabetic letters are continuous and in order (see Appendix C). Therefore, taking the numeric value of an uppercase letter such as `'E'` (which is 69) and subtracting the numeric value of the character `'A'` (which is 65) yields 4, which is the correct index for the counter of the character `'E'`. Note that nowhere in the program do we actually need to know the specific numeric values for each letter.

Alternate Array Syntax

Syntactically, there are two ways to declare an array reference in Java. The first technique, which is used in the previous examples and throughout this text, is to associate the brackets with the type of values stored in the array. The second technique is to associate the brackets with the name of the array. Therefore, the following two declarations are equivalent:

```
int[] grades;
int grades[];
```

Although there is no difference between these declaration techniques as far as the compiler is concerned, the first is consistent with other types of declarations. The declared type is explicit if the array brackets are associated with the element type, especially if there are multiple variables declared on the same line. Therefore we associate the brackets with the element type throughout this text.

Initializer Lists

You can use an *initializer list* to instantiate an array and provide the initial values for the elements of the array. It is essentially the same idea as initializing a variable of a primitive data type in its declaration except that an array requires several values.

The items in an initializer list are separated by commas and delimited by braces ({}). When an initializer list is used, the new operator is not used. The size of the array is determined by the number of items in the initializer list. For example, the following declaration instantiates the array scores as an array of eight integers, indexed from 0 to 7 with the specified initial values:

```
int[] scores = {87, 98, 69, 87, 65, 76, 99, 83};
```

An initializer list can be used only when an array is first declared.

The type of each value in an initializer list must match the type of the array elements. Let's look at another example:

```
char[] vowels = {'A', 'E', 'I', 'O', 'U'};
```

In this case, the variable vowels is declared to be an array of five characters, and the initializer list contains character literals.

The program shown in Listing 8.4 demonstrates the use of an initializer list to instantiate an array.

Arrays as Parameters

An entire array can be passed as a parameter to a method. Because an array is an object, when an entire array is passed as a parameter, a copy of the reference to the original array is passed. We discussed this issue as it applies to all objects in Chapter 7.

A method that receives an array as a parameter can permanently change an element of the array, because it is referring to the original element value. The method cannot permanently change the reference to the array itself, because a copy of the original reference is sent to the method. These rules are consistent with the rules that govern any object type.

An element of an array can be passed to a method as well. If the element type is a primitive type, a copy of the value is passed. If that element is a reference to an object, a copy of the object reference is passed. As always, the impact of changes made to a parameter inside the method depends on the type of the parameter. We discuss arrays of objects further in the next section.

LISTING 8.4

```java
//********************************************************************
//  Primes.java       Author: Lewis/Loftus
//
//  Demonstrates the use of an initializer list for an array.
//********************************************************************

public class Primes
{
   //-----------------------------------------------------------------
   //  Stores some prime numbers in an array and prints them.
   //-----------------------------------------------------------------
   public static void main (String[] args)
   {
      int[] primeNums = {2, 3, 5, 7, 11, 13, 17, 19};

      System.out.println ("Array length: " + primeNums.length);

      System.out.println ("The first few prime numbers are:");

      for (int prime : primeNums)
         System.out.print (prime + " ");
   }
}
```

OUTPUT

```
Array length: 8
The first few prime numbers are:
2  3  5  7  11  13  17  19
```

SELF-REVIEW QUESTIONS *(see answers in Appendix N)*

SR 8.4   What is an array's element type?

SR 8.5   Describe the process of creating an array. When is memory allocated for the array?

SR 8.6   Write an array declaration to represent the ages of all 100 children attending a summer camp.

SR 8.7   Write an array declaration to represent the counts of how many times each face appeared when a standard six-sided die is rolled.

SR 8.8   Explain the concept of array bounds checking. What happens when a Java array is indexed with an invalid value?

SR 8.9   What is an off-by-one error? How does it relate to arrays?

SR 8.10   Write code that increments (by one) each element of an array of integers named `values`.

SR 8.11   Write code that computes and prints the sum of the elements of an array of integers named `values`.

SR 8.12   What does an array initializer list accomplish?

SR 8.13   Can an entire array be passed as a parameter? How is this accomplished?

8.3 Arrays of Objects

In the previous examples in this chapter, we used arrays to store primitive types such as integers and characters. Arrays can also store references to objects as elements. Fairly complex information management structures can be created using only arrays and other objects. For example, an array could contain objects, and each of those objects could consist of several variables and the methods that use them. Those variables could themselves be arrays, and so on. The design of a program should capitalize on the ability to combine these constructs to create the most appropriate representation for the information.

Keep in mind that the array itself is an object. So it would be appropriate to picture an array of `int` values called `weight` as follows:

KEY CONCEPT

Instantiating an array of objects reserves room to store references only. The objects that are stored in each element must be instantiated separately.

When we store objects in an array, each element is a separate object. That is, an array of objects is really an array of object references. Consider the following declaration:

```
String[] words = new String[5];
```

The variable words is an array of references to String objects. The new operator in the declaration instantiates the array and reserves space for five String references. This declaration does not create any String objects; it merely creates an array that holds references to String objects. Initially, the array looks like this:

After a few String objects are created and put in the array, it might look like this:

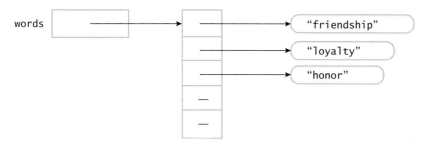

The words array is an object, and each character string it holds is its own object. Each object contained in an array has to be instantiated separately.

Keep in mind that String objects can be represented as string literals. So the following declaration creates an array called verbs and uses an initializer list to populate it with several String objects, each instantiated using a string literal:

```
String[] verbs = {"play", "work", "eat", "sleep"};
```

The program called GradeRange shown in Listing 8.5 creates an array of Grade objects, then prints them. The Grade objects are created using several new operators in the initialization list of the array.

The Grade class is shown in Listing 8.6. Each Grade object represents a letter grade for a school course and includes a numerical lower bound. The values for the grade name and lower bound can be set using the Grade constructor, or using appropriate mutator methods. Accessor methods are also defined, as is a toString method to return a string representation of the grade. The toString method is automatically invoked when the grades are printed in the main method.

Let's look at another example. Listing 8.7 shows the Movies class, which contains a main method that creates, modifies, and examines a DVD collection.

LISTING 8.5

```java
//********************************************************************
//  GradeRange.java       Author: Lewis/Loftus
//
// Demonstrates the use of an array of objects.
//********************************************************************

public class GradeRange
{
   //-----------------------------------------------------------------
   //  Creates an array of Grade objects and prints them.
   //-----------------------------------------------------------------
   public static void main (String[] args)
   {
      Grade[] grades =
      {
         new Grade("A", 95), new Grade("A-", 90),
         new Grade("B+", 87), new Grade("B", 85), new Grade("B-", 80),
         new Grade("C+", 77), new Grade("C", 75), new Grade("C-", 70),
         new Grade("D+", 67), new Grade("D", 65), new Grade("D-", 60),
         new Grade("F", 0)
      };

      for (Grade letterGrade : grades)
         System.out.println (letterGrade);
   }
}
```

OUTPUT

```
A        95
A-       90
B+       87
B        85
B-       80
C+       77
C        75
C-       70
D+       67
D        65
D-       60
F        0
```

LISTING 8.6

```java
//********************************************************************
//  Grade.java        Author: Lewis/Loftus
//
//  Represents a school grade.
//********************************************************************

public class Grade
{
    private String name;
    private int lowerBound;

    //-----------------------------------------------------------------
    //  Constructor: Sets up this Grade object with the specified
    //  grade name and numeric lower bound.
    //-----------------------------------------------------------------
    public Grade (String grade, int cutoff)
    {
        name = grade;
        lowerBound = cutoff;
    }

    //-----------------------------------------------------------------
    //  Returns a string representation of this grade.
    //-----------------------------------------------------------------
    public String toString()
    {
        return name + "\t" + lowerBound;
    }

    //-----------------------------------------------------------------
    //  Name mutator.
    //-----------------------------------------------------------------
    public void setName (String grade)
    {
        name = grade;
    }

    //-----------------------------------------------------------------
    //  Lower bound mutator.
    //-----------------------------------------------------------------
    public void setLowerBound (int cutoff)
    {
        lowerBound = cutoff;
    }
```

LISTING 8.6 *continued*

```java
    //----------------------------------------------------------
    // Name accessor.
    //----------------------------------------------------------
    public String getName()
    {
        return name;
    }

    //----------------------------------------------------------
    // Lower bound accessor.
    //----------------------------------------------------------
    public int getLowerBound()
    {
        return lowerBound;
    }
}
```

LISTING 8.7

```java
//********************************************************************
//  Movies.java       Author: Lewis/Loftus
//
//  Demonstrates the use of an array of objects.
//********************************************************************

public class Movies
{
    //----------------------------------------------------------------
    // Creates a DVDCollection object and adds some DVDs to it. Prints
    // reports on the status of the collection.
    //----------------------------------------------------------------
    public static void main (String[] args)
    {
        DVDCollection movies = new DVDCollection();

        movies.addDVD ("The Godfather", "Francis Ford Coppola", 1972, 24.95, true);
        movies.addDVD ("District 9", "Neill Blomkamp", 2009, 19.95, false);
        movies.addDVD ("Iron Man", "Jon Favreau", 2008, 15.95, false);
        movies.addDVD ("All About Eve", "Joseph Mankiewicz", 1950, 17.50, false);
        movies.addDVD ("The Matrix", "Andy & Lana Wachowski", 1999, 19.95, true);
```

LISTING 8.7   *continued*

```
        System.out.println (movies);

        movies.addDVD ("Iron Man 2", "Jon Favreau", 2010, 22.99, false);
        movies.addDVD ("Casablanca", "Michael Curtiz", 1942, 19.95, false);

        System.out.println (movies);
    }
}
```

OUTPUT

```
~~~~~~~~~~~~~~~~~~~~~~~~~~~~~~~~~~~~~~~~~~~
My DVD Collection

Number of DVDs: 5
Total cost: $98.30
Average cost: $19.66


DVD List:

$24.95  1972      The Godfather    Francis Ford Coppola     Blu-ray
$19.95  2009      District 9       Neill Blomkamp
$15.95  2008      Iron Man         Jon Favreau
$17.50  1950      All About Eve    Joseph Mankiewicz
$19.95  1999      The Matrix       Andy & Lana Wachowski    Blu-ray


~~~~~~~~~~~~~~~~~~~~~~~~~~~~~~~~~~~~~~~~~~~
My DVD Collection

Number of DVDs: 7
Total cost: $141.24
Average cost: $20.18

DVD List:

$24.95  1972      The Godfather    Francis Ford Coppola     Blu-ray
$19.95  2009      District 9       Neill Blomkamp
$15.95  2008      Iron Man         Jon Favreau
$17.50  1950      All About Eve    Joseph Mankiewicz
$19.95  1999      The Matrix       Andy & Lana Wachowski    Blu-ray
$22.99  2010      Iron Man 2       Jon Favreau
$19.95  1942      Casablanca       Michael Curtiz
```

Each DVD added to the collection is specified by its title, director, year of release, purchase price, and whether or not it is in Blu-ray format.

Listing 8.8 shows the DVDCollection class. It contains an array of DVD objects representing the collection. It maintains a count of the DVDs in the collection and their combined value. It also keeps track of the current size of the collection array so that a larger array can be created if too many DVDs are added to the collection.

LISTING 8.8

```java
//********************************************************************
//  DVDCollection.java          Author: Lewis/Loftus
//
//  Represents a collection of DVD movies.
//********************************************************************

import java.text.NumberFormat;

public class DVDCollection
{
   private DVD[] collection;
   private int count;
   private double totalCost;

   //-----------------------------------------------------------------
   // Constructor: Creates an initially empty collection.
   //-----------------------------------------------------------------
   public DVDCollection ()
   {
      collection = new DVD[100];
      count = 0;
      totalCost = 0.0;
   }

   //-----------------------------------------------------------------
   // Adds a DVD to the collection, increasing the size of the
   // collection array if necessary.
   //-----------------------------------------------------------------
   public void addDVD (String title, String director, int year,
                       double cost, boolean bluray)
   {
      if (count == collection.length)
        increaseSize();

      collection[count] = new DVD (title, director, year, cost, bluray);
```

LISTING 8.8   *continued*

```java
        totalCost += cost;
        count++;
    }

    //---------------------------------------------------------------
    // Returns a report describing the DVD collection.
    //---------------------------------------------------------------
    public String toString()
    {
        NumberFormat fmt = NumberFormat.getCurrencyInstance();

        String report = "~~~~~~~~~~~~~~~~~~~~~~~~~~~~~~~~~~~~~~~~~~~~~~\n";
        report += "My DVD Collection\n\n";

        report += "Number of DVDs: " + count + "\n";
        report += "Total cost: " + fmt.format(totalCost) + "\n";
        report += "Average cost: " + fmt.format(totalCost/count);

        report += "\n\nDVD List:\n\n";

        for (int dvd = 0; dvd < count; dvd++)
          report += collection[dvd].toString() + "\n";

        return report;
    }

    //---------------------------------------------------------------
    // Increases the capacity of the collection by creating a
    // larger array and copying the existing collection into it.
    //---------------------------------------------------------------
    private void increaseSize ()
    {
        DVD[] temp = new DVD[collection.length * 2];

        for (int dvd = 0; dvd < collection.length; dvd++)
           temp[dvd] = collection[dvd];

        collection = temp;
    }
}
```

The collection array is instantiated in the DVDCollection constructor. Every time a DVD is added to the collection (using the addDVD method), a new DVD object is created and a reference to it is stored in the collection array.

Each time a DVD is added to the collection, we check to see whether we have reached the current capacity of the collection array. If we didn't perform this check, an exception would eventually be thrown when we try to store a new DVD object at an invalid index. If the current capacity has been reached, the private increaseSize method is invoked, which first creates an array that is twice as big as the current collection array. Each DVD in the existing collection is then copied into the new array. Finally, the collection reference is set to the larger array. Using this technique, we theoretically never run out of room in our DVD collection. The user of the DVDCollection object (the main method in this case) never has to worry about running out of space, because it's all handled internally.

Figure 8.3 shows a UML class diagram of the Movies program. Recall that the open diamond indicates aggregation. The cardinality of the relationship is also noted: a DVDCollection object contains zero or more DVD objects.

The toString method of the DVDCollection class returns an entire report summarizing the collection. The report is created, in part, using calls to the toString method of each DVD object stored in the collection. Listing 8.9 shows the DVD class.

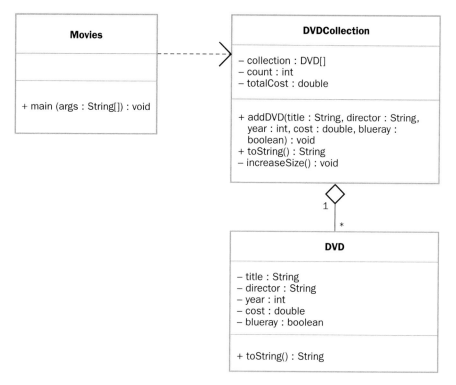

FIGURE 8.3   A UML class diagram of the Movies program

LISTING 8.9

```java
//********************************************************************
//  DVD.java          Author: Lewis/Loftus
//
//  Represents a DVD video disc.
//********************************************************************

import java.text.NumberFormat;

public class DVD
{
   private String title, director;
   private int year;
   private double cost;
   private boolean bluray;

   //-----------------------------------------------------------------
   // Creates a new DVD with the specified information.
   //-----------------------------------------------------------------
   public DVD (String title, String director, int year, double cost,
               boolean bluray)
   {
      this.title = title;
      this.director = director;
      this.year = year;
      this.cost = cost;
      this.bluray = bluray;
   }

   //-----------------------------------------------------------------
   // Returns a string description of this DVD.
   //-----------------------------------------------------------------
   public String toString()
   {
      NumberFormat fmt = NumberFormat.getCurrencyInstance();

      String description;

      description = fmt.format(cost) + "\t" + year + "\t";
      description += title + "\t" + director;
      if (bluray)
         description += "\t" + "Blu-ray";

      return description;
   }
}
```

SELF-REVIEW QUESTIONS *(see answers in Appendix N)*

SR 8.14 How is an array of objects created?

SR 8.15 Suppose `team` is an array of strings meant to hold the names of the six players on a volleyball team: Amanda, Clare, Emily, Julie, Katie, and Maria.

  a. Write an array declaration for `team`.
  b. Show how to both declare and populate `team` using an initializer list.

SR 8.16 Assume `Book` is a class whose objects represent books. Assume a constructor of the `Book` class accepts two parameters—the name of the book and the number of pages.

  a. Write a declaration for a variable named `library` that is an array of ten books.
  b. Write a `new` statement that sets the first book in the `library` array to `"Starship Troopers"`, which is 208 pages long.

8.4 Command-Line Arguments

The formal parameter to the `main` method of a Java application is always an array of `String` objects. We've ignored that parameter in previous examples, but now we can discuss how it might occasionally be useful.

KEY CONCEPT

Command-line arguments are stored in an array of `String` objects and are passed to the `main` method.

The Java run-time environment invokes the `main` method when an application is submitted to the interpreter. The `String[]` parameter, which we typically call `args`, represents *command-line arguments* that are provided when the interpreter is invoked. Any extra information on the command line when the interpreter is invoked is stored in the `args` array for use by the program. This technique is another way to provide input to a program.

The program shown in Listing 8.10 uses command-line arguments to print a nametag. It assumes the first argument represents some type of greeting and the second argument represents a person's name.

If two strings are not provided on the command line for the `NameTag` program, the `args` array will not contain enough (if any) elements, and the references in the program will cause an `ArrayIndexOutOfBoundsException` to be thrown. If extra information is included on the command line, it will be stored in the `args` array but ignored by the program.

LISTING 8.10

```
//********************************************************************
//  NameTag.java       Author: Lewis/Loftus
//
//  Demonstrates the use of command line arguments.
//********************************************************************

public class NameTag
{
   //-----------------------------------------------------------------
   // Prints a simple name tag using a greeting and a name that is
   // specified by the user.
   //-----------------------------------------------------------------
   public static void main (String[] args)
   {
      System.out.println ();
      System.out.println ("      " + args[0]);
      System.out.println ("My name is " + args[1]);
   }
}
```

O U T P U T

```
> java NameTag Howdy John

      Howdy
My name is John

> java NameTag Hello Bill

      Hello
My name is Bill
```

Remember that the parameter to the main method is always an array of String objects. If you want numeric information to be input as a command-line argument, the program has to convert it from its string representation.

You also should be aware that in some program development environments, a command line is not used to submit a program to the interpreter. In such situations, the command-line information can be specified in some other way. Consult the documentation for these specifics if necessary.

SELF-REVIEW QUESTIONS *(see answers in Appendix N)*

SR 8.17 What is a command-line argument?

SR 8.18 Write a `main` method for a program that outputs the sum of the string lengths of its first two command-line arguments.

SR 8.19 Write a `main` method for a program that outputs the sum of the values of its first two command-line arguments, which are integers.

8.5 Variable Length Parameter Lists

Suppose we wanted to design a method that processed a different amount of data from one invocation to the next. For example, let's design a method called `average` that accepts a few integer values and returns their average. In one invocation of the method we might pass in three integers to average:

```
mean1 = average(42, 69, 37);
```

In another invocation of the same method we might pass in seven integers to average:

```
mean2 = average(35, 43, 93, 23, 40, 21, 75);
```

> **KEY CONCEPT**
> A Java method can be defined to accept a varying number of parameters.

To accomplish this we could define overloaded versions of the `average` method, but that would require that we know the maximum number of parameters there might be and create a separate version of the method for each possibility. Alternatively, we could define the method to accept an array of integers, which could be of different sizes for each call. But that would require packaging the integers into an array in the calling method and passing in one parameter.

Java provides a way to define methods that accept variable-length parameter lists. By using some special syntax in the formal parameter list of the method, we can define the method to accept any number of parameters. The parameters are automatically put into an array for easy processing in the method. For example, the average method could be written as follows:

```
public double average (int ... list)
{
    double result = 0.0;

    if (list.length != 0)
```

```
    {
        int sum = 0;
        for (int num : list)
            sum += num;
        result = (double)sum / list.length;
    }

    return result;
}
```

Note the way the formal parameters are defined. The ellipsis (three periods in a row) indicates that the method accepts a variable number of parameters. In this case, the method accepts any number of int parameters, which it automatically puts into an array called list. In the method, we process the array normally.

We can now pass any number of int parameters to the average method, including none at all. That's why we check to see if the length of the array is zero before we compute the average.

The type of the multiple parameters can be any primitive or object type. For example, the following method accepts and prints multiple Grade objects (we defined the Grade class earlier in this chapter):

```
public void printGrades (Grade ... grades)
{
    for (Grade letterGrade : grades)
        System.out.println (letterGrade);
}
```

A method that accepts a variable number of parameters can also accept other parameters. For example, the following method accepts an int, a String object, and then a variable number of double values that will be stored in an array called nums:

```
public void test (int count, String name, double ... nums)
{
    // whatever
}
```

The varying parameters must come last in the formal arguments. A single method cannot accept two sets of varying parameters.

Constructors can also be set up to accept a varying number of parameters. The program shown in Listing 8.11 creates two Family objects, passing a varying number of strings (representing the family member names) into the Family constructor.

LISTING 8.11

```
//********************************************************************
//  VariableParameters.java        Author: Lewis/Loftus
//
//  Demonstrates the use of a variable length parameter list.
//********************************************************************

public class VariableParameters
{
   //  -----------------------------------------------------------
   //  Creates two Family objects using a constructor that accepts
   //  a variable number of String objects as parameters.
   //-------------------------------------------------------------
   public static void main (String[] args)
   {
      Family lewis = new Family ("John", "Sharon", "Justin", "Kayla",
         "Nathan", "Samantha");

      Family camden = new Family ("Stephen", "Annie", "Matt", "Mary",
         "Simon", "Lucy", "Ruthie", "Sam", "David");

      System.out.println(lewis);
      System.out.println();
      System.out.println(camden);
   }
}
```

OUTPUT

```
John
Sharon
Justin
Kayla
Nathan
Samantha


Stephen
Annie
Matt
Mary
Simon
Lucy
Ruthie
Sam
David
```

LISTING 8.12

```java
//********************************************************************
//  Family.java       Author: Lewis/Loftus
//
//  Demonstrates the use of variable length parameter lists.
//********************************************************************

public class Family
{
   private String[] members;

   //-----------------------------------------------------------------
   // Constructor: Sets up this family by storing the (possibly
   // multiple) names that are passed in as parameters.
   //-----------------------------------------------------------------
   public Family (String ... names)
   {
      members = names;
   }

   //-----------------------------------------------------------------
   //  Returns a string representation of this family.
   //-----------------------------------------------------------------
   public String toString()
   {
      String result = "";

      for (String name : members)
         result += name + "\n";

      return result;
   }
}
```

The `Family` class is shown in Listing 8.12. The constructor simply stores a reference to the array parameter until it is needed. By using a variable-length parameter list for the constructor, we make it easy to create a family of any size.

SELF-REVIEW QUESTIONS *(see answers in Appendix N)*

SR 8.20   How can Java methods have variable-length parameter lists?

SR 8.21   Write a method called `distance` that accepts a multiple number of integer parameters (each of which represents the distance of one leg of a journey) and returns the total distance of the trip.

SR 8.22 Write a method called `travelTime` that accepts an integer parameter indicating average speed followed by a multiple number of integer parameters (each of which represents the distance of one leg of a journey) and returns the total time of the trip.

8.6 Two-Dimensional Arrays

The arrays we've examined so far have all been *one-dimensional arrays* in the sense that they represent a simple list of values. As the name implies, a *two-dimensional array* has values in two dimensions, which are often thought of as the rows and columns of a table. Figure 8.4 graphically compares a one-dimensional array with a two-dimensional array. We must use two indexes to refer to a value in a two-dimensional array, one specifying the row and another the column.

Brackets are used to represent each dimension in the array. Therefore the type of a two-dimensional array that stores integers is `int[][]`. Technically, Java represents two-dimensional arrays as an array of arrays. A two-dimensional integer array is really a one-dimensional array of references to one-dimensional integer arrays.

The `TwoDArray` program shown in Listing 8.13 instantiates a two-dimensional array of integers. As with one-dimensional arrays, the size of the dimensions is specified when the array is created. The size of the dimensions can be different.

Nested `for` loops are used in the `TwoDArray` program to load the array with values and also to print those values in a table format. Carefully trace the processing to see how the nested loops eventually visit each element in the two-dimensional array. Note that the outer loops are governed by `table.length`, which represents the number of rows, and the inner loops are governed by `table[row].length`, which represents the number of columns in that row.

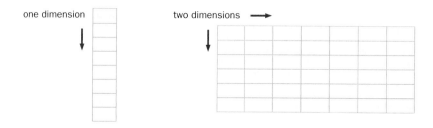

FIGURE 8.4   A one-dimensional array and a two-dimensional array

LISTING 8.13

```java
//********************************************************************
//  TwoDArray.java       Author: Lewis/Loftus
//
//  Demonstrates the use of a two-dimensional array.
//********************************************************************

public class TwoDArray
{
   //-----------------------------------------------------------------
   // Creates a 2D array of integers, fills it with increasing
   // integer values, then prints them out.
   //-----------------------------------------------------------------
   public static void main (String[] args)
   {
      int[][] table = new int[5][10];

      // Load the table with values
      for (int row=0; row < table.length; row++)
         for (int col=0; col < table[row].length; col++)
            table[row][col] = row * 10 + col;

      // Print the table
      for (int row=0; row < table.length; row++)
      {
         for (int col=0; col < table[row].length; col++)
            System.out.print (table[row][col] + "\t");
         System.out.println();
      }
   }
}
```

OUTPUT

0	1	2	3	4	5	6	7	8	9
10	11	12	13	14	15	16	17	18	19
20	21	22	23	24	25	26	27	28	29
30	31	32	33	34	35	36	37	38	39
40	41	42	43	44	45	46	47	48	49

As with one-dimensional arrays, an initializer list can be used to instanti-ate a two-dimensional array, where each element is itself an array initializer list. This technique is used in the SodaSurvey program, which is shown in Listing 8.14.

LISTING 8.14

```java
//********************************************************************
//  SodaSurvey.java       Author: Lewis/Loftus
//
//  Demonstrates the use of a two-dimensional array.
//********************************************************************

import java.text.DecimalFormat;

public class SodaSurvey
{
   //-----------------------------------------------------------------
   // Determines and prints the average of each row (soda) and each
   // column (respondent) of the survey scores.
   //-----------------------------------------------------------------
   public static void main (String[] args)
   {
      int[][] scores = { {3, 4, 5, 2, 1, 4, 3, 2, 4, 4},
                         {2, 4, 3, 4, 3, 3, 2, 1, 2, 2},
                         {3, 5, 4, 5, 5, 3, 2, 5, 5, 5},
                         {1, 1, 1, 3, 1, 2, 1, 3, 2, 4} };

      final int SODAS = scores.length;
      final int PEOPLE = scores[0].length;

      int[] sodaSum = new int[SODAS];
      int[] personSum = new int[PEOPLE];

      for (int soda=0; soda < SODAS; soda++)
         for (int person=0; person < PEOPLE; person++)
         {
            sodaSum[soda] += scores[soda][person];
            personSum[person] += scores[soda][person];
         }

      DecimalFormat fmt = new DecimalFormat ("0.#");
      System.out.println ("Averages:\n");
```

LISTING 8.14   *continued*

```
    for (int soda=0; soda < SODAS; soda++)
        System.out.println ("Soda #" + (soda+1) + ": " +
                fmt.format ((float)sodaSum[soda]/PEOPLE));

    System.out.println ();
    for (int person=0; person < PEOPLE; person++)
        System.out.println ("Person #" + (person+1) + ": " +
                fmt.format ((float)personSum[person]/SODAS));
    }
}
```

OUTPUT

```
Averages:

Soda #1: 3.2
Soda #2: 2.6
Soda #3: 4.2
Soda #4: 1.9

Person #1: 2.2
Person #2: 3.5
Person #3: 3.2
Person #4: 3.5
Person #5: 2.5
Person #6: 3
Person #7: 2
Person #8: 2.8
Person #9: 3.2
Person #10: 3.8
```

Suppose a soda manufacturer held a taste test for four new flavors to see how people liked them. The manufacturer got 10 people to try each new flavor and give it a score from 1 to 5, where 1 equals poor and 5 equals excellent. The two-dimensional array called scores in the SodaSurvey program stores the results of that survey. Each row corresponds to a soda and each column in that row corresponds to the person who tasted it. More generally, each row holds the responses that all testers gave for one particular soda flavor, and each column holds the responses of one person for all sodas.

The SodaSurvey program computes and prints the average responses for each soda and for each respondent. The sums of each soda and person are first stored in one-dimensional arrays of integers. Then the averages are computed and printed.

Multidimensional Arrays

An array can have one, two, three, or even more dimensions. Any array with more than one dimension is called a *multidimensional array*.

It's fairly easy to picture a two-dimensional array as a table. A three-dimensional array could be drawn as a cube. However, once you are past three dimensions, multidimensional arrays might seem hard to visualize. Yet, consider that each subsequent dimension is simply a subdivision of the previous one. It is often best to think of larger multidimensional arrays in this way.

For example, suppose we wanted to store the number of students attending universities across the United States, broken down in a meaningful way. We might represent it as a four-dimensional array of integers. The first dimension represents the state. The second dimension represents the universities in each state. The third dimension represents the colleges in each university. Finally, the fourth dimension represents departments in each college. The value stored at each location is the number of students in one particular department. Figure 8.5 shows these subdivisions.

> **KEY CONCEPT**
>
> Using an array with more than two dimensions is rare in an object-oriented system.

Two-dimensional arrays are fairly common. However, care should be taken when deciding to create multidimensional arrays in a program. When dealing with large amounts of data that are managed at multiple levels, additional information and the methods needed to manage that information will probably be required. It is far more likely, for instance, that in the previous example, each state would be represented by an object, which may contain, among other things, an array to store information about each university, and so on.

There is one other important characteristic of Java arrays to consider. As we established previously, Java does not directly support multidimensional

FIGURE 8.5   Visualization of a four-dimensional array

arrays. Instead, they are represented as arrays of references to array objects. Those arrays could themselves contain references to other arrays. This layering continues for as many dimensions as required. Because of this technique for representing each dimension, the arrays in any one dimension could be of different lengths. These are sometimes called *ragged arrays*. For example, the number of elements in each row of a two-dimensional array may not be the same. In such situations, care must be taken to make sure the arrays are managed appropriately.

SELF-REVIEW QUESTIONS *(see answers in Appendix N)*

SR 8.23 How are multidimensional arrays implemented in Java?

SR 8.24 A two-dimensional array named scores holds the test scores for a class of students for a semester. Write code that prints out a single value that represents the range of scores held in the array. It prints out the value of the highest score minus the value of the lowest score. Each test score is represented as an integer.

myprogramminglab

8.7 Polygons and Polylines

Arrays are helpful when drawing complex shapes. A polygon, for example, is a multisided shape that is defined in Java using a series of (x, y) points that indicate the vertices of the polygon. Arrays are often used to store the list of coordinates.

Polygons are drawn using methods of the Graphics class, similar to how we draw rectangles and ovals. Like these other shapes, a polygon can be drawn filled or unfilled. The methods used to draw a polygon are called drawPolygon and fillPolygon. Both of these methods are overloaded. One version uses arrays of integers to define the polygon, and the other uses an object of the Polygon class to define the polygon. We discuss the Polygon class later in this section.

In the version that uses arrays, the drawPolygon and fillPolygon methods take three parameters. The first is an array of integers representing the x coordinates of the points in the polygon, the second is an array of integers representing the corresponding y coordinates of those points, and the third is an integer that indicates how many points are used from each of the two arrays. Taken together, the first two parameters represent the (x, y) coordinates of the vertices of the polygons.

A polygon is always closed. A line segment is always drawn from the last point in the list to the first point in the list.

KEY CONCEPT

A polyline is similar to a polygon except that a polyline is not a closed shape.

Similar to a polygon, a *polyline* contains a series of points connected by line segments. Polylines differ from polygons in that the first and last coordinates are not automatically connected when it is drawn. Since a polyline is not closed, it cannot be filled. Therefore there is only one method, called drawPolyline, used to draw a polyline.

As with the drawPolygon method, the first two parameters of the drawPolyline method are both arrays of integers. Taken together, the first two parameters represent the (*x, y*) coordinates of the end points of the line segments of the polyline. The third parameter is the number of points in the coordinate list.

The program shown in Listing 8.15 uses polygons to draw a rocket. In the RocketPanel class, shown in Listing 8.16, the arrays called xRocket and yRocket define the points of the polygon that make up the main body of the rocket. The first point in the arrays is the upper tip of the rocket, and they progress clockwise from there. The xWindow and yWindow arrays specify the points for the polygon that form the window in the rocket. Both the rocket and the window are drawn as filled polygons.

LISTING 8.15

```
//********************************************************************
//  Rocket.java        Author: Lewis/Loftus
//
//  Demonstrates the use of polygons and polylines.
//********************************************************************

import javax.swing.JFrame;

public class Rocket
{
   //-----------------------------------------------------------
   //  Creates the main frame of the program.
   //-----------------------------------------------------------
   public static void main (String[] args)
   {
      JFrame frame = new JFrame ("Rocket");
      frame.setDefaultCloseOperation (JFrame.EXIT_ON_CLOSE);

      RocketPanel panel = new RocketPanel();

      frame.getContentPane().add(panel);
      frame.pack();
      frame.setVisible(true);
   }
}
```

LISTING 8.15   *continued*

DISPLAY

LISTING 8.16

```
//********************************************************************
//  RocketPanel.java       Author: Lewis/Loftus
//
//  Demonstrates the use of polygons and polylines.
//********************************************************************

import javax.swing.JPanel;
import java.awt.*;

public class RocketPanel extends JPanel
{
    private int[] xRocket = {100, 120, 120, 130, 130, 70, 70, 80, 80};
    private int[] yRocket = {15, 40, 115, 125, 150, 150, 125, 115, 40};

    private int[] xWindow = {95, 105, 110, 90};
    private int[] yWindow = {45, 45, 70, 70};
```

LISTING 8.16   *continued*

```
private int[] xFlame = {70, 70, 75, 80, 90, 100, 110, 115, 120,
                        130, 130};
private int[] yFlame = {155, 170, 165, 190, 170, 175, 160, 185,
                        160, 175, 155};

//-----------------------------------------------------------------
//  Constructor: Sets up the basic characteristics of this panel.
//-----------------------------------------------------------------
public RocketPanel()
{
    setBackground (Color.black);
    setPreferredSize (new Dimension(200, 200));
}

//-----------------------------------------------------------------
//  Draws a rocket using polygons and polylines.
//-----------------------------------------------------------------
public void paintComponent (Graphics page)
{
    super.paintComponent (page);
    page.setColor (Color.cyan);
    page.fillPolygon (xRocket, yRocket, xRocket.length);

    page.setColor (Color.gray);
    page.fillPolygon (xWindow, yWindow, xWindow.length);

    page.setColor (Color.red);
    page.drawPolyline (xFlame, yFlame, xFlame.length);
}
}
```

The xFlame and yFlame arrays define the points of a polyline that are used to create the image of flame shooting out of the tail of the rocket. Because it is drawn as a polyline, and not a polygon, the flame is not closed or filled.

The Polygon Class

A polygon can also be defined explicitly using an object of the Polygon class, which is defined in the java.awt package of the Java standard class library. Two versions of the overloaded drawPolygon and fillPolygon methods take a single Polygon object as a parameter.

```
Polygon ()
    Constructor: Creates an empty polygon.

Polygon (int[] xpoints, int[] ypoints, int npoints)
    Constructor: Creates a polygon using the (x, y) coordinate pairs
    in corresponding entries of xpoints and ypoints.

void addPoint (int x, int y)
    Appends the specified point to this polygon.

boolean contains (int x, int y)
    Returns true if the specified point is contained in this polygon.

boolean contains (Point p)
    Returns true if the specified point is contained in this polygon.

Rectangle getBounds ()
    Gets the bounding rectangle for this polygon.

void translate (int deltaX, int deltaY)
    Translates the vertices of this polygon by deltaX along the x axis
    and deltaY along the y axis.
```

FIGURE 8.6   Some methods of the Polygon class

A Polygon object encapsulates the coordinates of the polygon sides. The constructors of the Polygon class allow the creation of an initially empty polygon or one defined by arrays of integers representing the point coordinates. The Polygon class contains methods to add points to the polygon and to determine whether a given point is contained within the polygon shape. It also contains methods to get a representation of a bounding rectangle for the polygon, as well as a method to translate all of the points in the polygon to another position. Figure 8.6 lists these methods.

SELF-REVIEW QUESTIONS *(see answers in Appendix N)*

SR 8.25   What is a polyline? How do we specify its shape?

SR 8.26   What is the difference between a polygon and a polyline?

SR 8.27   What is the result of separately making each of the following changes to the RocketPanel class? You may make the change, compile and run the program, and observe and report the results. Briefly explain what you observe.

a. Change the `page.drawPolyline` method call to a `page.fillPolygon` method call.
b. Change the `fillPolygon` parameter `xWindow.length()` to the numeric literal `"2"`.
c. Switch the x and the y values in each of the arrays. For example `yWindow` becomes {95, 105, 110, 90}.
d. A new, filled yellow polygon is drawn first with coordinates (0, 100), (100, 0), (200, 100), and (100, 200).
e. A new, filled yellow polygon is drawn last with coordinates (0, 100), (100, 0), (200, 100), and (100, 200).

8.8 Mouse Events

Let's examine the events that are generated when using a mouse. Java divides these events into two categories: *mouse events* and *mouse motion events*. The table in Figure 8.7 defines these events.

When you click the mouse button over a Java GUI component, three events are generated: one when the mouse button is pushed down (*mouse pressed*) and two when it is let up (*mouse released* and *mouse clicked*). A mouse click is defined as pressing and releasing the mouse button in the same location. If you press the mouse button down, move the mouse, and then release the mouse button, a mouse clicked event is not generated.

Mouse Event	Description
mouse pressed	The mouse button is pressed down.
mouse released	The mouse button is released.
mouse clicked	The mouse button is pressed down and released without moving the mouse in between.
mouse entered	The mouse pointer is moved onto (over) a component.
mouse exited	The mouse pointer is moved off of a component.

Mouse Motion Event	Description
mouse moved	The mouse is moved.
mouse dragged	The mouse is moved while the mouse button is pressed down.

FIGURE 8.7   Mouse events and mouse motion events

A component will generate a *mouse entered* event when the mouse pointer passes into its graphical space. Likewise, it generates a *mouse exited* event when the mouse pointer leaves.

Mouse motion events, as the name implies, occur while the mouse is in motion. The *mouse moved* event indicates simply that the mouse is in motion. The *mouse dragged* event is generated when the user has pressed the mouse button down and moved the mouse without releasing the button. Mouse motion events are generated many times, very quickly, while the mouse is in motion.

> **KEY CONCEPT**
>
> Moving the mouse and clicking the mouse button generate events to which a program can respond.

In a specific situation, we may care about only one or two mouse events. What we listen for depends on what we are trying to accomplish.

The `Dots` program shown in Listing 8.17 responds to one mouse event. Specifically, it draws a green dot at the location of the mouse pointer whenever the mouse button is pressed.

The `main` method of the `Dots` class creates a frame and adds one panel to it. That panel is defined by the `DotsPanel` class shown in Listing 8.18.

LISTING 8.17

```
//********************************************************************
//  Dots.java       Author: Lewis/Loftus
//
//  Demonstrates mouse events.
//********************************************************************

import javax.swing.JFrame;

public class Dots
{
    //-----------------------------------------------------------------
    //  Creates and displays the application frame.
    //-----------------------------------------------------------------
    public static void main (String[] args)
    {
        JFrame frame = new JFrame ("Dots");
        frame.setDefaultCloseOperation (JFrame.EXIT_ON_CLOSE);

        frame.getContentPane().add (new DotsPanel());

        frame.pack();
        frame.setVisible(true);
    }
}
```

LISTING 8.17 *continued*

DISPLAY

LISTING 8.18

```
//********************************************************************
//  DotsPanel.java       Author: Lewis/Loftus
//
//  Represents the primary panel for the Dots program.
//********************************************************************

import java.util.ArrayList;
import javax.swing.JPanel;
import java.awt.*;
import java.awt.event.*;

public class DotsPanel extends JPanel
{
    private final int SIZE = 6; // radius of each dot
```

LISTING 8.18   *continued*

```java
    private ArrayList<Point> pointList;

    //-----------------------------------------------------------------
    // Constructor: Sets up this panel to listen for mouse events.
    //-----------------------------------------------------------------
    public DotsPanel()
    {
        pointList = new ArrayList<Point>();

        addMouseListener (new DotsListener());

        setBackground (Color.black);
        setPreferredSize (new Dimension(300, 200));
    }

    //-----------------------------------------------------------------
    // Draws all of the dots stored in the list.
    //-----------------------------------------------------------------
    public void paintComponent (Graphics page)
    {
        super.paintComponent(page);

        page.setColor (Color.green);

        for (Point spot : pointList)
            page.fillOval (spot.x-SIZE, spot.y-SIZE, SIZE*2, SIZE*2);

        page.drawString ("Count: " + pointList.size(), 5, 15);
    }

    //*****************************************************************
    // Represents the listener for mouse events.
    //*****************************************************************
    private class DotsListener implements MouseListener
    {
        //-------------------------------------------------------------
        // Adds the current point to the list of points and redraws
        // the panel whenever the mouse button is pressed.
        //-------------------------------------------------------------
        public void mousePressed (MouseEvent event)
        {
            pointList.add(event.getPoint());
            repaint();
        }
```

LISTING 8.18 *continued*

```java
//------------------------------------------------------------
// Provide empty definitions for unused event methods.
//------------------------------------------------------------
public void mouseClicked (MouseEvent event) {}
public void mouseReleased (MouseEvent event) {}
public void mouseEntered (MouseEvent event) {}
public void mouseExited (MouseEvent event) {}
    }
}
```

The DotsPanel class keeps track of a list of Point objects that represent all of the locations at which the user has clicked the mouse. A Point class represents the (*x*, *y*) coordinates of a given point in two-dimensional space. It provides public access to the instance variables x and y for the point. Each time the panel is painted, all of the points stored in the list are drawn.

The list of Point objects is maintained as an ArrayList object. More precisely, the type of the pointList object is ArrayList<Point>, specifying that only Point objects can be stored in that ArrayList. To draw the points, we use a for loop to iterate over all the points stored in the list.

The listener for the mouse pressed event is defined as a private inner class that implements the MouseListener interface. The mousePressed method is invoked by the panel each time the user presses down on the mouse button while it is over the panel.

A mouse event always occurs at some point in two-dimensional space, and the object that represents that event keeps track of that location. In a mouse listener, we can get and use that point whenever we need it. In the Dots program, each time the mousePressed method is called, the location of the event is obtained using the getPoint method of the MouseEvent object. That point is stored in the ArrayList, and the panel is then repainted.

KEY CONCEPT

A listener may have to provide empty method definitions for unheeded events to satisfy the interface.

Note that, unlike the listener interfaces that we've used in previous examples that contain one method each, the MouseListener interface contains five methods. For this program, the only event in which we are interested is the mouse pressed event. Therefore, the only method in which we have any interest is the mousePressed method. However, implementing an interface means we must provide definitions for all methods in the interface. Therefore we provide empty methods corresponding to the other events. When those events are generated, the empty methods are called, but no code is executed. In Chapter 9 we discuss a technique for creating listeners that lets us avoid creating such empty methods.

Let's look at an example that responds to two mouse-oriented events. The RubberLines program shown in Listing 8.19 draws a line between two points. The first point is determined by the location at which the mouse is first pressed down. The second point changes as the mouse is dragged while the mouse button is held down. When the button is released, the line remains fixed between the first and second points. When the mouse button is pressed again, a new line is started.

The panel on which the lines are drawn is represented by the RubberLinesPanel class shown in Listing 8.20. Because we need to listen for both a mouse pressed event and a mouse dragged event, we need a listener that responds to both mouse events and mouse motion events. Note that the listener class in this example implements both the MouseListener and MouseMotionListener interfaces. It must therefore implement all methods of both interfaces. The two methods of interest, mousePressed and mouseDragged, are implemented to accomplish our goals, and the other methods are given empty definitions to satisfy the interface contract.

When the mousePressed method is called, the variable point1 is set. Then, as the mouse is dragged, the variable point2 is continually reset and the panel repainted. Therefore, the line is constantly being redrawn as the mouse is dragged, giving the appearance that one line is being stretched between a fixed point and a moving point. This effect is called *rubberbanding* and is common in graphical programs.

> **KEY CONCEPT**
> Rubberbanding is the graphical effect caused when a shape seems to expand as the mouse is dragged.

Note that, in the RubberLinesPanel constructor, the listener object is added to the panel twice: once as a mouse listener and once as a mouse motion listener. The method called to add the listener must correspond to the object passed as the parameter. In this case, we had one object that served as a listener for both categories of events. We could have had two listener classes if desired: one listening for mouse events and one listening for mouse motion events. A component can have multiple listeners for various event categories.

VideoNote

Example using rubberbanding and arrays.

Also note that this program draws one line at a time. That is, when the user begins to draw another line with a new mouse click, the previous one disappears. This is because the paintComponent method redraws its background, eliminating the line every time. To see the previous lines, we'd have to keep track of them, perhaps using an ArrayList as was done in the Dots program. This modification to the RubberLines program is left as a programming project.

LISTING 8.19

```java
//********************************************************************
//  RubberLines.java       Author: Lewis/Loftus
//
//  Demonstrates mouse events and rubberbanding.
//********************************************************************

import javax.swing.JFrame;

public class RubberLines
{
   //-----------------------------------------------------------------
   // Creates and displays the application frame.
   //-----------------------------------------------------------------
   public static void main (String[] args)
   {
      JFrame frame = new JFrame ("Rubber Lines");
      frame.setDefaultCloseOperation (JFrame.EXIT_ON_CLOSE);

      frame.getContentPane().add (new RubberLinesPanel());

      frame.pack();
      frame.setVisible(true);
   }
}
```

DISPLAY

LISTING 8.20

```java
//********************************************************************
//  RubberLinesPanel.java       Author: Lewis/Loftus
//
//  Represents the primary drawing panel for the RubberLines program.
//********************************************************************

import javax.swing.JPanel;
import java.awt.*;
import java.awt.event.*;

public class RubberLinesPanel extends JPanel
{
    private Point point1 = null, point2 = null;

    //-----------------------------------------------------------------
    // Constructor: Sets up this panel to listen for mouse events.
    //-----------------------------------------------------------------
    public RubberLinesPanel()
    {
        LineListener listener = new LineListener();
        addMouseListener (listener);
        addMouseMotionListener (listener);

        setBackground (Color.black);
        setPreferredSize (new Dimension(400, 200));
    }

    //-----------------------------------------------------------------
    // Draws the current line from the initial mouse-pressed point to
    // the current position of the mouse.
    //-----------------------------------------------------------------
    public void paintComponent (Graphics page)
    {
        super.paintComponent (page);

        page.setColor (Color.yellow);
        if (point1 != null && point2 != null)
            page.drawLine (point1.x, point1.y, point2.x, point2.y);
    }

    //********************************************************************
    // Represents the listener for all mouse events.
    //********************************************************************
```

LISTING 8.20   *continued*

```
private class LineListener implements MouseListener,
                                      MouseMotionListener
{
   //---------------------------------------------------------------
   //  Captures the initial position at which the mouse button is
   //  pressed.
   //---------------------------------------------------------------
   public void mousePressed (MouseEvent event)
   {
      point1 = event.getPoint();
   }

   //---------------------------------------------------------------
   //  Gets the current position of the mouse as it is dragged and
   //  redraws the line to create the rubberband effect.
   //---------------------------------------------------------------
   public void mouseDragged (MouseEvent event)
   {
      point2 = event.getPoint();
      repaint();
   }

   //---------------------------------------------------------------
   //  Provide empty definitions for unused event methods.
   //---------------------------------------------------------------
   public void mouseClicked (MouseEvent event) {}
   public void mouseReleased (MouseEvent event) {}
   public void mouseEntered (MouseEvent event) {}
   public void mouseExited (MouseEvent event) {}
   public void mouseMoved (MouseEvent event) {}
}
}
```

myprogramming**lab**   **SELF-REVIEW QUESTIONS** *(see answers in Appendix N)*

SR 8.28   What is a mouse event?

SR 8.29   What sequence of mouse events is generated when the mouse button is clicked over a GUI component and then released?

SR 8.30   What sequence of mouse events is generated when the mouse button is clicked over a GUI component, the mouse is moved so it is no longer over that component, and then the mouse button is released?

SR 8.31   Which mouse events are responded to in the Dots program? Which are responded to in the RubberLines program?

SR 8.32   Suppose you are creating a GUI to support a program that plays Tic-Tac-Toe against the user. Describe how your program might respond to various mouse events.

8.9 Key Events

A *key event* is generated when a keyboard key is pressed. Key events allow a program to respond immediately to the user while he or she is typing or pressing other keyboard keys such as the arrow keys. If key events are being processed, the program can respond as soon as the key is pressed; there is no need to wait for the Enter key to be pressed or for some other component (like a button) to be activated.

> **KEY CONCEPT**
> Key events allow a program to respond immediately to the user pressing keyboard keys.

The Direction program shown in Listing 8.21 responds to key events. An image of an arrow is displayed, and the image moves across the screen as the arrow keys are pressed. Actually, four different images are used, one each for the arrow pointing in each of the primary directions (up, down, right, and left).

The DirectionPanel class, shown in Listing 8.22, represents the panel on which the arrow image is displayed. The constructor loads the four arrow images, one of which is always considered to be the current image (the one displayed). The current image is set based on the arrow key that was most recently pressed. For example, if the up arrow is pressed, the image with the arrow pointing up is displayed. If an arrow key is continually pressed, the appropriate image "moves" in the appropriate direction.

The arrow images are managed as ImageIcon objects. In this example, the image is drawn using the paintIcon method each time the panel is repainted. The paintIcon method takes four parameters: a component to serve as an *image observer*, the graphics context on which the image will be drawn, and the (*x*, *y*) coordinates where the image is drawn. An image observer is a component that serves to manage image loading; in this case we use the panel as the image observer.

The private inner class called DirectionListener is set up to respond to key events. It implements the KeyListener interface, which defines three methods that we can use to respond to keyboard activity. Figure 8.8 lists these methods.

Specifically, the Direction program responds to key pressed events. Because the listener class must implement all methods defined in the interface, we provide empty methods for the other events.

LISTING 8.21

```java
//********************************************************************
//  Direction.java        Author: Lewis/Loftus
//
//  Demonstrates key events.
//********************************************************************

import javax.swing.JFrame;

public class Direction
{
   //-----------------------------------------------------------------
   // Creates and displays the application frame.
   //-----------------------------------------------------------------
   public static void main (String[] args)
   {
      JFrame frame = new JFrame ("Direction");
      frame.setDefaultCloseOperation (JFrame.EXIT_ON_CLOSE);

      frame.getContentPane().add (new DirectionPanel());

      frame.pack();
      frame.setVisible(true);
   }
}
```

DISPLAY

LISTING 8.22

```java
//********************************************************************
//  DirectionPanel.java        Author: Lewis/Loftus
//
//  Represents the primary display panel for the Direction program.
//********************************************************************

import javax.swing.*;
import java.awt.*;
import java.awt.event.*;

public class DirectionPanel extends JPanel
{
   private final int WIDTH = 300, HEIGHT = 200;
   private final int JUMP = 10;  // increment for image movement

   private final int IMAGE_SIZE = 31;

   private ImageIcon up, down, right, left, currentImage;
   private int x, y;

   //-----------------------------------------------------------------
   //  Constructor: Sets up this panel and loads the images.
   //-----------------------------------------------------------------
   public DirectionPanel()
   {
      addKeyListener (new DirectionListener());

      x = WIDTH / 2;
      y = HEIGHT / 2;

      up = new ImageIcon ("arrowUp.gif");
      down = new ImageIcon ("arrowDown.gif");
      left = new ImageIcon ("arrowLeft.gif");
      right = new ImageIcon ("arrowRight.gif");

      currentImage = right;

      setBackground (Color.black);
      setPreferredSize (new Dimension(WIDTH, HEIGHT));
      setFocusable(true);
   }
```

LISTING 8.22 *continued*

```java
//-----------------------------------------------------------------
//  Draws the image in the current location.
//-----------------------------------------------------------------
public void paintComponent (Graphics page)
{
    super.paintComponent (page);
    currentImage.paintIcon (this, page, x, y);
}

//*****************************************************************
//  Represents the listener for keyboard activity.
//*****************************************************************
private class DirectionListener implements KeyListener
{
    //-------------------------------------------------------------
    // Responds to the user pressing arrow keys by adjusting the
    // image and image location accordingly.
    //-------------------------------------------------------------
    public void keyPressed (KeyEvent event)
    {
        switch (event.getKeyCode())
        {
            case KeyEvent.VK_UP:
                currentImage = up;
                y -= JUMP;
                break;
            case KeyEvent.VK_DOWN:
                currentImage = down;
                y += JUMP;
                break;
            case KeyEvent.VK_LEFT:
                currentImage = left;
                x -= JUMP;
                break;
            case KeyEvent.VK_RIGHT:
                currentImage = right;
                x += JUMP;
                break;
        }

        repaint();
    }
```

LISTING 8.22   *continued*

```
//---------------------------------------------------------------
// Provide empty definitions for unused event methods.
//---------------------------------------------------------------
public void keyTyped (KeyEvent event) {}
public void keyReleased (KeyEvent event) {}
    }
}
```

The KeyEvent object passed to the keyPressed method of the listener can be used to determine which key was pressed. In the example, we call the getKeyCode method of the event object to get a numeric code that represents the key that was pressed. We use a switch statement to determine which key was pressed and to respond accordingly. The KeyEvent class contains constants that correspond to the numeric code that is returned from the getKeyCode method. If any key other than an arrow key is pressed, it is ignored.

```
void keyPressed (KeyEvent event)
    Called when a key is pressed.

void keyReleased (KeyEvent event)
    Called when a key is released.

void keyTyped (KeyEvent event)
    Called when a pressed key or key combination produces
    a key character.
```

FIGURE 8.8   The methods of the KeyListener interface

Key events fire whenever a key is pressed, but most systems enable the concept of *key repetition*. That is, when a key is pressed and held down, it's as if that key is being pressed repeatedly and quickly. Key events are generated in the same way. In the Direction program, the user can hold down an arrow key and watch the image move across the screen quickly.

The component that generates key events is the one that currently has the *keyboard focus*. Usually the keyboard focus is held by the primary "active" component. A component usually gets the keyboard focus when the user clicks on it with the mouse. The call to the setFocusable method in the panel constructor sets the keyboard focus to the panel.

The Direction program sets no boundaries for the arrow image, so it can be moved out of the visible window, then moved back in if desired. You could add code to the listener to stop the image when it reaches one of the window boundaries. This modification is left as a programming project.

myprogramminglab

SELF-REVIEW QUESTIONS *(see answers in Appendix N)*

SR 8.33   What is a key event?

SR 8.34   Answer the following questions about our Direction program.

     a. Which key pressed events are responded to?
     b. Which key pressed events are not responded to?
     c. What is the key code for the up-arrow key?
     d. In what file do we store the left-arrow image?
     e. Which image is displayed when the program begins?

Summary of Key Concepts

- An array of size *N* is indexed from 0 to *N*–1.
- In Java, an array is an object that must be instantiated.
- Bounds checking ensures that an index used to refer to an array element is in range.
- An initializer list can be used to instantiate an array object instead of using the new operator.
- An entire array can be passed as a parameter, making the formal parameter an alias of the original.
- Instantiating an array of objects reserves room to store references only. The objects that are stored in each element must be instantiated separately.
- Command-line arguments are stored in an array of String objects and are passed to the main method.
- A Java method can be defined to accept a varying number of parameters.
- Using an array with more than two dimensions is rare in an object-oriented system.
- A polyline is similar to a polygon except that a polyline is not a closed shape.
- Moving the mouse and clicking the mouse button generate events to which a program can respond.
- A listener may have to provide empty method definitions for unheeded events to satisfy the interface.
- Rubberbanding is the graphical effect caused when a shape seems to expand as the mouse is dragged.
- Key events allow a program to respond immediately to the user pressing keyboard keys.

Exercises

Visit www.myprogramminglab.com to complete many of these Exercises online and get instant feedback.

myprogramminglab

EX 8.1   Which of the following are valid declarations? Explain your answers.

```
a. int [] num = {"1", "2", "3"};
b. int [] num = (1, 2, 3);
```

c. `int num [][]={1, 2, 3};`

d. `int num [] = {1, 2, 3};`

e. `int [] num [];`

f. `char [] name;`

g. `int [6] num;`

EX 8.2   Name three data structures that can be easily implemented using arrays.

EX 8.3   Describe how an element in an array is accessed in memory. For example, where is `myArray[25]` stored in memory?

EX 8.4   What would be the output of the following program? Describe the steps involved in obtaining this output.

```
class Sample
{
    public static void main(String[] args)
    {
        int[] ia = new int[101];
        for (int i = 0; i < ia.length; i++)
        ia[i] = i;
        int sum = 0;
        for (int i = 0; i < ia.length; i++)
        sum += ia[i];
        System.out.println(sum);
    }
}
```

EX 8.5   How do you write array declarations in a Java program to represent the following statements?

a. Students' marks for a class of 25 students.

b. The names of 50 employees in a company.

c. The capitals of ten countries.

EX 8.6   Write code to initialize an array so that the array elements have a value equal to their indices.

EX 8.7   Write a method called `palindrome` that accepts a `String` as parameter and returns true if the string is a palindrome, else it returns false.

EX 8.8   Write code that finds the largest number from an array of numbers entered by the user.

EX 8.9   Write a method called `AvgArray` that accepts an array of integers and returns the average of the values stored in the array.

EX 8.10 Write three assignment statements which try to swap the content of two variables without using a temporary variable.

EX 8.11 Write a method called `MinFinder` that reads 15 integer values from the user and prints the minimum value entered.

EX 8.12 Write a code fragment that reads a list of numbers from the user and prints them in the reverse order.

EX 8.13 The `Dots` program listens for a mouse pressed event to draw a dot. How would the program behave differently if it listened for a mouse released event instead? A mouse clicked event?

EX 8.14 What would happen if the call to `super.paintComponent` were removed from the `paintComponent` method of the `DotsPanel` class? Remove it and run the program to test your answer.

EX 8.15 What would happen if the call to `super.paintComponent` were removed from the `paintComponent` method of the `RubberLinesPanel` class? Remove it and run the program to test your answer. In what ways is the answer different from the answer to Exercise 8.13?

EX 8.16 Create a UML class diagram for the `Direction` program.

Programming Projects

Visit www.myprogramminglab.com to complete many of these Programming Projects online and get instant feedback.

myprogramminglab

PP 8.1 Twenty-five numbers are entered from the keyboard into an array. The number to be searched is entered through the keyboard by the user. Design and implement a program to find if the number is present in the array as well as display the number of occurrences of that number in the array.

PP 8.2 Modify the program from PP 8.1 so that it finds and displays how many of the numbers are positive, negative, even, and odd.

PP 8.3 Design and implement an application that creates a histogram that allows you to visually inspect the frequency distribution of a set of values. The program should read in an arbitrary number of integers that are in the range 1 to 100 inclusive; then produce a chart similar to the one below that indicates how many input values fell in the range 1 to 10, 11 to 20, and so on. Print one asterisk for each value entered.

```
┌─────────────────────────────────────────────────────┐
│  1  -  10  | *****                                    │
│ 11  -  20  | **                                       │
│ 21  -  30  | ************************                 │
│ 31  -  40  |                                          │
│ 41  -  50  | ***                                      │
│ 51  -  60  | *******                                  │
│ 61  -  70  | **                                       │
│ 71  -  80  | *****                                    │
│ 81  -  90  | *******                                  │
│ 91  - 100  | ********                                 │
└─────────────────────────────────────────────────────┘
```

VideoNote

Developing a solution of PP 8.5.

PP 8.4   The lines in the histogram in PP 8.3 will be too long if a large number of values is entered. Modify the program so that it prints an asterisk for every five values in each category. Ignore leftovers. For example, if a category had 17 values, print three asterisks in that row. If a category had 4 values, do not print any asterisks in that row.

PP 8.5   Design and implement an application that computes and prints the mean and standard deviation of a list of integers x1 through xn. Assume that there will be no more than 50 input values. Compute both the mean and standard deviation as floating point values, using the following formulas.

$$\text{mean} = \frac{\sum\limits_{i=1}^{n} X_i}{n}$$

$$\text{sd} = \sqrt{\sum\limits_{i=1}^{n} (X_i - \text{mean})^2}$$

PP 8.6   Design and implement a program that extracts part of a given string from the specified position. For example, if the string is "Working with strings is fun", and the given position is 4, 4 characters are to be extracted and the program should return the string "king". If the position of the string to be extracted is given and the number of characters to be extracted is 0, then the program should extract the entire string from the specified position.

PP 8.7   The programming projects of Chapter 4 discussed a Card class that represents a standard playing card. Create a class called DeckOfCards that stores 52 objects of the Card class. Include methods to shuffle the deck, deal a card, and report the number of cards left in the deck. The shuffle method should assume a full deck. Create a driver class with a main method that deals each card from a shuffled deck, printing each card as it is dealt.

PP 8.8   Design and implement an application that reads a sequence of up to 25 pairs of names and postal (ZIP) codes for individuals. Store the data in an object designed to store a first name (string), last name (string), and postal code (integer). Assume each line of input will contain two strings followed by an integer value, each separated by a tab character. Then, after the input has been read in, print the list in an appropriate format to the screen.

PP 8.9   Modify the program you created in PP 8.8 to accomplish the following:

- Support the storing of additional user information: street address (string), city (string), state (string), and 10 digit phone number (long integer, contains area code and does not include special characters such as '(', ')', or '-')

- Store the data in an ArrayList object.

PP 8.10 Use the Question class from Chapter 7 to define a Quiz class. A quiz can be composed of up to 25 questions. Define the add method of the Quiz class to add a question to a quiz. Define the giveQuiz method of the Quiz class to present each question in turn to the user, accept an answer for each one, and keep track of the results. Define a class called QuizTime with a main method that populates a quiz, presents it, and prints the final results.

PP 8.11 Modify your answer to PP 8.10 so that the complexity level of the questions given in the quiz is taken into account. Overload the giveQuiz method so that it accepts two integer parameters that specify the minimum and maximum complexity levels for the quiz questions and presents only questions in that complexity range. Modify the main method to demonstrate this feature.

PP 8.12 Design a class that represents a star with a specified radius and color. Use a filled polygon to draw the star. Design and implement a program that draws 10 stars of random radius in random locations.

PP 8.13 Design a class that represents the visual representation of a car. Use polylines and polygons to draw the car in any graphics context and at any location. Create a `main` driver to display the car.

PP 8.14 Modify the solution to PP 8.13 so that it uses the `Polygon` class to represent all polygons used in the drawing.

PP 8.15 Modify the `QuoteOptions` program from Chapter 5 so that it provides three additional quote options. Use an array to store all of the quote strings.

PP 8.16 Design and implement a program that draws 20 circles, with the radius and location of each circle determined at random. If a circle does not overlap any other circle, draw that circle in black. If a circle overlaps one or more other circles, draw it in cyan. Use an array to store a representation of each circle, then determine the color of each circle. Two circles overlap if the distance between their center points is less than the sum of their radii.

PP 8.17 Design and implement a program that draws a checkerboard with five red and eight black checkers on it in various locations. Store the checkerboard as a two-dimensional array.

PP 8.18 Modify the program from PP 8.17 so that the program determines whether any black checkers can jump any red checkers. Under the checkerboard, print (using `drawString`) the row and column position of all black checkers that have possible jumps.

PP 8.19 Modify the `RubberLines` program from this chapter so that it shows all of the lines drawn. Show only the final lines (from initial mouse press to mouse release), not the intermediate lines drawn to show the rubberbanding effect. *Hint*: Keep track of a list of objects that represent the lines similar to how the `Dots` program kept track of multiple dots.

PP 8.20 Design and implement a program that counts the number of times the mouse has been clicked. Display that number in the center of the applet window.

PP 8.21 Design and implement an application that creates a polyline shape dynamically using mouse clicks. Each mouse click adds a new line segment from the previous point. Include a button below the drawing area to clear the current polyline and begin another.

PP 8.22 Design and implement an application that draws a circle using a rubberbanding technique. The circle size is determined by a mouse drag. Use the original mouse click location as a fixed center point. Compute the distance between the current location of the mouse pointer and the center point to determine the current radius of the circle.

PP 8.23 Design and implement an application that serves as a mouse odometer, continually displaying how far, in pixels, the mouse has moved (while it is over the program window). Display the current odometer value using a label. *Hint*: Use the mouse movement event to determine the current position, and compare it to the last position of the mouse. Use the distance formula to see how far the mouse has traveled, and add that to a running total distance.

PP 8.24 Design and implement a program whose background changes color depending on where the mouse pointer is located. If the mouse pointer is on the left half of the program window, display red; if it is on the right half, display green.

PP 8.25 Design and implement a class that represents a spaceship, which can be drawn (side view) in any particular location. Create a program that displays the spaceship so that it follows the movement of the mouse. When the mouse button is pressed down, have a laser beam shoot out of the front of the spaceship (one continuous beam, not a moving projectile) until the mouse button is released.

PP 8.26 Design and implement a program that helps a hospital analyze the flow of patients through the emergency room. A text input file contains integers that represent the number of patients that entered the emergency room during each hour of each day for four weeks. Read the information and store it in a three dimensional array. Then analyze it to compare the total number of patients per week, per day, and per hour. Display the results of the analysis.

PP 8.27 Modify the `Direction` program from this chapter so that the image is not allowed to move out of the visible area of the panel. Ignore any key event that would cause that to happen.

PP 8.28 Modify the `Direction` program from this chapter so that, in addition to responding to the arrow keys, it also responds to four other keys that move the image in diagonal directions. When the `'t'` key is pressed, move the image up and to the left. Likewise, use `'u'` to move up and right, `'g'` to move down and left, and `'j'` to move down and right. Do not move the image if it has reached a window boundary.

LA Air Traffic Control

What Happened?

At about 5 pm on Tuesday, September 14, 2004, the Los Angeles air traffic-control center suddenly lost voice contact with 400 planes they were tracking in the southwestern United States. The Voice Switching and Control System (VSCS), designed by the Harris Corp. of Melbourne, Florida, had unexpectedly shut down. Then the backup system designed to take over when such a failure occurred crashed within a minute after it was activated. Without the controller's guidance, planes began coming dangerously close to each other, resulting in several near misses.

■ Air traffic controllers in action, using voice and imaging systems.

Collisions were avoided due in part to the quick thinking of some controllers, who used their cell phones to alert other traffic-control centers and the airlines. But the main reason the incident wasn't a disaster was the on-board collision avoidance systems now found in commercial jets. These systems track the transponders of nearby aircraft and give emergency instructions to the pilots to climb or descend at the last minute. It's likely that several midair collisions would have resulted if the problem had occurred 10 to 15 years earlier, before planes had such avoidance systems.

What Caused It?

Officially, the incident was blamed on human error. The FAA reported that the problem was "not the result of system reliability" and would have been avoided if FAA procedures had been followed. The key procedure in this case requires that the voice switching system be rebooted every 30 days.

The root cause, however, was traced to a software problem. The VSCS relies on a subsystem that periodically runs built-in tests. A countdown timer in the subsystem is used to determine when the tests will run. The timer counts down in milliseconds, starting at the highest numeric value that the system could handle: 2^{32}. That's just over four billion milliseconds. It takes just under 50 days for the timer to go from 2^{32} down to zero. Unfortunately, when the timer reaches zero, the tests cannot be run, and the system shuts down. By rebooting the system every 30 days, the timer is reset almost three weeks before it expires.

The FAA first discovered the problem when it ran tests on the system in the field. It ran for 49.7 days, and then crashed. After rebooting, everything seemed fine. When a similar crash happened with another system, the FAA instituted the 30-day reboot procedure.

After the incident in Los Angeles, the issue was tracked down, and a software patch was created to fix the problem. Now the system periodically resets the counter without the need for human intervention.

Lessons Learned

In this situation, the problem (if not its implications) was known beforehand. Harris (the manufacturer) knew about the potential for the timer to expire but hadn't determined the impact it might have on the system. The FAA discovered the problem during tests---although not the root cause. Instead of delving further, they instituted a human-based, manual solution---the ultimate "when in doubt, reboot" scenario.

It's true that the problem would have been avoided if the FAA procedures had been followed, but that's of little comfort when the software can make such procedures unnecessary. It's also true that the incident would have been negligible if the backup system had not failed. Having redundant backup systems would lessen the chance of complete failure.

In this case, though, the bottom line is that thorough testing and investigation would have brought the problem to light. In safety-critical systems, nothing less should be acceptable.

Source: IEEE Spectrum, November 2004

Inheritance

9

CHAPTER OBJECTIVES

- Explore the derivation of new classes from existing ones.
- Define the concept and purpose of method overriding.
- Discuss the design of class hierarchies.
- Discuss the issue of visibility as it relates to inheritance.
- Explore the ability to derive one interface from another.
- Discuss object-oriented design in the context of inheritance.
- Describe the inheritance structure for GUI components.
- Explore the creation of listeners by extending adaptor classes.

This chapter explains inheritance, a fundamental technique for organizing and creating classes. It is a simple but powerful idea that influences the way we design object-oriented software and enhances our ability to reuse classes in other situations and programs. In this chapter we explore the technique for creating subclasses and class hierarchies, and we discuss a technique for overriding the definition of an inherited method. We examine the protected modifier and discuss the effect all visibility modifiers have on inherited attributes and methods. Finally, we discuss how inheritance affects various issues related to graphical user interfaces (GUIs) in Java, such as the ability to extend an adaptor class to create a listener.

9.1 Creating Subclasses

In our introduction to object-oriented concepts in Chapter 1. we presented the analogy that a class is to an object what a blueprint is to a house. In subsequent chapters we've reinforced that idea, writing classes that define a set of similar objects. A class establishes the characteristics and behaviors of an object but reserves no memory space for variables (unless those variables are declared as static). Classes are the plan, and objects are the embodiment of that plan.

Many houses can be created from the same blueprint. They are essentially the same house in different locations with different people living in them. Now suppose you want a house that is similar to another but with some different or additional features. You want to start with the same basic blueprint but modify it to suit new, slightly different, needs. Many housing developments are created this way. The houses in the development have the same core layout, but they have unique features. For instance, they might all be split-level homes with the same basic room configuration, but some have a fireplace or full basement while others do not, or an upgraded gourmet kitchen instead of the standard version.

It's likely that the housing developer commissioned a master architect to create a single blueprint to establish the basic design of all houses in the development, then a series of new blueprints that include variations designed to appeal to different buyers. The act of creating the series of blueprints was simplified since they all begin with the same underlying structure, while the variations give them unique characteristics that may be important to the prospective owners.

> **KEY CONCEPT**
> Inheritance is the process of deriving a new class from an existing one.

Creating a new blueprint that is based on an existing blueprint is analogous to the object-oriented concept of *inheritance*, which is the process in which a new class is derived from an existing one. Inheritance is a powerful software development technique and a defining characteristic of object-oriented programming.

Via inheritance, the new class automatically contains the variables and methods in the original class. Then, to tailor the class as needed, the programmer can add new variables and methods to the derived class or modify the inherited ones.

> **KEY CONCEPT**
> One purpose of inheritance is to reuse existing software.

In general, new classes can be created via inheritance faster, easier, and cheaper than by writing them from scratch. Inheritance is one way to support the idea of *software reuse*. By using existing software components to create new ones, we capitalize on the effort that went into the design, implementation, and testing of the existing software.

Keep in mind that the word *class* comes from the idea of classifying groups of objects with similar characteristics. Classification schemes often use levels of classes that relate to each other. For example, all mammals share certain characteristics: They are warmblooded, have hair, and produce milk to feed their young. Now consider a subset of mammals, such as horses. All horses are mammals and have all of the characteristics of mammals, but they also have unique features that make them different from other mammals such as dogs.

If we translate this idea into software terms, an existing class called Mammal would have certain variables and methods that describe the state and behavior of mammals. A Horse class could be derived from the existing Mammal class, automatically inheriting the variables and methods contained in Mammal. The Horse class can refer to the inherited variables and methods as if they had been declared locally in that class. New variables and methods can then be added to the derived class to distinguish a horse from other mammals.

The original class that is used to derive a new one is called the *parent class, superclass,* or *base class.* The derived class is called a *child class,* or *subclass.* Java uses the reserved word extends to indicate that a new class is being derived from an existing class.

> **KEY CONCEPT**
>
> Inheritance creates an is-a relationship between the parent and child classes.

The process of inheritance should establish an *is-a relationship* between two classes. That is, the child class should be a more specific version of the parent. For example, a horse is a mammal. Not all mammals are horses, but all horses are mammals. For any class X that is derived from class Y, you should be able to say that "X is a Y." If such a statement doesn't make sense, then that relationship is probably not an appropriate use of inheritance.

Let's look at an example. The program shown in Listing 9.1 instantiates an object of class Dictionary, which is derived from a class called Book. In the main method, three methods are invoked through the Dictionary object: two that were declared locally in the Dictionary class and one that was inherited from the Book class.

The Book class (see Listing 9.2) is used to derive the Dictionary class (see Listing 9.3) using the reserved word extends in the header of Dictionary. The Dictionary class automatically inherits the definition of the setPages and getPages methods, as well as the pages variable. It is as if those methods and the pages variable were declared inside the Dictionary class. Note that, in the Dictionary class, the computeRatio method explicitly references the pages variable, even though the variable is declared in the Book class.

Also note that although the Book class is needed to create the definition of Dictionary, no Book object is ever instantiated in the program. An instance of a child class does not rely on an instance of the parent class.

Inheritance is a one-way street. The Book class cannot use variables or methods that are declared explicitly in the Dictionary class. For instance, if we created an object from the Book class, it could not be used to invoke the setDefinitions method. This restriction makes sense, because a child class is a more specific

LISTING 9.1

```java
//********************************************************************
//  Words.java       Author: Lewis/Loftus
//
//  Demonstrates the use of an inherited method.
//********************************************************************

public class Words
{
   //-----------------------------------------------------------------
   //  Instantiates a derived class and invokes its inherited and
   //  local methods.
   //-----------------------------------------------------------------
   public static void main (String[] args)
   {
      Dictionary webster = new Dictionary();

      System.out.println ("Number of pages: " + webster.getPages());

      System.out.println ("Number of definitions: " +
                          webster.getDefinitions());

      System.out.println ("Definitions per page: " +
                          webster.computeRatio());
   }
}
```

OUTPUT

```
Number of pages: 1500
Number of definitions: 52500
Definitions per page: 35.0
```

version of the parent class. A dictionary has pages, because all books have pages; but although a dictionary has definitions, not all books do.

Inheritance relationships are often represented in UML class diagrams. Figure 9.1 shows the inheritance relationship between the Book and Dictionary classes. An arrow with an open arrowhead is used to show inheritance in a UML diagram, with the arrow pointing from the child class to the parent class.

LISTING 9.2

```java
//********************************************************************
//  Book.java         Author: Lewis/Loftus
//
//  Represents a book. Used as the parent of a derived class to
//  demonstrate inheritance.
//********************************************************************

public class Book
{
    protected int pages = 1500;

    //-----------------------------------------------------------------
    //  Pages mutator.
    //-----------------------------------------------------------------
    public void setPages (int numPages)
    {
        pages = numPages;
    }

    //-----------------------------------------------------------------
    //  Pages accessor.
    //-----------------------------------------------------------------
    public int getPages ()
    {
        return pages;
    }
}
```

The protected Modifier

As we've seen, visibility modifiers are used to control access to the members of a class. This effect extends into the process of inheritance as well. Any public method or variable in a parent class can be explicitly referenced by name in the child class and through objects of that child class. On the other hand, private methods and variables of the parent class cannot be referenced in the child class or through an object of the child class.

However, if we declare a variable with public visibility so that a derived class can reference it, we violate the principle of encapsulation. Therefore, Java provides a third visibility modifier: protected. Note that the variable pages is declared with protected visibility in the Book class. When a variable or method is

LISTING 9.3

```java
//********************************************************************
//  Dictionary.java       Author: Lewis/Loftus
//
//  Represents a dictionary, which is a book. Used to demonstrate
//  inheritance.
//********************************************************************

public class Dictionary extends Book
{
   private int definitions = 52500;

   //------------------------------------------------------
   //  Prints a message using both local and inherited values.
   //------------------------------------------------------
   public double computeRatio ()
   {
      return (double) definitions/pages;
   }

   //------------------------------------------------------
   //  Definitions mutator.
   //------------------------------------------------------
   public void setDefinitions (int numDefinitions)
   {
      definitions = numDefinitions;
   }

   //------------------------------------------------------
   //  Definitions accessor.
   //------------------------------------------------------
   public int getDefinitions ()
   {
      return definitions;
   }
}
```

declared with protected visibility, a derived class can reference it. And protected visibility allows the class to retain some encapsulation properties. The encapsulation with protected visibility is not as tight as it would be if the variable or method were declared private, but it is better than if it were declared public. Specifically, a

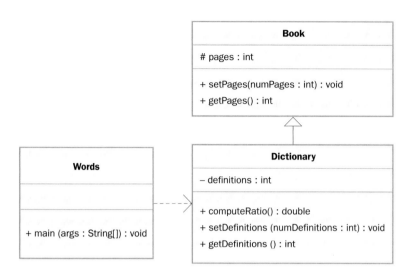

FIGURE 9.1   A UML class diagram showing an inheritance relationship

variable or method declared with protected visibility may be accessed by any class in the same package, in addition to being accessible by any derived classes. The relationships among all Java modifiers are explained completely in Appendix E.

In a UML diagram, protected visibility can be indicated by preceding the protected member with a hash mark (#). The pages variable of the Book class has this annotation in Figure 9.1.

> **KEY CONCEPT**
> Protected visibility provides the best possible encapsulation that permits inheritance.

Each variable or method retains the effect of its original visibility modifier. For example, the setPages method is still considered to be public in its inherited form in the Dictionary class.

Let's be clear about our terms. All methods and variables, even those declared with private visibility, are inherited by the child class. That is, their definitions exist and memory space is reserved for the variables. It's just that they can't be referenced by name. This issue is explored in more detail in section 9.4.

VideoNote

Overview of inheritance.

Constructors, however, are not inherited. Constructors are special methods that are used to set up a particular type of object, so it doesn't make sense for a class called Dictionary to have a constructor called Book. But you can imagine that a child class may want to refer to the constructor of the parent class, which is one of the reasons for the super reference, described next.

The super Reference

The reserved word super can be used in a class to refer to its parent class. Using the super reference, we can access a parent's members. Like the this reference, what the word super refers to depends on the class in which it is used.

One use of the super reference is to invoke a parent's constructor. Let's look at an example. Listing 9.4 shows a modification of the original Words program from Listing 9.1. Similar to the original version, we use a class called Book2

LISTING 9.4

```java
//********************************************************************
//  Words2.java        Author: Lewis/Loftus
//
//  Demonstrates the use of the super reference.
//********************************************************************

public class Words2
{
   //-----------------------------------------------------------------
   //  Instantiates a derived class and invokes its inherited and
   //  local methods.
   //-----------------------------------------------------------------
   public static void main (String[] args)
   {
      Dictionary2 webster = new Dictionary2 (1500, 52500);

      System.out.println ("Number of pages: " + webster.getPages());

      System.out.println ("Number of definitions: " +
                          webster.getDefinitions());

      System.out.println ("Definitions per page: " +
                          webster.computeRatio());
   }
}
```

OUTPUT

```
Number of pages: 1500
Number of definitions: 52500
Definitions per page: 35.0
```

LISTING 9.5

```java
//********************************************************************
//  Book2.java        Author: Lewis/Loftus
//
//  Represents a book. Used as the parent of a derived class to
//  demonstrate inheritance and the use of the super reference.
//********************************************************************

public class Book2
{
   protected int pages;

   //-----------------------------------------------------------------
   //  Constructor: Sets up the book with the specified number of
   //  pages.
   //-----------------------------------------------------------------
   public Book2 (int numPages)
   {
      pages = numPages;
   }

   //-----------------------------------------------------------------
   //  Pages mutator.
   //-----------------------------------------------------------------
   public void setPages (int numPages)
   {
      pages = numPages;
   }

   //-----------------------------------------------------------------
   //  Pages accessor.
   //-----------------------------------------------------------------
   public int getPages ()
   {
      return pages;
   }
}
```

(see Listing 9.5) as the parent of the derived class Dictionary2 (see Listing 9.6). However, unlike earlier versions of these classes, Book2 and Dictionary2 have explicit constructors used to initialize their instance variables. The output of the Words2 program is the same as it is for the original Words program.

LISTING 9.6

```
//********************************************************************
//  Dictionary2.java       Author: Lewis/Loftus
//
//  Represents a dictionary, which is a book. Used to demonstrate
//  the use of the super reference.
//********************************************************************

public class Dictionary2 extends Book2
{
   private int definitions;

   //---------------------   -----------------------------------------
   //  Constructor: Sets up the dictionary with the specified number
   //  of pages and definitions.
   //-----------------------------------------------------------------
   public Dictionary2 (int numPages, int numDefinitions)
   {
      super(numPages);

      definitions = numDefinitions;
   }

   //-----------------------------------------------------------------
   //  Prints a message using both local and inherited values.
   //-----------------------------------------------------------------
   public double computeRatio ()
   {
      return (double) definitions/pages;
   }

   //-----------------------------------------------------------------
   //  Definitions mutator.
   //-----------------------------------------------------------------
   public void setDefinitions (int numDefinitions)
   {
      definitions = numDefinitions;
   }

   //-----------------------------------------------------------------
   //  Definitions accessor.
   //-----------------------------------------------------------------
```

LISTING 9.6   *continued*

```
    public int getDefinitions ()
    {
        return definitions;
    }
}
```

The Dictionary2 constructor takes two integer values as parameters, representing the number of pages and definitions in the book. Because the Book2 class already has a constructor that performs the work to set up the parts of the dictionary that were inherited, we rely on that constructor to do that work. However, since the constructor is not inherited, we cannot invoke it directly, and so we use the super reference to get to it in the parent class. The Dictionary2 constructor then proceeds to initialize its definitions variable.

In this case, it would have been just as easy to set the pages variable explicitly in the Dictionary2 constructor instead of using super to call the Book2 constructor. However, it is good practice to let each class "take care of itself." If we choose to change the way that the Book2 constructor sets up its pages variable, we would also have to remember to make that change in Dictionary2. By using the super reference, a change made in Book2 is automatically reflected in Dictionary2.

A child's constructor is responsible for calling its parent's constructor. Generally, the first line of a constructor should use the super reference call to a constructor of the parent class. If no such call exists, Java will automatically make a call to super() at the beginning of the constructor. This rule ensures that a parent class initializes its variables before the child class constructor begins to execute. Using the super reference to invoke a parent's constructor can be done only in the child's constructor, and if included it must be the first line of the constructor.

The super reference can also be used to reference other variables and methods defined in the parent's class. We use this technique in later sections of this chapter.

Multiple Inheritance

Java's approach to inheritance is called *single inheritance*. This term means that a derived class can have only one parent. Some object-oriented languages allow a

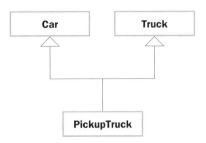

FIGURE 9.2   A UML class diagram showing multiple inheritance

child class to have multiple parents. This approach is called *multiple inheritance* and is occasionally useful for describing objects that are in between two categories or classes. For example, suppose we had a class Car and a class Truck and we wanted to create a new class called PickupTruck. A pickup truck is somewhat like a car and somewhat like a truck. With single inheritance, we must decide whether it is better to derive the new class from Car or Truck. With multiple inheritance, it can be derived from both, as shown in Figure 9.2.

Multiple inheritance works well in some situations, but it comes with a price. What if both Truck and Car have methods with the same name? Which method would PickupTruck inherit? The answer to this question is complex, and it depends on the rules of the language that supports multiple inheritance.

The designers of the Java language explicitly decided not to support multiple inheritance. Instead, we can rely on interfaces to provide the best features of multiple inheritance without the added complexity. Although a Java class can be derived from only one parent class, it can implement multiple interfaces. Therefore, we can interact with a particular class in specific ways while inheriting the core information from one parent class.

myprogramming**lab**

SELF-REVIEW QUESTIONS *(see answers in Appendix N)*

SR 9.1   Describe the relationship between a parent class and a child class.

SR 9.2   How does inheritance support software reuse?

SR 9.3   What relationship should every class derivation represent?

SR 9.4   What does the protected modifier accomplish?

SR 9.5   Why is the super reference important to a child class?

SR 9.6   Define a class SchoolBook2 that extends Book2 to include an attribute indicating the age (4 through 16) that a book targets. The constructor accepts the age as a parameter. The class also provides a level method that returns a string as follows: "Pre-school" if the target age is 4 through 6, "Early" if the target age is 7 through 9, "Middle" if the target age is 10 through 12, and "Upper" if the target age is 13 through 16.

SR 9.7   What is the difference between single inheritance and multiple inheritance?

9.2 Overriding Methods

When a child class defines a method with the same name and signature as a method in the parent class, we say that the child's version *overrides* the parent's version in favor of its own. The need for overriding occurs often in inheritance situations.

> **KEY CONCEPT**
>
> A child class can override (redefine) the parent's definition of an inherited method.

The program in Listing 9.7 provides a simple demonstration of method overriding in Java. The Messages class contains a main method that instantiates two objects: one from class Thought and one from class Advice. The Thought class is the parent of the Advice class.

LISTING 9.7

```java
//********************************************************************
//  Messages.java       Author: Lewis/Loftus
//
//  Demonstrates the use of an overridden method.
//********************************************************************
public class Messages
{
   //-----------------------------------------------------------------
   //  Creates two objects and invokes the message method in each.
   //-----------------------------------------------------------------
   public static void main (String[] args)
   {
      Thought parked = new Thought();
      Advice dates = new Advice();

      parked.message();

      dates.message();   // overridden
   }
}
```

LISTING 9.7   *continued*

OUTPUT

```
I feel like I'm diagonally parked in a parallel universe.

Warning: Dates in calendar are closer than they appear.

I feel like I'm diagonally parked in a parallel universe.
```

Both the Thought class (see Listing 9.8) and the Advice class (see Listing 9.9) contain a definition for a method called message. The version of message defined in the Thought class is inherited by Advice, but Advice overrides it with an alternative version. The new version of the method prints out an entirely different message and then invokes the parent's version of the message method using the super reference.

The object that is used to invoke a method determines which version of the method is actually executed. When message is invoked using the parked object in

LISTING 9.8

```java
//********************************************************************
//  Thought.java        Author: Lewis/Loftus
//
//  Represents a stray thought. Used as the parent of a derived
//  class to demonstrate the use of an overridden method.
//********************************************************************

public class Thought
{
   //-----------------------------------------------------------
   //  Prints a message.
   //-----------------------------------------------------------
   public void message()
   {
      System.out.println ("I feel like I'm diagonally parked in a " +
                          "parallel universe.");

      System.out.println();
   }
}
```

LISTING 9.9

```java
//********************************************************************
//  Advice.java        Author: Lewis/Loftus
//
//  Represents some thoughtful advice. Used to demonstrate the use
//  of an overridden method.
//********************************************************************

public class Advice extends Thought
{
   //-----------------------------------------------------------------
   //  Prints a message. This method overrides the parent's version.
   //-----------------------------------------------------------------
   public void message()
   {
      System.out.println ("Warning: Dates in calendar are closer " +
                          "than they appear.");

      System.out.println();

      super.message();   // explicitly invokes the parent's version
   }
}
```

the main method, the Thought version of message is executed. When message is invoked using the dates object, the Advice version of message is executed.

A method can be defined with the final modifier. A child class cannot override a final method. This technique is used to ensure that a derived class uses a particular definition of a method.

Method overriding is a key element in object-oriented design. It allows two objects that are related by inheritance to use the same naming conventions for methods that accomplish the same general task in different ways. Overriding becomes even more important when it comes to polymorphism, which is discussed in Chapter 10.

Shadowing Variables

It is possible, although not recommended, for a child class to declare a variable with the same name as one that is inherited from the parent. Note the distinction between redeclaring a variable and simply giving an inherited variable a particular value. If a variable of the same name is declared in a child class, it is called a *shadow variable*. It is similar in concept to the process of overriding methods but creates confusing subtleties.

Because an inherited variable is already available to the child class, there is usually no good reason to redeclare it. Someone reading code with a shadowed variable will find two different declarations that seem to apply to a variable used in the child class. This confusion causes problems and serves no useful purpose. A redeclaration of a particular variable name could change its type, but that is usually unnecessary. In general, shadowing variables should be avoided.

myprogramminglab

SELF-REVIEW QUESTIONS *(see answers in Appendix N)*

SR 9.8   Why would a child class override one or more of the methods of its parent class?

SR 9.9   True or False? Explain.

    a. A child class may define a method with the same name as a method in the parent class.
    b. A child class can override the constructor of the parent class.
    c. A child class can override a `final` method of the parent class.
    d. It is considered poor design when a child class overrides a method from the parent class.
    e. A child class may define a variable with the same name as a variable in the parent class.

9.3 Class Hierarchies

KEY CONCEPT
The child of one class can be the parent of one or more other classes, creating a class hierarchy.

A child class derived from one parent can be the parent of its own child class. Furthermore, multiple classes can be derived from a single parent. Therefore, inheritance relationships often develop into *class hierarchies*. The diagram in Figure 9.3 shows a class

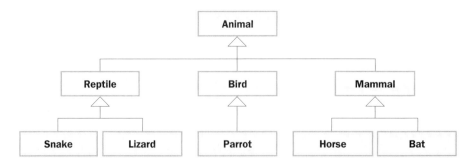

FIGURE 9.3   A UML class diagram showing a class hierarchy

hierarchy that includes the inheritance relationship between the Mammal and Horse classes.

There is no limit to the number of children a class can have or to the number of levels to which a class hierarchy can extend. Two children of the same parent are called *siblings*. Although siblings share the characteristics passed on by their common parent, they are not related by inheritance, because one is not used to derive the other.

In class hierarchies, common features should be kept as high in the hierarchy as reasonably possible. That way, the only characteristics explicitly established in a child class are those that make the class distinct from its parent and from its siblings. This approach maximizes the potential to reuse classes. It also facilitates maintenance activities, because when changes are made to the parent, they are automatically reflected in the descendents. Always remember to maintain the is-a relationship when building class hierarchies.

The inheritance mechanism is transitive. That is, a parent passes along a trait to a child class, and that child class passes it along to its children, and so on. An inherited feature might have originated in the immediate parent or possibly several levels higher in a more distant ancestor class.

> **KEY CONCEPT**
> Common features should be located as high in a class hierarchy as is reasonably possible.

There is no single best hierarchy organization for all situations. The decisions you make when you are designing a class hierarchy restrict and guide more detailed design decisions and implementation options, so you must make them carefully.

Earlier in this chapter we discussed a class hierarchy that organized animals by their major biological classifications, such as Mammal, Bird, and Reptile. However, in a different situation, the same animals might logically be organized in a different way. For example, as shown in Figure 9.4, the class hierarchy might be organized around a function of the animals, such as their ability to fly. In this case, a Parrot class and a Bat class would be siblings derived from a general FlyingAnimal class. This class hierarchy is as valid and reasonable as the original one. The needs of the programs that use the classes will determine which is best for the particular situation.

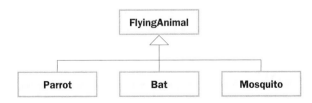

FIGURE 9.4   An alternative hierarchy for organizing animals

The Object Class

In Java, all classes are derived ultimately from the Object class. If a class definition doesn't use the extends clause to derive itself explicitly from another class, then that class is automatically derived from the Object class by default. Therefore, the following two class definitions are equivalent:

```
class Thing
{
    //  whatever
}
```

and

```
class Thing extends Object
{
    //  whatever
}
```

> **KEY CONCEPT**
>
> All Java classes are derived, directly or indirectly, from the Object class.

Because all classes are derived from Object, all public methods of Object are inherited by every Java class. They can be invoked through any object created in any Java program. The Object class is defined in the java.lang package of the Java standard class library. Figure 9.5 lists some of the methods of the Object class.

As it turns out, we've been using Object methods quite often in our examples. The toString method, for instance, is defined in the Object class, so the toString method can be called on any object. As we've seen several times, when a println method is called with an object parameter, toString is called to determine what to print.

> **KEY CONCEPT**
>
> The toString and equals methods are inherited by every class in every Java program.

Therefore, when we define a toString method in a class, we are actually overriding an inherited definition. The definition for toString that is provided by the Object class returns a string containing the

```
boolean equals (Object obj)
    Returns true if this object is an alias of the specified object.

String toString ()
    Returns a string representation of this object.

Object clone ()
    Creates and returns a copy of this object.
```

FIGURE 9.5   Some methods of the Object class

object's class name followed by a numeric value that is unique for that object. Usually, we override the Object version of toString to fit our own needs. The String class has overridden the toString method so that it returns its stored string value.

We are also overriding an inherited method when we define an equals method for a class. As we've discussed previously, the purpose of the equals method is to determine whether two objects are equal. The definition of the equals method provided by the Object class returns true if the two object references actually refer to the same object (that is, if they are aliases). Classes often override the inherited definition of the equals method in favor of a more appropriate definition. For instance, the String class overrides equals so that it returns true only if both strings contain the same characters in the same order.

Abstract Classes

An *abstract class* represents a generic concept in a class hierarchy. An abstract class cannot be instantiated and usually contains one or more *abstract methods*, which have no definition. We've discussed abstract methods in Chapter 7 when they are used to define a Java interface. An abstract class is similar to an interface in some ways. However, unlike interfaces, an abstract class can contain methods that are not abstract. It can also contain data declarations other than constants.

A class is declared as abstract by including the abstract modifier in the class header. Any class that contains one or more abstract methods must be declared as abstract. In abstract classes (unlike interfaces), the abstract modifier must be applied to each abstract method. A class declared as abstract does not have to contain abstract methods.

> **KEY CONCEPT**
>
> An abstract class cannot be instantiated. It represents a concept on which other classes can build their definitions.

Abstract classes serve as placeholders in a class hierarchy. As the name implies, an abstract class represents an abstract entity that is usually insufficiently defined to be useful by itself. Instead, an abstract class may contain a partial description that is inherited by all of its descendants in the class hierarchy. Its children, which are more specific, fill in the gaps.

Consider the class hierarchy shown in Figure 9.6. The Vehicle class at the top of the hierarchy may be too generic for a particular application. Therefore we may choose to implement it as an abstract class. In UML diagrams, abstract class names are shown in italic.

Concepts that apply to all vehicles can be represented in the Vehicle class and are inherited by its descendants. That way, each of its descendants doesn't have to define the same concept redundantly (and perhaps inconsistently). For example, we may say that all vehicles have a particular speed. Therefore we declare a speed variable in the Vehicle class, and all specific vehicles below it in the hierarchy

VideoNote

Example using a class hierarchy.

FIGURE 9.6   A vehicle class hierarchy

automatically have that variable because of inheritance. Any change we make to the representation of the speed of a vehicle is automatically reflected in all descendant classes. Similarly, we may declare an abstract method called `fuelConsumption`, whose purpose is to calculate how quickly fuel is being consumed by a particular vehicle. The details of the `fuelConsumption` method must be defined by each type of vehicle, but the `Vehicle` class establishes that all vehicles consume fuel and provides a consistent way to compute that value.

Some concepts don't apply to all vehicles, so we wouldn't represent those concepts at the `Vehicle` level. For instance, we wouldn't include a variable called `numberOfWheels` in the `Vehicle` class, because not all vehicles have wheels. The child classes for which wheels are appropriate can add that concept at the appropriate level in the hierarchy.

There are no restrictions as to where in a class hierarchy an abstract class can be defined. Usually they are located at the upper levels of a class hierarchy. However, it is possible to derive an abstract class from a nonabstract parent.

Usually, a child of an abstract class will provide a specific definition for an abstract method inherited from its parent. Note that this is just a specific case of overriding a method, giving a different definition than the one the parent provides. If a child of an abstract class does not give a definition for every abstract method that it inherits from its parent, then the child class is also considered abstract.

> **KEY CONCEPT**
> A class derived from an abstract parent must override all of its parent's abstract methods, or the derived class will also be considered abstract.

Note that it would be a contradiction for an abstract method to be modified as `final` or `static`. Because a final method cannot be overridden in subclasses, an abstract final method would have no way of being given a definition in subclasses. A static method can be invoked using the class name without declaring an object of the class. Because abstract methods have no implementation, an abstract static method would make no sense.

Choosing which classes and methods to make abstract is an important part of the design process. You should make such choices only after careful consideration. By using abstract classes wisely, you can create flexible, extensible software designs.

Interface Hierarchies

The concept of inheritance can be applied to interfaces as well as classes. That is, one interface can be derived from another interface. These relationships can form an *interface hierarchy*, which is similar to a class hierarchy. Inheritance relationships between interfaces are shown in UML diagrams using the same connection (an arrow with an open arrowhead) as they are with classes.

> **KEY CONCEPT**
>
> Inheritance can be applied to interfaces so that one interface can be derived from another.

When a parent interface is used to derive a child interface, the child inherits all abstract methods and constants of the parent. Any class that implements the child interface must implement all of the methods. There are no visibility issues when dealing with inheritance between interfaces (as there are with protected and private members of a class), because all members of an interface are public.

Class hierarchies and interface hierarchies do not overlap. That is, an interface cannot be used to derive a class, and a class cannot be used to derive an interface. A class and an interface interact only when a class is designed to implement a particular interface.

SELF-REVIEW QUESTIONS *(see answers in Appendix N)*

myprogramminglab

SR 9.10 Draw a UML class diagram showing an inheritance hierarchy containing classes that represent different types of food. Show some appropriate variables and method names for at least two of these classes.

SR 9.11 What is the significance of the `Object` class?

SR 9.12 Which is the only Java class that does not have a parent class? Explain.

SR 9.13 What is the role of an abstract class?

SR 9.14 Why is it a contradiction to define a `final`, `abstract` class?

SR 9.15 What is an interface hierarchy?

9.4 Visibility

As we discussed earlier in this chapter, all variables and methods, even private members, that are defined in a parent class are inherited by a child class. They exist for an object of a derived class, even though they can't be referenced directly. They can, however, be referenced indirectly.

> **KEY CONCEPT**
>
> Private members are inherited by the child class, but cannot be referenced directly by name. They may be used indirectly, however.

Let's look at an example that demonstrates this situation. The program shown in Listing 9.10 contains a `main` method that instantiates a `Pizza`

LISTING 9.10

```
//********************************************************************
//  FoodAnalyzer.java        Author: Lewis/Loftus
//
//  Demonstrates indirect access to inherited private members.
//********************************************************************

public class FoodAnalyzer
{
   //-----------------------------------------------------------------
   //  Instantiates a Pizza object and prints its calories per
   //  serving.
   //-----------------------------------------------------------------
   public static void main (String[] args)
   {
      Pizza special = new Pizza (275);

      System.out.println ("Calories per serving: " +
                          special.caloriesPerServing());
   }
}
```

OUTPUT

```
Calories per serving: 309
```

object and invokes a method to determine how many calories the pizza has per serving due to its fat content.

The FoodItem class shown in Listing 9.11 represents a generic type of food. The constructor of FoodItem accepts the number of grams of fat and the number of servings of that food. The calories method returns the number of calories due to fat, which the caloriesPerServing method invokes to help compute the number of fat calories per serving.

The Pizza class, shown in Listing 9.12, is derived from the FoodItem class, but it adds no special functionality or data. Its constructor calls the constructor of FoodItem using the super reference, asserting that there are eight servings per pizza.

The Pizza object called special in the main method is used to invoke the method caloriesPerServing, which is defined as a public method of FoodItem. Note that caloriesPerServing calls calories, which is declared with private visibility. Furthermore, calories references the variable fatGrams and the constant CALORIES_PER_GRAM, which are also declared with private visibility.

LISTING 9.11

```java
//********************************************************************
//  FoodItem.java       Author: Lewis/Loftus
//
//  Represents an item of food. Used as the parent of a derived class
//  to demonstrate indirect referencing.
//********************************************************************

public class FoodItem
{
   final private int CALORIES_PER_GRAM = 9;
   private int fatGrams;
   protected int servings;

   //-----------------------------------------------------------------
   //  Sets up this food item with the specified number of fat grams
   //  and number of servings.
   //-----------------------------------------------------------------
   public FoodItem (int numFatGrams, int numServings)
   {
      fatGrams = numFatGrams;
      servings = numServings;
   }

   //-----------------------------------------------------------------
   //  Computes and returns the number of calories in this food item
   //  due to fat.
   //-----------------------------------------------------------------
   private int calories()
   {
      return fatGrams * CALORIES_PER_GRAM;
   }

   //-----------------------------------------------------------------
   //  Computes and returns the number of fat calories per serving.
   //-----------------------------------------------------------------
   public int caloriesPerServing()
   {
      return (calories() / servings);
   }
}
```

```
LISTING  9.12

//************************************************************************
//  Pizza.java        Author: Lewis/Loftus
//
//  Represents a pizza, which is a food item. Used to demonstrate
//  indirect referencing through inheritance.
//************************************************************************

public class Pizza extends FoodItem
{
   //----------------------------------------------------------------
   //  Sets up a pizza with the specified amount of fat (assumes
   //  eight servings).
   //----------------------------------------------------------------
   public Pizza (int fatGrams)
   {
      super (fatGrams, 8);
   }
}
```

Even though the Pizza class cannot explicitly reference calories, fatGrams, or CALORIES_PER_GRAM, they are available for use indirectly when the Pizza object needs them. A Pizza object cannot be used to invoke the calories method, but it can call a method that can. Note that a FoodItem object was never created or needed.

myprogramminglab | SELF-REVIEW QUESTIONS *(see answers in Appendix N)*

SR 9.16 Are all members of a parent class inherited by the child? Explain.

SR 9.17 Could the Pizza class refer to the variable servings explicitly? What about the calories method? Explain.

9.5 Designing for Inheritance

KEY CONCEPT

Software design must carefully and specifically address inheritance.

As a major characteristic of object-oriented software, inheritance must be carefully and specifically addressed during software design. A little thought about inheritance relationships can lead to a far more elegant design, which pays huge dividends in the long term.

Throughout this chapter, several design issues have been addressed in the discussion of the nuts and bolts of inheritance in Java. The following list summarizes some of the inheritance issues that you should keep in mind during the program design stage:

■ Every derivation should be an is-a relationship. The child should be a more specific version of the parent.

■ Design a class hierarchy to capitalize on reuse, and potential reuse in the future.

■ As classes and objects are identified in the problem domain, find their commonality. Push common features as high in the class hierarchy as appropriate for consistency and ease of maintenance.

■ Override methods as appropriate to tailor or change the functionality of a child.

■ Add new variables to the child class as needed, but don't shadow (redefine) any inherited variables.

■ Allow each class to manage its own data. Therefore use the super reference to invoke a parent's constructor and to call overridden versions of methods if appropriate.

■ Use interfaces to create a class that serves multiple roles (simulating multiple inheritance).

■ Design a class hierarchy to fit the needs of the application, with attention to how it may be useful in the future.

■ Even if there are no current uses for them, override general methods such as toString and equals appropriately in child classes so that the inherited versions don't cause unintentional problems later.

■ Use abstract classes to specify a common class interface for the concrete classes lower in the hierarchy.

■ Use visibility modifiers carefully to provide the needed access in derived classes without violating encapsulation.

Restricting Inheritance

We've seen the final modifier used in declarations to create constants many times. The other uses of the final modifier involve inheritance and can have a significant influence on software design. Specifically, the final modifier can be used to curtail the abilities related to inheritance.

Earlier in this chapter we mentioned that a method can be declared as final, which means it cannot be overridden in any classes that extend the one it is in. A final method is often used to insist that particular functionality be used in all child classes.

> **KEY CONCEPT**
> The final modifier can be used to restrict inheritance.

The `final` modifier can also be applied to an entire class. A final class cannot be extended at all. Consider the following declaration:

```
public final class Standards
{
    //  whatever
}
```

Given this declaration, the `Standards` class cannot be used in the `extends` clause of another class. The compiler will generate an error message in such a case. The `Standards` class can be used normally, but it cannot be the parent of another class.

Using the `final` modifier to restrict inheritance abilities is a key design decision. It should be done in situations in which a child class could possibly be used to change functionality that you, as the designer, specifically want to be handled a certain way. This issue comes up again in the discussion of polymorphism in Chapter 10.

myprogramminglab

SELF-REVIEW QUESTIONS *(see answers in Appendix N)*

SR 9.18 What does it mean for an inheritance derivation to represent an is-a relationship?

SR 9.19 Where should common features of classes appear in a class hierarchy? Why?

SR 9.20 How can you define a class with multiple roles?

SR 9.21 Why should you override the `toString` method of a parent in its child class, even when the method is not invoked through the child by your current applications?

SR 9.22 How can the `final` modifier be used to restrict inheritance? Why would you do this?

9.6 The Component Class Hierarchy

KEY CONCEPT

The classes that represent Java GUI components are organized into a class hierarchy.

All of the Java classes that define GUI components are part of a class hierarchy, shown in part in Figure 9.7. Almost all Swing GUI components are derived from the `JComponent` class, which defines how all components work in general. `JComponent` is derived from the `Container` class, which in turn is derived from the `Component` class.

You'll recall that there are two primary GUI APIs used in Java: the Abstract Windowing Toolkit (AWT) and the Swing classes. The AWT is the original set of

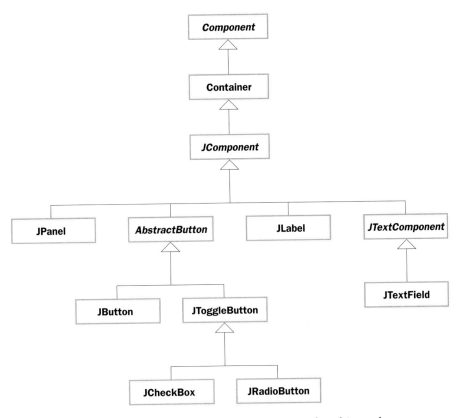

FIGURE 9.7   Part of the GUI component class hierarchy

graphics classes in Java. Swing classes were introduced later, adding components that provided much more functionality than their AWT counterparts. We use Swing components in our examples in this book. In the component class hierarchy, some Swing classes are ultimately derived from AWT classes.

Both Container and Component are original AWT classes. The Component class contains much of the general functionality that applies to all GUI components, such as basic painting and event handling. So although we may prefer to use some of the specific Swing components, they are based on core AWT concepts and respond to the same events as AWT components. Because they are derived from Container, many Swing components can serve as containers, though in most circumstances those abilities are curtailed. For example, we've seen that a JLabel object can contain an image, but it cannot be used as a generic container to which any component can be added.

Many features that apply to all Swing components are defined in the JComponent class and are inherited into its descendants. For example, we have the ability to put a border on any Swing component (as we saw in Chapter 6). This ability is defined once in the JComponent class and is inherited by any class that is derived, directly or indirectly, from it.

Some component classes, such as JPanel and JLabel, are derived directly from JComponent. Other component classes are nested further down in the inheritance hierarchy structure. For example, the AbstractButton class is an abstract class that defines the functionality that applies to all types of GUI buttons. JButton is derived directly from it. However, note that JCheckBox and JRadioButton are both derived from a class called JToggleButton, which embodies the common characteristics for buttons that can be in one of two states. The set of classes that define GUI buttons shows once again how common characteristics are put at appropriately high levels of the class hierarchy rather than duplicated in multiple classes.

The world of text components demonstrates this as well. The JTextField class that we've used in previous examples is one of many Java GUI components that support the management of text data. They are organized under a class called JTextComponent. Keep in mind that there are many GUI component classes that are not shown in the diagram in Figure 9.7.

In previous chapters we've extended the component class hierarchy further by defining panel and applet classes of our own using inheritance. By extending the JPanel or JApplet class, we create our own classes that automatically have all the characteristics of those components. Sometimes we then overrode the definition of a method, such as the paintComponent method, to behave in a particular way.

Creating our own panel and applet classes is a classic use of inheritance, allowing the parent class to shoulder the responsibilities that apply to all of its descendants. For example, the JApplet class is already designed to handle all of the details concerning applet creation and execution. An applet interacts with a browser, can accept parameters through HTML code, and is constrained by certain security limitations. The JApplet class already takes care of these details in a generic way that applies to all applets. The applet class that we write (the one derived from JApplet) is ready to focus on the purpose of that particular program. In other words, the only issues that we address in our applet code are those that make it different from other applets.

SELF-REVIEW QUESTIONS *(see answers in Appendix N)*

SR 9.23   True or False, based on the GUI component class hierarchy diagram displayed in this section.

a. A JCheckBox object is a JToggleButton.
b. A JCheckBox object is an AbstractButton.
c. A JTextField object is a JLabel.

    d. A `JComponent` object is a `JPanel`.

    e. A `JToggleButton` object is a `JButton`.

    f. A `JRadioButton` is a `Component`.

SR 9.24 What benefits do you derive by having your applet class extend the Java library's `JApplet` class?

9.7 Extending Adapter Classes

In previous event-based examples, we've created the listener classes by implementing a particular listener interface. For instance, to create a class that listens for mouse events, we created a listener class that implements the `MouseListener` interface. As we saw in the `Dots` and `RubberLines` programs in Chapter 8, a listener interface often contains event methods that are not important to a particular program, in which case we provided empty definitions to satisfy the interface requirement.

> **KEY CONCEPT**
>
> A listener class can be created by deriving it from an event adapter class.

An alternative technique for creating a listener class is to extend an *event adapter class*. Each listener interface that contains more than one method has a corresponding adapter class that already contains empty definitions for all of the methods in the interface. To create a listener, we can derive a new listener class from the appropriate adapter class and override any event methods in which we are interested. Using this technique, we no longer need to provide empty definitions for unused methods.

The program shown in Listing 9.13 displays a panel that responds to mouse click events. Whenever the mouse button is clicked over the panel, a line is drawn from the location of the mouse pointer to the center of the panel. The distance that line represents in pixels is displayed.

The listener class is implemented as an inner class of the `OffCenterPanel` class, shown in Listing 9.14. Instead of implementing the `MouseListener` interface directly as we have done in previous examples, this listener extends the `MouseAdapter` class, which is defined in the `java.awt.event` package of the Java standard class library. The `MouseAdapter` class implements the `MouseListener` interface and contains empty definitions for all of the mouse event methods. In our listener class, we override the definition of the `mouseClicked` method to suit our needs. Because we inherit the other empty methods corresponding to the rest of the mouse events, we don't have to provide our own empty definitions.

Because of inheritance, we now have a choice when it comes to creating event listeners. We can implement an event listener interface, or we can extend an event adapter class. This is a design decision that should be considered carefully. The best technique depends on the situation.

LISTING 9.13

```java
//********************************************************************
//  OffCenter.java        Author: Lewis/Loftus
//
//  Demonstrates the use of an event adapter class.
//********************************************************************

import javax.swing.*;

public class OffCenter
{
   //-----------------------------------------------------------------
   //  Creates the main frame of the program.
   //-----------------------------------------------------------------
   public static void main (String[] args)
   {
      JFrame frame = new JFrame ("Off Center");
      frame.setDefaultCloseOperation (JFrame.EXIT_ON_CLOSE);

      frame.getContentPane().add(new OffCenterPanel());
      frame.pack();
      frame.setVisible(true);
   }
}
```

DISPLAY

LISTING 9.14

```
//********************************************************************
//  OffCenterPanel.java        Author: Lewis/Loftus
//
//  Represents the primary drawing panel for the OffCenter program.
//********************************************************************

import java.awt.*;
import java.awt.event.*;
import java.text.DecimalFormat;
import javax.swing.*;

public class OffCenterPanel extends JPanel
{
    private final int WIDTH=300, HEIGHT=300;

    private DecimalFormat fmt;
    private Point current;
    private int centerX, centerY;
    private double length;

    //-----------------------------------------------------------
    //  Constructor: Sets up the panel and necessary data.
    //-----------------------------------------------------------
    public OffCenterPanel()
    {
        addMouseListener (new OffCenterListener());

        centerX = WIDTH / 2;
        centerY = HEIGHT / 2;

        fmt = new DecimalFormat ("0.##");

        setPreferredSize (new Dimension(WIDTH, HEIGHT));
        setBackground (Color.yellow);
    }

    //-----------------------------------------------------------
    //  Draws a line from the mouse pointer to the center point of
    //  the panel and displays the distance.
    //-----------------------------------------------------------
    public void paintComponent (Graphics page)
    {
        super.paintComponent (page);
```

LISTING 9.14 *continued*

```
        page.setColor (Color.black);
        page.drawOval (centerX-3, centerY-3, 6, 6);

        if (current != null)
        {
            page.drawLine (current.x, current.y, centerX, centerY);
            page.drawString ("Distance: " + fmt.format(length), 10, 15);
        }
    }

    //*********************************************************************
    //   Represents the listener for mouse events.  Demonstrates the
    //   ability to extend an adapter class.
    //*********************************************************************
    private class OffCenterListener extends MouseAdapter
    {
        //----------------------------------------------------------------
        //   Computes the distance from the mouse pointer to the center
        //   point of the applet.
        //----------------------------------------------------------------
        public void mouseClicked (MouseEvent event)
        {
            current = event.getPoint();
            length = Math.sqrt(Math.pow((current.x-centerX), 2) +
                            Math.pow((current.y-centerY), 2));
            repaint();
        }
    }
}
```

myprogramminglab **SELF-REVIEW QUESTIONS** *(see answers in Appendix N)*

SR 9.25 What is an adapter class?

SR 9.26 Is an OffCenterPanel object a JPanel? Is it a JComponent? Is it a Container? Is it an Object? Explain.

SR 9.27 In the private listener class defined for the RubberLinesPanel class in Chapter 8, five empty mouse event methods were included. Why are there no such methods included for the private OffCenterListener class defined in this section?

9.8 The Timer Class

A *timer* object, created from the Timer class of the javax. swing package, can be thought of as a GUI component. However, unlike other components, it does not have a visual representation that appears on the screen. Instead, as the name implies, it helps us manage an activity over time.

> **KEY CONCEPT**
>
> A Timer object generates action events at regular intervals and can be used to control an animation.

A timer object generates an action event at regular intervals. To perform an animation, we set up a timer to generate an action event periodically, then update the animation graphics in the action listener. The methods of the Timer class are shown in Figure 9.8.

The program shown in Listing 9.15 displays the image of a smiling face that seems to glide across the program window at an angle, bouncing off of the window edges.

The constructor of the ReboundPanel class, shown in Listing 9.16, creates a Timer object. The first parameter to the Timer constructor is the delay in milliseconds. The second parameter to the constructor is the listener that handles the action events of the timer. The constructor also sets up the initial position for the image and the number of pixels it will move, in both the vertical and horizontal directions, each time the image is redrawn.

VideoNote

Example using the Timer class.

```
Timer (int delay, ActionListener listener)
    Constructor: Creates a timer that generates an action event at
    regular intervals, specified by the delay. The event will be handled
    by the specified listener.

void addActionListener (ActionListener listener)
    Adds an action listener to the timer.

boolean isRunning ()
    Returns true if the timer is running.

void setDelay (int delay)
    Sets the delay of the timer.

void start ()
    Starts the timer, causing it to generate action events.

void stop ()
    Stops the timer, causing it to stop generating action events.
```

FIGURE 9.8   Some methods of the Timer class

LISTING 9.15

```java
//********************************************************************
//  Rebound.java        Author: Lewis/Loftus
//
//   Demonstrates an animation and the use of the Timer class.
//********************************************************************

import java.awt.*;
import java.awt.event.*;
import javax.swing.*;

public class Rebound
{
   //-----------------------------------------------------------------
   // Displays the main frame of the program.
   //-----------------------------------------------------------------
   public static void main (String[] args)
   {
      JFrame frame = new JFrame ("Rebound");
      frame.setDefaultCloseOperation (JFrame.EXIT_ON_CLOSE);

      frame.getContentPane().add(new ReboundPanel());
      frame.pack();
      frame.setVisible(true);
   }
}
```

DISPLAY

LISTING 9.16

```java
//********************************************************************
//  ReboundPanel.java       Author: Lewis/Loftus
//
//  Represents the primary panel for the Rebound program.
//********************************************************************

import java.awt.*;
import java.awt.event.*;
import javax.swing.*;

public class ReboundPanel extends JPanel
{
    private final int WIDTH = 300, HEIGHT = 100;
    private final int DELAY = 20, IMAGE_SIZE = 35;

    private ImageIcon image;
    private Timer timer;
    private int x, y, moveX, moveY;

    //-----------------------------------------------------------------
    //  Sets up the panel, including the timer for the animation.
    //-----------------------------------------------------------------
    public ReboundPanel()
    {
        timer = new Timer(DELAY, new ReboundListener());

        image = new ImageIcon ("happyFace.gif");

        x = 0;
        y = 40;
        moveX = moveY = 3;

        setPreferredSize (new Dimension(WIDTH, HEIGHT));
        setBackground (Color.black);
        timer.start();
    }

    //-----------------------------------------------------------------
    //  Draws the image in the current location.
    //-----------------------------------------------------------------
    public void paintComponent (Graphics page)
    {
        super.paintComponent (page);
        image.paintIcon (this, page, x, y);
    }
```

LISTING 9.16   *continued*

```
//************************************************************
//  Represents the action listener for the timer.
//************************************************************
private class ReboundListener implements ActionListener
{
    //----------------------------------------------------------
    //  Updates the position of the image and possibly the direction
    //  of movement whenever the timer fires an action event.
    //----------------------------------------------------------
    public void actionPerformed (ActionEvent event)
    {
        x += moveX;
        y += moveY;

        if (x <= 0 || x >= WIDTH-IMAGE_SIZE)
            moveX = moveX * -1;

        if (y <= 0 || y <= HEIGHT-IMAGE_SIZE)
            moveY = moveY * -1;

        repaint();
    }
}
}
```

The actionPerformed method of the listener updates the current *x* and *y* coordinate values, then checks to see if those values cause the image to "run into" the edge of the panel. If so, the movement is adjusted so that the image will make future moves in the opposite direction horizontally, vertically, or both. Note that this calculation takes the image size into account.

The speed of the animation in this program is a function of two factors: the pause between the action events and the distance the image is shifted each time. In this example, the timer is set to generate an action event every 20 milliseconds, and the image is shifted 3 pixels each time it is updated. You can experiment with these values to change the speed of the animation. The goal should be to create the illusion of movement that is pleasing to the eye.

SELF-REVIEW QUESTIONS *(see answers in Appendix N)*

SR 9.28 What does a Timer object do?

SR 9.29 List each of the Timer methods used in the Rebound program, and describe how they are used.

SR 9.30 Describe how you would change the ReboundPanel class to provide each of the following changes to the Rebound program:

   a. The smiling face moves faster.
   b. The smiling face moves slower.
   c. A different image bounces around.
   d. Larger "jumps" are made by the smiling face.
   e. Each time the smiling face "hits" a window edge it speeds up.

Summary of Key Concepts

- Inheritance is the process of deriving a new class from an existing one.
- One purpose of inheritance is to reuse existing software.
- Inheritance creates an is-a relationship between the parent and child classes.
- Protected visibility provides the best possible encapsulation that permits inheritance.
- A parent's constructor can be invoked using the `super` reference.
- A child class can override (redefine) the parent's definition of an inherited method.
- The child of one class can be the parent of one or more other classes, creating a class hierarchy.
- Common features should be located as high in a class hierarchy as is reasonably possible.
- All Java classes are derived, directly or indirectly, from the `Object` class.
- The `toString` and `equals` methods are inherited by every class in every Java program.
- An abstract class cannot be instantiated. It represents a concept on which other classes can build their definitions.
- A class derived from an abstract parent must override all of its parent's abstract methods, or the derived class will also be considered abstract.
- Inheritance can be applied to interfaces so that one interface can be derived from another.
- Private members are inherited by the child class, but cannot be referenced directly by name. They may be used indirectly, however.
- Software design must carefully and specifically address inheritance.
- The `final` modifier can be used to restrict inheritance.
- The classes that represent Java GUI components are organized into a class hierarchy.
- A listener class can be created by deriving it from an event adapter class.
- A `Timer` object generates action events at regular intervals and can be used to control an animation.

Exercises

Visit www.myprogramminglab.com to complete many of these Exercises online and get instant feedback.

EX 9.1   Draw a UML class diagram showing an inheritance hierarchy containing classes that represent different types of calculating devices. Provide class members for at least one of these classes.

EX 9.2   Draw a UML class diagram showing inheritance between the various types of writing instruments. Discuss the structure of the hierarchy drawn.

EX 9.3   Draw a UML class diagram showing an inheritance hierarchy containing classes that represent different types of cars, organized first by manufacturer. Show some appropriate variables and method names for at least two of these classes.

EX 9.4   Show an alternative diagram for the hierarchy in Exercise 9.3 in which the cars are organized first by type (sports car, sedan, SUV, etc.). Show some appropriate variables and method names for at least two of these classes. Compare and contrast the two approaches.

EX 9.5   Draw a UML class diagram showing an inheritance hierarchy containing classes that represent different types of airplanes. Show some appropriate variables and method names for at least two of these classes.

EX 9.6   Draw a UML class diagram showing an inheritance hierarchy containing classes that represent different types of trees (oak, elm, etc.). Show some appropriate variables and method names for at least two of these classes.

EX 9.7   Draw a UML class diagram showing an inheritance hierarchy containing classes that represent different types of payment transactions at a store (cash, credit card, etc). Show some appropriate variables and method names for at least two of these classes.

EX 9.8   Experiment with a simple derivation relationship between two classes. Put `println` statements in constructors of both the parent and child classes. Do not explicitly call the constructor of the parent in the child. What happens? Why? Change the child's constructor to explicitly call the constructor of the parent. Now what happens?

Programming Projects

Visit www.myprogramminglab.com to complete many of these Programming Projects online and get instant feedback.

PP 9.1   Design and implement a class called MonetaryCoin that is derived from the Coin class presented in Chapter 5. Store an integer in the MonetaryCoin that represents its value and add a method that returns its value. Create a main driver class to instantiate and compute the sum of several MonetaryCoin objects. Demonstrate that a monetary coin inherits its parent's ability to be flipped.

PP 9.2   Design and implement a set of classes that defines the components of a personal computer: processor, input devices, output devices, main memory and secondary memory. Include methods in each class that are named according to their services and print an appropriate message. Create a main driver class to instantiate these classes and draw a UML class diagram which depicts this hierarchy.

PP 9.3   Using the concept of inheritance, design and implement a set of classes that defines various types of reading material: books, novels, magazines, technical journals, textbooks, and so on. Create a main driver class to instantiate and exercise several of the classes. Draw a UML class diagram which depicts this inheritance concept.

PP 9.4   Design and implement a set of classes that keeps track of various sports statistics. Have each low-level class represent a specific sport. Tailor the services of the classes to the sport in question, and move common attributes to the higher-level classes as appropriate. Create a main driver class to instantiate and exercise several of the classes.

PP 9.5   Design and implement a set of classes that keeps track of demographic information about a set of people, such as age, nationality, occupation, income, and so on. Design each class to focus on a particular aspect of data collection. Create a main driver class to instantiate and exercise several of the classes.

PP 9.6   Modify the Rebound program from this chapter such that when the mouse button is clicked the animation stops, and when it is clicked again the animation resumes.

PP 9.7   Design and implement an application that displays an animation of a car (side view) moving across the screen from left to right. Create a Car class that represents the car (or use one that was created for a programming project in Chapter 8).

PP 9.8   Design and implement an application that displays an animation of a horizontal line segment moving across the screen, eventually passing across a vertical line. As the vertical line is passed, the horizontal line should change color. The change of color should occur while the horizontal line crosses the vertical one; therefore, while crossing, the horizontal line will be two different colors.

PP 9.9   Design and implement an application that plays a game called Catch-the-Creature. Use an image to represent the creature. Have the creature appear at a random location for a random duration, then disappear and reappear somewhere else. The goal is to "catch" the creature by pressing the mouse button while the mouse pointer is on the creature image. Create a separate class to represent the creature, and include in it a method that determines if the location of the mouse click corresponds to the current location of the creature. Display a count of the number of times the creature is caught.

VideoNote

Developing a solution of PP 9.8.

PP 9.10   Design and implement an application that works as a stopwatch. Include a display that shows the time (in seconds) as it increments. Include buttons that allow the user to start and stop the time, and reset the display to zero. Arrange the components to present a nice interface. *Hint*: use the Timer class to control the timing of the stopwatch.

PP 9.11   Design and implement a set of classes that define a series of three-dimensional geometric shapes. For each, store fundamental data about their size and provide methods to access and modify this data. In addition, provide appropriate methods to compute each shape's circumference, area, and volume. In your design, consider how shapes are related and thus where inheritance can be implemented. Create a main driver class to instantiate several shapes of differing types and exercise the behavior you provided.

PP 9.12   Design and implement a set of classes that define various types of electronics equipment (computers, cell phones, pagers, digital cameras, etc.). Include data values that describe various attributes of the electronics, such as the weight, cost, power usage, and the names of the manufacturers. Include methods that are named appropriately for each class and that print an appropriate message. Create a `main` driver class to instantiate and exercise several of the classes.

PP 9.13   Design and implement a set of classes that define various courses in your curriculum. Include information about each course such as the title, number, description, and department that teaches the course. Consider the categories of classes that constitutes your curriculum when designing your inheritance structure. Create a `main` driver class to instantiate and exercise several of the classes.

SOFTWARE FAILURE

Ariane 5 Flight 501

What Happened?

Ariane 5 is an expendable launch system designed by the European Space Agency (ESA) to deliver payloads into earth orbit. On June 4, 1996, the first flight of the rocket (Flight 501) exploded 37 seconds after liftoff.

The control system had malfunctioned, causing the rocket to veer off course. Strong aerodynamic forces caused the main portion of the rocket to break apart. An on-board monitor detected the break up and initiated an automatic destruct system to destroy the vehicle in the air.

Flight 501 was carrying four unmanned spacecraft designed to study the magnetic field of the Earth. The rocket's destruction resulted in a complete loss of the payload at an estimated cost of $370 million.

■ The first flight of the Ariane 5 rocket exploded shortly after liftoff.

What Caused It?

The Ariane 5 rocket reused some of the software that was used to control its predecessor, the Ariane 4. That software contained a segment for converting a floating-point number to a signed 16-bit integer. On Flight 501, this value was outside of the range that a 16-bit integer could represent, causing an overflow error. In the Ariane 4, the converted value had always been small enough to avoid this problem.

The overflow error would have been caught by an exception handler, but that part of the system had been disabled for efficiency reasons. The error occurred almost simultaneously in both the main and backup computers, causing them to shut down. This led to the rocket veering off course and its destruction.

Lessons Learned

The success of the Ariane 4 gave the designers of the Ariane 5 confidence in the software. Therefore, minimal testing was done for some parts of the system. The potential problem had always existed in the previous system, but the data (which represented a measurement) was always small. The varying parameters of the new system were not taken into account. So while the root cause was a software bug, the failure resulted from changes in the dynamics of the system and its environment. It is a failure of design and testing---more so than a software bug.

Better reactions to such a problem would have been helpful as well. The exception handling system, if left in place, could have handled the problem more gracefully, rather than simply shutting down the control computer. Ironically, in this case, the measurement in question wasn't even needed after liftoff.

Sources: IEEE Software, cnn.com

Polymorphism

CHAPTER OBJECTIVES

- Define polymorphism and explore its benefits.
- Discuss the concept of dynamic binding.
- Use inheritance relationships to create polymorphic references.
- Use interfaces to create polymorphic references.
- Explore sorting and searching using polymorphic implementations.
- Discuss object-oriented design in the context of polymorphism.
- Discuss the processing of events as an example of polymorphism.
- Examine more GUI components.

This chapter discusses polymorphism, another fundamental principle of object-oriented software. We first explore the concept of binding and discuss how it relates to polymorphism. Then we examine how polymorphic references can be accomplished using either inheritance or interfaces. Design issues related to polymorphism are examined. The Graphics Track of this chapter discusses how event processing in a graphical user interface is an example of polymorphism. We also examine several new GUI components.

10.1 Late Binding

Often, the type of a reference variable matches the class of the object to which it refers exactly. For example, consider the following reference:

```
ChessPiece bishop;
```

The `bishop` variable may be used to point to an object that is created by instantiating the `ChessPiece` class. However, it doesn't have to. The variable type and the object it refers to must be compatible, but their types need not be exactly the same. The relationship between a reference variable and the object it refers to is more flexible than that.

> **KEY CONCEPT**
>
> A polymorphic reference can refer to different types of objects over time.

The term *polymorphism* can be defined as "having many forms." A *polymorphic reference* is a reference variable that can refer to different types of objects at different points in time. The specific method invoked through a polymorphic reference can change from one invocation to the next.

Consider the following line of code:

```
obj.doIt();
```

If the reference `obj` is polymorphic, it can refer to different types of objects at different times. So if that line of code is in a loop, or if it's in a method that is called more than once, that line of code could call a different version of the `doIt` method each time it is invoked.

At some point, the commitment is made to execute certain code to carry out a method invocation. This commitment is referred to as *binding* a method invocation to a method definition. In many situations, the binding of a method invocation to a method definition can occur at compile time. For polymorphic references, however, the decision cannot be made until run time. The method definition that is used is based on the object that is being referred to by the reference variable at that moment. This deferred commitment is called *late binding* or *dynamic binding*. It is less efficient than binding at compile time, because the decision must be made during the execution of the program. This overhead is generally acceptable in light of the flexibility that a polymorphic reference provides.

> **KEY CONCEPT**
>
> The binding of a method invocation to its definition is performed at run time for a polymorphic reference.

We can create a polymorphic reference in Java in two ways: using inheritance and using interfaces. Let's look at each in turn.

SELF-REVIEW QUESTIONS *(see answers in Appendix N)*

myprogramminglab

SR 10.1   What is polymorphism?

SR 10.2   Why is compile time binding considered more efficient than dynamic binding?

10.2 Polymorphism via Inheritance

When we declare a reference variable using a particular class name, it can be used to refer to any object of that class. In addition, it can also refer to any object of any class that is related to its declared type by inheritance. For example, if the class `Mammal` is the parent of the class `Horse`, then a `Mammal` reference can be used to refer to any object of class `Horse`. This ability is shown in the following code segment:

> **KEY CONCEPT**
> A reference variable can refer to any object created from any class related to it by inheritance.

```
Mammal pet;
Horse secretariat = new Horse();
pet = secretariat;  // a valid assignment
```

The reverse operation, assigning the `Mammal` object to a `Horse` reference, can also be done but it requires an explicit cast. Assigning a reference in this direction is generally less useful and more likely to cause problems, because although a horse has all the functionality of a mammal (because a horse *is-a* mammal), the reverse is not necessarily true.

This relationship works throughout a class hierarchy. If the `Mammal` class were derived from a class called `Animal`, the following assignment would also be valid:

```
Animal creature = new Horse();
```

Carrying this to the limit, an `Object` reference can be used to refer to any object, because ultimately all classes are descendants of the `Object` class. An `ArrayList`, for example, uses polymorphism in that it is designed to hold `Object` references. That's why an `ArrayList` that doesn't specify an element type can be used to store any kind of object. In fact, a particular `ArrayList` can be used to hold several different types of objects at one time, because, by inheritance, they are all `Object` objects.

The reference variable `creature` can be polymorphic, because at any point in time it can refer to an `Animal` object, a `Mammal` object, or a `Horse` object. Suppose that all three of these classes have a method called `move` that is implemented in different ways (because

> **KEY CONCEPT**
> The type of the object, not the type of the reference, is used to determine which version of a method to invoke.

the child class overrode the definition it inherited). The following invocation calls the move method, but the particular version of the method it calls is determined at run time:

```
creature.move();
```

When this line is executed, if creature currently refers to an Animal object, the move method of the Animal class is invoked. Likewise, if creature currently refers to a Mammal object, the Mammal version of move is invoked. Likewise if it currently refers to a Horse object.

Of course, since Animal and Mammal represent general concepts, they may be defined as abstract classes. This situation does not eliminate the ability to have polymorphic references. Suppose the move method in the Mammal class is abstract and is given unique definitions in the Horse, Dog, and Whale classes (all derived from Mammal). A Mammal reference variable can be used to refer to any objects created from any of the Horse, Dog, and Whale classes, and can be used to execute the move method on any of them.

Let's look at another situation. Consider the class hierarchy shown in Figure 10.1. The classes in it represent various types of employees that might be employed at a particular company. Let's explore an example that uses this hierarchy to pay a set of employees of various types.

The Firm class shown in Listing 10.1 contains a main driver that creates a Staff of employees and invokes the payday method to pay them all. The program output includes information about each employee and how much each is paid (if anything).

The Staff class shown in Listing 10.2 maintains an array of objects that represent individual employees of various kinds. Note that the array is declared to hold StaffMember references, but it is actually filled with objects created from several other classes, such as Executive and Employee. These classes are all descendants of the StaffMember class, so the assignments are valid. The staffList array is filled with polymorphic references.

The payday method of the Staff class scans through the list of employees, printing their information and invoking their pay methods to determine how much each employee should be paid. The invocation of the pay method is polymorphic, because each class has its own version of the pay method.

The StaffMember class shown in Listing 10.3 is abstract. It does not represent a particular type of employee and is not intended to be instantiated. Rather, it serves as the ancestor of all employee classes and contains information that applies to all employees. Each employee has a name, address, and phone number, so variables to store these values are declared in the StaffMember class and are inherited by all descendants.

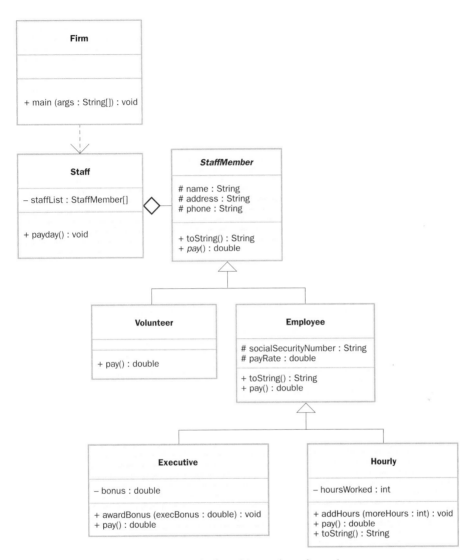

FIGURE 10.1   A class hierarchy of employees

The StaffMember class contains a toString method to return the information managed by the StaffMember class. It also contains an abstract method called pay, which takes no parameters and returns a value of type double. At the generic StaffMember level, it would be inappropriate to give a definition for this method.

LISTING 10.1

```java
//***********************************************************************
//  Firm.java        Author: Lewis/Loftus
//
//  Demonstrates polymorphism via inheritance.
//***********************************************************************

public class Firm
{
   //-----------------------------------------------------------------
   //  Creates a staff of employees for a firm and pays them.
   //-----------------------------------------------------------------
   public static void main (String[] args)
   {
      Staff personnel = new Staff();

      personnel.payday();
   }
}
```

OUTPUT

```
Name: Sam
Address: 123 Main Line
Phone: 555-0469
Social Security Number: 123-45-6789
Paid: 2923.07
----------------------------------
Name: Carla
Address: 456 Off Line
Phone: 555-0101
Social Security Number: 987-65-4321
Paid: 1246.15
----------------------------------
Name: Woody
Address: 789 Off Rocker
Phone: 555-0000
Social Security Number: 010-20-3040
Paid: 1169.23
----------------------------------
Name: Diane
Address: 678 Fifth Ave.
Phone: 555-0690
```

LISTING 10.1   *continued*

```
Social Security Number: 958-47-3625
Current hours: 40
Paid: 422.0
------------------------------------
Name: Norm
Address: 987 Suds Blvd.
Phone: 555-8374
Thanks!
------------------------------------
Name: Cliff
Address: 321 Duds Lane
Phone: 555-7282
Thanks!
------------------------------------
```

LISTING 10.2

```java
//********************************************************************
//  Staff.java        Author: Lewis/Loftus
//
//  Represents the personnel staff of a particular business.
//********************************************************************

public class Staff
{
   private StaffMember[] staffList;

   //-----------------------------------------------------------------
   //  Constructor: Sets up the list of staff members.
   //-----------------------------------------------------------------
   public Staff ()
   {
      staffList = new StaffMember[6];

      staffList[0] = new Executive ("Sam", "123 Main Line",
         "555-0469", "123-45-6789", 2423.07);
```

L I S T I N G   1 0 . 2   *continued*

```
      staffList[1] = new Employee ("Carla", "456 Off Line",
         "555-0101", "987-65-4321", 1246.15);
      staffList[2] = new Employee ("Woody", "789 Off Rocker",
         "555-0000", "010-20-3040", 1169.23);

      staffList[3] = new Hourly ("Diane", "678 Fifth Ave.",
         "555-0690", "958-47-3625", 10.55);

      staffList[4] = new Volunteer ("Norm", "987 Suds Blvd.",
         "555-8374");
      staffList[5] = new Volunteer ("Cliff", "321 Duds Lane",
         "555-7282");

      ((Executive)staffList[0]).awardBonus (500.00);

      ((Hourly)staffList[3]).addHours (40);
   }

   //-----------------------------------------------------------
   //  Pays all staff members.
   //-----------------------------------------------------------
   public void payday ()
   {
      double amount;

      for (int count=0; count < staffList.length; count++)
      {
         System.out.println (staffList[count]);

         amount = staffList[count].pay();  // polymorphic

         if (amount == 0.0)
            System.out.println ("Thanks!");
         else
            System.out.println ("Paid: " + amount);

         System.out.println ("-----------------------------------");
      }
   }
}
```

LISTING 10.3

```java
//********************************************************************
//  StaffMember.java       Author: Lewis/Loftus
//
//  Represents a generic staff member.
//********************************************************************

abstract public class StaffMember
{
   protected String name;
   protected String address;
   protected String phone;

   //-----------------------------------------------------------------
   //  Constructor: Sets up this staff member using the specified
   //  information.
   //-----------------------------------------------------------------
   public StaffMember (String eName, String eAddress, String ePhone)
   {
      name = eName;
      address = eAddress;
      phone = ePhone;
   }

   //-----------------------------------------------------------------
   //  Returns a string including the basic employee information.
   //-----------------------------------------------------------------
   public String toString()
   {
      String result = "Name: " + name + "\n";

      result += "Address: " + address + "\n";
      result += "Phone: " + phone;

      return result;
   }

   //-----------------------------------------------------------------
   //  Derived classes must define the pay method for each type of
   //  employee.
   //-----------------------------------------------------------------
   public abstract double pay();
}
```

However, the descendants of StaffMember each provide their own specific definition for pay. By defining pay abstractly in StaffMember, the payday method of Staff can polymorphically pay each employee.

This is the essence of polymorphism. Each class knows best how it should handle a specific behavior, in this case paying an employee. Yet in one sense it's all the same behavior—the employee is getting paid. Polymorphism lets us treat similar objects in consistent but unique ways.

The Volunteer class shown in Listing 10.4 represents a person that is not compensated monetarily for his or her work. We keep track only of a volunteer's basic information, which is passed into the constructor of Volunteer, which in turn passes it to the StaffMember constructor using the super reference. The pay method of Volunteer simply returns a zero pay value. If pay had not been

LISTING 10.4

```
//********************************************************************
//  Volunteer.java       Author: Lewis/Loftus
//
//  Represents a staff member that works as a volunteer.
//********************************************************************

public class Volunteer extends StaffMember
{
   //-----------------------------------------------------------------
   //  Constructor: Sets up this volunteer using the specified
   //  information.
   //-----------------------------------------------------------------
   public Volunteer (String eName, String eAddress, String ePhone)
   {
      super (eName, eAddress, ePhone);
   }

   //-----------------------------------------------------------------
   //  Returns a zero pay value for this volunteer.
   //-----------------------------------------------------------------
   public double pay()
   {
      return 0.0;
   }
}
```

overridden, the Volunteer class would have been considered abstract and could not have been instantiated.

Note that when a volunteer gets "paid" in the payday method of Staff, a simple expression of thanks is printed. In all other situations, where the pay value is greater than zero, the payment itself is printed.

The Employee class shown in Listing 10.5 represents an employee that gets paid at a particular rate each pay period. The pay rate, as well as the employee's Social Security number, is passed along with the other basic information to the Employee constructor. The basic information is passed to the constructor of StaffMember using the super reference.

The toString method of Employee is overridden to concatenate the additional information that Employee manages to the information returned by the parent's version of toString, which is called using the super reference. The pay method of an Employee simply returns the pay rate for that employee.

The Executive class shown in Listing 10.6 represents an employee that may earn a bonus in addition to his or her normal pay rate. The Executive class is derived from Employee and therefore inherits from both StaffMember and Employee. The constructor of Executive passes along its information to the Employee constructor and sets the executive bonus to zero.

A bonus is awarded to an executive using the awardBonus method. This method is called in the Staff constructor for the only executive that is part of the staffList array. Note that the generic StaffMember reference must be cast into an Executive reference to invoke the awardBonus method (which doesn't exist for a StaffMember).

The Executive class overrides the pay method so that it first determines the payment as it would for any employee, then adds the bonus. The pay method of the Employee class is invoked using super to obtain the normal payment amount. This technique is better than using just the payRate variable, because if we choose to change how Employee objects get paid, the change will automatically be reflected in Executive. After the bonus is awarded, it is reset to zero.

The Hourly class shown in Listing 10.7 represents an employee whose pay rate is applied on an hourly basis. It keeps track of the number of hours worked in the current pay period, which can be modified by calls to the addHours method. This method is called from the payday method of Staff. The pay method of Hourly determines the payment based on the number of hours worked and then resets the hours to zero.

LISTING 10.5

```java
//********************************************************************
//  Employee.java       Author: Lewis/Loftus
//
//  Represents a general paid employee.
//********************************************************************

public class Employee extends StaffMember
{
   protected String socialSecurityNumber;
   protected double payRate;

   //-----------------------------------------------------------------
   //  Constructor: Sets up this employee with the specified
   //  information.
   //-----------------------------------------------------------------
   public Employee (String eName, String eAddress, String ePhone,
                    String socSecNumber, double rate)
   {
      super (eName, eAddress, ePhone);

      socialSecurityNumber = socSecNumber;
      payRate = rate;
   }

   //-----------------------------------------------------------------
   //  Returns information about an employee as a string.
   //-----------------------------------------------------------------
   public String toString()
   {
      String result = super.toString();

      result += "\nSocial Security Number: " + socialSecurityNumber;

      return result;
   }

   //-----------------------------------------------------------------
   //  Returns the pay rate for this employee.
   //-----------------------------------------------------------------
   public double pay()
   {
      return payRate;
   }
}
```

LISTING 10.6

```java
//********************************************************************
//  Executive.java       Author: Lewis/Loftus
//
//  Represents an executive staff member, who can earn a bonus.
//********************************************************************

public class Executive extends Employee
{
   private double bonus;

   //-----------------------------------------------------------------
   //  Constructor: Sets up this executive with the specified
   //  information.
   //-----------------------------------------------------------------
   public Executive (String eName, String eAddress, String ePhone,
                     String socSecNumber, double rate)
   {
      super (eName, eAddress, ePhone, socSecNumber, rate);

      bonus = 0;  // bonus has yet to be awarded
   }

   //-----------------------------------------------------------------
   //  Awards the specified bonus to this executive.
   //-----------------------------------------------------------------
   public void awardBonus (double execBonus)
   {
      bonus = execBonus;
   }

   //-----------------------------------------------------------------
   //  Computes and returns the pay for an executive, which is the
   //  regular employee payment plus a one-time bonus.
   //-----------------------------------------------------------------
   public double pay()
   {
      double payment = super.pay() + bonus;

      bonus = 0;

      return payment;
   }
}
```

LISTING 10.7

```java
//********************************************************************
//  Hourly.java         Author: Lewis/Loftus
//
//  Represents an employee that gets paid by the hour.
//********************************************************************

public class Hourly extends Employee
{
   private int hoursWorked;

   //-----------------------------------------------------------------
   //  Constructor: Sets up this hourly employee using the specified
   //  information.
   //-----------------------------------------------------------------
   public Hourly (String eName, String eAddress, String ePhone,
                  String socSecNumber, double rate)
   {
      super (eName, eAddress, ePhone, socSecNumber, rate);

      hoursWorked = 0;
   }

   //-----------------------------------------------------------------
   //  Adds the specified number of hours to this employee's
   //  accumulated hours.
   //-----------------------------------------------------------------
   public void addHours (int moreHours)
   {
      hoursWorked += moreHours;
   }

   //-----------------------------------------------------------------
   //  Computes and returns the pay for this hourly employee.
   //-----------------------------------------------------------------
   public double pay()
   {
      double payment = payRate * hoursWorked;

      hoursWorked = 0;

      return payment;
   }
```

LISTING 10.7 *continued*

```java
//---------------------------------------------------------------
//  Returns information about this hourly employee as a string.
//---------------------------------------------------------------
public String toString()
{
    String result = super.toString();

    result += "\nCurrent hours: " + hoursWorked;

    return result;
}
}
```

SELF-REVIEW QUESTIONS *(see answers in Appendix N)*

myprogramminglab

SR 10.3 How does inheritance support polymorphism?

SR 10.4 Suppose the class MusicPlayer is the parent of the class CDPlayer. Is the following sequence of statements legal? Explain.

```java
MusicPlayer mplayer = new MusicPlayer();
CDPlayer cdplayer = new CDPlayer();
mplayer = cdplayer;
```

SR 10.5 Suppose the class MusicPlayer is the parent of the class CDPlayer. Is the following sequence of statements legal? Explain.

```java
MusicPlayer mplayer = new MusicPlayer();
CDPlayer cdplayer = new CDPlayer();
cdplayer = mplayer;
```

SR 10.6 How is overriding related to polymorphism?

SR 10.7 Why is the StaffMember class in the Firm example declared as abstract?

SR 10.8 Why is the pay method declared in the StaffMember class, given that it is abstract and has no body at that level?

SR 10.9 Which pay method is invoked by the following line from the payday method of the Staff class?

```java
amount = staffList[count].pay();
```

10.3 Polymorphism via Interfaces

Now let's examine how we can create polymorphic references using interfaces. As we've seen many times, a class name can be used to declare the type of an object reference variable. Similarly, an interface name can be used as the type of a reference variable as well. An interface reference variable can be used to refer to any object of any class that implements that interface.

Suppose we declare an interface called Speaker as follows:

```java
public interface Speaker
{
    public void speak();
    public void announce (String str);
}
```

The interface name, Speaker, can now be used to declare an object reference variable:

```java
Speaker current;
```

The reference variable current can be used to refer to any object of any class that implements the Speaker interface. For example, if we define a class called Philosopher such that it implements the Speaker interface, we can then assign a Philosopher object to a Speaker reference as follows:

```java
current = new Philosopher();
```

This assignment is valid, because a Philosopher is a Speaker. In this sense the relationship between a class and its interface is the same as the relationship between a child class and its parent. It is an is-a relationship. And that relationship forms the basis of the polymorphism.

The flexibility of an interface reference allows us to create polymorphic references. As we saw earlier in this chapter, using inheritance, we can create a polymorphic reference that can refer to any one of a set of objects as long as they are related by inheritance. Using interfaces, we can create similar polymorphic references among objects that implement the same interface.

For example, if we create a class called Dog that also implements the Speaker interface, it can be assigned to a Speaker reference variable as well. The same reference variable, in fact, can at one point refer to a Philosopher object and then later refer to a Dog object. The following lines of code illustrate this:

```
Speaker guest;
guest = new Philosopher();
guest.speak();
guest = new Dog();
guest.speak();
```

In this code, the first time the `speak` method is called, it invokes the `speak` method defined in the `Philosopher` class. The second time it is called, it invokes the `speak` method of the `Dog` class. As with polymorphic references via inheritance, it is not the type of the reference that determines which method gets invoked; it is based on the type of the object that the reference points to at the moment of invocation.

Note that when we are using an interface reference variable, we can invoke only the methods defined in the interface, even if the object it refers to has other methods to which it can respond. For example, suppose the `Philosopher` class also defined a public method called `pontificate`. The second line of the following code would generate a compiler error, even though the object can in fact respond to the `pontificate` method:

```
Speaker special = new Philosopher();
special.pontificate();   // generates a compiler error
```

The problem is that the compiler can determine only that the object is a `Speaker`, and therefore can guarantee only that the object can respond to the `speak` and `announce` methods. Because the reference variable `special` could refer to a `Dog` object (which cannot pontificate), it does not allow the invocation. If we know in a particular situation that such an invocation is valid, we can cast the object into the appropriate reference so that the compiler will accept it, as follows:

```
((Philosopher)special).pontificate();
```

As we can with polymorphic references based in inheritance, an interface name can be used as the type of a method parameter. In such situations, any object of any class that implements the interface can be passed into the method. For example, the following method takes a `Speaker` object as a parameter. Therefore both a `Dog` object and a `Philosopher` object can be passed into it in separate invocations:

> **KEY CONCEPT**
> A parameter to a method can be polymorphic, giving the method flexible control of its arguments.

```
public void sayIt (Speaker current)
{
    current.speak();
}
```

Using a polymorphic reference as the formal parameter to a method is a powerful technique. It allows the method to control the types of parameters passed into it, yet gives it the flexibility to accept arguments of various types.

SELF-REVIEW QUESTIONS *(see answers in Appendix N)*

SR 10.10 How can polymorphism be accomplished using interfaces?

SR 10.11 Suppose that the `Speaker` interface and the `Philosopher` and `Dog` classes are as described in this section. Are the following sequences of statements legal? Explain.

```
a. Speaker current = new Speaker();
```

```
b. Speaker current = new Dog();
```

```
c. Speaker first, second;
   first = new Dog();
   second = new Philosopher();
   first.speak();
   first = second;
```

```
d. Speaker first = new Dog();
   Philospher second = new Philosopher();
   second.pontificate();
   first = second;
```

```
e. Speaker first = new Dog();
   Philospher second = new Philosopher();
   first = second;
   second.pontificate();
   first.pontificate();
```

10.4 Sorting

Let's examine a problem that lends itself to a polymorphic solution. *Sorting* is the process of arranging a list of items in a well-defined order. For example, you may want to alphabetize a list of names or put a list of survey results into descending numeric order. Many sorting algorithms have been developed and critiqued over the years. In fact, sorting is considered to be a classic area of study in computer science.

This section examines two sorting algorithms: selection sort and insertion sort. Complete coverage of various sorting techniques is beyond the scope of this text. Instead we introduce the topic and establish some of the fundamental ideas involved. We do not delve into a detailed analysis of the algorithms but instead focus on the strategies involved and general characteristics.

Selection Sort

The *selection sort* algorithm sorts a list of values by successively putting particular values in their final, sorted positions. In other words, for each position in the list, the algorithm selects the value that should go in that position and puts it there. Let's consider the problem of putting a list of numeric values into ascending order.

The general strategy of selection sort is: Scan the entire list to find the smallest value. Exchange that value with the value in the first position of the list. Scan the rest of the list (all but the first value) to find the smallest value, then exchange it with the value in the second position of the list. Scan the rest of the list (all but the first two values) to find the smallest value, then exchange it with the value in the third position of the list. Continue this process for all but the last position in the list (which will end up containing the largest value). When the process is complete, the list is sorted. Figure 10.2 demonstrates the use of the selection sort algorithm.

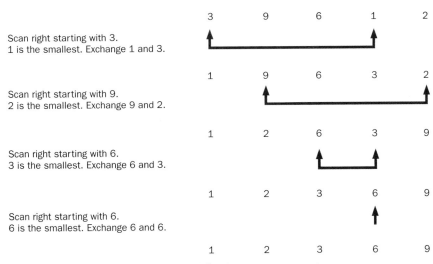

FIGURE 10.2   Selection sort processing

Let's look at an example. The program shown in Listing 10.8 uses a selection sort to arrange a list of Contact objects into ascending order.

Listing 10.9 shows the Sorting class. It contains two static sorting algorithms. The PhoneList program uses only the selectionSort method. The other method is discussed later in this section.

The selectionSort method accepts an array of Comparable objects to sort. Recall that Comparable is an interface that includes only one method, compareTo, which is designed to return an integer that is less than zero, equal to zero, or greater than zero if the executing object is less than, equal to, or greater than the object to which it is being compared, respectively.

Any class that implements the Comparable interface must define the compareTo method. Therefore any such object can be compared to another object to determine their relative order.

The selectionSort method is polymorphic. Note that it doesn't refer to Contact objects at all and yet is used to sort an array of Contact objects. The selectionSort method is set up to sort any array of objects, as long as those objects can be compared to determine their order. You can call selectionSort multiple times, passing in arrays of different types of objects, as long as they are Comparable.

> **KEY CONCEPT**
>
> Implementing a sort algorithm polymorphically allows it to sort any comparable set of objects.

Each Contact object represents a person with a last name, a first name, and a phone number. Listing 10.10 shows the Contact class.

The Contact class implements the Comparable interface and therefore provides a definition of the compareTo method. In this case, the contacts are sorted by last name; if two contacts have the same last name, their first names are used.

The implementation of the selectionSort method uses two for loops to sort the array. The outer loop controls the position in the array where the next smallest value will be stored. The inner loop finds the smallest value in the rest of the list by scanning all positions greater than or equal to the index specified by the outer loop. When the smallest value is determined, it is exchanged with the value stored at the index. This exchange is done in three assignment statements by using an extra variable called temp. This type of exchange is often called *swapping*.

VideoNote

Sorting Comparable objects.

Note that because this algorithm finds the smallest value during each iteration, the result is an array sorted in ascending order (that is, smallest to largest). The algorithm can easily be changed to put values in descending order by finding the largest value each time.

Also note that we've set up the sorting methods to sort arrays of objects. Therefore, if your goal is to sort an array of a primitive type, such as an array of integer values, they would have to be put into an array of Integer objects to be processed. All of the wrapper classes implement the Comparable interface.

LISTING 10.8

```java
//********************************************************************
//  PhoneList.java          Author: Lewis/Loftus
//
//  Driver for testing a sorting algorithm.
//********************************************************************

public class PhoneList
{
    //-----------------------------------------------------------------
    //  Creates an array of Contact objects, sorts them, then prints
    //  them.
    //-----------------------------------------------------------------
    public static void main (String[] args)
    {
        Contact[] friends = new Contact[8];

        friends[0] = new Contact ("John", "Smith", "610-555-7384");
        friends[1] = new Contact ("Sarah", "Barnes", "215-555-3827");
        friends[2] = new Contact ("Mark", "Riley", "733-555-2969");
        friends[3] = new Contact ("Laura", "Getz", "663-555-3984");
        friends[4] = new Contact ("Larry", "Smith", "464-555-3489");
        friends[5] = new Contact ("Frank", "Phelps", "322-555-2284");
        friends[6] = new Contact ("Mario", "Guzman", "804-555-9066");
        friends[7] = new Contact ("Marsha", "Grant", "243-555-2837");

        Sorting.selectionSort(friends);

        for (Contact friend : friends)
            System.out.println (friend);
    }
}
```

OUTPUT

```
Barnes, Sarah    215-555-3827
Getz, Laura      663-555-3984
Grant, Marsha    243-555-2837
Guzman, Mario    804-555-9066
Phelps, Frank    322-555-2284
Riley, Mark      733-555-2969
Smith, John      610-555-7384
Smith, Larry     464-555-3489
```

LISTING 10.9

```java
//********************************************************************
//  Sorting.java        Author: Lewis/Loftus
//
//  Demonstrates the selection sort and insertion sort algorithms.
//********************************************************************

public class Sorting
{
   //-----------------------------------------------------------------
   //  Sorts the specified array of objects using the selection
   //  sort algorithm.
   //-----------------------------------------------------------------
   public static void selectionSort (Comparable[] list)
   {
      int min;
      Comparable temp;

      for (int index = 0; index < list.length-1; index++)
      {
         min = index;
         for (int scan = index+1; scan < list.length; scan++)
            if (list[scan].compareTo(list[min]) < 0)
               min = scan;

         // Swap the values
         temp = list[min];
         list[min] = list[index];
         list[index] = temp;
      }
   }

   //-----------------------------------------------------------------
   //  Sorts the specified array of objects using the insertion
   //  sort algorithm.
   //-----------------------------------------------------------------
   public static void insertionSort (Comparable[] list)
   {
      for (int index = 1; index < list.length; index++)
      {
         Comparable key = list[index];
         int position = index;
```

LISTING 10.9   *continued*

```
        // Shift larger values to the right
        while (position > 0 && key.compareTo(list[position-1]) < 0)
        {
            list[position] = list[position-1];
            position--;
        }

        list[position] = key;
    }
}
}
```

LISTING 10.10

```
//********************************************************************
//  Contact.java        Author: Lewis/Loftus
//
//  Represents a phone contact.
//********************************************************************

public class Contact implements Comparable
{
    private String firstName, lastName, phone;

    //-----------------------------------------------------------------
    //  Constructor: Sets up this contact with the specified data.
    //-----------------------------------------------------------------
    public Contact (String first, String last, String telephone)
    {
        firstName = first;
        lastName = last;
        phone = telephone;
    }

    //-----------------------------------------------------------------
    //  Returns a description of this contact as a string.
    //-----------------------------------------------------------------
    public String toString ()
    {
        return lastName + ", " + firstName + "\t" + phone;
    }
```

LISTING 10.10   *continued*

```
//---------------------------------------------------------------
//  Returns true if the first and last names of this contact match
//  those of the parameter.
//---------------------------------------------------------------
public boolean equals (Object other)
{
   return (lastName.equals(((Contact)other).getLastName()) &&
           firstName.equals(((Contact)other).getFirstName()));
}


//---------------------------------------------------------------
//  Uses both last and first names to determine ordering.
//---------------------------------------------------------------
public int compareTo (Object other)
{
   int result;

   String otherFirst = ((Contact)other).getFirstName();
   String otherLast = ((Contact)other).getLastName();

   if (lastName.equals(otherLast))
      result = firstName.compareTo(otherFirst);
   else
      result = lastName.compareTo(otherLast);

   return result;
}

//---------------------------------------------------------------
//  First name accessor.
//---------------------------------------------------------------
public String getFirstName ()
{
   return firstName;
}

//---------------------------------------------------------------
//  Last name accessor.
//---------------------------------------------------------------
public String getLastName ()
{
   return lastName;
}
}
```

Insertion Sort

The Sorting class also contains a method that performs an insertion sort on an array of Comparable objects. If used to sort the array of Contact objects in the PhoneList program, it would produce the same results as the selection sort did. However, the logic used to put the objects in order is different.

The *insertion sort* algorithm sorts a list of values by repetitively inserting a particular value into a subset of the list that has already been sorted. One at a time, each unsorted element is inserted at the appropriate position in that sorted subset until the entire list is in order.

The general strategy of insertion sort is: Begin with a "sorted" list containing only one value. Sort the first two values in the list relative to each other by exchanging them if necessary. Insert the list's third value into the appropriate position relative to the first two (sorted) values. Then insert the fourth value into its proper position relative to the first three values in the list. Each time an insertion is made, the number of values in the sorted subset increases by one. Continue this process until all values are inserted in their proper places, at which point the list is completely sorted.

The insertion process requires that the other values in the array shift to make room for the inserted element. Figure 10.3 demonstrates the behavior of the insertion sort algorithm with integers.

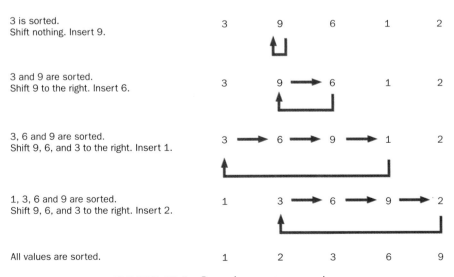

FIGURE 10.3   Insertion sort processing

Similar to the selection sort implementation, the `insertionSort` method uses two `for` loops to sort the array. In the insertion sort, however, the outer loop controls the index in the array of the next value to be inserted. The inner loop compares the current insert value with values stored at lower indexes (which make up a sorted subset of the entire list). If the current insert value is less than the value at `position`, that value is shifted to the right. Shifting continues until the proper position is opened to accept the insert value. Each iteration of the outer loop adds one more value to the sorted subset of the list, until the entire list is sorted.

Comparing Sorts

There are various reasons for choosing one sorting algorithm over another, including the algorithm's simplicity, its level of efficiency, and the amount of memory it uses. An algorithm that is easier to understand is also easier to implement and debug. However, often the simplest sorts are the most inefficient ones. Efficiency is usually considered to be the primary criterion when comparing sorting algorithms. In general, one sorting algorithm is less efficient than another if it performs more comparisons than the other. There are several algorithms that are more efficient than the two we examined, but they are also more complex.

Both selection sort and insertion sort have essentially the same level of efficiency. Both have an outer loop and an inner loop with similar properties, if not purposes. The outer loop is executed once for each value in the list, and the inner loop compares the value in the outer loop with most, if not all, of the values in the rest of the list. Therefore, both algorithms perform approximately n^2 number of comparisons, where n is the number of values in the list. We say that both selection sort and insertion sort are algorithms of *order n^2*. More efficient sorts perform fewer comparisons and are of a smaller order, such as $n \log_2 n$.

Because both selection sort and insertion sort have the same general efficiency, the choice between them is almost arbitrary. However, there are some additional issues to consider. Selection sort is usually easy to understand and will often suffice in many situations. Further, each value moves exactly once to its final place in the list. That is, although the selection and insertion sorts are equivalent (generally) in the number of comparisons made, selection sort makes fewer swaps.

myprogramminglab

SELF-REVIEW QUESTIONS *(see answers in Appendix N)*

SR 10.12   Describe the `Comparable` interface.

SR 10.13   Show the sequence of changes the selection sort algorithm makes to the following list of numbers:

5   7   1   8   2   4   3

SR 10.14   Show the sequence of changes the insertion sort algorithm makes to the following list of numbers:

5   7   1   8   2   4   3

SR 10.15   In what way are the sort methods defined in this chapter polymorphic?

SR 10.16   Which is better: selection sort or insertion sort? Explain.

10.5 Searching

Like sorting, searching for an item is another classic computing problem, and also lends itself to a polymorphic solution. *Searching* is the process of finding a designated *target element* within a group of items. For example, we may need to search for a person named Vito Andolini in a club roster.

The group of items to be searched is sometimes called the *search pool*. The search pool is usually organized into a collection of objects of some kind, such as an array.

Whenever we perform a search, we must consider the possibility that the target is not present in the group. Furthermore, we would like to perform a search efficiently. We don't want to make any more comparisons than we have to.

In this section we examine two search algorithms, linear search and binary search. We explore versatile, polymorphic implementations of these algorithms and compare their efficiency.

Linear Search

If the search pool can be examined one element at a time in any order, one straightforward way to perform the search is to start at the beginning of the list and compare each value in turn to the target element. Eventually, either the target element will be found or we will come to the end of the list and conclude that the target doesn't exist in the group.

This approach is called a *linear search,* because it begins at one end and scans the search pool in a linear manner. This process is depicted in Figure 10.4. When items are stored in an array, a linear search is relatively simple.

The program shown in Listing 10.11 is similar to the PhoneList program from the previous section. It begins with the same, unsorted array of Contact objects. It then performs a linear search for a contact and prints the result. Then it calls the selectionSort method, which was discussed in the previous section, to sort the contacts. It then searches for another contact using a binary search, which is discussed later in this section.

FIGURE 10.4   A linear search

LISTING 10.11

```
//********************************************************************
//  PhoneList2.java        Author: Lewis/Loftus
//
//  Driver for testing searching algorithms.
//********************************************************************

public class PhoneList2
{
   //-----------------------------------------------------------------
   //  Creates an array of Contact objects, sorts them, then prints
   //  them.
   //-----------------------------------------------------------------
   public static void main (String[] args)
   {
      Contact test, found;
      Contact[] friends = new Contact[8];

      friends[0] = new Contact ("John", "Smith", "610-555-7384");
      friends[1] = new Contact ("Sarah", "Barnes", "215-555-3827");
      friends[2] = new Contact ("Mark", "Riley", "733-555-2969");
      friends[3] = new Contact ("Laura", "Getz", "663-555-3984");
      friends[4] = new Contact ("Larry", "Smith", "464-555-3489");
      friends[5] = new Contact ("Frank", "Phelps", "322-555-2284");
      friends[6] = new Contact ("Mario", "Guzman", "804-555-9066");
      friends[7] = new Contact ("Marsha", "Grant", "243-555-2837");

      test = new Contact ("Frank", "Phelps", "");
      found = (Contact) Searching.linearSearch(friends, test);
      if (found != null)
         System.out.println ("Found: " + found);
      else
```

LISTING 10.11   *continued*

```
        System.out.println ("The contact was not found.");
        System.out.println ();

        Sorting.selectionSort(friends);

        test = new Contact ("Mario", "Guzman", "");
        found = (Contact) Searching.binarySearch(friends, test);
        if (found != null)
            System.out.println ("Found: " + found);
        else
            System.out.println ("The contact was not found.");
    }
}
```

OUTPUT

```
Found: Phelps, Frank    322-555-2284

Found: Guzman, Mario    804-555-9066
```

Listing 10.12 shows the Searching class. It contains two static searching algorithms.

In the linearSearch method, the while loop steps through the elements of the array, terminating either when the target is found or the end of the array is reached. The boolean variable found is initialized to false and is only changed to true if the target element is located.

Note that we'll have to examine every element before we can conclude that the target doesn't exist in the array. On average, the linear search approach will look through half the data before finding a target that is present in the array.

The linearSearch method is implemented to process an array of Comparable objects. For this algorithm, however, which relies only on the equals method, that restriction is not necessary.

Binary Search

If the elements in an array are sorted, in either ascending or descending order, then our approach to searching can be much more efficient than the linear search algorithm. A *binary search* eliminates large parts of the search pool with each comparison by capitalizing on the fact that the search pool is ordered.

LISTING 10.12

```java
//********************************************************************
//  Searching.java       Author: Lewis/Loftus
//
//  Demonstrates the linear search and binary search algorithms.
//********************************************************************

public class Searching
{
   //-----------------------------------------------------------------
   //  Searches the specified array of objects for the target using
   //  a linear search. Returns a reference to the target object from
   //  the array if found, and null otherwise.
   //-----------------------------------------------------------------
   public static Comparable linearSearch (Comparable[] list,
                                           Comparable target)
   {
      int index = 0;
      boolean found = false;

      while (!found && index < list.length)
      {
         if (list[index].compareTo(target) == 0)
            found = true;
         else
            index++;
      }

      if (found)
         return list[index];
      else
         return null;
   }

   //-----------------------------------------------------------------
   //  Searches the specified array of objects for the target using
   //  a binary search. Assumes the array is already sorted in
   //  ascending order when it is passed in. Returns a reference to
   //  the target object from the array if found, and null otherwise.
   //-----------------------------------------------------------------
   public static Comparable binarySearch (Comparable[] list,
                                           Comparable target)
   {
      int min=0, max=list.length-1, mid=0;
      boolean found = false;
```

LISTING 10.12 *continued*

```
        while (!found && min <= max)
        {
            mid = (min+max) / 2;
            if (list[mid].compareTo(target) == 0)
                found = true;
            else
                if (target.compareTo(list[mid]) < 0)
                    max = mid-1;
                else
                    min = mid+1;
        }

        if (found)
            return list[mid];
        else
            return null;
    }
}
```

Consider the following sorted array of integers:

0	1	2	3	4	5	6	7	8	9	10	11	12	13	14
10	12	18	22	31	34	40	46	59	67	69	72	82	84	98

Suppose we were trying to determine if the number 67 is in this list. Initially, the target might be anywhere in the list, or not at all. That is, at first, all items in the search pool are *viable candidates*.

Instead of starting the search at one end or the other, a binary search begins in the middle of the sorted list. If the target element is not found at that middle element, then the search continues. The middle element of this list is 46, which is not our target, so we must search on. However, since the list is sorted, we know that if 67 is in the list, it will be in the later half of the array. All values at lower indexes are less than 46. Thus, with one comparison, we've taken half of the data out of consideration, and we are left with the following viable candidates:

Viable Candidates

0	1	2	3	4	5	6	7	8	9	10	11	12	13	14
10	12	18	22	31	34	40	46	59	67	69	72	82	84	98

To search the remaining candidates, we once again examine the "middle" element. The middle element is 72, and thus we have still not found the target. But once again, we can eliminate half of the viable candidates (those greater than 72) and we are left with:

Viable Candidates

0	1	2	3	4	5	6	7	8	9	10	11	12	13	14
10	12	18	22	31	34	40	46	59	67	69	72	82	84	98

Employing the same approach again, we select the middle element, 67, and find the element we are seeking. If it had not been our target, we would have continued with this process until we either found the value or eliminated all possible data.

With each comparison, a binary search eliminates approximately half of the remaining data to be searched (it also eliminates the middle element as well). That is, a binary search eliminates half of the data with the first comparison, another quarter of the data with the second comparison, another eighth of the data with the third comparison, and so on. The binary search approach is pictured in Figure 10.5.

The binarySearch method from the Searching class performs a binary search by looping until the target element is found or until the viable candidates drop to zero. Two integer indexes, min and max, are used to define the portion of the array that is still considered viable. When min becomes greater than max, then the viable candidates have been exhausted.

On each iteration of the loop, the midpoint is calculated by dividing the sum of min and max by two. If there are currently an even number of viable candidates, and thus two "middle" values, this calculation discards the fractional remainder and picks the first of the two.

If the target element is not found, the value of min or max is modified to eliminate the appropriate half of the viable candidates. Then the search continues.

start

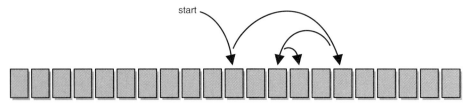

FIGURE 10.5   A binary search

Comparing Searches

As far as the search algorithms go, there is no doubt that the binary search approach is far more efficient than the linear search. However, the binary search requires that the data be sorted. So once again, the algorithm to choose depends on the situation.

If it's relatively easy to keep the data sorted, or if there will be a lot of searching, it will likely be more appropriate to use a binary search. On the other hand, a linear search is quite simple to implement and may be the best choice when long-term efficiency is not an issue.

SELF-REVIEW QUESTIONS *(see answers in Appendix N)*   myprogramminglab

SR 10.17   Given the following list of numbers, how many elements of the list would be examined by the linear search algorithm to determine if each of the indicated target elements are on the list?

15   21   4   17   8   27   1   22   43   57   25   7   53   12   16

a. 17
b. 15
c. 16
d. 45

SR 10.18   Describe the general concept of a binary search.

SR 10.19   Given the following list of numbers, how many elements of the list would be examined by the binary search algorithm to determine if each of the indicated target elements are on the list?

1   4   7   8   12   15   16   17   21   22   25   27   43   53   57

a. 17
b. 15
c. 57
d. 45

10.6 Designing for Polymorphism

We've been evolving the concepts underlying good software design throughout this book. For every aspect of object-oriented software, we should make decisions, consciously and carefully, that lead to well-structured, flexible, and elegant code. We want to define appropriate classes and objects, with proper encapsulation. We want to define appropriate relationships among the classes and objects, including leveraging the powerful aspects of inheritance when possible. Now we can add polymorphism to our set of intellectual tools for thinking about software design.

Polymorphism provides a means to create elegant versatility in our software. It allows us to apply a consistent approach to inconsistent but related behaviors. We should try to find opportunities in our software systems that lend themselves to polymorphic solutions. We should seek them out, actively and deliberately, before we begin to write code.

Whenever you find situations in which different types of objects perform the same type of behavior, there is an opportunity for a polymorphic solution. The more experience you get, the easier it will be to detect such situations. See if you recognize the opportunity for polymorphism in the following situations:

- Different types of vehicles move in different ways.
- All business transactions for a company must be logged.
- All products produced by a company must meet certain quality standards.
- A hotel needs to plan their remodeling efforts for every room.
- A casino wants to analyze the profit margin for their games.
- A dispatcher must schedule moving vans and personnel based on the job size.
- A drawing program allows the user to draw various shapes.

The common theme in these examples is that the same basic behavior applies to multiple objects, and those behaviors are accomplished differently depending on the specific type of object. Every circle is drawn using the same basic techniques and information, which is different from the information needed and the steps taken to draw a rectangle. Yet both types of shapes get drawn. Different, but similar. Polymorphic.

The example of a drawing program is explored in more detail in the `PaintBox` case study presented in Appendix J. It follows the refinement of a large program through various stages of its development. The heart of its design is a polymorphic approach to handling the various types of shapes that the user can draw.

Once a polymorphic situation is identified, the specifics of the design can be addressed. In particular, should you use inheritance or interfaces as the mechanism to define polymorphic references? The answer to that question lies in the relationships among the different types of objects involved. If those objects can be related naturally by inheritance, with true is-a relationships, then polymorphism via inheritance is probably the way to go. But if the main thing the objects have in common is their need to be processed in a particular way, then perhaps using an interface to create the polymorphic references is the better solution.

SR 10.20   Suppose you are designing classes for a banking-related system. Both checking accounts and savings accounts require deposit and withdraw operations. You decide to provide these behaviors using polymorphism. Which polymorphic mechanism (inheritance or interfaces) is best suited for this situation? Provide support for your choice.

SR 10.21   Suppose you are designing classes to help create aquarium-based screen savers. At times, you will want some aquarium objects to "float" from wherever they are to the top of the tank. You decide to provide this behavior using polymorphism. Which polymorphic mechanism (inheritance or interfaces) is best suited for this situation? Provide support for your choice.

SR 10.22   Suppose you are designing classes to support the modeling of rain forest environments. Animal objects, such as butterflies and monkeys, need to grow older periodically. You decide to provide this behavior using polymorphism. Which polymorphic mechanism (inheritance or interfaces) is best suited for this situation? Provide support for your choice.

10.7 Event Processing

Let's revisit the concept of event processing in a Java GUI and see how it relates to polymorphism. As we've seen many times in previous examples, in order to respond to an event, we must establish a relationship between an event listener object and a particular component that may fire the event. We establish the relationship between the listener and the component it listens to by making a method call that adds the listener to the component.

For example, suppose a class called MyButtonListener represents an action listener. To set up a listener to respond to a JButton object, we might do the following:

```
JButton button = new JButton();
button.addActionListener (new MyButtonListener());
```

Once this relationship is established, the listener will respond whenever the button fires an action event (because the user pressed it). Now think about the addActionListener method carefully. It is a method of the JButton class, which was written by someone at Sun Microsystems years ago. On the other hand, we might have written the MyButtonListener class today. So how can a method written years ago take a parameter whose class was just written?

The answer is polymorphism. If you examine the source code for the addActionListener method, you'll discover that it accepts a parameter of type ActionListener, the interface. Therefore, instead of accepting a parameter of only one object type, the addActionListener method can accept any object of any class that implements the ActionListener interface. All other add listener methods work in similar ways.

The JButton object doesn't know anything particular about the object that is passed to the addActionListener method, except for the fact that it implements the ActionListener interface (otherwise the code wouldn't compile). The JButton object simply stores the listener object and invokes its actionPerformed method when the event occurs.

In Chapter 9 we discussed that we can also create a listener by extending an adapter class. Well, it turns out that using an adapter class isn't really a new way to create a listener after all. Each adapter class is written to implement the appropriate listener interface, providing empty methods for all event handlers. So by extending an adapter class, the new listener class automatically implements the corresponding listener interface. And that is what really makes it a listener such that it can be passed to an appropriate add listener method.

Thus, no matter how a listener object is created, we are using polymorphism via interfaces to set up the relationship between a listener and the component it listens to. GUI events are a wonderful example of the power and versatility provided by polymorphism.

10.8 File Choosers

Dialog boxes were introduced in Chapter 6. We used the JOptionPane class to create several dialog boxes to present information, accept input, and confirm actions.

The JFileChooser class represents another specialized dialog box, a *file chooser*, which allows the user to select a file from a hard disk or other storage medium. You have probably run many programs that allow you to open a file using a similar dialog box.

The program shown in Listing 10.13 uses a JFileChooser dialog box to select a file. This program also demonstrates the use of another GUI component, a *text area*, which is similar to a text field but can display multiple lines of text at one time. After the user selects a file using the file chooser dialog box, the text contained in that file is displayed in a text area.

LISTING 10.13

```java
//********************************************************************
//  DisplayFile.java       Author: Lewis/Loftus
//
//  Demonstrates the use of a file chooser and a text area.
//********************************************************************

import java.util.Scanner;
import java.io.*;
import javax.swing.*;

public class DisplayFile
{
   //-----------------------------------------------------------------
   //  Opens a file chooser dialog, reads the selected file and
   //  loads it into a text area.
   //-----------------------------------------------------------------
   public static void main (String[] args) throws IOException
   {
      JFrame frame = new JFrame ("Display File");
      frame.setDefaultCloseOperation (JFrame.EXIT_ON_CLOSE);

      JTextArea ta = new JTextArea (20, 30);
      JFileChooser chooser = new JFileChooser();

      int status = chooser.showOpenDialog (null);

      if (status != JFileChooser.APPROVE_OPTION)
         ta.setText ("No File Chosen");
      else
      {
         File file = chooser.getSelectedFile();
         Scanner scan = new Scanner(file);

         String info = "";
         while (scan.hasNext())
            info += scan.nextLine() + "\n";

         ta.setText (info);
      }

      frame.getContentPane().add (ta);
      frame.pack();
      frame.setVisible(true);
   }
}
```

LISTING 10.13 *continued*

DISPLAY

The file chooser dialog box is displayed when the showOpenDialog method is invoked. It automatically presents the list of files contained in a particular directory. The user can use the controls on the dialog box to navigate to other directories, change the way the files are viewed, and specify which types of files are displayed.

The showOpenDialog method returns an integer representing the status of the operation, which can be checked against constants defined in the JFileChooser class. In this program, if a file was not selected (perhaps by pressing the Cancel button), a default message is displayed in the text area. If the user chose a file, it is opened and its contents are read using the Scanner class. Note that this program assumes the selected file contains text. It does not catch any exceptions, so if the user selects an inappropriate file, the program will terminate when the exception is thrown.

A text area component is defined by the JTextArea class. In this program, we pass two parameters to its constructor, specifying the size of the text area in terms of the number of characters (rows and columns) it should display. The text to display is set using the setText method.

A text area component, like a text field, can be set so that it is either editable or noneditable. The user can change the contents of an editable text area by clicking on the text area and typing with the keyboard. If the text area is noneditable, it is used to display text only. By default, a JTextArea component is editable.

A JFileChooser component makes it easy to allow users to specify a specific file to use. Another specialized dialog box—one that allows the user to choose a color—is discussed in the next section.

10.9 Color Choosers

In many situations we may want to give the user of a program the ability to choose a color. We could accomplish this in various ways. For instance, we could provide a list of colors using a set of radio buttons. However, with the wide variety of colors available, it's nice to have an easier and more flexible technique to accomplish this common task. A specialized dialog box, often referred to as a *color chooser*, is a graphical component that serves this purpose.

> **KEY CONCEPT**
>
> A color chooser allows the user to select a color from a palette or use RGB values.

The JColorChooser class represents a color chooser. It can be used to display a dialog box that lets the user click on a color of choice from a palette presented for that purpose. The user could also specify a color using RGB values or other color representation techniques.

The program shown in Listing 10.14 uses a color chooser dialog box to specify the color of a panel that is displayed in a separate frame.

After a color has been chosen. the new color is displayed in the primary frame and another dialog box (this one was created using JOptionPane as discussed in Chapter 6) is used to determine if the user wants to change the color again. If so, another color chooser dialog box is displayed. This cycle can continue as long as the user desires.

Invoking the static showDialog method of the JColorChooser class causes the color chooser dialog box to appear. The parameters to that method specify the parent component for the dialog box, the title that appears in the dialog box frame, and the initial color showing in the color chooser. By using the variable shade as the third parameter, the color initially showing in the color chooser when it first appears will coincide with the current color of the panel.

LISTING 10.14

```java
//********************************************************************
//  DisplayColor.java          Author: Lewis/Loftus
//
//  Demonstrates the use of a color chooser.
//********************************************************************

import javax.swing.*;
import java.awt.*;

public class DisplayColor
{
   //-----------------------------------------------------------------
   //  Presents a frame with a colored panel, then allows the user
   //  to change the color multiple times using a color chooser.
   //-----------------------------------------------------------------
   public static void main (String[] args)
   {
      JFrame frame = new JFrame ("Display Color");
      frame.setDefaultCloseOperation (JFrame.EXIT_ON_CLOSE);

      JPanel colorPanel = new JPanel();
      colorPanel.setBackground (Color.white);
      colorPanel.setPreferredSize (new Dimension (300, 100));

      frame.getContentPane().add (colorPanel);
      frame.pack();
      frame.setVisible(true);

      Color shade = Color.white;
      int again;

      do
      {
         shade = JColorChooser.showDialog (frame, "Pick a Color!",
                                           shade);

         colorPanel.setBackground (shade);

         again = JOptionPane.showConfirmDialog (null,
            "Display another color?");
      }
      while (again == JOptionPane.YES_OPTION);
   }
}
```

LISTING 10.14   *continued*

DISPLAY

10.10 Sliders

A *slider* is a component that allows the user to specify a numeric value within a bounded range. A slider can be presented either vertically or horizontally and can have optional tick marks and labels indicating the range of values.

> **KEY CONCEPT**
>
> A slider lets the user specify a numeric value within a bounded range.

A program called SlideColor is shown in Listing 10.15. In one sense, this program is an improvement over the DisplayColor program from the previous section in that it allows the user to constantly change the displayed color without using a color chooser each time. This program presents three sliders that control the RGB components of a color. The color specified by the values of the sliders is shown in a square that is displayed to the right of the sliders.

The SlideColorPanel class shown in Listing 10.16 is a panel used to display the three sliders. Each is created from the JSlider class, which accepts four parameters. The first determines the orientation of the slider using one of two JSlider constants (HORIZONTAL or VERTICAL). The second and third parameters specify the maximum and minimum values of the slider, which are set to 0 and 255 for each of the sliders in the example. The last parameter of the JSlider

LISTING 10.15

```java
//********************************************************************
//  SlideColor.java       Author: Lewis/Loftus
//
//  Demonstrates the use of slider components.
//********************************************************************

import java.awt.*;
import javax.swing.*;

public class SlideColor
{
    //-----------------------------------------------------------------
    //  Presents a frame with a control panel and a panel that
    //  changes color as the sliders are adjusted.
    //-----------------------------------------------------------------
    public static void main (String[] args)
    {
        JFrame frame = new JFrame ("Slide Colors");
        frame.setDefaultCloseOperation (JFrame.EXIT_ON_CLOSE);

        frame.getContentPane().add(new SlideColorPanel());

        frame.pack();
        frame.setVisible(true);
    }
}
```

DISPLAY

LISTING 10.16

```java
//********************************************************************
//  SlideColorPanel.java       Author: Lewis/Loftus
//
//  Represents the slider control panel for the SlideColor program.
//********************************************************************

import java.awt.*;
import javax.swing.*;
import javax.swing.event.*;

public class SlideColorPanel extends JPanel
{
   private JPanel controls, colorPanel;
   private JSlider rSlider, gSlider, bSlider;
   private JLabel rLabel, gLabel, bLabel;

   //-----------------------------------------------------------------
   //  Sets up the sliders and their labels, aligning them along
   //  their left edge using a box layout.
   //-----------------------------------------------------------------
   public SlideColorPanel()
   {
      rSlider = new JSlider (JSlider.HORIZONTAL, 0, 255, 0);
      rSlider.setMajorTickSpacing (50);
      rSlider.setMinorTickSpacing (10);
      rSlider.setPaintTicks (true);
      rSlider.setPaintLabels (true);
      rSlider.setAlignmentX (Component.LEFT_ALIGNMENT);

      gSlider = new JSlider (JSlider.HORIZONTAL, 0, 255, 0);
      gSlider.setMajorTickSpacing (50);
      gSlider.setMinorTickSpacing (10);
      gSlider.setPaintTicks (true);
      gSlider.setPaintLabels (true);
      gSlider.setAlignmentX (Component.LEFT_ALIGNMENT);

      bSlider = new JSlider (JSlider.HORIZONTAL, 0, 255, 0);
      bSlider.setMajorTickSpacing (50);
      bSlider.setMinorTickSpacing (10);
      bSlider.setPaintTicks (true);
      bSlider.setPaintLabels (true);
      bSlider.setAlignmentX (Component.LEFT_ALIGNMENT);
```

LISTING 10.16 *continued*

```java
      SliderListener listener = new SliderListener();
      rSlider.addChangeListener (listener);
      gSlider.addChangeListener (listener);
      bSlider.addChangeListener (listener);

      rLabel = new JLabel ("Red: 0");
      rLabel.setAlignmentX (Component.LEFT_ALIGNMENT);
      gLabel = new JLabel ("Green: 0");
      gLabel.setAlignmentX (Component.LEFT_ALIGNMENT);
      bLabel = new JLabel ("Blue: 0");
      bLabel.setAlignmentX (Component.LEFT_ALIGNMENT);

      controls = new JPanel();
      BoxLayout layout = new BoxLayout (controls, BoxLayout.Y_AXIS);
      controls.setLayout (layout);
      controls.add (rLabel);
      controls.add (rSlider);
      controls.add (Box.createRigidArea (new Dimension (0, 20)));
      controls.add (gLabel);
      controls.add (gSlider);
      controls.add (Box.createRigidArea (new Dimension (0, 20)));
      controls.add (bLabel);
      controls.add (bSlider);

      colorPanel = new JPanel();
      colorPanel.setPreferredSize (new Dimension (100, 100));
      colorPanel.setBackground (new Color (0, 0, 0));

      add (controls);
      add (colorPanel);
   }

   //*****************************************************************
   //  Represents the listener for all three sliders.
   //*****************************************************************
   private class SliderListener implements ChangeListener
   {
      private int red, green, blue;
```

LISTING 10.16   *continued*

```
//----------------------------------------------------------
//  Gets the value of each slider, then updates the labels and
//  the color panel.
//----------------------------------------------------------
public void stateChanged (ChangeEvent event)
{
    red = rSlider.getValue();
    green = gSlider.getValue();
    blue = bSlider.getValue();

    rLabel.setText ("Red: " + red);
    gLabel.setText ("Green: " + green);
    bLabel.setText ("Blue: " + blue);

    colorPanel.setBackground (new Color (red, green, blue));
    }
  }
}
```

constructor specifies the slider's initial value. In our example, the initial value of each slider is zero, which puts the slider knob to the far left when the program initially executes.

The panel called `colorPanel` is used to display the color specified by the sliders by setting its background color. Initially, the settings of the sliders are all zero, which correspond to the initial color displayed (black).

The `JSlider` class has several methods that allow the programmer to tailor the look of a slider. Major tick marks can be set at specific intervals using the `setMajorTickSpacing` method. Intermediate minor tick marks can be set using the `setMinorTickSpacing` method. Neither is displayed, however, unless the `setPaintTicks` method, with a parameter of `true`, is invoked as well. Labels indicating the value of the major tick marks are displayed if indicated by a call to the `setPaintLabels` method.

Note that in this example, the major tick spacing is set to 50. Starting at zero, each increment of 50 is labeled. The last label is therefore 250, even though the slider value can reach 255.

A slider produces a *change event*, indicating that the position of the slider and the value it represents has changed. The ChangeListener interface contains a single method called stateChanged. In the SlideColor program, the same listener object is used for all three sliders. In the stateChanged method, which is called whenever any of the sliders is adjusted, the value of each slider is obtained, the labels of all three are updated, and the background color of the display panel is revised. It is actually only necessary to update one of the labels (the one whose corresponding slider changed). However, the effort to determine which slider was adjusted is not warranted. It's easier—and probably more efficient—to update all three labels each time. Another alternative is to have a unique listener for each slider, though that extra coding effort is not needed either.

A slider is often a good choice when a large range of values is possible but strictly bounded on both ends. Compared to alternatives such as a text field, sliders convey more information to the user and eliminate input errors.

Summary of Key Concepts

- A polymorphic reference can refer to different types of objects over time.
- The binding of a method invocation to its definition is performed at run time for a polymorphic reference.
- A reference variable can refer to any object created from any class related to it by inheritance.
- The type of the object, not the type of the reference, is used to determine which version of a method to invoke.
- An interface name can be used to declare an object reference variable.
- An interface reference can refer to any object of any class that implements that interface.
- A parameter to a method can be polymorphic, giving the method flexible control of its arguments.
- Implementing a sort algorithm polymorphically allows it to sort any comparable set of objects.
- Polymorphism allows us to apply a consistent approach to inconsistent behaviors.
- We should hone our design senses to identify situations that lend themselves to polymorphic solutions.
- Establishing the relationship between a listener and the component it listens to is accomplished using polymorphism.
- A file chooser allows the user to browse a disk and select a file to be processed.
- A color chooser allows the user to select a color from a palette or use RGB values.
- A slider lets the user specify a numeric value within a bounded range.

Exercises

Visit www.myprogramminglab.com to complete many of these Exercises online and get instant feedback.   myprogramminglab

EX 10.1   Draw and annotate a class hierarchy that represents various types of faculty at a university. Show what characteristics would be represented in the various classes of the hierarchy. Explain how polymorphism could play a role in the process of assigning courses to each faculty member.

EX 10.2   Draw and annotate a class hierarchy that represents various types of employees who are working in the public sector. Show what characteristics could be represented in the various classes of employees. Explain how polymorphism can play a role in calculating the salary of each employee.

EX 10.3   Draw and annotate a class hierarchy that represents various types of transactions in a bank. Show what characteristics could be represented in the various classes of the hierarchy Explain how polymorphism can play a role in maintaining various customer accounts.

EX 10.4   What would happen if the pay method were not defined as an abstract method in the StaffMember class of the Firm program?

EX 10.5   Explain how a call to the addkeylistener represents a polymorphic situation.

EX 10.6   Draw the containment hierarchy tree for a FormDesign program.

Programming Projects

VideoNote

Developing a solution of PP 10.1.

Visit www.myprogramminglab.com to complete many of these Programming Projects online and get instant feedback.

PP 10.1   A class called Shapes represents abstract classes for all objects that have a defined shape. Shapes has a method called draw. All real objects will derive characteristics from Shapes. Would you use an interface to define the method draw? How and why? If yes, would having a class called Shapes serve any purpose?

PP 10.2   Modify the Firm example from this chapter such that all employees can be given different vacation options depending on their classification. Modify the driver program to demonstrate this new functionality.

PP 10.3   Implement the Speaker interface described in Section 10.3, and create three classes that implement Speaker in various ways. Create a driver class whose main method instantiates some of these objects and tests their abilities.

PP 10.4   Rewrite the Sorting class so that both sorting algorithms put the values in descending order. Create a driver class with a main method to exercise the modifications.

PP 10.5   Modify the Movies program from Chapter 8 so that it keeps the DVDs sorted by title.

PP 10.6   Design and implement a program that graphically displays the processing of a selection sort. Use bars of various heights to represent the values being sorted. Display the set of bars after each swap. Put a delay in the processing of the sort to give the human observer a chance to see how the order of the values changes.

PP 10.7   Repeat PP 10.6 using an insertion sort.

PP 10.8   Design and implement a program that combines the functionality of the `StyleOptions` and `QuoteOptions` programs from Chapter 5. That is, the new program should present the appropriate quote (using radio buttons) whose style can be changed (using checkboxes). Also include a slider that regulates the size of the quotation font. Design the containment hierarchy carefully and use layout managers as appropriate to create a nice interface.

PP 10.9   Design and implement an application that draws the graph of the equation $ax^2 + bx + c$, where the values of a, b, and c are set using three sliders.

Exceptions

11

Exception handling is an important part of an object-oriented software system. Exceptions represent problems or unusual situations that may occur in a program. Java provides various ways to handle exceptions when they occur. We explore the class hierarchy from the Java standard library used to define exceptions, as well as the ability to define our own exception objects. This chapter also discusses the use of exceptions when dealing with input and output, and examines an example that writes a text file. The Graphics Track sections of this chapter explore some special features of Swing components, as well as a few additional components and containers.

11.1 Exception Handling

As we've discussed briefly in other parts of the text, problems that arise in a Java program may generate exceptions or errors. An *exception* is an object that defines an unusual or erroneous situation. An exception is thrown by a program or the run-time environment and can be caught and handled appropriately if desired. An *error* is similar to an exception except that an error generally represents an unrecoverable situation and should not be caught. Java has a predefined set of exceptions and errors that may occur during the execution of a program.

> **KEY CONCEPT**
>
> Errors and exceptions are objects that represent unusual or invalid processing.

Problem situations represented by exceptions and errors can have various kinds of root causes. Here are some situations that cause exceptions to be thrown:

- Attempting to divide by zero.
- An array index that is out of bounds.
- A specified file that could not be found.
- A requested I/O operation that could not be completed normally.
- An attempt was made to follow a null reference.
- An attempt was made to execute an operation that violates some kind of security measure.

These are just a few examples. There are dozens of others that address very specific situations.

As many of these examples show, an exception can represent a truly erroneous situation. But as the name implies, they may simply represent an exceptional situation. That is, an exception may represent a situation that won't occur under usual conditions. Exception handling is set up to be an efficient way to deal with such situations, especially given that they don't happen too often.

We have several options when it comes to dealing with exceptions. A program can be designed to process an exception in one of three ways. It can:

- not handle the exception at all,
- handle the exception where it occurs, or
- handle the exception at another point in the program.

We explore each of these approaches in the following sections.

myprogramming**lab**

SELF-REVIEW QUESTIONS *(see answers in Appendix N)*

SR 11.1   What is the difference between an error and an exception?

SR 11.2   In what ways might a thrown exception be handled?

11.2 Uncaught Exceptions

If a program does not handle the exception at all, it will terminate abnormally and produce a message that describes what exception occurred and where it was produced. The information associated with an exception is often helpful in tracking down the cause of a problem.

Let's look at the output of an exception. The program shown in Listing 11.1 throws an ArithmeticException when an invalid arithmetic operation is attempted. In this case, the program attempts to divide by zero.

Because there is no code in this program to handle the exception explicitly, it terminates when the exception occurs, printing specific information about the exception. Note that the last println statement in the program never executes, because the exception occurs first.

LISTING 11.1

```java
//********************************************************************
//  Zero.java        Author: Lewis/Loftus
//
//  Demonstrates an uncaught exception.
//********************************************************************

public class Zero
{
   //-----------------------------------------------------------------
   //  Deliberately divides by zero to produce an exception.
   //-----------------------------------------------------------------
   public static void main (String[] args)
   {
      int numerator = 10;
      int denominator = 0;

      System.out.println (numerator / denominator);

      System.out.println ("This text will not be printed.");
   }
}
```

OUTPUT

```
Exception in thread "main" java.lang.ArithmeticException: / by zero
        at Zero.main(Zero.java:17)
```

The first line of the exception output indicates which exception was thrown and provides some information about why it was thrown. The remaining lines are the *call stack trace*; they indicate where the exception occurred. In this case, there is only one line in the call stack trace, but there may be several depending on where the exception originated. The first trace line indicates the method, file, and line number where the exception occurred. The other trace lines, if present, indicate the methods that were called to get to the method that produced the exception. In this program, there is only one method, and it produced the exception; therefore there is only one line in the trace.

The call stack trace information is also available by calling methods of the exception class that is being thrown. The method `getMessage` returns a string explaining the reason the exception was thrown. The method `printStackTrace` prints the call stack trace.

myprogramminglab

SELF-REVIEW QUESTION *(see answer in Appendix N)*

SR 11.3 True or False. Explain.

a. An exception and an error are the same thing.
b. An attempt to divide by zero will cause an exception to be thrown.
c. If a program does not handle a raised exception, the exception is ignored and nothing happens.
d. If a program does not handle an exception, a message related to the exception will be produced.
e. A call stack trace shows the sequence of method calls that led to the code where an exception occurred.

11.3 The try-catch Statement

Let's now examine how we catch and handle an exception when it is thrown. The *try-catchstatement* identifies a block of statements that may throw an exception. A *catch clause*, which follows a `try` block, defines how a particular kind of exception is handled. A `try` block can have several `catch` clauses associated with it. Each `catch` clause is called an *exception handler*.

When a `try` statement is executed, the statements in the `try` block are executed. If no exception is thrown during the execution of the `try` block, processing continues with the statement following the `try` statement (after all of the `catch` clauses). This situation is the normal execution flow and should occur most of the time.

If an exception is thrown at any point during the execution of the try block, control is immediately transferred to the appropriate catch handler if it is present. That is, control transfers to the first catch clause whose exception class corresponds to the exception that was thrown. After executing the statements in the catch clause, control transfers to the statement after the entire try-catch statement.

> **KEY CONCEPT**
> Each catch clause handles a particular kind of exception that may be thrown within the try block.

Let's look at an example. Suppose a hypothetical company uses codes to represent its various products. A product code includes, among other information, a character in the tenth position that represents the zone from which that product was made, and a four-digit integer in positions 4 through 7 that represents the district in which it will be sold. Due to some reorganization, products from zone R are banned from being sold in districts with a designation of 2000 or higher. The program shown in Listing 11.2 reads product codes from the user and counts the number of banned codes entered.

Try Statement

A try statement contains a block of code followed by one or more catch clauses. If an exception occurs in the try block, the code of the corresponding catch clause is executed. The finally clause, if present, is executed no matter how the try block is exited.

Example:

```
try
{
    System.out.println (Integer.parseInt(numString));
}
catch (NumberFormatException exception)
{
    System.out.println ("Caught an exception.");
}
finally
{
    System.out.println ("Done.");
}
```

LISTING 11.2

```
//********************************************************************
//  ProductCodes.java        Author: Lewis/Loftus
//
//  Demonstrates the use of a try-catch block.
//********************************************************************

import java.util.Scanner;

public class ProductCodes
{
   //-----------------------------------------------------------------
   //  Counts the number of product codes that are entered with a
   //  zone of R and and district greater than 2000.
   //-----------------------------------------------------------------
   public static void main (String[] args)
   {
      String code;
      char zone;
      int district, valid = 0, banned = 0;

      Scanner scan = new Scanner (System.in);

      System.out.print ("Enter product code (XXX to quit): ");
      code = scan.nextLine();

      while (!code.equals ("XXX"))
      {
         try
         {
            zone = code.charAt(9);
            district = Integer.parseInt(code.substring(3, 7));
            valid++;
            if (zone == 'R' && district > 2000)
               banned++;
         }
         catch (StringIndexOutOfBoundsException exception)
         {
            System.out.println ("Improper code length: " + code);
         }
         catch (NumberFormatException exception)
         {
            System.out.println ("District is not numeric: " + code);
         }
```

LISTING 11.2   *continued*

```
        System.out.print ("Enter product code (XXX to quit): ");
        code = scan.nextLine();
    }

    System.out.println ("# of valid codes entered: " + valid);
    System.out.println ("# of banned codes entered: " + banned);
    }
}
```

OUTPUT

```
Enter product code (XXX to quit): TRV2475A5R-14
Enter product code (XXX to quit): TRD1704A7R-12
Enter product code (XXX to quit): TRL2k74A5R-11
District is not numeric: TRL2k74A5R-11
Enter product code (XXX to quit): TRQ2949A6M-04
Enter product code (XXX to quit): TRV2105A2
Improper code length: TRV2105A2
Enter product code (XXX to quit): TRQ2778A7R-19
Enter product code (XXX to quit): XXX
# of valid codes entered: 4
# of banned codes entered: 2
```

The programming statements in the try block attempt to pull out the zone and district information, and then determine whether it represents a banned product code. If there is any problem extracting the zone and district information, the product code is considered to be invalid and is not processed further. For example, a StringIndexOutOfBoundsException could be thrown by either the charAt or substring methods. Furthermore, a NumberFormatException could be thrown by the parseInt method if the substring does not contain a valid integer. A particular message is printed depending on which exception is thrown. In either case, since the exception is caught and handled, processing continues normally.

Note that, for each code examined, the integer valid is incremented only if no exception is thrown. If an exception is thrown, control transfers immediately to the appropriate catch clause. Likewise, the zone and district are tested by the if statement only if no exception is thrown.

The finally Clause

A try-catch statement can have an optional *finally clause*. The finally clause defines a section of code that is executed no matter how the try block is exited. Most often, a finally clause is used to manage resources or to guarantee that particular parts of an algorithm are executed.

If no exception is generated, the statements in the finally clause are executed after the try block is complete. If an exception is generated in the try block, control first transfers to the appropriate catch clause. After executing the exception-handling code, control transfers to the finally clause and its statements are executed. A finally clause, if present, must be listed following the catch clauses.

Note that a try block does not need to have a catch clause at all. If there are no catch clauses, a finally clause may used by itself if that is appropriate for the situation.

myprogramminglab

SELF-REVIEW QUESTIONS *(see answers in Appendix N)*

SR 11.4   What is a catch clause?

SR 11.5   What is a finally clause?

SR 11.6   What output is produced by the following code fragment under each of the stated conditions?

```
try
{
    review.question();
}
catch (Exception1 exception)
{
    System.out.println ("one caught");
}
catch (Exception2 exception)
{
    System.out.println ("two caught");
}
finally
{
    System.out.println ("finally");
}
System.out.println ("the end");
```

a. No exception is thrown by the review.question() method.

    b. An `Exception1` exception is thrown by the `review.question()` method.

    c. An `Exception2` exception is thrown by the `review.question()` method.

    d. An `Exception3` exception is thrown by the `review.question()` method.

11.4 Exception Propagation

If an exception is not caught and handled where it occurs, control is immediately returned to the method that invoked the method that produced the exception. We can design our software so that the exception is caught and handled at this outer level. If it isn't caught there, control returns to the method that called it. This process is called *propagating the exception*. This propagation continues until the exception is caught and handled or until it is passed out of the `main` method, which terminates the program and produces an exception message. To catch an exception at an outer level, the method that produces the exception must be invoked inside a `try` block that has `catch` clauses to handle it.

> **KEY CONCEPT**
>
> If an exception is not caught and handled where it occurs, it is propagated to the calling method.

The `Propagation` program shown in Listing 11.3 succinctly demonstrates the process of exception propagation. The `main` method invokes method `level1` in the `ExceptionScope` class (see Listing 11.4), which invokes `level2`, which invokes `level3`, which produces an exception. Method `level3` does not catch and handle the exception, so control is transferred back to `level2`. The `level2` method does not catch and handle the exception either, so control is transferred back to `level1`. Because the invocation of `level2` is made inside a `try` block (in method `level1`), the exception is caught and handled at that point.

Note that the output does not include the messages indicating that the methods `level3` and `level2` are ending. These `println` statements are never executed, because an exception occurred and had not yet been caught. However, after method `level1` handles the exception, processing continues normally from that point, printing the messages indicating that method `level1` and the program are ending.

VideoNote

Proper exception handling.

Note also that the `catch` clause that handles the exception uses the `getMessage` and `printStackTrace` methods to output that information. The stack trace shows the methods that were called when the exception occurred.

LISTING 11.3

```
//********************************************************************
//  Propagation.java       Author: Lewis/Loftus
//
//  Demonstrates exception propagation.
//********************************************************************

public class Propagation
{
   //-----------------------------------------------------------------
   // Invokes the level1 method to begin the exception demonstration.
   //-----------------------------------------------------------------
   public static void main (String[] args)
   {
      ExceptionScope demo = new ExceptionScope();

      System.out.println("Program beginning.");
      demo.level1();
      System.out.println("Program ending.");
   }
}
```

OUTPUT

```
Program beginning.
Level 1 beginning.
Level 2 beginning.
Level 3 beginning.

The exception message is: / by zero

The call stack trace:
java.lang.ArithmeticException: / by zero
        at ExceptionScope.level3(ExceptionScope.java:54)
        at ExceptionScope.level2(ExceptionScope.java:41)
        at ExceptionScope.level1(ExceptionScope.java:18)
        at Propagation.main(Propagation.java:17)

Level 1 ending.
Program ending.
```

LISTING 11.4

```java
//********************************************************************
//  ExceptionScope.java        Author: Lewis/Loftus
//
//  Demonstrates exception propagation.
//********************************************************************

public class ExceptionScope
{
   //-----------------------------------------------------------------
   // Catches and handles the exception that is thrown in level3.
   //-----------------------------------------------------------------
   public void level1()
   {
      System.out.println("Level 1 beginning.");

      try
      {
         level2();
      }
      catch (ArithmeticException problem)
      {
         System.out.println ();
         System.out.println ("The exception message is: " +
                             problem.getMessage());
         System.out.println ();
         System.out.println ("The call stack trace:");
         problem.printStackTrace();
         System.out.println ();
      }

      System.out.println("Level 1 ending.");
   }

   //-----------------------------------------------------------------
   //  Serves as an intermediate level. The exception propagates
   //  through this method back to level1.
   //-----------------------------------------------------------------
   public void level2()
   {
      System.out.println("Level 2 beginning.");
      level3 ();
      System.out.println("Level 2 ending.");
   }
```

LISTING 11.4   *continued*

```
//-----------------------------------------------------------------
// Performs a calculation to produce an exception. It is not
// caught and handled at this level.
//-----------------------------------------------------------------
public void level3 ()
{
    int numerator = 10, denominator = 0;

    System.out.println("Level 3 beginning.");
    int result = numerator / denominator;
    System.out.println("Level 3 ending.");
}
}
```

KEY CONCEPT

A programmer must carefully consider how and where exceptions should be handled, if at all.

A programmer must pick the most appropriate level at which to catch and handle an exception. There is no single best answer as to how to do this. It depends on the situation and the design of the system. Sometimes the right approach will be not to catch an exception at all and let the program terminate.

myprogramming**lab**

SELF-REVIEW QUESTIONS *(see answers in Appendix N)*

SR 11.7   What happens if an exception is not caught?

SR 11.8   How would the result of the Propagation program change if the following code fragment was placed in the level2 method just before the call to the level3 method?

```
int num = 10, den = 0;
int res = num / den;
```

SR 11.9   How would the result of the Propagation program change if the following code fragment was placed in the level2 method just after the call to the level3 method?

```
int num = 10, den = 0;
int res = num / den;
```

11.5 The Exception Class Hierarchy

The classes that define various exceptions are related by inheritance, creating a class hierarchy that is shown in part in Figure 11.1

The Throwable class is the parent of both the Error class and the Exception class. Many types of exceptions are derived from the Exception class, and these classes also have many children. Though these high-level classes are defined in the java.lang package, many child classes that define specific exceptions are part of several other packages. Inheritance relationships can span package boundaries.

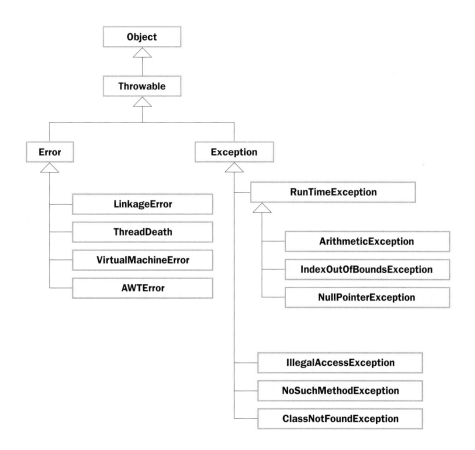

FIGURE 11.1   Part of the Error and Exception class hierarchy

We can define our own exceptions by deriving a new class from Exception or one of its descendants. The class we choose as the parent depends on what situation or condition the new exception represents.

> **KEY CONCEPT**
>
> A new exception is defined by deriving a new class from the Exception class or one of its descendants.

The program in Listing 11.5 instantiates an exception object and throws it. The exception is created from the OutOfRangeException class, which is shown in Listing 11.6. Note that this exception is not part of the Java standard class library. It was created to represent the situation in which a value is outside a particular valid range.

LISTING 11.5

```java
//********************************************************************
//  CreatingExceptions.java       Author: Lewis/Loftus
//
//  Demonstrates the ability to define an exception via inheritance.
//********************************************************************

import java.util.Scanner;

public class CreatingExceptions
{
    //-----------------------------------------------------------------
    // Creates an exception object and possibly throws it.
    //-----------------------------------------------------------------
    public static void main (String[] args) throws OutOfRangeException
    {
        final int MIN = 25, MAX = 40;

        Scanner scan = new Scanner (System.in);

        OutOfRangeException problem =
            new OutOfRangeException ("Input value is out of range.");

        System.out.print ("Enter an integer value between " + MIN +
                          " and " + MAX + ", inclusive: ");
        int value = scan.nextInt();

        //  Determine if the exception should be thrown
        if (value < MIN || value > MAX)
            throw problem;

        System.out.println ("End of main method.");   // may never reach
    }
}
```

LISTING 11.5   *continued*

OUTPUT

```
Enter an integer value between 25 and 40, inclusive: 69
Exception in thread "main" OutOfRangeException:
    Input value is out of range.
    at CreatingExceptions.main(CreatingExceptions.java:20)
```

After reading in an input value, the main method evaluates it to see whether it is in the valid range. If not, the *throw statement* is executed. A throw statement is used to begin exception propagation. Because the main method does not catch and handle the exception, the program will terminate if the exception is thrown, printing the message associated with the exception.

We create the OutOfRangeException class by extending the Exception class. Often, a new exception is nothing more than what you see in this example:

LISTING 11.6

```java
//********************************************************************
//  OutOfRangeException.java       Author: Lewis/Loftus
//
//  Represents an exceptional condition in which a value is out of
//  some particular range.
//********************************************************************

public class OutOfRangeException extends Exception
{
   //-----------------------------------------------------------------
   // Sets up the exception object with a particular message.
   //-----------------------------------------------------------------
   OutOfRangeException (String message)
   {
      super (message);
   }
}
```

an extension of some existing exception class that stores a particular message describing the situation it represents. The important point is that the class is ultimately a descendant of the Exception class and the Throwable class, which gives it the ability to be thrown using a throw statement.

The type of situation handled by this program, in which a value is out of range, does not need to be represented as an exception. We've previously handled such situations using conditionals or loops. Whether you handle a situation using an exception or whether you take care of it in the normal flow of your program is an important design decision.

Checked and Unchecked Exceptions

Some exceptions are checked, whereas others are unchecked. A *checked exception* must either be caught by a method or it must be listed in the *throws clause* of any method that may throw or propagate it. A throws clause is appended to the header of a method definition to formally acknowledge that the method will throw or propagate a particular exception if it occurs. An *unchecked exception* requires no throws clause.

> **KEY CONCEPT**
>
> The throws clause on a method header must be included for checked exceptions that are not caught and handled in the method.

The only unchecked exceptions in Java are objects of type RuntimeException or any of its descendants. All other exceptions are considered checked exceptions. The main method of the CreatingExceptions program has a throws clause, indicating that it may throw an OutOfRangeException. This throws clause is required because the OutOfRangeException was derived from the Exception class, making it a checked exception.

myprogramminglab

SELF-REVIEW QUESTIONS *(see answers in Appendix N)*

SR 11.10 What is a checked exception?

SR 11.11 True or False? Explain.

> a. An ArithmeticException is an Exception.
> b. An ArithmeticException is Throwable.
> c. An ArithmeticException is a checked exception.
> d. A NoSuchMethodException is a checked exception.
> e. We can create our own exceptions by extending the Exception class.
> f. A throws clause must be appended to the header of a method definition if the method may potentially throw an ArithmeticException.

SR 11.12 What happens if the input to the CreatingExceptions program is 42? What if it is –3?

11.6 I/O Exceptions

Processing input and output is a task that often produces unforeseeable situations, leading to exceptions being thrown. Let's explore some I/O issues and the problems that may arise.

A *stream* is an ordered sequence of bytes. The term stream comes from the analogy that as we read and write information, the data flows from a source to a destination (or *sink*) as water flows down a stream. The source of the information is like a spring filling the stream, and the destination is like a cave into which the stream flows.

In a program, we treat a stream as either an *input stream*, from which we read information, or as an *output stream*, to which we write information. That is, a program serves either as the spring filling the stream or as the cave receiving the stream. A program can deal with multiple input and output streams at one time. A particular store of data, such as a file, can serve either as an input stream or as an output stream to a program, but it generally cannot be both at the same time.

There are three streams that are referred to as the *standard I/O streams*. They are listed in Figure 11.2. The System class contains three object reference variables (in, out, and err) that represent the three standard I/O streams. These references are declared as both public and static, which allows them to be accessed directly through the System class.

We've been using the standard output stream, with calls to System.out. println for instance, in examples throughout this book. We've also used the standard input stream to create a Scanner object when we want to process input read interactively from the user. The Scanner class manages the input read from the standard input stream in various ways that makes our programming tasks easier. It also processes various I/O exceptions internally, creating an InputMismatchException when needed.

The standard I/O streams, by default, represent particular I/O devices. System.in typically represents keyboard input, whereas System.out and System.err typi-

Standard I/O Stream	Description
System.in	Standard input stream.
System.out	Standard output stream.
System.err	Standard error stream (output for error messages)

FIGURE 11.2 Standard I/O streams

cally represent a particular window on the monitor screen. The System.out and System.err streams write output to the same window by default (usually the one in which the program was executed), though they could be set up to write to different places. The System.err stream is usually where error messages are sent.

In addition to the standard input streams, the java.io package of the Java standard class library provides many classes that let us define streams with particular characteristics. Some of the classes deal with files, others with memory, and others with strings. Some classes assume that the data they handle consists of characters, whereas others assume the data consists of raw bytes of binary information. Some classes provide the means to manipulate the data in the stream in some way, such as buffering the information or numbering it. By combining classes in appropriate ways, we can create objects that represent a stream of information that has the exact characteristics we want for a particular situation.

> **KEY CONCEPT**
>
> The Java class library contains many classes for defining I/O streams with various characteristics.

The broad topic of Java I/O, along with the sheer number of classes in the java.io package, prohibits us from covering it in detail in this book. Our focus for the moment is on I/O exceptions.

Many operations performed by I/O classes can potentially throw an IOException. The IOException class is the parent of several exception classes that represent problems when trying to perform I/O.

An IOException is a checked exception. As described earlier in this chapter, that means that either the exception must be caught, or all methods that propagate it must list it in a throws clause of the method header.

Because I/O often deals with external resources, many problems can arise in programs that attempt to perform I/O operations. For example, a file from which we want to read might not exist; when we attempt to open the file, an exception will be thrown, because that file can't be found. In general, we should try to design programs to be as robust as possible when dealing with potential problems.

We've seen in previous examples how we can use the Scanner class to read and process input read from a text file. Now let's explore an example that writes data to a text output file. Writing output to a text file requires simply that we use the appropriate classes to create the output stream, then call the appropriate methods to write the data.

Suppose we want to test a program we are writing, but don't have the real data available. We could write a program that generates a test data file that contains random values. The program shown in Listing 11.7 generates a file that contains random integer values within a particular range. It also writes one line of standard output, confirming that the data file has been written.

LISTING 11.7

```java
//********************************************************************
//  TestData.java       Author: Lewis/Loftus
//
//  Demonstrates I/O exceptions and the use of a character file
//  output stream.
//********************************************************************

import java.util.Random;
import java.io.*;

public class TestData
{
   //-----------------------------------------------------------------
   //  Creates a file of test data that consists of ten lines each
   //  containing ten integer values in the range 10 to 99.
   //-----------------------------------------------------------------
   public static void main (String[] args) throws IOException
   {
      final int MAX = 10;

      int value;
      String file = "test.dat";

      Random rand = new Random();

      FileWriter fw = new FileWriter (file);
      BufferedWriter bw = new BufferedWriter (fw);
      PrintWriter outFile = new PrintWriter (bw);

      for (int line=1; line <= MAX; line++)
      {
         for (int num=1; num <= MAX; num++)
         {
            value = rand.nextInt (90) + 10;
            outFile.print (value + "  ");
         }
         outFile.println ();
      }
```

LISTING 11.7 *continued*

```
        outFile.close();
        System.out.println ("Output file has been created: " + file);
    }
}
```

OUTPUT

```
Output file has been created: test.dat
```

The FileWriter class represents a text output file, but has minimal method support for manipulating data. The PrintWriter class provides print and println methods similar to the standard I/O PrintStream class.

The data that is contained in the file test.dat after the TestData program is run might look like this:

```
85  90  93  15  82  79  52  71  70  98
74  57  41  66  22  16  67  65  24  84
86  61  91  79  18  81  64  41  68  81
98  47  28  40  69  10  85  82  64  41
23  61  27  10  59  89  88  26  24  76
33  89  73  36  54  91  42  73  95  58
19  41  18  14  63  80  96  30  17  28
24  37  40  64  94  23  98  10  78  50
89  28  64  54  59  23  61  15  80  88
51  28  44  48  73  21  41  52  35  38
```

Although we do not need to do so for the program to work, we have added a layer in the file stream configuration to include a BufferedWriter. This addition simply gives the output stream buffering capabilities, which makes the processing more efficient. While buffering is not crucial in this situation, it is usually a good idea when writing text files.

Note that in the TestData program, we have eliminated explicit exception handling. That is, if something goes wrong, we simply allow the program to terminate instead of specifically catching and handling the problem. Because all IOExceptions are checked exceptions, we must include the throws clause on the method header to indicate that they may be thrown. For each program, we must carefully consider how best to handle the exceptions that may be thrown. This requirement is especially important when dealing with I/O, which is fraught with potential problems that cannot always be foreseen.

The TestData program uses nested for loops to compute random values and write them to the output file. After all values are printed, the file is closed. Output files must be closed explicitly to ensure that the data is retained. In general, it is good practice to close all file streams explicitly when they are no longer needed.

SELF-REVIEW QUESTIONS *(see answers in Appendix N)*

SR 11.13   What is a stream?

SR 11.14   What are the standard I/O streams?

SR 11.15   What Stream class object have we been using explicitly throughout this book?

SR 11.16   An I/O exception, the InputMismatchException, will occur during the main method of the CreatingExceptions program (see Listing 11.5) if the user enters an alphabetic character. Why doesn't the main method definition include a throws InputMismatchException clause?

SR 11.17   An I/O exception, the FileNotFoundException, will occur during the main method of the TestData program if the test.dat is not writable. Why doesn't the main method definition include a throws FileNotFoundException clause?

SR 11.18   What happens if the PrintWriter constructor of the TestDate class is passed the fw object instead of the bw object?

11.7 Tool Tips and Mnemonics

Let's take a look at a some special features that can be used with any Swing component. Appropriate application of these features can enhance the user interface and facilitate the use of the components. This section describes the use of tool tips and mnemonics, as well as the ability to disable components, then explores an example that uses these features.

Any Swing component can be assigned a *tool tip*, which is a short line of text that will appear when the cursor is rested momentarily on top of the component. Tool tips are usually used to inform the user about the component, such as the purpose of a button.

> **KEY CONCEPT**
>
> Tool tips and mnemonics can enhance the functionality of a graphical user interface.

A tool tip can be assigned using the setToolTipText method of a Swing component. For example:

```
JButton button = new JButton ("Compute");
button.setToolTipText ("Calculates the area under the curve.");
```

When the button is added to a container and displayed, it appears normally. When the user rolls the mouse pointer over the button, hovering there momentarily, the tool tip text pops up. When the user moves the mouse pointer off of the button, the tool tip text disappears.

A *mnemonic* is a character that allows the user to push a button or make a menu choice using the keyboard in addition to the mouse. For example, when a mnemonic has been defined for a button, the user can hold down the ALT key and press the mnemonic character to activate the button. Using a mnemonic to activate the button causes the system to behave just as it would if the user had used the mouse to press the button.

A mnemonic character should be chosen from the label on a button or menu item. Once the mnemonic has been established using the setMnemonic method, the character in the label will be underlined to indicate that it can be used as a shortcut. If a letter is chosen that is not in the label, nothing will be underlined and the user won't know how to use the shortcut. You can set a mnemonic as follows:

```
JButton button = new JButton ("Calculate");
button.setMnemonic ('C');
```

When the button is displayed, the letter C in Calculate is underlined on the button label. When the user presses ALT-C, the button is activated as if the user had pressed it with the mouse.

Some components can be *disabled* if they should not be used. A disabled component will appear "grayed out," and nothing will happen if the user attempts to interact with it. To disable and enable components, we invoke the setEnabled method of the component, passing it a boolean value to indicate whether the component should be disabled (false) or enabled (true). For example:

```
JButton button = new JButton ("Do It");
button.setEnabled (false);
```

Disabling components is a good idea when users should not be allowed to use the functionality of a component. The grayed appearance of the disabled component is an indication that using the component is inappropriate (and, in fact, impossible) at the current time. Disabled components not only convey to the user which actions are appropriate and which aren't, they also prevent erroneous situations from occurring.

> **KEY CONCEPT**
> Components should be disabled when their use is inappropriate.

Let's look at an example that uses tool tips, mnemonics, and disabled components. The program in Listing 11.8 presents the image of a light bulb and provides a button to turn the light bulb on and a button to turn the light bulb off.

There are actually two images of the light bulb: one showing it turned on and one showing it turned off. These images are brought in as `ImageIcon` objects. The `setIcon` method of the label that displays the image is used to set the appropriate image, depending on the current status. This processing is controlled in the `LightBulbPanel` class shown in Listing 11.9.

LISTING 11.8

```java
//************************************************************
//  LightBulb.java        Author: Lewis/Loftus
//
//  Demonstrates mnemonics and tool tips.
//************************************************************

import javax.swing.*;
import java.awt.*;

public class LightBulb
{
    //----------------------------------------------------------
    //  Sets up a frame that displays a light bulb image that can be
    //  turned on and off.
    //----------------------------------------------------------
    public static void main (String[] args)
    {
        JFrame frame = new JFrame ("Light Bulb");
        frame.setDefaultCloseOperation (JFrame.EXIT_ON_CLOSE);

        LightBulbPanel bulb = new LightBulbPanel();
        LightBulbControls controls = new LightBulbControls (bulb);

        JPanel panel = new JPanel();
        panel.setBackground (Color.black);
        panel.setLayout (new BoxLayout(panel, BoxLayout.Y_AXIS));
        panel.add (Box.createRigidArea (new Dimension (0, 20)));
        panel.add (bulb);
        panel.add (Box.createRigidArea (new Dimension (0, 10)));
        panel.add (controls);
        panel.add (Box.createRigidArea (new Dimension (0, 10)));

        frame.getContentPane().add(panel);
        frame.pack();
        frame.setVisible(true);
    }
}
```

LISTING 11.8 *continued*

DISPLAY

LISTING 11.9

```
//********************************************************************
//  LightBulbPanel.java          Author: Lewis/Loftus
//
//  Represents the image for the LightBulb program.
//********************************************************************

import javax.swing.*;
import java.awt.*;

public class LightBulbPanel extends JPanel
{
    private boolean on;
    private ImageIcon lightOn, lightOff;
    private JLabel imageLabel;

    //-----------------------------------------------------------------
    //  Constructor: Sets up the images and the initial state.
    //-----------------------------------------------------------------
```

LISTING 11.9   *continued*

```java
public LightBulbPanel()
{
    lightOn = new ImageIcon ("lightBulbOn.gif");
    lightOff = new ImageIcon ("lightBulbOff.gif");

    setBackground (Color.black);

    on = true;
    imageLabel = new JLabel (lightOff);
    add (imageLabel);
}

//------------------------------------------------------------
//  Paints the panel using the appropriate image.
//------------------------------------------------------------
public void paintComponent (Graphics page)
{
    super.paintComponent(page);

    if (on)
        imageLabel.setIcon (lightOn);
    else
        imageLabel.setIcon (lightOff);
}

//------------------------------------------------------------
//  Sets the status of the light bulb.
//------------------------------------------------------------
public void setOn (boolean lightBulbOn)
{
    on = lightBulbOn;
}
}
```

The LightBulbControls class shown in Listing 11.10 is a panel that contains the on and off buttons. Both of these buttons have tool tips assigned to them, and both use mnemonics. Also, when one of the buttons is enabled, the other is disabled, and vice versa. When the light bulb is on, there is no reason for the On button to be enabled. Likewise, when the light bulb is off, there is no reason for the Off button to be enabled.

VideoNote

Exploring GUI design details.

LISTING 11.10

```java
//********************************************************************
//  LightBulbControls.java        Author: Lewis/Loftus
//
//  Represents the control panel for the LightBulb program.
//********************************************************************

import javax.swing.*;
import java.awt.*;
import java.awt.event.*;

public class LightBulbControls extends JPanel
{
    private LightBulbPanel bulb;
    private JButton onButton, offButton;

    //-----------------------------------------------------------------
    //  Sets up the lightbulb control panel.
    //-----------------------------------------------------------------
    public LightBulbControls (LightBulbPanel bulbPanel)
    {
        bulb = bulbPanel;

        onButton = new JButton ("On");
        onButton.setEnabled (false);
        onButton.setMnemonic ('n');
        onButton.setToolTipText ("Turn it on!");
        onButton.addActionListener (new OnListener());

        offButton = new JButton ("Off");
        offButton.setEnabled (true);
        offButton.setMnemonic ('f');
        offButton.setToolTipText ("Turn it off!");
        offButton.addActionListener (new OffListener());

        setBackground (Color.black);
        add (onButton);
        add (offButton);
    }

    //********************************************************************
    // Represents the listener for the On button.
    //********************************************************************
    private class OnListener implements ActionListener
    {
```

LISTING 11.10   *continued*

```java
      //-----------------------------------------------------------
      // Turns the bulb on and repaints the bulb panel.
      //-----------------------------------------------------------
      public void actionPerformed (ActionEvent event)
      {
         bulb.setOn (true);
         onButton.setEnabled (false);
         offButton.setEnabled (true);
         bulb.repaint();
      }
   }

   //*************************************************************
   //  Represents the listener for the Off button.
   //*************************************************************
   private class OffListener implements ActionListener
   {
      //-----------------------------------------------------------
      // Turns the bulb off and repaints the bulb panel.
      //-----------------------------------------------------------
      public void actionPerformed (ActionEvent event)
      {
         bulb.setOn (false);
         onButton.setEnabled (true);
         offButton.setEnabled (false);
         bulb.repaint();
      }
   }
}
```

Each button has its own listener class. The `actionPerformed` method of each sets the bulb's status, toggles the enabled state of both buttons, and causes the panel with the image to repaint itself.

Note that the mnemonic characters used for each button are underlined in the display. When you run the program, note that the tool tips automatically include an indication of the mnemonic that can be used for the button.

SELF-REVIEW QUESTIONS *(see answers in Appendix N)*   myprogramminglab

SR 11.19   What is a tool tip?

SR 11.20   What is a mnemonic and how is it used?

SR 11.21   Why might you want to disable a component?

SR 11.22 Identify the class(es) and the line(s) of code from the class(es) that provide each of the following for the Lightbulb program.

a. The background is black.
b. The message "Turn it off!" appears when you put the mouse over the off button.
c. An off bulb will turn on if the user enters ALT-n.
d. The on button is grayed out when the bulb is turned on.
e. Originally the bulb is on.

11.8 Combo Boxes

A *combo box* allows the user to select one of several options from a "drop down" menu. When the user presses a combo box using the mouse, a list of options is displayed from which the user can choose. The current choice is displayed in the combo box. A combo box is defined by the JComboBox class.

A combo box can be either *editable* or *uneditable*. By default, a combo box is uneditable. Changing the value of an uneditable combo box can be accomplished only by selecting an item from the list. If the combo box is editable, however, the user can change the value either by selecting an item from the list or by typing a particular value into the combo box area.

The options in a combo box list can be established in one of two ways. We can create an array of strings and pass it into the constructor of the JComboBox class. Alternatively, we can use the addItem method to add an item to the combo box after it has been created. A JComboBox can also display ImageIcon objects as options as well.

The JukeBox program shown in Listing 11.11 demonstrates the use of a combo box. The user chooses a song to play using the combo box and then presses the Play button to begin playing the song. The Stop button can be pressed at any time to stop the song. Selecting a new song while one is playing also stops the current song.

The JukeBoxControls class shown in Listing 11.12 is a panel that contains the components that make up the jukebox GUI. The constructor of the class also loads the audio clips that will be played. An audio clip is obtained first by creating a URL object that corresponds to the wav or au file that defines the clip. The first two parameters to the URL constructor should be "file" and "localhost", respectively, if the audio clip is stored on the same machine on which the program is executing. Creating URL objects can potentially throw a checked exception; therefore they are created in a try block. However, this program assumes the audio clips will be loaded successfully and therefore does nothing if an exception is thrown.

LISTING 11.11

```java
//********************************************************************
//  JukeBox.java        Author: Lewis/Loftus
//
//  Demonstrates the use of a combo box.
//********************************************************************

import javax.swing.*;

public class JukeBox
{
   //-----------------------------------------------------------------
   //  Creates and displays the controls for a juke box.
   //-----------------------------------------------------------------
   public static void main (String[] args)
   {
      JFrame frame = new JFrame ("Java Juke Box");
      frame.setDefaultCloseOperation (JFrame.EXIT_ON_CLOSE);

      JukeBoxControls controlPanel = new JukeBoxControls();

      frame.getContentPane().add(controlPanel);
      frame.pack();
      frame.setVisible(true);
   }
}
```

DISPLAY

Once created, the URL objects are used to create AudioClip objects using the static newAudioClip method of the JApplet class. The audio clips are stored in an array. The first entry in the array, at index 0, is set to null. This entry corresponds to the initial combo box option, which simply encourages the user to make a selection.

LISTING 11.12

```java
//********************************************************************
//  JukeBoxControls.java        Author: Lewis and Loftus
//
//  Represents the control panel for the juke box.
//********************************************************************

import java.awt.*;
import java.awt.event.*;
import javax.swing.*;
import java.applet.AudioClip;
import java.net.URL;

public class JukeBoxControls extends JPanel
{
   private JComboBox musicCombo;
   private JButton stopButton, playButton;
   private AudioClip[] music;
   private AudioClip current;

   //-----------------------------------------------------------------
   //  Sets up the GUI for the juke box.
   //-----------------------------------------------------------------
   public JukeBoxControls()
   {
      URL url1, url2, url3, url4, url5, url6;
      url1 = url2 = url3 = url4 = url5 = url6 = null;

      // Obtain and store the audio clips to play
      try
      {
         url1 = new URL ("file", "localhost", "westernBeat.wav");
         url2 = new URL ("file", "localhost", "classical.wav");
         url3 = new URL ("file", "localhost", "jeopardy.au");
         url4 = new URL ("file", "localhost", "newAgeRythm.wav");
         url5 = new URL ("file", "localhost", "eightiesJam.wav");
         url6 = new URL ("file", "localhost", "hitchcock.wav");
      }
      catch (Exception exception) {}

      music = new AudioClip[7];
      music[0] = null;  // Corresponds to "Make a Selection..."
      music[1] = JApplet.newAudioClip (url1);
      music[2] = JApplet.newAudioClip (url2);
      music[3] = JApplet.newAudioClip (url3);
```

LISTING 11.12   *continued*

```
music[4] = JApplet.newAudioClip (url4);
music[5] = JApplet.newAudioClip (url5);
music[6] = JApplet.newAudioClip (url6);

JLabel titleLabel = new JLabel ("Java Juke Box");
titleLabel.setAlignmentX (Component.CENTER_ALIGNMENT);

// Create the list of strings for the combo box options
String[] musicNames = {"Make A Selection...", "Western Beat",
        "Classical Melody", "Jeopardy Theme", "New Age Rythm",
        "Eighties Jam", "Alfred Hitchcock's Theme"};

musicCombo = new JComboBox (musicNames);
musicCombo.setAlignmentX (Component.CENTER_ALIGNMENT);

// Set up the buttons
playButton = new JButton ("Play", new ImageIcon ("play.gif"));
playButton.setBackground (Color.white);
playButton.setMnemonic ('p');
stopButton = new JButton ("Stop", new ImageIcon ("stop.gif"));
stopButton.setBackground (Color.white);
stopButton.setMnemonic ('s');

JPanel buttons = new JPanel();
buttons.setLayout (new BoxLayout (buttons, BoxLayout.X_AXIS));
buttons.add (playButton);
buttons.add (Box.createRigidArea (new Dimension(5,0)));
buttons.add (stopButton);
buttons.setBackground (Color.cyan);

// Set up this panel
setPreferredSize (new Dimension (300, 100));
setBackground (Color.cyan);
setLayout (new BoxLayout (this, BoxLayout.Y_AXIS));
add (Box.createRigidArea (new Dimension(0,5)));
add (titleLabel);
add (Box.createRigidArea (new Dimension(0,5)));
add (musicCombo);
add (Box.createRigidArea (new Dimension(0,5)));
add (buttons);
add (Box.createRigidArea (new Dimension(0,5)));

musicCombo.addActionListener (new ComboListener());
stopButton.addActionListener (new ButtonListener());
```

LISTING 11.12   *continued*

```
      playButton.addActionListener (new ButtonListener());

      current = null;
   }

   //***********************************************************************
   //  Represents the action listener for the combo box.
   //***********************************************************************
   private class ComboListener implements ActionListener
   {
      //--------------------------------------------------------------
      //  Stops playing the current selection (if any) and resets
      //  the current selection to the one chosen.
      //--------------------------------------------------------------
      public void actionPerformed (ActionEvent event)
      {
         if (current != null)
            current.stop();

         current = music[musicCombo.getSelectedIndex()];
      }
   }

   //***********************************************************************
   //  Represents the action listener for both control buttons.
   //***********************************************************************
   private class ButtonListener implements ActionListener
   {
      //--------------------------------------------------------------
      //  Stops the current selection (if any) in either case. If
      //  the play button was pressed, start playing it again.
      //--------------------------------------------------------------
      public void actionPerformed (ActionEvent event)
      {
         if (current != null)
            current.stop();

         if (event.getSource() == playButton)
            if (current != null)
               current.play();
      }
   }
}
```

The list of songs that is displayed in the combo box is defined in an array of strings. The first entry of the array will appear in the combo box by default and is often used to direct the user. We must take care that the rest of the program does not try to use that option as a valid song.

The play and stop buttons are displayed with both a text label and an image icon. They are also given mnemonics so that the jukebox can be controlled partially from the keyboard.

A combo box generates an action event whenever the user makes a selection from it. The JukeBox program uses one action listener class for the combo box and another for both of the push buttons. They could have been combined, using code to distinguish which component fired the event.

The actionPerformed method of the ComboListener class is executed when a selection is made from the combo box. The current audio selection that is playing, if any, is stopped. The current clip is then updated to reflect the new selection. Note that the audio clip is not immediately played at that point. The way this program is designed, the user must press the play button to hear the new selection.

The actionPerformed method of the ButtonListener class is executed when either of the buttons is pushed. The current audio selection that is playing, if any, is stopped. If it was the stop button that was pressed, the task is complete. If the play button was pressed, the current audio selection is played again from the beginning.

SELF-REVIEW QUESTIONS (see answers in Appendix N)

SR 11.23   What is a combo box?

SR 11.24   How does the JukeBox program ensure that it doesn't try to play
           a song associated with the "Make a Selection. . ." combo box
           option?

SR 11.25   How many action listeners are defined in the JukeBox program, and
           what do they each listen for?

SR 11.26   Describe in detail how the JukeBox program associates the combo
           box selection made by the user with a specific audio clip.

11.9 Scroll Panes

Sometimes we need to deal with images or information that is too large to fit in a reasonable area. A *scroll pane* is often helpful in these situations. A scroll pane is a container that offers a limited view of a component, and provides vertical or horizontal scroll bars to change that view. At any point, only part of the underlying component can be seen, but the scroll bars allow the user to navigate to any part of the component. Scroll bars are useful when space within a GUI is limited or when the component being viewed is large or can change in size dynamically.

The program in Listing 11.13 presents a frame that contains a single scroll pane. The scroll pane is used to view an image of a fairly large subway map for Philadelphia and the surrounding areas. The image is put into a label, and the label is added to the scroll pane using the JScrollPane constructor.

LISTING 11.13

```java
//********************************************************************
//  TransitMap.java         Author: Lewis/Loftus
//
//  Demonstrates the use of a scroll pane.
//********************************************************************

import java.awt.*;
import javax.swing.*;

public class TransitMap
{
   //-----------------------------------------------------------------
   //  Presents a frame containing a scroll pane used to view a large
   //  map of the Philadelphia subway system.
   //-----------------------------------------------------------------
   public static void main (String[] args)
   {
      // SEPTA = SouthEast Pennsylvania Transit Authority
      JFrame frame = new JFrame ("SEPTA Transit Map");

      frame.setDefaultCloseOperation (JFrame.EXIT_ON_CLOSE);

      ImageIcon image = new ImageIcon ("septa.jpg");
      JLabel imageLabel = new JLabel (image);

      JScrollPane sp = new JScrollPane (imageLabel);
      sp.setPreferredSize (new Dimension (450, 400));
      frame.getContentPane().add (sp);
      frame.pack();
      frame.setVisible(true);
   }
}
```

LISTING 11.13   *continued*

DISPLAY

A scroll pane can have a vertical scroll bar on the right of the container as well as a horizontal scroll bar at the bottom of the container. For each of these, the programmer can specify that the scroll bars are always used, never used, or used as needed to view the underlying component. By default, both the vertical and horizontal scroll bars are used as needed. The TransitMap program relies on these defaults, and both scroll bars appear because the image is too large in both height and width.

To move a scroll bar, the user can click on and drag the box, called the *knob*, in the scroll bar that indicates its current location (in that dimension: up/down or right/left). Alternatively, the user can click in the bar to the right or left of the knob, or on the arrows at either end of the scroll bar, to adjust the location. The programmer can determine how much each of these actions changes the viewing area.

Note that no event listeners need to be set up to use a scroll pane in this manner. A scroll pane responds automatically to the adjustments of its scroll bars.

myprogramminglab

SELF-REVIEW QUESTIONS *(see answers in Appendix N)*

SR 11.27 Describe the use of scroll bars on a scroll pane.

SR 11.28 What happens if you change the first parameter passed to the `Dimension` constructor within the `TransitMap` program to 1000? Explain.

11.10 Split Panes

A *split pane* is a container that displays two components separated by a moveable divider bar. Depending on how the split pane is set up, the two components are displayed either side by side or one on top of the other, as shown in Figure 11.3. In Java, we can create a split pane using the `JSplitPane` class.

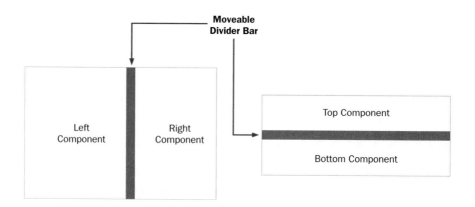

FIGURE 11.3   The configurations of a split pane

The orientation of a split pane is set using constants in the JSplitPane class and can be set when the container is created or explicitly later on. The constant HORIZONTAL_SPLIT specifies that the components be displayed side by side. In contrast, VERTICAL_SPLIT specifies that the components be displayed one on top of the other.

> **KEY CONCEPT**
>
> A split pane displays two components side by side or one on top of the other.

The location of the divider bar determines how much visible area is devoted to each component in the split pane. The divider bar can be dragged across the container area using the mouse. As it moves, the visible space is increased for one component and decreased for the other. The total space allotted for both components changes only if the size of the entire split pane changes.

A JSplitPane respects the minimum size set for the components it displays. Therefore, the divider bar may not allow a section to be reduced in size beyond a particular point. To adjust this aspect, the minimum sizes of the components displayed can be changed.

The divider bar of a JSplitPane object can be set so that it can be expanded, one direction or the other, with one click of the mouse. By default, the divider bar does not have this feature and can be moved only by dragging it. If this feature is turned on, the divider bar appears with two small arrows pointing in opposite directions. Clicking either of these arrows causes the divider bar to move fully in that direction, maximizing the space allotted to one of the components. This feature is set using the setOneTouchExpandable method, which takes a boolean parameter. The size of the divider bar and the initial location of the divider bar can be set explicitly as well.

Another feature that can be set on a JSplitPane is whether or not the components are continuously adjusted and repainted as the divider bar is being moved. If this feature is not set, the components' layout managers will be consulted only after the divider bar stops moving. This feature is off by default and can be turned on when the JSplitPane object is created or by using the setContinuousLayout method.

Split panes can be nested by putting a split pane into one or both sides of another split pane. For example, we could divide a container into three sections by putting a split pane into the top component of another split pane. There would then be two divider bars, one that separates the total area into two main sections and another that separates one of those sections into two others. How much visible area is shown in each would depend on where the divider bars are placed.

The program shown in Listing 11.14 presents a list of image file names to the user. When one of the file names is selected, the corresponding image is displayed in the right side of the split pane.

The split pane is created in the main method and added to the frame to be displayed. The split pane is oriented, using the HORIZONTAL_SPLIT constant, such that the panel containing the list and the label containing the image to be displayed are side by side. The call to the `setOneTouchExpandable` method causes the divider bar of the split pane to display the arrows that permit the user to expand the panes one way or the other with one click of the mouse.

LISTING 11.14

```java
//********************************************************************
//  PickImage.java        Author: Lewis/Loftus
//
//  Demonstrates the use of a split pane and a list.
//********************************************************************

import java.awt.*;
import javax.swing.*;

public class PickImage
{
    //-----------------------------------------------------------------
    //  Creates and displays a frame containing a split pane. The
    //  user selects an image name from the list to be displayed.
    //-----------------------------------------------------------------
    public static void main (String[] args)
    {
        JFrame frame = new JFrame ("Pick Image");
        frame.setDefaultCloseOperation (JFrame.EXIT_ON_CLOSE);

        JLabel imageLabel = new JLabel();
        JPanel imagePanel = new JPanel();
        imagePanel.add (imageLabel);
        imagePanel.setBackground (Color.white);

        ListPanel imageList = new ListPanel (imageLabel);

        JSplitPane sp = new JSplitPane(JSplitPane.HORIZONTAL_SPLIT,
                                       imageList, imagePanel);

        sp.setOneTouchExpandable (true);

        frame.getContentPane().add (sp);
        frame.pack();
        frame.setVisible(true);
    }
}
```

LISTING 11.14   *continued*

DISPLAY

The `ListPanel` class shown in Listing 11.15 defines the panel that contains the list of file names. We use a *list* component, defined by the `JList` class, to display the list of file names. The list contents are set up as an array of `String` objects, which are passed into the `JList` constructor.

LISTING 11.15

```
//********************************************************************
//  ListPanel.java        Author: Lewis/Loftus
//
//  Represents the list of images for the PickImage program.
//********************************************************************

import java.awt.*;
import javax.swing.*;
import javax.swing.event.*;

public class ListPanel extends JPanel
{
    private JLabel label;
```

LISTING 11.15 *continued*

```java
    private JList list;

    //-----------------------------------------------------------------
    // Loads the list of image names into the list.
    //-----------------------------------------------------------------
    public ListPanel (JLabel imageLabel)
    {
        label = imageLabel;

        String[] fileNames = { "circuit.gif",
                               "duke.gif",
                               "hammock.gif",
                               "justin.jpg",
                               "kayla.jpg",
                               "tiger.jpg",
                               "toucan.gif",
                               "worldmap.gif" };

        list = new JList (fileNames);
        list.addListSelectionListener (new ListListener());
        list.setSelectionMode (ListSelectionModel.SINGLE_SELECTION);

        add (list);
        setBackground (Color.white);
    }

    //*****************************************************************
    //  Represents the listener for the list of images.
    //*****************************************************************
    private class ListListener implements ListSelectionListener
    {
        public void valueChanged (ListSelectionEvent event)
        {
            if (list.isSelectionEmpty())
                label.setIcon (null);
            else
            {
                String fileName = (String)list.getSelectedValue();
                ImageIcon image = new ImageIcon (fileName);
                label.setIcon (image);
            }
        }
    }
}
```

In general, all of the options in a JList component are visible. When the user selects an item using the mouse, it is highlighted. When a new item is selected, the previously selected item is automatically unhighlighted.

The contents of a JList can be specified using an array of objects passed into the constructor. Methods of the JList class are used to manage the list in various ways, including retrieving the currently selected item.

Note the similarities and differences between a combo box (described in Section 11.8) and a JList object. Both allow the user to select an item from a set of choices. However, the choices on a list are always displayed, with the current choice highlighted, whereas a combo box presents its options only when the user presses it with the mouse. The only item displayed all the time in a combo box is the current selection.

A JList object generates a *list selection event* whenever the current selection of the list changes. The ListSelectionListener interface contains one method called valueChanged. In this program, the private inner class called ListListener defines the listener for the list of file names.

The valueChanged method of the listener calls the isSelectionEmpty method of the JList object to determine if there is any value currently selected. If not, the icon of the label is set to null. If so, the file name is obtained using the getSelectedValue method. Then the corresponding image icon is created and displayed in the label.

A JList object can be set so that multiple items can be selected at the same time. The *list selection mode* can be one of three options, as shown in the table in Figure 11.4.

The list selection mode is defined by a ListSelectionModel object. By default, a list allows multiple interval selection. A call to the setSelectionMode method, using a constant defined in the ListSelectionModel class, will explicitly set the list selection mode.

In the PickImage program, we set the list selection mode to single selection because only one image can be displayed at a time. However, even if multiple

List Selection Mode	Description
Single Selection	Only one item can be selected at a time.
Single Interval Selection	Multiple, contiguous items can be selected at a time.
Multiple Interval Selection	Any combination of items can be selected.

FIGURE 11.4   List selection modes

selections were allowed in this program, the getSelectedValue method returns the first item selected, so that would be the image displayed. A similar method called getSelectedValues returns an array of objects representing the items selected when multiple selections are permitted.

Instead of an array of String objects, the JList constructor could be passed an array of ImageIcon objects instead. In that case, the images would be displayed in the list.

SELF-REVIEW QUESTIONS *(see answers in Appendix N)*

SR 11.29 Describe the use of the divider bar on a split pane.

SR 11.30 What is the difference between how a combo box (Section 11.8) is displayed and how a JList object is displayed?

Summary of Key Concepts

- Errors and exceptions are objects that represent unusual or invalid processing.
- The messages printed when an exception is thrown provide a method call stack trace.
- Each `catch` clause handles a particular kind of exception that may be thrown within the `try` block.
- The `finally` clause is executed whether the `try` block is exited normally or because of a thrown exception.
- If an exception is not caught and handled where it occurs, it is propagated to the calling method.
- A programmer must carefully consider how and where exceptions should be handled, if at all.
- A new exception is defined by deriving a new class from the `Exception` class or one of its descendants.
- The `throws` clause on a method header must be included for checked exceptions that are not caught and handled in the method.
- A stream is a sequential sequence of bytes; it can be used as a source of input or a destination for output.
- Three public reference variables in the `System` class represent the standard I/O streams.
- Output file streams should be explicitly closed or they may not correctly retain the data written to them.
- The Java class library contains many classes for defining I/O streams with various characteristics.
- Tool tips and mnemonics can enhance the functionality of a graphical user interface.
- Components should be disabled when their use is inappropriate.
- A combo box provides a drop down menu of options for the user.
- A scroll pane is useful for viewing large objects or large amounts of data.
- A split pane displays two components side by side or one on top of the other.

Exercises

Visit www.myprogramminglab.com to complete many of these Exercises online and get instant feedback.

EX 11.1 What are the two categories of exceptions that arise in Java programs? Differentiate an exception from an error.

EX 11.2 Write code in Java to catch the NumberFormatException, which arises when the given input is not a numeric value.

EX 11.3 How do you avoid a ClassCastException in a Java program? Explain this concept with an example program.

EX 11.4 Look up the following exception classes in the online Java API documentation and describe their purposes:

    a. IllegalAccessException
    b. NegativeArraySizeException
    c. ArrayStoreException
    d. NoSuchMethodException

EX 11.5 When would the finally statement following a try-catch block be executed? Illustrate with an example.

EX 11.6 Draw the containment hierarchy for an application which uses an applet, root pane, panel and text area.

EX 11.7 Draw the containment hierarchy tree for the JukeBox program.

EX 11.8 What effect would removing the call to setSelectionMode in the ListPanel class have? Make the change to test your answer.

Programming Projects

Visit www.myprogramminglab.com to complete many of these Programming Projects online and get instant feedback.

PP 11.1 Design and implement a program that creates an exception class called StringTooLongException, designed to be thrown when a string is discovered that has too many characters in it. In the main driver of the program, read strings from the user until the user enters "DONE". If a string is entered that has too many characters (say 20), throw the exception. Allow the thrown exception to terminate the program.

VideoNote
Developing a solution
of PP 11.1.

PP 11.2 Modify the solution to PP 11.1 such that it catches and handles the exception if it is thrown. Handle the exception by printing an appropriate message, and then continue processing more strings.

PP 11.3 Design and implement a program that creates an exception class called `InvalidDocumentCodeException`, designed to be thrown when an improper designation for a document is encountered during processing. Suppose in a particular business all documents are given a two-character designation starting with either U, C, or P, standing for unclassified, confidential, or proprietary. If a document designation is encountered that doesn't fit that description, the exception is thrown. Create a driver program to test the exception, allowing it to terminate the program.

PP 11.4 Design and implement a program that creates an array index `OutOfRangeException` whenever a formula references an array with an index that is outside the valid boundaries of the array. Handle the exception by printing an appropriate message and continue processing.

PP 11.5 Modify the `DisplayFile` program from Chapter 10 to add a button labeled `Save` above the text area. When the button is pushed, write the contents back out to the file.

PP 11.6 Modify the `JukeBox` program such that it plays a song immediately after it has been selected using the combo box. Combine the two listeners into one.

PP 11.7 Modify the `StyleOptions` program from Chapter 5 so that it uses a split pane. Orient the split pane such that the label is on the top and the style check boxes are in the bottom. Add tool tips to the check boxes to explain their purpose.

PP 11.8 Modify the `PickImage` program so that it presents several additional image options. Display the list within a scroll pane with a vertical scroll bar that is always displayed. Display the image in a scroll pane that uses both horizontal and vertical scroll bars, but only when necessary.

PP 11.9 Design and implement an application that performs flashcard testing of simple mathematical problems. Allow the user to pick the category. Repetitively display a problem and get the user's answer. Indicate whether the user's answer is right or wrong for each problem, and display an ongoing score.

Recursion

12

CHAPTER OBJECTIVES

- Explain the underlying concepts of recursion.
- Explore examples that promote recursive thinking.
- Examine recursive methods and unravel their processing steps.
- Define infinite recursion and discuss ways to avoid it.
- Explain when recursion should and should not be used.
- Demonstrate the use of recursion to solve problems.
- Explore the use of recursion in graphics-based programs.
- Define the concept of a fractal and its relationship to recursion.

Recursion is a powerful programming technique that provides elegant solutions to certain problems. This chapter provides an introduction to recursive processing. It contains an explanation of the basic concepts underlying recursion and then explores the use of recursion in programming. Several specific problems are solved using recursion, demonstrating its versatility, simplicity, and elegance.

12.1 Recursive Thinking

We've seen many times in previous examples that one method can call another method to accomplish a goal. What we haven't seen yet, however, is that a method can call itself. *Recursion* is a programming technique in which a method calls itself in order to fulfill its purpose. But before we get into the details of how we use recursion in a program, we need to explore the general concept of recursion. The ability to think recursively is essential to being able to use recursion as a programming technique.

In general, recursion is the process of defining something in terms of itself. For example, consider the following definition of the word *decoration*:

decoration: n. any ornament or adornment used to decorate something

The word *decorate* is used to define the word *decoration*. You may recall your grade school teacher telling you to avoid such recursive definitions when explaining the meaning of a word. However, in many situations, recursion is an appropriate way to express an idea or definition. For example, suppose we wanted to formally define a list of one or more numbers, separated by commas. Such a list can be defined recursively as either a number or as a number followed by a comma followed by a list. This definition can be expressed as follows:

A *List* is a: number

 or a: number   comma   *List*

This recursive definition of *List* defines each of the following lists of numbers:

```
24, 88, 40, 37
96, 43
14, 64, 21, 69, 32, 93, 47, 81, 28, 45, 81, 52, 69
70
```

No matter how long a list is, the recursive definition describes it. A list of one element, such as in the last example, is defined completely by the first (non-recursive) part of the definition. For any list longer than one element, the recursive part of the definition (the part which refers to itself) is used as many times as necessary until the last element is reached. The last element in the list is always defined by the non-recursive part of the definition. Figure 12.1 shows how one particular list of numbers corresponds to the recursive definition of *List*.

Infinite Recursion

Note that the definition of *List* contains one option that is recursive and one option that is not. The part of the definition that is not recursive is called the *base*

```
LIST: number   comma   LIST
        24        ,      88,  40,  37
                        number   comma   LIST
                          88        ,      40,  37
                                         number   comma   LIST
                                           40        ,      37
                                                           number
                                                             37
```

FIGURE 12.1 Tracing the recursive definition of *List*

case. If all options had a recursive component, the recursion would never end. For example, if the definition of *List* was simply "a number followed by a comma followed by a *List*," no list could ever end. This problem is called *infinite recursion*. It is similar to an infinite loop except that the "loop" occurs in the definition itself.

As in the infinite loop problem, a programmer must be careful to design algorithms so that they avoid infinite recursion. Any recursive definition must have a base case that does not result in a recursive option. The base case of the *List* definition is a single number that is not followed by anything. In other words, when the last number in the list is reached, the base case option terminates the recursive path.

Recursion in Math

Let's look at an example of recursion in mathematics. The value referred to as $N!$ (pronounced N *factorial*) is defined for any positive integer N as the product of all integers between 1 and N inclusive. Therefore, 3! is defined as:

```
3!  =  3*2*1  =  6
```

and 5! is defined as:

```
5!  =  5*4*3*2*1  =  120.
```

Mathematical formulas are often expressed recursively. The definition of $N!$ can be expressed recursively as:

```
1! = 1
N! = N * (N-1)! for N > 1
```

KEY CONCEPT

Mathematical problems and formulas are often expressed recursively.

The base case of this definition is 1!, which is defined as 1. All other values of $N!$ (for $N > 1$) are defined recursively as N times the value $(N–1)!$. The recursion is that the factorial function is defined in terms of the factorial function.

Using this definition, 50! is equal to 50 * 49!. And 49! is equal to 49 * 48!. And 48! is equal to 48 * 47!. This process continues until we get to the base case of 1. Because $N!$ is defined only for positive integers, this definition is complete and will always conclude with the base case.

The next section describes how recursion is accomplished in programs.

myprogramminglab

SELF-REVIEW QUESTIONS *(see answers in Appendix N)*

SR 12.1 What is recursion?

SR 12.2 How many times is the recursive part of the definition of a *List* used to define a list of 10 numbers? How many times is the base case used?

SR 12.3 What is infinite recursion?

SR 12.4 When is a base case needed for recursive processing?

SR 12.5 Write a recursive definition of 5 * n (integer multiplication), where n > 0. Define the multiplication process in terms of integer addition. For example, 5 * 7 is equal to 5 added to itself 7 times.

12.2 Recursive Programming

Let's use a simple mathematical operation to demonstrate the concept of recursive programming. Consider the process of summing the values between 1 and N inclusive, where N is any positive integer. The sum of the values from 1 to N can be expressed as N plus the sum of the values from 1 to $N–1$. That sum can be expressed similarly, as shown in Figure 12.2.

$$\sum_{i=1}^{N} i \;=\; N + \sum_{i=1}^{N-1} i \;=\; N + N - 1 + \sum_{i=1}^{N-2} i$$

$$=\; N + N - 1 + N - 2 + \sum_{i=1}^{N-3} i$$

$$\vdots$$

$$=\; N + N - 1 + N - 2 + \cdots + 2 + 1$$

FIGURE 12.2   The sum of the numbers 1 through N, defined recursively

For example, the sum of the values between 1 and 20 is equal to 20 plus the sum of the values between 1 and 19. Continuing this approach, the sum of the values between 1 and 19 is equal to 19 plus the sum of the values between 1 and 18. This may sound like a strange way to think about this problem, but it is a straightforward example that can be used to demonstrate how recursion is programmed.

As we mentioned earlier, in Java, as in many other programming languages, a method can call itself. Each call to the method creates a new environment in which to work. That is, all local variables and parameters are newly defined with their own unique data space every time the method is called. Each parameter is given an initial value based on the new call. Each time a method terminates, processing returns to the method that called it (which may be an earlier invocation of the same method). These rules are no different from those governing any "regular" method invocation.

> **KEY CONCEPT**
>
> Each recursive call to a method creates new local variables and parameters.

A recursive solution to the summation problem is defined by the following recursive method called sum:

```java
// This method returns the sum of 1 to num
public int sum (int num)
{
    int result;
    if (num == 1)
        result = 1;
    else
        result = num + sum (num-1);
    return result;
}
```

Note that this method essentially embodies our recursive definition that the sum of the numbers between 1 and N is equal to N plus the sum of the numbers between 1 and $N-1$. The sum method is recursive, because sum calls itself. The parameter passed to sum is decremented each time sum is called until it reaches the base case of 1. Recursive methods invariably contain an if-else statement, with one of the branches, usually the first one, representing the base case, as in this example.

Suppose the main method calls sum, passing it an initial value of 1, which is stored in the parameter num. Since num is equal to 1, the result of 1 is returned to main and no recursion occurs.

Now let's trace the execution of the sum method when it is passed an initial value of 2. Since num does not equal 1, sum is called again with an argument of num−1, or 1. This is a new call to the method sum, with a new parameter num and a new local variable result. Since this num is equal to 1 in this invocation, the result of 1 is returned without further recursive calls. Control returns to the first version of sum that was invoked. The return value of 1 is added to the initial value of num in that call to sum, which is 2. Therefore, result is assigned the value 3, which is returned to the main method. The method called from main correctly calculates the sum of the integers from 1 to 2 and returns the result of 3.

The base case in the summation example is when N equals 1, at which point no further recursive calls are made. The recursion begins to fold back into the earlier versions of the sum method, returning the appropriate value each time. Each return value contributes to the computation of the sum at the higher level. Without the base case, infinite recursion would result. Each call to a method requires additional memory space; therefore infinite recursion often results in a run-time error indicating that memory has been exhausted.

Trace the sum function with different initial values of num until this processing becomes familiar. Figure 12.3 illustrates the recursive calls when main invokes sum to determine the sum of the integers from 1 to 4. Each box represents a copy of the method as it is invoked, indicating the allocation of space to store the formal parameters and any local variables. Invocations are shown as solid lines,

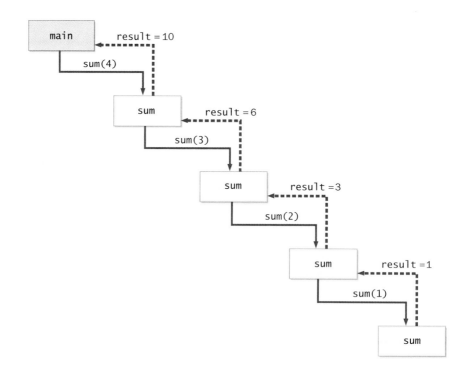

FIGURE 12.3   Recursive calls to the sum method

and returns as dotted lines. The return value `result` is shown at each step. The recursive path is followed completely until the base case is reached; the calls then begin to return their result up through the chain.

Recursion vs. Iteration

Of course, there is a non-recursive solution to the summation problem we just explored. One way to compute the sum of the numbers between 1 and `num` inclusive in an iterative manner is as follows:

> **KEY CONCEPT**
> Recursion is the most elegant and appropriate way to solve some problems, but for others it is less intuitive than an iterative solution.

```
sum = 0;
for (int number = 1; number <= num; number++)
    sum += number;
```

This solution is certainly more straightforward than the recursive version. We used the summation problem to demonstrate recursion because it is simple, not because you would use recursion to solve it under normal conditions. Recursion has the overhead of multiple method invocations and, in this case, presents a more complicated solution than its iterative counterpart.

A programmer must learn when to use recursion and when not to use it. Determining which approach is best depends on the problem being solved. All problems can be solved in an iterative manner, but in some cases the iterative version is much more complicated. Recursion, for some problems, allows us to create relatively short, elegant programs.

Direct vs. Indirect Recursion

Direct recursion occurs when a method invokes itself, such as when `sum` calls `sum`. *Indirect recursion* occurs when a method invokes another method, eventually resulting in the original method being invoked again. For example, if method `m1` invokes method `m2`, and `m2` invokes method `m1`, we can say that `m1` is indirectly recursive. The amount of indirection could be several levels deep, as when `m1` invokes `m2`, which invokes `m3`, which invokes `m4`, which invokes `m1`. Figure 12.4 depicts a situation with indirect recursion. Method invocations are shown with solid lines, and returns are shown with dotted lines. The entire invocation path is followed, and then the recursion unravels following the return path.

Indirect recursion requires all of the same attention to base cases that direct recursion requires. Furthermore, indirect recursion can be more difficult to trace because of the intervening method calls. Therefore extra care is warranted when designing or evaluating indirectly recursive methods. Ensure that the indirection is truly necessary and clearly explained in documentation.

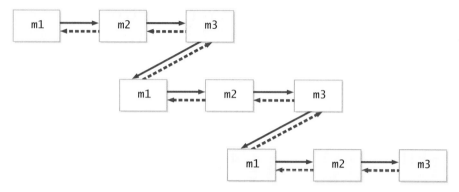

FIGURE 12.4   Indirect recursion

SELF-REVIEW QUESTIONS *(see answers in Appendix N)*

SR 12.6   Is recursion necessary?

SR 12.7   When should recursion be avoided?

SR 12.8   Describe what is returned by the following recursive method.

```
private static int exercise (int n)
{
    if (n < 0)
        return −1;
    else
        if (n < 10)
            return 1;
        else
            return 1 + exercise (n/10);
}
```

SR 12.9   Write a recursive method that returns the value of 5 * n, where n > 0. See Self-Review Question 12.5. Explain why you would not normally use recursion to solve this problem.

SR 12.10   What is indirect recursion?

12.3 Using Recursion

Each of the following sections describes a particular recursive problem. For each one, we examine exactly how recursion plays a role in the solution and how a base case is used to terminate the recursion. As you examine these examples, consider how complicated a non-recursive solution for each problem would be.

Traversing a Maze

Solving a maze involves a great deal of trial and error: following a path, backtracking when you cannot go farther, and trying other untried options. Such activities often are handled nicely using recursion. The program shown in Listing 12.1 creates a Maze object and attempts to traverse it.

LISTING 12.1

```java
//********************************************************************
//  MazeSearch.java       Author: Lewis/Loftus
//
//  Demonstrates recursion.
//********************************************************************
public class MazeSearch
{
   //-----------------------------------------------------------------
   //  Creates a new maze, prints its original form, attempts to
   //  solve it, and prints out its final form.
   //-----------------------------------------------------------------
   public static void main (String[] args)
   {
      Maze labyrinth = new Maze();

      System.out.println (labyrinth);

      if (labyrinth.traverse (0, 0))
         System.out.println ("The maze was successfully traversed!");
      else
         System.out.println ("There is no possible path.");

      System.out.println (labyrinth);
   }
}
```

OUTPUT

```
1110110001111
1011101111001
0000101010100
1110111010111
1010000111001
1011111101111
1000000000000
1111111111111
```

LISTING 1 2 . 1   *continued*

```
The maze was successfully traversed!

7770110001111
3077707771001
0000707070300
7770777070333
7070000773003
7077777703333
7000000000000
7777777777777
```

The Maze class shown in Listing 12.2 uses a two-dimensional array of integers to represent the maze. The goal is to move from the top-left corner (the entry point) to the bottom-right corner (the exit point). Initially, a 1 indicates a clear path and a 0 indicates a blocked path. As the maze is solved, these array elements are changed to other values to indicate attempted paths and ultimately a successful path through the maze if one exists.

LISTING 1 2 . 2

```java
//********************************************************************
//  Maze.java          Author: Lewis/Loftus
//
//  Represents a maze of characters. The goal is to get from the
//  top left corner to the bottom right, following a path of 1s.
//********************************************************************

public class Maze
{
   private final int TRIED = 3;
   private final int PATH = 7;

   private int[][] grid = { {1,1,1,0,1,1,0,0,0,1,1,1,1},
                            {1,0,1,1,1,0,1,1,1,1,0,0,1},
                            {0,0,0,0,1,0,1,0,1,0,1,0,0},
                            {1,1,1,0,1,1,1,0,1,0,1,1,1},
```

LISTING 12.2   *continued*

```
                  {1,0,1,0,0,0,0,1,1,1,0,0,1},
                  {1,0,1,1,1,1,1,1,0,1,1,1,1},
                  {1,0,0,0,0,0,0,0,0,0,0,0,0},
                  {1,1,1,1,1,1,1,1,1,1,1,1,1} };

   //----------------------------------------------------------------
   //  Attempts to recursively traverse the maze. Inserts special
   //  characters indicating locations that have been tried and that
   //  eventually become part of the solution.
   //----------------------------------------------------------------
   public boolean traverse (int row, int column)
   {
      boolean done = false;

      if (valid (row, column))
      {
         grid[row][column] = TRIED;  // this cell has been tried

         if (row == grid.length-1 && column == grid[0].length-1)

            done = true;  // the maze is solved
         else
         {
            done = traverse (row+1, column);      // down
            if (!done)
               done = traverse (row, column+1);  // right
            if (!done)
               done = traverse (row-1, column);  // up
            if (!done)
               done = traverse (row, column-1);  // left
         }

         if (done)  // this location is part of the final path
            grid[row][column] = PATH;
      }
      return done;
   }

   //----------------------------------------------------------------
   //  Determines if a specific location is valid.
   //----------------------------------------------------------------
   private boolean valid (int row, int column)
   {
      boolean result = false;
```

LISTING 12.2 *continued*

```
    // check if cell is in the bounds of the matrix
    if (row >= 0 && row < grid.length &&
        column >= 0 && column < grid[row].length)

        // check if cell is not blocked and not previously tried
        if (grid[row][column] == 1)
            result = true;

    return result;
}

//----------------------------------------------------------------
//  Returns the maze as a string.
//----------------------------------------------------------------
public String toString ()
{
    String result = "\n";
    for (int row=0; row < grid.length; row++)
    {
        for (int column=0; column < grid[row].length; column++)
            result += grid[row][column] + "";
        result += "\n";
    }

    return result;
}
}
```

VideoNote

Tracing the
MazeSearch program.

The only valid moves through the maze are in the four primary directions: down, right, up, and left. No diagonal moves are allowed. In this example, the maze is 8 rows by 13 columns, although the code is designed to handle a maze of any size.

Let's think this through recursively. The maze can be traversed successfully if it can be traversed successfully from position (0, 0). Therefore, the maze can be traversed successfully if it can be traversed successfully from any positions adjacent to (0, 0), namely position (1, 0), position (0, 1), position (–1, 0), or position (0, –1). Picking a potential next step, say (1, 0), we find ourselves in the same type of situation we did before. To successfully traverse the maze from the new current position, we must successfully traverse it from an adjacent position. At any point, some of the adjacent positions may be invalid, may be blocked, or may represent a possible successful path. We continue this process recursively. If the base case, position (7, 12) is reached, the maze has been traversed successfully.

The recursive method in the `Maze` class is called `traverse`. It returns a boolean value that indicates whether a solution was found. First the method determines whether a move to the specified row and column is valid. A move is considered valid if it stays within the grid boundaries and if the grid contains a 1 in that location, indicating that a move in that direction is not blocked. The initial call to `traverse` passes in the upper-left location (0, 0).

If the move is valid, the grid entry is changed from a 1 to a 3, marking this location as visited so that later we don't retrace our steps. The `traverse` method then determines whether the maze has been completed by having reached the bottom-right location. Therefore, there are actually three possibilities of the base case for this problem that will terminate any particular recursive path:

- an invalid move because the move is out of bounds
- an invalid move because the move has been tried before
- a move that arrives at the final location

If the current location is not the bottom-right corner, we search for a solution in each of the primary directions, if necessary. First, we look down by recursively calling the `traverse` method and passing in the new location. The logic of the `traverse` method starts all over again using this new position. A solution is either ultimately found by first attempting to move down from the current location, or it's not found. If it's not found, we try moving right. If that fails, we try up. Finally, if no other direction has yielded a correct path, we try left. If no direction from the current location yields a correct solution, then there is no path from this location, and `traverse` returns false.

If a solution is found from the current location, the grid entry is changed to a 7. The first 7 is placed in the bottom-right corner. The next 7 is placed in the location that led to the bottom-right corner, and so on until the final 7 is placed in the upper-left corner. Therefore, when the final maze is printed, the zeros still indicate a blocked path, a 1 indicates an open path that was never tried, a 3 indicates a path that was tried but failed to yield a correct solution, and a 7 indicates a part of the final solution of the maze.

Note that there are several opportunities for recursion in each call to the `traverse` method. Any or all of them might be followed, depending on the maze configuration. Although there may be many paths through the maze, the recursion terminates when a path is found. Carefully trace the execution of this code while following the maze array to see how the recursion solves the problem. Then consider the difficulty of producing a non-recursive solution.

FIGURE 12.5   The Towers of Hanoi puzzle

The Towers of Hanoi

The *Towers of Hanoi* puzzle was invented in the 1880s by Edouard Lucas, a French mathematician. It has become a favorite among computer scientists, because its solution is an excellent demonstration of recursive elegance.

The puzzle consists of three upright pegs and a set of disks with holes in the middle so that they slide onto the pegs. Each disk has a different diameter. Initially, all of the disks are stacked on one peg in order of size such that the largest disk is on the bottom, as shown in Figure 12.5.

The goal of the puzzle is to move all of the disks from their original (first) peg to the destination (third) peg. We can use the "extra" peg as a temporary place to put disks, but we must obey the following three rules:

- We can move only one disk at a time.
- We cannot place a larger disk on top of a smaller disk.
- All disks must be on some peg except for the disk in transit between pegs.

These rules imply that we must move smaller disks "out of the way" in order to move a larger disk from one peg to another. Figure 12.6 shows the step-by-step solution for the Towers of Hanoi puzzle using three disks. In order to ultimately move all three disks from the first peg to the third peg, we first have to get to the point where the smaller two disks are out of the way on the second peg so that the largest disk can be moved from the first peg to the third peg.

The first three moves shown in Figure 12.6 can be thought of as moving the smaller disks out of the way. The fourth move puts the largest disk in its final place. The last three moves then put the smaller disks to their final place on top of the largest one.

Let's use this idea to form a general strategy. To move a stack of N disks from the original peg to the destination peg:

- Move the topmost $N-1$ disks from the original peg to the extra peg.
- Move the largest disk from the original peg to the destination peg.
- Move the $N-1$ disks from the extra peg to the destination peg.

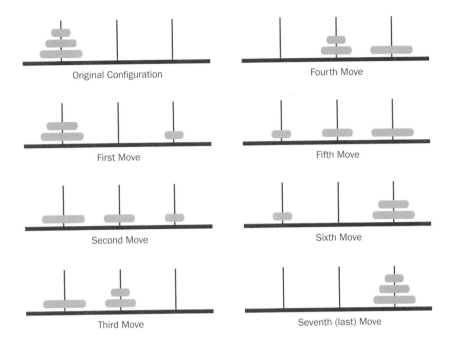

FIGURE 12.6   A solution to the three-disk Towers of Hanoi puzzle

This strategy lends itself nicely to a recursive solution. The step to move the N–1 disks out of the way is the same problem all over again: moving a stack of disks. For this subtask, though, there is one less disk, and our destination peg is what we were originally calling the extra peg. An analogous situation occurs after we've moved the largest disk and we have to move the original N–1 disks again.

The base case for this problem occurs when we want to move a "stack" that consists of only one disk. That step can be accomplished directly and without recursion.

The program in Listing 12.3 creates a TowersOfHanoi object and invokes its solve method. The output is a step-by-step list of instructions that describe how the disks should be moved to solve the puzzle. This example uses four disks, which is specified by a parameter to the TowersOfHanoi constructor.

The TowersOfHanoi class shown in Listing 12.4 uses the solve method to make an initial call to moveTower, the recursive method. The initial call indicates that all of the disks should be moved from peg 1 to peg 3, using peg 2 as the extra position.

The moveTower method first considers the base case (a "stack" of one disk). When that occurs, it calls the moveOneDisk method that prints a single line

VideoNote

Exploring the Towers of Hanoi.

LISTING 12.3

```
//********************************************************************
//  SolveTowers.java        Author: Lewis/Loftus
//
//  Demonstrates recursion.
//********************************************************************

public class SolveTowers
{
    //-----------------------------------------------------------------
    // Creates a TowersOfHanoi puzzle and solves it.
    //-----------------------------------------------------------------
    public static void main (String[] args)
    {
        TowersOfHanoi towers = new TowersOfHanoi (4);

        towers.solve();
    }
}
```

OUTPUT

```
Move one disk from 1 to 2
Move one disk from 1 to 3
Move one disk from 2 to 3
Move one disk from 1 to 2
Move one disk from 3 to 1
Move one disk from 3 to 2
Move one disk from 1 to 2
Move one disk from 1 to 3
Move one disk from 2 to 3
Move one disk from 2 to 1
Move one disk from 3 to 1
Move one disk from 2 to 3
Move one disk from 1 to 2
Move one disk from 1 to 3
Move one disk from 2 to 3
```

describing that particular move. If the stack contains more than one disk, we call moveTower again to get the N-1 disks out of the way, then move the largest disk, then move the N-1 disks to their final destination with yet another call to moveTower.

LISTING 12.4

```java
//********************************************************************
//  TowersOfHanoi.java        Author: Lewis/Loftus
//
//  Represents the classic Towers of Hanoi puzzle.
//********************************************************************

public class TowersOfHanoi
{
   private int totalDisks;

   //-----------------------------------------------------------------
   //  Sets up the puzzle with the specified number of disks.
   //-----------------------------------------------------------------
   public TowersOfHanoi (int disks)
   {
      totalDisks = disks;
   }

   //-----------------------------------------------------------------
   //  Performs the initial call to moveTower to solve the puzzle.
   //  Moves the disks from tower 1 to tower 3 using tower 2.
   //-----------------------------------------------------------------
   public void solve ()
   {
      moveTower (totalDisks, 1, 3, 2);
   }

   //-----------------------------------------------------------------
   //  Moves the specified number of disks from one tower to another
   //  by moving a subtower of n-1 disks out of the way, moving one
   //  disk, then moving the subtower back. Base case of 1 disk.
   //-----------------------------------------------------------------
   private void moveTower (int numDisks, int start, int end, int temp)
   {
      if (numDisks == 1)
         moveOneDisk (start, end);
      else
      {
         moveTower (numDisks-1, start, temp, end);
         moveOneDisk (start, end);
         moveTower (numDisks-1, temp, end, start);
      }
   }
```

LISTING 12.4 *continued*

```
//-----------------------------------------------------------------
//  Prints instructions to move one disk from the specified start
//  tower to the specified end tower.
//-----------------------------------------------------------------
private void moveOneDisk (int start, int end)
{
    System.out.println ("Move one disk from " + start + " to " +
                        end);
}
}
```

Note that the parameters to moveTower describing the pegs are switched around as needed to move the partial stacks. This code follows our general strategy and uses the moveTower method to move all partial stacks. Trace the code carefully for a stack of three disks to understand the processing. Compare the processing steps to Figure 12.6.

> **KEY CONCEPT**
>
> The Towers of Hanoi solution has exponential complexity, which is very inefficient. Yet the implementation of the solution is incredibly short and elegant.

Contrary to its short and elegant implementation, the solution to the Towers of Hanoi puzzle is terribly inefficient. To solve the puzzle with a stack of N disks, we have to make 2^N-1 individual disk moves. This situation is an example of *exponential complexity*. As the number of disks increases, the number of required moves increases exponentially.

Legend has it that priests of Brahma are working on this puzzle in a temple at the center of the world. They are using 64 gold disks, moving them between pegs of pure diamond. The downside is that when the priests finish the puzzle, the world will end. The upside is that even if they move one disk every second of every day, it will take them over 584 billion years to complete it. That's with a puzzle of only 64 disks! It is certainly an indication of just how intractable exponential algorithmic complexity is.

myprogramminglab

SELF-REVIEW QUESTIONS *(see answers in Appendix N)*

SR 12.11   Under what conditions does the recursion stop in the MazeSearch program?

SR 12.12   Identify where in the MazeSearch program each of the following is provided.

a. The original maze is defined.
b. A test to see if we have arrived at the goal occurs.
c. A location is marked as having been tried.
d. A test to see if we already tried a location occurs.

SR 12.13 Trace the `MazeSearch` program to determine the series of calls to the method `valid` (including the values of the parameters that are passed) that would occur if the original maze is as shown.

a. 1 1   b. 0 0   c. 1 1
   1 1   0 0   1 0

SR 12.14 Explain the general approach to solving the Towers of Hanoi puzzle. How does it relate to recursion?

SR 12.15 Trace the `SolveTowers` code for an initial stack of 1 disk. How many calls to the `moveTower` method are made? How many calls are made for an initial stack of 2 disks? How many for 3 disks? Describe a pattern related to the number of calls made to the `moveTower` method as the number of disks increases.

12.4 Recursion in Graphics

The concept of recursion has several uses in images and graphics. The following section explores some image and graphics-based recursion examples.

Tiled Pictures

Carefully examine the display for the `TiledPictures` applet shown in Listing 12.5. There are actually three unique images among the menagerie. The entire area is divided into four equal quadrants. A picture of the world (with a circle indicating the Himalayan mountain region) is shown in the bottom-right quadrant. The bottom-left quadrant contains a picture of Mt. Everest. In the top-right quadrant is a picture of a mountain goat.

The interesting part of the picture is the top-left quadrant. It contains a copy of the entire collage, including itself. In this smaller version you can see the three simple pictures in their three quadrants. And again, in the top-left corner, the picture is repeated (including itself). This repetition continues for several levels. It is similar to the effect you can create when looking at a mirror in the reflection of another mirror.

LISTING 12.5

```java
//********************************************************************
//  TiledPictures.java        Author: Lewis/Loftus
//
//  Demonstrates the use of recursion.
//********************************************************************

import java.awt.*;
import javax.swing.JApplet;

public class TiledPictures extends JApplet
{
   private final int APPLET_WIDTH = 320;
   private final int APPLET_HEIGHT = 320;
   private final int MIN = 20;  // smallest picture size

   private Image world, everest, goat;

   //-----------------------------------------------------------------
   //  Loads the images.
   //-----------------------------------------------------------------
   public void init()
   {
      world = getImage (getDocumentBase(), "world.gif");
      everest = getImage (getDocumentBase(), "everest.gif");
      goat = getImage (getDocumentBase(), "goat.gif");

      setSize (APPLET_WIDTH, APPLET_HEIGHT);
   }

   //-----------------------------------------------------------------
   //  Draws the three images, then calls itself recursively.
   //-----------------------------------------------------------------
   public void drawPictures (int size, Graphics page)
   {
      page.drawImage (everest, 0, size/2, size/2, size/2, this);
      page.drawImage (goat, size/2, 0, size/2, size/2, this);
      page.drawImage (world, size/2, size/2, size/2, size/2, this);

      if (size > MIN)
         drawPictures (size/2, page);
   }

   //-----------------------------------------------------------------
   //  Performs the initial call to the drawPictures method.
   //-----------------------------------------------------------------
```

LISTING 12.5   *continued*

```
    public void paint (Graphics page)
    {
        drawPictures (APPLET_WIDTH, page);
    }
}
```

DISPLAY

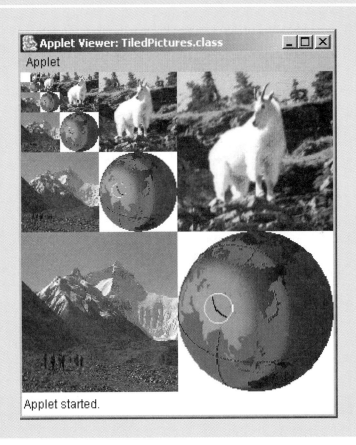

This visual effect is created quite easily using recursion. The applet's `init` method initially loads the three images. The `paint` method then invokes the `drawPictures` method, which accepts a parameter that defines the size of the area in which pictures are displayed. It draws the three images using the `drawImage`

method, with parameters that scale the picture to the correct size and location. The drawPictures method is then called recursively to draw the upper-left quadrant.

On each invocation, if the drawing area is large enough, the drawPictures method is invoked again, using a smaller drawing area. Eventually, the drawing area becomes so small that the recursive call is not performed. Note that draw-Pictures assumes the origin (0, 0) coordinate as the relative location of the new images, no matter what their size is.

The base case of the recursion in this problem specifies a minimum size for the drawing area. Because the size is decreased each time, the base case eventually is reached and the recursion stops. This is why the upper-left corner is empty in the smallest version of the collage.

Fractals

> **KEY CONCEPT**
>
> A fractal is a geometric shape that is defined naturally in a recursive manner.

A *fractal* is a geometric shape that can be made up of the same pattern repeated at different scales and orientations. The nature of a fractal lends itself to a recursive definition. Interest in fractals has grown immensely in recent years, largely due to Benoit Mandelbrot, a Polish mathematician born in 1924. He demonstrated that fractals occur in many places in mathematics and nature. Computers have made fractals much easier to generate and investigate. Over the past quarter century, the bright, interesting images that can be created with fractals have come to be considered as much an art form as a mathematical interest.

One particular example of a fractal is called the *Koch snowflake,* named after Helge von Koch, a Swedish mathematician. It begins with an equilateral triangle, which is considered to be the Koch fractal of order 1. Koch fractals of higher orders are constructed by repeatedly modifying all of the line segments in the shape.

To create the next higher order Koch fractal, each line segment in the shape is modified by replacing its middle third with a sharp protrusion made of two line segments, each having the same length as the replaced part. Relative to the entire shape, the protrusion on any line segment always points outward. Figure 12.7 shows several orders of Koch fractals. As the order increases, the shape begins to look like a snowflake.

The applet shown in Listing 12.6 draws a Koch snowflake of several different orders. The buttons at the top of the applet allow the user to increase and decrease the order of the fractal. Each time a button is pressed, the fractal image is redrawn. The applet serves as the listener for the buttons.

FIGURE 12.7   Several orders of the Koch snowflake

LISTING 12.6

```java
//********************************************************************
//  KochSnowflake.java        Author: Lewis/Loftus
//
//  Demonstrates the use of recursion.
//********************************************************************

import java.awt.*;
import java.awt.event.*;
import javax.swing.*;

public class KochSnowflake extends JApplet implements ActionListener
{
   private final int APPLET_WIDTH = 400;
   private final int APPLET_HEIGHT = 440;

   private final int MIN = 1, MAX = 9;

   private JButton increase, decrease;
   private JLabel titleLabel, orderLabel;
   private KochPanel drawing;
   private JPanel appletPanel, tools;

   //-----------------------------------------------------------
   // Sets up the components for the applet.
   //-----------------------------------------------------------
   public void init()
   {
      tools = new JPanel ();
      tools.setLayout (new BoxLayout(tools, BoxLayout.X_AXIS));
      tools.setBackground (Color.yellow);
      tools.setOpaque (true);
```

LISTING 12.6   *continued*

```
      titleLabel = new JLabel ("The Koch Snowflake");
      titleLabel.setForeground (Color.black);

      increase = new JButton (new ImageIcon ("increase.gif"));
      increase.setPressedIcon (new ImageIcon ("increasePressed.gif"));
      increase.setMargin (new Insets (0, 0, 0, 0));
      increase.addActionListener (this);
      decrease = new JButton (new ImageIcon ("decrease.gif"));
      decrease.setPressedIcon (new ImageIcon ("decreasePressed.gif"));
      decrease.setMargin (new Insets (0, 0, 0, 0));
      decrease.addActionListener (this);

      orderLabel = new JLabel ("Order: 1");
      orderLabel.setForeground (Color.black);

      tools.add (titleLabel);
      tools.add (Box.createHorizontalStrut (20));
      tools.add (decrease);
      tools.add (increase);
      tools.add (Box.createHorizontalStrut (20));
      tools.add (orderLabel);

      drawing = new KochPanel (1);

      appletPanel = new JPanel();
      appletPanel.add (tools);
      appletPanel.add (drawing);

      getContentPane().add (appletPanel);

      setSize (APPLET_WIDTH, APPLET_HEIGHT);
   }

   //-----------------------------------------------------------------
   //  Determines which button was pushed, and sets the new order
   //  if it is in range.
   //-----------------------------------------------------------------
   public void actionPerformed (ActionEvent event)
   {
      int order = drawing.getOrder();

      if (event.getSource() == increase)
         order++;
      else
         order--;
```

LISTING 12.6 *continued*

```
    if (order >= MIN && order <= MAX)
    {
        orderLabel.setText ("Order: " + order);
        drawing.setOrder (order);
        repaint();
    }
  }
}
```

DISPLAY

The fractal image is drawn on a canvas defined by the KochPanel class shown in Listing 12.7. The paint method makes the initial calls to the recursive method drawFractal. The three calls to drawFractal in the paint method represent the original three sides of the equilateral triangle that make up a Koch fractal of order 1.

LISTING 12.7

```java
//********************************************************************
//  KochPanel.java         Author: Lewis/Loftus
//
//  Represents a drawing surface on which to paint a Koch Snowflake.
//********************************************************************

import java.awt.*;
import javax.swing.JPanel;

public class KochPanel extends JPanel
{
   private final int PANEL_WIDTH = 400;
   private final int PANEL_HEIGHT = 400;

   private final double SQ = Math.sqrt(3.0) / 6;

   private final int TOPX = 200, TOPY = 20;
   private final int LEFTX = 60, LEFTY = 300;
   private final int RIGHTX = 340, RIGHTY = 300;

   private int current;   // current order

   //-----------------------------------------------------------------
   //  Sets the initial fractal order to the value specified.
   //-----------------------------------------------------------------
   public KochPanel (int currentOrder)
   {
      current = currentOrder;
      setBackground (Color.black);
      setPreferredSize (new Dimension(PANEL_WIDTH, PANEL_HEIGHT));
   }

   //-----------------------------------------------------------------
   //  Draws the fractal recursively. Base case is an order of 1 for
   //  which a simple straight line is drawn. Otherwise three
```

LISTING 12.7   *continued*

```
//   intermediate points are computed, and each line segment is
//   drawn as a fractal.
//----------------------------------------------------------------
public void drawFractal (int order, int x1, int y1, int x5, int y5,
                         Graphics page)
{
   int deltaX, deltaY, x2, y2, x3, y3, x4, y4;

   if (order == 1)
      page.drawLine (x1, y1, x5, y5);
   else
   {
      deltaX = x5 - x1;   // distance between end points
      deltaY = y5 - y1;

      x2 = x1 + deltaX / 3;   // one third
      y2 = y1 + deltaY / 3;

      x3 = (int) ((x1+x5)/2 + SQ * (y1-y5));   // tip of projection
      y3 = (int) ((y1+y5)/2 + SQ * (x5-x1));

      x4 = x1 + deltaX * 2/3;   // two thirds
      y4 = y1 + deltaY * 2/3;

      drawFractal (order-1, x1, y1, x2, y2, page);
      drawFractal (order-1, x2, y2, x3, y3, page);
      drawFractal (order-1, x3, y3, x4, y4, page);
      drawFractal (order-1, x4, y4, x5, y5, page);
   }
}

//----------------------------------------------------------------
//   Performs the initial calls to the drawFractal method.
//----------------------------------------------------------------
public void paintComponent (Graphics page)
{
   super.paintComponent (page);

   page.setColor (Color.green);

   drawFractal (current, TOPX, TOPY, LEFTX, LEFTY, page);
   drawFractal (current, LEFTX, LEFTY, RIGHTX, RIGHTY, page);
   drawFractal (current, RIGHTX, RIGHTY, TOPX, TOPY, page);
}
```

LISTING 12.7   *continued*

```
//-----------------------------------------------------------
//  Sets the fractal order to the value specified.
//-----------------------------------------------------------
public void setOrder (int order)
{
    current = order;
}

//-----------------------------------------------------------
//  Returns the current order.
//-----------------------------------------------------------
public int getOrder ()
{
    return current;
}
}
```

The variable current represents the order of the fractal to be drawn. Each recursive call to drawFractal decrements the order by 1. The base case of the recursion occurs when the order of the fractal is 1, which results in a simple line segment between the coordinates specified by the parameters.

If the order of the fractal is higher than 1, three additional points are computed. In conjunction with the parameters, these points form the four line segments of the modified fractal. Figure 12.8 shows the transformation.

Based on the position of the two end points of the original line segment, a point one-third of the way and a point two-thirds of the way between them are computed. The calculation of $<x_3, y_3>$, the point at the tip of the protrusion, is more convoluted and uses a simplifying constant that incorporates multiple geometric relationships. The calculations to determine the three new points actually have nothing to do with the recursive technique used to draw the fractal, and so we won't discuss the details of these computations here.

An interesting mathematical feature of a Koch snowflake is that it has an infinite perimeter but a finite area. As the order of the fractal increases, the perimeter grows exponentially larger, with a mathematical limit of infinity. However, a rectangle large enough to surround the second-order fractal for the Koch snowflake is large enough to contain all higher-order fractals. The shape is restricted forever in area, but its perimeter gets infinitely longer.

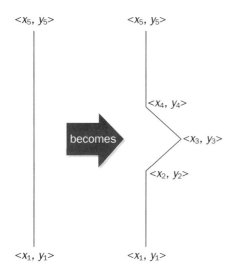

FIGURE 12.8   The transformation of each line segment of a Koch snowflake

SR 12.16   What is the base case for the `TiledPictures` program?

SR 12.17   What is a fractal? What does it have to do with recursion?

Summary of Key Concepts

- Recursion is a programming technique in which a method calls itself. A key to being able to program recursively is to be able to think recursively.

- Any recursive definition must have a non-recursive part, called the base case, which permits the recursion to eventually end.

- Mathematical problems and formulas are often expressed recursively.

- Each recursive call to a method creates new local variables and parameters.

- A careful trace of recursive processing can provide insight into the way it is used to solve a problem.

- Recursion is the most elegant and appropriate way to solve some problems, but for others it is less intuitive than an iterative solution.

- The Towers of Hanoi solution has exponential complexity, which is very inefficient. Yet the implementation of the solution is incredibly short and elegant.

- A fractal is a geometric shape that is defined naturally in a recursive manner.

Exercises

myprogramminglab

Visit www.myprogramminglab.com to complete many of these Exercises online and get instant feedback.

EX 12.1 Describe the problem of infinite recursion and explain why it occurs.

EX 12.2 When would you use direct recursion? In which situations would indirect recursion be a better choice?

EX 12.3 Write a recursive definition to compute the following series:

$$x^n + x^{n-1} + x^{n-2} + \dots x^1$$

Accept values for x and n from the user.

EX 12.4 Write a recursive definition to find the sum of the squares of n numbers. Accept a value for n from the user, and compute the sum of the squares of the numbers from 1 to n using recursive calls. What is the advantage of using recursion in this problem?

EX 12.5   Modify the method that calculates the sum of the integers between 1 and N shown in this chapter. Have the new version match the following recursive definition: The sum of 1 to N is the sum of 1 to $(N/2)$ plus the sum of $(N/2 + 1)$ to N. Trace your solution using an N of 7.

EX 12.6   Write a recursive method that returns the value of $N!$ (N factorial) using the definition given in this chapter. Explain why you would not normally use recursion to solve this problem.

EX 12.7   Write a recursive method that computes the number of times the character 'r' occurs in a given string. Your method should accept an input string from the user and return the number of occurrences of 'r' in it.

EX 12.8   Design and generate a recursive PerfectSquare program which generates all the perfect square numbers which lie in the range of 1 to 30. [A positive integer is perfect if the sum of its factors (excluding the integer itself) is equal to the integer. For example, 6 is perfect, since the numbers that divide it exactly are 1, 2, 3, and 6, and the sum of 1, 2, and 3 is 6].

EX 12.9   Annotate the lines of output of the SolveTowers program in this chapter to show the recursive steps.

EX 12.10   Produce a chart showing the number of moves required to solve the Towers of Hanoi puzzle using the following number of disks: 2, 3, 4, 5, 6, 7, 8, 9, 10, 15, 20, and 25.

EX 12.11   How many line segments are used to construct a Koch snowflake of order N? Produce a chart showing the number of line segments that make up a Koch snowflake for orders 1 through 9.

Programming Projects

Visit www.myprogramminglab.com to complete many of these Programming Projects online and get instant feedback.

PP 12.1   Design and implement a recursive version of the PalindromeTester program from Chapter 5.

myprogramminglab

VideoNote

Developing a solution of PP 12.1.

PP 12.2 Design and implement a program that implements Euclid's algorithm for finding the greatest common divisor of two positive integers. The greatest common divisor is the largest integer that divides both values without producing a remainder. An iterative version of this method was part of the `RationalNumber` class presented in Chapter 7. In a class called `DivisorCalc`, define a `static` method called `gcd` that accepts two integers, num1 and num2. Create a driver to test your implementation. The recursive algorithm is defined as follows:

- gcd (num1, num2) is num2 if num2 <= num1 and num2 divides num1

- gcd (num1, num2) is gcd (num2, num1) if num1 < num2

- gcd (num1, num2) is gcd (num2, num1%num2) otherwise

PP 12.3 Modify the `Maze` class so that it prints out the path of the final solution as it is discovered without storing it.

PP 12.4 Design and implement a program that traverses a 3D maze.

PP 12.5 Modify the `TiledPictures` program so that the repeated images appear in the lower-right quadrant.

PP 12.6 Design and implement a recursive program that solves the Non-Attacking Queens problem. That is, write a program to determine how eight queens can be positioned on an eight-by-eight chessboard so that none of them are in the same row, column, or diagonal as any other queen. There are no other chess pieces on the board.

PP 12.7 In the language of an alien race, all words take the form of Blurbs. A Blurb is a Whoozit followed by one or more Whatzits. A Whoozit is the character 'x' followed by zero or more 'y's. A Whatzit is a 'q' followed by either a 'z' or a 'd', followed by a Whoozit. Design and implement a recursive program that generates random Blurbs in this alien language.

PP 12.8 Design and implement a recursive program to list all the files present in a tree-based directory structure.

PP 12.9 Design and implement a recursive program to determine and print the Nth line of Pascal's Triangle, as shown below. Each interior value is the sum of the two values above it. *Hint*: use an array to store the values on each line.

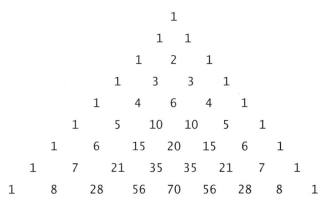

```
                        1
                    1       1
                1       2       1
            1       3       3       1
        1       4       6       4       1
    1       5       10      10      5       1
1       6       15      20      15      6       1
1   7       21      35      35      21      7       1
1   8   28      56      70      56      28  8   1
```

PP 12.10 Design and implement an applet that generalizes the KochSnowflake program. Allow the user to choose a fractal design from a menu item and to pick the background and drawing colors. The buttons to increase and decrease the order of the fractal will apply to whichever fractal design is chosen. In addition to the Koch snowflake, include a *C-curve fractal* whose order 1 is a straight line. Each successive order is created by replacing all line segments by two line segments, both half of the size of the original, and which meet at a right angle. Specifically, a C-curve of order N from $<x_1, y_1>$ to $<x_3, y_3>$ is replaced by two C-curves from to and from $<x_2, y_2>$ to $<x_3, y_3>$ where:

- $x2 = (x1 + x3 + y1 - y3) / 2;$
- $y2 = (x3 + y1 + y3 - x1) / 2;$

PP 12.11 Design and implement a graphic version of the Towers of Hanoi puzzle. Allow the user to set the number of disks used in the puzzle. The user should be able to interact with the puzzle in two main ways. The user can move the disks from one peg to another using the mouse, in which case the program should ensure that each move is legal. The user can also watch a solution take place as an animation, with pause/resume buttons. Permit the user to control the speed of the animation.

PP 12.12   Write a program that implements a recursive search of a sorted list of strings. Your program should include a recursive method that determines whether or not a given String is present within a sorted array (or, if you choose, an ArrayList) by searching successively smaller segments of the list.

Include a test driver that prompts the user for strings to be searched. The user should enter one string per line, with an empty line indicating the end of the series. After the sorted list of strings has been entered, the program should prompt the user for a search string. The program should then print a message stating whether or not the search string was found in the list, the total number of strings in the list, and the number of comparisons made while looking for the search string.

PP 12.13   Write a program that prompts the user for a list of cities, where each city has a name and x and y coordinates. After all cities have been entered, the program should use a recursive algorithm to print the length of all possible routes that start at the first city entered, end at the last city entered, and visit every city in the list. For each route, the program should print the name of each city visited, followed by length of the route.

PP 12.14   Design and implement a program named ExpressionEvaluator using recursion. ExpressionEvaluator computes simple arithmetic expressions recursively and returns the result. [ExpressionEvaluator can compute addition, subtraction, multiplication and division operations present in an arithmetic expression on its own to produce the appropriate results. For example, if the arithmetic expression (1.5 + 3.0 * (0.5 + 1.5)) is given as input, ExpressionEvaluator returns the output 7.5, after the computation of 1.5 + 3.0 * (0.5 + 1.5) = 7.5].

Collections

13

CHAPTER OBJECTIVES

- Explore the concept of a collection.
- Stress the importance of separating the interface from the implementation.
- Examine the difference between fixed and dynamic implementations.
- Define and use dynamically linked lists.
- Introduce classic linear data such as queues and stacks.
- Introduce classic nonlinear data structures such as trees and graphs.
- Discuss the Java Collections API.
- Define the use of generic types and their use in collection classes.

Problem solving often requires techniques for organizing and managing information. This chapter explores objects that store information, called collections, as well as various ways to implement them. Many collections have been developed over the years, and some of them have become classics. This chapter explains how collections can be implemented using references to link one object to another.

13.1 Collections and Data Structures

A *collection* is an object that serves as a repository for other objects. It is a generic term that can be applied to many situations, but we usually use it when discussing an object whose specific role is to provide services to add, remove, and otherwise manage the elements that are contained within. For example, the ArrayList class (discussed in Chapter 5) represents a collection. It provides methods to add elements to the end of a list or to a particular location in the list based on an index value. It provides methods to remove specific elements as needed.

Some collections maintain their elements in a specific order, while others do not. Some collections are *homogeneous,* meaning that they can contain all of the same type of object; other collections are *heterogeneous,* which means they can contain objects of various types. An ArrayList that doesn't specify an explicit element type can be thought of as heterogeneous because it can hold an object of any type. Its heterogeneous nature comes from the fact that an ArrayList stores Object references, which means it can store any object because of inheritance and polymorphism.

Separating Interface from Implementation

A crucial aspect of collections is that they can be implemented in a variety of ways. That is, the underlying *data structure* that stores the objects can be implemented using various techniques. The ArrayList class from the Java standard library, for instance, is implemented using an array. All operations on an ArrayList are accomplished by invoking methods that perform the appropriate operations on the underlying array.

An *abstract data type* (ADT) is a collection of data and the particular operations that are allowed on that data. An ADT has a name, a domain of values, and a set of operations that can be performed. An ADT is considered abstract, because the operations you can perform on it are separated from the underlying implementation. That is, the details of how an ADT stores its data and accomplishes its methods are separate from the concept that it embodies. Essentially, the terms *collection* and *abstract data type* are interchangeable.

Objects are perfectly suited for defining collections. An object, by definition, has a well-defined interface whose implementation is hidden in the class. The way the data is represented, and the operations that manage the data, are encapsulated inside the object. This type of object is reusable and reliable, because its interaction with the rest of the system is controlled.

KEY CONCEPT

An object, with its well-defined interface, is a perfect mechanism for implementing a collection.

SELF-REVIEW QUESTIONS *(see answers in Appendix N)*

SR 13.1   What is a collection?

SR 13.2   Does the `ArrayList` class provide an abstract data type?

SR 13.3   Why are objects particularly well suited for implementing abstract data types?

`myprogramminglab`

13.2 Dynamic Representations

An array is only one way in which a `list` can be represented. Arrays are limited in one sense, because they have a fixed size throughout their existence. Sometimes we don't know how big to make an array, because we don't know how much information we will store. The `ArrayList` class handles this by creating a larger array and copying everything over whenever necessary. This is not necessarily an efficient implementation.

A *dynamic data structure* is implemented using links. Using references as links between objects, we can create whatever type of structure is appropriate for the situation. If implemented carefully, the structure can be quite efficient to search and modify. Structures created this way are considered to be dynamic, because their size is determined dynamically, as they are used, and not by their declaration.

> **KEY CONCEPT**
> The size of a dynamic data structure grows and shrinks as needed.

Dynamic Structures

Recall that the variable used to keep track of an object is actually a reference to the object, meaning that it stores the address of the object. A declaration such as

```
House home = new House ("602 Greenbriar Court");
```

actually accomplishes two things: it declares `home` to be a reference to a `House` object, and it instantiates an object of class `House`. Now consider an object that contains a reference to another object of the same type. For example:

```
class Node
{
    int info;
    Node next;
}
```

Two objects of this class can be instantiated and chained together by having the `next` reference of one `Node` object refer to the other `Node` object. The second

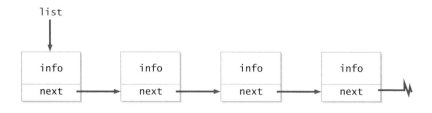

FIGURE 13.1   A linked list

object's next reference can refer to a third Node object, and so on, creating a *linked list*. The first node in the list could be referenced using a separate variable. The last node in the list would have a next reference that is null, indicating the end of the list. Figure 13.1 depicts this situation.

In this example, the information stored in each Node class is a simple integer, but keep in mind that we could define a class to contain any amount of information of any type.

A Dynamically Linked List

The program in Listing 13.1 sets up a list of Magazine objects and then prints the list. The list of magazines is encapsulated inside the MagazineList class shown in Listing 13.2 and is maintained as a dynamically linked list.

The MagazineList class represents the list of magazines. From outside of the class (an external view), we do not focus on how the list is implemented. We don't know, for instance, whether the list of magazines is stored in an array or in a linked list. The MagazineList class provides a set of methods that allows the user to maintain the list of magazines. That set of methods, specifically add and toString, defines the operations to the MagazineList ADT.

The MagazineList class uses an inner class called MagazineNode to represent a node in the linked list. Each node contains a reference to one magazine and a reference to the next node in the list. Because MagazineNode is an inner class, it is reasonable to allow the data values in the class to be public. Therefore, the code in the MagazineList class refers to those data values directly.

The Magazine class shown in Listing 13.3 is well encapsulated, with all data declared as private and methods provided to accomplish any updates necessary. Note that because we use a separate class to represent a node in the list, the Magazine class itself does not need to contain a link to the next Magazine in the list. That allows the Magazine class to be free of any issues regarding its containment in a list.

VideoNote

Example using a linked list.

LISTING 13.1

```
//********************************************************************
//  MagazineRack.java        Author: Lewis/Loftus
//
//  Driver to exercise the MagazineList collection.
//********************************************************************

public class MagazineRack
{
   //-----------------------------------------------------------------
   //  Creates a MagazineList object, adds several magazines to the
   //  list, then prints it.
   //-----------------------------------------------------------------
   public static void main (String[] args)
   {
      MagazineList rack = new MagazineList();

      rack.add (new Magazine("Time"));
      rack.add (new Magazine("Woodworking Today"));
      rack.add (new Magazine("Communications of the ACM"));
      rack.add (new Magazine("House and Garden"));
      rack.add (new Magazine("GQ"));

      System.out.println (rack);
   }
}
```

OUTPUT

```
Time
Woodworking Today
Communications of the ACM
House and Garden
GQ
```

Other methods could be included in the MagazineList ADT. For example, in addition to the add method provided, which always adds a new magazine to the end of the list, another method called insert could be defined to add a node anywhere in the list (to keep it sorted, for instance). A parameter to insert could indicate the value of the node after which the new node should be inserted. Figure 13.2 shows how the references would be updated to insert a new node.

KEY CONCEPT

Insert and delete operations can be implemented by carefully manipulating object references.

LISTING 13.2

```java
//********************************************************************
//  MagazineList.java       Author: Lewis/Loftus
//
//  Represents a collection of magazines.
//********************************************************************

public class MagazineList
{
   private MagazineNode list;

   //-----------------------------------------------------------------
   //  Sets up an initially empty list of magazines.
   //-----------------------------------------------------------------
   public MagazineList()
   {
      list = null;
   }

   //-----------------------------------------------------------------
   //  Creates a new MagazineNode object and adds it to the end of
   //  the linked list.
   //-----------------------------------------------------------------
   public void add (Magazine mag)
   {

      MagazineNode node = new MagazineNode (mag);
      MagazineNode current;

      if (list == null)
         list = node;
      else
      {
         current = list;
         while (current.next != null)
            current = current.next;
         current.next = node;
      }
   }

   //-----------------------------------------------------------------
   //  Returns this list of magazines as a string.
   //-----------------------------------------------------------------
   public String toString ()
```

LISTING 13.2   *continued*

```java
   {
      String result = "";

      MagazineNode current = list;

      while (current != null)
      {
         result += current.magazine + "\n";
         current = current.next;
      }

      return result;
   }

   //*********************************************************************
   //   An inner class that represents a node in the magazine list.
   //   The public variables are accessed by the MagazineList class.
   //*********************************************************************
   private class MagazineNode
   {
      public Magazine magazine;
      public MagazineNode next;

      //-----------------------------------------------------------
      // Sets up the node
      //-----------------------------------------------------------
      public MagazineNode (Magazine mag)
      {
         magazine = mag;
         next = null;
      }
   }
}
```

```java
//********************************************************************
//  Magazine.java       Author: Lewis/Loftus
//
//  Represents a single magazine.
//********************************************************************

public class Magazine
{
   private String title;

   //-----------------------------------------------------------------
   //  Sets up the new magazine with its title.
   //-----------------------------------------------------------------
   public Magazine (String newTitle)
   {
      title = newTitle;
   }

   //-----------------------------------------------------------------
   //  Returns this magazine as a string.
   //-----------------------------------------------------------------
   public String toString ()
   {
      return title;
   }
}
```

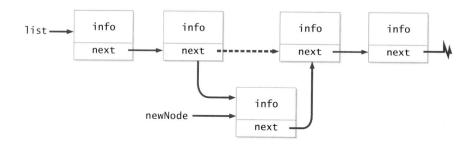

FIGURE 13.2   Inserting a node into the middle of a list

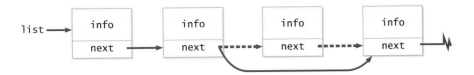

FIGURE 13.3   Deleting a node from a list

Another operation that would be helpful in the list ADT would be a `delete` method to remove a particular node. Recall from our discussion in Chapter 3 that by removing all references to an object, it becomes a candidate for garbage collection. Figure 13.3 shows how references would be updated to delete a node from a list. Care must be taken to accomplish the modifications to the references in the proper order to ensure that other nodes are not lost and that references continue to refer to valid, appropriate nodes in the list.

Other Dynamic List Representations

You can use different list implementations, depending on the specific needs of the program you are designing. For example, in some situations it may make processing easier to implement a *doubly linked list* in which each node has not only a reference to the next node in the list but another reference to the previous node in the list. Our generic `Node` class might be declared as follows:

> **KEY CONCEPT**
>
> Many variations on the implementation of dynamically linked lists can be defined.

```
class Node
{
    int info;
    Node next, prev;
}
```

Figure 13.4 shows a doubly linked list. Note that, like a single linked list, the next reference of the last node is `null`. Similarly, the previous node of the first node is `null` since there is no node that comes before the first one. This type of structure makes it easy to move back and forth between nodes in the list but requires more effort to set up and modify.

FIGURE 13.4   A doubly linked list

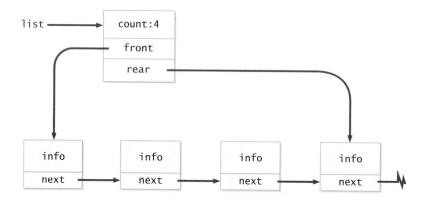

FIGURE 13.5   A list with front and rear references

Another implementation of a linked list could include a *header node* for the list that has a reference to the front of the list and another reference to the rear of the list. A rear reference makes it easier to add new nodes to the end of the list. The header node could contain other information, such as a count of the number of nodes currently in the list. The declaration of the header node would be similar to the following:

```
class ListHeader
{
    int count;
    Node front, rear;
}
```

Note that the header node is not of the same class as the Node class to which it refers. Figure 13.5 depicts a linked list that is implemented using a header node.

Still other linked list implementations can be created. For instance, the use of a header can be combined with a doubly linked list, or the list can be maintained in sorted order. The implementation should cater to the type of processing that is required. Some extra effort to maintain a more complex data structure may be worthwhile if it makes common operations on the structure more efficient.

myprogramminglab   SELF-REVIEW QUESTIONS *(see answers in Appendix N)*

SR 13.4   What is a dynamic data structure?

SR 13.5   Describe the steps depicted in Figure 13.2 to insert a node into a list. What special cases exist?

SR 13.6   Describe the steps depicted in Figure 13.3 to delete a node from a list. What special cases exist?

SR 13.7 Suppose `first` is a reference to a `Node` object, and that it refers to the first node in a linked list. Show, in pseudocode, the steps that would count and return the number of nodes on the list.

SR 13.8 What is a doubly linked list?

SR 13.9 What is a header node for a linked list?

13.3 Linear Data Structures

In addition to lists, some data structures have become classic in that they represent important generic situations that commonly occur in computing. Like lists, a queue and a stack are *linear data structures*, meaning that the data they represent is organized in a linear fashion. This section explores some linear data structures in more detail.

Queues

A *queue* is similar to a list except that it has restrictions on the way you put items in and take items out. Specifically, a queue uses *first-in, first-out* (FIFO) processing. That is, the first item put in the list is the first item that comes out of the list. Figure 13.6 depicts the FIFO processing of a queue.

> **KEY CONCEPT**
>
> A queue is a linear data structure that manages data in a first-in, first-out manner.

Any waiting line is a queue. Think about a line of people waiting for a teller at a bank. A customer enters the queue at the back and moves forward as earlier customers are serviced. Eventually, each customer comes to the front of the queue to be processed.

Note that the processing of a queue is conceptual. We may speak in terms of people moving forward until they reach the front of the queue, but the reality might be that the front of the queue moves as elements come off. That is, we are

Items go on the queue
at the rear (enqueue)

Items come off the queue
at the front (dequeue)

FIGURE 13.6 A queue data structure

VideoNote

Implementing a queue.

not concerned at this point with whether the queue of customers moves toward the teller, or remains stationary as the teller moves when customers are serviced.

A queue data structure typically has the following operations:

- enqueue—adds an item to the rear of the queue
- dequeue—removes an item from the front of the queue
- empty—returns true if the queue is empty

Stacks

> **KEY CONCEPT**
>
> A stack is a linear data structure that manages data in a last-in, first-out manner.

A *stack* is similar to a queue except that its elements go on and come off at the same end. The last item to go on a stack is the first item to come off, like a stack of plates in the cupboard or a stack of hay bales in the barn. A stack, therefore, processes information in a *last-in, first-out* (LIFO) manner, as shown in Figure 13.7.

A typical stack ADT contains the following operations:

- push—pushes an item onto the top of the stack
- pop—removes an item from the top of the stack
- peek—retrieves information from the top item of the stack without removing it
- empty—returns true if the stack is empty

The `java.util` package of the API contains a class called `Stack` that implements a stack data structure. It contains methods that correspond to the standard stack operations, plus a method that searches for a particular object in the stack.

The `Stack` class has a `search` method that returns an integer corresponding to the position in the stack of the particular object. This type of searching is not usually considered to be part of the classic stack ADT.

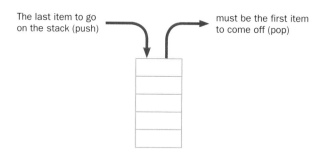

FIGURE 13.7　A stack data structure

Like ArrayList operations, the Stack operations operate on Object references. Because all objects are derived from the Object class, any object can be pushed onto a stack. If primitive types are to be stored, they must be treated as objects using the corresponding wrapper class. Unlike the Stack class, no class implementing a queue is defined in the Java API.

Let's look at an example that uses a stack to solve a problem. The program in Listing 13.4 accepts a string of characters that represents a secret message. The program decodes and prints the message.

LISTING 13.4

```java
//********************************************************************
//  Decode.java        Author: Lewis/Loftus
//
//  Demonstrates the use of the Stack class.
//********************************************************************

import java.util.*;

public class Decode
{
   //-----------------------------------------------------------------
   //  Decodes a message by reversing each word in a string.
   //-----------------------------------------------------------------
   public static void main (String[] args)
   {
      Scanner scan = new Scanner (System.in);

      Stack word = new Stack();

      String message;
      int index = 0;

      System.out.println ("Enter the coded message:");
      message = scan.nextLine();
      System.out.println ("The decoded message is:");

      while (index < message.length())
      {
         // Push word onto stack
         while (index < message.length() && message.charAt(index) != ' ')
         {
            word.push (new Character(message.charAt(index)));
            index++;
         }
```

> **LISTING 13.4**   *continued*
>
> ```
>         // Print word in reverse
>         while (!word.empty())
>            System.out.print ((((Character)word.pop()).charValue()));
>         System.out.print (" ");
>         index++;
>      }
>
>      System.out.println();
>    }
> }
> ```

OUTPUT

```
Enter the coded message:
artxE eseehc esaelp
The decoded message is:
Extra cheese please
```

A message that has been encoded has each individual word in the message reversed. Words in the message are separated by a single space. The program uses the Stack class to push the characters of each word on the stack. When an entire word has been read, each character appears in reverse order as it is popped off the stack and printed.

myprogramminglab | **SELF-REVIEW QUESTIONS** *(see answers in Appendix N)*

SR 13.10   How is a queue different from a list?

SR 13.11   Show the contents of a queue after the following operations are performed. Assume the queue is initially empty.

```
enqueue (5);
enqueue (21);
dequeue();
enqueue (72);
enqueue (37);
enqueue (15);
dequeue();
```

SR 13.12   What is a stack?

SR 13.13   Show the contents of a stack after the following operations are per-
           formed. Assume the stack is initially empty.

```
push (5);
push (21);
pop();
push (72);
push (37);
push (15);
pop();
```

SR 13.14   What is the Stack class?

13.4 Non-Linear Data Structures

Some data structures are considered to be *non-linear data structures*, because
their data is not organized linearly. This section examines two types of non-linear
structures: trees and graphs.

Trees

A *tree* is a non-linear data structure that consists of a *root node* and
potentially many levels of additional nodes that form a hierarchy. All
nodes other than the root are called *internal nodes*. Nodes that have no
children are called *leaf nodes*. Figure 13.8 depicts a tree. Note that we
draw a tree "upside down," with the root at the top and the leaves at
the bottom.

> **KEY CONCEPT**
>
> A tree is a non-linear data structure
> that organizes data into a hierarchy.

In a general tree like the one in Figure 13.8, each node could have many child
nodes. As we mentioned in Chapter 9, the inheritance relationships among classes
can be depicted using a general tree structure.

In a *binary tree*, each node can have no more than two child nodes. Binary trees
are useful in various programming situations and usually are easier to implement
than general trees. Technically, binary trees are a subset of general trees, but they
are so important in the computing world that they usually are thought of as their
own data structure.

The operations on trees and binary trees vary, but minimally include adding
and removing nodes from the tree or binary tree. Because of their non-linear
nature, trees and binary trees are implemented nicely using references as dynamic
links. However, it is possible to implement a tree data structure using a fixed
representation such as an array.

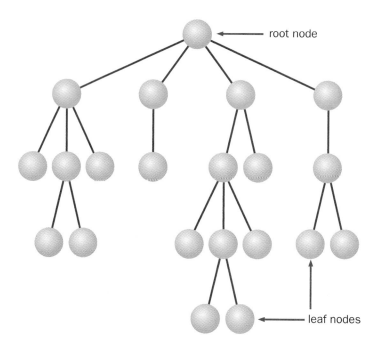

FIGURE 13.8 A tree data structure

Graphs

Like a tree, a *graph* is a non-linear data structure. Unlike a tree, a graph does not have a primary entry point like the tree's root node. In a graph, a node is linked to another node by a connection called an *edge*. Generally there are no restrictions on the number of edges that can be made between nodes in a graph. Figure 13.9 presents a graph data structure.

Graphs are useful when representing relationships for which linear paths and strict hierarchies do not suffice. For instance, the highway system connecting cities on a map and airline connections between airports are better represented as graphs than by any other data structure discussed so far.

In a general graph, the edges are bi-directional, meaning that the edge connecting nodes A and B can be followed from A to B and also from B to A. In a *directed graph*, or *digraph*, each edge has a specific direction. Figure 13.10 shows a digraph, in which each edge indicates the direction using an arrowhead.

A digraph might be used, for instance, to represent airline flights between airports. Unlike highway systems, which are in almost all cases bi-directional, having a flight from one city to another does not necessarily mean there is a

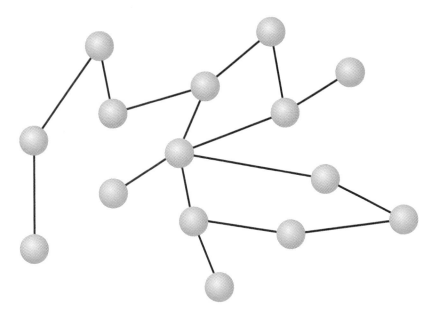

FIGURE 13.9   A graph data structure

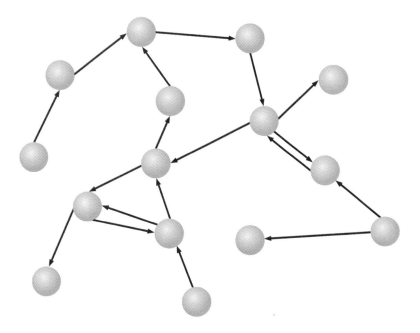

FIGURE 13.10   A directed graph

corresponding flight going the other way. Or, if there is, we may want to associate different information with it, such as cost.

Like trees, graphs often are implemented using dynamic links, although they can be implemented using arrays as well.

myprogramminglab

SELF-REVIEW QUESTIONS *(see answers in Appendix N)*

SR 13.15   What do trees and graphs have in common?

SR 13.16   Which structure (a tree or a graph) would be a good choice to represent each of the following.

    a. The directories and files on a computer system.
    b. Airplane routes.
    c. An "is a friend of" relationship among a group of people.
    d. An "is a boss of" relationship in a company.

13.5 The Java Collections API

The Java standard class library contains several classes that represent collections of various types. These are often referred to as the *Java Collections API* (Application Programming Interface).

KEY CONCEPT

The Java Collections API defines several collection classes implemented in various ways.

Most of the names of the classes in this set indicate both the collection type and the underlying implementation. One example is the ArrayList class, which is discussed in some detail in Chapter 5. It represents a list collection, implemented using an underlying array. Similarly, the LinkedList class represents a list collection with a dynamically linked internal implementation.

The Vector class and the Stack class are carried over from earlier Java incarnations, which is why their names aren't consistent with the newer collection classes.

Several interfaces are used to define the collection operations themselves. These interfaces include List, Set, SortedSet, Map, and SortedMap. A Set is consistent with its normal interpretation as a collection of elements without duplicates. A Map is a group of elements that can be referenced by a key value.

Generics

As we mentioned in Chapter 5 during the discussion of the ArrayList class, the classes in the Java Collections API are implemented as *generic types*, meaning that the type of object that the collection manages can be established when an object of that collection type is instantiated.

> **KEY CONCEPT**
> The classes of the Java Collections API are implemented as generic types.

For example, to create a LinkedList of String objects, we would instantiate a collection object in the following way:

```
LinkedList<String> myStringList = new LinkedList<String>();
```

Similarly, to create a LinkedList of Book objects, we would instantiate the collection as follows:

```
LinkedList<Book> myBookList = new LinkedList<Book>();
```

By specifying the type stored in the collection, we gain two advantages:

- Only objects of the appropriate type can be added to the collection.
- When an object is removed from the collection, its type is already established, avoiding the need to cast it to an appropriate type.

The myStringList object can store only String objects, and the myBookList collection can store only Book objects. Keep in mind that these include objects related to the specified type by inheritance. For example, if a Dictionary class is derived from Book, then we could store a Dictionary object in the myBookList collection. After all, if we're using inheritance correctly, a Dictionary is-a Book.

> **KEY CONCEPT**
> Generic classes ensure type compatibility among the objects stored by the collection.

If no specific type is specified when the collection object is created, the collection is defined as containing references of the Object class, which means they can store any type of object. This makes the use of the collections classes consistent with earlier versions of Java that did not include generic specifications.

The details of the collection classes and the techniques for defining a generic class go beyond the scope of this book and so are not explored further here.

SELF-REVIEW QUESTIONS *(see answers in Appendix N)*

SR 13.17 What is the Java Collections API?

SR 13.18 What is a generic type, and how does it relate to the Java Collections API?

myprogramminglab

Summary of Key Concepts

- An object, with its well-defined interface, is a perfect mechanism for implementing a collection.
- The size of a dynamic data structure grows and shrinks as needed.
- A dynamically linked list is managed by storing and updating references to objects.
- Insert and delete operations can be implemented by carefully manipulating object references.
- Many variations on the implementation of dynamically linked lists can be defined.
- A queue is a linear data structure that manages data in a first-in, first-out manner.
- A stack is a linear data structure that manages data in a last-in, first-out manner.
- A tree is a non-linear data structure that organizes data into a hierarchy.
- A graph is a non-linear data structure that connects nodes using generic edges.
- The Java Collections API defines several collection classes implemented in various ways.
- The classes of the Java Collections API are implemented as generic types.
- Generic classes ensure type compatibility among the objects stored by the collection.

Exercises

Visit www.myprogramminglab.com to complete many of these Exercises online and get instant feedback.

EX 13.1   Suppose LINK is a reference to a Node object and it is currently pointing to a specific node in a linked list. Using pseudocode, show the steps involved in deleting LINK from the list irrespective of its position in the list.

EX 13.2   Modify your answer to Exercise 13.1 to delete the list, assuming it was set up as a doubly linked list with both prev and next references.

EX 13.3   Suppose current and newNode are references to Node objects. Assume current currently refers to a specific node in a linked list and `newNode` refers to an unattached `Node` object. Show, in pseudocode, the steps that would insert `newNode` behind current in the list. Carefully consider the cases in which `current` is referring to the first and last nodes in the list.

EX 13.4   Modify your answer to Exercise 13.3 assuming that the list was set up as a doubly linked list, with both `next` and `prev` references.

EX 13.5   Would the front and rear references in the header node of a linked list ever refer to the same node? Would they ever both be null? Would one ever be null if the other was not? Explain your answers using examples.

EX 13.6   Show the contents of a queue after the following operations are performed. Assume the queue is initially empty.

```
enqueue (10);
enqueue (20);
enqueue (30);
enqueue (40);
enqueue (50);
dequeue();
dequeue();
dequeue();
enqueue (10);
dequeue();
enqueue (20);
dequeue();
dequeue();
```

EX 13.7   In terms of the final state of a queue, does it matter how dequeue operations are intermixed with enqueue operations? Does it matter how the enqueue operations are intermixed among themselves? Explain using examples.

EX 13.8   Show the contents of a stack after the following operations are performed. Assume the stack is initially empty.

```
push (10);
push (20);
push (30);
push (40);
push (50);
pop();
pop();
pop();
push (10);
```

```
pop();
push (20);
pop();
pop();
```

EX 13.9   Which package in Java enables the implementation of Stack data structure? Write code to implement a stack data structure, which will search for an element in a stack and return its position.

EX 13.10   Would it be possible to implement a tree data structure using an array? If so, draw an array representation that shows the hierarchy of a binary tree. What relationship do a parent and a child share in an array representation?

EX 13.11   What data structure would be a good choice to represent the links between various Web sites? Give an example.

Programming Projects

Visit www.myprogramminglab.com to complete many of these Programming Projects online and get instant feedback.

PP 13.1   Consistent with the example from Chapter 8, design and implement an application that maintains a collection of DVDs using a linked list. In the main method of the driver class, add various DVDs to the collection and print the list when complete.

PP 13.2   Modify the MagazineRack program presented in this chapter by adding delete and insert operations into the MagazineList class. Have the Magazine class implement the Comparable interface, and base the processing of the insert method on calls to the compareTo method in the Magazine class that determines whether one Magazine title comes before another alphabetically. In the driver, exercise various insertion and deletion operations. Print the list of magazines when complete.

PP 13.3   Design and implement a version of selection sort (from Chapter 10) that operates on a linked list of nodes that each contain an integer.

PP 13.4   Design and implement a version of bubble sort for a linked list. Assume that each node in the list contains an integer value.

VideoNote

Developing a solution of PP 13.3.

PP 13.5   Design and implement an application that simulates the customers waiting in line at a bank. Use a queue data structure to represent the line. As customers arrive at the bank, customer objects are put in the rear of the queue with an enqueue operation. When the teller is ready to service another customer, the customer object is removed from the front of the queue with a dequeue operation. Randomly determine when new customers arrive at the bank and when current customers are finished at the teller window. Print a message each time an operation occurs during the simulation.

PP 13.6   Modify the solution to the PP 13.5 so that it represents eight tellers and therefore eight customer queues. Have new customers go to the shortest queue. Determine which queue had the shortest waiting time per customer on average.

PP 13.7   Design and implement an application that evaluates a postfix expression that operates on integer operands using the arithmetic operators +, –, *, /, and %. We are already familiar with infix expressions, in which an operator is positioned between its two operands. A *postfix expression* puts the operators after its operands. Keep in mind that an operand could be the result of another operation. This eliminates the need for parentheses to force precedence. For example, the following infix expression:

(5 + 2) * (8 – 5)

is equivalent to the following postfix expression.

5 2 + 8 5 – *

The evaluation of a postfix expression is facilitated by using a stack. As you process a postfix expression from left to right, you encounter operands and operators. If you encounter an operand, push it on the stack. If you encounter an operator, pop two operands off the stack, perform the operation, and push the result back on the stack. When you have processed the entire expression, there will be one value on the stack, which is the result of the entire expression.

You may want to use a `StringTokenizer` object to assist in the parsing of the expression. You can assume the expression will be in valid postfix form.

PP 13.8   Design and implement a program to create a dictionary, which consists of all the index terms in a sorted order using binary trees. Each index term has been encapsulated in a `Node` object with a reference to its left child and right child. The program must accept new index terms from the user, insert them into the appropriate positions, and display the dictionary to the user in sorted order after constructing it.

PP 13.9 Design and implement a class named `StringTree`, a binary tree for storing `String` objects in alphabetic order. Each node in the tree should be represented by a `Node` class, which stores the string value and pointers to the right and left child nodes. For any node value in the tree, the value of its left child should come before that value, and the value of its right child should come after that value. The `StringTree` class should contain both a method for adding strings to the tree and a method for printing the tree's value in alphabetic order. Write a driver program that prompts the user for strings and adds them to the tree. After processing the input, print the tree values.

PP 13.10 Design and implement an application to support a moderated question-and-answer session in which audience members submit questions to a queue. The question at the front of the queue may be answered by the speaker or panel, and a list of answered or unanswered questions may be retrieved at any time.

The program should accept the following simple commands: 'Q' will allow an audience member to submit a question, along with their name; 'A' will allow the speaker to enter an answer to the question currently at the top of the queue; 'P' will allow the speaker to pass on a question, moving it from the front of the queue to the end of the queue; 'R' will allow the speaker to mark a question as rejected, removing it from the queue; 'LA' will print a numbered list of answered questions, along with the answers; 'LU' will print a numbered list of unanswered questions; finally, 'X' will print numbered lists of answered and unanswered questions, then exit the program.

You should create a `Question` class to store each question, its answer, and any other question state information. The answered and unanswered queues should be implemented using the `java.util.LinkedList` class. You must use only the methods in the class that provide Queue functionality: remove the first element, append an element to the end, retrieve the queue size, and iterate over the list.

Glossary

abstract—A Java reserved word that serves as a modifier for classes, interfaces, and methods. An abstract class cannot be instantiated and is used to specify bodiless abstract methods that are given definitions by derived classes. Interfaces are inherently abstract.

abstract class—*See* abstract.

abstract data type (ADT)—A collection of data and the operations that are defined on that data. An abstract data type might be implemented in a variety of ways, but the interface operations are consistent.

abstract method—*See* abstract.

Abstract Windowing Toolkit (AWT)—The package in the Java API (java.awt) that contains classes related to graphics and graphical user interfaces. *See also* Swing.

abstraction—The concept of hiding details. If the right details are hidden at the right times, abstraction can significantly help control complexity and focus attention on appropriate issues.

access—The ability to reference a variable or invoke a method from outside the class in which it is declared. Controlled by the visibility modifier used to declare the variable or method. Also called the level of encapsulation. *See also* visibility modifier.

access modifier—*See* visibility modifier.

actual parameter—The value passed to a method as a parameter. *See also* formal parameter.

adaptor class—*See* listener adaptor class.

address—(1) A numeric value that uniquely identifies a particular memory location in a computer's main memory. (2) A designation that uniquely identifies a computer among all others on a network.

ADT—*See* abstract data type.

aggregate object—An object that contains variables that are references to other objects. *See also* has-a relationship.

aggregation—Something that is composed, at least in part, of other things. *See also* aggregate object.

algorithm—A step-by-step process for solving a problem. A program is based on one or more algorithms.

alias—A reference to an object that is currently also referred to by another reference. Each reference is an alias of the other.

analog—A representation that is in direct proportion to the source of the information. *See also* digital.

animation—A series of images or drawings that give the appearance of movement when displayed in order at a particular speed.

API—*See* Application Programming Interface.

applet—A Java program that is linked into an HTML document, then retrieved and executed using a Web browser, as opposed to a standalone Java application.

appletviewer—A software tool that interprets and displays Java applets through links in HTML documents. Part of the Java Development Kit.

application—(1) A generic term for any program. (2) A Java program that can be run without the use of a Web browser, as opposed to a Java applet.

Application Programming Interface (API)—A set of classes that defines services for a programmer. Not part of the language itself, but often relied on to perform even basic tasks. *See also* class library.

arc angle—When defining an arc, the radial distance that defines the arc's length. *See also* start angle.

architectural design—A high-level design that identifies the large portions of a software system and key data structures. *See also* detailed design.

architecture—*See* computer architecture.

architecture neutral—Not specific to any particular hardware platform. Java code is considered architecture neutral because it is compiled into bytecode and then interpreted on any machine with a Java interpreter.

arithmetic operator—An operator that performs a basic arithmetic computation, such as addition or multiplication.

arithmetic promotion—The act of promoting the type of a numeric operand to be consistent with the other operand.

array—A programming language construct used to store an ordered list of primitive values or objects. Each element in the array is referenced using a numerical index from 0 to $N-1$, where N is the size of the array.

array element—A value or object that is stored in an array.

array element type—The type of the values or objects that are stored in an array.

ASCII—A popular character set used by many programming languages. ASCII stands for American Standard Code for Information Interchange. It is a subset of the Unicode character set, which is used by Java.

assembly language—A low-level language that uses mnemonics to represent program commands.

assignment conversion—Some data types can be converted to another in an assignment statement. *See* widening conversion.

assignment operator—An operator that results in an assignment to a variable. The = operator performs basic assignment. Many other assignment operators perform additional operations prior to the assignment, such as the *= operator.

association—A relationship between two classes in which one uses the other or relates to it in some way. *See also* operator association, use relationship.

AWT—*See* Abstract Windowing Toolkit.

background color—(1) The color of the background of a graphical user interface component. (2) The color of the background of an HTML page. *See also* foreground color.

base—The numerical value on which a particular number system is based. It determines the number of digits available in that number system and the place value of each digit in a number. *See also* binary, decimal, hexadecimal, octal, place value.

base 2—*See* binary.

base 8—*See* octal.

base 10—*See* decimal.

base 16—*See* hexadecimal.

base case—The situation that terminates recursive processing, allowing the active recursive methods to begin returning to their point of invocation.

base class—*See* superclass.

behavior—The functional characteristics of an object, defined by its methods. *See also* identity, state.

binary—The base-2 number system. Modern computer systems store information as strings of binary digits (bits).

binary operator—An operator that uses two operands.

binary search—A searching algorithm that requires that the list be sorted. It repetitively compares the "middle" element of the list to the target value, narrowing the scope of the search each time. *See also* linear search.

binary string—A series of binary digits (bits).

binary tree—A tree data structure in which each node can have no more than two child nodes.

binding—The process of associating an identifier with the construct that it represents. For example, the process of binding a method name to the specific definition that it invokes.

bit—A binary digit, either 0 or 1.

bit shifting—The act of shifting the bits of a data value to the left or right, losing bits on one end and inserting bits on the other.

bits per second (bps)—A measurement rate for data transfer devices.

bitwise operator—An operator that manipulates individual bits of a value, either by calculation or by shifting.

black-box testing—Producing and evaluating test cases based on the input and expected output of a software component. The test cases focus on covering the equivalence categories and boundary values of the input. *See also* white-box testing.

block—A group of programming statements and declarations delimited by braces ({}).

boolean—A Java reserved word representing a logical primitive data type that can only take the values `true` or `false`.

boolean expression—An expression that evaluates to a true or false result, primarily used as conditions in selection and repetition statements.

boolean operator—Any of the bitwise operators AND (&), OR (|), or XOR (^) when applied to `boolean` operands. The results are equivalent to their logical counterparts, except that boolean operators are not short-circuited.

border—A graphical edge around a graphical user interface component to enhance its appearance or to group components visually. An empty border creates a buffer of space around a component.

bounding rectangle—A rectangle that delineates a region in which an oval or arc is defined.

boundary values—The input values corresponding to the edges of equivalence categories. Used in black-box testing.

bounds checking—The process of determining whether an array index is in bounds, given the size of the array. Java performs automatic bounds checking.

bps—*See* bits per second.

break—A Java reserved word used to interrupt the flow of control by breaking out of the current loop or `switch` statement.

browser—Software that retrieves HTML documents and other resources across a network and formats them for viewing. A browser is the primary vehicle for accessing the World Wide Web.

bug—A slang term for a defect or error in a computer program.

build-and-fix approach—An approach to software development in which a program is created without any significant planning or design, then modified until it reaches some level of acceptance. It is a prevalent, but unwise, approach.

bus—A group of wires in the computer that carry data between components such as the CPU and main memory.

button—A graphical user interface component that allows the user to initiate an action, set a condition, or choose an option with a mouse click. There are several kinds of GUI buttons. *See also* check box, push button, radio button.

byte—(1) A unit of binary storage equal to eight bits. (2) A Java reserved word that represents a primitive integer type, stored using eight bits in two's complement format.

byte stream—An I/O stream that manages 8-bit bytes of raw binary data. *See also* character stream.

bytecode—The low-level format into which the Java compiler translates Java source code. The bytecodes are interpreted and executed by the Java interpreter, perhaps after transportation over the Internet.

capacity—*See* storage capacity.

case—(1) A Java reserved word that is used to identify each unique option in a `switch` statement. (2) The orientation of an alphabetic character (uppercase or lowercase).

case sensitive—Differentiating between the uppercase and lowercase versions of an alphabetic letter. Java is case sensitive; therefore the identifier total and the identifier Total are considered to be different identifiers.

cast—A Java operation expressed using a type or class name in parentheses to explicitly convert and return a value of one data type into another.

catch—A Java reserved word that is used to specify an exception handler, defined after a `try` block.

CD-Recordable (CD-R)—A compact disc on which information can be stored once using a home computer with an appropriate drive. *See also* CD-Rewritable, CD-ROM.

CD-Rewritable (CD-RW)—A compact disc on which information can be stored and rewritten multiple times using a home computer with an appropriate drive. *See also* CD-Recordable, CD-ROM.

CD-ROM—An optical secondary memory medium that stores binary information in a manner similar to a musical compact disc.

central processing unit (CPU)—The hardware component that controls the main activity of a computer, including the flow of information and the execution of commands.

char—A Java reserved word that represents the primitive character type. All Java characters are members of the Unicode character set and are stored using 16 bits.

character font—A specification that defines the distinct look of a character when it is printed or drawn.

character set—An ordered list of characters, such as the ASCII or Unicode character sets. Each character corresponds to a specific, unique numeric value within a given character set. A programming language adopts a particular character set to use for character representation and management.

character stream—An I/O stream that manages 16-bit Unicode characters. *See also* byte stream.

character string—A series of ordered characters. Represented in Java using the `String` class and string literals such as `"hello"`.

check box—A graphical user interface component that allows the user to set a boolean condition with a mouse click. A check box can be used alone or independently among other check boxes. *See also* radio button.

checked exception—A Java exception that must be either caught or explicitly thrown to the calling method. *See also* unchecked exception.

child class—*See* subclass.

class—(1) A Java reserved word used to define a class. (2) The blueprint of an object—the model that defines the variables and methods an object will contain when instantiated.

class diagram—A diagram that shows the relationships between classes, including inheritance and use relationships. *See also* Unified Modeling Language.

class hierarchy—A tree-like structure created when classes are derived from other classes through inheritance. *See also* interface hierarchy.

class library—A set of classes that define useful services for a programmer. *See also* Application Programming Interface.

class method—A method that can be invoked using only the class name. An instantiated object is not required as it is with instance methods. Defined in a Java program by using the `static` reserved word.

CLASSPATH—An operating system setting that determines where the Java interpreter searches for class files.

class variable—A variable that is shared among all objects of a class. It can also be referenced through the class name, without instantiating any object of that class. Defined in a Java program by using the `static` reserved word.

client-server model—A manner in which to construct a software design based on objects (clients) making use of the services provided by other objects (servers).

coding guidelines—A series of conventions that describe how programs should be constructed. They make programs easier to read, exchange, and integrate. Sometimes referred to as coding standards, especially when they are enforced.

coding standard—*See* coding guidelines.

cohesion—The strength of the relationship among the parts within a software component. *See also* coupling.

collision—The process of two hash values producing the same hash code. *See also* hash code, hashing.

color chooser—A graphical user interface component, often displayed as a dialog box, that allows the user to select or specify a color.

combo box—A graphical user interface component that allows the user to select one of several options. A combo box displays the most recent selection. *See also* list.

command-line arguments—The values that follow the program name on the command line. Accessed within a Java program through the String array parameter to the main method.

comment—A programming language construct that allows a programmer to embed human-readable annotations into the source code. *See also* documentation.

compiler—A program that translates code from one language to equivalent code in another language. The Java compiler translates Java source code into Java bytecode. *See also* interpreter.

compile-time error—Any error that occurs during the compilation process, often indicating that a program does not conform to the language syntax or that an operation was attempted on an inappropriate data type. *See also* logical error, run-time error, syntax error.

component—Any portion of a software system that performs a specific task, transforming input to output. *See also* GUI component.

computer architecture—The structure and interaction of the hardware components of a computer.

concatenation—*See* string concatenation.

condition—A `boolean` expression used to determine whether the body of a selection or repetition statement should be executed.

conditional coverage—A strategy used in white-box testing in which all conditions in a program are executed, producing both `true` and `false` results. *See also* statement coverage.

conditional operator—A Java ternary operator that evaluates one of two expressions based on a condition.

conditional statement—*See* selection statement.

const—A Java reserved word that is not currently used.

constant—An identifier that contains a value that cannot be modified. Used to make code more readable and to facilitate changes. Defined in Java using the `final` modifier.

constructor—A special method in a class that is invoked when an object is instantiated from the class. Used to initialize the object.

container—A Java graphical user interface component that can hold other components. *See also* containment hierarchy.

containment hierarchy—The relationships among graphical components of a user interface. *See also* container.

content pane—The part of a top-level container to which components are added.

control characters—*See* nonprintable characters.

controller—Hardware devices that control the interaction between a computer system and a particular kind of peripheral.

coupling—The strength of the relationship between two software components. *See also* cohesion.

CPU—*See* central processing unit.

data stream—An I/O stream that represents a particular source or destination for data, such as a file. *See also* processing stream.

data structure—Any programming construct, either defined in the language or by a programmer, used to organize data into a format to facilitate access and processing. Arrays, linked lists, and stacks can all be considered data structures.

data type—A designation that specifies a set of values (which may be infinite). For example, each variable has a data type that specifies the kinds of values that can be stored in it.

data transfer device—A hardware component that allows information to be sent between computers, such as a modem.

debugger—A software tool that allows a programmer to step through an executing program and examine the value of variables at any point. *See also* jdb.

decimal—The base-10 number system, which humans use in everyday life. *See also* binary.

default—A Java reserved word that is used to indicate the default case of a `switch` statement, used if no other cases match.

default visibility—The level of access designated when no explicit visibility modifier is used to declare a class, interface, method, or variable. Sometimes referred to as package visibility. Anything declared with default visibility is visible only to classes in the same package.

defect testing—Testing designed to uncover errors in a program.

delimiter—Any symbol or word used to set the boundaries of a programming language construct, such as the braces ({}) used to define a Java block.

deprecated—Something, such as a particular method in the Java API, that is considered out-of-favor and should not be used.

derived class—*See* subclass.

design—(1) The plan for implementing a program, which includes a specification of the classes and objects used and an expression of the important program algorithms. (2) The process of creating a program design.

desk check—A type of review in which a developer carefully examines a design or program to find errors.

detailed design—(1) The low-level algorithmic steps of a method. (2) The development stage at which low-level algorithmic steps are determined.

development stage—The software life-cycle stage in which a software system is first created, preceding use, maintenance, and eventual retirement.

dialog box—A graphical window that pops up to allow brief, specific user interaction.

digital—A representation that breaks information down into pieces, which are in turn represented as numbers. All modern computer systems are digital.

digitize—The act of converting an analog representation into a digital one by breaking it down into pieces.

digraph—A graph data structure in which each edge has a specific direction.

dimension—The number of index levels of a particular array.

direct recursion—The process of a method invoking itself. *See also* indirect recursion.

disable—Make a graphical user interface component inactive so that it cannot be used. A disabled component is grayed to indicate its disabled status. *See also* enable.

DNS—*See* Domain Name System.

do—A Java reserved word that represents a repetition construct. A do statement is executed one or more times. *See also* for, while.

documentation—Supplemental information about a program, including comments in a program's source code and printed reports such as a user's guide.

domain name—The portion of an Internet address that specifies the organization to which the computer belongs.

Domain Name System (DNS)—Software that translates an Internet address into an IP address using a domain server.

domain server—A file server that maintains a list of Internet addresses and their corresponding IP addresses.

double—A Java reserved word that represents a primitive floating point numeric type, stored using 64 bits in IEEE 754 format.

doubly linked list—A linked list with two references in each node: one that refers to the next node in the list and one that refers to the previous node in the list.

dynamic binding—The process of associating an identifier with its definition during run time. *See also* binding.

dynamic data structure—A set of objects that are linked using references, which can be modified as needed during program execution.

editor—A software tool that allows the user to enter and store a file of characters on a computer. Often used by programmers to enter the source code of a program.

efficiency—The characteristic of an algorithm that specifies the required number of a particular operation in order to complete its task. For example, the efficiency of a sort can be measured by the number of comparisons required to sort a list. *See also* order.

element—A value or object stored in another object such as an array.

element type—*See* array element type.

else—A Java reserved word that designates the portion of code in an `if` statement that will be executed if the condition is false.

enable—Make a graphical user interface component active so that it can be used. *See also* disable.

encapsulation—The characteristic of an object that limits access to the variables and methods contained in it. All interaction with an object occurs through a well-defined interface that supports a modular design.

equality operator—One of two Java operators that returns a boolean result based on whether two values are equal (==) or not equal (!=).

equivalence category—A range of functionally equivalent input values as specified by the requirements of the software component. Used when developing black-box test cases.

error—(1) Any defect in a design or program. (2) An object that can be thrown and processed by special `catch` blocks, though usually errors should not be caught. *See also* compile-time error, exception, logical error, run-time error, syntax error.

escape sequence—In Java, a sequence of characters beginning with the backslash character (\), used to indicate a special situation when printing values. For example, the escape sequence \t specifies that a horizontal tab should be printed.

exception—(1) A situation that arises during program execution that is erroneous or out of the ordinary. (2) An object that can be thrown and processed by special `catch` blocks. *See also* error.

exception handler—The code in a `catch` clause of a `try` statement, executed when a particular type of exception is thrown.

exception propagation—The process that occurs when an exception is thrown: control returns to each calling method in the stack trace until the exception is caught and handled or until the exception is thrown from the main method, terminating the program.

exponent—The portion of a floating point value's internal representation that specifies how far the decimal point is shifted. *See also* mantissa.

expression—A combination of operators and operands that produce a result.

extends—A Java reserved word used to specify the parent class in the definition of a child class.

event—(1) A user action, such as a mouse click or key press. (2) An object that represents a user action, to which the program can respond. *See also* event-driven programming.

event-driven programming—An approach to software development in which the program is designed to acknowledge that an event has occurred and to act accordingly. *See also* event.

false—A Java reserved word that serves as one of the two boolean literals (`true` and `false`).

fetch-decode-execute—The cycle through which the CPU continually obtains instructions from main memory and executes them.

FIFO—*See* first-in, first-out.

file—A named collection of data stored on a secondary storage device such as a disk. *See also* text file.

file chooser—A graphical user interface component, usually displayed as a dialog box, that allows the user to select a file from a storage device.

file server—A computer in a network, usually with a large secondary storage capacity, that is dedicated to storing software needed by many network users.

filtering stream—*See* processing stream.

final—A Java reserved word that serves as a modifier for classes, methods, and variables. A `final` class cannot be used to derive a new class. A `final` method cannot be overridden. A `final` variable is a constant.

finalize—A Java method defined in the Object class that can be overridden in any other class. It is called after the object becomes a candidate for garbage collection and before it is destroyed. It can be used to perform "clean-up" activity that is not performed automatically by the garbage collector.

finalizer method—A Java method, called finalize, that is called before an object is destroyed. *See also* finalize.

finally—A Java reserved word that designates a block of code to be executed when an exception is thrown, after any appropriate catch handler is processed.

first-in, first-out (FIFO)—A data management technique in which the first value that is stored in a data structure is the first value that comes out. *See also* last-in, first-out; queue.

float—A Java reserved word that represents a primitive floating point numeric type, stored using 32 bits in IEEE 754 format.

flushing—The process of forcing the contents of the output buffer to be displayed on the output device.

font—*See* character font.

for—A Java reserved word that represents a repetition construct. A `for` statement is executed zero or more times and is usually used when a precise number of iterations is known.

foreground color—The color in which any current drawing will be rendered. *See also* background color.

formal parameter—An identifier that serves as a parameter name in a method. It receives its initial value from the actual parameter passed to it. *See also* actual parameter.

fourth-generation language—A high-level language that provides built-in functionality such as automatic report generation or database management, beyond that of traditional high-level languages.

function—A named group of declarations and programming statements that can be invoked (executed) when needed. A function that is part of a class is called a method. Java has no functions because all code is part of a class.

garbage—(1) An unspecified or uninitialized value in a memory location. (2) An object that cannot be accessed anymore because all references to it have been lost.

garbage collection—The process of reclaiming unneeded, dynamically allocated memory. Java performs automatic garbage collection of objects that no longer have any valid references to them.

gigabyte (GB)—A unit of binary storage, equal to 2^{30} (approximately 1 billion) bytes.

goto—(1) A Java reserved word that is not currently used. (2) An unconditional branch.

grammar—A representation of language syntax that specifies how reserved words, symbols, and identifiers can be combined into valid programs.

graph—A nonlinear data structure made up of nodes and edges that connect the nodes. *See also* digraph.

graphical user interface (GUI)—Software that provides the means to interact with a program or operating system by making use of graphical images and point-and-click mechanisms, such as buttons and text fields.

graphics context—The drawing surface and related coordinate system on which a drawing is rendered or graphical user interface components are placed.

GUI component—A visual element, such as a button or text field, that is used to make up a graphical user interface (GUI).

hardware—The tangible components of a computer system, such as the keyboard, monitor, and circuit boards.

has-a relationship—The relationship between two objects in which one is composed, at least in part, of one or more of the other. *See also* aggregate object, is-a relationship.

hash code—An integer value calculated from any given data value or object, used to determine where a value should be stored in a hash table. Also called a hash value. *See also* hashing.

hash method—A method that calculates a hash code from a data value or object. The same data value or object will always produce the same hash code. Also called a hash function. *See also* hashing.

hash table—A data structure in which values are stored for efficient retrieval. *See also* hashing.

hashing—A technique for storing items so that they can be found efficiently. Items are stored in a hash table at a position specified by a calculated hash code. *See also* hash method.

hexadecimal—The base-16 number system, often used as an abbreviated representation of binary strings.

hierarchy—An organizational technique in which items are layered or grouped to reduce complexity.

high-level language—A programming language in which each statement represents many machine-level instructions.

HTML—*See* HyperText Markup Language.

hybrid object-oriented language—A programming language that can be used to implement a program in a procedural manner or an object-oriented manner, at the programmer's discretion. *See also* pure object-oriented language.

hypermedia—The concept of hypertext extended to include other media types such as graphics, audio, video, and programs.

hypertext—A document representation that allows a user to easily navigate through it in other than a linear fashion. Links to other parts of the document are embedded at the appropriate places to allow the user to jump from one part of the document to another. *See also* hypermedia.

HyperText Markup Language (HTML)—The notation used to define Web pages. *See also* browser, World Wide Web.

icon—A small, fixed-sized picture, often used to decorate a graphical interface. *See also* image.

identifier—Any name that a programmer makes up to use in a program, such as a class name or variable name.

identity—The designation of an object, which, in Java, is an object's reference name. *See also* state, behavior.

IEEE 754—A standard for representing floating point values. Used by Java to represent `float` and `double` data types.

if—A Java reserved word that specifies a simple conditional construct. *See also* else.

image—A picture, often specified using the GIF, JPEG, or PING formats. *See also* icon.

immutable—The characteristic of something that does not change. For example, the contents of a Java character string are immutable once the string has been defined.

implementation—(1) The process of translating a design into source code. (2) The source code that defines a method, class, abstract data type, or other programming entity.

implements—A Java reserved word that is used in a class declaration to specify that the class implements the methods specified in a particular interface.

import—A Java reserved word that is used to specify the packages and classes that are used in a particular Java source code file.

index—The integer value used to specify a particular element in an array.

index operator—The brackets ([]) in which an array index is specified.

indirect recursion—The process of a method invoking another method, which eventually results in the original method being invoked again. *See also* direct recursion.

infinite loop—A loop that does not terminate because the condition controlling the loop never becomes false.

infinite recursion—A recursive series of invocations that does not terminate because the base case is never reached.

infix expression—An expression in which the operators are positioned between the operands on which they work. *See also* postfix expression.

inheritance—The ability to derive a new class from an existing one. Inherited variables and methods of the original (parent) class are available in the new (child) class as if they were declared locally.

initialize—To give an initial value to a variable.

initializer list—A comma-separated list of values, delimited by braces ({}), used to initialize and specify the size of an array.

inline documentation—Comments that are included in the source code of a program.

inner class—A nonstatic, nested class.

input/output buffer—A storage location for data on its way from the user to the computer (input buffer) or from the computer to the user (output buffer).

input/output devices—Hardware components that allow the human user to interact with the computer, such as a keyboard, mouse, and monitor.

input/output stream—A sequence of bytes that represents a source of data (input stream) or a destination for data (output stream).

insertion sort—A sorting algorithm in which each value, one at a time, is inserted into a sorted subset of the entire list. *See also* selection sort.

inspection—*See* walkthrough.

instance—An object created from a class. Multiple objects can be instantiated from a single class.

instance method—A method that must be invoked through a particular instance of a class, as opposed to a class method.

instance variable—A variable that must be referenced through a particular instance of a class, as opposed to a class variable.

instanceof—A Java reserved word that is also an operator, used to determine the class or type of a variable.

instantiation—The act of creating an object from a class.

int—A Java reserved word that represents a primitive integer type, stored using 32 bits in two's complement format.

integration test—The process of testing software components that are made up of other interacting components. Stresses the communication between components rather than the functionality of individual components.

interface—(1) A Java reserved word that is used to define a set of abstract methods that will be implemented by particular classes. (2) The set of messages to which an object responds, defined by the methods that can be invoked from outside of the object. (3) The techniques through which a human user interacts with a program, often graphically. *See also* graphical user interface.

interface hierarchy—A tree-like structure created when interfaces are derived from other interfaces through inheritance. *See also* class hierarchy.

interpreter—A program that translates and executes code on a particular machine. The Java interpreter translates and executes Java bytecode. *See also* compiler.

Internet—The most pervasive wide-area network in the world; it has become the primary vehicle for computer-to-computer communication.

Internet address—A designation that uniquely identifies a particular computer or device on the Internet.

invisible component—A graphical user interface component that can be added to a container to provide buffering space between other components.

invocation—*See* method invocation.

I/O devices—*See* input/output devices.

IP address—A series of several integer values, separated by periods (.), that uniquely identifies a particular computer or device on the Internet. Each Internet address has a corresponding IP address.

is-a relationship—The relationship created through properly derived classes via inheritance. The subclass *is-a* more specific version of the superclass. *See also* has-a relationship.

ISO-Latin-1—A 128-character extension to the ASCII character set defined by the International Standards Organization (ISO). The characters correspond to the numeric values 128 through 255 in both ASCII and Unicode.

iteration—(1) One execution of the body of a repetition statement. (2) One pass through a cyclic process, such as an iterative development process.

iteration statement—*See* repetition statement.

iterative development process—A step-by-step approach for creating software, which contains a series of stages that are performed repetitively.

Java Virtual Machine (JVM)—The conceptual device, implemented in software, on which Java bytecode is executed. Bytecode, which is architecture neutral, does not run on a particular hardware platform; instead, it runs on the JVM.

java—The Java command-line interpreter, which translates and executes Java bytecode. Part of the Java Development Kit.

Java—The programming language used throughout this text to demonstrate software development concepts. Described by its developers as object oriented, robust, secure, architecture neutral, portable, high-performance, interpreted, threaded, and dynamic.

Java API—*See* Application Programming Interface.

Java Development Kit (JDK)—A collection of basic software tools, including a compiler and interpreter, for developing Java software. *See also* Software Development Kit.

javac—The Java command-line compiler, which translates Java source code into Java bytecode. Part of the Java Development Kit.

javadoc—A software tool that creates external documentation in HTML format about the contents and structure of a Java software system. Part of the Java Development Kit.

javah—A software tool that generates C header and source files, used for implementing `native` methods. Part of the Java Development Kit.

javap—A software tool that disassembles a Java class file, containing unreadable bytecode, into a human-readable version. Part of the Java Development Kit.

jdb—The Java command-line debugger. Part of the Java Development Kit.

JDK—*See* Java Development Kit.

JVM—*See* Java Virtual Machine.

kilobit (Kb)—A unit of binary storage, equal to 2^{10}, or 1024 bits.

kilobyte (K or KB)—A unit of binary storage, equal to 2^{10}, or 1024 bytes.

label—(1) A graphical user interface component that displays text, an image, or both. (2) An identifier in Java used to specify a particular line of code. The `break` and `continue` statements can jump to a specific, labeled line in the program.

LAN—*See* local-area network.

last-in, first-out (LIFO)—A data management technique in which the last value that is stored in a data structure is the first value that comes out. *See also* first-in, first-out; stack.

layout manager—An object that specifies the presentation of graphical user interface components. Each container is governed by a particular layout manager.

lexicographic ordering—The ordering of characters and strings based on a particular character set such as Unicode.

life cycle—The stages through which a software product is developed and used.

LIFO—*See* last-in, first-out.

linear search—A search algorithm in which each item in the list is compared to the target value until the target is found or the list is exhausted. *See also* binary search.

link—(1) A designation in a hypertext document that "jumps" to a new document (or to a new part of the same document) when followed. (2) A connection between two items in a dynamically linked structure, represented as an object reference.

linked list—A dynamic data structure in which objects are linked using references.

list—A graphical user interface component that presents a list of items from which the user can choose. The current selection is highlighted in the list. *See also* combo box.

listener—An object that is set up to respond to an event when it occurs.

listener adaptor class—A class defined with empty methods corresponding to the methods invoked when particular events occur. A listener object can be derived from an adaptor class. *See also* listener interface.

listener interface—A Java interface that defines the methods invoked when particular events occur. A listener object can be created by implementing a listener interface. *See also* listener adaptor class.

literal—A primitive value used explicitly in a program, such as the numeric literal 147 or the string literal "hello".

local-area network (LAN)—A computer network designed to span short distances and connect a relatively small number of computers. *See also* wide-area network.

local variable—A variable defined within a method, which does not exist except during the execution of the method.

logical error—A problem stemming from inappropriate processing in the code. It does not cause an abnormal termination of the program, but it produces incorrect results. *See also* compile-time error, run-time error, syntax error.

logical line of code—A logical programming statement in a source code program, which may extend over multiple physical lines. *See also* physical line of code.

logical operator—One of the operators that perform a logical NOT (!), AND (&&), or OR (||), returning a boolean result. The logical operators are short-circuited, meaning that if their left operand is sufficient to determine the result, the right operand is not evaluated.

long—A Java reserved word that represents a primitive integer type, stored using 64 bits in two's complement format.

loop—*See* repetition statement.

loop control variable—A variable whose value specifically determines how many times a loop body is executed.

low-level language—Either machine language or assembly language, which are not as convenient to construct software in as high-level languages are.

machine language—The native language of a particular CPU. Any software that runs on a particular CPU must be translated into its machine language.

main memory—The volatile hardware storage device where programs and data are held when they are actively needed by the CPU. *See also* secondary memory.

maintenance—(1) The process of fixing errors in or making enhancements to a released software product. (2) The software life-cycle phase in which the software is in use and changes are made to it as needed.

mantissa—The portion of a floating point value's internal representation that specifies the magnitude of the number. *See also* exponent.

megabyte (MB)—A unit of binary storage, equal to 2^{20} (approximately 1 million) bytes.

member—A variable or method in an object or class.

memory—Hardware devices that store programs and data. *See also* main memory, secondary memory.

memory location—An individual, addressable cell inside main memory into which data can be stored.

memory management—The process of controlling dynamically allocated portions of main memory, especially the act of returning allocated memory when it is no longer required. *See also* garbage collection.

method—A named group of declarations and programming statements that can be invoked (executed) when needed. A method is part of a class.

method call conversion—The automatic widening conversion that can occur when a value of one type is passed to a formal parameter of another type.

method definition—The specification of the code that gets executed when the method is invoked. The definition includes declarations of local variables and formal parameters.

method invocation—A line of code that causes a method to be executed. It specifies any values that are passed to the method as parameters.

method overloading—*See* overloading.

mnemonic—(1) A word or identifier that specifies a command or data value in an assembly language. (2) A keyboard character used as a alternative means to activate a graphical user interface component such as a button.

modal—Having multiple modes (such as a dialog box).

modem—A data transfer device that allows information to be sent along a telephone line.

modifier—A designation used in a Java declaration that specifies particular characteristics to the construct being declared.

monitor—The screen in the computer system that serves as an output device.

multidimensional array—An array that uses more than one index to specify a value stored in it.

multiple inheritance—Deriving a class from more than one parent, inheriting methods and variables from each. Multiple inheritance is not supported in Java.

multiplicity—The numeric relationship between two objects, often shown in class diagrams.

NaN—An abbreviation that stands for "not a number," which is the designation for an inappropriate or undefined numeric value.

narrowing conversion—A conversion between two values of different but compatible data types. Narrowing conversions could lose information because the converted type usually has an internal representation smaller than the original storage space. *See also* widening conversion.

native—A Java reserved word that serves as a modifier for methods. A native method is implemented in another programming language.

natural language—A language that humans use to communicate, such as English or French.

negative infinity—A special floating point value that represents the "lowest possible" value. *See also* positive infinity.

nested class—A class declared within another class in order to facilitate implementation and restrict access.

nested if statement—An `if` statement that has as its body another `if` statement.

network—Two or more computers connected together so that they can exchange data and share resources.

network address—*See* address.

new—A Java reserved word that is also an operator, used to instantiate an object from a class.

newline character—A nonprintable character that indicates the end of a line.

nonprintable characters—Any character, such as escape or newline, that does not have a symbolic representation that can be displayed on a monitor or printed by a printer. *See also* printable characters.

nonvolatile—The characteristic of a memory device that retains its stored information even after the power supply is turned off. Secondary memory devices are nonvolatile. *See also* volatile.

null—A Java reserved word that is a reference literal, used to indicate that a reference does not currently refer to any object.

number system—A set of values and operations defined by a particular base value that determines the number of digits available and the place value of each digit.

object—(1) The primary software construct in the object-oriented paradigm. (2) An encapsulated collection of data variables and methods. (3) An instance of a class.

object diagram—A visual representation of the objects in a program at a given point in time, often showing the status of instance data.

object-oriented programming—An approach to software design and implementation that is centered around objects and classes. *See also* procedural programming.

octal—The base-8 number system, sometimes used to abbreviate binary strings. *See also* binary, hexadecimal.

off-by-one error—An error caused by a calculation or condition being off by one, such as when a loop is set up to access one too many array elements.

operand—A value on which an operator performs its function. For example, in the expression 5 + 2, the values 5 and 2 are operands.

operating system—The collection of programs that provide the primary user interface to a computer and manage its resources, such as memory and the CPU.

operator—A symbol that represents a particular operation in a programming language, such as the addition operator (+).

operator association—The order in which operators within the same precedence level are evaluated, either right to left or left to right. *See also* operator precedence.

operator overloading—Assigning additional meaning to an operator. Operator overloading is not supported in Java, though method overloading is.

operator precedence—The order in which operators are evaluated in an expression as specified by a well- defined hierarchy.

order—The dominant term in an equation that specifies the efficiency of an algorithm. For example, selection sort is of order n^2.

overflow—A problem that occurs when a data value grows too large for its storage size, which can result in inaccurate arithmetic processing. *See also* underflow.

overloading—Assigning additional meaning to a programming language construct, such as a method or operator. Method overloading is supported by Java, but operator overloading is not.

overriding—The process of modifying the definition of an inherited method to suit the purposes of the subclass. *See also* shadowing variables.

package—A Java reserved word that is used to specify a group of related classes.

package visibility—*See* default visibility.

panel—A graphical user interface (GUI) container that holds and organizes other GUI components.

parameter—(1) A value passed from a method invocation to its definition. (2) The identifier in a method definition that accepts the value passed to it when the method is invoked. *See also* actual parameter, formal parameter.

parameter list—The list of actual or formal parameters to a method.

parent class—*See* superclass.

pass by reference—The process of passing a reference to a value into a method as the parameter. In Java, all objects are managed using references, so an object's formal parameter is an alias to the original. *See also* pass by value.

pass by value—The process of making a copy of a value and passing the copy into a method. Therefore, any change made to the value inside the method is not reflected in the original value. All Java primitive types are passed by value.

PDL—*See* Program Design Language.

peripheral—Any hardware device other than the CPU or main memory.

persistence—The ability of an object to stay in existence after the executing program that creates it terminates. *See also* serialize.

physical line of code—A line in a source code file, terminated by a newline or similar character. *See also* logical line of code.

pixel—A picture element. A digitized picture is made up of many pixels.

place value—The value of each digit position in a number, which determines the overall contribution of that digit to the value. *See also* number system.

pointer—A variable that can hold a memory address. Instead of pointers, Java uses references, which provide essentially the same functionality as pointers but without the need for explicit dereferencing.

point-to-point connection—The link between two networked devices that are connected directly by a wire.

polyline—A shape made up of a series of connected line segments. A polyline is similar to a polygon, but the shape is not closed.

polymorphism—An object-oriented technique by which a reference that is used to invoke a method can result in different methods being invoked at different times. All Java method invocations are potentially polymorphic in that they invoke the method of the object type, not the reference type.

portability—The ability of a program to be moved from one hardware platform to another without having to change it. Because Java bytecode is not related to any particular hardware environment, Java programs are considered portable. *See also* architecture neutral.

positive infinity—A special floating point value that represents the "highest possible" value. *See also* negative infinity.

postfix expression—An expression in which an operator is positioned after the operands on which it works. *See also* infix expression.

postfix operator—In Java, an operator that is positioned behind its single operand, whose evaluation yields the value prior to the operation being performed. Both the increment (++) and decrement (– –) operators can be applied postfix. *See also* prefix operator.

precedence—*See* operator precedence.

prefix operator—In Java, an operator that is positioned in front of its single operand, whose evaluation yields the value after the operation has been performed. Both the increment (++) and decrement (– –) operators can be applied prefix. *See also* postfix operator.

primitive data type—A data type that is predefined in a programming language.

printable characters—Any character that has a symbolic representation that can be displayed on a monitor or printed by a printer. *See also* nonprintable characters.

private—A Java reserved word that serves as a visibility modifier for inner classes as well as methods and variables. A private inner class is accessible only to members of the class in which it is declared. Private methods and variables are visible only in the class in which they are declared.

procedural programming—An approach to software design and implementation that is centered around procedures (or functions) and their interaction. *See also* object-oriented programming.

processing stream—An I/O stream that performs some type of manipulation on the data in the stream. Sometimes called a filtering stream. *See also* data stream.

program—A series of instructions executed by hardware, one after another.

Program Design Language (PDL)—A language in which a program's design and algorithms are expressed. *See also* pseudocode.

programming language—A specification of the syntax and semantics of the statements used to create a program.

programming language statement—An individual instruction in a given programming language.

prompt—A message or symbol used to request information from the user.

propagation—*See* exception propagation.

protected—A Java reserved word that serves as a visibility modifier for inner classes as well as methods and variables. A protected inner class is visible to classes in the same package and to all classes in other packages that extend the class in which it is declared. Protected methods and variables are visible to all classes in the same package and to classes outside the package that extend the class.

prototype—A program used to explore an idea or prove the feasibility of a particular approach.

pseudocode—Structured and abbreviated natural language used to express the algorithmic steps of a program. *See also* Program Design Language.

pseudorandom number—A value generated by software that performs extensive calculations based on an initial seed value. The result is not truly random because it is based on a calculation, but it is usually random enough for most purposes.

public—A Java reserved word that serves as a visibility modifier for classes, interfaces, methods, and variables. Anything declared public is visible to all classes.

pure object-oriented language—A programming language that enforces, to some degree, software development using an object-oriented approach. *See also* hybrid object-oriented language.

push button—A graphical user interface component that allows the user to initiate an action with a mouse click. *See also* check box, radio button.

queue—An abstract data type that manages information in a first-in, first-out manner.

radio button—A graphical user interface component that allows the user choose one of a set of options with a mouse click. A radio button is useful only as part of a group of other radio buttons. *See also* check box.

RAM—*See* random access memory.

random access device—A memory device whose information can be directly accessed. *See also* random access memory, sequential access device.

random access memory (RAM)—A term basically interchangeable with main memory. Should probably be called read-write memory, to distinguish it from read-only memory.

random number generator—Software that produces a pseudorandom number, generated by calculations based on a seed value.

read-only memory (ROM)—Any memory device whose stored information is stored permanently when the device is created. It can be read from, but not written to.

recursion—The process of a method invoking itself, either directly or indirectly. Recursive algorithms sometimes provide elegant, though perhaps inefficient, solutions to a problem.

reference—A variable that holds the address of an object. In Java, a reference can be used to interact with an object, but its numeric address cannot be accessed, set, or operated on directly.

register—A small area of storage in the CPU of the computer.

relational operator—One of several operators that determine the ordering relationship between two values: less than (<), less than or equal to (<=), greater than (>), and greater than or equal to (>=). *See also* equality operator.

release—A version of a software product that is made available to the customer.

repetition statement—A programming construct that allows a set of statements to be executed repetitively as long as a particular condition is true. The body of the repetition statement should eventually make the condition false. Also called an iteration statement or loop. *See also* do, for, while.

requirements—(1) The specification of what a program must and must not do. (2) An early phase of the software development process in which the program requirements are established.

reserved word—A word that has special meaning in a programming language and cannot be used for any other purpose.

retirement—The phase of a program's life cycle in which the program is taken out of active use.

return—A Java reserved word that causes the flow of program execution to return from a method to the point of invocation.

return type—The type of value returned from a method, specified before the method name in the method declaration. Could be void, which indicates that no value is returned.

reuse—Using existing software components to create new ones.

review—The process of critically examining a design or program to discover errors. There are many types of review. *See also* desk check, walkthrough.

RGB value—A collection of three values that define a color. Each value represents the contribution of the primary colors red, green, and blue.

ROM—*See* read-only memory.

run-time error—A problem that occurs during program execution that causes the program to terminate abnormally. *See also* compile-time error, logical error, syntax error.

scope—The areas within a program in which an identifier, such as a variable, can be referenced. *See also* access.

scroll pane—A graphical user interface container that offers a limited view of a component and provides horizontal and/or vertical scroll bars to change that view.

SDK—*See* Software Development Kit.

searching—The process of determining the existence or location of a target value within a list of values. *See also* binary search, linear search.

secondary memory—Hardware storage devices, such as magnetic disks or tapes, which store information in a relatively permanent manner. *See also* main memory.

seed value—A value used by a random number generator as a base for the calculations that produce a pseudo-random number.

selection sort—A sorting algorithm in which each value, one at a time, is placed in its final, sorted position. *See also* insertion sort.

selection statement—A programming construct that allows a set of statements to be executed if a particular condition is true. *See also* if, switch.

semantics—The interpretation of a program or programming construct.

sentinel value—A specific value used to indicate a special condition, such as the end of input.

serialize—The process of converting an object into a linear series of bytes so it can be saved to a file or sent across a network. *See also* persistence.

service methods—Methods in an object that are declared with public visibility and define a service that the object's client can invoke.

shadowing variables—The process of defining a variable in a subclass that supersedes an inherited version.

short—A Java reserved word that represents a primitive integer type, stored using 16 bits in two's complement format.

sibling—Two items in a tree or hierarchy, such as a class inheritance hierarchy, that have the same parent.

sign bit—A bit in a numeric value that represents the sign (positive or negative) of that value.

signed numeric value—A value that stores a sign (positive or negative). All Java numeric values are signed. A Java character is stored as an unsigned value.

signature—The number, types, and order of the parameters of a method. Overloaded methods must each have a unique signature.

slider—A graphical user interface component that allows the user to specify a numeric value within a bounded range by moving a knob to the appropriate place in the range.

software—(1) Programs and data. (2) The intangible components of a computer system.

software component—*See* component.

Software Development Kit (SDK)—A collection of software tools that assist in the development of software. The Java Software Development Kit is another name for the Java Development Kit.

software engineering—The discipline within computer science that addresses the process of developing high-quality software within practical constraints.

sorting—The process of putting a list of values into a well-defined order. *See also* insertion sort, selection sort.

split pane—A graphical user interface container that displays two components, either side by side or one on top of the other, separated by a moveable divider bar.

stack—An abstract data type that manages data in a last-in, first-out manner.

stack trace—The series of methods called to reach a certain point in a program. The stack trace can be analyzed when an exception is thrown to assist the programmer in tracking down the problem.

standard I/O stream—One of three common I/O streams representing standard input (usually the keyboard), standard output (usually

the monitor screen), and standard error (also usually the monitor). *See also* stream.

start angle—When defining an arc, the angle at which the arc begins. *See also* arc angle.

state—The state of being of an object, defined by the values of its data. *See also* behavior, identity.

statement—*See* programming language statement.

statement coverage—A strategy used in white-box testing in which all statements in a program are executed. *See also* condition coverage.

static—A Java reserved word that serves as a modifier for methods and variables. A static method is also called a class method and can be referenced without an instance of the class. A static variable is also called a class variable and is common to all instances of the class.

static data structure—A data structure that has a fixed size and cannot grow and shrink as needed. *See also* dynamic data structure.

storage capacity—The total number of bytes that can be stored in a particular memory device.

stream—A source of input or a destination for output.

strictfp—A Java reserved word that is used to control certain aspects of floating point arithmetic.

string—*See* character string.

string concatenation—The process of attaching the beginning of one character string to the end of another, resulting in one longer string.

strongly typed language—A programming language in which each variable is associated with a particular data type for the duration of its existence. Variables are not allowed to take on values or be used in operations that are inconsistent with their type.

structured programming—An approach to program development in which each software component has one entry and exit point and in which the flow of control does not cross unnecessarily.

stub—A method that simulates the functionality of a particular software component. Often used during unit testing.

subclass—A class derived from another class via inheritance. Also called a derived class or child class. *See also* superclass.

subscript—*See* index.

super—A Java reserved word that is a reference to the parent class of the object making the reference. Often used to invoke a parent's constructor.

super reference—*See* super.

superclass—The class from which another class is derived via inheritance. Also called a base class or parent class. *See also* subclass.

support methods—Methods in an object that are not intended for use outside the class. They provide support functionality for service methods. As such, they are usually not declared with public visibility.

swapping—The process of exchanging the values of two variables.

swing—The package in the Java API (javax. swing) that contains classes related to graphical user interfaces. Swing provides alternative components than the Abstract Windowing Toolkit package, but does not replace it.

switch—A Java reserved word that specifies a compound conditional construct.

synchronization—The process of ensuring that data shared among multiple threads cannot be accessed by more than one thread at a time. *See also* synchronized.

synchronized—A Java reserved word that serves as a modifier for methods. Separate threads of a process can execute concurrently in a method, unless the method is synchronized, making it a mutually exclusive resource. Methods that access shared data should be synchronized.

syntax rules—The set of specifications that govern how the elements of a programming language can be put together to form valid statements.

syntax error—An error produced by the compiler because a program did not conform to the syntax of the programming language. Syntax errors are a subset of compile-time errors. *See also* compile-time error, logical error, run-time error, syntax rules.

tabbed pane—A graphical user interface (GUI) container that presents a set of cards from which the user can choose. Each card contains its own GUI components.

target value—The value that is sought when performing a search on a collection of data.

TCP/IP—Software that controls the movement of messages across the Internet. The acronym stands for Transmission Control Protocol/Internet Protocol.

terabyte (TB)—A unit of binary storage, equal to 2^{40} (approximately 1 trillion) bytes.

termination—The point at which a program stops executing.

ternary operator—An operator that uses three operands.

test case—A set of input values and user actions, along with a specification of the expected output, used to find errors in a system.

testing—(1) The process of running a program with various test cases in order to discover problems. (2) The process of critically evaluating a design or program.

text area—A graphical user interface component that displays, or allows the user to enter, multiple lines of data.

text field—A graphical user interface component that displays, or allows the user to enter, a single line of data.

text file—A file that contains data formatted as ASCII or Unicode characters.

this—A Java reserved word that is a reference to the object executing the code making the reference.

thread—An independent process executing within a program. A Java program can have multiple threads running in a program at one time.

throw—A Java reserved word that is used to start an exception propagation.

throws—A Java reserved word that specifies that a method may throw a particular type of exception.

timer—An object that generates an event at regular intervals.

token—A portion of a string defined by a set of delimiters.

tool tip—A short line of text that appears when the mouse pointer is allowed to rest on top of a particular component. Usually, tool tips are used to inform the user of the component's purpose.

top-level domain—The last part of a network domain name, such as edu or com.

transient—A Java reserved word that serves as a modifier for variables. A transient variable does not contribute to the object's persistent state and therefore does not need to be saved. *See also* serialize.

tree—A nonlinear data structure that forms a hierarchy stemming from a single root node.

true—A Java reserved word that serves as one of the two boolean literals (`true` and `false`).

truth table—A complete enumeration of all permutations of values involved in a boolean expression, as well as the computed result.

try—A Java reserved word that is used to define the context in which certain exceptions will be handled if they are thrown.

two-dimensional array—An array that uses two indices to specify the location of an element. The two dimensions are often thought of as the rows and columns of a table. *See also* multidimensional array.

two's complement—A technique for representing numeric binary data. Used by all Java integer primitive types (`byte`, `short`, `int`, `long`).

type—*See* data type.

UML—*See* Unified Modeling Language.

unary operator—An operator that uses only one operand.

unchecked exception—A Java exception that does not need to be caught or dealt with if the programmer so chooses.

underflow—A problem that occurs when a floating point value becomes too small for its storage size, which can result in inaccurate arithmetic processing. *See also* overflow.

Unicode—The international character set used to define valid Java characters. Each character is represented using a 16-bit unsigned numeric value.

Unified Modeling Language (UML)—A graphical notation for visualizing relationships among classes and objects. Abbreviated UML. There are many types of UML diagrams. *See also* class diagrams.

uniform resource locator (URL)—A designation for a resource that scan be located through a World Wide Web browser.

unit test—The process of testing an individual software component. May require the creation of stub modules to simulate other system components.

unsigned numeric value—A value that does not store a sign (positive or negative). The bit usually reserved to represent the sign is included in the value, doubling the magnitude of the number that can be stored. Java characters are stored as unsigned numeric values, but there are no primitive numeric types that are unsigned.

URL—*See* uniform resource locator.

use relationship—A relationship between two classes, often shown in a class diagram, that establishes that one class uses another in some way, such as relying on its services. *See also* association.

user interface—The manner in which the user interacts with a software system, which is often graphical. *See also* graphical user interface.

variable—An identifier in a program that represents a memory location in which a data value is stored.

visibility modifier—A Java modifier that defines the scope in which a construct can be accessed. The Java visibility modifiers are public, protected, private, and default (no modifier used).

void—A Java reserved word that can be used as a return value for a method, indicating that no value is returned.

volatile—(1) A Java reserved word that serves as a modifier for variables. A volatile variable might be changed asynchronously and therefore indicates that the compiler should not attempt optimizations on it. (2) The characteristic of a memory device that loses stored information when the power supply is interrupted. Main memory is a volatile storage device. *See also* nonvolatile.

von Neumann architecture—The computer architecture named after John von Neumann, in which programs and data are stored together in the same memory devices.

walkthrough—A form of review in which a group of developers, managers, and quality assurance personnel examine a design or program in order to find errors. Sometimes referred to as an inspection. *See also* desk check.

WAN—*See* wide-area network.

waterfall model—One of the earliest software development process models. It defines a basically linear interaction between the requirements, design, implementation, and testing stages.

Web—*See* World Wide Web.

while—A Java reserved word that represents a repetition construct. A while statement is executed zero or more times. *See also* do, for.

white-box testing—Producing and evaluating test cases based on the interior logic of a software component. The test cases focus on stressing decision points and ensuring coverage. *See also* black-box testing, condition coverage, statement coverage.

white space—Spaces, tabs, and blank lines that are used to set off sections of source code to make programs more readable.

wide-area network (WAN)—A computer network that connects two or more local area networks, usually across long geographic distances. *See also* local-area network.

widening conversion—A conversion between two values of different but compatible data types. Widening conversions usually leave the data value intact because the converted type has an internal representation equal to or larger than the original storage space. *See also* narrowing conversion.

word—A unit of binary storage. The size of a word varies by computer, and is usually two, four, or eight bytes. The word size indicates the amount of information that can be moved through the machine at one time.

World Wide Web (WWW or Web)—Software that makes the exchange of information across a network easier by providing a common user interface for multiple types of information. Web browsers are used to retrieve and format HTML documents.

wrapper class—A class designed to store a primitive type in an object. Usually used when an object reference is needed and a primitive type would not suffice.

WWW—*See* World Wide Web.

Number Systems

B

This appendix contains a detailed introduction to number systems and their under-lying characteristics. The particular focus is on the binary number system, its use with computers, and its similarities to other number systems. This introduction also covers conversions between bases.

In our everyday lives, we use the *decimal number system* to represent values, to count, and to perform arithmetic. The decimal system is also referred to as the *base-10 number system*. We use 10 digits (0 through 9) to represent values in the decimal system.

Computers use the *binary number system* to store and manage information. The binary system, also called the *base-2 number system*, has only two digits (0 and 1). Each 0 and 1 is called a *bit*, short for binary digit. A series of bits is called a *binary string*.

There is nothing particularly special about either the binary or decimal systems. Long ago, humans adopted the decimal number system probably because we have 10 fingers on our hands. If humans had 12 fingers, we would probably be using a base-12 number system regularly and find it as easy to deal with as we do the decimal system now. It all depends on what you get used to. As you explore the binary system, it will become more familiar and natural.

Binary is used for computer processing because the devices used to manage and store information are less expensive and more reliable if they have to represent only two possible values. Computers have been made that use the decimal system, but they are not as convenient.

There are an infinite number of number systems, and they all follow the same basic rules. You already know how the binary number system works, but you just might not be aware that you do. It all goes back to the basic rules of arithmetic.

Place Value

In decimal, we represent the values of 0 through 9 using only one digit. To rep-resent any value higher than 9, we must use more than one digit. The position of each digit has a *place value* that indicates the amount it contributes to the overall value. In decimal, we refer to the one's column, the ten's column, the hundred's column, and so on forever.

FIGURE B.1   Place values in the decimal system

Each place value is determined by the *base* of the number system, raised to increasing powers as we move from right to left. In the decimal number system, the place value of the digit furthest to the right is 10^0, or 1. The place value of the next digit is 10^1, or 10. The place value of the third digit from the right is 10^2, or 100, and so on. Figure B.1 shows how each digit in a decimal number contributes to the value.

The binary system works the same way except that we exhaust the available digits much sooner. We can represent 0 and 1 with a single bit, but to represent any value higher than 1, we must use multiple bits.

The place values in binary are determined by increasing powers of the base as we move right to left, just as they are in the decimal system. However, in binary, the base value is 2. Therefore the place value of the bit furthest to the right is 2^0, or 1. The place value of the next bit is 2^1, or 2. The place value of the third bit from the right is 2^2, or 4, and so on. Figure B.2 shows a binary number and its place values.

The number 1101 is a valid binary number, but it is also a valid decimal number as well. Sometimes to make it clear which number system is being used, the

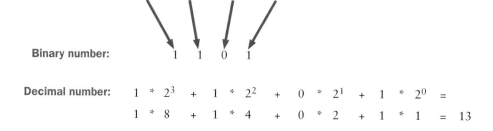

FIGURE B.2   Place values in the binary system

base value is appended as a subscript to the end of a number. Therefore you can distinguish between 1101_2, which is equivalent to 13 in decimal, and 1101_{10} (one thousand, one hundred and one), which in binary is represented as 10001001101_2.

A number system with base N has N digits (0 through $N-1$). As we have seen, the decimal system has 10 digits (0 through 9), and the binary system has two digits (0 and 1). They all work the same way. For instance, the base-5 number system has five digits (0 to 4).

Note that, in any number system, the place value of the digit furthest to the right is 1, since any base raised to the zero power is 1. Also notice that the value 10, which we refer to as "ten" in the decimal system, always represents the base value in any number system. In base 10, 10 is one 10 and zero 1's. In base 2, 10 is one 2 and zero 1's. In base 5, 10 is one 5 and zero 1's.

Bases Higher Than 10

Since all number systems with base N have N digits, then base 16 has 16 digits. But what are they? We are used to the digits 0 through 9, but in bases higher than 10, we need a single digit, a single symbol, that represents the decimal value 10. In fact, in *base 16*, which is also called *hexadecimal,* we need digits that represent the decimal values 10 through 15.

For number systems higher than 10, we use alphabetic characters as single digits for values greater than 9. The hexadecimal digits are 0 through F, where 0 through 9 represent the first 10 digits, and A represents the decimal value 10, B represents 11, C represents 12, D represents 13, E represents 14, and F represents 15.

Therefore the number 2A8E is a valid hexadecimal number. The place values are determined as they are for decimal and binary, using increasing powers of the base. So in hexadecimal, the place values are powers of 16. Figure B.3 shows how the place values of the hexadecimal number 2A8E contribute to the overall value.

FIGURE B.3   Place values in the hexadecimal system

All number systems with bases greater than 10 use letters as digits. For example, base 12 has the digits 0 through B and base 19 has the digits 0 through I. However, beyond having a different set of digits and a different base, the rules governing each number system are the same.

Keep in mind that when we change number systems, we are simply changing the way we represent values, not the values themselves. If you have 18_{10} pencils, it may be written as 10010 in binary or as 12 in hexadecimal, but it is still the same number of pencils.

Figure B.4 shows the representations of the decimal values 0 through 20 in several bases, including *base 8*, which is also called *octal*. Note that the larger the base, the higher the value that can be represented in a single digit.

Binary (base 2)	Octal (base 8)	Decimal (base 10)	Hexadecimal (base 16)
0	0	0	0
1	1	1	1
10	2	2	2
11	3	3	3
100	4	4	4
101	5	5	5
110	6	6	6
111	7	7	7
1000	10	8	8
1001	11	9	9
1010	12	10	A
1011	13	11	B
1100	14	12	C
1101	15	13	D
1110	16	14	E
1111	17	15	F
10000	20	16	10
10001	21	17	11
10010	22	18	12
10011	23	19	13
10100	24	20	14

FIGURE B.4   Counting in various number systems

Conversions

We've already seen how a number in another base is converted to decimal by determining the place value of each digit and computing the result. This process can be used to convert any number in any base to its equivalent value in base 10.

Now let's reverse the process, converting a base-10 value to another base. First, find the highest place value in the new number system that is less than or equal to the original value. Then divide the original number by that place value to determine the digit that belongs in that position. The remainder is the value that must be represented in the remaining digit positions. Continue this process, position by position, until the entire value is represented.

For example, Figure B.5 shows the process of converting the decimal value 180 into binary. The highest place value in binary that is less than or equal to 180 is 128 (or 2^7), which is the eighth bit position from the right. Dividing 180 by 128 yields 1 with 52 remaining. Therefore the first bit is 1, and the decimal value 52 must be represented in the remaining seven bits. Dividing 52 by 64, which is the next place value (2^6), yields 0 with 52 remaining. So the second bit is 0. Dividing 52 by 32 yields 1 with 20 remaining. So the third bit is 1, and the remaining five bits must represent the value 20. Dividing 20 by 16 yields 1 with 4 remaining. Dividing 4 by 8 yields 0 with 4 remaining. Dividing 4 by 4 yields 1 with 0 remaining.

Since the number has been completely represented, the rest of the bits are zero. Therefore 180_{10} is equivalent to 10110100 in binary. This can be confirmed by

Place value	Number	Digit
128	180	1
64	52	0
32	52	1
16	20	1
8	4	0
4	4	1
2	0	0
1	0	0

$$180_{10} = 10110100_2$$

FIGURE B.5   Converting a decimal value into binary

Place value	Number	Digit	
256	1967	7	
16	175	A	$1967_{10} = 7AF_{16}$
1	15	F	

FIGURE B.6   Converting a decimal value into hexadecimal

converting the new binary number back to decimal to make sure we get the original value.

This process works to convert any decimal value to any target base. For each target base, the place values and possible digits change. If you start with the correct place value, each division operation will yield a valid digit in the new base.

In the example in Figure B.5, the only digits that could have resulted from each division operation would have been 1 or 0, since we were converting to binary. However, when we are converting to other bases, any valid digit in the new base could result. For example, Figure B.6 shows the process of converting the decimal value 1967 into hexadecimal.

The place value of 256, which is 16^2, is the highest place value less than or equal to the original number, since the next highest place value is 16^3 or 4096. Dividing 1967 by 256 yields 7 with 175 remaining. Dividing 175 by 16 yields 10 with 15 remaining. Remember that 10 in decimal can be represented as the single digit A in hexadecimal. The 15 remaining can be represented as the digit F. Therefore 1967_{10} is equivalent to 7AF in hexadecimal.

Shortcut Conversions

We have established techniques for converting any value in any base to its equivalent representation in base 10, and from base 10 to any other base. Therefore. you can now convert a number in any base to any other base by going through base 10. However, an interesting relationship exists between the bases that are powers of 2, such as binary, octal, and hexadecimal, which allows very quick conversions between them.

To convert from binary to hexadecimal, for instance, you can simply group the bits of the original value into groups of four, starting from the right, then convert each group of four into a single hexadecimal digit. The example in Figure B.7 demonstrates this process.

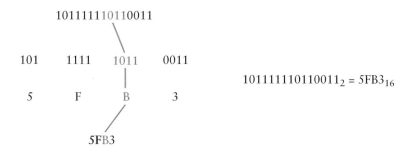

FIGURE B.7   Shortcut conversion from binary to hexadecimal

FIGURE B.8   Shortcut conversion from hexadecimal to binary

To go from hexadecimal to binary, we reverse this process, expanding each hexadecimal digit into four binary digits. Note that you may have to add leading zeros to the binary version of each expanded hexadecimal digit if necessary to make four binary digits. Figure B.8 shows the conversion of the hexadecimal value 40C6 to binary.

Why do we section the bits into groups of four when converting from binary to hexadecimal? The shortcut conversions work between binary and any base that is a power of 2. We section the bits into groups of that power. Since $2^4 = 16$, we section the bits in groups of four.

Converting from binary to octal is the same process except that the bits are sectioned into groups of three, since $2^3 = 8$. Likewise, when converting from octal to binary, we expand each octal digit into three bits.

To convert between, say, hexadecimal and octal is now a process of doing two shortcut conversions. First convert from hexadecimal to binary, then take that result and perform a shortcut conversion from binary to octal.

By the way, these types of shortcut conversions can be performed between any base B and any base that is a power of B. For example, conversions between base 3 and base 9 can be accomplished using the shortcut grouping technique, sectioning or expanding digits into groups of two, since $3^2 = 9$.

The Unicode Character Set

The Java programming language uses the Unicode character set for managing text. A *character set* is simply an ordered list of characters, each corresponding to a particular numeric value. Unicode is an international character set that contains letters, symbols, and ideograms for languages all over the world. Each character is represented as a 16-bit unsigned numeric value. Unicode, therefore, can support over 65,000 unique characters. Only about half of those values have characters assigned to them at this point. The Unicode character set continues to be refined as characters from various languages are included.

Many programming languages still use the ASCII character set. ASCII stands for the American Standard Code for Information Interchange. The 8-bit extended ASCII set is quite small, so the developers of Java opted to use Unicode in order to support international users. However, ASCII is essentially a subset of Unicode, including corresponding numeric values, so programmers used to ASCII should have no problems with Unicode.

Figure C.1 shows a list of commonly used characters and their Unicode numeric values. These characters also happen to be ASCII characters. All of the characters in Figure C.1 are called *printable characters* because they have a symbolic representation that can be displayed on a monitor or printed by a printer. Other characters are called *nonprintable characters* because they have no such symbolic representation. Note that the space character (numeric value 32) is considered a printable character, even though no symbol is printed when it is displayed. Nonprintable characters are sometimes called *control characters* because many of them can be generated by holding down the control key on a keyboard and pressing another key.

The Unicode characters with numeric values 0 through 31 are nonprintable characters. Also, the delete character, with numeric value 127, is a nonprintable

Value	Char	Value	Char	Value	Char	Value	Char	Value	Char
32	space	51	3	70	F	89	Y	108	l
33	!	52	4	71	G	90	Z	109	m
34	"	53	5	72	H	91	[	110	n
35	#	54	6	73	I	92	\	111	o
36	$	55	7	74	J	93	]	112	p
37	%	56	8	75	K	94	^	113	q
38	&	57	9	76	L	95	–	114	r
39	'	58	:	77	M	96	'	115	s
40	(	59	;	78	N	97	a	116	t
41	)	60	<	79	O	98	b	117	u
42	*	61	=	80	P	99	c	118	v
43	+	62	>	81	Q	100	d	119	w
44	'	63	?	82	R	101	e	120	x
45	–	64	@	83	S	102	f	121	y
46	.	65	A	84	T	103	g	122	z
47	/	66	B	85	U	104	h	123	{
48	0	67	C	86	V	105	i	124		
49	1	68	D	87	W	106	j	125	}
50	2	69	E	88	X	107	k	126	~

FIGURE C.1 A small portion of the Unicode character set

character. All of these characters are ASCII characters as well. Many of them have fairly common and well-defined uses, while others are more general. The table in Figure C.2 lists a small sample of the nonprintable characters.

Nonprintable characters are used in many situations to represent special conditions. For example, certain nonprintable characters can be stored in a text document to indicate, among other things, the beginning of a new line. An editor will process these characters by starting the text that follows it on a new line, instead of printing a symbol to the screen. Various types of computer systems use different nonprintable characters to represent particular conditions.

Except for having no visible representation, nonprintable characters are essentially equivalent to printable characters. They can be stored in a Java character variable and be part of a character string. They are stored using 16 bits, can be converted to their numeric value, and can be compared using relational operators.

Value	Character
0	*null*
7	*bell*
8	*backspace*
9	*tab*
10	*line feed*
12	*form feed*
13	*carriage return*
27	*escape*
127	*delete*

FIGURE C.2   Some nonprintable characters in the Unicode character set

The first 128 characters of the Unicode character set correspond to the common ASCII character set. The first 256 characters correspond to the ISO-Latin-1 extended ASCII character set. Many operating systems and Web browsers will handle these characters, but they may not be able to print the other Unicode characters.

The Unicode character set contains most alphabets in use today, including Greek, Hebrew, Cyrillic, and various Asian ideographs. It also includes Braille, and several sets of symbols used in mathematics and music. Figure C.3 shows a few characters from non-Western alphabets.

Value	Character	Source
1071	Я	Russian (Cyrillic)
3593	ฝ	Thai
5098	Ꮹ	Cherokee
8478	℞	Letterlike Symbols
8652	⇌	Arrows
10287	⠿	Braille
13407	侜	Chinese/Japanese/Korean (Common)

FIGURE C.3   Some non-Western characters in the Unicode character set

Java Operators

Java operators are evaluated according to the precedence hierarchy shown in Figure D.1 Operators at low precedence levels are evaluated before operators at higher levels. Operators within the same precedence level are evaluated according to the specified association, either right to left (R to L) or left to right (L to R). Operators in the same precedence level are not listed in any particular order.

The order of operator evaluation can always be forced by the use of parentheses. It is often a good idea to use parentheses even when they are not required, to make it explicitly clear to a human reader how an expression is evaluated.

For some operators, the operand types determine which operation is carried out. For instance, if the + operator is used on two strings, string concatenation is performed, but if it is applied to two numeric types, they are added in the arithmetic sense. If only one of the operands is a string, the other is converted to a string, and string concatenation is performed. Similarly, the operators &, ∧, and | perform bitwise operations on numeric operands but boolean operations on boolean operands.

The boolean operators & and | differ from the logical operators && and || in a subtle way. The logical operators are "short-circuited" in that if the result of an expression can be determined by evaluating only the left operand, the right operand is not evaluated. The boolean versions always evaluate both sides of the expression. There is no logical operator that performs an exclusive OR (XOR) operation.

Java Bitwise Operators

The Java *bitwise operators* operate on individual bits within a primitive value. They are defined only for integers and characters. They are unique among all Java operators, because they let us work at the lowest level of binary storage. Figure D.2 lists the Java bitwise operators.

Three of the bitwise operators are similar to the logical operators !, &&, and ||. The bitwise NOT, AND, and OR operations work basically the same way as their logical counterparts, except they work on individual bits of a value. The

Precedence Level	Operator	Operation	Associates
1	[] . (*parameters*) ++ --	array indexing object member reference parameter evaluation and method invocation postfix increment postfix decrement	L to R
2	++ -- + - ~ !	prefix increment prefix decrement unary plus unary minus bitwise NOT logical NOT	R to L
3	new (*type*)	object instantiation cast	R to L
4	* / %	multiplication division remainder	L to R
5	+ + -	addition string concatenation subtraction	L to R
6	<< >> >>>	left shift right shift with sign right shift with zero	L to R
7	< <= > >= instanceof	less than less than or equal greater than greater than or equal type comparison	L to R
8	== !=	equal not equal	L to R
9	& &	bitwise AND boolean AND	L to R
10	^ ^	bitwise XOR boolean XOR	L to R
11	| |	bitwise OR boolean OR	L to R
12	&&	logical AND	L to R
13	||	logical OR	L to R

FIGURE D.1   Java operator precedence

Precedence Level	Operator	Operation	Associates
14	?:	conditional operator	R to L
15	=	assignment	R to L
	+=	addition, then assignment	
	+=	string concatenation, then assignment	
	-=	subtraction, then assignment	
	*=	multiplication, then assignment	
	/=	division, then assignment	
	%=	remainder, then assignment	
	<<=	left shift, then assignment	
	>>=	right shift (sign), then assignment	
	>>>=	right shift (zero), then assignment	
	&=	bitwise AND, then assignment	
	&=	boolean AND, then assignment	
	^=	bitwise XOR, then assignment	
	^=	boolean XOR, then assignment	
	|=	bitwise OR, then assignment	
	|=	boolean OR, then assignment	

FIGURE D.1   Java operator precedence, continued

rules are essentially the same. Figure D.3 shows the results of bitwise operators on all combinations of two bits. Compare this chart to the truth tables for the logical operators in Chapter 5 to see the similarities.

The bitwise operators include the XOR operator, which stands for *exclusive OR*. The logical || operator is an *inclusive OR* operation, which means it returns true if both operands are true. The | bitwise operator is also inclusive and yields a

Operator	Description
~	bitwise NOT
&	bitwise AND
		bitwise OR
^	bitwise XOR
<<	left shift
>>	right shift with sign
>>>	right shift with zero fill

FIGURE D.2   Java bitwise operators

a	b	~ a	a & b	a | b	a ^ b
0	0	1	0	0	0
0	1	1	0	1	1
1	0	0	0	1	1
1	1	0	1	1	0

FIGURE D.3   Bitwise operations on individual bits

1 if both corresponding bits are 1. However, the exclusive OR operator (^) yields a 0 if both operands are 1. There is no logical exclusive OR operator in Java.

When the bitwise operators are applied to integer values, the operation is performed individually on each bit in the value. For example, suppose the integer variable number is declared to be of type byte and currently holds the value 45. Stored as an 8-bit byte, it is represented in binary as 00101101. When the bitwise complement operator (~) is applied to number, each bit in the value is inverted, yielding 11010010. Since integers are stored using two's complement representation, the value represented is now negative, specifically –46.

Similarly, for all bitwise operators, the operations are applied bit by bit, which is where the term "bitwise" comes from. For binary operators (with two operands), the operations are applied to corresponding bits in each operand. For example, assume num1 and num2 are byte integers, num1 holds the value 45, and num2 holds the value 14. Figure D.4 shows the results of several bitwise operations.

The operators &, |, and ^ can also be applied to boolean values, and they have basically the same meaning as their logical counterparts. When used with boolean values, they are called *boolean operators*. However, unlike the operators && and ||, which are "short-circuited," the boolean operators are not short-circuited. Both sides of the expression are evaluated every time.

num1 & num2	num1 | num2	num1 ^ num2
00101101	00101101	00101101
& 00001110	| 00001110	^ 00001110
= 00001100	= 00101111	= 00100011

FIGURE D.4   Bitwise operations on bytes

Like the other bitwise operators, the three bitwise shift operators manipulate the individual bits of an integer value. They all take two operands. The left operand is the value whose bits are shifted; the right operand specifies how many positions they should move. Prior to performing a shift, byte and short values are promoted to int for all shift operators. Furthermore, if either of the operands is long, the other operand is promoted to long. For readability, we use only 16 bits in the examples in this section, but the concepts are the same when carried out to 32- or 64-bit strings.

When bits are shifted, some bits are lost off one end, and others need to be filled in on the other. The *left-shift* operator (<<) shifts bits to the left, filling the right bits with zeros. For example, if the integer variable number currently has the value 13, then the statement

```
number = number << 2;
```

stores the value 52 into number. Initially, number contains the bit string 0000000000001101. When shifted to the left, the value becomes 0000000000110100, or 52. Notice that for each position shifted to the left, the original value is multiplied by 2.

The sign bit of a number is shifted along with all of the others. Therefore the sign of the value could change if enough bits are shifted to change the sign bit. For example, the value –8 is stored in binary two's complement form as 1111111111111000. When shifted left two positions, it becomes 1111111111100000, which is –32. However, if enough positions are shifted, a negative number can become positive and vice versa.

There are two forms of the right-shift operator: one that preserves the sign of the original value (>>) and one that fills the leftmost bits with zeros (>>>).

Let's examine two examples of the *right-shift-with-sign-fill* operator. If the int variable number currently has the value 39, the expression (number >> 2) results in the value 9. The original bit string stored in number is 0000000000100111, and the result of a right shift two positions is 0000000000001001. The leftmost sign bit, which in this case is a zero, is used to fill from the left.

If number has an original value of –16, or 1111111111110000, the right-shift (with sign fill) expression (number >> 3) results in the binary string 1111111111111110, or –2. The leftmost sign bit is a 1 in this case and is used to fill in the new left bits, maintaining the sign.

If maintaining the sign is not desirable, the *right-shift-with-zero-fill* operator (>>>) can be used. It operates similarly to the >> operator but fills with zero no matter what the sign of the original value is.

Java Modifiers

This appendix summarizes the modifiers that give particular characteristics to Java classes, interfaces, methods, and variables. For discussion purposes, the set of all Java modifiers is divided into two groups: visibility modifiers and all others.

Java Visibility Modifiers

The table in Figure E.1 describes the effect of Java visibility modifiers on various constructs. Visibility modifiers operate in the same way on classes and interfaces and in the same way on methods and variables.

Default visibility means that no visibility modifier was explicitly used. Default visibility is sometimes called *package visibility,* but you cannot use the reserved word package as a modifier.

Note that only inner classes can have private or protected visibility.

Modifier	Classes and interfaces	Methods and variables
default (no modifier)	Visible in its package.	Visible to any class in the same package as its class.
public	Visible anywhere.	Visible anywhere.
protected	Can only be applied to inner classes. Visible in its package and to classes that extend the class in which it is declared.	Visible to any class in the same package and to any derived classes.
private	Can only be applied to inner classes. Visible to the enclosing class only.	Not visible by any other class.

FIGURE E.1   Java visibility modifiers

A Visibility Example

Consider the highly contrived situation depicted in the Figure E.2 Class P is the parent class that is used to derive child classes C1 and C2. Class C1 is in the same package as P, but C2 is not. Class P contains four methods, each with different visibility modifiers. One object has been instantiated from each of these classes.

The public method a() has been inherited by C1 and C2, and any code with access to object x can invoke x.a(). The private method d() is not visible to C1 or C2, so objects y and z have no such method available to them. Furthermore, d() is fully encapsulated and can be invoked only from within object x.

The protected method b() is visible in both C1 and C2. A method in y could invoke x.b(), but a method in z could not. Furthermore, an object of any class in package One could invoke x.b(), even those that are not related to class P by inheritance, such as an object created from class Another1.

Method c() has default visibility, since no visibility modifier was used to declare it. Therefore object y can refer to the method c() as if it were declared locally, but object z cannot. Object y can invoke x.c(), as can an object instantiated from any class in package One, such as Another1. Object z cannot invoke x.c().

These rules generalize in the same way for variables. The visibility rules may appear complicated initially, but they can be mastered with a little effort.

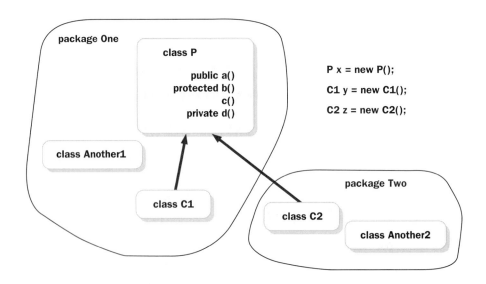

FIGURE E.2   A situation demonstrating Java visibility modifiers

Other Java Modifiers

Figure E.3 summarizes the rest of the Java modifiers, which address a variety of issues. Furthermore, a modifier has different effects on classes, interfaces, methods, and variables. Some modifiers cannot be used with certain constructs and therefore are listed as not applicable (N/A).

The `transient` modifier is used to indicate data that need not be stored in a persistent (serialized) object. That is, when an object is written to a serialized stream, the object representation will include all data that is not specified as transient.

Modifier	Class	Interface	Method	Variable
abstract	The class may contain abstract methods. It cannot be instantiated.	All interfaces are inherently abstract. The modifier is optional.	No method body is defined. The method requires implementation when inherited.	N/A
final	The class cannot be used to drive new classes.	N/A	The method cannot be overridden.	The variable is a constant, whose value cannot be changed once initially set.
native	N/A	N/A	No method body is necessary since implementation is in another language.	N/A
static	N/A	N/A	Defines a class method. It does not require an instantiated object to be invoked. It cannot reference non-static methods or variables. It is implicitly final.	Defines a class variable. It does not require an instantiated object to be referenced. It is shared (common memory space) among all instances of the class.
synchronized	N/A	N/A	The execution of the method is mutually exclusive among all threads.	N/A
transient	N/A	N/A	N/A	The variable will not be serialized.
volatile	N/A	N/A	N/A	The variable is changed asynchronously. The compiler should not perform optimizations on it.

FIGURE E.3   The rest of the Java modifiers

Java Coding Guidelines

F

This appendix contains a series of guidelines that describe how to organize and format Java source code. They are designed to make programs easier to read and maintain. Some guidelines can be attributed to personal preferences and could be modified. However, it is important to have a standard set of practices that make sense and to follow them carefully. The guidelines presented here are followed in the example code throughout the text and are consistent with the Java naming conventions.

Consistency is half the battle. If you follow the same rules throughout a program and follow them from one program to another, you make the effort of reading and understanding your code easier for yourself and others. It is not unusual for a programmer to develop software that seems straightforward at the time, only to revisit it months later and have difficulty remembering how it works. If you follow consistent development guidelines, you reduce this problem considerably.

When an organization adopts a coding standard, it is easier for people to work together. A software product is often created by a team of cooperating developers, each responsible for a piece of the system. If they all follow the same development guidelines, they facilitate the process of integrating the separate pieces into one cohesive entity.

You may have to make tradeoffs between some guidelines. For example, you may be asked to make all of your identifiers easy to read yet keep them to a reasonably short length. Use common sense on a case-by-case basis to embrace the spirit of all guidelines as much as possible.

You may choose, or be asked, to follow this set of guidelines as presented. If changes or additions are made, make sure they are clear and that they represent a conscious effort to use good programming practices. Most of these issues are discussed further in appropriate areas of the text but are presented succinctly here, without elaboration.

Design Guidelines

A. Design Preparation
1. The ultimate guideline is to develop a clean design. Think before you start coding. A working program is not necessarily a good program.
2. Express and document your design with consistent, clear notation.

B. Structured Programming
1. Do not use the `continue` statement.
2. Use the `break` statement only to terminate cases of a `switch` statement.
3. Have only one `return` statement in a method as the last line, unless it unnecessarily complicates the method.

C. Classes and Packages
1. Do not have additional methods in the class that contains the `main` method.
2. Define the class that contains the `main` method at the top of the file it is in, followed by other classes if appropriate.
3. If only one class is used from an imported package, import that class by name. If two or more are imported, use the * symbol.

D. Modifiers
1. Do not declare variables with `public` visibility.
2. Do not use modifiers inside an interface.
3. Always use the most appropriate modifiers for each situation. For example, if a variable is used as a constant, explicitly declare it as a constant using the `final` modifier.

E. Exceptions
1. Use exception handling only for truly exceptional conditions, such as terminating errors, or for significantly unusual or important situations.
2. Do not use exceptions to disguise or hide inappropriate processing.
3. Handle each exception at the appropriate level of design.

F. Miscellaneous
1. Use constants instead of literals in almost all situations.
2. Design methods so that they perform one logical function. As such, the length of a method will tend to be no longer than 50 lines of code, and usually much shorter.
3. Keep the physical lines of a source code file to less than 80 characters in length.
4. Extend a logical line of code over two or more physical lines only when necessary. Divide the line at a logical place.

Style Guidelines

A. Identifier Naming

1. Give identifiers semantic meaning. For example, do not use single letter names such as a or i unless the single letter has semantic meaning.
2. Make identifiers easy to read. For example, use `currentValue` instead of `curval`.
3. Keep identifiers to a reasonably short length.
4. Use the underscore character to separate words of a constant.

B. Identifier Case

1. Use UPPERCASE for constants.
2. Use Title Case for class, package, and interface names.
3. Use lowercase for variable and method names, except for the first letter of each word other than the first word. For example, `minTaxRate`. Note that all reserved words must be lowercase.

C. Indentation

1. Indent the code in any block by three or four spaces (be consistent).
2. If the body of a loop, `if` statement, or `else` clause is a single statement (not a block), indent the statement three spaces on its own line.
3. Put the left brace ({) starting each new block on a new line. Line up the terminating right brace (}) with the opening left brace. For example:

```
while (value < 25)
{
    value += 5;
    System.out.println ("The value is " + value);
}
```

4. In a `switch` statement, indent each `case` label three spaces. Indent all code associated with a `case` three additional spaces.

D. Spacing

1. Carefully use white space to draw attention to appropriate features of a program.
2. Put one space after each comma in a parameter list.
3. Put one space on either side of a binary operator.
4. Do not put spaces immediately after a left parenthesis or before a right parenthesis.
5. Do not put spaces before a semicolon.
6. Put one space before a left parenthesis, except before an empty parameter list.

7. When declaring arrays, associate the brackets with the element type, as opposed to the array name, so that it applies to all variables on that line. For example:

```
int[30] list1, list2;
```

8. When referring to the type of an array, do not put any spaces between the element type and the square brackets, such as `int[]`.

E. Messages and Prompts
1. Do not condescend.
2. Do not attempt to be humorous.
3. Be informative, but succinct.
4. Define specific input options in prompts when appropriate.
5. Specify default selections in prompts when appropriate.

F. Output
1. Label all output clearly.
2. Present information to the user in a consistent manner.

Documentation Guidelines

A. The Reader
1. Write all documentation as though the reader is computer literate and basically familiar with the Java language.
2. Assume the reader knows almost nothing about what the program is supposed to do.
3. Remember that a section of code that seems intuitive to you when you write it might not seem so to another reader or to yourself later. Document accordingly.

B. Content
1. Make sure comments are accurate.
2. Keep comments updated as changes are made to the code.
3. Be concise but thorough.

C. Header Blocks
1. Every source code file should contain a header block of documentation providing basic information about the contents and the author.
2. Each class and interface, and each method in a class, should have a small header block that describes its role.
3. Each header block of documentation should have a distinct delimiter on the top and bottom so that the reader can visually scan from one construct to the next easily. For example:

```
//********************************************
//              header block
//********************************************
```

D. In-Line Comments

1. Use in-line documentation as appropriate to clearly describe interesting processing.
2. Put a comment on the same line with code only if the comment applies to one line of code and can fit conveniently on that line. Otherwise, put the comment on a separate line above the line or section of code to which it applies.

E. Miscellaneous

1. Avoid the use of the /* */ style of comment except to conform to the javadoc (/** */) commenting convention.
2. Don't wait until a program is finished to insert documentation. As pieces of your system are completed, comment them appropriately.

Java Applets

In Chapter 2 we presented the basic concept of an applet, including how an applet differs from an application and how an applet is referenced in an HTML page so that it can be executed in a browser. The applet examples in Chapter 2 present simple drawings. We revisited the concept of an applet in Chapter 9, exploring how applets are a good example of inheritance. This appendix fills in some other details about Java applets.

The example applets in Chapter 2 override the paint method of the JApplet class. An applet has several other methods that perform specific duties. Because an applet is designed to work with Web pages, some applet methods are specifically designed with that concept in mind. Figure G.1 lists several applet methods.

```
public void init ()
    Initializes the applet. Called just after the applet is loaded.

public void start ()
    Starts the applet. Called just after the applet is made active.

public void stop ()
    Stops the applet. Called just after the applet is made inactive.

public void destroy ()
    Destroys the applet. Called when the browser is exited.

public URL getCodeBase ()
    Returns the URL at which this applet's bytecode is located.

public URL getDocumentBase ()
    Returns the URL at which the HTML document containing this applet is
    located.

public AudioClip getAudioClip (URL url, String name)
    Retrieves an audio clip from the specified URL.

public Image getImage (URL url, String name)
    Retrieves an image from the specified URL.
```

FIGURE G.1   Some methods of the Applet class

The `init` method is executed once when the applet is first loaded, such as when the browser or appletviewer initially views the applet. Therefore the `init` method is the place to initialize the applet's environment and permanent data.

The `start` and `stop` methods of an applet are called when the applet becomes active or inactive, respectively. For example, after we use a browser to initially load an applet, the applet's `start` method is called. We may then leave that page to visit another one, at which point the applet becomes inactive and the `stop` method is called. If we return to the applet's page, the applet becomes active again and the `start` method is called again.

Note that the `init` method is called once when the applet is loaded, but `start` may be called several times as the page is revisited. It is good practice to implement `start` and `stop` for an applet if it actively uses CPU time, such as when it is showing an animation, so that CPU time is not wasted on an applet that is not visible.

Also note that reloading the Web page in the browser does not necessarily reload the applet. To force the applet to reload, most browsers provide some key combination for that purpose. For example, in Netscape Navigator, holding down the Shift key while clicking the Reload button with the mouse not only reloads the Web page but also reloads (and reinitializes) all applets linked to that page.

The `getCodeBase` and `getDocumentBase` methods are useful to determine where the applet's bytecode or HTML document resides. An applet could use the appropriate URL to retrieve additional resources, such as an image or audio clip by using the applet methods `getImage` or `getAudioClip`, respectively.

Security is an issue with applets. As you browse Web pages, you may open a page containing an applet, and suddenly an unknown program is executing on your machine. Because of the dangers inherent in that process, applets are restricted in the kinds of operations they can perform. For instance, an applet cannot write data to a local drive.

In the Graphics Track sections throughout this book, we explore issues related to the development of programs that use graphical user interfaces (GUIs). The examples in those sections are presented as Java applications, using `JFrame` components as the primary heavyweight container. An applet can also be used to present GUI-based programs. Like a `JFrame`, a `JApplet` is a heavyweight container.

Applets are useful for small, isolated programs, such as a game or calculator. Because of their security restrictions and processing overhead, they are not frequently used for larger systems. Generally, other technologies are used to support fully integrated, dynamic Web sites.

Regular Expressions

Throughout the book we've used the Scanner class to read interactive input from the user and parse strings into individual tokens such as words. In Chapter 5 we also used it to read input from a data file. Usually we used the default whitespace delimiters for tokens in the scanner input.

The Scanner class can also be used to parse its input according to a *regular expression,* which is a character string that represents a pattern. A regular expression can be used to set the delimiters used when extracting tokens, or it can be used in methods like findInLine to match a particular string.

Some of the general rules for constructing regular expressions include:

- The dot (.) character matches any single character.
- The * character, which is called the Kleene star, matches zero or more characters.
- A string of characters in square brackets ([ ]) matches any single character in the string.
- The \ character followed by a special character (such as the ones in this list) matches the character itself.
- The \ character followed by a character matches the pattern specified by that character (see the following table).

For example, the regular expression B.b* matches Bob, Bubba, and Baby. The regular expression T[aei]*ing matches Taking, Tickling, and Telling.

These examples are just a few of many. Figure H.1 specifies some of the patterns that can be matched in a Java regular expression, and this list is not complete. See the online documentation for the Pattern class for a complete list.

Regular Expression	Matches
x	The character x
.	Any character
[abc]	a, b, or c
[^abc]	Any character except a, b, or c (negation)
[a-z][A-Z]	a through z or A through Z, inclusive (range)
[a-d[m-p]]	a through d or m through p (union)
[a-z&&[def]]	d, e, or f (intersection)
[a-z&&[^bc]]	a through z, except for b and c (subtraction)
[a-z&&[^m-p]]	a through z but not m through p (subtraction)
\d	A digit: [0–9]
\D	A non-digit: [^0–9]
\s	A whitespace character
\S	A non-whitespace character
^	The beginning of a line
$	The end of a line

FIGURE H.1   Some patterns that can be matched in a Java regular expression

Javadoc Documentation Generator

Javadoc is a tool for creating documentation in HTML format from Java source code. The utility examines the source code, extracts specially marked information in the documentation, and then produces Web pages that summarize the software.

Documentation comments, also referred to as doc comments, specify the format for comments to be processed by the javadoc tool. Special labels called *tags* are also parsed by javadoc. Together, doc comments and tags can be used to construct a complete Java application programming interface (API) specification. A Java API is a specification of how to work with a class.

Javadoc can be run on packages or individual files (or both). It produces a well-structured, single document each time. However, javadoc does not support incremental additions.

Javadoc comes as a standard part of the Java Software Development Kit (SDK). The tool executable, javadoc.exe, resides in the bin folder of the installation directory along with the javac compiler and java execution tool. Therefore, if you are able to compile and execute your code using the command line, javadoc should also work.

Using javadoc is simple in its plain form; it is very much like compiling a java source file. For example:

```
javadoc myfile.java
```

The javadoc command may also specify options and package names. The source file name must contain the .java extension (similar to the javac compiler command).

Doc Comments

The document comments are subdivided into descriptions and tags. Descriptions should provide an overview of the functionality of the explained code. Tags address the specifics of the functionality such as code version (for classes or interfaces) or return types (for methods).

Javadoc processes code comments placed between /**, the beginning tag, and */, the end tag. The comments are allowed to span multiple lines where each line begins with a * character, which are, along with any white space before them, discarded by the tool. These comments are allowed to contain HTML tags. For example:

```
/**
*    This is an <strong>example</strong> document comment.
*/
```

Comment placement should be considered carefully. The javadoc tool automatically copies the first sentence from each doc to a summary at the top of the HTML document. The sentence begins after any white space following the * character and ends at the first period. The description that follows should be concise and complete. Document comments are recognized only if they are placed immediately before a class, constructor, method, interface, or field declaration.

The use of HTML inside the description should be limited to proper comment separation and display rather than styling. Javadoc automatically structures the document using certain tags—for example, heading tags. Appropriate use of paragraph or list tags (ordered/unordered) should provide satisfactory formatting.

Tags

Tags are included in a doc comment. Each tag must start on a separate line, hence it must be preceded by the * character. Tags are case sensitive and begin with the @ symbol.

Certain tags are required in some situations. The @param tag must be supplied for every parameter and is used to describe the purpose of the parameter. The @return tag must be supplied for every method that returns anything other than void, to describe what the method returns. The @author class and the @version tags are required for classes and interfaces only.

Figure I.1 lists the various tags used in javadoc comments.

Note the two different types of tags listed in Figure I.1. The *block tags,* which begin with the @ symbol (e.g., @author), must be placed in the tag section

Tag Name	Description
@author	Inserts an "Author" entry with the specified text.
{ @code}	Same as `<code>{@literal}</code>`.
@deprecated	Inserts a bold "Deprecated" entry with the specified text.
{ @docRoot}	Relative link to the root of the document.
@exception	See @throws.
{ @inheritDoc}	Copies documentation from the closest inherited class or implemented interface where used allowing for more general comments of hierarchically higher classes to be reused.
{ @link}	Inserts a hyperlink to an HTML document. Use: `{@link name url}`.
{ @linkPlain}	Same as `{@link}` but is displayed as plain text. Use: `{@linkPlain link label}`.
{ @literal}	Text enclosed in the tag is denoted literally, as containing any HTML. For example, `{@literal <td> TouchDown}` would be displayed as `<td> TouchDown` (`<td>` not interpreted as a table cell).
@param	Inserts a "Parameters" section, which lists and describes parameters for a particular constructor/method.
@return	Inserts a "Returns" section, which lists and describes any return values for a particular constructor/method. Use: `@return description`. An error will be thrown if included in a comment of a method with the void return type.
@see	Included a "See Also" comment with a link pointing to a document with more information. Use: `@see link`.
@serial	Used for a serializable field. Use: `@serial text`.
@serialData	Used to document used to describe data written by the `writeObject`, `readObject`, `writeExternal`, and `readExternal` methods. Use: `@serialdata text`.
@serialField	Used to comment on the `ObjectStreamField`. Use: `@serialField name type description`.
@since	Inserts a new "Since" heading that is used to denote when particular features were first introduced. Use: `@since text`.
@throws	Includes a "Throws" heading. Use: `@throws name description`.
{ @value}	Returns the value of a code element it refers to. Use: `@value code-member label`.
@version	Add a "Version" heading when the –version command–line option is used. Use: `@version text`.

FIGURE I.1   Various tags used in javadoc comments

following the main description. The *inline tags*, enclosed in the { and } delimiters, can be placed anywhere in the description section or in the comments for block tags. For example:

```
/**
 * This is an <strong>example</strong> document comment.
 * The {@link Glossary} provides definitions of types used.
 *
 * @author Sebastian Niezgoda
 */
```

Files Generated

The javadoc tool analyzes a java source file or package and produces a three-part HTML document for each class. The HTML file is often referred to as a documentation file. It contains cleanly organized information about the class file derived from the doc comments included in the code.

The first part of the document contains an overall description of the class. The class name appears first followed by a graphical representation of the inheritance relationships. A general description is displayed next, which is extracted from the first sentence of each doc comment entity (as discussed previously).

Next, a list of constructors and methods is provided. The signatures of all the constructors and methods included in the source file are listed along with one-sentence descriptions. The name of the constructor/method is a hyperlink to a more detailed description in the third part of the document.

Third, complete descriptions of the methods are provided. Again, the signature is provided first followed by an explanation of the entity, this time without the one-sentence limit, which is obtained from the doc comments. If applicable, a list of parameters and return values, along with their descriptions, is provided in the respective sections.

The HTML document makes extensive use of hyperlinks to provide necessary additional information, using the @see tag for example, and for navigational purposes. The header and the footer of the page are navigation bars, with the following links:

- *Package* provides a list of classes included in the package along with a short purpose and description of each class.
- *Tree* presents a visual hierarchy of the classes within the package. Each class name is a link to the appropriate documentation HTML file.
- *Deprecated* lists functionality that is considered deprecated that is used in any of the class files contained in the package.

- *Index* provides an alphabetical listing of classes, constructors, and methods in the package. The class name is also associated with a short purpose and description of the class. Each appearance of the class name is a link to the appropriate HTML documentation. The signature of every constructor and method is a link to the appropriate detailed description. A one-sentence description presented next to the signature listing associates the constructor/ method with the appropriate class.

- *Help* loads a help page with how-to instructions for using and navigating the HTML documentation.

All pages could be viewed with or without frames. Each class summary has links that can be used to quickly access any of the parts of the document (as described above).

The output content could be somewhat generated by command-line options (see above) used when executing the javadoc tool. By default, if no options are specified, the output returned is equivalent to using the -protected option. The options include:

- private shows all classes, methods, and variables.
- public shows only public classes, methods, and variables.
- protected shows only protected and public classes, methods, and variables.
- help presents the online help.
- keywords includes HTML meta tags to the output file generated to assist with searching.

The PaintBox Project

J

In this appendix we examine a software development project that is larger than any other described in this text. Our example program allows the user to create drawings with various shapes and colors. This type of project encompasses a variety of issues that are commonly found in large-scale software development and provides a good basis for exploring our development model. We call this example the PaintBox project.

PaintBox Requirements

Suppose the client provides the following set of initial requirements. The program will:

- Present a graphical user interface that is primarily mouse driven for all user actions.
- Allow the user to draw lines, ovals, circles, rectangles, and squares.
- Allow the user to change the drawing color.
- Display the current drawing color.
- Allow the user to fill a shape, except for a line, with a color.
- Allow the user to select a shape in order to move it, modify its color, or reshape it.
- Allow the user to cut, copy, and paste individual shapes in a drawing.
- Allow the user to save a drawing in a file and load a previously stored drawing from a file for further editing.
- Allow the user to begin a new drawing at any time.

After examining these general requirements, we might sit down with the client and discuss some of the details to ensure that there are no misunderstandings. We might create a new requirements document that is much more specific about the issues involved.

During these interactions with the client, we might create a sketch, such as the one shown in Figure J.1, of a user interface for the system. This sketch serves as a basic prototype of the interface, and gives us something to refer to in our discussions

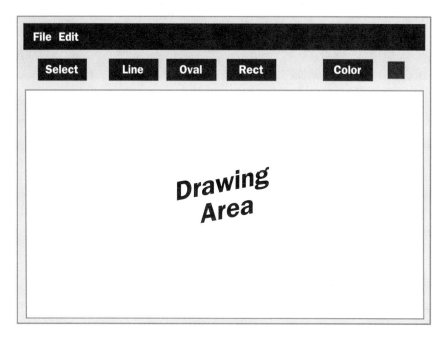

with the client. For other systems there may be many such sketches for each screen of the program.

The interface sketch shows a main drawing area where the user will create a drawing. The top edge contains a set of buttons used to select various tools, such as the oval tool to draw an oval or circle, the color tool to change the current drawing color, and a select tool to select a previously drawn shape to modify or move it. Two menu headings are shown along the top edge. The File menu contains operations to begin a new drawing, save a drawing, and exit the program. The Edit menu contains editing operations such as cut, copy, and paste.

As a result of the discussions with the client, several additional requirements issues are established:

- There is no need to have separate user interactions for circles or squares because they are subsets of ovals and rectangles, respectively.
- The user should also be able to create polyline shapes.
- The buttons used to select drawing tools should have icons instead of words.

- The system should make a distinction between the stroke color (the outline) and the fill color (the interior) of a shape. Therefore, each shape will have a separate stroke and fill color. Lines and polylines will have only a stroke color because they cannot be filled.

- An option to save a drawing under a particular name should be provided (the traditional "save as" operation).

- Traditional keyboard shortcuts for operations such as cut, copy, and paste should be included.

- The system should perform checks to ensure that the user does not lose unsaved changes to a drawing.

- The system should present an initial "splash screen" to introduce the program when it is executed.

These issues must be integrated into the formal description of the requirements document for the project. Several discussions with the client, with additional screen sketches, may be necessary before we have an accurate and solid set of program requirements.

PaintBox Architectural Design

After we have clarified the requirements with the client, we can begin to think about some of the elements of the high-level *architectural design* of the system. For example, many of the classes needed for the user interface can come from the Java standard class library in the Swing package.

It also seems reasonable that a separate class could be used to represent each shape type. Further, each individually drawn shape should be an instantiation of the appropriate shape class. For example, we could define an Oval class to represent an oval, a Line class to represent a line, and so on. Each class should be responsible for keeping track of the information it needs to define it, and it should provide methods to draw itself.

A drawing may be composed of many shapes, so we need a way to keep track of all of them. An ArrayList might be a good choice for this. As each new shape is drawn, we can add the object that represents it to the list. The list will also inherently define the order in which shapes are drawn. Since some shapes will be drawn on top of others, the list will also keep track of the order in which shapes are "stacked."

The process of defining an architectural design could take a while. The key is to make the most important and fundamental decisions that will affect the entire system without skipping ahead to decisions that are better left to individual refinements of the system.

PaintBox Refinements

After some consideration, we might decide that the evolution of the PaintBox project could be broken down into the following refinement steps:

- Establish the basic user interface.
- Allow the user to draw basic shapes using different stroke colors.
- Allow the user to cut, copy, and paste shapes.
- Allow the user to select, move, and fill shapes.
- Allow the user to modify the dimensions of shapes.
- Allow the user to save and reload drawings.
- Include final touches such as the splash screen.

Note, first of all, that these refinements focus on breaking down the functionality of the system. Additional refinements may be necessary as we get into the iterative process. For instance, we may decide that we need a refinement to address problems that were discovered in previous refinements.

The listed refinements could have been broken down further. For example, one refinement could have been devoted to the ability to draw one particular type of shape. The level of refinement, just like many other decisions when developing a software system, is a judgment call. The developer must decide what is best in any particular situation.

The order in which we tackle the refinements is also important. The user interface refinement seems to be a logical first step because all other activity relies on it. We may decide that the ability to save and reload a drawing would be nice to have early for testing purposes. We might also note that being able to select an object is fundamental to operations such as move and cut/copy/paste. After further analysis, we end up with the set of refinements shown in Figure J.2.

PaintBox Refinement #1

Most of the classes used for the interface come from predefined libraries. We use Swing technology whenever reasonable. For example, we can use a JPanel for the overall interface space, as well as separate JPanel objects to organize the button tools and the drawing area. The JButton class will serve well for the buttons. Classes such as JMenuBar and JMenuItem will serve to implement the menus.

Figure J.3 shows a class diagram that represents the classes that are important to the first refinement of the PaintBox project. Note that it does not include all classes that might be needed, nor does it address anything other than the needs

Refinement	Description
1	Present the basic graphical user interface, including the main frame, buttons, menus, menu items, and the drawing area. The select and shape buttons work together as a radio button set (only one can be chosen at a time). No functionality for these interface elements is included at this time. Exiting the program is provided only by the frame's window close button.
2	Add support for drawing the four basic shapes: lines, ovals, rectangles, and polylines. The chosen shape button determines what shape is drawn. The stroke color button can be used to set the stroke color for the next shape drawn. The color button causes a separate dialog box to appear to allow color selection.
3	Add support for saving and loading drawings. This includes the functionality of the *open, save,* and *save as* File menu items. When the *open, new,* or *exit* File menu options are chosen, check to see if the current drawing has been modified since last saved, and if so prompt to see if the user wants to save the drawing.
4	Provide the ability to select and move shapes on the drawing surface. Simple graphic selection blocks should be presented on the shape's outline to indicate the currently selected shape. Once selected, the mouse can be used to drag the shape to another location on the drawing surface.
5	Add the functionality for the *cut, copy* and *paste* Edit menu items. Once selected, a shape can be cut or copied. Once a shape has been cut or copied, it can be pasted (perhaps multiple times) onto the drawing surface at a fixed offset to the original position. Edit menu items that are not valid at any given time are disabled. For example, unless a shape is selected, the cut and copy menu items cannot be chosen.
6	Add support for filling and reshaping a shape. Once a shape has been selected, the fill color button can be used to determine its fill color. A menu item on the Edit menu can be used to remove the fill of any filled object (make it transparent). The currently selected shape will now have a reshape handle that can be used to change the dimensions of the shape.
7	Add some extra functionality to the program. These additions include a splash screen that appears when the system is initially executed, an *about* dialog box, keyboard shortcuts for all menu items, and packaging the application into an executable JAR file.

FIGURE J.2 Functional refinements for the PaintBox project

of this one refinement. We'll create additional diagrams that augment our understanding of the system design as further refinements are developed.

The detailed design and implementation for the interface refinement might
develop similarly to other graphical projects we've developed in previous chapters.

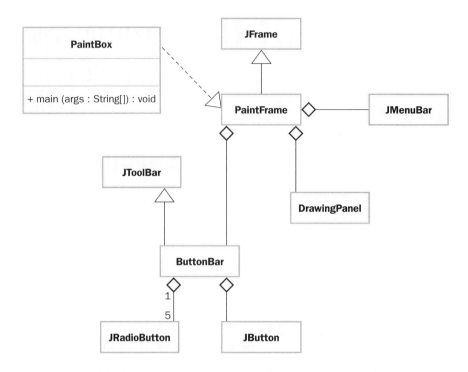

FIGURE J.3 A class diagram for the interface refinement of the PaintBox project

We can create listener objects and methods as appropriate but not concern ourselves with their inner workings at this time. That is, our focus in this refinement is to present the user interface, not to create any of the functionality behind the interface. During the development of this refinement, we modify the details of the user interface until it appears just the way we'd like it.

At the end of the first refinement, we are left with a completely implemented program that presents only the user interface. The buttons do nothing when pushed, and the menu items do nothing when selected. We have no way of creating a drawing yet.

What we do have, however, is a complete entity that has been debugged and tested to the level of this refinement. We may show it to the client at this point and get further input. Any changes that result from these discussions can be incorporated into future refinements. Figure J.4 shows the PaintBox program after the first refinement has been completed.

FIGURE J.4   The PaintBox application after refinement #1

PaintBox Refinement #2

The next refinement to address is the ability to draw basic shapes, because all other operations use drawn shapes in one way or another. Therefore, in this refinement we focus on providing the processing power behind the buttons that draw shapes and specify color.

Most of the objects and classes that we will use in this refinement are not predefined as they were in the interface refinement. We might consider using the

`Rectangle` class from the Java standard class library, but on further investigation we realize that its role is not really consistent with our goals. In addition, no other classes are defined for the other shapes we need.

So, as we envisioned in our architectural design, we consider having one class per shape type: `Line`, `Oval`, `Rect`, and `Poly`. Remember that circles and squares will just be specific instances of the `Oval` and `Rect` classes, respectively. Each shape class will have a `draw` method that draws that kind of shape on the screen.

Now let's consider the kind of information that each shape needs to store to be able to draw itself. A line needs two points: a starting point and an ending point. Each polyline, on the other hand, needs a list of points to define the start and end points of each line segment. Both ovals and rectangles are defined by a bounded rectangle, storing an upper-left corner and the width and height of the shape.

This analysis leads to the conclusion that `Oval` and `Rect` objects have some common characteristics that we could exploit using inheritance. They could both, for instance, be derived from a class called `BoundedShape`. Furthermore, because all shapes have to be stored in the `ArrayList` object that we'll use to keep track of the entire drawing, it would simplify the refinement to have a generic `Shape` class from which all drawn shapes are derived.

The `Shape` and `BoundedShape` classes are used for organizational purposes. We do not intend to instantiate them; therefore they probably should be abstract classes. In fact, if we define an `abstract` method called `draw` in the `Shape` class, we could capitalize on polymorphism to simplify the drawing of the shapes in the drawing area. A loop can move through the `ArrayList`, having each shape (whatever it may be) draw itself.

After some consideration, we achieve the class diagram shown in Figure J.5. This diagram specifically represents the classes that are important to the second refinement of the `PaintBox` project.

Selecting a current color can be relegated to the `JColorChooser` component provided by the Swing package. The color button will bring up the `JColorChooser` dialog box and respond accordingly to the user's selection.

Multiple shapes will accumulate on the drawing surface. We could define a class to serve as a collection of the drawn shape objects. It could use an `ArrayList` to keep track of the list of shapes. Whenever the drawing area needs to be refreshed, we can iterate through the list of shapes and draw each one in turn.

Figure J.6 shows the `PaintBox` program after the first two refinements have been completed. Once again, we could visit with the client at this point to determine whether the evolution of the system meets with his or her satisfaction.

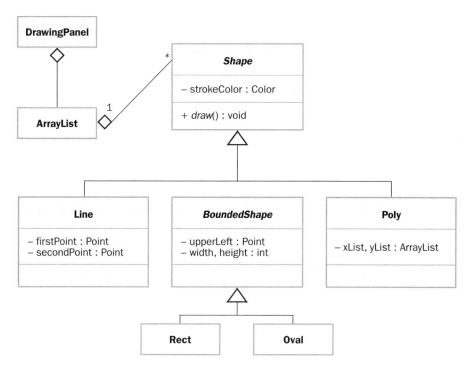

FIGURE J.5 A class diagram for the second refinement of the PaintBox project

Remaining PaintBox Refinements

For space reasons, the code for the various PaintBox refinements is not presented in the text. The full implementation of the first two refinements can be downloaded with the rest of the book's examples. The remaining refinements are left as projects.

The refinements of the PaintBox program continue until all requirements issues and problems have been addressed. This type of evolutionary development is crucial for medium- and large-scale development efforts. Figure J.7 shows the PaintBox program after all of the seven refinements have been completed.

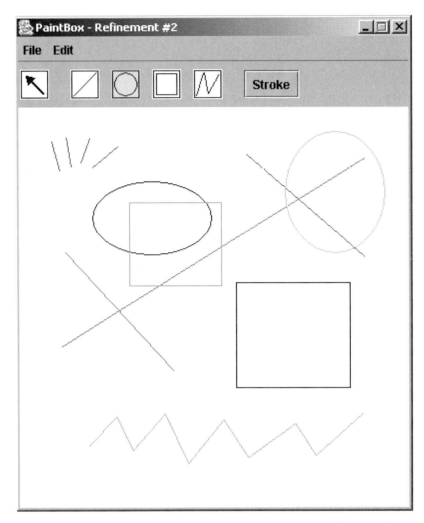

FIGURE J.6   The PaintBox program after the interface and shapes refinements

FIGURE J.7   The completed PaintBox program

GUI Events

K

Throughout the Graphics Track sections of this book, we've discussed various events that components might generate. The goal of this appendix is to put the event/component relationship into context.

The events listed in Figure K.1 are generated by every Swing component. That is, we can set up a listener for any of these events on any component.

Some events are generated only by certain components. The table in Figure K.2 maps the components to the events that they can generate. Keep in mind that these events are in addition to the ones that all components generate. If a component does not generate a particular kind of event, a listener for that event cannot be added to that component.

We have discussed some of the events in Figures K.1 and K.2 at appropriate points in this text; we have left others for your independent exploration. Applying the basic concept of component/event/listener interaction is often just a matter of knowing which components generate which events under which circumstances.

Of course, many events occur in a GUI that have no bearing on the current program. For example, every time a mouse is moved across a component, many mouse motion events are generated. However, this doesn't mean we must listen for them. A GUI is defined in part by the events to which we choose to respond.

Despite our heavy coverage of GUI development in this book, we've still only scratched the surface. The following list describes a few other Java GUI containers and components that are not covered in depth in this text:

Event	Represents
Component Event	Changing a component's size, position, or visibility.
Focus Event	Gaining or losing the keyboard focus.
Key Event	Pressing, releasing, and clicking keyboard keys.
Mouse Event	Clicking the mouse button and moving the mouse into and out of a component's drawing area.
Mouse Motion Event	Moving or dragging a mouse over a component.

FIGURE K.1 Events that are generated by every Swing component

Component	Action	Caret	Change	Document	Item	List Selection	Window	Other
JButton	√		√		√			
JCheckBox	√		√		√			
JColorChooser			√					
JComboBox	√				√			
JDialog							√	
JEditorPane		√		√				√
JFileChooser	√							
JFrame							√	
JInternalFrame								√
JList						√		√
JMenu								√
JMenuItem	√		√		√			√
JOptionPane								
JPasswordField	√	√		√				
JPopupMenu								√
JProgessBar			√		√			
JRadioButton	√		√					
JSlider			√					
JTabbedPane			√					
JTable						√		√
JTextArea		√		√				
JTextField	√	√		√				
JTextPane		√		√				√
JToggleButton	√		√		√			
JTree								√

FIGURE K.2   Specific events generated by specific components

- A *tool bar* is a container that groups several components into a row or column. A tool bar usually contains buttons that correspond to tasks that can also be accomplished in other ways. Tool bars can be dragged away from the container in which they initially exist into their own window.
- An *internal frame* is a container that operates like a regular frame but only within another window. An internal frame can be moved around within the window and overlapped with other internal frames. Internal frames can be used to create the feel of a GUI desktop in which components can be arranged as the user chooses.

- A *layered pane* is a container that takes into account a third dimension, depth, for organizing the components it contains. When a component is added to a layered pane, its depth is specified. If components overlap, the depth value of each component determines which is on top.

- A *progress bar* can be used to indicate the progress of a particular activity. The user does not generally interact with a progress bar other than to view it to determine how far along a task, such as the loading of images, has progressed.

- A *table* is a Java GUI component that displays data in a table format. A Java table can be completely tailored to provide a precise organization and presentation. It can allow the user to edit the data as well. A Java table does not actually contain or store the data; it simply presents it to the user in an organized manner.

- A *tree* is a component that presents a hierarchical view of data. Like a table, it doesn't actually store the data; it provides an organized view that allows the user to traverse the data from a high-level root node down through the various branches.

- Another area for which Java provides rich support is *text processing.* We've made use of basic text components such as text fields and text areas, but that's only the beginning. The Java standard class library (and particularly the Swing API) has a huge number of classes that support the display, editing, and manipulation of text.

As with all topics introduced in this book, we encourage you to explore these issues in more detail. The world of Java GUIs, in particular, offers many opportunities for you to discover.

Java Syntax

This appendix contains syntax diagrams that collectively describe the way in which Java language elements can be constructed. Rectangles indicate something that is further defined in another syntax diagram, and ovals indicate a literal word or character.

Compilation Unit

```
●──┬────────────────────┬──┬───────────────────┬──┬──────────────────┬──►●
   └─►[Package Declaration]─┘  └─►[Import Declaration]─┘  └─►[Type Declaration]─┘
```

Package Declaration

```
●──►(package)──►[Name]──►(;)──►●
```

Import Declaration

```
●──►(import)──►[Name]──►(.)──┬─►[Identifier]─┬──►(;)──►●
                             └─►(*)──────────┘
```

Type Declaration

```
●──┬─►[Class Declaration]────┬──►●
   └─►[Interface Declaration]─┘
```

Class Declaration

Class Associations

Class Body

Class Member

Interface Declaration

Interface Body

Interface Member

Field Declaration

Variable Declarator

Type

Modifier   **Primitive Type**

Array Initializer

Name   **Name List**

Method Declaration

Parameters

Throws Clause

Method Body

Constructor Declaration

Constructor Body

Constructor Invocation

Block

Block Statement

Local Variable Declaration

Statement

If Statement

Switch Statement

Switch Case

While Statement

Do Statement

For Statement

For Init

For Update

Basic Assignment

Return Statement

Throw Statement

Try Statement

Synchronized Statement

Empty Statement

Break Statement

Continue Statement

Labeled Statement

Expression

Primary Expression

Primary Suffix

Arguments

Allocation

Array Dimensions

Statement Expression

Assignment

Arithmetic Expression

Equality Expression

Relational Expression

Logical Expression

Bitwise Expression

Conditional Expression

Instance Expression

Cast Expression

Unary Expression

Prefix Expression

Postfix Expression

Literal

Integer Literal

Decimal Integer Literal

Octal Integer Literal   **Hex Digit**

Hex Integer Literal

Floating Point Literal

Exponent Part

Float Suffix

Character Literal

Boolean Literal

String Literal

Escape Sequence

Identifier

Java Letter

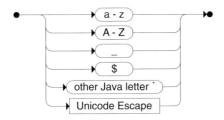

* The "other Java letter" category includes letters
   from many languages other than English.

Java Digit

* The "other Java digit" category includes
   additional digits defined in Unicode.

Unicode Escape*

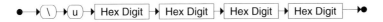

* In some contexts, the character represented
   by a Unicode Escape is restricted.

The Java Class Library

In previous editions of this book, this appendix included abbreviated reference material for the Java API. This appendix is still available at ftp://ftp.aw.com/cseng/authors/lewis/jss7/ for anyone who would like to download and make use of it.

A better solution, however, is to become familiar with the official and complete online API documentation, as shown in Figure M.1. It contains a description of every class, interface, and method available to every Java development environment. We encourage you to spend some time becoming familiar with the organization and layout of that documentation. It is a valuable tool to rely on during program development.

FIGURE M.1   The online Java API documentation

Answers to Self-Review Questions

Chapter 1 Introduction

1.1 Computer Processing

SR 1.1   The hardware of a computer system consists of its physical components such as a circuit board, monitor, or keyboard. Computer software consists of the programs that are executed by the hardware and the data that those programs use. Hardware is tangible, whereas software is intangible. In order to be useful, hardware requires software and software requires hardware.

SR 1.2   The operating system provides a user interface and efficiently coordinates the use of resources such as main memory and the CPU.

SR 1.3   It takes 7,200,000 numbers for a 3-minute song ($40,000 \times 60 \times 3$) and 144,000,000 numbers for 1 hour of music ($40,000 \times 60 \times 60$).

SR 1.4   The information is broken into pieces, and those pieces are represented as numbers.

SR 1.5   In general, N bits can represent 2^N unique items. Therefore:

a. 2 bits can represent 4 items because $2^2 = 4$.
b. 4 bits can represent 16 items because $2^4 = 16$.
c. 5 bits can represent 32 items because $2^5 = 32$.
d. 7 bits can represent 128 items because $2^7 = 128$.

SR 1.6   It would take 6 bits to represent each of the 50 states. Five bits is not enough because $2^5 = 32$ but six bits would be enough because $2^6 = 64$.

1.2 Hardware Components

SR 1.7   A kilobyte (KB) is $2^{10} = 1{,}024$ bytes, a megabyte (MB) is $2^{20} = 1{,}048{,}576$ bytes, and a gigabyte (GB) is $2^{30} = 1{,}073{,}741{,}824$ bytes. Therefore:

a. 3 KB = 3 * 1,024 bytes = 3,072 bytes = approximately 3 thousand bytes

b. 2 MB = 2 * 1,048,576 bytes = 2,097,152 bytes = approximately 2.1 million bytes

c. 4 GB = 4 * 1,073,741,824 bytes = 4,294,967,296 bytes = approximately 4.3 billion bytes

SR 1.8   There are eight bits in a byte. Therefore:

a. 8 bytes = 8 * 8 bits = 64 bits

b. 2 KB = 2 * 1,024 bytes = 2,048 bytes = 2,048 * 8 bits = 16,384 bits

c. 4 MB = 4 * 1,048,576 bytes = 4,194,304 bytes = 4,194,304 * 8 bits = 33,554,432 bits

SR 1.9   Under the stated conditions, one hour of music would require 288,000,000 bytes (40,000 × 60 × 60 × 2). Dividing this number by the number of bytes in a megabyte (1,048,576 bytes) gives approximately 275 MB. Note that a typical audio CD has a capacity of about 650 MB and can store about 70 minutes of music. This coincides with an actual sampling rate of 41,000 measurements per second, two bytes of storage space per measurement, and the need to store two streams of music to produce a stereo effect.

SR 1.10 The two primary hardware components are main memory and the CPU. Main memory holds the currently active programs and data. The CPU retrieves individual program instructions from main memory, one at a time, and executes them.

SR 1.11 A memory address is a number that uniquely identifies a particular memory location in which a value is stored.

SR 1.12 Main memory is volatile, which means the information that is stored in it will be lost if the power supply to the computer is turned off. Secondary memory devices are nonvolatile; therefore, the information that is stored on them is retained even if the power goes off.

SR 1.13 The word that best matches is

a. peripheral   b. controller   c. modem   d. main or RAM
e. secondary or ROM   f. RAM   g. CPU

1.3 Networks

SR 1.14 A file server is a network computer that is dedicated to storing and providing programs and data that are needed by many network users.

SR 1.15 Counting the number of unique connections in Figure 1.16, there are 10 communication lines needed to fully connect a point-to-point network of five computers. Adding a sixth computer to the network will require that it be connected to the original five, bringing the total to 15 communication lines.

SR 1.16 Having computers on a network share a communication line is cost effective because it cuts down on the number of connections needed and it also makes it easier to add a new computer to the network. Sharing lines, however, can mean delays in communication if the network is busy.

SR 1.17 The word Internet comes from the word internetworking, a concept related to wide-area networks (WANs). An internetwork connects one network to another. The Internet is a WAN.

SR 1.18 TCP stands for *Transmission Control Protocol*. IP stands for *Internet Protocol*. A protocol is a set of rules that govern how two things communicate.

SR 1.19 Breaking down the parts of each URL:

a. `duke` is the name of a computer within the `csc` subdomain (the Department of Computing Sciences) of the `villanova.edu` domain, which represents Villanova University. The `edu` top-level domain indicates that it is an educational organization. This URL is requesting a file called `examples.html` from within a subdirectory called `jss`.

b. `java` is the name of a computer (Web server) at the `sun.com` domain, which represents Sun Microsystems, Inc. The `com` top-level domain indicates that it is a commercial business. This URL is requesting a file called `index.html` from within a subdirectory called `products`.

1.4 The Java Programming Language

SR 1.20 The Java programming language was developed in the early 1990s by James Gosling at Sun Microsystems. It was introduced to the public in 1995.

SR 1.21 The processing of a Java application begins with the `main` method.

SR 1.22 The characters "Hello" will be printed on the computer screen.

SR 1.23 The entire line of code is a comment, so there is no result.

SR 1.24 All of the identifiers shown are valid except `12345` (since an identifier cannot begin with a digit) and `black&white` (since an identifier cannot contain the character &). The identifiers RESULT and result are both valid, but should not be used together in a program because they differ only by case. The underscore character (as in answer_7) is a valid part of an identifier.

SR 1.25 Although any of the listed names *could* be used as the required identifier, the only "good" choice is scoreSum. The identifier x is not descriptive and is meaningless, the identifier sumOfTheTestScoresOfTheStudents is unnecessarily long, and the identifier smTstScr is unclear.

SR 1.26 White space is a term that refers to the spaces, tabs, and newline characters that separate words and symbols in a program. The compiler ignores extra white space; therefore, it doesn't affect execution. However, it is crucial to use white space appropriately to make a program readable to humans.

1.5 Program Development

SR 1.27 At the lowest level, a computer's instructions perform only simple tasks, such as copying a value or comparing two numbers. However, by putting together millions of these simple instructions every second, a computer can perform complex tasks.

SR 1.28 High-level languages allow a programmer to express a series of program instructions in English-like terms that are relatively easy to read and use. However, in order to execute, a program must be expressed in a particular computer's machine language, which consists of a series of bits that are basically unreadable by humans. A high-level language program must be translated into machine language before it can be run.

SR 1.29 Java bytecode is a low-level representation of a Java source code program. The Java compiler translates the source code into bytecode, which can then be executed using the Java interpreter. The bytecode might be transported across the Web before being executed by a Java interpreter that is part of a Web browser.

SR 1.30 The word that best matches is

a. machine   b. assembly   c. high-level   d. high-level
e. compiler   f. interpreter

SR 1.31 Syntax rules define how the symbols and words of a programming language can be put together. The semantics of a programming language instruction determine what will happen when that instruction is executed.

SR 1.32 a. Compile-time error   b. Run-time error (you cannot divide by zero)   c. Logical error

1.6 Object-Oriented Programming

SR 1.33 1. Understand the problem.
2. Design a solution.
3. Consider alternatives and refinements to the solution.
4. Implement the solution.
5. Test the solution.

SR 1.34 The first solution to a problem that we think of may not be a good one. By considering alternative solutions before expending too much energy implementing our first idea, we can often save overall time and effort.

SR 1.35 The primary elements that support object-oriented programming are objects, classes, encapsulation, and inheritance. An object is defined by a class, which contains methods that define the operations on those objects (the services that they perform). Objects are encapsulated such that they store and manage their own data. Inheritance is a reuse technique in which one class can be derived from another.

Chapter 2 Data and Expressions

2.1 Character Strings

SR 2.1 A string literal is a sequence of characters delimited by double quotes.

SR 2.2 Both the `print` and `println` methods of the `System.out` object write a string of characters to the monitor screen. The difference is that, after printing the characters, the `println` performs a carriage return so that whatever's printed next appears on the next line. The `print` method allows subsequent output to appear on the same line.

SR 2.3 A parameter is data that is passed into a method when it is invoked. The method usually uses that data to accomplish the service that it provides. For example, the parameter to the `println` method indicates what characters should be printed.

SR 2.4 The output produced by the code fragment is

```
One
Two Three
```

SR 2.5 The output produced by the code fragment is

```
Ready
Set

Go
```

SR 2.6   The output produced by the statement is

It is good to be 10

The + operator in the sub-expression (5 + 5) represents integer addition, since both of its operands are integers. If the inner parentheses are removed, the + operators represent string concatenation and the output produced is

It is good to be 55

SR 2.7   An escape sequence is a series of characters that begins with the backslash (\) and that implies that the following characters should be treated in some special way. Examples: \n represents the newline character, \t represents the tab character, and \" represents the quotation character (as opposed to using it to terminate a string).

SR 2.8   System.out.println ("\"I made this letter longer than "
         + "usual because I lack the time to\nmake it short.\""
         + "\n\tBlaise Pascal");

2.2 Variables and Assignment

SR 2.9   A variable declaration establishes the name of a variable and the type of data that it can contain. A declaration may also have an optional initialization, which gives the variable an initial value.

SR 2.10 Given those variable declarations, the answers are:
         a. Five variables are declared: count, value, total, MAX_VALUE, and myValue.
         b. They are all of type int.
         c. count, MAX_VALUE, and myValue are each given an initial value.
         d. Yes, it is legal. myValue is a variable of type int and 100 is an int literal.
         e. No, it is not legal. MAX_VALUE is declared as a final variable and therefore it cannot be assigned a value other than its initial value.

SR 2.11 The variable name you choose should reflect the purpose of the variable. For example:

int numCDs = 0;

SR 2.12 The variable name you choose should reflect the purpose of the variable. Since the number of feet in a mile will not change, it is a good idea to declare a constant. For example:

final int FT_PER_MILE = 5280;

SR 2.13 First, by carefully choosing the name of the constant, you can make your program more understandable than if you just use the literal value. Second, using a constant ensures that the literal value represented by the variable will not be inadvertently changed somewhere in the program. Third, if you ever do have to rewrite the program using a different literal value, you will only need to change that value once, as the initial value of the constant, rather than many places throughout the program.

2.3 Primitive Data Types

SR 2.14 Primitive data are basic values such as numbers or characters. Objects are more complex entities that usually contain primitive data that help define them.

SR 2.15 An integer variable can store only one value at a time. When a new value is assigned to it, the old one is overwritten and lost.

SR 2.16 The four integer data types in Java are byte, short, int, and long. They differ in how much memory space is allocated for each and therefore how large a number they can hold.

SR 2.17 Java automatically assigns an integer literal the data type int. If you append an L or an l on the end of an integer literal, for example 1234L, Java will assign it the type long.

SR 2.18 Java automatically assigns a floating point literal the data type double. If you append an F or an f on the end of a floating point literal, for example 12.34f, Java will assign it the type float.

SR 2.19 A character set is a list of characters in a particular order. A character set defines the valid characters that a particular type of computer or programming language will support. Java uses the Unicode character set.

SR 2.20 The original ASCII character set supports $2^7 = 128$ characters, the extended ASCII character set supports $2^8 = 256$ characters, and the UNICODE character set supports $2^{16} = 65,536$ characters.

2.4 Expressions

SR 2.21 The result of 19%5 in a Java expression is 4. The remainder operator % returns the remainder after dividing the second operand into the first. The remainder when dividing 19 by 5 is 4.

SR 2.22 The result of 13/4 in a Java expression is 3 (not 3.25). The result is an integer because both operands are integers. Therefore, the / operator performs integer division, and the fractional part of the result is truncated.

SR 2.23 After executing the statement, `diameter` holds the value 20. First, the current value of `diameter` (5) is multiplied by 4, and then the result is stored back in `diameter`.

SR 2.24 Operator precedence is the set of rules that dictates the order in which operators are evaluated in an expression.

SR 2.25 The evaluations of the expressions are

```
a. 15 + 7 * 3           = 15 + 21       = 36
b. (15 + 7) * 3         = 22 * 3        = 66
c. 3 * 6 + 10 / 5 + 5   = 18 + 2 + 5    = 25
d. 27 % 5 + 7 % 3       = 2 + 1         = 3
e. 100 / 2 / 2 / 2      = 50 / 2 / 2    = 25 / 2  = 12
f. 100 / ( 2 / 2) / 2   = 100 / 1 / 2   = 100 / 2 = 50
```

SR 2.26 Expression a is valid. Expression b is invalid because there are two open parentheses but only one close parenthesis. Similarly with expression c, where there are two open parentheses but no close parenthesis. Expression d might be a valid algebraic expression in an algebra book, but it is not a valid expression in Java. There is no operator between the operands 2 and (4).

SR 2.27 After the sequence of statements, the value in `result` is 8.

SR 2.28 After the sequence of statements, the value in `result` is 8. Note that even though `result` was set to `base + 3`, changing the value of `base` to 7 does not retroactively change the value of `result`.

SR 2.29 An assignment operator combines an operation with assignment. For example, the `+=` operator performs an addition, then stores the value back into the variable on the left-hand side.

SR 2.30 After executing the statement, `weight` holds the value 83. The assignment operator `-=` modifies `weight` by first subtracting 17 from the current value (100), then storing the result back into `weight`.

2.5 Data Conversion

SR 2.31 A widening conversion tends to go from a small data value, in terms of the amount of space used to store it, to a larger one. A narrowing conversion does the opposite. Information is more likely to be lost in a narrowing conversion, which is why narrowing conversions are considered to be less safe than widening ones.

SR 2.32 The conversions are: a. widening, b. narrowing, c. widening, d. widening, e. widening.

SR 2.33 During the execution of the statement, the `value` stored in value is read and transformed into a `float` as it is being copied into the memory location represented by `result`. But the `value` variable itself is not changed, so `value` will remain an `int` variable after the assignment statement.

SR 2.34 During the execution of the statement, the value stored in `result` is read and then transformed into an `int` as it is being copied into the memory location represented by `value`. But the `result` variable itself is not changed, so it remains equal to 27.32, whereas `value` becomes 27.

SR 2.35 The results stored are

    a. 3   integer division is used since both operands are integers.

    b. 3.0   integer division is used since both operands are integers, but then assignment conversion converts the result of 3 to 3.0.

    c. 2.4   floating point division is used since one of the operands is a floating point.

    d. 3.4   `num1` is first cast as a `double`; therefore, floating point division is used since one of the operands is a floating point.

    e. 2   `val1` is first cast as an `int`; therefore, integer division is used since both operands are integers.

2.6 Interactive Programs

SR 2.36 The corresponding lines of the `GasMileage` program are

```
a. import java.util.Scanner;
b. Scanner scan = new Scanner (System.in);
c. Scanner scan = new Scanner (System.in);
d. miles = scan.nextInt();
```

SR 2.37 Under the stated assumptions, the following code will ask users to enter their age and store their response in value.

```
System.out.print ("Enter your age in years: ");
value = myScanner.nextInt();
```

2.7 Graphics

SR 2.38 A black and white picture can be drawn using a series of dots, called pixels. Pixels that correspond to a value of 0 are displayed in white, and pixels that correspond to a value of 1 are displayed in black. By using thousands of pixels, a realistic black and white photo can be produced on a computer screen.

SR 2.39 The coordinates of the fourth corner are (3, 7), which is the top right corner.

SR 2.40 We can tell from the given information that the side of the square has length 3. Therefore, the other two corners are (5, 13) and (8, 13).

SR 2.41 Eight bits per number, three numbers per pixel, and 300 by 200 pixels gives

$$8 \times 3 \times 300 \times 200 = 1,440,000 \text{ bits}$$

2.8 Applets

SR 2.42 A Java applet is a Java program that can be executed using a Web browser. Usually, the bytecode form of the Java applet is pulled across the Internet from another computer and executed locally. A Java application is a Java program that can stand on its own. It does not require a Web browser in order to execute.

SR 2.43 An applet's `paint` method is invoked by the system whenever the applet's graphic element needs to be displayed (or "painted") on the screen. Examples include when the applet first runs or when a window that was covering the applet's window is removed.

SR 2.44 The code tag should indicate a bytecode file, such as `DrawHouse.class`, and not a source code file. The file indicated by the tag is supposed to be "ready to run" on a Java interpreter.

2.9 Drawing Shapes

SR 2.45 A bounding rectangle is an imaginary rectangle that surrounds a curved shape, such as an oval, in order to define the shape's width, height, and upper left corner.

SR 2.46 `page.drawRect (16, 12, 50, 50);`

SR 2.47 `page.setColor (Color.blue);`
`page.fillRect (30, 35, 40, 20);`

SR 2.48 The results of the changes are

a. Since the value of `MID` is added to all the horizontal components of the snowman figure, the snowman shifts a little bit to the left.
b. Since the value of `TOP` is added to all the vertical components of the snowman figure, the snowman shifts upwards a little bit.
c. The hat is now blue.

d. By changing the start angle of the smile arc to 10, the starting point is now on the right side of the snowman's face instead of the left. The "direction" of the arc is still counterclockwise. Thus, the arc curves downward instead of upward and the happy snowman is now sad.

e. The upper torso "disappears" since it merges with the background.

Chapter 3 Using Classes and Objects

3.1 Creating Objects

SR 3.1   A null reference is a reference that does not refer to any object. The reserved word `null` can be used to check for null references before following them.

SR 3.2   The `new` operator creates a new instance (an object) of the specified class. The constructor of the class is then invoked to help set up the newly created object.

SR 3.3   The following declaration creates a String variable called `author` and initializes it:

```
String author = new String ("Fred Brooks");
```

For strings, this declaration could have been abbreviated as follows:

```
String author = "Fred Brooks";
```

This object reference variable and its value can be depicted as follows:

SR 3.4   To set an integer variable `size` to the length of a `String` object called `name`, you code:

```
size = name.length();
```

SR 3.5   Two references are aliases of each other if they refer to the same object. Changing the state of the object through one reference changes it for the other because there is actually only one object. An object is marked for garbage collection only when there are no valid references to it.

3.2 The String Class

SR 3.6   Strings are immutable. The only way to change the value of a `String` variable is to reassign it a new object. Therefore, the variables changed by the statements are: a. none, b. s1, c. none, d. s3.

SR 3.7   The output produced is:

```
o
Found
11
5
```

SR 3.8   The following statement prints the value of a `String` object in all upper-case letters:

```
System.out.println (title.toUpperCase());
```

SR 3.9   The following declaration creates a `String` object and sets it equal to the first 10 characters of the `String` description;

```
String front = description.substring(0, 10);
```

3.3 Packages

SR 3.10   A Java package is a collection of related classes. The Java standard class library is a group of packages that support common programming tasks.

SR 3.11   Each package contains a set of classes that support particular programming activities. The classes in the `java.net` package support network communication and the classes in the `javax.swing` class support the development of graphical user interfaces.

SR 3.12   The `Scanner` class and the `Random` class are part of the `java.util` package. The `String` and `Math` classes are part of the `java.lang` package.

SR 3.13   The `Point` class, according to the online Java API documentation, represents a location with coordinates (x, y) in two-dimensional space.

SR 3.14   An `import` statement establishes the fact that a program uses a particular class, specifying what package that class is a part of. This allows the programmer to use the class name (such as `Random`) without having to fully qualify the reference (such as `java.util.Random`) every time.

SR 3.15   The `String` class is part of the `java.lang` package, which is automatically imported into any Java program. Therefore, no separate import declaration is needed.

3.4 The Random Class

SR 3.16   A call to the `nextInt` method of a `Random` object returns a random integer in the range of all possible `int` values, both positive and negative.

SR 3.17 Passing a positive integer parameter x to the `nextInt` method of a Random object returns a random number in the range of 0 to $x-1$. So a call to `nextInt(20)` will return a random number in the range 0 to 19, inclusive.

SR 3.18 The ranges of the expressions are:

a. From 0 to 49   b. From 10 to 14   c. From 5 to 14
d. From -25 to 24

SR 3.19 The expressions to generate the given ranges are:

```
a. generator.nextInt (31);        // range is 0 to 30
b. generator.nextInt (10) + 10;   // range is 10 to 19
c. generator.nextInt (11) - 5;    // range is -5 to 5
```

3.5 The Math Class

SR 3.20 A class or static method can be invoked through the name of the class that contains it, such as `Math.abs`. If a method is not static, it can be executed only through an instance (an object) of the class.

SR 3.21 The values of the expressions are:

a. 20   b. 16.0   c. 16.0   d. 243.0   e. 125.0   f. 4.0

SR 3.22 The following statement prints the sine of an angle measuring 1.23 radians:

```
System.out.println (Math.sin(1.23));
```

SR 3.23 The following declaration creates a `double` variable and initializes it to 5 raised to the power 2.5:

```
double result = Math.pow(5, 2.5);
```

SR 3.24 Examples of methods that are not listed in Figure 3.5 include:

```
static int min(int a, int b)
static float max(long a, long b)
static long round(double a)
```

3.6 Formatting Output

SR 3.25 To obtain a `NumberFormat` object for use within a program, you request an object using one of the static methods provided by the `NumberFormat` class. The method you invoke depends upon your intended use of the object. For example, if you intend to use it for formatting percentages, you might code:

```
NumberFormat fmt = NumberFormat.getPercentInstance();
```

SR 3.26   a. The statement is:

```
NumberFormat moneyFormat = NumberFormat.getCurrencyInstance();
```

Do not forget, you also must import java.text.NumberFormat into your program.

b. The statement is:

```
System.out.println(moneyFormat.format(cost));
```

c. If the locale is the United States, the output will be $54.89. If the locale is the United Kingdom, the output will be £54.89.

SR 3.27   To output a floating point value as a percentage, you first obtain a NumberFormat object using a call to the static method getPercentage-Instance of the NumberFormat class. Then, you pass the value to be formatted to the format method of the formatter object, which returns a properly formatted string. For example:

```
NumberFormat fmt = NumberFormat.getPercentageInstance();
System.out.println (fmt.format(value));
```

SR 3.28   The following code will prompt for and read in a double value from the user and then print the result of taking the square root of the absolute value of the input value to two decimal places:

```
Scanner scan = new Scanner (System.in);
DecimalFormat fmt = new DecimalFormat("0.00");
double value, result;
System.out.print ("Enter a double value: ");
value = scan.nextDouble();
result = Math.sqrt(Math.abs(value));
System.out.println (fmt.format(result));
```

3.7 Enumerated Types

SR 3.29   The following is a declaration of an enumerated type for movie ratings:

```
enum Ratings {G, PG, PG13, R, NC17}
```

SR 3.30   Under the listed assumptions, the output is:

```
clubs
hearts
0
2
```

SR 3.31 By using an enumerated type, you guarantee that variables of that type will only take on the enumerated values.

3.8 Wrapper Classes

SR 3.32 A wrapper class is defined in the Java standard class library for each primitive type. In situations where objects are called for, an object created from a wrapper class may suffice.

SR 3.33 The corresponding wrapper classes are `Byte`, `Integer`, `Double`, `Character`, and `Boolean`.

SR 3.34 One approach is to use the constructor of `Integer`, as follows:

```
holdNumber = new Integer(number);
```

Another approach is to take advantage of autoboxing, as follows:

```
holdNumber = number;
```

SR 3.35 The following statement uses the `MAX_VALUE` constant of the `Integer` class to print the largest possible `int` value:

```
System.out.println (Integer.MAX_VALUE);
```

3.9 Components and Containers

SR 3.36 Both a frame and a panel are containers that can hold GUI elements. However, a frame is displayed as a separate window with a title bar, whereas a panel cannot be displayed on its own. A panel is often displayed inside a frame.

SR 3.37 The term that best matches is

a. container   b. frame   c. panel   d. heavyweight
e. lightweight   f. content pane   g. label   h. layout manager

SR 3.38 If you resize the frame by dragging the bottom right corner toward the right, the saying changes from being spread across two lines to being on one line. This happens because no special instructions were included to describe the layout of the container, in which case components of a panel arrange themselves next to each other if the size of the panel allows.

SR 3.39 The best description is "Labels are added to a panel, which is added to a content pane of a frame."

SR 3.40 The results of the changes are

a. Due to the new dimensions the panel is larger and square.

  b. The saying is not visible. You just see a black panel because the saying, which is written in black, blends in with the background.

  c. There is no change.

  d. Since the labels are added in the opposite order, the saying is "backwards"—that is, it reads "but raise your hand first." followed by "Question authority."

3.10 Nested Panels

SR 3.41 The containment hierarchy of a graphical user interface identifies the nesting of elements within the GUI. For example, in a particular GUI, suppose some labels and buttons are contained within a panel that is contained within another panel that is contained within a frame. The containment hierarchy can be represented as a tree that indicates how all the elements of a GUI are nested within each other.

SR 3.42 In the `NestedPanels` program, there are three panels created: sub-Panel1, subPanel2, and primary.

SR 3.43 In the `NestedPanels` program, subPanel1 and subPanel2 are added to the primary panel. The primary panel is explicitly added to the content pane of the frame.

3.11 Images

SR 3.44 One frame, one panel, one image icon, and three labels are declared in the `LabelDemo` program.

SR 3.45 In the label instantiation statement from the `LabelDemo` program:

```
label2 = new JLabel ("Devil Right", icon, SwingConstants.CENTER);
```

  the first parameter defines the text, the second parameter provides the image, and the third parameter indicates the horizontal alignment of the label.

SR 3.46 The results of the changes are:

  a. Changing the horizontal alignment of the labels has no visual effect. The horizontal alignment describes only how text and icons are aligned *within* a label. Since a label's area is typically exactly the size needed to display the label, label alignment within that area is irrelevant.

  b. The change in the text position results in the text "Devil Right" appearing to the right of the second image, instead of to its left.

c. The change in the text position results in a run-time error—
"Bottom" is not a valid argument for the `setHorizontalTextPosition` method.

d. Since you changed the vertical position of the text within the label, the text "Devil Above" appears directly on the third image.

Chapter 4 Writing Classes

4.1 Classes and Objects Revisited

SR 4.1   An attribute is a data value stored in an object and defines a particular characteristic of that object. For example, one attribute of a `Student` object might be that student's current grade point average. Collectively, the values of an object's attributes determine that object's current state.

SR 4.2   An operation is a function that can be done to or done by an object. For example, one operation of a `Student` object might be to compute that student's current grade point average. Collectively, an object's operations are referred to as the object's behaviors.

SR 4.3   Some attributes and operations that might be defined for a class called `Book` that represents a book in a library are:

Attributes	Operations
idNumber	checkOut
onShelfStatus	checkIn
readingLevel	isAvailable
dueDate	placeOnHold
	setStatus

SR 4.4   The answers are:

a. False – Identifying classes to help us solve a problem is a key step in object-oriented programming. In addition to identifying classes that already exist, we also identify, design, and implement new classes, as needed.

b. True – We call such operations mutators.

c. True – The result of many operations depends on the current state of the object on which they are operating.

d. False – In Java, the state of an object is represented by its instance data.

4.2 Anatomy of a Class

SR 4.5   A class is the blueprint of an object. It defines the variables and methods that will be a part of every object that is instantiated from it. But a class reserves no memory space for variables. Each object has its own data space and, therefore, its own state.

SR 4.6   The instance data of the Die class are MAX, an integer constant equal to 6 that represents the number of faces on the die and therefore the maximum value of the die, and faceValue, an integer variable that represents the current "up" or face value of the die.

SR 4.7   The methods defined for the Die class that can change the state of a Die object are roll and setFaceValue.

SR 4.8   When you pass an object to a print or println method, the toString method of the object is called automatically to obtain a string description of the object. If no toString method is defined for the object, then a default string is used. Therefore, it is usually a good idea to define a toString method when defining classes.

SR 4.9   The scope of a variable is the area within a program in which the variable can be referenced. An instance variable, declared at the class level, can be referenced in any method of the class. Local variables, including the formal parameters, declared within a particular method, can be referenced only in that method.

SR 4.10   A UML diagram helps us visualize the entities (classes and objects) in a program as well as the relationships among them. UML diagrams are tools that help us capture the design of a program prior to writing it.

4.3 Encapsulation

SR 4.11   A self-governing object is one that controls the values of its own data. Encapsulated objects, which don't allow an external client to reach in and change its data, are self-governing.

SR 4.12   An object's interface is the set of public operations (methods) defined on it. That is, the interface establishes the set of services the object will perform for the rest of the system.

SR 4.13   A modifier is a Java reserved word that can be used in the definition of a variable or method and that specifically defines certain characteristics of its use. For example, by declaring a variable with private visibility, the variable cannot be directly accessed outside of the object in which it is defined.

SR 4.14   A constant might be declared with public visibility, because that would not violate encapsulation. Because the value of a constant cannot be changed, it is not generally a problem for another object to access it directly.

SR 4.15   The modifiers affect the methods and variables in the following ways:

a. A public method is called a service method for an object because it defines a service that the object provides.

b. A private method is called a support method because it cannot be invoked from outside the object and is used to support the activities of other methods in the class.

c. A public variable is a variable that can be directly accessed and modified by a client. This explicitly violates the principle of encapsulation and therefore should be avoided.

d. A private variable is a variable that can be accessed and modified only from within the class. Variables almost always are declared with private visibility.

4.4 Anatomy of a Method

SR 4.16   Although a method is defined in a class, it is invoked through a particular object to indicate which object of that class is being affected. For example, the Student class may define the operation that computes the grade point average (GPA) of a student, but the operation is invoked through a particular Student object to compute the GPA for that student. The exception to this rule is the invocation of a static method (see Chapter 3), which is executed through the class name and does not affect any particular object.

SR 4.17   An invoked method may return a value, which means it computes a value and provides that value to the calling method. The calling method usually uses the invocation and thus its return value, as part of a larger expression.

SR 4.18   An explicit return statement is used to specify the value that is returned from a method. The type of the return value must match the return type specified in the method definition.

SR 4.19   A return statement is required in methods that have a return type other than void. A method that does not return a value could use a return statement without an expression, but it is not necessary. Only one return statement should be used in a method.

SR 4.20   An actual parameter is a value sent to a method when it is invoked. A formal parameter is the corresponding variable in the header of the method declaration; it takes on the value of the actual parameter so that it can be used inside the method.

SR 4.21 The following code implements the requested getFaceDown method.:

```
//---------------------------------------------------
//  Face down value accessor.
//---------------------------------------------------
public int getFaceDown()
{
    return (MAX + 1) - faceValue;
}
```

SR 4.22 In the Transactions program

a. Three Account objects are created.

b. Two arguments (actual parameters) are passed to the withdraw method when it is invoked on the acct2 object.

c. No arguments (actual parameters) are passed to the addInterest method when it is invoked on the acct3 object.

SR 4.23 The method getBalance is a classic accessor method. One can also classify the toString method as an accessor, since it returns information about the object. The deposit, withdraw, and addInterest methods all provide both mutator and accessor capabilities, because they can be used to change the account balance and also return the value of the balance after the change is made. All of the methods mentioned above are service methods—they all have public visibility and provide a service to the client.

4.5 Constructors Revisited

SR 4.24 Constructors are special methods in an object that are used to initialize the object when it is instantiated.

SR 4.25 A constructor has the same name as its class, and it does not return a value.

4.6 Graphical Objects

SR 4.26 The "content" of the panel created in the SmilingFace program is defined in the SmilingFacePanel class.

SR 4.27 In the SmilingFace program, the paintComponent method of the panel object is invoked automatically when the panel object SmilingFacePanel is instantiated.

SR 4.28 There are many ways to add a pair of eyeglasses to the smiling face. The following code, inserted after the code that draws the nose and mouth, is one approach.

```
page.drawOval (BASEX+17, BASEY+23, 21, 21);   // glasses
page.drawOval (BASEX+42, BASEY+23, 21, 21);
page.drawLine (BASEX+3,  BASEY+27, BASEX+17, BASEY+27);
page.drawLine (BASEX+62, BASEY+27, BASEX+76, BASEY+27);
page.drawLine (BASEX+39, BASEY+29, BASEX+42, BASEY+29);
```

SR 4.29 The following code implements the requested constructor:

```
//-----------------------------------------------------
//  Constructor: Sets up this circle with the
//  specified values.
//-----------------------------------------------------
public Circle (Color shade, int upperX, int upperY)
{
    diameter = (int) (Math.random() * 180) + 20;
    color = shade;
    x = upperX;
    y = upperY;
}
```

It might be better to define and use constants of 180 and 20 in the Circle class, or perhaps pass those values to the constructor from the client as arguments.

4.7 Graphical User Interfaces

SR 4.30 Events usually represent user actions. A listener object is set up to listen for a certain event to be generated from a particular component.

SR 4.31 No, we cannot add any listener to any component. Each component generates a certain set of events, and only listeners of those types can be added to the component.

4.8 Buttons

SR 4.32 A JButton object generates an action event when the button is pushed. When that occurs, the actionPerformed method of the action listener associated with that button is invoked.

SR 4.33 To change the PushCounterPanel class so that instead of displaying a count of how many times the button was pushed it displays a count "trail," you can define a new instance variable of the PushCounterPanel class as follows:

```
private String display = "0";
```

Then change the code in the actionPerformed method to be:

```
count++;
display = display + count;
label.setText("Pushes: " + display);
```

4.9 Text Fields

SR 4.34 In the Fahrenheit program, when a user types a number into the text box of the interface and presses the Enter (or Return) key, the text field component generates an action event. The TempListener class that is listening for that event reacts by getting the text from the text box, transforming the text into an integer that represents the given Fahrenheit temperature, calculating the corresponding Celsius temperature and saving it to the resultLabel. The contents of the resultLabel then appear on the screen.

SR 4.35 To make the change to the FahrenheitPanel class, first remove the outputLabel from the class since it is no longer needed. Then, change the code that sets the result label to:

```
String hold = text + " degrees Fahrenheit = ";
hold += celsiusTemp + " degrees Celsius";
resultLabel.setText (hold);
```

Chapter 5 Conditionals and Loops

5.1 Boolean Expressions

SR 5.1 The flow of control through a program determines the program statements that will be executed on a given run of the program.

SR 5.2 Each conditional and loop is based on a boolean condition that evaluates to either true or false.

SR 5.3 The equality operators are equal (==) and not equal (!=). The relational operators are less than (<), less than or equal to (<=), greater than (>), and greater than or equal to (>=). The logical operators are not (!), and (&&) and or (||).

SR 5.4   Assuming the given declarations, the values are: a. true, b. true, c. false, d. true, e. true, f. true, g. true, h. false, i. true, j. true

SR 5.5   A truth table is a table that shows all possible results of a boolean expression, given all possible combinations of variables and conditions.

SR 5.6   The truth table is:

value > 0	done	!done	(value > 0) || !done
true	true	false	true
true	false	true	true
false	true	false	false
false	false	true	true

SR 5.7   The truth table is:

c1	c2	!c1	!c2	c1 && !c2	!c1 && c2	c1 && !c2 || !c1 && c2
true	true	false	false	false	false	false
true	false	false	true	true	false	true
false	true	true	false	false	true	true
false	false	true	true	false	false	false

5.2 The if Statement

SR 5.8   Based on the given assumptions, the output would be:

a. red   white   yellow
b. blue   yellow
c. blue   yellow

SR 5.9   A block statement groups several statements together. We use them to define the body of an if statement or loop when we want to do multiple things based on the boolean condition.

SR 5.10   A nested if occurs when the statement inside an if or else clause is an if statement. A nested if lets the programmer make a series of decisions. Similarly, a nested loop is a loop within a loop.

SR 5.11 Based on the given assumptions, the output would be:

      a. red   orange   white   yellow
      b. black   blue   green
      c. yellow   green

SR 5.12
```
if (temperature <= 50)
{
    System.out.println ("It is cool.");
    System.out.println ("Dress warmly.");
}
else
    if (temperature > 80)
    {
        System.out.println ("It is warm.");
        System.out.println ("Dress cooly.");
    }
    else
    {
        System.out.println ("It is pleasant.");
        System.out.println ("Dress pleasantly.");
    }
```

5.3 Comparing Data

SR 5.13 Because they are stored internally as binary numbers, comparing floating point values for exact equality will be true only if they are the same
bit-by-bit. It's better to use a reasonable tolerance value and consider
the difference between the two values.

SR 5.14 We compare strings for equality using the equals method of the String
class, which returns a boolean result. The compareTo method of the String
class can also be used to compare strings. It returns a positive, 0, or negative integer result depending on the relationship between the two strings.

SR 5.15
```
//---------------------------------------------------------
//  Returns true if this Die equals die, otherwise
//  returns false.
//---------------------------------------------------------
public boolean equals(Die die)
{
    return (this.faceValue == die.faceValue);
}
```

SR 5.16
```
if (s1.compareTo(s2) < 0)
    System.out.println (s1 + "\n" + s2);
else
    System.out.println (s2 + "\n" + s1);
```

5.4 The `while` Statement

SR 5.17   An infinite loop is a repetition statement that never terminates. Specifically, the body of the loop never causes the condition to become false.

SR 5.18   The output is the integers 0 through 9, printed one integer per line.

SR 5.19   The loop is not entered, so there is no output.

SR 5.20   Since the value of `high` always remains larger than the value of `low`, the code loops continuously, producing many lines of zeros, until the program is terminated.

SR 5.21   The output is:

```
0 1 2 3 4 5 6 7 8 9 10
1 2 3 4 5 6 7 8 9 10
2 3 4 5 6 7 8 9 10
3 4 5 6 7 8 9 10
4 5 6 7 8 9 10
5 6 7 8 9 10
6 7 8 9 10
7 8 9 10
8 9 10
9 10
10
```

SR 5.22
```java
int count = 1;
System.out.print ("divisors of " + value + ":");
while (count <= value)
{
    if ((value % count) == 0)
        System.out.print(" " + count);
    count++;
}
```

SR 5.23
```java
int count1 = 1, count2;
while (count1 <= value)
{
    System.out.print ("divisors of " + count1 + ":");
    count2 = 1;
    while (count2 <= count1)
    {
        if ((count1 % count2) == 0)
            System.out.print(" " + count2);
        count2++;
    }
    System.out.println ();
    count1++;
}
```

5.5 Iterators

SR 5.24 a. Scanner user = new Scanner (System.in);
         b. Scanner infoFileScan = new Scanner (new
            File("info.dat"));
         c. Scanner infoStringScan = new Scanner (infoString);

SR 5.25 The following code prints out the average number of characters per
         line:

```
int numChars = 0;
int numLines = 0;
String holdLine;

// Read and process each line of the file
while (fileScan.hasNext())
{
   numLines++;
   holdLine = fileScan.nextLine();
   numChars += holdLine.length();
}
System.out.println ((double)numChars/numLines);
```

5.6 The ArrayList Class

SR 5.26 An ArrayList stores and manages multiple objects at one time. It allows
         you to access the objects by a numeric index and keeps the indexes of
         its objects continuous as they are added and removed. An ArrayList
         dynamically increases its capacity as needed.

SR 5.27 An ArrayList generally holds references to the Object class, which
         means that it can hold any type of object at all (this is discussed
         further in Chapter 8). A specific type of element can and should be
         specified in the ArrayList declaration to restrict the type of objects
         that can be added and eliminate the need to cast the type when
         extracted.

SR 5.28 ArrayList<Die> dice = new ArrayList<Die>();

SR 5.29 [Andy, Don, Betty]

Chapter 6 More Conditionals and Loops

6.1 The `switch` Statement

SR 6.1   When a Java program is running, if the expression evaluated for a `switch` statement does not match any of the case values associated with the statement, execution continues with the `default` case. If no `default` case exists, processing continues with the statement following the `switch` statement.

SR 6.2   If a case does not end with a `break` statement, processing continues into the statements of the next case. We usually want to use `break` statements in order to jump to the end of the `switch`.

SR 6.3   If the user enters 72, the output is: That grade is average. If the user enters 46, the output is: That grade is not passing. If the user enters 123, the output is: That grade is not passing.

SR 6.4   An equivalent `switch` statement is:

```
switch (num1)
{
    case 5:
        myChar = 'W';
        break;
    case 6:
        myChar = 'X';
        break;
    case 7:
        myChar = 'Y';
        break;
    default:
        myChar = 'Z';
}
```

6.2 The Conditional Operator

SR 6.5   The conditional operator is a trinary operator that evaluates a condition and produces one of two possible results. A conditional statement, such as the `if` and `switch` statements, is a category of statements that allow conditions to be evaluated and the appropriate statements executed as a result.

SR 6.6   `char id = (first) ? 'A' : 'B';`

SR 6.7   `System.out.println ("The value is " + ((val <= 10) ? "not" : "") + "greater than 10.");`

6.3 The do Statement

SR 6.8   A `while` loop evaluates the condition first. If it is true, it executes the loop body. The `do` loop executes the body first and then evaluates the condition. Therefore, the body of a `while` loop is executed zero or more times, and the body of a `do` loop is executed one or more times.

SR 6.9   The output is the integers 0 through 9, printed one integer per line.

SR 6.10   The code contains an infinite loop. The numbers 10, 11, 12, and so on will be printed until the program is terminated or until the number gets too large to be held by the `int` variable `low`.

SR 6.11
```
Scanner scan = new Scanner (System.in);
int num, sum = 0;
do
{
    System.out.print ("enter next number (0 to quit) > ");
    num = scan.nextInt ();
    sum += num;
} while (num != 0);
System.out.println (sum);
```

6.4 The for Statement

SR 6.12   A `for` loop is usually used when we know, or can calculate, how many times we want to iterate through the loop body. A `while` loop handles a more generic situation.

SR 6.13   The output is: 100

SR 6.14   The output is: 60

SR 6.15   The output is:

```
        *
      ***
     *****
    *******
   *********
  ***********
```

SR 6.16
```
final int NUMROLLS = 100;
int sum = 0;
for (int i = 1; i <= NUMROLLS; i++)
{
    sum += die.roll();
}
System.out.println((double)sum/NUMROLLS);
```

Chapter 7 Object-Oriented Design

7.1 Software Development Activities

SR 7.1   The four basic activities in software development are requirements analysis (deciding what the program should do), design (deciding how to do it), implementation (writing the solution in source code), and testing (validating the implementation).

SR 7.2   Typically the client provides an initial set of requirements or a description of a problem they would like to have solved. It is the responsibility of the software developer to work with the client to make sure the requirements or problem statement is correct and unambiguous.

SR 7.3   Software development is a problem-solving activity. Therefore, it is not surprising that the four basic development activities presented in this section are essentially the same as the five general problem-solving steps presented in Section 1.6. "Establishing the requirements" directly corresponds to "understanding the problem." "Designing a solution" and "considering alternative designs" taken together correspond to "creating a design"—in the case of software, the design is the solution. Finally, in both approaches we include "implementation" and "testing" stages.

7.2 Identifying Classes and Objects

SR 7.4   Identifying the nouns in a problem specification can help you identify potential classes to use when developing an object-oriented solution to a problem. The nouns in the specification often correspond to objects that should be represented in the solution.

SR 7.5   It is not crucial to identify and define all the methods that a class will contain during the early stages of problem solution design. It is often sufficient to just identify those methods that provide the primary responsibilities of the class. Additional methods can be added to a class as needed, when you evolve and add detail to your design.

7.3 Static Class Members

SR 7.6   Memory space for an instance variable is created for each object that is instantiated from a class. A static variable is shared among all objects of a class.

SR 7.7   Assuming you decide to use the identifier totalBalance, the declaration is:

```
private static int totalBalance = 0;
```

SR 7.8   Assuming that the minimum required is 100 and you decide to use the identifier MIN_BALANCE, the declaration is:

```
public static final int MIN_BALANCE = 100;
```

SR 7.9   The main method of any program is static, and can refer only to static or local variables. Therefore, a main method could not refer to instance variables declared at the class level.

7.4 Class Relationships

SR 7.10   A dependency relationship between two classes occurs when one class relies on the functionality of the other. It is often referred to as a "uses" relationship.

SR 7.11   A method executed through an object might take as a parameter another object created from the same class. For example, the concat method of the String class is executed through one String object and takes another String object as a parameter.

SR 7.12   An aggregate object is an object that has other objects as instance data. That is, an aggregate object is one that is made up of other objects.

SR 7.13   The this reference always refers to the currently executing object. A non-static method of a class is written generically for all objects of the class, but it is invoked through a particular object. The this reference, therefore, refers to the object through which that method is currently being executed.

7.5 Interfaces

SR 7.14   A class can be instantiated; an interface cannot. An interface contains a set of abstract methods for which a class provides the implementation.

SR 7.15

```
public interface Nameable
{
    public void setName (String name);
    public String getName();
}
```

SR 7.16 a. False – An interface can also include constants.

b. True – There is no body of code defined for an abstract method.

c. True – An interface is a collection of constants and abstract methods.

d. False – Although the class must define the methods that are included in the interface, the class can also define additional methods.

e. True – As long as each of the implementing classes provides the required methods.

f. True – As long as the class provides the required methods for each interface it implements.

g. False – Although the signatures of the methods must be the same, the implementations of the methods can be different.

7.6 Enumerated Types Revisited

SR 7.17 Using the enumerated type `Season` as defined in this section, the output is

```
winter
summer
0
June through August
```

7.7 Method Design

SR 7.18 Method decomposition is the process of dividing a complex method into several support methods to get the job done. This simplifies and facilitates the design of the program.

SR 7.19 Based on the `PigLatinTranslator` class:

a. The service provided by the class, namely to translate a string into Pig Latin, is accessed through a static method. Therefore, there is no need to create an object of the class. It follows that there is no need for a constructor.

b. The methods defined as private methods do not provide services directly to clients of the class. Instead, they are used to support the public method `translate`.

c. The Scanner object declared in the `translate` method is used to scan the string `sentence`, which is passed to the method by the client.

SR 7.20 The sequence of calls is:

a. `translate` – `translateWord` – `beginsWithVowel`

b. `translate` – `translateWord` – `beginsWithVowel` – `beginsWithBlend`

    c. `translate – translateWord – beginsWithVowel–beginsWithBl`
       `end – translateWord – beginsWithVowel – translateWord`
       `– beginsWithVowel – beginsWithBlend – translateWord –`
       `beginsWithVowel – beginsWithBlend`

SR 7.21 Objects are passed to methods by copying the reference to the object (its address). Therefore, the actual and formal parameters of a method become aliases of each other.

7.8 Method Overloading

SR 7.22 Overloaded methods are distinguished by having a unique signature, which includes the number, order, and type of the parameters. The return type is not part of the signature.

SR 7.23 a. They are distinct.
        b. They are not distinct. The return type of a method is not part of its signature.
        c. They are not distinct. The names of a method's parameters are not part of its signature.
        d. They are distinct.

SR 7.24
```
//-------------------------------------------------------
//  Sets up the new Num object, storing a default value
//  of 0.
//-------------------------------------------------------
public Num ()
{
    value = 0;
}
```

7.9 Testing

SR 7.25 The word that best matches is

      a. regression   b. review   c. walkthrough   d. defects
      e. test case   f. test suite   g. black-box   h. white-box

7.10 GUI Design

SR 7.26 The general guidelines for GUI design include: know the needs and characteristics of the user, prevent user errors when possible, optimize user abilities by providing shortcuts and other redundant means to accomplish a task, and be consistent in GUI layout and coloring schemes.

SR 7.27   A good user interface design is very important because to the user, the interface *is* the program. Since it is the only way the user interacts with the program, in the user's mind the interface represents the entire program.

7.11 Layout Managers

SR 7.28   A layout manager is consulted whenever the visual appearance of its components might be affected, such as when the container is resized or when a new component is added to the container.

SR 7.29   Flow layout attempts to put as many components on a row as possible. Multiple rows are created as needed.

SR 7.30   Border layout is divided into five areas: North, South, East, West, and Center. The North and South areas are at the top and bottom of the container, respectively, and span the entire width of the container. Sandwiched between them, from left to right, are the West, Center, and East areas. Any unused area takes up no space, and the others fill in as needed.

SR 7.31   A glue component in a box layout dictates where any extra space in the layout should go. It expands as necessary, but takes up no space if there is no extra space to distribute.

7.12 Borders

SR 7.32   The `BorderFactory` class contains several methods used to create borders that can be applied to components.

SR 7.33   The border types presented in this section are: empty—buffering space only, line—a simple line, etched—etched groove, bevel—component appears raised or sunken, titled—text title, matte—edges may have separate sizes, and compound—a combination of two borders.

7.13 Containment Hierarchies

SR 7.34   The containment hierarchy for a GUI is the set of nested containers and the other components they contain. The containment hierarchy can be described as a tree.

SR 7.35 The containment hierarchy tree for the LeftRight application GUI presented in Chapter 5 is:

Chapter 8 Arrays

8.1 Array Elements

SR 8.1   An array is an object that stores a list of values. The entire list can be referenced by its name, and each element in the list can be referenced individually based on its position in the array.

SR 8.2   Each element in an array can be referenced by its numeric position, called an index, in the array. In Java, all array indexes begin at zero. Square brackets are used to specify the index. For example, nums[5] refers to the sixth element in the array called nums.

SR 8.3   a. 61, b. 139, c. 73, d. 79, e. 74, f. 11

8.2 Declaring and Using Arrays

SR 8.4   An array's element type is the type of values that the array can hold. All values in a particular array have the same type, or are at least of compatible types. So we might have an array of integers, or an array of boolean values, or an array of Dog objects, etc.

SR 8.5   Arrays are objects. Therefore, as with all objects, to create an array we first create a reference to the array (its name). We then instantiate the array itself, which reserves memory space to store the array elements. The only difference between a regular object instantiation and an array instantiation is the bracket syntax.

SR 8.6   int[] ages = new int[100];

SR 8.7   int[] faceCounts = new int[6];

SR 8.8   Whenever a reference is made to a particular array element, the index operator (the brackets that enclose the subscript) ensures that the value of the index is greater than or equal to zero and less than the size of the array. If it is not within the valid range, an `ArrayIndexOutOfBoundsException` is thrown.

SR 8.9   An off-by-one error occurs when a program's logic exceeds the boundary of an array (or similar structure) by one. These errors include forgetting to process a boundary element as well as attempting to process a nonexistent element. Array processing is susceptible to off-by-one errors because their indexes begin at zero and run to one less than the size of the array.

SR 8.10
```
for (int index = 0; index < values.length; index++)
{
    values[index]++;
}
```

SR 8.11
```
int sum = 0;
for (int index = 0; index < values.length; index++)
{
    sum += values[index];
}
System.out.println(sum);
```

SR 8.12   An array initializer list is used in the declaration of an array to set up the initial values of its elements. An initializer list instantiates the array object, so the `new` operator is not needed.

SR 8.13   An entire array can be passed as a parameter. Specifically, because an array is an object, a reference to the array is passed to the method. Any changes made to the array elements will be reflected outside of the method.

8.3 Arrays of Objects

SR 8.14   An array of objects is really an array of object references. The array itself must be instantiated, and the objects that are stored in the array must be created separately.

SR 8.15   a. `String[] team = new String[6];`

b. `String[] team = {"Amanda", "Clare", "Emily", "Julie", "Katie", "Maria"};`

SR 8.16   a. `Book[] library = new Book[10];`

b. `library[0] = new Book("Starship Troopers", 208);`

8.4 Command-Line Arguments

SR 8.17 A command-line argument is data that is included on the command line when the interpreter is invoked to execute the program. Command-line arguments are another way to provide input to a program. They are accessed using the array of strings that is passed into the `main` method as a parameter.

SR 8.18
```java
//-----------------------------------------------------
//   Prints the sum of the string lengths of the first
//   two command line arguments.
//-----------------------------------------------------
public static void main (String[] args)
{
    System.out.println (args[0].length() +
    args[1].length());
}
```

SR 8.19
```java
//-----------------------------------------------------
//   Prints the sum of the first two command line
//   arguments, assuming they are integers.
//-----------------------------------------------------
public static void main (String[] args)
{
    System.out.println (Integer.parseInt(args[0])
                        + Integer.parseInt(args[1]));
}
```

8.5 Variable Length Parameter Lists

SR 8.20 A Java method can be defined to accept a variable number of parameters by using ellipses (...) in the formal parameter list. When a set of values is passed to the method, they are automatically converted to an array. This allows the method to be written in terms of array processing without forcing the calling method to create the array.

SR 8.21
```java
public int distance (int ... legs)
{
    int sum = 0;
    for (int leg : legs)
    {
        sum += leg;
    }
    return sum;
}
```

SR 8.22
```java
double travelTime (int speed, int ... legs)
{
    int sum = 0;
```

```
        for (int leg : legs)
        {
            sum += leg;
        }
        return (double)sum/speed;
    }
```

8.6 Two-Dimensional Arrays

SR 8.23 A multidimensional array is implemented in Java as an array of array objects. The arrays that are elements of the outer array could also contain arrays as elements. This nesting process could continue for as many levels as needed.

SR 8.24
```
int high = scores[0][0];
int low = high;
for (int row = 0; row < scores.length; row++)
    for (int col = 0; col < scores[row].length; col++)
    {
        if (scores[row][col] < low)
            low = scores[row][col];
        if (scores[row][col] > high)
            high = scores[row][col];
    }
System.out.println (high - low);
```

8.7 Polygons and Polylines

SR 8.25 A polyline is defined by a series of points that represent its vertices. The drawPolyline method takes three parameters to specify its shape. The first is an array of integers that represent the x coordinates of the points. The second is an array of integers that represent the y coordinates of the points. The third parameter is a single integer that indicates the number of points to be used from the arrays.

SR 8.26 A polygon is always closed, whereas a polyline may be open. The first and last coordinates of a polygon are automatically connected; that is not the case for polylines.

SR 8.27 The results of the changes are:

a. The flame below the rocket is now solid red, because a polygon is always closed and we specified it to be filled in.
b. The rocket ship's window disappears, because only the first two points are used to draw the polygon, which results in an "invisible" line being drawn instead of the window.

   c. The rocket ship and flames now appear sideways (i.e., horizontal),
      because exchanging the x and y coordinates of all of the points
      reflects the drawing across the line $x = y$.
   d. The rocket ship and flames are framed by a yellow diamond;
      because the yellow polygon is drawn first, everything else is visible
      on top of it.
   e. Almost all of the picture is hidden by the yellow polygon; because
      the yellow polygon is drawn last, it hides the other components of
      the drawing that fall within its coordinates.

8.8 Mouse Events

SR 8.28 A mouse event is an event generated when the user manipulates the
         mouse in various ways. There are several types of mouse events that
         may be of interest in a particular situation, including the mouse being
         moved, a mouse button being pressed, the mouse entering a particular
         component, and the mouse being dragged.

SR 8.29 The sequence of events is mouse pressed, mouse released, and mouse
         clicked.

SR 8.30 The sequence of events is mouse pressed, mouse exited, and mouse
         clicked. There are also a series of mouse motion events generated.

SR 8.31 The mouse event responded to in the Dots program is mouse pressed.
         The mouse events responded to in the RubberLines program are mouse
         pressed and mouse dragged.

SR 8.32 Some possible responses are: highlight a game square when a mouse
         enters its space, if it represents a legal move; place an X (or an O) in a
         game square if the user clicks on it at the appropriate time; allow the
         user to drag an X (or an O) to a square.

8.9 Key Events

SR 8.33 A key event is generated when a keyboard key is pressed, which allows
         a listening program to respond immediately to the user input. The object
         representing the event holds a code that specifies which key was pressed.

SR 8.34 a. keyPressed
         b. keyTyped, keyReleased
         c. VK_UP
         d. arrowLeft.gif
         e. arrowRight.gif

Chapter 9 Inheritance

9.1 Creating Subclasses

SR 9.1   A child class is derived from a parent class using inheritance. The methods and variables of the parent class automatically become a part of the child class, subject to the rules of the visibility modifiers used to declare them.

SR 9.2   Because a new class can be derived from an existing class, the characteristics of the parent class can be reused without the error-prone process of copying and modifying code.

SR 9.3   Each inheritance derivation should represent an *is-a* relationship: the child *is-a* more specific version of the parent. If this relationship does not hold, then inheritance is being used improperly.

SR 9.4   The protected modifier establishes a visibility level (like public and private) that takes inheritance into account. A variable or method declared with protected visibility can be referenced by name in the derived class, while retaining some level of encapsulation. Protected visibility allows access from any class in the same package.

SR 9.5   The super reference can be used to call the parent's constructor, which cannot be invoked directly by name. It can also be used to invoke the parent's version of an overridden method.

SR 9.6
```java
public class SchoolBook2 extends Book2
{
    private int ageLevel;

    //-------------------------------------------------
    // Constructor: Sets up the schoolbook with the
    // specified number of pages and age level (assumed
    // to be between 4 and 16 inclusive).
    //-------------------------------------------------
    public SchoolBook2 (int numPages, int age)
    {
        super(numPages);
        ageLevel = age;
    }

    //-------------------------------------------------
    // Returns a string that describes the age level.
    //-------------------------------------------------
    public String level ()
    {
        if (ageLevel <= 6)
            return "Pre-school";
```

```
                else
                    if (ageLevel <= 9)
                        return "Early";
                    else
                        if (ageLevel <= 12)
                            return "Middle";
                        else
                            return "Upper";
        }
    }
```

SR 9.7   With single inheritance, a class is derived from only one parent, whereas with multiple inheritance, a class can be derived from multiple parents, inheriting the properties of each. The problem with multiple inheritance is that collisions must be resolved in the cases when two or more parents contribute an attribute or method with the same name. Java supports only single inheritance.

9.2 Overriding Methods

SR 9.8   A child class may prefer its own definition of a method in favor of the definition provided for it by its parent. In this case, the child overrides (redefines) the parent's definition with its own.

SR 9.9   The answers are:

  a. True – The child "overrides" the parent's definition of the method if both methods have the same signature.
  b. False – A constructor is a special method with no return type which has the same name as its class. If you tried to override the parent's constructor, you would create a syntax error since all methods except constructors must have a return type.
  c. False – A `final` method cannot be overridden (that's why it is "final").
  d. False – On the contrary, the need to override methods of a parent class occurs often when using inheritance.
  e. True – Such a variable is called a *shadow* variable. You can do this, but it may lead to confusing situations and its use is discouraged.

9.3 Class Hierarchies

SR 9.10 There are many potential answers to this problem.

SR 9.11 All classes in Java are derived, directly or indirectly, from the `Object` class. Therefore, all public methods of the `Object` class, such as `equals` and `toString`, are available to every object.

SR 9.12   The only Java class that does not have a parent class is the `Object` class. As mentioned in the previous answer, all other classes are derived from `Object` either directly or indirectly. `Object` is the root of the Java inheritance tree.

SR 9.13   An abstract class is a representation of a general concept. Common characteristics and method signatures can be defined in an abstract class so that they are inherited by child classes derived from it.

SR 9.14   It is a contradiction to define an abstract class as `final`. An abstract class is "incomplete" because it contains abstract methods. Typically the definitions of these methods are completed by one or more classes that extend the abstract class. But a `final` class cannot be extended, so there would be no way to complete its definition.

SR 9.15   A new interface can be derived from an existing interface using inheritance, just as a new class can be derived from an existing class.

9.4 Visibility

SR 9.16   A class member is not inherited if it has private visibility, meaning that it cannot be referenced by name in the child class. However, such members do exist for the child and can be referenced indirectly.

SR 9.17   The `Pizza` class can refer to the variable servings explicitly, because it is declared with `protected` visibility. It cannot, however, refer to the `calories` method explicitly, because the `calories` method is declared as `private`.

9.5 Designing for Inheritance

SR 9.18   An inheritance derivation represents an "is-a" relationship when the child class represents a more specific version of the parent class. For example, a dictionary is a type of book, so if a `Dictionary` class extends a `Book` class, the inheritance represents an "is-a" relationship.

SR 9.19   Common features of classes should appear as high as possible in a class hierarchy, as long as it is appropriate for the features to be at the level where they are defined. This approach supports understandability, consistency, and reuse.

SR 9.20   You can define a class with multiple roles by having the class implement more than one interface.

SR 9.21   You should override the `toString` method of a parent in its child class, even when the method is not invoked through the child by your current applications, to avoid problems at a later time. Someone who later uses the class directly or extends the class may assume the existence of a valid `toString` method.

SR 9.22 The `final` modifier can be applied to a particular method, which keeps that method from being overridden in a child class. It can also be applied to an entire class, which keeps that class from being extended at all.

9.6 The Component Class Hierarchy

SR 9.23 a. True, b. True, c. False, d. False, e. False, f. True

SR 9.24 The benefits include not having to worry about the details of applet creation and execution, or how the applet interacts with the browser, or security concerns. Essentially, you do not have to worry about anything that would be a common concern across all applets; such concerns have already been handled. You just have to worry about what makes your applet different from other applets.

9.7 Extending Adapter Classes

SR 9.25 An adapter class is a class that implements a listener interface, providing empty definitions for all of its methods. A listener class can be created by extending the appropriate adapter class and overriding the methods of interest.

SR 9.26 The `OffCenterPanel` class extends the `JPanel` class. The `JPanel` class inherits from all of the other classes mentioned. Therefore, an `OffCenterPanel` object "is" a `JPanel`, and a `JComponent`, and a `Container`, and an `Object`.

SR 9.27 The `OffCenterListener` class extends the `MouseAdapter` class. Since the `MouseAdapter` class includes methods for each of the mouse events, the `OffCenterListener` class inherits those methods and does not need to define them directly.

9.8 The `Timer` Class

SR 9.28 An object created from the `Timer` class produces an action event at regular intervals. It can be used to control the speed of an animation.

SR 9.29 The `Timer` constructor is called in the `ReboundPanel` constructor to set the initial delay and to associate a listener with the timer. The `start` method is also called in the ReboundPanel constructor to begin the timer countdown initially. The timer is never stopped in the Rebound program.

SR 9.30 a. The smiling face would move faster if the timer delay were decreased. b. The smiling face would move slower if the timer delay were increased. c. The image could be changed by specifying a new file in the call to the ImageIcon constructor. d. The smiling face would make larger jumps if the values of moveX and moveY were increased. e. The smiling face would move faster when it hits the edge if, in the action-Performed method, the timer delay were decreased in both of the if statements.

Chapter 10 Polymorphism

10.1 Late Binding

SR 10.1 Polymorphism is the ability of a reference variable to refer to objects of various types at different times. A method invoked through such a reference is bound to different method definitions at different times, depending on the type of the object referenced.

SR 10.2 Compile time binding is considered more efficient than dynamic binding. Compile time binding occurs before the program is executed and therefore does not delay the execution progress of the program. Dynamic binding occurs while the program is running and therefore does affect the runtime efficiency of the program.

10.2 Polymorphism via Inheritance

SR 10.3 In Java, a reference variable declared using a parent class can be used to refer to an object of the child class. If both classes contain a method with the same signature, the parent reference can be polymorphic.

SR 10.4 Yes, the statements are legal. Since a CDPlayer is a MusicPlayer, it is legal to assign an object of class CDPlayer to a variable of class MusicPlayer.

SR 10.5 No, the third statement is not legal. A MusicPlayer is not necessarily a CDPlayer. It is not legal to perform cdplayer = mplayer without using an explicit cast operation. Consider that the mplayer variable could potentially represent many different kinds of music players: CD players, record players, mp3 players, etc. Suppose at the time of the assignment statement, it represents an mp3 player. Then, you would be assigning an mp3 player object to a `CDPlayer` variable. That, most likely, doesn't make sense and would cause problems if it was allowed to happen.

SR 10.6   When a child class overrides the definition of a parent's method, two versions of that method exist. If a polymorphic reference is used to invoke the method, the version of the method that is invoked is determined by the type of the object being referred to, not by the type of the reference variable.

SR 10.7   The `StaffMember` class is abstract because it is not intended to be instantiated. It serves as a placeholder in the inheritance hierarchy to help organize and manage the objects polymorphically.

SR 10.8   The pay method has no meaning at the `StaffMember` level, so is declared as abstract. But by declaring it there we guarantee that every object of its children will have a pay method. This allows us to create an array of `StaffMember` objects, which is actually filled with various types of staff members, and pay each one. The details of being paid are determined by each class as appropriate.

SR 10.9   It depends. The pay method invocation is polymorphic. The actual method that is invoked is determined at run time and is based on the class of the object referenced by the current (according to the value of `count`) element of the staff list.

10.3 Polymorphism via Interfaces

SR 10.10   An interface name can be used as the type of a reference. Such a reference variable can refer to any object of any class that implements that interface. Because all classes implement the same interface, they have methods with common signatures, which can be dynamically bound.

SR 10.11   a. illegal – Speaker is an interface and interfaces do not have constructors.

      b. legal – the Dog class implements Speaker.
      c. legal – note that all the classes involved implement Speaker.
      d. legal – Philosopher implements Speaker, so it is legal to assign a philosopher object to a speaker variable.
      e. illegal – first is declared to be a Speaker, so we cannot invoke the Philosopher method pontificate through first.

10.4 Sorting

SR 10.12   The `Comparable` interface contains a single method called `compareTo`, which should return an integer that is less than zero, equal to zero, or greater than zero if the executing object is less than, equal to, or greater than the object to which it is being compared, respectively.

SR 10.13   The sequence of changes the selection sort algorithm makes to the list of numbers is:

5	7	1	8	2	4	3
1	7	5	8	2	4	3
1	2	5	8	7	4	3
1	2	3	8	7	4	5
1	2	3	4	7	8	5
1	2	3	4	5	8	7
1	2	3	4	5	7	8

SR 10.14   The sequence of changes the insertion sort algorithm makes to the list of numbers is:

5	7	1	8	2	4	3
5	7	1	8	2	4	3
1	5	7	8	2	4	3
1	5	7	8	2	4	3
1	2	5	7	8	4	3
1	2	4	5	7	8	3
1	2	3	4	5	7	8

SR 10.15   The sorting methods in this chapter all operate on an array of Comparable objects. So the sorting method doesn't really "know" what the objects are, other than that they are comparable and therefore have a compareTo method that can be invoked.

SR 10.16   Selection sort and insertion sort are generally equivalent in efficiency, because they both take about n^2 number of comparisons to sort a list of n numbers. Selection sort, though, generally makes fewer swaps. Several sorting algorithms are more efficient than either of these.

10.5 Searching

SR 10.17   a. 4, b. 1, c. 15, d. 15

SR 10.18   A binary search assumes that the search pool is already sorted and begins by examining the middle element. Assuming the target is not found, approximately half of the data is eliminated as viable candidates. Then, the middle element of the remaining candidates is examined, eliminating another quarter of the data. This process continues until the element is found or all viable data has been examined.

SR 10.19   a. 1, b. 3, c. 4, d. 4

10.6 Designing for Polymorphism

SR 10.20–SR 10.22 For the questions in this section, reasonable arguments can be made for using either inheritance or interfaces in each of the situations described. The point of the questions is to have students think about choices, consider alternative approaches, and practice making technical arguments to support their decisions.

Chapter 11 Exceptions

11.1 Exception Handling

SR 11.1 An exception is an object that defines an unusual or erroneous situation. An error is similar, except that an error generally represents an unrecoverable situation and should not be caught.

SR 11.2 A thrown exception can be handled in one of three ways: it can be ignored, which will cause a program to terminate; it can be handled where it occurs using a `try` statement; or it can be caught and handled higher in the method calling hierarchy.

11.2 Uncaught Exceptions

SR 11.3 a. False – Exceptions and errors are related but are not always the same thing.
b. True – Division by zero is invalid, so an exception is thrown.
c. False – An exception must be either handled or thrown.
d. True – If the exception is not handled, the program will terminate and display a message.
e. True – That is the purpose of the call stack trace.

11.3 The `try-catch` Statement

SR 11.4 A `catch` phrase of a `try` statement defines the code that will handle a particular type of exception.

SR 11.5 The `finally` clause of a `try` statement is executed no matter how the `try` block is exited. If no exception is thrown, the `finally` clause is executed after the `try` block is complete. If an exception is thrown, the appropriate `catch` clause is executed; then the `finally` clause is executed.

SR 11.6   The output produced is:

a. `finally`
   `the end`

b. `one caught`
   `finally`
   `the end`

c. `two caught`
   `finally`
   `the end`

d. `finally`

11.4 Exception Propagation

SR 11.7   If an exception is not caught immediately when thrown, it begins to propagate up through the methods that were called to get to the point where it was generated. The exception can be caught and handled at any point during that propagation. If it propagates out of the `main` method, the program terminates.

SR 11.8   If the exception generating code was added to the `level2` method, just before the call to the `level3` method, then the output would not include any mention of "Level 3" – this is because the call to level 3 does not occur since the exception is raised before the call is made.

SR 11.9   There is no change. The exception is still raised in level 3. The new code in level 2 does not get executed.

11.5 The Exception Class Hierarchy

SR 11.10   A checked exception is an exception that must be either (1) caught and handled or (2) listed in the `throws` clause of any method that may throw or propagate it. This establishes a set of exceptions that must be formally acknowledged in the program one way or another. Unchecked exceptions can be ignored completely in the code if desired.

SR 11.11   a. True – It inherits from `RunTimeException` which inherits from `Exception`.

b. True – It inherits from `Throwable` through `RunTimeException` and `Exception`.

c. False – It inherits from `RunTimeException` so it is unchecked.

d. True – It does not inherit from `RunTimeException`.

e. True – See, for example, the `OutOfRangeException` defined in this section.

f. False – The `ArithmeticException` is unchecked.

SR 11.12   If the input is 42 the program defined `OutOfRangeException` is thrown in main, the message "Input value is out of range." is printed along with the stack trace that consists of just information about `CreatingExceptions.main`, and the program terminates. If the input is -3, the same thing happens. If the input is the string "thirty," then a library defined `InputMismatchException` is thrown, a stack trace that consists of information about five methods is printed, and the program terminates. I/O exceptions are the topic of the next section of this textbook.

11.6 I/O Exceptions

SR 11.13   A stream is a sequential series of bytes that serves as a source of input or a destination for output.

SR 11.14   The standard I/O streams in Java are `System.in`, the standard input stream; `System.out`, the standard output stream; and `System.err`, the standard error stream. Usually, standard input comes from the keyboard and standard output and error go to a default window on the monitor screen.

SR 11.15   The `Stream` object we have been using explicitly throughout this book is the `System.out` object. We have used it when printing output from our programs. Sometimes we have also used the `System.in` object, to create `Scanner` objects for reading input from the user.

SR 11.16   The `main` method definition of the `CreatingExceptions` program does not include a `throws InputMismatchException` clause, because the `Scanner` class takes care of that—there is no need to repeat code in the `main` method when it is already included in a helper class.

SR 11.17   The `main` method definition of the `TestData` program does not include a `throws FileNotFoundException` clause, because the `FileWriter` class takes care of that that—there is no need to repeat code in the `main` method when it is already included in a helper class.

SR 11.18   If the `PrintWriter` constructor of the `TestDate` class is passed the `fw` object instead of the `bw` object, the program still works. The only difference is that the program does not use the buffering capabilities of the `BufferedWriter` class and therefore the processing may not be as efficient.

11.7 Tool Tips and Mnemonics

SR 11.19   A tool tip is a small amount of text that can be set up to appear when the cursor comes to rest on a component. It usually gives information about that component.

SR 11.20   A mnemonic is a character that can be used to activate a control
             such as a button as if the user had used to mouse to do so. The user
             activates a mnemonic by holding down the ALT key and pressing the
             appropriate character.

SR 11.21   A component should be disabled if it is not a viable option for the user
             at a given time. Not only does this prevent user error, but also it helps
             clarify what the current valid actions are.

SR 11.22   The class(es), and the line(s) of code from the class(es), that provide
             the listed functionality are:

   a. `LightBulb` - `panel.setBackground (Color.black)`
   b. `LightBulbControls` - `offButton.setToolTipText ("Turn it off!")`
   c. `LightBulbControls` - `onButton.setMnemonic ('n')`
      `OffListener` - `onButton.setEnabled (true)`
   d. `OnListener` - `onButton.setEnabled (false)`
   e. `LightBulbPanel` - `on = true`

11.8 Combo Boxes

SR 11.23   A combo box is a component that allows the user to choose from a
             set of options in a pull-down list. An editable combo box also allows
             the user to enter a specific value.

SR 11.24   The `JukeBox` program ensures that it doesn't try to play a song associ-
             ated with the `"Make a Selection. . ."` combo box option by setting
             the corresponding entry in the `music` array to `null`.

SR 11.25   There are two action listeners defined in the `JukeBox` program. The
             `ComboListener` listens for a mouseclick on the combo box selection
             list. The `ButtonListener` listens for a mouseclick on one of the two
             buttons (play and stop).

SR 11.26   The `JukeBox` program associates the combo box selection made by the
             user with a specific audio clip by storing the audio clips in an array
             `music`; storing the descriptions of the music, in the same order, in an
             array `musicNames`; generating the combo box used to make music selec-
             tions based on the array `musicNames`; and using the index returned from
             a combo box selection to set the current audio clip from the `music` array.

11.9 Scroll Panes

SR 11.27   A scroll pane can have a vertical scroll bar on the right side and/or a hor-
             izontal scroll bar along the bottom. The programmer can determine, in

either case, whether the scroll bar should always appear, never appear, or appear as needed to be able to view the underlying component.

SR 11.28 If you change the first parameter passed to the Dimension constructor within the TransitMap program to 1000, when the map appears, it is in a wider container—there is no horizontal scroll bar at the bottom of the map, because the entire width of the map already fits in the container.

11.10 Split Panes

SR 11.29 Divider bars separate split panes into distinct right/left or top/bottom sections. The bars can be dragged to make one section larger and the other section smaller so that users can control what they see.

SR 11.30 In general, all of the options of a JList object are visible to the user, whereas with a combo box the user must "open" the box to see the options.

Chapter 12 Recursion

12.1 Recursive Thinking

SR 12.1 Recursion is a programming technique in which a method calls itself, solving a smaller version of the problem each time, until the terminating condition is reached.

SR 12.2 The recursive part of the definition of a List is used nine times to define a list of 10 numbers. The base case is used once.

SR 12.3 Infinite recursion occurs when there is no base case that serves as a terminating condition or when the base case is improperly specified. The recursive path is followed forever. In a recursive program, infinite recursion will often result in an error that indicates that available memory has been exhausted.

SR 12.4 A base case is always required to terminate recursion and begin the process of returning through the calling hierarchy. Without the base case, infinite recursion results.

SR 12.5 $5 * n = 5$ if $n = 1$, $5 * n = 5 + (5 * (n - 1))$ if $n > 1$

12.2 Recursive Programming

SR 12.6 Recursion is not necessary. Every recursive algorithm can be written in an iterative manner. However, some problem solutions are much more elegant and straightforward when written recursively.

SR 12.7   Avoid recursion when the iterative solution is simpler and more easily understood and programmed. Recursion has the overhead of multiple method calls and is not always intuitive.

SR 12.8   If n < 0 a –1 is returned; otherwise the number of digits in the integer n is returned.

SR 12.9   The recursive solution below is more complicated than the iterative version, so it normally would not be done in this way.

```
// Returns 5 * num, assumes num > 0
private static int multByFive (int num)
{
    int result = 5; // when num == 1
    if (num > 1)
        result = 5 + multByFive(num - 1);
    return result;
}
```

SR 12.10   Indirect recursion occurs when a method calls another method, which calls another method, and so on until one of the called methods invokes the original. Indirect recursion is usually more difficult to trace than direct recursion, in which a method calls itself.

12.3 Using Recursion

SR 12.11   The MazeSearch program recursively processes each of the four positions adjacent to the "current" one unless either (1) the current position is outside of the playing grid or (2) the final destination position is reached.

SR 12.12   a. The original maze is defined when the grid array is declared and initialized.
b. A test to see if we have arrived at the goal occurs at the second if statement in the traverse method.
c. A location is marked as having been tried in the first statement in the first if block of the traverse method.
d. A test to see if we already tried a location occurs in the second if statement of the valid method.

SR 12.13   a. valid 0,0   valid 1,0   valid 2,0   valid 1,1
b. valid 0,0
c. valid 0,0 valid 1,0 valid 2,0 valid 1,1 valid 0,0 valid 1,-1
   valid 0,1   valid 1,1   valid 0,2   valid -1,1 valid 0,0
   valid -1,0   valid 0,-1

SR 12.14   The Towers of Hanoi puzzle of N disks is solved by moving N–1 disks out of the way onto an extra peg, moving the largest disk to its destination, then moving the N–1 disks from the extra peg to the destination. This solution is inherently recursive because, to move the substack of N–1 disks, we can use the same process.

SR 12.15 For an initial stack of 1 disk there is 1 call to the moveTower method. For an initial stack of 2 disks there are 3 calls. For 3 disks there are 7 calls. For every disk added, the number of calls increases by double the previous number, plus one.

12.4 Recursion in Graphics

SR 12.16 The base case of the TiledPictures program is a minimal size for the images to be produced. If the size of the area is smaller than the preset minimum, the recursion terminates.

SR 12.17 A fractal is a geometric shape that can be composed of multiple versions of the same shape at different scales and different angles of orientation. Recursion can be used to draw the repetitive shapes over and over again.

Chapter 13 Collections

13.1 Collections and Data Structures

SR 13.1 A collection is an object whose purpose is to store and organize primitive data or other objects. Some collections represent classic data structures that are helpful in particular problem-solving situations.

SR 13.2 Yes, the ArrayList class provides an abstract data type. The ArrayList class provides a collection of information. It provides operations for storing and accessing the information. The implementation details are hidden from us—that is, we do not need to know anything about how the information is stored or how the operations are implemented in order to use an ArrayList object.

SR 13.3 An abstract data type (ADT) is a collection of data and the operations that can be performed on that data. An object is essentially the same thing in that we encapsulate related variables and methods in an object. The object hides the underlying implementation of the ADT, separating the interface from the underlying implementation, permitting the implementation to be changed without affecting the interface.

13.2 Dynamic Representations

SR 13.4 A dynamic data structure is constructed using references to link various objects together into a particular organization. It is dynamic in that it can grow and shrink as needed. New objects can be added to the structure, and obsolete objects can be removed from the structure at run time by adjusting references between objects in the structure.

SR 13.5 To insert a node into a list, first find the node that comes before the new node (let's call it beforeNode). Then, set the new node's next pointer equal to beforeNode's next pointer. Then, set beforeNode's next pointer to the new node. A special case exists when inserting a node at the beginning of the list.

SR 13.6 To delete a node from a list, first find the node that comes before the node to be deleted (let's call it beforeNode). Then, set beforeNode's next pointer to the deleted node's next pointer. A special case exists when deleting the first node of the list.

SR 13.7
```
set count = 0;
current = first;
while current != null
    count++;
    current = current.next;
return count;
```

SR 13.8 Each node in a doubly linked list has references to both the node that comes before it in the list and the node that comes after it in the list. This organization allows for easy movement forward and backward in the list, and simplifies some operations.

SR 13.9 A header node for a linked list is a special node that holds information about the list, such as references to the front and rear of the list and an integer to keep track of how many nodes are currently in the list.

13.3 Linear Data Structures

SR 13.10 A queue is a linear data structure like a list, but it has more constraints on its use. A general list can be modified by inserting or deleting nodes anywhere in the list, but a queue only adds nodes to one end (enqueue) and takes them off of the other (dequeue). Thus, a queue uses a first-in, first-out (FIFO) approach.

SR 13.11 The contents of the queue from front to rear are: 72 37 15

SR 13.12   A stack is a linear data structure that adds (pushes) and removes (pops) nodes from one end. It manages information using a last-in, first-out (LIFO) approach.

SR 13.13   The contents of the stack from top to bottom are: 37 72 5

SR 13.14   The Stack class is defined in the java.util package of the Java standard class library. It implements a generic stack ADT. The Stack class stores Object references, so the stack can be used to store any kind of object.

13.4 Non-Linear Data Structures

SR 13.15   Trees and graphs are both non-linear data structures, meaning that the data they store is not organized in a linear fashion. Trees create a hierarchy of nodes. The nodes in a graph are connected using general edges.

SR 13.16   a. tree, b. graph, c. graph, d. tree

13.5 The Java Collections API

SR 13.17   The Java Collections API is a set of classes in the Java standard class library that represents collections of various types, such as ArrayList and LinkedList.

SR 13.18   A generic type is a collection object that is implemented such that the type of objects it manages can be established when the collection is created. This allows some compile-time control over the types of objects that are added to the collection and eliminates the need to cast the objects when they are removed from the collection. All collections in the Java Collections API have been implemented as generic types.

Index

Symbols

-- (decrement operator), 106–107
' ' (single quotes for character literals), 99
- (subtraction operator), 101
!== (equal to operator), 235–236
" " (double quotes for character string literals), 55, 84, 89
$ (dollar sign character), 57–58
% (remainder operator), 101, 303–304
%= (remainder assignment operator), 107–108
& (AND bitwise operator), 693
&& (AND logical operator), 236–238
() (parentheses), 88–89, 103–104, 111–112, 141, 239
  arithmetic expressions, 103–104
  boolean expressions, 239
  casting data conversion, 111–112
  invoking methods, 141
  operator precedence using, 88–89, 103–104
* (asterisk for Import declaration), 151
*- (multiplication assignment operator), 107
* (multiplication operator), 101
. (dot operator for accessing methods), 141
/ (division operator), 101–102
/ (slash for path separation), 270
/* and */ (multiple line comments), 56
/** and */ (external comments), 56
// (comments), 54, 56
/= (division assignment operator), 107

? : (conditional operator), 300–301
[] (square brackets for arrays), 406–407, 410
\' (single quote escape sequence), 89
\" (double quote escape sequence), 89
\\ (backslash escape sequence), 89
\b (backspace escape sequence), 89
\n (newline escape sequence), 89
\r (carriage return escape sequence), 89
\t (tab escape sequence), 89
^ (XOR bitwise operator), 693–704
_ (underscore character), 57–58
{ } (class definition), 54–55
{} (braces for if statements), 247, 251
| (NOT logical operator), 236–238
| (OR bitwise operator), 693–704
|| (OR logical operator), 236–238
~ (NOT bitwise operator), 693
+ (plus symbol), 86–88, 101
  addition operator, 101
  string concatenation, 86–88
++ (increment operator), 106–107
+= (addition assignment operator), 107
< (less than relational operator), 235–236
<< (left–shift bitwise operator), 695
<= (less than or equal to relational operator), 235–236
<> (HTML tags), 124

-= (subtraction assignment operator), 107
== (not equal to operator), 235–236
> (greater than relational operator), 235–236
>= (greater than or equal to relational operator), 235–236
>> (right–shift bitwise operator), 695
>>> (right–shift with zeros bitwise operator), 695

A

abstract classes, 487–488
abstract data types (ADT), 644
abstract methods, 349
abstract modifier (reserved word), 349, 487–488, 699
Abstract Windowing Toolkit (AWT), 170, 494–495
accessor methods, encapsulation, 197–198
action events, 221–222, 274–277, 283–285
actual parameters (arguments), 201
adapter classes, extended events using, 497–500
add method, 171
addresses, 39, 47, 49–50
  Internet, 47, 49–50
  memory, 39
  network, 47
Advanced Research Projects Agency (ARPA) network (ARAPNET), 49
aggregation, 342–346
algorithms, 358–359
aliases, 142–144
analog signals, 30–31
AND bitwise operator (&), 693

applets, 121–129, 627–637,
    707–708
    appletviewer tool for,
        121–122
    applications compared to,
        121–122
    bytecode for, 122
    drawing shapes, 125–129
    executing, 122–124
    fractals, 630–637
    Graphics class, 125–129
    HTML tags <> for, 124
    import statements for,
        122–123
    Java programming, 121–129,
        707–708
    methods for, 123, 707–708
    paint method, 123
    public declaration of, 123
    recursion used for, 627–637
    tiled pictures, 627–630
    World Wide Web execution
        of, 124
application programming
    interfaces (API), 53,
    148–149, 660–661
applications, 30, 121–122
arc angle, 127
architecture, computer
    hardware functions,
    37–39
arg identifier, 57, 428–429
arguments, command-line,
    428–429. *See also*
    parameters
arithmetic/logic unit, 43
ArrayList class, 271–273
arrays, 271, 405–468,
    601–604
    bounds checking, 410–415
    characters in, 412–415
    command-line arguments,
        428–429
    constructors and, 424–426,
        431–433
    declaration, 407–427
    elements, 406–407
    event-driven programs using,
        444–458, 601–604
    graphical user interfaces
        (GUIs), 439–458,
        601–604
    index (subscript) values, 271,
        406–407, 410–415
    initializer lists, 415–416

instantiation, 407–408,
    418–420, 424–426
int[] declaration,
    407–408, 434
integers in, 410–412
key events using,
    453–458
lists as, 601–604
mouse events using, 444–452
multidimensional, 438–439
new operator, 407–408,
    418–419
objects and, 407–410,
    418–427
off-by-one errors, 410
parameters as, 416–417,
    428–433
polygons drawn using,
    439–443
polylines drawn using,
    440–442
ragged, 439
square brackets [] used for,
    406–407, 410
syntax, 415
two-dimensional, 434–438
variable-length parameter
    lists, 430–433
variables in, 407–410,
    415–416
ASCII character set, 99–100,
    687–688
assembly language, 63
assignment, 93–95, 103–104,
    107–108, 111
    arithmetic operator
        precedence and, 103–104
    addition (+=), 107
    data conversion by, 111
    data values and, 93–95
    division (/=), 107
    expressions and, 93, 103–
        104, 107–108
    Java defined operations,
        107–108
    multiplication (*=), 107
    operators (=), 93, 103–104,
        107–108
    remainder (%=), 107–108
    statements, 93–95
    subtraction (–=), 107
    variables and, 93–95
asterisk (*) for Import
    declaration, 151
autoboxing, 169

B
background color, 127
base case, 610–611
base value, 33
bevel borders, 393–394
binary operators, 102
binary search, 541–544
binary trees, 657
binary values, 33–36, 679
bits, 35–36, 679
black–box testing, 373–374
block statements, 245–249
boolean expressions,
    234–239, 252–255
    conditional statement
        decisions and, 234
    data comparison using,
        252–255
    equality operators, 235–236
    if statements, 234,
        238–239, 252–255
    logical operators, 236–238
    loop execution time using,
        235
    parentheses () for, 239
    relational operators,
        235–236
    short-circuited operations,
        237–238
    truth tables, 236–238
boolean literals, 100
boolean operators, 694
boolean primitive data types,
    100, 111, 167
borders, 382–385, 391–395
    bevel, 393–394
    compound, 394
    empty, 393–394
    etched, 393–394
    GUI programs for, 391–395
    layout manager for, 382–385
    line, 393–394
    matte, 394–395
    Swing components use of,
        391–395
    titled, 394
boundaries, 373–374
    black-box testing, 373–374
    equivalence categories for,
        373–374
bounding rectangle, 125–127
bounds checking, 410–415
    array index (subscript)
        values, 410–415
    characters, 412–415

integers, 410–412
off-by-one errors, 410
box layout, 387–390
break statements, 265, 296–297
browser, 51
bus, 37
buttons, 218–222, 274–285
action events, 221–222, 274–277, 283–285
check boxes, 277–281
conditional statements for, 274–285
event sources, 274–277
GUI programs for, 218–222, 274–277
item events, 278–281
label font styles, 277–281
listener objects, 217–225, 274–277
push, 218–222, 274–277
radio, 281–285
toggle, 285
by value parameter passing, 364–368
byte integer data type, 97–98, 109–111, 167–168
bytecode, Java programming, 65–66, 122
bytes, 40

C
cache, 41
call stack trace, 566
case sensitivity, Java programming, 58–59
casting (), data conversion by, 111–112
catch clause, 566–570
CD (compact disc) devices, 42–43
CD-ROM device, 42
central processing unit (CPU), 28–29, 38, 41, 43–45
arithmetic/logic unit, 43
cache, 41
computer hardware functions, 28–29, 38, 43–45
control unit, 43
fetch-decode-execute cycle, 44
main memory and, 28–29, 41
microprocessor, 44–45
registers, 43–44
system clock, 45

von Neumann architecture, 44
change events, 558
char character data type, 100, 110–111, 167
character strings, 55, 84–91, 142, 254–255
data comparison, 254–255
escape sequences, 89–90
if statements for, 254–255
Java programming, 55, 84
literals (" "), 55, 84, 89, 142
object data and, 84–91, 142, 254–255
parameters of, 84
print and println methods for, 84–85
string concatenation, 86–89
Unicode relationships, 254–255
characters, 99–100, 109–111, 253, 412–415, 687–689
array index values, 412–415
ASCII character set, 99–100, 687–688
assignment conversion for, 111
bounds checking, 412–415
char, 100, 110–111
control characters, 99, 687–689
conversion of, 109–112
data comparisons, 253
if statements for, 253
literals (' '), 99
narrowing conversion for, 109–110
nonprintable (control), 687–689
primitive data as, 99–100
printable, 687–688
Unicode character set, 100, 687–689
widening conversion for, 109–110
check boxes, GUI creation of, 277–281
checked exceptions, 578
child class, 471, 479–485. See also subclasses
Circle class, 214–216
class definition ({}), 54–55
class hierarchies, 484–488, 494–496, 516–517, 575–578
abstract classes, 487–488

child class and, 484–485
Component class, 494–496
exceptions, 575–578
inheritance and, 484–488, 494–496
Object class, 486–487
polymorphism and, 516–517
classes, 53, 57, 73–75, 139–184, 185–232, 329–369, 469–512, 516–517
adapter classes, 497–500
abstract, 487–488
aggregation, 342–346
assigning responsibilities to, 331
child, 471, 479–484
Component, 494–496
constructors, 207–208
DecimalFormat, 160–161
dependency, 336–342
encapsulation, 195–198
enumerated types, 164–166, 355–358
event adapter, 497–500
formatting output using, 158–163
graphical objects, 208–216
graphic-user interfaces (GUIs), 169–179, 217–225
identification of, 329–331
import declaration, 150–151
inheritance, 74, 469–512
instance data, 193
interfaces, implementation of, 348–355
Java programming and, 73–75
Java standard class library, 53, 57, 148–151
JButton, 219–221
JFrame, 170–173, 211–212
JPanel, 170–173, 208–213
JTextField, 222–225
listener, 221
main method, 188–189
Math, 155–158
methods for, 186–192, 195–208, 358–369
NumberFormat, 158–160
Object, 486–487
object-oriented (OO) programming and, 73–75, 329–348

classes *(continued)*
  objects and, 73–74,
    139–184, 186–187,
    195–198, 207–216,
    329–331, 336–343,
    346–348
  packages, 148–151
  parent (base), 471, 476–479
  polymorphism and, 516–517
  qualified names, 150
  Random, 152–155
  relationships, 336–348
  returned values from,
    141–142, 152–153,
    155–158
  software design, 329–348
  static members, 331–335
  String, 144–147
  subclasses, 470–473
  System, 161–163
  this method for, 346–348
  Timer, 501–504
  use of, 139–184
  visibility modifiers, 196
  wrapper, 167–169
  writing, 185–232
clients, 195, 328
clock speed, 45
coding guidelines, 701–705
  design, 702
  documentation, 704–705
  Java programming, 701–705
  style, 703–704
collections, 643–666
  abstract data types (ADT),
    644
  data structures for, 644–660
  dynamic representations,
    645–652
  generic types, 660–661
  graphs, 658–660
  heterogeneous, 644
  homogeneous, 644
  implementation of, 644
  interfaces for, 644
  Java Collections API,
    660–661
  linked lists, 646–652
  linear data structures,
    653–656
  nonlinear data structures,
    657–660
  queues, 653–654
  stacks, 654–656
  trees, 657–658

color choosers, GUI programs
    for, 552–553
Color class, 120–121
color representation, Java
    graphics, 120–121, 127
combo boxes, GUI programs
    for, 590–595
command-line applications,
    170
command-line arguments,
    428–429
comments, 54–57, 711–714
  documentation, 54, 56–57,
    711–714
  double slash (//) symbols for,
    54, 56
  inline documentation,
    54, 57
  javadoc, 56, 711–714
  javadoc (/** and */)
    symbols for, 56
  newline character, 56
  multiple line (/* and */)
    symbols for, 56
  tags, 712–714
Comparable interface, 354
compile–time error, 68
compilers, 65–66
Component class, 494–496
compound borders, 394
computer systems, 27–82
  architecture, 37–38
  central processing unit (CPU),
    28, 43–45
  development environments,
    66–67
  digital technology for, 30–36
  errors, 68–69, 71–72
  hardware components, 28–
    29, 36–45
  information storage and
    management, 30–36, 39–43
  input/output (I/O) devices,
    28, 38–39
  Internet, 49–50
  Java programming, 52–61,
    65–67, 70–75
  local area network (LAN),
    48–49
  memory, 28, 39–43
  networks, 46–52
  object–oriented (OO)
    programming, 53,
    70–75
  processing, 28–36

programming languages,
    52–67
programs, 28, 52–75
  semantics, 67–68
  software, 28–30, 50–51,
    64–69, 70–75
  syntax, 67–68
  Uniform Resource Locators
    (URL), 51–52
  wide area network (WAN),
    48–49
  World Wide Web (WWW),
    51–52
conditional operator (? :),
    300–301
conditional statements,
    233–294, 295–325
  boolean expressions for,
    234–238
  break, 265, 296–297
  buttons developed using,
    274–285
  continue, 265
  data comparison using,
    252–255
  decisions from, 234
  dialog box development
    using, 317–319
  do loops, 235, 301–304,
    318–319
  drawing programs using,
    311–317
  events determined using,
    274–277
  flow of control, 234
  for loops, 235, 305–310
  graphical user interfaces
    (GUI), 274–285, 311–319
  if, 234, 239–252
  if–else, 234, 242–251,
    300–301
  iterators, 267–270, 308–310
  loops, 235–238, 256–265,
    295, 301–319
  nested, 249–251, 262–265
  object management using,
    271–273
  objects and, 267–285
  switch, 234, 296–299
  ternary operator (? :) for,
    300–301
  while loops, 235,
    256–265, 267–270
confirm dialog box,
    318–319

connections, 46–48
constants, data value as,
    95–96
constructors, 113–115, 141, 190,
    201, 207–216, 424–426,
    431–433
    arrays using, 424–426,
        431–433
    default, 207
    graphical object
        characteristics from,
        208–216
    instantiation using, 113–115,
        207, 424–426
    invoking (calling), 190, 207
    Java programming use of,
        113–115, 207–208
    new operator for, 113–115,
        141, 190
    parameters and, 431–433
    void modifier, 201,
        207–208
containers, 170–176, 217,
    376–391, 395–397
    add method for, 171
    content panes, 171–173
    GUI components, 170–176,
        217, 376–391, 395–397
    heavyweight, 170–171
    hierarchy for, 174–176,
        395–397
    labels, 171–172, 177–179
    layout manager for, 173,
        376–391
    lightweight, 170–171
    panels, 170–176
    panes, 171–173
    top-level, 395
containment hierarchy,
    174–176, 395–397
content panes, 171–173
continue statements, 265
control (nonprintable)
    characters, 99, 687–689
control flow statements, 374
control unit, 43
controllers, 38
coordinate systems, Java
    graphics, 118–120, 125

D
data, 83–136, 164–166,
    189–190, 193, 201–202,
    252–255, 296–297,
    355–348, 430–433

applets, 121–129
assignment statements, 93–95
boolean, 100, 111
character strings (" "),
    84–91, 254–255
characters, 99–100, 109–112,
    253
comparison of types,
    252–255
constants, 95–96
constructor, 113–115
conversion, 109–112
declarations, 189–190, 193,
    201–202
enumerated types, 164–166,
    355–358
escape sequences, 89–90
expressions, 101–109
floating point, 97–98,
    109–112, 252–253
Graphics class, 125–129
graphics, 118–129
if statements for, 252–255
input, 115, 117
instance, 193
integers, 97–98, 109–112
interactive programs for,
    113–117
lexicographic order, 255
literals, 84, 89, 98–100
local, 201–202
method declaration and,
    201–202
new operator, 113–115
object comparisons, 254–255
operators, 86–88, 93, 95,
    101–108
output, 116
parameters, 84, 430–433
primitive types, 97–101,
    109–113
Scanner class, 113–117
switch statement types,
    296–297
Unicode relationships,
    254–255
variable-length parameter
    lists, 430–433
variables, 91–95, 193,
    201–202
data conversion, 109–113, 169
    assignment, 111
    autoboxing, 169
    casting (), 111–112
    narrowing, 110–111

primitive data types and,
    109–111, 169
promotion, 111
widening, 109–110
wrapper class objects and,
    169
data structures, 644–660
    collections and, 644,
        653–660
    doubly linked lists, 651
    dynamic, 645–652
    graphs, 658–660
    header nodes, 652
    linear, 653–656
    linked lists, 646–652
    nodes, 657–658
    nonlinear, 657–660
    object storage using, 644
    queues, 653–654
    stacks, 654–656
    trees, 657–658
data transfer devices, 38
debugging software, 66–67, 69
decimal values, 679
DecimalFormat class,
    160–161
declaration, 91–93, 95–96,
    113–115, 140–142,
    150–151, 189–193,
    198–199, 201–202,
    407–426, 515–516, 528
    arrays, 407–426
    asterisk (*) for, 151
    bounds checking, 400–415
    classes, 150–151
    constants, 95–96
    constructors and, 115, 141,
        207, 424–426
    data, 189–190, 193,
        201–202
    import, 150–151
    initializer lists, 415–416
    instance data, 193
    instantiation and, 113–115,
        141, 207, 407–408,
        418–420, 424–426
    int, 91–93, 140, 407–408
    java.util packages,
        150–151
    local data, 201–202
    methods, 189–192,
        198–199, 201–202
    new operator and, 113–115,
        141–142, 407–408,
        418–420

declaration *(continued)*
  objects, 113–115, 140–142,
    407–410, 418–426
  parameters and, 416–417
  polymorphism and,
    515–516, 528
  reference variables,
    514–516, 528
  square brackets [] used for,
    407–410, 415
  String methods for,
    140–142, 418–423
  syntax and, 415
  variables, 92–93, 140–142,
    193, 201–202, 408–410,
    415–416
decomposition of methods,
  359–364
decrement (–) operator, 106–107
default visibility, 697–698
defect testing, 372–374
delimiters, 115, 270
dependency, 336–342
development environments,
  66–67
diagraph, 658–659
dialog boxes, 317–319,
  548–553
  color choosers, 552–553
  conditional statements used
    for, 317–319
  confirm, 318–319
  creation of, 317–319
  file choosers, 548–551
  input, 318–319
  loops for creation of, 317–319
  message, 318–319
  polymorphism used for,
    548–553
  Swing package for, 317
digital computers, 30–36
  analog information
    compared to, 30–31
  binary values, 33–36
  digitized process, 32–33
  sampling rate, 31–33
  signals, 32–36
direct access storage devices,
  41–42
direct recursion, 615–616
directed graph, 658–659
divide–by–zero error, 258–259
do loop statements, 301–304,
  318–319
  infinite, 304

remainder operator (%) for,
  303–304
  repetition of, 302–304
  while clause for, 301–302
documentation, 54, 56–57,
  704–705, 711–715
  coding guidelines, 704–705
  comments, 54, 56–57,
    711–714
  HTML file generation,
    714–715
  programming style, 54,
    56–57, 704–705
  inline, 54, 56
  javadoc generator, 56,
    711–715
  tags, 712–714
Domain Name System (DNS),
  50
domain names, 49–50
domain server, 50
dot (.) operator for accessing
  methods, 141
double floating–point data type,
  97–98, 110–111, 167–168
doubly linked lists, 651
drawing, 125–129, 208–216,
  311–317, 439–443
  arc angle, 127
  arrays used for, 439–443
  background color, 127
  bounding rectangle, 125–127
  bull's–eye, 311–314
  Circle class, 214–216
  conditional statements used
    for, 311–317
  constructors for, 208–216
  drawing programs using,
    311–317
  foreground color, 127
  graphical objects, 208–216
  Graphics class, 125–129,
    439–442
  Java standard class library
    for, 442–443
  loops used for, 311–317
  ovals, 125–127
  paintComponent method,
    208, 211, 213–214,
    311–314
  polygons, 439–443
  polylines, 440–442
  rectangles, 314–317
  shapes, 125–129
  start angle, 127

DVD devices, 43
dynamic data structures,
  645–652

E
Eclipse IDE software, 67
editors, 64–65
else clause, 249–251
empty borders, 393–394
encapsulation, 74, 195–198,
  473–475
  accessor methods, 197–198
  client, 195
  inheritance and, 473–475
  modifiers for, 196–198
  mutator methods, 197–198
  objects, 74, 195–198
  service (support) methods,
    196
  visibility modifiers,
    196–197, 473–475
enumerated types, 164–166,
  355–358
equality operators, 235–236
equivalence categories,
  373–374
errors, 66–69, 258–259,
  371–374, 410, 564
  black-box testing, 373
  compile-time, 68
  debugging software for,
    66–67, 69
  defect testing, 372–374
  divide-by-zero, 258–259
  exceptions and, 69, 564
  logical, 69
  off-by-one, 410
  programming, 68–69
  run-time, 69, 564
  syntax, 69
  testing programs for,
    371–374
  white-box (glass-box)
    testing, 374
escape sequences, 89–90
etched borders, 393–394
event adapter classes,
  497–500
event-driven programs,
  217–218, 221–222,
  274–285, 444–458,
  497–500, 547–548,
  553–558, 590–604
  action events, 221–222

adapter classes, 497–500
arrays used for, 444–458
buttons, 218–222, 274–285
change events, 558
combo boxes, 590–595
conditional statements used
for, 274–285
determining event sources,
274–277
graphical-user interfaces
(GUIs) as, 217–218
inheritance used for,
497–500
item events, 278–281
key events, 453–458
list selection events,
598–604
listeners, 217–225, 274–277,
448–452, 453–457,
497–500, 595
mouse events, 444–452,
497–500
mouse motion events,
444–445
polymorphism used for,
547–548, 553–558
rubberbanding, 449–452
scroll panes, 595–598
sliders, 553–558
split panes, 598–604
event generation, 729–731
event processing, 547–548
event sources, 274–277,
444–458
exceptions, 69, 563–607
call stack trace, 566
catch clause, 566–570
checked, 578
class hierarchy, 575–578
combo boxes, 590–595
finally clause, 570
graphic user interfaces (GUI),
583–604
handling, 564, 566–570
inheritance and, 575–578
input/output (I/O), 579–583
mnemonics and, 583–589
propagation, 571–574
run-time errors, 69, 564
scroll panes, 595–598
split panes, 598–604
streams in, 579–580
throw statements,
577–578, 580–582
tool tips and, 583–589

try blocks, 566–570
try-catch statements,
566–570
uncaught, 565–566
unchecked, 578
exponential complexity, 626
expressions, 101–109, 235–
238, 270, 709–710
arithmetic operators, 101–102
assignment (=) operators,
103–104, 107–108
boolean, 235–238
data and, 101–109
decrement (–) operator,
106–107
equality operators, 235–236
increment (++) operator,
106–107
logical operators, 236–238
operator precedence, 102–106
parentheses () in, 103–104
postfix operator, 106–107
prefix operator, 106–107
regular, 270, 709–710
relational operators, 235–236
trees, 103
extends modifier (reserved
word), 208, 471, 486

F
false boolean value, 100
fetch-decode-execute cycle, 44
file choosers, GUI programs
for, 548–551
file generation (HTML),
714–715
file servers, 46
final modifier (reserved
word), 95–96, 196, 483,
493–494, 699
finally clause, 570
first-in, first-out (fifo)
processing, 653
float floating-point data type,
97–98, 110–111, 167
floating-point data types,
97–98, 109–113, 252–253
assignment conversion for, 111
casting (), 111–112
conversion of, 109–113
data comparison, 252–253
if statements for, 252–253
narrowing conversion of,
109–110

literals, 98
primitive data as, 97–98
promotion conversion
for, 111
widening conversion of,
110–111
flow layout, 378–382
font styles, GUI programming
for, 277–281
for loop statements, 235,
305–310, 434–438
for-each version, 308–310
increment code for,
305–307
initialization of, 305–308
iterators and, 308–310
nested, 434–438
repetition of, 305–306
two–dimensional arrays
using, 434–438
for-each loop, 308–310
foreground color, 127
formal parameters, 201
formatting output, 158–163
DecimalFormat class,
160–161
NumberFormat class,
158–160
printf method, 161–163
fourth–generation language
(30GL), 64
fractals, 630–637
frames, 170–176
containment hierarchy,
174–176
content pane, 171–173
Jframe class, 170–173
panes, 171
functional specification, 328

G
garbage, object references,
143–144
generic types, 660–661
graph data structures, 658–660
graphic applications, 627–637
graphical user interfaces (GUIs),
30, 170–179, 217–225,
274–285, 311–319,
375–397, 439–458,
494–504, 547–558,
583–604, 729–731. *See
also* event-driven programs
Abstract Windowing Toolkit
(AWT), 170, 494–495

graphical user interfaces *(GUIs)* *(continued)*
action events, 221–222, 274–277, 283–285
arrays used for, 439–458, 600–604
borders, 382–385, 391–395
buttons, 218–222, 274–277
change events, 558
classes used for, 169–179, 217–225
color choosers and, 552–553
combo boxes, 590–595
components, 170, 217, 376–391, 494–496, 583–589, 729–731
computer systems and, 30
conditional statements used for, 274–285, 311–319
containers, 170–176, 217, 376–391, 395–397
containment hierarchies, 174–176, 395–397
dialog boxes, 317–319
disabling components, 584, 587–589
drawing programs, 311–317, 439–443
event adapter classes, 497–500
event generation, 729–731
event processing, 547–548
event sources, 274–277, 444–458
exceptions used for, 583–604
file choosers, 548–551
frames, 170–173
inheritance used for, 494–504
interaction of, 217–225
interface implementation, 221
item events, 278–281
key events, 453–458
labels, 171–172, 177–179
layout managers, 173, 376–391
list components, 601–604
listener objects, 217–225, 274–277, 448–452, 453–457, 497–504, 595
loops used for, 311–317
mnemonics and, 583–589
mouse events, 444–452
object-oriented programming and, 375–397
panels, 170–176

polymorphism used for, 547–558
scroll panes, 595–598
sliders, 553–558
software design and, 375–397
split panes, 598–604
Swing package, 170, 317, 494–496, 583
text fields, 222–225
timer objects, 501–504
tool tips and, 583–589
graphics, 118–121, 121–129, 169–179, 208–216, 627–637
applets used for, 121–129
color representation, 120–121, 127
constructors for, 208–216
coordinate systems, 118–120, 125
drawing, 125–129, 208–216
fractals, 630–637
GUI containers for, 170–176
images, 177–179
Java programming, 117–129
Koch snowflakes, 630–637
labels, 171–172, 177–179
monitor resolution, 118
objects as, 208–216
`paint` method, 123
panels, 170–176
picture resolution, 118
pixels, 118
recursion used for, 627–637
RGB (red-green-blue) values, 120
tiled pictures and, 627–630
Graphics class, 125–129
grid layout, 385–387
GUI, *see* graphical user interfaces (GUIs)

H
hard disks, 41
hardware components, 28–29, 36–45
central processing unit (CPU), 28–29, 38, 41, 43–45
computer architecture, 37–39
computer processing functions, 28–29
input/output (I/O) devices, 28, 38–39

main memory, 28–29, 39–41
memory, 28–29, 39–43
secondary memory, 28, 41–43
software and, 28
has-a relationships, 342–343
header nodes, 652
Heavyweight containers, 170–171
hexadecimal values, 681
high-level languages, 63–64
HTML file generation, 714–715
HTML tags (<>), 124
hypermedia, 51
hypertext, 50–52
HyperText Markup Language (HTML), 51
HyperText Transfer Protocol (http), 52

I
identifiers, 57–59, 703
abbreviations for, 59
case sensitivity of, 58–59
coding guidelines, 703
naming, 59
reserved words, 57–58
title case for, 59
`if` statements, 234, 239–255
boolean expressions () for, 234, 238–239, 252–255
braces {} used in, 247, 251
character data comparisons, 253
data comparison using, 252–255
`else` clause, 242–251
floating-point data comparisons, 252–253
indentation for, 239–240, 242, 247, 251
nested, 249–251
object comparisons, 254–255
`if-else` statements, 234, 242–251, 300–301
block statements, 245–249
conditional (ternary) operators as, 300–301
nested, 249–251
true/false conditions of, 242–245
image observer, 453
`ImageIcon` class, 177–179

images, 118–121, 177–179, 627–637. *See also* drawing
  color representation, 120–121
  coordinate systems, 118–120
  fractals, 630–637
  Java programming for, 118–121
  labels with, 177–179
  picture resolution, 118
  pixels, 118
  recursion used for, 627–637
  tiled pictures, 627–630
immutable objects, 144
implementation, 221, 329, 349–354, 644
  classes, 349–354
  collections, 644
  interfaces, 221, 349–354
  software design and, 329, 349–354
implements reserved word, 348–354
import statement, 115, 122–123, 150–151
  asterisk (*) for, 151
  class declaration, 115, 150–151
  java.util packages and, 122–123, 150–151
increment code, 305–307
increment (++) operator, 106–107
indentation, 239–240, 242, 247, 251, 703
  coding guidelines, 703
  if statements, 239–240, 242, 247, 251
  nested statements, 251
index values, 271, 406–407, 410–415
  array elements, 271, 406–407, 410–415
  ArrayList class, 271–273
  bounds checking, 410–415
  characters, 412–415
  integers, 410–412
indirect recursion, 615–616
infinite loops, 260–261, 304
infinite recursion, 610–611
information storage and management, 30–36, 39–43
  analog, 30–31
  binary values, 33–36
  bits, 35–36
  capacity of devices, 40–43
  digital, 32–36

main memory, 28–29, 39–41
memory devices, 39–43
sampling rate, 31–33
secondary memory, 28, 41–43
signals, 30–36
inheritance, 74, 469–512, 514–527, 575–578
  abstract classes, 487–488
  child class, 471, 479–484
  class hierarchies, 484–488, 494–496, 575–578
  Component class, 494–496
  encapsulation and, 473–475
  event adapter classes, 497–500
  exceptions and, 575–578
  extends modifier used for, 471, 486
  final modifier used for, 483, 493–494
  graphical-user interfaces (GUIs), 494–504
  interface hierarchies, 489
  is-a relationship of, 471–472
  multiple, 479–480
  Object class, 486–487
  object-oriented programming and, 74, 469–512
  overriding methods, 481–483, 523
  parent (base) class, 471, 476–479
  polymorphism via, 514–527
  protected modifier used for, 473–475
  reference variables, 514–516
  reserved words for, 471, 473–479, 483, 486–488, 490, 493–494
  restricting, 493–494
  shadow variables, 483–484
  siblings, 485
  software design for, 492–494
  software reuse, 74, 470
  subclasses, 470–480
  super modifier used for, 476–479, 490, 493
  Timer class, 501–504
  UML diagrams for, 472, 475
  visibility and, 473–475, 489–492
initializer lists, 415–416
input data, 115, 117

input dialog box, 318–319
input/output (I/O), 28, 38–39, 579–583
  computer devices, 28, 38–39
  exceptions and, 579–583
  Java standard class library for, 580
  streams, 579–583
input validation, 260
insertion sort, 537–538
instance data, 193
instantiation, 113–115, 141, 207, 407–408, 418–420, 424–426
  arrays, 407–408, 418–420, 424–426
  constructors, 113–115, 207, 424–426
  object declaration and, 141, 407–408, 418–420, 424–426
instruction register, 43
int integer data type, 91–93, 97–98, 110–111, 167–169, 407–408, 434
  array declaration using, 407–408, 434
  autoboxing, 169
  conversion for, 110–111
  primitive data, as, 97–98
  square brackets ([]) for, 407–408, 434
  variable value declaration using, 91–93
  wrapper classes for, 167–168
integer data types, 97–98, 109–113, 410–412
  array index values, 410–412
  assignment conversion of, 111
  bounds checking, 410–412
  casting () conversion of, 111–112
  conversion of, 109–113
  literals, 98
  narrowing conversion for, 109–110
  primitive data as, 97–98
  promotion conversion of, 111
  widening conversion for, 110–111
integrated development environments (IDEs), 66–67

interactive programming, 113–115

`new` operator, 113–115, 141, 407–408, 418–420

interfaces, 221, 349–355, 489, 528–530. *See also* graphical user interfaces (GUIs)

`Comparable`, 354

hierarchies, 489

implementation for, 221, 349–354

inheritance and, 489

`Iterator`, 354–355

methods for, 348–354, 528–530

polymorphism via, 528–530

reference variables for, 528–530

software design and, 349–355

internal frame, 730

internal nodes, 657

Internet, 49–52

addresses, 47, 49–50

Advanced Research Projects Agency (ARAPA), 49

domain names, 49–50

domain server, 50

hypertext, 50–52

protocol (IP), 49

search engines, 51–52

subdomains, 50

top-level domain (TLD), 50

Transmission Control Protocol (TCP), 49

Uniform Resource Locators (URL), 51–52

World Wide Web (WWW), 51–52

interpreters, 75–66

invisible components, 388–390

invoking (calling) methods, 55, 141, 198–199, 369–371

is-a relationship, 471–472

`Iterator` interface, 354–355

iterators, 267–270, 308–310, 615

conditional statements and, 267–270, 308–310

delimiters, 270

`for-each` statements for, 308–310

path separation (/), 270

reading text files using, 268–270

recursion versus, 615

`Scanner` class for, 267–270

J

Java Collections API, 660–661

Java Development Kit (JDK), 67

Java programming, 52–61, 65–67, 70–75, 107–108, 113–117, 118–121, 121–129, 143–144, 148–151, 163–166, 196, 207–208, 376–391, 691–708, 717–745

applets, 121–129, 707–708

application programming interfaces (API), 53, 148–149

applications, 121–122

assignment operators 107–108

bytecode, 65–66, 122

character strings (" "), 55

class definition ({ }), 54–55

classes, 73–75, 148–151, 207–208

coding guidelines, 701–705

color representation, 120–121

coordinate systems, 118–120

comments, 54–57

compilers, 65–66

constructors, 113–115, 207–208

deprecated, 53

documentation, 54, 56–57, 704–705

encapsulation, 74

enumerated types, 164–166

event generation, 729–731

garbage collection, 143–144

graphics, 118–129

identifiers, 57–59, 703

inheritance, 74

inline documentation, 54, 57

integrated development environments (IDEs), 66–67

interactive, 113–117

invoking (calling) methods, 55

language, 52–61

layout managers, 376–391

legacy system, 163

`main` method, 54

methods, 55, 73

modifiers, 697–699, 702

`new` operator, 113–115

object-oriented (OO) language, 53, 72–75

objects, 72–75, 113–115, 207–208

operators, 691–695

packages, 148–151

`PaintBox` project, 717–727

polymorphism, 74

primitive data, 72

`println` method, 55

reserved words, 57–59

`Scanner` class, 113–117

semantics, 67–68

Software Development Kit (SDK), 67

standard class library, 53, 57

syntax, 67–68, 733–745

terminating, 55

visibility modifiers, 196

white space, 59–61, 115, 703

Java standard class library, 53, 57, 148–151, 158–161, 167–168, 271–273, 442–443, 486–487, 660–661, 697–698, 747

application programming interfaces (API), 53, 148–149, 660–661

`ArrayList` class, 271–273

collections, 660–661

formatting data output, 158–161

generic types, 660–661

identifiers in, 57

`import` declaration, 150–151

`java` packages, 150–151, 442–443

modifiers, 697–699

`Object` class, 486–487

online API documentation, 149–150, 747

packages, 148–151

`Polygon` class, 442–443

input/output (I/O) streams, 580

visibility modifiers, 697–698

wrapper classes, 167–168

`java.util` packages, 150–151

javadoc, 56, 711–715

comments, 56, 711–714

documentation generation, 56, 711–715

files generated for, 714–715

tags, 712–714

JButton class, 219–221
JColorChooser class, 551–553
JComboBox class, 590–595
JFileChooser class,
      548–551
JFrame class, 170–173,
      211–212
JList class, 601–604
JOptionPane class, 317–319
JPanel class, 170–173,
      208–213
JScrollBar class, 595–598
JSlider class, 553–558
JSplitPane class, 598–604
JTextField class, 222–225

K

key events, GUI programs for,
      453–458
key repetition, 458
keyboard focus, 458
kilobyte (KB), 40

L

labels, 171–172, 177–179,
      277–281
   font styles, 277–281
   GUI containers, 171–172
   images and, 176–179
   JLabel class, 171–172, 177
languages, *see* programming
      languages
last-in, first–out (lifo)
      processing, 654
late (dynamic) binding, 514
layered pane, 731
layout managers, 173,
      376–391
   border, 382–385
   box, 387–390
   containers and, 173, 376–391
   flow, 378–382
   grid, 385–387
   GUI components using,
      376–391
   invisible components,
      388–390
   tabbed panes, 377–378
leaf nodes, 657–658
left-shift operator (<<), 695
legacy systems, 163
lexicographic order, 255
lightweight containers,
      170–171

line borders, 393–394
linear search, 539–541
linked lists, 646–652
list components, 601–604
listener objects, 217–225,
      274–277, 448–452,
      453–457, 497–500,
      547–548, 553–558
   adapter classes extended for,
      497–500
   buttons, 218–222, 274–285
   key events, 453–457
   mouse events, 448–452
   polymorphism and,
      547–548, 553–558
   sliders, 553–558
ListPanel class, 600–604
literals, data types as, 84, 89,
      98–100, 142, 419
local area network (LAN),
      48–49
local data, 201–202
logical error, 69
logical operators, 236–238
long integer data type, 97, 110
loops, 235–238, 256–265, 295,
      301–319
   boolean expressions for,
      235–238
   comparison of, 310
   dialog box creation using,
      317–319
   do statements, 235,
      301–304, 318–319
   drawing programs using,
      311–317
   execution time, 238
   for statements, 235,
      305–310
   for-each statements,
      308–310
   graphical user interfaces
      (GUI), 311–319
   infinite, 260–261, 304
   nested, 262–265
   while statements, 235,
      256–265
low–level languages, 63

M

machine language, 63
magnetic storage devices,
      41–42
main memory, 28–29, 39–41
   addresses, 39

cache, 41
central processing unit (CPU)
      and, 28–29, 41
   locations, 39–40
   storage capacity, 40–41
main method, 54, 188–189,
      428–429
Math class, 155–158
matte borders, 394–395
megabyte (MB), 40
memory, 28–29, 39–43
   address, 39
   bytes, 40
   capacity, 40–43
   computer hardware
      functions, 28–29, 39–43
   direct access devices,
      41–42
   locations, 39–40
   magnetic devices, 41–42
   main, 28–29, 39–41
   random access (RAM), 40
   read-only (ROM), 40
   secondary, 28, 41–43
   sequential access devices, 40
   storage devices, 40–43
   volatility of, 40
message dialog box, 318–319
methods, 55, 73, 84–85,
      140–142, 144–147,
      152–155, 155–158,
      161–163, 168, 186–192,
      195–208, 332–335,
      348–355, 358–371,
      430–433, 481–483,
      514–530, 707–708. *See
      also* recursion
   abstract, 349
   accessor, 197–198
   algorithms for, 358–359
   applets, 123, 707–708
   classes and, 186–192,
      195–208
   constructors as, 141, 190,
      207–208
   declaration of, 189–192,
      198–199
   decomposition, 359–364
   dot (.) operator for
      accessing, 141
   encapsulation of objects,
      195–198
   header, 198, 200–201
   inheritance and, 481–483,
      514–527

methods *(continued)*
  interfaces and, 348–354,
    528–530
  invoking (calling), 55, 141,
    198–199, 369–371
  late (dynamic) binding, 514
  local, 201–202
  main, 54, 188–189
  Math class, 155–158
  mutator, 197–198
  object behavior and, 73,
    186–187, 189
  object declaration, 140–142
  object-oriented
    programming and,
    332–335, 348–355,
    358–371
  object reference variables, 73,
    140–142
  operations as, 186–187
  overloading, 369–371
  overriding, 481–483, 523
  parameter passing,
    201–202, 364–368,
    430–433
  parentheses ( ) for
    invoking, 141
  polymorphism and,
    514–530
  print, 84–85
  printf, 161–163
  println, 55, 84–85
  pseudorandom number
    generator, 152–155
  Random class, 152–155
  reference variables, 73,
    140–142, 514–516,
    528–530
  return statement, 200–201
  returned values, 141–142,
    152–153, 155–158
  signature, 370
  static, 155, 168, 332–335
  String class, 140–142,
    144–147
  terminating programs, 55
  UML class diagrams for,
    363–364
  variable–length parameter
    lists, 430–433
  variables in, 73, 140–142,
    201–202, 514–516,
    528–530
  wrapper classes and, 168
microprocessor, 44–45

mnemonics, 63
mnemonics, GUI programs for,
  583–589
modifiers, 196–197,
    473–475, 489–492,
    697–699. *See also*
    reserved words
  encapsulation and, 196–198
  inheritance and, 473–475,
    489–492
  Java programming, 697–699
  visibility, 196–197, 473–475,
    489–492, 697–698
  use of, 699
monitor resolution, 118
mouse events, GUI programs
  for, 444–452, 497–500
mouse motion events,
  444–445
multidimensional arrays,
  438–439
multiple inheritance, 479–480
mutator methods,
  encapsulation, 197–198

N

narrowing conversions, 110–111
native modifier (reserved
  word), 699
nested panels, 174–176
nested statements, 249–251,
    262–265, 434–438
  boolean expressions, 249–251
  else clause applications,
    249–251
  for loop statements,
    249–251
  if statements, 249–251
  indentation for, 251
  palindrome example,
    262–265
  two-dimensional arrays using,
    434–438
  while loops, 262–265
networks, 46–52
  computer systems, 46–52
  addresses, 47, 49–50
  connections, 46–48
  file servers, 46
  Internet, 49–52
  local-area (LAN), 48–49
  packets, 47–48
  point-to-point connection,
    46–47
  protocol, 49

Uniform Resource Locators
    (URL), 51–52
  wide area (WAN), 48–49
  World Wide Web, 51–52
new operator, 113–115,
    141–142, 190, 407–408,
    418–420
  array declaration, 407–408,
    418–420
  constructors and, 113–115,
    141, 190
  instantiation using, 113–115,
    141, 407–408, 418–420
  object data and, 113–115,
    141–142, 418–420
  String objects and,
    141–142, 418–420
nextLine method, 115
nodes, non-linear data
    structures, 657–658
nonprintable (control)
    characters, 687–689
NOT bitwise operator (~), 693
null value setting,
    141, 651
number systems, 679–685
  base-28, 679
  bases higher than ten,
    681–682
  binary, 679
  bits, 679
  conversions, 683–685
  decimal, 679
  hexadecimal, 681
  place value, 679–681
NumberFormat class,
    158–160

O

object-oriented (OO)
    programming, 53,
    70–75, 193–194,
    327–404, 492–494,
    545–546
  aggregation and, 342–346
  assigning responsibilities, 331
  borders, 382–385, 391–395
  classes and, 73–75, 329–331
  containment hierarchies,
    395–397
  dependency and, 336–342
  encapsulation, 74
  enumerated types, 355–358
  graphical user interfaces
    (GUI), 375–397

inheritance for, 74, 492–494
interfaces, 348–355
language, 53
layout managers, 376–391
methods, 73, 332–335,
    358–371
objects and, 72–74, 113–115,
    329–331, 342–343,
    346–348
overloading methods,
    369–371
polymorphism for, 74,
    545–546
problem solving, 71–72
software design, 70–75,
    327–404, 492–494,
    545–546
static class members,
    331–335
testing, 371–375
this reserved word and,
    346–348
Unified Modeling Language
    (UML) diagrams,
    193–194, 472, 475
objects, 72–74, 113–115,
    139–184, 207–225,
    254–255, 267–285,
    329–331, 336–343,
    346–348, 407–410,
    418–427, 501–504,
    643–666
action events for, 221
aggregate, 342–343
aliases of, 142–144
ArrayList class, 271–273
arrays as, 407–410,
    418–427
attributes, 73, 186–187
autoboxing, 169
behavior, 72–73, 186
buttons, 218–222,
    274–285
character strings (" ") for,
    84–91, 142, 254–255
classes and, 73–74, 139–184,
    186–187, 195–198,
    207–216, 329–331,
    336–343, 346–348
client, 195
collections, 643–666
conditional statements for,
    267–285
constructors for, 113–115,
    141, 207–216, 424–426

containers, 170–171
creating, 140–144
data comparisons, 254–255
declaration of, 113–115,
    140–141, 407–410,
    418–427
dependencies among,
    336–342
dot (.) operator for accessing
    methods, 141
encapsulation, 74, 195–198
enumerated types, 164–166
event-driven programs,
    217–218
events, 217–225, 274–277
frames for, 169–173
frames, 170–173
garbage, 143–144
graphical, 170–179, 208–216
GUI-based classes for,
    170–179, 217–225,
    274–285
has-a relationships, 342–343
identification of, 329–331
images, 177–179
immutable, 144
index value, 271–273
inheritance and, 74, 501–504
instantiation, 141, 407–410,
    418–420, 424–426
iterators, 267–270
labels, 171–172, 177–179
listeners for GUI interfaces,
    217–225, 274–277
methods and, 73, 141–142,
    195–198
new operator, 113–115,
    141–142, 407–408,
    418–420
object-oriented programming
    and, 72–73, 113–115,
    329–331, 342–343,
    346–348
operations for, 186–187
ordinal values, 164–165
parentheses ( ) for
    invoking methods, 141
pointers, 141
reference variables, 140–144
returned values, 141–142
software design and, 329–
    331, 342–343, 346–348
state, 72, 186
String class, 140–142,
    144–147, 418–423

string literals ("") for, 142,
    419
text fields, 222–225
this reference for, 346–348
timers, 501–504
variables as, 140–144,
    164–166
wrapper classes, 167–169
off-by-one errors, 410
operating systems, 29–30
operations, object behavior
    and, 186–187. See also
    methods
operators, 86–88, 93, 95,
    101–108, 141, 235–238,
    300–301, 691–695
addition (+), 101, 107
arithmetic, 101–102
assignment (=), 93, 107–108
binary, 102
bitwise, 691–695
boolean values, 694
boolean expression
    conditions, 235–238
conditional (? :), 300–301
conditional statements and,
    235–238, 300–301
decrement (–), 106–107
division (/), 101–102, 107
dot (.) for accessing
    methods, 141
equality, 235–236
increment (++), 106–107
Java programming, 691–695
logical, 236–238
looping statements and,
    235–238
multiplication (*), 101, 107
parentheses () for, 88,
    103–104
postfix form, 106–107
precedence, 88, 102–106,
    691–693
prefix form, 106–107
relational, 235–236
remainder (%), 101, 107–108,
    303–304
string concatenation (+),
    86–88
subtraction (–), 101, 107
ternary (conditional), 300–301
unary, 102
OR bitwise operator (|),
    693–704
ordinal value, 164–165

output data, 55, 84–85, 116, 158–163
  DecimalFormat class, 160–161
  formatting, 158–163
  interactive programming, 116
  Java standard class library packages, 158–161
  NumberFormat class, 158–160
  print method, 84–85
  printf method, 161–163
  println method, 55, 84–85
overloading methods, 369–371
overriding methods, 481–483, 523

P
packages, 148–151, 697
  application programming interfaces (API), 148–149
  import declaration, 150–151
  java.util, 150–151
  visibility of, 697
packets, 47–48
paint method, 123
PaintBox project, 717–727
paintComponent method, 208, 211, 213–214, 311–314
palindrome, nested loop example of, 262–265
panels, 170–176
  containment hierarchy, 174–176
  Jpanel class, 170–173
  nested, 174–176
panes, 171–173, 377–378, 595–604
  content, 171–173
  exceptions used for, 595–604
  frames and, 171
  GUI programs for, 171–173, 377–378, 595–604
  layout manager and, 377–378
  list components for, 601–604
  scrolls, 595–598
  split, 598–604
  tabbed, 377–378
parameters, 84, 201–202, 364–368, 416–417, 428–433
  actual (arguments), 201
  arg identifier, 428–429
  arrays as, 416–417, 428–433

by value passing, 364–368
character strings as, 84
command-line arguments, 428–433
constructors and, 431–433
data as, 84
formal, 201
header specification, 201–202
lists, 201
main method and, 428–429
methods, 201–201, 364–368, 430–433
multiple, 428–433
passing, 201–202, 364–368, 416–417, 430–433
software design and, 364–368
String objects and, 428–429
variable–length lists, 430–433
parent (base) class, 471, 476–479
path separation (/), 270
peripherals, 38
petabyte (PB), 40
picture resolution, 118
pixels, 118
place value, 679–681
point-to-point connection, 46–47
pointers, 141
polygons, drawing, 439–443
polylines, drawing, 440–442
polymorphism, 74, 513–561
  class hierarchy and, 516–517
  color choosers and, 552–553
  event processing using, 547–548
  file choosers and, 548–551
  graphical user interfaces (GUI), 547–558
  inheritance and, 74, 514–527
  interfaces and, 528–530
  late (dynamic) binding, 514
  methods and, 514–527
  reference variables, 514–516, 528–530
  searching, 539–545
  sliders and, 553–558
  software design for, 545–546
  sorting, 530–538
  super reserved word used for, 523
postfix operator form, 106–107
prefix operator form, 106–107
primary colors, 120

primitive data types, 72, 97–101, 109–113, 167–169, 252–253, 410–415, 687–689
  array index values, 410–415
  assignment conversion of, 111
  autoboxing, 169
  booleans, 100, 167
  bounds checking, 410–415
  casting () conversion of 111–112
  char, 100, 110–111
  characters, 99–100, 109–112, 412–415, 687–689
  conversion of, 109–113
  data values as, 97–101
  double, 97–98, 110–111
  false, 100
  float, 97–98, 110–111
  floating point, 97–98, 109–112, 252–253
  int, 97–98, 110–111, 167–169
  integers, 97–98, 109–113, 410–412
  Java programming and, 72
  literals, 98
  long, 97, 110
  narrowing conversion of, 110–111
  promotion conversion of, 111
  short, 97–98, 109–111
  true, 100
  types, 97–101
  widening conversion for, 109–110
  wrapper classes, 167–169
print method, 84–85
printable characters, 687–688
printf method12, 161–163
println method, 55, 84–85
private modifier, 196, 697–698
program counter, 43
programming languages, 52–69
  assembly, 63
  character strings (" "), 55
  class definition ({ }), 54–55
  comments, 54–57
  compilers for, 65–66
  computer error and, 68–69
  documentation, 54, 57
  fourth-generation (30GL), 64
  high-level, 63–64
  identifiers, 57–59
  interpreters for, 65–66

invoking (calling) methods, 55
Java, 52–61
low-level, 63
machine, 63
methods and, 55
mnemonics, 63
object-oriented (OO), 53
reserved words, 57–58
semantics, 67–68
statements and, 52
syntax, 67–68
target, 65
translating code for, 64–66
programs, 28, 52–75
class definition ({ }), 54–55
comments, 54–57
compilers, 65–66
computer hardware and, 28
debuggers, 66–67
development environments, 66–67
development of, 62–69
documentation, 54, 56–57
editors, 64–65
errors, 66–69
integrated development environments (IDEs), 66–67
interpreters, 75–76
invoking (calling) methods, 55
Java, 52–61, 66–69
languages, 52–69
methods, 55, 73
object-oriented (OO), 53, 70–75
semantics, 67–68
software tools for, 28, 64–67
source code, 65
statements, 52
syntax, 67–68
terminating, 55
progress bar, 731
promotion, data conversion by, 111
propagating the exception, 571–574
protected modifier, 196, 473–475, 697–698
protocol, 49
pseudocode, 359
pseudorandom number generator, 152–155
public modifier, 55, 57, 123, 196, 697–698

push buttons, GUI creation of, 218–222, 274–277

Q
queues, 653–654

R
radio buttons, GUI creation of, 281–285
ragged arrays, 439
random access memory (RAM), 40
Random class, 152–155
read-only memory (ROM), 40
recordable CD (CD–R) devices, 42
recursion, 609–642
direct, 615–616
fractals and, 630–637
graphic applications, 627–637
indirect, 615–616
infinite, 610–611
iteration versus, 615
math use of, 611–612
problem-solving use of, 616–626
programming, 612–616
recursive thinking, 610–612
tiled pictures and, 627–630
Towers of Hanoi problem, 621–626
traversing a maze, 617–621
reference variables, 73, 140–144, 515–516, 528–530
garbage, 143–144
inheritance and, 515–516
interfaces and, 528–530
object aliases for, 142–144
object declaration and, 140–142
polymorphic, 514–516, 528–530
string methods, 140–142
registers, 43–44
regular expressions, 117, 709–710
relational operators, 235–236
remainder (%) operator, 101, 107–108, 303–304
repetition statements, *see* loops

reserved words, 57–58, 95–96, 100, 196–197, 200–201, 207–208, 331–335, 346–354, 473–479, 483, 486–488, 493–494, 697–699, 702
abstract, 349, 487–488, 699
extends, 471, 486
boolean, 100
class, 57
constants declared using, 95–96
false, 100
final, 95–96, 196, 483, 493–494, 354, 699
identifiers, 57–58
implements, 348–354
inheritance using, 471, 473–479, 486–488, 490, 493–494
interfaces and, 348–354
Java modifiers, 697–699, 702
Java programming, 57–58
object-oriented design using, 331–335, 346–354
private modifier, 196, 697–698
protected modifier, 196, 473–475, 697–698
public modifier, 57, 196, 697–698
return, 200–201, 207
static modifier, 57, 331–335, 699
super, 476–479, 490, 493, 523
this reserved word and, 346–348
true, 100
visibility modifiers, 196–197, 473–475
void, 57, 200–201, 207–208
return statement, 200–201
returned values, 141–142, 152–153, 155–158
Math class, 155–158
Random class, 152–155
String class, 141–142
review, code evaluation by, 372
rewritable CD (CD–RW) devices, 42
RGB (red-green-blue) values, 120
right-shift operator (>>), 695

right-shift with zeros operator
    (>>>), 695
robust programs, 260
root nodes, 657–658
rubberbanding, 449–452
run-time error, 69
running sums, 259

S
sampling rate, 31–33
Scanner class, 113–117,
    267–270
scope of a variable, 193
scroll panes, GUI programs for,
    595–598
search engines, 51–52
searching, 539–545
    binary, 541–544
    comparison of approaches,
        545
    linear, 539–541
    polymorphism and, 539–545
secondary memory, 28, 41–43
    direct access storage devices,
        41–42
    magnetic storage devices,
        41–42
    random access memory
        (RAM), 40
    read-only memory (ROM), 40
    sequential access storage
        devices, 40
    storage capacity, 41–43
seed value, 152–153
selection sort, 531–533
selection statements, *see*
        conditional statements
semantics, 67–68
sentinel values, 257–259
sequential access storage
        devices, 40
service (support) methods,
        encapsulation, 196
shadow variables, 483–484
short integer data type,
        97–98, 109–111
siblings, 485
signals, 30–36
    analog, 30–31
    digital, 32–36
    sampling rate, 31–33
signature, method invocation
        and, 370
sliders, GUI programs for,
        553–558

software, 28–30, 50–51, 64–
        69, 70–75, 492–494,
        545–546
    application, 30
    compilers, 65–66
    compile-time error, 68
    computer system functions,
        28–30
    debugging, 66–67, 69
    development environments,
        66–67
    editors, 64–65
    errors, 66–69
    graphical user interface
        (GUI), 30
    hardware components and, 30
    inheritance and design of,
        492–494
    interpreters, 65–66
    Java Development Kit (JDK),
        67
    logical error, 69
    object-oriented
        programming, 70–75
    operating systems, 29–30
    polymorphism and design of,
        545–546
    program development tools,
        64–67
    run-time error, 69
    user interface, 29
software design, 70–75,
        327–404, 492–494,
        545–546
    polymorphism and,
        545–546
    aggregation and, 342–346
    borders, 382–385, 391–395
    boundaries, 373–374
    classes and, 329–369
    clients, 328
    containment hierarchies,
        395–397
    dependency and, 336–342
    development activities,
        328–329
    enumerated types, 355–358
    functional specification, 328
    graphical user interfaces
        (GUIs), 375–397
    identification of objects and
        classes, 329–331
    implementation, 329, 349–354
    inheritance and, 492–494
    interfaces and, 348–355

    layout managers, 376–391
    methods, 332–335, 358–371
    objects and, 72–74, 329–331,
        342–343, 346–348
    parameter passing, 364–368
    principles of, 70–75
    static class members,
        331–335
    testing programs for, 329,
        371–374
    this reserved word and,
        346 348
Software Development Kit
        (SDK), 67
software failure, 137–138,
        231–232, 293–294,
        403–404, 467–468,
        511–512
    Ariane 31 Fight 527,
        511–512
    Denver Airport Baggage
        Handling System,
        231–232
    LA Air Traffic Control,
        467–468
    NASA Mars Climate Orbiter
        and Polar Lander,
        137–138
    Therac-51, 293–294
    2029 Northeast blackout,
        403–404
software reuse, 74, 470
sorting, 530–538
    comparison of approaches,
        538
    insertion, 537–538
    polymorphism and, 530–538
    selection, 531–533
source code, 65
spacing, coding guidelines for,
        703
split panes, GUI programs for,
        598–604
stack data structures, 654–656
standard input stream, 115
start angle, 127
statement coverage, 374
static class members, 55, 57,
        155, 168, 326, 331–335,
        699
    methods, 155, 168,
        332–335
    static modifier, 55, 57,
        331–335, 699
    variables, 326, 332

streams, exceptions and, 579–580
string concatenation, 86–89
string literals (" "), 55, 84, 142, 419
String objects, 140–142, 144–147, 418–423, 428–429
  arg identifier, 428–429
  arrays of, 418–423, 428–429
  command–line arguments for, 428–429
  declaration of objects using, 140–142, 418–423
  immutable objects in, 144
  index of characters, 144
  instantiation using, 141, 418–420
  main method and, 428–429
  methods, 142–142, 144–147
  new operator for, 141–142, 418–420
  parameters as, 428–429
  reference variables, 140–142
  returned values, 141–142
subclasses, 470–484
  child class as, 471
  creating, 470–473
  extends reserved word used for, 471
  multiple inheritance, 479–480
  overriding methods, 481–483
  parent (base) class, 471
  protected modifier used for, 473–475
  shadow variables, 483–484
  super reserved word used for, 476–479
  UML class diagrams for, 472, 475
subdomains, 50
subscript values, *see* index values
super modifier (reserved word), 476–479, 490, 493, 523
Swing packages, 170, 317, 391–395, 494–496, 583
switch statements, 234, 296–299
  break statement and, 296–297
  data types for, 297

  default case, 296–297
  equal conditions of, 298–299
  single value cases of, 296
synchronized modifier (reserved word), 699
syntax, 67–68, 415, 733–745
syntax error, 69
System class, 161–163
system clock, 45
System.err standard I/O stream, 579–580
System.in standard I/O stream, 579
System.out standard I/O stream, 579–580

T
tabbed panes, 377–378
tables, 731
tags, javadoc comments, 712–714
target language, 65
terabyte (TB), 40
test case, 373
test suite, 373
testing programs, 329, 371–374
  black–box, 373–374
  boundaries, 373–374
  defect, 372–374
  equivalence categories, 373–374
  review, 372
  software design and, 329, 371–374
  statement coverage, 374
  walkthrough, 372
  white-box (glass-box), 374
text fields, 222–225
text files, reading using iterators, 268–270
text processing, 731
this reserved word, 346–348
throws clause, 269–270, 576–581
throw statements, 577–578, 580–582
tiled pictures and, 627–630
Timer class, 501–504
title case, 59
titled borders, 394
toggle buttons, 285
tokens, 115
tool bar, 730
tool tips and, GUI programs for, 583–589

top-level containers, 395
top-level domain (TLD), 50
touch screen systems, 39
Towers of Hanoi recursion problem, 621–626
transient modifier (reserved word), 699
Transmission Control Protocol (TCP), 49
traversing a maze recursion problem, 617–621
tree component, 731
tree data structures, 657–658
true boolean value, 100
truth tables, 236–238
try blocks, 566–570
try-catch statements, 566–570
two–dimensional arrays, 434–438

U
unary operators, 102
unchecked exceptions, 578
Unicode Character Set, 100, 687–689
Unified Modeling Language (UML) diagrams, 193–194, 472, 475
Uniform Resource Locators (URL), 51–52
uninitialized variables, 140
USB flash drives, 41
user interface, 29

V
variable-length parameter lists, 430–433
variables, 91–95, 140–144, 164–166, 193, 201–202, 332, 355–358, 407–410, 415–416, 483–484, 514–516, 528–530
  aliases of, 142–144
  arrays, 407–410, 415–416
  assignment statements, 93–95
  data value as, 91–95
  declarations, 92–93, 140–142, 193, 201–202, 407–410, 415–416, 515–516, 528
  enumerated types, 164–166, 355–358
  inheritance and, 483–484, 515–516

variables *(continued)*
  initializer lists, 415–416
  instance data, 193
  instantiation, 141, 193
  int value declaration of,
    91–93, 140, 407–408,
    415–416
  interfaces and, 528–530
  interfaces for, 528–530
  late binding, 514
  local data, 201–202
  method declaration of,
    201–202, 407–410
  new operator for, 141–142
  null value setting, 141
  objects and, 140–144,
    164–166
  ordinal value, 164–165
  polymorphism and,
    514–516, 528–530
  reference, 140–142, 514–516,
    528–530
  scope of, 223
  shadowing, 483–484
  static (class), 326, 332
  uninitialized, 140
  visibility modifiers, 196–197,
    473–475, 489–492,
    697–698
  default, 697–698

encapsulation and, 196–197,
    473–475
inheritance and, 473–475,
    489–492
Java programming, 697–698
package, 697
private, 196, 697–698
protected, 473–475,
    697–698
public, 196, 697–698
void modifier, 55, 57, 167,
    200–201, 207–208
Java programming use of, 55,
    57, 207–208
  method header specification,
    200–201
  return statement and,
    200–201, 207
  wrapper class for, 167
volatile modifier (reserved
    word), 699
von Neumann architecture,
    44

W
walkthrough, code evaluation
    by, 372
while clause for do statements,
    301–302

while loop statements, 235,
    256–265, 267–270
  break statements for,
    265
  continue statements for,
    265
  divide-by-zero error,
    258–259
  infinite, 260–261
  input validation, 260
  iteration using, 267–270
  nested, 262–295
  repetition of, 256–257
  running sums, 259
  sentinel values, 257–259
white-box (glass-box)
    testing, 374
white space, 59–61, 115, 703
wide area network (WAN),
    48–49
widening conversions, 109–110
World Wide Web (WWW),
    51–52, 124
wrapper classes, 167–169
writing classes, 185–232

X
XOR bitwise operator (^),
    693–704